THE HARDING ERA

PUBLISHED WITH ASSISTANCE FROM THE
ROGER E. JOSEPH MEMORIAL FUND FOR GREATER UNDERSTANDING OF
PUBLIC AFFAIRS, A CAUSE IN WHICH ROGER JOSEPH BELIEVED

The
Harding Era

*Warren G. Harding and His
Administration*

by ROBERT K. MURRAY

UNIVERSITY OF MINNESOTA PRESS • MINNEAPOLIS

Published in Great Britain, India, and Pakistan by the Oxford
University Press, London, Bombay, and Karachi, and in Canada
by the Copp Clark Publishing Co. Limited, Toronto

Library of Congress Catalog Card Number: 74-91797

Preface

THE decade of the 1920's offers the American historian an excellent opportunity for research, reevaluation, and reinterpretation. Too long has this period been viewed simply as a deplorable interim between the Progressive Era and the New Deal. Too frequently has it been the subject of superficial judgments and cliché-ridden condemnation. Although exciting nostalgia, the frivolity and ballyhoo of the twenties have normally been used to prove the decade's utter bankruptcy, and this shallow image of the period has remained to the present day. For most Americans the twenties represent little more than a wasteland of trivia and immorality.

Recently American historians have begun to reexamine this era in order to challenge and, where warranted, to substantiate the traditional view. The goal is to place the 1920's in a broader perspective and uncover the era's own uniqueness as well as any characteristics of political continuity. Careful examination reveals that the twenties, as with any period in history, defies glib analysis and flashy generalities.

This book examines the beginning years of the decade and its most controversial and misunderstood figure, Warren G. Harding. In part this work is biographical. In part it deals with legislative programs and the aspirations of an administration. And in part it recounts a sordid story of government corruption and degeneracy. It is hoped, however, that the result is more than mere biography, or the listing of the events of a single presidential administration, or the reiteration of scandals already well known. It is an attempt to blend personalities, circumstances, economic challenges, individual ambition, human motivation, political ideas, domestic and international politics, and public attitudes into a related whole which for lack of a better name can be called the Harding era.

I fully realize that dangers exist. Although the Harding years beg for reinterpretation, nothing is more intellectually dishonest than historical revisionism for revisionism's sake. This activity may gain an author a certain notoriety, but it rarely results in sound scholarship. Unfortunately, the careful reconstruction of historical truth is often a dull business and not very earthshaking. An open-minded investigator must always revise his hypotheses to fit the facts and not vice versa. This oftentimes requires a sober admission that what predecessors believed and wrote had considerable validity.

What I hope to achieve here is both the excitement of revisionist history and the soundness of careful historical scholarship. To this end I relied heavily on the growing number of excellent monographs which have appeared recently on various aspects of the twenties. At the same time, I examined all the older traditional writings and attempted to merge the value of their contemporaneity with the detachment and critical insight of the more recent accounts. Published government documents, as well as material in the National Archives, I mined to the best of my ability and within the time limits I had available. To expand my comprehension of the period, and especially of the human element, I surveyed over threescore biographies and some fifty memoirs. More than twenty newspapers and periodicals also became important eyes through which I glimpsed the early twenties more clearly.

Of all the sources, none was more significant than the thirty-three manuscript collections which I was privileged to use. Three of these were never before seen by a historian; twelve had been examined in their entirety by only two colleagues. If the newspapers, memoirs, government documents, biographies, monographic studies, and periodicals provided the warp of my effort, these manuscripts supplied the woof. Of them all, by far the most important was the Harding collection in the Ohio Historical Society Library, Columbus, Ohio. These Harding manuscripts have as yet received only limited use by scholars—a pity, since this collection more than fulfills curator Kenneth W. Duckett's prophecy upon its acquisition in 1964 that "this wealth of unexpected detail may amaze even those who feel they know him [Harding] and his times well."

No author works in isolation and I am no exception. It would be impossible to single out all those whose time, energy, and talents contributed in some way to this book. While remaining nameless here, they know who they are. Nameless, too, must remain those innumerable library employees at the Pennsylvania State University, at Rutgers, at Princeton, at Columbia, at Ohio State, and at the New York Public Library who were badgered by my endless and sometimes unreasonable requests. A few require a special word of gratitude: David C. Mearns and his cooperative staff at the Manuscript Division of the Library of Congress; Mrs. Elizabeth B. Mason, assistant director of the Oral History Research Office, Columbia University; Dwight M. Miller, archivist, and Charles W. Corkran, assistant archivist, Hoover Presidential Library; Mrs. Elizabeth Martin, David Larson, Conrad Weitzel, and Dr. Allen T. Price, all of the Ohio Historical Society Library; Dr. Warren C. Sawyer, president of the Harding Memorial Association; Professor David Jennings, Ohio Wesleyan University; Professor Randolph C. Downes, University of Toledo; and Mrs. Audrey Key, who more than once saved the day with her typing. My thanks are also due the following for permission to quote either printed or manuscript materials: *Ohio History* for portions of Chapter IV; Dr. George T. Harding, the Harding Memorial Association, and the Ohio Historical Society Library for the Harding Papers; Mrs. William T. Gossett for the Hughes Papers; and the literary administrators of the Hoover manuscripts and memoirs for the various Hoover materials. A word of appreciation must also be expressed to my colleagues in the History Department of the Pennsylvania State University who were willing to tolerate a less-than-effective chairman during the better part of three years while this book was in preparation. Their patience and forbearance will not soon be forgotten.

For my family I can only express the warm tribute of a husband and father who painfully observed the knowing smiles and sly winks that met his grumblings about doing even the most minor household chores, and the uncomplaining manner in which all those formerly enjoyed trailer trips and Sunday afternoon mountain explorations were deferred because "Dad is writing another book."

To the two named in the dedication, who annually drove by the Harding Memorial with me as a boy as we proceeded on our way to fairyland Christmases at Grandmother's farm, I wish to express a son's gratitude for those things which are felt and known but cannot be adequately described.   R. K. M.

State College, Pennsylvania
December 1968

Contents

Illustrations between pages 52 and 53

THE HARDING ERA

I

The Making of a President

THE convention reconvened at 10 A.M. Hot and sweaty delegates filtered back to their seats as rumors swept the floor that the stalemate was about to be broken. From his place on the rostrum, the chairman, Senator Henry Cabot Lodge, gaveled the assembly to order and asked that the balloting begin. Four times on the day before, Friday, June 11, 1920, this procedure had resulted in no decision and the delegates had adjourned to swelter through a humid Chicago night amid intense political maneuvering and confusion.[1]

Saturday morning brought no immediate clearing of the air either climatically or politically. As raw pitch oozed from the new pine boards of the chair seats in the auditorium, delegation chairmen bawled out their votes from behind crumpled shirts and loosened neckties. In Saturday's first ballot, the fifth of the convention, the voting pattern differed but little from the previous day's roll calls as Frank O. Lowden barely edged past General Leonard Wood 303–299, picking up fourteen votes; Hiram Johnson dropped seven to 133½; and fourth-place Warren G. Harding climbed 16½ to 78. The seventh ballot, however, produced the first solid evidence of a swing in convention sentiment. While Lowden and Wood virtually deadlocked, at 311½ to 312, Harding moved into third place, with 105 to Johnson's 90½. By the eighth ballot it was unmistakably clear that a switch was on as Lowden dropped to 307 and Wood to 299,

Johnson was virtually eliminated, and Harding's total reached 133½. This surge to Harding was not an isolated phenomenon; new votes came from Missouri, Indiana, New York, Wyoming, Alabama, and Texas. Indeed, at the end of the eighth ballot Missouri attempted to change all its votes to Harding amid indications that a bandwagon was in the making. But Chairman Lodge headed it off by quickly recognizing Alvin T. Hert, Lowden's campaign manager, who moved for immediate adjournment. Backed by a scattering of "ayes" which were drowned in a chorus of "noes," Lodge arbitrarily declared the convention adjourned until 4 P.M.[2]

Despite bitter protests from Harding supporters who crowded the platform, Lodge refused to change his ruling; besides, most of the delegates were already rushing for the exits to cooler temperatures outside — and to whatever liquid refreshments prohibition Chicago had to offer. For some there were no moments of relaxation. The Wood and Lowden forces held anxious conferences. The only agreement they could reach was to urge a further postponement, and through the mediation of the national chairman, Will H. Hays, secured from Lodge a brief delay in reconvening the delegates. But finally a restless and badgered Lodge called the convention to order at 4:46 P.M.

The ninth ballot began. Alabama, Arizona, Arkansas, California, and Colorado remained essentially the same. Then came Connecticut which had cast most of its fourteen votes for Lowden in previous ballots and whose senator, Frank B. Brandegee, had been encouraged by some leaders during the recess to start a "Draft Hays" movement.[3] Connecticut suddenly switched all but one of its votes to Harding. Shortly thereafter Florida changed its support from Wood to Harding. Kansas, whose governor had placed Wood's name in nomination and whose delegation had previously been split among the candidates, gave twenty votes to Harding. Just before Kentucky's name was called, Hert, who was chairman of the Kentucky delegation as well as Lowden's manager, notified Colonel William C. Procter, Wood's manager, that any deal between the Wood and Lowden forces was impossible and that the Lowden group intended to free its votes. A moment later, Kentucky turned its bloc of twenty-six Lowden votes over to Harding. Louisiana added twelve more; Missouri contributed thirty-six. But the real sensation was New York: sixty-six of its eighty-eight delegates voted for the candidate from Ohio. The ninth-

4

ballot total read Harding 374½, Wood 249, Lowden 121½, and Johnson 82.

Bandwagon psychology now took charge. Ohio delegates whooped and hollered for the undecided to jump on before it was too late. Harry M. Daugherty, Harding's manager, rushed up to the balcony to tell Mrs. Harding that her husband would probably be nominated on the next ballot. She was pale with anticipation, and as they clutched each other her hatpins gouged him unmercifully. Daugherty gasped with the pain and thought he felt blood running down his side. Later he realized it was only perspiration from the excitement.[4] On the floor, Procter vainly attempted to catch Lodge's eye and secure another adjournment. But Lodge studiously avoided him, knowing another delay would produce insurrection among the frustrated delegates. The tenth ballot began.

There was no doubt about the outcome. As the roll call proceeded, one state delegation after another joined the Harding drive — and when Pennsylvania threw most of its sizable vote to him, it was over. The time was 6:05 P.M. The cheering delegates barely listened to the final count: Harding 692 1/5, Wood 156, Johnson 80 4/5, and Lowden 11.

During the fateful tenth ballot, Warren Harding was sitting with Nicholas Murray Butler and Frank Lowden in one of the small rooms behind the platform of convention hall. They were alone. Suddenly a roar went up from the floor and the door was flung open by Charles B. Warren of Michigan who shouted, "Pennsylvania has voted for you, Harding, and you are nominated!" Harding rose, and with one hand in Lowden's and one in Butler's, said: "I shall need all the help that you two friends can give me." Immediately Daugherty appeared, seized him, and whisked him back to his hotel before a crowd could assemble. Later, when asked by reporters how he would describe his phenomenal success in capturing the nomination, Harding allegedly replied, "We drew to a pair of deuces, and filled."[5]

The statement was apocryphal, but the condition was true.

⌈ 2

WARREN GAMALIEL HARDING was born on November 2, 1865, in a tiny clapboard house on the edge of the small Ohio village of Blooming Grove. The Hardings had moved into the gentle-rolling, lush frontierland

5

of Ohio from Pennsylvania's Wyoming Valley some decades before. Harding's great-great-grandfather had cleared a small homestead near Blooming Grove which thereafter had been passed from father to son and finally came to Harding's father, Dr. George Tryon Harding.

Tryon, as he was familiarly called, had been a drummer in the Civil War and had married a neighborhood girl, Phoebe E. Dickerson, in 1864. Warren was the first of eight children born to the couple, two of whom died in childhood.[6] Several years after Warren's birth, his father, who was a self-educated veterinarian, began to "read medicine" and in 1873 received a degree after attending two sessions of the Homeopathic Hospital College in Cleveland. He thereafter turned his attention from animals to humans and moved his family first to the outskirts of Caledonia and later to Marion, some twenty-five miles away. In these early years his medical practice was never good; Phoebe was more in demand as a midwife than he was as a physician.

Warren Harding was reared in a strait-laced Christian home. His father was a Baptist and his mother a Methodist who later became a convert to the Seventh-Day Adventist faith. She, especially, provided the family with a fundamentalist background and devoutly read her Bible as her son's middle name suggested. Indeed, she selected the name "Gamaliel" carefully. She always hoped he would become a minister and a "teacher of God's people." She taught him the alphabet and gave him his first reading lessons from the Bible and from a copy of the *Marion County Sentinel* which was pasted on a woodbox beside the kitchen stove. Until her death she remained the most vital influence in his life. As long as she was alive Warren Harding was, to some extent, "momma's boy."[7]

According to one of his closest contemporaries, Harding was not unusual as a child. Nicknamed "Winnie" by his family and friends, he attended the village school, swam in the local creek, loved animals, played scrub baseball, and got into the normal boyhood scrapes. He was never the "leader," but always "one of the boys" who possessed a good sense of humor and who was universally liked because of his friendliness and amenability.[8]

Like most boys, Harding preferred play to work, but he worked hard "when there was money in it." At ten he made his first dollar cutting corn; at fourteen he was earning money by painting houses and barns, and helping local farmers thrash. When the Ohio Central Railroad came through

6

the area, he briefly joined a construction gang. He also served as a printer's helper in the nearby office of the *Caledonia Argus* and learned how to "stick type, feed press, make up forms, and wash rollers." Of all his work experiences, this last was the most satisfying.

In 1882 Harding graduated from Ohio Central College in nearby Iberia. The college's major educational function was to prepare students for rural school teaching. Like so many other normal schools of the era, its curriculum was meager and its level of instruction poor. Yet the exposure to arithmetic, world and American history, grammar, and some science was sufficient to meet the local criterion of being "well educated."

There were just three graduates in 1882 and no records exist to indicate whether Harding stood at the head, the middle, or the foot of his class. Other evidence, however, supports the belief that he did not take his studies too seriously. He never mentioned the excitement of the classroom but instead the joy of making new friends, debating, and editing the school paper, the *Iberian Spectator*. Founded through the joint efforts of a classmate and himself, this paper unfortunately lasted only six issues. Yet it was enough to mark the highlight of his stay at Ohio Central College.[9]

Upon graduation Harding began a short-lived teaching career at the White Schoolhouse just north of Marion. He required but a few months to determine that the life of the rural teacher was not to his liking and someone else should assume the battle against juvenile ignorance. Toward the end of the school year in 1883, he wrote his aunt, "Next Friday, one week . . . my career as pedagogue will close, and—oh, the joy! I believe my calling to be in some other sphere and will follow out the belief."[10]

Not yet eighteen, Harding dabbled for a short time in other vocational pursuits. He tried selling insurance and also toyed with the idea of reading law. Finally, he returned to the one activity that had always held a fascination for him—printing.

In 1884 Harding and two partners bought for $300 a decrepit five-column, four-page newspaper which was called the *Marion Star*. Starting with a subscription list of 700 the *Star* under Harding's direction ultimately surpassed the stronger Democratic *Mirror* in influence and forced its Republican rival, the *Marion Independent*, out of business entirely by capturing the county printing contract and by charging the *Independent*'s

7

owner, George Crawford, with being "a liar," "a lickspittle," "a moral leper," and "a disgruntled and disappointed old ass." Such vicious name calling was hardly in keeping with the amiable and genial personality that Harding normally showed to the world. But for the moment it was instrumental in giving to the *Star* a reputation for aggressiveness and by the mid-nineties assured the paper an unchallenged position in the growing and bustling community of Marion.[11]

Seven years after taking over the *Star*, Warren Harding married Florence Kling DeWolfe. Flossie, as she was called, obviously had set her cap for the young editor and pursued him vigorously. Five years older than Warren, she was plain-featured, somewhat ungraceful, and had a reputation for a sharp tongue. He, on the other hand, was strikingly handsome and was eyed longingly by the local Marion belles. That Flossie DeWolfe should land him was something of a surprise.

What Flossie lacked in beauty she compensated for in stubbornness, determination, and ambition. At nineteen she had defied her autocratic father by eloping with the flashy Henry A. (Pete) DeWolfe, the son of a prosperous neighboring Marion family, with whom she had often gone to the nearby roller-skating rink. A ne'er-do-well, Pete DeWolfe later died of alcoholism, but not before abandoning Florence with a year-old son, named Marshall, who was thereafter raised by his Kling grandparents. Amos Kling, who was vain and tyrannical and who had built a modest fortune by selling hardware supplies and real estate, absolutely forbade his daughter to marry again, especially the *Marion Star* editor. Kling did not approve of Harding, mainly because of a local rumor that the Harding line contained Negro blood. Once he and the young editor almost came to blows over the matter. After the marriage Kling renounced his daughter and for fourteen years would not permit her to cross his threshold.[12]

The couple had no need of Amos Kling or his money. They immediately moved into a house which Harding had built at 380 Mount Vernon Avenue. From the outset Florence Harding took more interest in the newspaper business than in housework, and she soon became a permanent fixture around the *Star* offices. As she later said, she went down to the office to help out temporarily but "remained fourteen years." Some Marion tongue-waggers claimed she went there to keep an eye on her handsome husband. If so, that was not all she did. She reorganized the carrier delivery system and introduced a streamlined bookkeeping arrangement. This freed Harding to concentrate on editorial matters and on advertising. He solicited advertisements himself, thus getting to know all the important businessmen in the area.

Under the Hardings' joint nurture, the *Star* prospered. Although for Florence the *Star* remained a business venture, to Warren it became his life. As reporter Mark Sullivan once commented: "The Marion *Star* was Warren Harding."[13] Never did Mrs. Harding intrude into the policy of the paper, do any reporting, or write editorials. Her contributions were confined to the office, and despite legend, she was not responsible for the paper's growing influence. She was, as her husband later said, simply a "good businesswoman." But whatever the peculiar alchemy of their joint relationship with the *Marion Star*, it paid off handsomely. Having already bought out his partners before his marriage, by 1914 Warren Harding was making between $15,000 and $20,000 annually from the paper which by now had a circulation of 10,000.[14]

As the *Star* prospered, so also expanded the importance and influence of its editor. When Harding first acquired the *Star*, Marion was a sleepy town of 4000. From the beginning he became one of Marion's chief boosters, played B-flat cornet in the marching band, and pushed every commercial, religious, and philanthropic endeavor. He joined the Elks and the Rotarians, maintained a respectable membership in the Baptist church, and at one time or other served as chairman of all the important committees of the Marion Chamber of Commerce. He also became a director of the Marion County Bank and a member of the board of directors of the Marion Lumber Company, the Telephone Company, and the Home Building and Loan.[15]

Harding's journalistic activity, his community endeavors, and his wide social acquaintance provided him with an excellent base from which to launch a political career. Marion, in turn, offered him a suitable background against which he could project his personality and ideas successfully. For him, the small midwestern town, like Marion, was the common denominator of the nation. Here conflict was harmonized; here the farmer and the businessman met on equal ground; here there was no great gulf between employer and employee; here even the differences between East and West were seemingly resolved. The small town was the healer of divisions and yet was also the primary agent of national progress. Cooperation, friendship, loyalty, and local pride were all ingredients for a splendid harmony—a harmony which to Harding was absolutely essential for both economic and political success.[16]

[3

THEODORE ROOSEVELT once remarked that he could not understand Ohio Republican politics. He was not alone. From the 1880's to World War I, Ohio politics was a tangled jumble of temporary and fluid coalitions usually controlled by bosses or strong party leaders who knew no political morality and who were motivated solely by their instinct for survival. During these years Senator Marcus A. Hanna, Senator Joseph B. Foraker, and Boss George B. Cox dominated the Republican party in the Buckeye State. When their interests coalesced, they pooled their collective majorities to achieve stunning victories. At other times they leaped at each other's throat, precipitating defeat through violent intraparty feuds.

Warren Harding became a part of this political intrigue and confusion. As a schoolboy he had shown an interest in "declaiming" and as a young man attended county caucuses and mass political meetings. His father was a Republican, and after buying the *Marion Star* Harding quickly announced its adherence to Republican doctrines. As the *Star* grew, its owner's influence in Republican party circles also increased. By 1900 Harding was the undisputed spokesman of the party in Marion County.

In 1899 Harding ran for his first elective office—the Ohio Senate—as a Foraker man, and won. In an age of wide-scale corruption he made a mark by being reasonably honest. While not a fighter against graft, he did not encourage it himself and mildly rebuked those who did. His vote was not purchasable by money even though he worked within a political framework that condoned at least limited bribery. He did not object basically to the dictum "to the victor belongs the spoils," although, again, by no stretch of contemporary standards could he have been called a spoilsman.[17] On legislative issues he generally stuck to middle ground and somehow retained the good will of both reformers and standpatters. In 1901 he was easily returned to the Senate for a second term and was elected floor leader, a post reserved only for the most loyal.

Harding's political philosophy was not yet completely formed, but several trends were emerging. On the tariff he was a protectionist, believing high duties increased workers' wages and protected the American standard of living. He was suspicious of foreign immigration, especially the "newer" immigrant, and feared that the recent influx was leading America to ruin. He distrusted labor unions although he was not violent on the subject. With regard to anarchists, his solution was simple: hang or shoot them. On the question of prohibition he vacillated. He was no "dry" himself, but he early recognized the potent political power of the dry element in Ohio. Hence, he voted on prohibition in whatever way was expedient at the moment. Like most Ohio politicians, Harding never let his personal convictions stand in the way of political survival.[18]

One facet of Harding's political philosophy was definitely formed: a firm belief that conciliation and harmony were superior political weapons to obstruction and strife. This trait made him increasingly valuable in the acrimonious environment of Ohio politics. As one contemporary said, "In the Ohio Senate, Harding proved a great harmonizer. He had the unusual gift of getting people together and inducing them to patch up differences."[19] His methods of personal contact, of convivial association, and of gentle persuasion certainly enabled him to advance in party councils beyond the level warranted by his other contributions or by his intellect.

In 1903 Harding was nominated for the post of lieutenant governor on a ticket headed by Myron T. Herrick. Harding was a sop to the Foraker forces, since Herrick was a Cleveland man and acceptable to Hanna. This coalition was successful at the polls and for the next two years Harding served as the amiable moderator of the Ohio Senate, broadening his circle of friends and enhancing his public image. However, he was blocked from higher office because Herrick wished to run again for governor in 1905, and, feeling pressure in managing his newspaper at long range, he decided to return to Marion to attend more closely to his personal affairs. He ended his stay in Columbus without remorse, leaving behind a huge reservoir of party good will.

Harding's political career had a residual effect on his position as an editor. First, he continued to play the role of a mediator in party circles; second, he retained a close contact with political trends in the state. In his *Star* editorials he continued to preach party harmony and with considerable apprehension viewed from his Marion sanctuary the changing and disruptive pattern of Ohio politics from 1906 to 1908. The old was making way for the new: Hanna and McKinley were already gone, while

Foraker and Cox were slowly losing their power. Blending prescience with reality, Harding gingerly began to lean toward the emerging Roosevelt-Taft element and in 1908 boldly left the Foraker fold to support Taft for president. Again, conviction was not the critical factor in determining his action, but political success. As he explained in one of his editorials, the anti-Taft elements would surely be "licked" and "the trend in Ohio politics is for Taft."[20] Harding did not intend to be left behind.

Taft carried Ohio for the presidency in 1908, although the state Republican ticket lost and Judson Harmon, a Democrat, became governor. Two years later, Harding, who was looking for the right moment to re-enter the political game, was induced to leave his retirement and run against Harmon as a compromise gubernatorial candidate. But Harding made a weak showing as Ohio Republicans split badly between progressives and regulars. Harding, with his earlier Foraker connections, was regarded as being too "conservative" and boss-controlled by progressives, who deserted the party in droves. The Democrats reaped the rewards. Harmon's plurality was over 100,000 and the Democrats captured a majority of the legislature and sixteen of twenty-one congressmen.[21]

Discouraging as it was, the 1910 gubernatorial race had one important result. It ingratiated Harding with William Howard Taft. Seeking someone to place his name in nomination at the Republican National Convention in 1912, Taft turned to Harding because he was a respected orator and because he had proved his loyalty. Harding later said, "I think I was more honored by that request than I was in my own nomination [in 1920]. . . ."[22] Although he hoped to electrify the convention with his speech, Harding's effort for Taft was met with sullen disapproval by the supporters of Theodore Roosevelt. Angered by the rude audience which at times hissed and booed him, Harding momentarily lost his penchant for amiability and compromise, bitterly attacking the Roosevelt faction and condemning the Rough Rider as "utterly without conscience . . . the greatest faker of all times." On the other hand, Harding described Taft as the "greatest progressive of the age."[23] Roosevelt's daughter, Alice Longworth, later described this speech as "run-of-the-mill stuff," but neither she nor other Roosevelt supporters ever really forgave him.

Despite the continuing split in party ranks, Harding returned to Ohio from the 1912 national convention a much bigger political figure than when he left. For the first time he had faced a national audience and his performance had shown him to be reliable. He had called for party loyalty in the face of insurrection, and in Ohio politics such action was worthy of reward. Harding quickly became the favorite of many regular elements to be the party's candidate for the United States Senate in 1914.

No sooner had incumbent Republican Senator Theodore E. Burton announced in early 1914 that he did not wish to run for reelection than a mad scramble began for his post. Joseph Foraker immediately came out of retirement and proclaimed his intention to regain this position which he had held twice before. Repelled by Foraker's unsavory past, many Republicans anxiously sought a strong opponent to face him in the primaries and they found such a person in the Marion editor. Ironically, this former Foraker supporter now became the rallying point for all anti-Foraker sentiment ranging from Dan Hanna, son of Mark Hanna and long-time Foraker foe, to Harry Daugherty, an erstwhile Foraker lieutenant who saw an upset in the making. Both men encouraged Harding to run as did Burton, who much preferred Harding to Foraker as his successor.[24]

On August 11, 1914, Ohio held its first statewide direct primary in history. The Democrats endorsed James M. Cox for governor and Attorney General Timothy S. Hogan for senator. The Progressives, still nursing wounds from 1912 and refusing to rejoin the GOP, named James R. Garfield for governor and Arthur L. Garford for senator. The Republicans chose Frank B. Willis as their candidate for governor while Warren Harding defeated Foraker in the latter's bid for the Senate nomination. This victory brought joy to anti-Foraker circles, the Hanna-controlled *Cleveland Leader* stating: "[Harding] will help draw back to the Republican ranks the few progressives who have not yet decided to return, and he will aid in keeping the Republican party of this state always safely and soundly progressive. . . . "[25] Obviously Harding's ability to effect compromise was still valuable and it played no small role in his primary victory.

Both the Democrats and the Progressives ran a poor campaign in 1914, and in the November election the Republicans won handily, capturing all the state offices and control of both houses of the legislature. Harding defeated both Garford and Hogan easily in a dirty campaign which centered around Hogan's Roman Catholicism and Irish background. While Harding personally did not stoop to such tactics, he unquestionably bene-

13

fited from them and his 100,000-vote majority was a stunning eyeopener for a state which under the Seventeenth Amendment was popularly electing senators for the first time. It proved Harding was a strong vote-getter and possessed a broad popular appeal.

Harding found himself United States senator in 1914 because of his artful playing of the game of compromise politics. He had not been too forward or "pushy." He had never assaulted any group unless it was already on its way to oblivion. He had succeeded in acquiring a minimum number of enemies. He had judged changing political conditions in Ohio extremely well. He had concentrated on the theme of party harmony and loyalty. And he had utilized to the maximum his major assets—a golden voice, an amiable personality, and an imposing physical appearance. To be sure, at critical junctures he had received important help and advice—from Burton, Willis, Daugherty, and others. But he was master of his own fate and up to 1914, contrary to the opinion of some critics, had rather skillfully combined luck with prescience and opportunity to advance his political career.

Nineteen hundred and fifteen was not a propitious year to enter the United States Senate. The major legislative battles over Wilson's New Freedom program had already been fought and war fears were beginning to transcend normal partisan activities. During the war period, 1917–18, there was little opportunity for a junior senator to make much of a reputation. Not until the League question emerged in 1919 was there an issue capable of evoking sustained partisan debate or providing a test of senatorial leadership.

What prominence Harding acquired before 1919 he secured within the fold of the party rather than on the floor of the Senate. In 1916 he was selected to deliver the Republican National Convention's keynote address and then was elected permanent chairman. As a member of the Ohio delegation he voted on the first ballot for a favorite son, former Senator Burton, but thereafter he supported the ultimate nominee, Charles Evans Hughes. Harding's keynote speech was too long and metropolitan newspapers derided it. Still it was good enough to be remembered favorably by some delegates four years later when he was a candidate himself. What was especially memorable about the speech was his usual call for unity, for conciliation, and for moderation. It struck just the proper chord for a party still suffering from the Bull Moose split of 1912.[26]

14

In the Senate, Harding passed the years 1915–19 unspectacularly. While he was not the nonentity which some observers later called him, he certainly was not obtrusive nor did he appear to be presidential timber. He carried his committee load, shunned acrimonious debate, made an occasional formal speech, and enjoyed immensely the prestige of being a senator. In general, he followed the Old Guard, or popular opinion if that proved more beneficial. He trimmed where necessary and never openly challenged the party. His legislative record was mediocre, but satisfactory to his Ohio constituents. He introduced 134 bills of which 122 were local in nature. None of the remaining 12 was of national importance. His attendance record was poor. He missed 43 percent of all quorum or roll calls; there were only eighteen senators who missed more.[27]

As in the Ohio Senate, Harding was most successful in making himself agreeable to party leaders and to his colleagues. His popularity extended to both sides of the aisle. Among his close friends were powerful Democratic senators, such as Oscar W. Underwood, and when he infrequently engaged them in debate, he included the requisite number of compliments. Along with Mrs. Harding, he occupied a spot in Washington society's "four hundred," a position no doubt enhanced by his close relationship with Edward B. and Evalyn Walsh McLean, the multimillionaire owners of the *Washington Post* and the Hope Diamond, whom he first met at a poker party at Nicholas Longworth's house. Harding's own Washington home was a mecca for weekend entertaining and his poker table frequently attracted such Senate colleagues as Albert B. Fall, Frederick Hale, and Joseph S. Frelinghuysen.

Many critics have concluded that Harding as a senator was simply a stooge of the Old Guard element headed by Boies Penrose—that he had no mind of his own and was incapable of independent judgment. This is an oversimplification of the truth. Harding usually found himself on the side of the Old Guard, but it was because of his own inclinations and not as a result of manipulation. He was, to be sure, probusiness. He voted for returning the railroads to their private owners after the war, pushed for high tariffs, was dubious about government subsidies to agriculture, and opposed excess-profits taxes and high surtax rates. But he was too much the product of the small town to be a true spokesman for big business or for Wall Street.[28] On labor he was ambivalent. His record in three Congresses showed ten votes unfavorable to labor and seven favorable.

On the question of congressional authority vis-à-vis the executive, he was also inconsistent. As a freshman senator he had defended the principle of legislative supremacy; but then during the war he diverged from the Old Guard position and spoke in favor of broad presidential powers. Moreover, unlike many Old Guard members, he was not swept off his feet by the Red Scare which followed the war. Although this phenomenon nudged him into a more conservative position, he did not share the belief that the country was about to succumb to radicalism or that a stringent curtailment of civil liberties was necessary to eliminate the menace. True, he continued to attack radical philosophies, as he always had done, but he was no superpatriot and refused to join the witch-hunting.[29]

Nor was Harding a fervent isolationist, as were many in the Old Guard. Although his world view was admittedly a naive, "be-good-to-your-neighbor" variety, he did not believe that America could live by itself alone and his strong support of intervention in World War I was his testimony to that belief. Moreover, his senatorial committee assignments on the Philippines, on the territories, on naval affairs, and on the Pacific Islands gave him some appreciation of America's worldwide position.

On two important issues Harding looked to the Old Guard for no guidance whatsoever. However, in neither case did he vote his real convictions. He supported woman suffrage even though he was not personally committed to it. He simply swam with public opinion. On prohibition he had a momentary crisis of conscience, but this did not deter him from finally voting on the basis of sheer expediency. In a curious sort of way, his prohibition position was logical. In one Senate speech he admitted that he was "not a prohibitionist . . . and never pretended to be. . . . I do not approach this question from a moral viewpoint, because I am unable to see it as a great moral question." But, he continued, he was tired of the issue's being a political football and therefore would support the Eighteenth Amendment in order to refer the question "to the people who must make the ultimate decision."[30] While later historians were quick to label this stand as equivocation and evasion of responsibility, it was shrewd politics.

By the early spring of 1919 many Republican politicians began to concentrate on the League question as the best means of embarrassing the Wilson administration. Harding was one of them, but he was never a leader in the anti-League movement. By signing Lodge's "round robin" against

16

the League in March 1919, he found himself among strange partners. William E. Borah and old progressives such as Hiram Johnson and Robert M. LaFollette joined with anti-League elements of the Old Guard to attack the Versailles Treaty but retained contempt for them otherwise. This mixture was explosive and remained stable only so long as the chief concern was the League fight.

Harding has usually been portrayed as simply being "towed along" on the League issue by the stronger Republican senators. When in May 1919 he finally decided to oppose the League, the primary reason was not pressure from Lodge or the Old Guard. It was a calculated decision of political expediency. As he explained it to his close friend F. E. Scobey, "My own judgement is that in the long run this country will be very hostile to this venture into the unknown."[31] During the course of the subsequent debates, he mentioned many other reasons for his objection to the League. None, however, was more basic than the simple fact that he believed his Ohio constituents were against it.

As a member of the powerful Foreign Relations Committee, Harding was privy to all discussions regarding the League and was also one of the group that called on the White House in mid-August 1919 to air their differences with Woodrow Wilson. At that confrontation, Harding asked Wilson if the implementation of Article X involved a legal commitment on the part of League members or only a moral one. If merely moral, as some pro-Leaguers were saying, queried Harding, then was not the whole peace-keeping structure reduced to nothing? It was a shrewd question and Wilson never really answered it, averring only that each nation would have to search its own conscience on the matter and act accordingly. Harding returned to this point somewhat later in the White House conversation and asked again how the peace of the world could be maintained if the obligation under Article X was merely moral. Wilson denied that whether it was moral or not the United States was in any danger of submitting its interests "to the prejudices or necessities of the nations of the Old World."[32]

Harding's exposure to Wilson in this conference confirmed him in his opposition to the League. If Wilson thought Harding "dull," as he later remarked to his cabinet, Harding thought Wilson obtuse. In a major speech before the Senate on September 11, 1919, the Ohioan gave expression to his doubts about the League and concentrated his fire on the ambiguity of Article X. Declaring himself in favor of the Lodge reservations, he said they were necessary in order "to protect America first."[33]

Yet political expediency was still his primary touchstone. Two days after his Senate speech he wrote his friend Charles E. Hard, "If my correspondence is any index to the sentiment of the country, I think there has been an overwhelming change in the past sixty days and the popular sentiment is strongly against the League covenant in the form presented."[34] From this fact he deduced that his position was "right," and held to his reservationist convictions. At the same time he renounced an irreconcilable stand. He was never too comfortable with Borah and Johnson and retained vague and somewhat pious hopes for some kind of international cooperation.

In the final voting Harding arrayed himself beside Lodge and other reservationists. But he did not approve of the badgering tactics which some Republicans employed against Wilson in the summer and fall of 1919 or the "truth squads" that they sent out to harass him on his western trip.[35] Secretly he rather admired Wilson's courage and felt genuinely sorry when a stroke cut him down. This did not prevent him, however, from joining the diverse crowd—Borah, Brandegee, Frelinghuysen, Lodge, Medill McCormick, James A. Reed, and others—that gathered at Nicholas Longworth's house after the anti-League vote on November 19, 1919, to eat scrambled eggs and celebrate their victory. Mrs. Harding cooked the eggs.[36]

[4

HARRY MICAJAH DAUGHERTY was born on January 26, 1860, in Washington Court House, Ohio, a county seat thirty-five miles southwest of Columbus. When he was but four years old, severe attacks of diphtheria killed his father and left him with physical weaknesses that plagued him the rest of his life. He graduated from the local high school, obtained a law degree from the University of Michigan, and then returned to Washington Court House to practice. As he often said, "Law and politics, you know, go hand in hand" and soon he was both an important lawyer and an influential Republican politician in the area. Meanwhile, his brother Mal became a local banker and by the early 1890's the two Daughertys were on their way to becoming the town's leading citizens.

First elected to the state legislature in 1889 as a Foraker man, Daugherty served two terms and then opened a law office in Columbus in order to remain near the scene of political activity. He was shrewd and aggressive. He did not have a scholar's mind and cared little for poring over legal briefs or unearthing musty precedents. He liked the world of action, and wherever resourcefulness and intrigue counted Daugherty was at his best.[37]

When not serving in the legislature or running for office, Daugherty engaged in lobbying. He always knew what wire to pull and assiduously maintained the widest possible contacts. He was careful to stay inside the law, yet was remarkably successful in securing political advantages for his clients. In Columbus political circles his reputation was two-sided. He was regarded with some contempt for engaging in ruthless and rather unsavory activities, but he was begrudgingly admired for his skill in delivering votes.

Daugherty's insight into men was something of an art. Instinctively he knew just when to cajole, when to bluster, when to seize the initiative, when to retreat. He could, when necessary, take on the coloration of his object, like a chameleon. Daugherty stated that he never met a man who, from his point of view, was unfathomable.[38]

From their first meeting, Daugherty claimed to "know" Warren Harding. As he later remembered it, the two met in the backyard of a small hotel in Richwood, Ohio, around the turn of the century. Both were attending a Republican campaign rally. They were on their way to use the outdoor privy when they ran into one another, and chatted briefly as they stopped to employ the services of a shoeshine boy who had stationed himself there to catch the traffic. As the handsome Marion editor turned to leave and flicked a tip to the bootblack, the Columbus lawyer thought to himself, "What a President he'd make!"[39]

Myth has it that from that moment on Daugherty was fired by the dream of making Harding president.[40] If so, their relationship was a bit curious before 1919. Contact between them was only casual and while a state senator Harding was important to lobbyist Daugherty as a vote rather than as a potential presidential aspirant. Indeed, it is clear that from the beginning of their relationship Daugherty always needed Harding more than Harding needed Daugherty. It was Daugherty who did the wooing and not the other way around. Even after Daugherty rose through

19

his legislative and lobbying activities to be chairman of the Republican party in the Ohio legislature and then supported Harding in the senatorial campaign of 1914, Harding still did not feel beholden to him in any significant way.

Between 1914 and 1919 the relationship between the two men deepened, although not without difficulty. In 1918, for example, Harding almost broke off with Daugherty altogether. Daugherty's penchant for intrigue and his intense combativeness antagonized the senator. To Charles Hard, Harding wrote, "[Daugherty] is a brilliant and resourceful man but his political hatreds have come to a point where they bias his judgment and I do not think him always a trustworthy adviser." A week later, on December 20, 1918, he wrote to Daugherty, "The trouble with you, my dear Daugherty, in your political relations with me, is that you appraise my political sense so far below par that you have no confidence in me or my judgment. Pray do not think because I can and do listen in politeness to much that is said to me, that I am always being 'strung.' I cannot and will not suspect everyone of wanting to use me."[41]

Strained relations might have increased between the two men had it not been for two important circumstances. First, Daugherty came to the realization that he, personally, had no political future in Ohio. While he had risen to be a Republican national committeeman, his defeat for the United States Senate by Myron Herrick in the Republican primary in 1916 had sealed his political fate. Second, Theodore Roosevelt died in January 1919, and with his death the entire Ohio political picture changed.

It had been assumed that the Rough Rider would declare for the presidential nomination in 1920 and Ohio probably would support him. This had caused regular Republicans in the state to treat their progressive brethren with some deference and to deemphasize the importance of the regular state organization. With Roosevelt's death this tack was no longer necessary and Daugherty saw an opportunity to establish an immediate position of strength for the regular faction by advancing Senator Warren Harding as a favorite son. His main problem was to convince Harding to run.

Daugherty was neither the first to think of Harding in this connection nor alone in his efforts to make him a candidate. Indeed, by the time Daugherty got the idea of seriously promoting Harding for the presidency, others had already laid the groundwork. Even before Roosevelt's death,

20

a few of Harding's close friends had indicated a reluctance to support Roosevelt and had prodded Harding from the sidelines. Harding, in turn, was in a difficult situation. While displaying no specific presidential aspirations himself, he was concerned about his reelection to the Senate in 1920 and viewed the Roosevelt candidacy as weakening his own hold on the party in Ohio. His intemperate remarks about Teddy in 1912 now returned to haunt him.

Two early Harding boosters were Charles Hard and George B. Christian, Jr. Owner of the *Portsmouth Daily Blade*, Hard was a long-time Harding friend and secretary of the pro-Harding Republican State Advisory Committee. Christian was Harding's next-door neighbor in Marion whom he had taken to Washington as his private secretary after his election to the Senate. Neither of these men needed the death of Roosevelt to spark their interest in Harding as a presidential candidate. Throughout 1918 both urged him to use his influence to block the Roosevelt movement in Ohio. Rather suggestively, Hard wrote him in August 1918, "If Ohio intends to have a candidate for the Presidency in 1920, it hardly [seems] necessary to build up . . . Roosevelt."[42] Of course, following Roosevelt's death Hard increased his pressure on Harding while Christian, close to Harding in Washington, gave Hard substantial aid.[43]

Hard and Christian were greatly helped by an influential voice from Texas—that of F. E. Scobey. Ed Scobey was one of Harding's oldest political friends. A former Miami County sheriff, Scobey had been clerk of the Ohio Senate when Harding was a freshman senator. Even after Scobey moved to Texas for his health, their relationship had remained close. Their correspondence was frequent and intimate, filled with references to poker parties and occasional off-color jokes. Some suspicious-minded readers might find a female-chasing escapade or two hidden between the lines, but the jocularity was apparently all in fun because there was evidence that they gave their wives these letters to read.[44]

In the fall of 1918 Scobey mentioned to Harding in a half-joking, half-serious manner that he ought to run for the presidency despite Roosevelt's intentions. Then on November 27, Scobey bluntly wrote that although Roosevelt would be a formidable opponent, "I believe you have a good chance to secure that nomination, provided you do certain things."[45] After Roosevelt's death, the Texan hammered away at Harding and by the early summer of 1919 became insistent that Harding throw

21

his hat in the ring. As Scobey read the signs, there were two compelling reasons for Harding to do so: (1) the country needed a "good conservative" to save it from the excesses of Wilsonism and (2) only by running could Harding hope to keep control of the local situation in Ohio and prevent a takeover by the "non-regular" Republican crowd.

There was still another voice which during this early period called upon Harding to declare himself—E. Mont Reily's. Reily was somewhat of an enigma. He and Harding were not friends. Indeed, they had never met. Reily was a young Kansas City newspaperman who had been dabbling in local Missouri politics for several years. Currently he was a member of the Republican State Committee. Suffering from delusions of grandeur, Reily thought of himself as a "king-maker" but until January 1919 had never found a king to make. Suddenly, with the death of Roosevelt, he decided to move into the "big game," and seized upon Harding as a presidential possibility. In later years, one of Reily's most cherished distinctions was his self-acclaimed title of the "original Harding man." [46]

A political opportunist, Reily boosted Harding in order to boost himself. He was persistent, and he was shrewd. On January 20, 1919, he issued a circular letter to "My Fellow Republicans" in which he analyzed why Warren G. Harding of Ohio was the logical Republican nominee: (1) Harding was only fifty-three, thus young and in his prime; (2) Governor Cox of Ohio would probably be the Democratic candidate and this "means the loss of Ohio if we fail to nominate Senator Harding"; (3) the senator was "not too far West to upset the traditions of the effete East, neither is he too far East to be unsatisfactory to the sturdy West"; (4) Harding came from a state which was "the mother of Republican presidents"; (5) he could "make a greater campaign than even McKinley could [because] he is a more attractive orator"; (6) he "remained 'regular' and supported Taft" in 1912; (7) and he believed "in normal things, normal thinking and normal legislation." Concluded Reily, "Our motto for 1920 should be, 'Harding and Back to Normal.' "[47]

Throughout 1919 Harding's position on his availability was anomalous. To these numerous friends he presented a reluctant stance, but there was little question that he was flattered. Most observers took his negative responses at face value and later asserted that he was forced into the presidency. One recent writer has claimed that his unwillingness to run was actually a sham and masked a carefully calculated and ambitious

22

plan to gain the top prize.[48] Either makes a good story, but neither is accurate for neither makes allowances for the intricate psychology of a man who wanted to run and yet did not want to run. There was no calculated plan on Harding's part other than a willingness to surrender his destiny to the "fates." That way he did not have to make any decision. Events would make one for him. All he had to do was remain pliable and not close any doors.

Harding's first negative responses were more direct than his later ones and his reluctance to run shifted from a moderately firm "No" to a mild "No" by the fall of 1919. Earlier in the year he had written to Reily that he had "no desire in the world" to be a candidate, and to Scobey's first entreaties he had replied that he would be "unhappy every hour" if he entered the race.[49] However, his friends detected a growing receptivity on his part by September—a receptivity which was only lightly masked in his later replies. On October 21, 1919, Harding wrote to Hard, "I am confident that I shall not be persuaded to change my mind . . . but I shall not act hastily because I do want to do that which seems to suggest the greatest possible good for the party in Ohio." Five days later he wrote Scobey, "I have not decided definitely on what course to pursue. . . ."[50]

Actually, it was not Harding who represented the greatest obstacle to his candidacy, but his wife. As he was swept along by the enthusiasm of his friends, Mrs. Harding sought to stem the tide. Commonly referred to by her husband and her closest friends as the "Duchess" (and not always endearingly), Florence Harding was a formidable opponent. Belligerent and outspoken in her opposition, she threatened to undo the persuasive work of Daugherty, Reily, Scobey, Hard, Christian, and others. While she was ambitious for her husband, at the moment that ambition did not extend to the presidency. Rather she was protective of Harding's position in the Senate and wished nothing to interfere with his life there.

Florence and Warren Harding undoubtedly had a number of heated discussions over his availability as a presidential candidate. Both Hard and Daugherty implied as much. Until the late fall of 1919, she remained absolutely opposed to his candidacy and once verbally attacked Hard for pressing the issue. "With tears in her eyes and in her voice," claimed Hard, she urged him to leave her husband alone.[51] In reply to those who later claimed that she pushed Harding into the presidency, Daugherty flatly stated: "She never once begged her husband to enter the race. She op-

23

posed it from the beginning. . . . She feared the tragic struggle in which he was entering with a dread that was pathetic."[52]

The most critical factor in Harding's final decision was not the appeals of his friends or the fears of his wife, but the local political situation in Ohio. Contrary to earlier expectations, Roosevelt's death did not clear the political air in the state nor did it reduce intraparty friction. Instead, a bitter struggle ensued for control of Ohio's Republican machinery. Harding found himself caught in the middle between Roosevelt progressives, the Cincinnati crowd led by Rudolph (Rud) Hynicka and Colonel William C. Procter, and Harry Daugherty's burgeoning desire to be Ohio's undisputed political boss. In addition, there was a continuing struggle between the wets and the drys, as well as a policy split within the party on whether primary control should rest with the State Advisory Committee (run by pro-Harding forces), or the State Central Committee (packed with anti-Harding men). Obviously the outcome was of momentous importance to Harding if he wished reelection to the Senate let alone nomination for the presidency.

Conversely, to all these various groups Harding's intentions were important. In October 1919, Walter F. Brown, leader of the progressives, tried to smoke out Harding on his presidential ambitions but failed. In November, Colonel Procter, tired of waiting on Harding to declare himself, announced that his faction was for General Wood and urged Brown to enter the fight on Wood's side. This produced panic among upstate Ohio politicians and anti-progressives who now feared that a coalition of Cincinnati and progressive forces might sweep the state and seize the party machinery. Daugherty, whose political neck was directly endangered by these maneuverings, redoubled his efforts to induce Harding to run and pointed out to him the disastrous ramifications of this turn of events. Harding realized that he was in a bind. To his old friend Malcolm Jennings he declared, "It is unthinkable that Walter Brown and his crew should be allowed to seize the helm and undertake to pilot the Republican party in our State."[53] To declare for the presidency seemed to be the only sure way to prevent this seizure and at the same time protect his position in the Senate. As Harding wrote Scobey, "The only thing disagreeable about it is that I despise being forced into the position of being a presidential aspirant."[54]

As Harding edged toward a formal announcement, friends such as

Scobey rejoiced. They were convinced that it was the proper move. Scobey wrote that not only did it mean saving "your Ohio situation," but in the long run "you will have a better chance of winning this nomination than any of the rest."[55] Still Harding moved slowly. He left few stones unturned in protecting his Ohio base. Writing to political contacts throughout the state, he satisfied himself that the reception of his candidacy would be favorable. Before formally announcing, he even got in touch with Walter Brown and asked whether he could count on Brown's support in the interests of "party harmony." Brown, who, unknown to Harding, had already told Procter that he would not help Wood's cause, indicated he would do what he could.[56]

On December 17, 1919, Harding formally announced his intention to run. The day before, he wrote Scobey, "You will have read by this time that I have decided to take the plunge and play the big game. You know how reluctant I was to take this step, but it looked like I needed to do so to preserve my political life and influence in Ohio."[57] To another friend he wrote on that same day, "I have always been quite sincere in insisting that I should prefer to remain in the Senate than to be the recipient of the higher honor. However, there were political developments which necessitated my entering the contest. . . ."[58]

Daugherty later asserted that he alone was responsible for getting Harding into the race. " 'I found him,' said Daugherty, 'sunning himself, like a turtle on a log, and I pushed him into the water,' "[59] Clearly, Daugherty exaggerated and clearly the Ohio senator needed no other prodding than the force of circumstances. There was no deep-seated hidden motivation in his final decision, nor was it primarily the result of irresistible pressure by Daugherty or others. It was mainly a matter of political survival. In Ohio politics that was motive enough.

[5

"THE only thing I really worry about is that I might be nominated and elected. That's an awful thing to contemplate."[60] These were Harding's words to Scobey as the year 1919 faded into the fateful presidential year of 1920.

If Harding was "really worried" his close friends did not add to his peace of mind. Whatever Harding's own ambitions were, his supporters

25

were in the fight to win and brought to the battle great enthusiasm and dedication. This was especially true of Harry Daugherty. Even before Harding's formal announcement, Daugherty was busy laying plans. In early November 1919, he wrote to Christian, "Now I think we should without Harding knowing it canvass and keep in touch with the big field."[61] Thus, from the beginning, Daugherty assumed responsibility for the direction of the Harding candidacy. The Ohio lawyer stepped boldly to the front as coordinator of *all* pro-Harding activities. This caused a flurry among Harding supporters. They were skeptical of Daugherty's qualifications. Ed Scobey was not at all convinced that Daugherty was the man for the job, and Malcolm Jennings openly and bitterly disliked him. Charles Hard also had his doubts, which he had earlier expressed to Harding: "[Harry] always 'busts up' anything he is in because he plays it too hard and is too combative. That is the Irish in him."[62]

Daugherty was aware that he might encounter criticism and quickly took steps to disarm it. In seeking the managerial role he wisely made assets out of his alleged weaknesses. To Harding, he argued: "I am far more comfortable as to your ability to cope with great public questions and public appearances, positions and utterances, than I am for you to deal with those who are engaged in intrigue. I will take care of the latter and together we will make a fair combination in this great enterprise."[63] George Christian, meanwhile, came to Daugherty's defense by telling Scobey, "I do not know what you think of Daugherty. I know Jennings dislikes him very much, but Harry is loyal, very alert, does his sleeping at nights, and there is no double-geared political trickster in Ohio or any other state who can put anything over on him."[64]

The opinion that really counted was Harding's and he did not equivocate. He let it be known that despite the opposition, Daugherty was his choice. He wrote to Scobey, "[Daugherty] is vastly much the smartest politician in the bunch and the only one with vision and acquaintance to carry on a nation-wide campaign. More than that," added Harding, "he is the only big fellow in Ohio who doesn't find his system more or less tinctured with jealousy of me."[65] This latter asset alone was enough to commend him.

Daugherty threw himself into the campaign. After January 1 he set up the main "Harding for President" headquarters in Washington, D.C., with his close confidant and general factotum, Jesse (Jess) W. Smith, in

26

charge. On the first letterhead appeared two slogans: "Think of America First" and "Harding and Back to Normal." Daugherty divided his time between the capital and New York, Chicago, Columbus, and Marion. He assumed the responsibility of soliciting money and of writing letters, inviting support for Harding from all sources. Already prone to hypertension and nervous disorders, Daugherty pushed himself to the limit. During the hectic months of January to June 1920, he would often take to his bed, only to hurry back up and hold the Harding preconvention operation together. Even severe family illness in the spring of 1920 did not swerve him from his course. Sick with worry over his wife and daughter, both of whom were at one point near death, he spared neither himself nor those around him. As he wrote to Scobey, "Work; write letters; drive." [66]

Daugherty had some dedicated help. Three weeks after Harding's announcement E. Mont Reily opened a "Harding for President" headquarters in Missouri. Thereafter he traveled throughout the state singing Harding's praises, buttonholing prospective contributors and supporters, and by clever manipulation preventing an early slide to Wood. In Texas, Ed Scobey sought to unite a badly splintered Republican state organization around Harding's candidacy. In Washington, George Christian borrowed time from his job as secretary to the senator to write letters to his friends urging them to keep Harding's interests uppermost in their minds. In Ohio, a triumvirate labored to hold the state in line—Newton H. Fairbanks, Charles Hard, and Alfred W. (Hoke) Donithen. As chairman of the Republican State Central Committee, Fairbanks immediately declared for Harding and worked diligently to swing the committee's anti-Harding members into the senator's column. Hard, secretary of the Republican State Advisory Committee, began a publicity campaign, circulating Harding's various speeches with a covering letter stating that Ohio had secured the presidency for Hayes in the 1870's, Garfield in the 1880's, McKinley in the 1890's, Taft in the next decade, and was "now due to repeat." Hoke Donithen, a Marion attorney and civic leader, kept Harding's home base in central Ohio inviolable and maintained tight control of the Marion County political machine.

During these early months of 1920 no one worked harder for Harding than he did for himself. Daugherty later took too much personal credit when he labeled the Harding operation as "a one-man [Daugherty] man-

27

aged campaign," or when he stated that "Harding did not know much about what I was doing."[67] Not only did Harding know what Daugherty was doing, but Daugherty was often ignorant of what Harding was accomplishing for himself. The senator kept up a torrent of correspondence with old friends, especially newspapermen, in various states. He personally replied to every offer of support and boldly, but nonetheless humbly, solicited help from every source. A typical Harding letter would begin, "The fates . . . have drawn me into the Presidential race" and would conclude by requesting the recipient "to say the word here and there which would lead to a favorable consideration of my ambitions."[68]

The major weakness of the Harding preconvention campaign was not a lack of worker dedication but the emptiness of the campaigners' pockets. Harding had no angel, as Wood had in Colonel Procter, or personal fortune, as Lowden possessed in his wife's Pullman money. The entire Harding operation was financed on a shoestring through voluntary contributions. At one point Harding's brother, George ("Deac") T. Harding III, made $500 available to keep the campaign rolling. The biggest contributor was Carmi Thompson, a northern Ohio political boss and millionaire, who financed a publicity man for Harding in late January 1920 and who ultimately spent $13,950 in one way or another. No other contributor came close to that figure. L. H. Brush, who later bought the *Marion Star* from Harding, gave $800. Ed Scobey put up $500. Hoke Donithen enticed Harvey S. Firestone to contribute $1000. But Daugherty's attempt to secure a contribution from oilman Harry F. Sinclair was unsuccessful. Sinclair believed that Harding "did not stand a Chinaman's chance" and supported Wood throughout the campaign.[69]

This lack of funds became critical in view of Wood's challenge to Harding in Ohio. The Wood forces, led by Procter and relying on the soap king's millions, were not prepared to surrender Ohio to Harding without a struggle. Besides, they did not take the Harding candidacy seriously, believing that his primary purpose was simply to assure his reelection to the Senate. As a result, Procter in mid-January offered Harding a deal whereby the Wood forces would support him for reelection to the Senate if, after a courtesy first-ballot favorite-son vote, he would throw the Ohio delegation to Wood.

With this offer, a crucial point in Harding's candidacy was reached. What, up to this moment, had been a strategy for political survival in

28

Ohio was now transformed into a drive for national political power. Ambition, pride, the constant prodding of his friends, the excitement of a great gamble—all these, and perhaps many other hidden motives, caused Harding to reject the Procter offer. On January 19, 1920, the senator, somewhat recklessly, challenged Wood to settle the state's choice at the April primaries. "I will not be a mere favorite son," said Harding. To Malcolm Jennings, the senator wrote that he had "decided to take the bull by the horns" in order to rid himself completely of the charge that he was not a serious candidate. He knew the dangers of an election contest with Wood but fatalistically declared, "I am quite content to abide loyally by the result. In simple truth, if the Republicans of Ohio do not cordially wish me to be a candidate, I want to have nothing to do with the matter." [70]

At Daugherty's suggestion, Harding also entered the Indiana primary and in the late winter and early spring made a few speaking tours outside Ohio in Texas, Missouri, Kansas, and Colorado. Again the purpose was to underscore the seriousness of his candidacy. But Harding was careful not to spread himself too thin. Traveling too far afield might arouse the ire of other favorite sons—and he did not have the money. Besides, the Ohio primary was *the* great test for him and he knew it.

Wood realized that a defeat for Harding in Ohio would eliminate him from the race. Therefore Wood poured money into the state. This unnerved Harding who watched helplessly as Procter directed the golden flood. Indeed, near-panic gripped the Harding forces as rumors circulated of "deals" and "double-crosses." Robert F. Wolfe, owner of the *Columbus Dispatch* and bitterly anti-Daugherty, announced for Wood; the Negro vote was said to support Wood; the veteran vote supposedly belonged to Wood; even the union vote was declared to be "in the bag" for the general.

On election day neither side won. Wood did not succeed in taking the state from Harding; Harding, in turn, could not prevent Wood from capturing nine of the state's forty-eight delegates. The greatest blow to the Harding cause was Daugherty's failure to be elected as one of the four delegates-at-large. In Indiana the election result was even more discouraging. Harding carried only two of fifty-six counties and ran far behind the other major contenders, Wood, Johnson, and Lowden. Neither

29

of Indiana's two senators—Harry New and James E. Watson—supported their Ohio colleague. They voted for Wood.[71]

In the post-mortems Harding was declared dead. The *New York Times* solemnly announced: "Harding is eliminated. Even if his name is presented to the convention . . . everyone will know that he is an impossible candidate. . . ."[72] Reportedly, certain Republican bosses who earlier had been favorably inclined toward Harding's candidacy grew cool after the Ohio primary and quietly switched their support to Lowden. Political pundits, such as David Lawrence, who before the April election had spoken of Harding as a "real presidential possibility," now dropped his name from the list. Even the Republican party chairman, Will Hays, who up to this time had engaged in a growing correspondence with Harding, suddenly broke off his letter writing.[73]

But the corpse quickly revived. Although disheartened, both Harding and his followers believed that they had won a victory of a sort. Wood had hurt himself by challenging a favorite son on his own home ground. This reeked of overweening ambition and political treachery. Moreover, voter reaction to Wood had shown that the use of money to buy an election was more widely resented than admired. After all, the capture of only nine delegates in view of the lavish expenditure of talent and treasure represented an uneconomical political "success." Therefore, Scobey and other Harding leaders could console themselves about "the magnificent fight" in Ohio, and Harding could assert that on the whole he was "pretty well satisfied with the result in our State."[74]

Ohio was only one of many places where Wood campaign money flowed so freely that much bitterness ensued. Hiram Johnson's chief lieutenant, Senator Borah, angered by the money being spent by the Wood forces against his candidate in the West, secured a Senate resolution on May 20, 1920, which directed the Committee on Privileges and Elections to inquire into *all* campaign expenditures. Chairmaned by Senator William S. Kenyon, this committee uncovered not only huge outlays by the Wood forces but also monetary irregularities in the Lowden operation. Between charges that the Lowden group was bribing individual delegates and countercharges that the Wood element was buying the whole nomination, Wood and Lowden supporters developed such an animosity for each other that it was obvious that theirs was a fight to the death. Johnson, meanwhile, was splashed with some of the spillover hatred since it was his manager who had opened up the Pandora's Box of campaign financing in the first place. Harding, on the other hand, escaped unscathed, especially since his campaign expenses were the lowest of all the major candidates—a mere $113,109 to Wood's $1,773,303.[75]

The political situation just before the opening of the Republican convention in June was confusing. While Lowden and Wood were the top contenders they were so evenly matched that many observers doubted whether either of them could secure the nomination. Of the two, Wood was more popular with the public and had the most delegates. Claiming to be Teddy Roosevelt's legitimate successor, he had attempted to unite all progressive elements behind him and had stumped the entire country for support. Campaigning in his uniform and speaking on the Red menace and military preparedness, he aroused some enthusiasm. But he also betrayed an appalling lack of knowledge about social and economic problems. Indeed, as a "liberal" he was ludicrous and on many matters had "no philosophy but the soldier's one of force." [76]

While not the most popular, Lowden was basically the strongest candidate. He had the support of the regular organization and possessed a distinguished record as governor of Illinois. Born in a log cabin, yet possessing a fortune through his marriage to a Pullman heiress, Lowden appealed to conservative northern business interests. But Lowden was dour, undramatic, and not a genial candidate. Furthermore, his primary delegate strength was in Illinois, Iowa, and certain areas of the South. This was not a broad enough base from which to storm the convention and force a quick nomination.

Among the other candidates considered as possibilities—Herbert Hoover, Philander C. Knox, Charles Evans Hughes, Calvin Coolidge— Hiram Johnson was rated as having the best outside chance. Unlike Wood, Johnson was a "true" progressive, yet he was also a League irreconcilable. Therefore, while he had strong agrarian liberal support he did not appeal to eastern liberals. Short, heavyset, and spectacled, he was best known for his oratory and his bombast. Johnson followers insisted that he, not Wood, was the real successor to Theodore Roosevelt and would follow in the Rough Rider's hoofprints. With no regular support at all, Johnson had entered eleven of twenty-one state primaries and had made a creditable showing in each. The number of preconvention delegates committed to him was second only to that committed to Wood.

Harding's name was all but lost in the preconvention guessing and hoopla. In committed first-ballot delegates he had the smallest number of any of the major contenders. But his actual strength resembled an iceberg; only the smaller portion was visible. The submerged part represented a huge accumulation of good will which he, Daugherty, and his supporters had carefully nurtured over several months. The Harding forces had steered clear of poaching on favorite-son preserves or strong-arming delegates into the Harding fold. In every case where a first-ballot preference was not possible the Harding group asked for consideration on the second, third, or later ballots. Thus, in the Texas, Colorado, Kansas, Missouri, Alabama, Oklahoma, and Kentucky delegations Harding had considerable hidden support by convention time.

While Daugherty later claimed credit for this "second-choice" approach, it really belonged to Harding, and it was Harding's amiable personality which made it work.[77] This nonaggressive and low-key attitude was especially important in maintaining a working relationship with the Lowden forces. The Ohio senator had earlier assured Lowden that he would not compete for delegates in Lowden territory. Lowden had made a similar pledge and the two men kept their word.[78] In case of a convention deadlock, the Lowden element was much more inclined to move toward Harding than toward any other candidate.

This quiet "strategy of conciliation" was worth more than any primary victory or any amount of preconvention publicity. And Harding's close friends knew it. As Albert Fall snorted to a worried Harding supporter just before the convention, "They say Warren Harding is not getting newspaper publicity. Well, I'm glad he isn't. But you haven't heard anyone say that Warren Harding is making any enemies anywhere, have you? That's the answer. Harding will be nominated."[79]

[6

THE Republican National Convention opened on Tuesday, June 8, in the barnlike Chicago Coliseum with a band playing snappy foxtrots as the delegates straggled in. After "The Star-Spangled Banner," the director of community singing of the Republican League of Massachusetts shouted, "Now give three cheers and a tiger for the greatest country on earth—the United States of America!" The cheers went up: "Hurrah for the United States! And a long-tailed T-I-G-E-R!"

Meeting in the midst of a torrid Chicago heat wave, this convention quickly elected Senator Henry Cabot Lodge chairman, and then for the next two days turned its attention to the platform and allied matters. The platform excited little interest, except for the plank on the League. When it was read the entire convention rose with applause. Well it might. The plank was a masterful job of reconciling diametrically opposing views. Written by Elihu Root, who was preparing to sail for Europe but postponed his plans in order to work this miracle, the resolution first criticized Wilson's League, and then stated: "The Republican party stands for agreement among the nations to preserve the peace of the world. We believe that such an international association must be based upon international justice and must provide methods which shall maintain the rule of public right by the development of law and the decision of impartial courts, and which shall secure instant and general international conference whenever peace shall be threatened . . ."[80] All shades of opinion were satisfied. Irreconcilable Hiram Johnson was "delighted," while pro-League Nicholas Murray Butler found it "perfectly satisfactory." William Allen White, editor of the famous Kansas *Emporia Gazette* and a member of the platform committee, later claimed that the Root plank "was fearfully and wonderfully made. It meant nothing except that it frankly did mean nothing, and we accepted it."[81]

With the platform and other housekeeping matters out of the way, on Friday, June 11, the convention got down to the serious business of presidential nominations and balloting. At this moment the convention, unlike some earlier ones, had no boss or bosses. No one dominated the proceedings. There was no leader, only a mass of conflicts. Of the 984 voting delegates, almost half were uninstructed and, without firm direction, often voted as they pleased. Since the Democrats had controlled the national patronage for the past eight years, the leaders of the Republican party had few levers of national power to keep restive delegates in line. Of necessity, they had to look to local party chieftains to deliver votes and maintain delegate discipline. Moreover, the introduction of the direct presidential primary in twenty-one states had effectively reduced the possibility of old-time boss control. Significantly, however, for Harding's chances, over 22 percent of the delegates had been present at the 1916 convention

33

when the Ohioan had delivered the keynote address, and almost 10 percent had attended the 1912 gathering and had heard him nominate Taft. In some southern delegations over 50 percent had participated either in 1912 or in 1916.[82]

Against this background the nominations began. At one point during the afternoon the temperature on the floor hit 106°, but that did not prevent the delegates from stomping, parading, and shouting for their favorite candidates. After General Wood's name was presented, a forty-two-minute demonstration ensued that left the participants limp and exhausted. Not to be outdone, the Lowden forces greeted their champion's name with a forty-six-minute orgy.

To present his name to the convention, Harding, with the endorsement of Daugherty, had selected Frank Willis, former governor of Ohio and current United States congressman. He was a master orator, specializing in long "o's" and rolling "r's." Reporter Mark Sullivan, who heard the speech, said it contained a splendid combination of "oratory, grand opera, and hog-calling."[83] Whatever its forensic qualities, it certainly created a feeling of friendliness for Harding. Leaning over the platform railing, Willis concluded with colloquial intimacy, "Say, boys—and girls too—why not name Warren Harding?" There was laughing and applause from a convention which had just officially recognized women delegates for the first time.[84] However, the resultant Harding demonstration lasted only ten minutes, barely long enough to be worthwhile.

When the nominations were concluded, the convention began to ballot. After the first four ballots, it was hopelessly deadlocked with the front runners, Wood (314½) and Lowden (289), having no immediate prospects of securing the necessary 493 votes for the nomination. At this moment, about 7 P.M., Senator Reed Smoot of Utah moved for a recess until 10 A.M. the next day, and Chairman Lodge, amid a chorus of "noes" from Wood and Lowden supporters, declared the convention adjourned.[85]

Up to this time, Harding had vacillated between a cautious optimism and a fatalistic pessimism about his chances. Although he still retained some of the affectations of a reluctant candidate, he now badly wanted the nomination. To observers he presented a contradictory picture, depending upon who saw him and at what time. At his modest headquarters in the Florentine Room of the Congress Hotel, he had greeted delegates jovially during the early part of the week and was described as being

34

optimistic. But by Thursday his headquarters was almost deserted as convention interest centered on Wood and Lowden. By Friday, according to Nicholas Murray Butler, he had become so discouraged that he was prepared to withdraw his name from further consideration. William Allen White later contended that on Friday Harding had "a two days' beard and was disheveled. His eyes were bloodshot. He evidently had been drinking. . . . He was discouraged." On the other hand, Harding's Senate colleague James W. Wadsworth recalled that by Friday the Ohioan had become truly excited about his chances for the nomination and "was anxious to win." [86]

Mrs. Harding remained pessimistic throughout. Although she presented a bold front "for Warren's sake," she wished that they could somehow escape the whole ordeal. But now that he had come this far, she did not want him to quit. [87] Actually she relished the thought of neither victory nor defeat. The day before the balloting, she complained to a friend, "I don't know why we're keeping the headquarters. It's simply a needless expense." On Friday morning, she told her brother-in-law "Deac" Harding that she wished Warren were not a candidate and that it was a mistake for them to be there. In the papers that day she was quoted as saying: "I cannot see why anyone should want to be President. . . . I can see but one word written over the head of my husband if he is elected, and that word is 'Tragedy.' " [88]

On one point Florence Harding was insistent—that her husband file for reelection to the Senate before it was too late. Under Ohio law the deadline for such action was midnight on June 11, 1920. That was Friday midnight, some ten hours before the deadlocked convention would reconvene. This presented a ticklish problem. Should the news of Harding's filing leak out, it would be regarded as an admission that he considered himself out of the presidential race. Not only might the other candidates make political capital out of such information but his own delegate strength might quickly disappear. Daugherty counseled against it and "urged putting everything on red." But Mrs. Harding was not willing to gamble her husband's Senate seat on a long-shot chance at the White House. Warren agreed with her, although Daugherty extracted a promise that filing would not be done until the very last minute. On June 11, an agent for Harding, George B. Harris, stationed himself in the Deshler Hotel in Columbus and, after receiving telephoned instructions from the

35

senator, delivered Harding's Declaration of Candidacy to the secretary of state's office in Columbus, Ohio, at 11:58 P.M.[89]

If the Hardings were discouraged and uneasy, Harry Daugherty was not. Although he later admitted that he was not "absolutely sure" of a Harding victory "until the night before he actually was nominated," Daugherty never once gave up hope.[90] He sensed that the strategy of conciliation was paying dividends and, as the deadlock between Wood and Lowden deepened, Daugherty increased these efforts. He catered especially to the press; he offended no one. He even imported a seventy-five-voice glee club from Columbus to visit all the enemy headquarters and serenade the candidates. At every opportunity he emphasized Harding's availability to party regulars as an alternate possibility. To Mark Sullivan he confided: ". . . those two armies [Wood's and Lowden's] will battle each other to a standstill. When both realize they can't win, when they're tired and hot and sweaty and discouraged, both the armies will remember me and this little headquarters [Harding's]. They'll be like soldiers after a battle, who recall a shady spring along a country road, where they got a drink as they marched to the front. When they remember me that way, maybe both sides will turn to Harding—I don't know—it's just a chance."[91]

Some four months before, Daugherty had made another prophetic statement which, in view of the activities of Friday night, June 11, gave birth to one of the most pervasive myths in modern American history. Said Daugherty: "I don't expect Senator Harding to be nominated on the first, second or third ballot, but I think we can well afford to take chances that about eleven minutes after 2 o'clock on Friday morning at the convention, when fifteen or twenty men, somewhat weary, are sitting around a table, some one of them will say: 'Who will we nominate?' At that decisive time the friends of Senator Harding can suggest him and can afford to abide by the result."[92] What this statement itself did not supply, others, especially Colonel George Harvey and his biographer, Willis F. Johnson, later added. According to the Harvey story, which was widely popularized, a group of senators met in Harvey's suite in the Blackstone Hotel late on Friday night and, after considering possibilities, settled on Harding who was then called into the room and apprised of the situation. Asked if there was any reason why he should not be nominated, Harding disappeared into a bedroom for ten or fifteen minutes and then returned with

36

a negative reply. The word was passed along to the various delegations that Harding was the selection of the group and on Saturday he was nominated.[93]

As with most myths, this one contained elements of truth. Friday night was a bedlam of confusion. The Wood group was anxiously attempting to effect a liaison with the Johnson forces by offering Johnson the vice-presidency. Harding was busily engaged in meeting with the Ohio delegation which, because of rumors of his filing for the Senate, was threatening to bolt to Wood. Lowden, learning of these events, dispatched Hert to the Blackstone Hotel to prowl around and discover what was happening.

At the Blackstone there was much milling about. The main center of activity was a suite rented by Chairman Will Hays, consisting of a parlor and two bedrooms, one of which was occupied by George Harvey. Harvey, a former Democrat but now bitterly anti-Wilson, was at Chicago covering the Republican convention for his magazine, *Harvey's Weekly*. Friday night he dined with Senators Brandegee and Charles Curtis (head of the Kansas delegation). Then the four adjourned to the Hays-Harvey suite where between 8 P.M. and 2 A.M. a constant parade of party leaders moved in and out. Among those who came and went were Senator James Watson (Indiana), Senator Reed Smoot (Utah), Senator Medill McCormick (Illinois), Senators James Wadsworth and William M. Calder (both of New York), Senator Selden P. Spencer (Missouri), Senator Joseph Frelinghuysen (New Jersey), former Senators W. Murray Crane and John W. Weeks (both of Massachusetts), and Joseph R. Grundy (Pennsylvania).

They held a floating and freewheeling discussion, not a formal or cabal meeting. As Wadsworth recalled it, those who were present "did not know what to do. Some would say, 'Wouldn't it be a good thing to do this? Wouldn't it be a good thing to do that?' " Wadsworth stated positively that "they never got together on anything in the way of a program for the nomination. . . ."[94] Most of the time was spent in attempting to fathom what the individual state delegations would do on Saturday morning as well as to evaluate the strength of the respective candidates. But "all was confusion, puzzlement and divided councils."[95] With respect to the various candidates, Harvey was apparently for Hays but was mainly interested in keeping Johnson and Wood off the ticket, both of whom he despised. Lodge was ambivalent, showing no real enthusiasm for anyone. Wadsworth had been supporting Nicholas Murray Butler. Watson and Frelinghuysen were Wood men. McCormick still hoped for Lowden's selection. Penrose was ill at home but was connected with the convention by a private wire and was backing Knox through the voice of Grundy. Only Reed Smoot pushed for Harding.[96]

By the time that Wadsworth and most of the others left the suite shortly before 1 A.M., no decision of any kind had been reached although Harding's name constantly popped up as the best compromise possibility. On his way to bed the New York senator met Harding in the hall, returning from his discussions with the Ohio delegation. They exchanged brief comments, Harding saying that he thought his chances were improving.[97] Sometime shortly thereafter, Harvey informed two reporters that he believed the convention would ultimately turn to Harding because of the liabilities of all the other candidates. At about 3:30 A.M. Senator Curtis told another reporter the same thing. Reed Smoot, a Harding partisan anyway, prophesied to still another reporter later in the morning that it was "probable" the convention would endorse Harding as the most available choice. Meanwhile, Senator Weeks, who had remained in the Harvey suite somewhat longer than Wadsworth, confided to a friend that although no definite decision had been made, it was his private opinion that if Wood and Lowden failed to break their deadlock the convention would shift to Harding.[98] If any meeting was held between Harding and Harvey, as Harvey later claimed, it had to have occurred sometime between 2 A.M. and 4 A.M. Such a meeting was possible, but there is only Harvey's word for it. No one else mentioned Harding's being in the suite at all. Indeed, Senator Watson, one of the chief participants in the Blackstone discussions, later wrote, "[There] is not a thing to the story that Colonel Harvey . . . got Harding in a corner and questioned him as to his fitness to be President."[99] Daugherty also later denied this portion of the "smoke-filled room" tale.[100]

After the Harvey, Smoot, and Curtis statements to the press early Saturday morning, the rumor spread that a "Senate cabal" had arrived at a decision for Harding. Later on Saturday afternoon when the convention swung to Harding, most observers were convinced of it. Said the *New York Evening World*, "The Republicans did not nominate a man; they nominated a group, an oligarchy."[101] The charge stuck even though it was spurious. There were sixteen senators (including the ill Penrose) who were delegates to the 1920 convention. Thirteen of them voted *against* Harding until the ninth ballot. Only Senators Reed Smoot and Lawrence C. Phipps (Colorado) were Harding men on the early ballots. Senator Lodge cast his vote for Coolidge, then for Wood, then Lowden—indeed, Massachusetts did not give a single vote to Harding until the ninth ballot, when only one was cast for him (and it was not Lodge's). Senators Wadsworth and Calder (both of New York) voted for Butler until the eighth ballot and thereafter for Lowden. Senators Watson and New (both of Indiana) voted for Wood until the eighth when New went for Harding while Watson continued with Wood. Senator Spencer (Missouri), a Lowden man, did not shift his vote to Harding until the ninth ballot. The same was true of Senator Curtis (Kansas) who remained with Wood until the ninth ballot. Senators Frelinghuysen and Walter E. Edge (both of New Jersey) supported Wood to the end, while Senators Lawrence Y. Sherman and McCormick (both of Illinois) cast all their votes for Lowden. Senator Borah, Johnson's campaign manager, and Senator L. Heisler Ball (Delaware) never voted for Harding at any time.

If a definite pro-Harding decision had been reached in the Blackstone suite the night before, thirteen senators inexplicably continued to vote against him on the first four ballots on Saturday morning. Even after the convention reconvened for the ninth ballot late on Saturday afternoon and rumors were flying of an impending Harding victory, only three of the thirteen switched to Harding, leaving ten still voting for other candidates. Far from supporting Harding, a few of these, such as Lodge, used the Saturday recess to attempt the creation of a stop-Harding movement. Senator Boies Penrose, who continued to support Knox before belatedly turning to Harding, did not agree to free the Pennsylvania delegation for the Ohioan until after the eighth roll call. Even this move was not fully consummated until the final ballot.[102]

Both later and at the time, observers and delegates alike nevertheless remained convinced that a senatorial "cabal" had forced Harding's nomination. The senatorial delegates themselves encouraged this belief by quickly spreading the word *after* Harding's victory that their Ohio colleague had always been their choice. So sure were many ordinary delegates that a conspiracy had occurred that they immediately reacted against any further signs of dictation. After Harding's nomination, when it appeared that the Senate leaders were going to support another of their

Senate colleagues, Irvine L. Lenroot of Wisconsin, for Vice-President, the convention rebelled. No sooner had Senator McCormick begun his nominating speech for Lenroot than a voice from the Oregon delegation cried out the name "Coolidge!" Soon other delegates picked it up. McCormick managed to finish but now a dozen delegations were shouting "Coolidge!" Thereupon, the Oregon delegate who started it all, Wallace McCamant, simply stood on his chair and nominated Coolidge. A Coolidge boom followed, which finally resulted in the unanimous endorsement of the Massachusetts governor while surprised and shocked Senate leaders looked on.[103]

Regarded as a stunning defeat for the Senate oligarchy that allegedly had engineered Harding's nomination, Coolidge's selection was trumpeted as the exasperated independent action of a convention which to that moment had been "boss" controlled. Even if this were so, it is rather ironic that this "free and spontaneous" action should have resulted in the selection of a vice-presidential candidate no more liberal, no more progressive, and much less charismatic than Warren Harding.

There were also subsequent charges that money and oil forced the Harding nomination at the convention. Most of these claims were made through hindsight after the Teapot Dome scandals of 1924. The fact that monied interests and some oil manipulators were known to be partial to the Republican party in 1920 served as the real basis for such a belief. During the convention, men like Harry F. Sinclair (oil), Edward L. Doheny (oil), Herbert L. Satterlee (finance), William Boyce Thompson (copper), Frank A. Vanderlip (banking), Cornelius Vanderbilt (railroads), and Elbert Gary (steel) were in Chicago and showed interest in the outcome. Their interest, however, was more general than specific. They were mainly concerned with a Republican victory in November and not so much with individual nominees. Those who were known to have candidate preferences did not support Harding. General Wood had the backing of most financiers, while Lowden was the businessman's candidate.

If there was any oil chicanery at the convention, it has managed to elude the searching eye of historical research. Sinclair supported Wood, and Doheny was willing to back anyone in either party who could win the presidency in November. But there were no "oil deals" with any candidate. The only connection between oil and Harding was the fact that Jake Hamon, an oil manipulator and boss of the Oklahoma delegation, quickly climbed on the Harding bandwagon on Saturday morning. At no time, however, was his support decisive. After Harding's nomination, Hamon offered through Daugherty to pay some of Harding's preconvention campaign debts. But Daugherty smelled trouble, and bluntly refused. Shortly thereafter Hamon was shot by his mistress in an ugly brawl. Whatever schemes or aspirations he may have had died with him.[104]

[7

THE success of Warren Gamaliel Harding at the Republican convention in 1920 was no mystery. Yet the fact that his nomination could come about so naturally, given the circumstances, prompted many to disbelieve its simplicity. After all, Harding was eminently available. He had been on the winning side of most national questions and had rarely taken a stand antithetical to political trends. He was small-town America personified— so much so that when the Lynds performed their famous study of Muncie, Indiana, they uncovered the exact beliefs which Harding displayed. He was genial and open, making few enemies and hosts of friends. He had political experience both at the state and the national level. He was known personally—more than either Wood or Lowden—to the delegates, many of whom had seen him in earlier conventions. He had traveled the preconvention presidential trail carefully and had displayed just the proper amount of reluctance and humility to offset his mounting ambition. He possessed a campaign manager who was quick and daring and complemented Harding's own affinity for conciliation and compromise. Finally Harding was from Ohio, the mother of presidents and a pivotal state in any national election. Ohio had already provided six out of ten presidents since 1869. Ohio candidates had a reputation for victory.

Convention circumstances coalesced to favor Harding's cause. The Wood-Lowden deadlock was an important factor in his ultimate success. So also were the disclosures of the Kenyon committee on preconvention campaign spending. Meanwhile, all the other candidates possessed insurmountable liabilities. Hoover was not yet enough of a Republican. Knox came from the wrong state politically and had voted against the Eighteenth and Nineteenth amendments. Will Hays was too young and known only for his party work. Eastern liberals could not swallow Johnson. Charles Evans Hughes, having lost four years before, had the smell of defeat.

Lodge was too partisan to be considered and Coolidge was too lackluster to command a presidential following.

Rather than boss control, *no* control was the final key to Harding's nomination success. On the last day (Saturday), the delegates, as well as their leaders, were confused and disoriented. They were seeking a friendly face. Connecticut's refusal to join a stop-Harding movement was important. So was the inability of the Wood and Lowden forces to reach any kind of a compromise. Kentucky's move to Harding on the ninth ballot was the final catalytic agent which fused all the other factors into a chain reaction leading to victory.

Contrary to myths stressing smoke-filled-room intrigues, oil deals, and the like, Harding's nomination was perfectly natural. His name was certainly not pulled out of a hat. From the Friday deadlock on, he *had actually become the most available candidate.* At that moment, his rejection would have been more surprising than his selection. The move toward his banner happened spontaneously; there were no orders and, as Senator Wadsworth later analyzed it, the motivation was "psychological not hysterical. . . . The delegates did it themselves!" [105]

Political commentators and historians sometimes display short memories. In the face of later scandal it was forgotten that the bulk of the Republican party and of the Republican press quickly endorsed the decision of the convention. Aside from Democratic sniping, some talk about "second-raters," and the disappointment of Roosevelt liberals, the rank and file accepted the convention's verdict willingly and believed that it had chosen a winner. The *Baltimore American* claimed that Harding was the "best aspirant for the honor" while the *Chicago Tribune* called him "worthy of unhesitant confidence." [106] It was the *Atlanta Constitution*, however, which summed it up best: "As for Senator Harding, he will unquestionably make a strong candidate. His chief strength lies in the fact that he has been a sort of a middle-of-the-roader. . . . The Republicans might have gone further and done much worse." [107]

II

Not Nostrums but
Normalcy

[1

ON JULY 6 in the cooler climate of San Francisco, the Democratic party nominated James M. Cox, governor of Ohio, as its candidate for president, and Franklin D. Roosevelt, a New Yorker and currently assistant secretary of the navy, for vice-president. After forty-four ballots, Cox defeated the preconvention favorites, A. Mitchell Palmer and William G. McAdoo, in a struggle marked by bitterness and strife. Although a "mildly progressive" Democrat, Cox received his nomination at the hands of a convention which was much more tightly controlled than the Chicago Republican conclave. A wet and just pro-League enough to satisfy Wilsonian liberals, Governor Cox was Tammany's choice and the choice of other northern big-city politicians.

A newspaper editor and publisher of the *Dayton Daily News*, Cox had served two terms in Congress before becoming governor. Possessing a solid record as Ohio's chief executive, he went into the 1920 convention as a strong candidate but not one identified with Wilson's New Freedom, and therefore he was not expected to win. His somewhat surprising victory was tempered by the selection of the thirty-eight-year-old Roosevelt, who was directly connected with the incumbent administration.

President Wilson's insistence that the campaign be a "great and solemn referendum" on the League, and the convention's own action in endorsing the League unreservedly, gave neither Democratic candidate much maneuverability. As a result, the League issue, as well as Wilsonism itself, became the overriding concern of the 1920 campaign. From the outset, Roosevelt championed both the League and the Wilson administration's record. So did Cox, but he never felt really comfortable supporting either.[1]

With the conventions over, the acceptance speeches were carefully watched as a clue to the direction of the campaign as well as a gauge of the stature of the two presidential aspirants. On July 22, with a gala atmosphere permeating Marion, Republican leaders gathered in the town's Garfield Park to hear Senator Lodge officially notify the Republican candidate of his nomination. Lodge's speech was laced with cantankerous malice and snide allusions to President Wilson. But it also contained some subtle warnings to Harding. Reminding the audience that the Constitution provided for three coordinate branches of government, no one of which was to usurp the powers of the other two, Lodge asserted that Harding would run the executive branch "in that spirit" and maintain that condition. As for opposition to the League, the Massachusetts senator concluded: "Such has been the policy of the Republican party as represented in the Senate and such its policy will remain. We are certain that you [Harding] who helped so largely to frame this policy will, when the executive authority comes into your hands, carry it out."[2] The Lodge notification message to Harding was clear: do not oppose the will of the Senate, and campaign against the League.

Harding's acceptance speech struck a different note. Rather than intensify emotions, his address was designed to soothe and pacify. One newspaperman described it as creating "an atmosphere usually associated with churches and with ceremonies that have to do with eternity."[3] Not especially noteworthy in content, the speech was humble, reverent, and nondisputatious. Harding said the right things, stuck to middle ground, and gave the appearance of being his own man. He agreed with Lodge's assessment of the check and balance system and foreshadowed the fact that he would not be a strong executive of the Theodore Roosevelt or Woodrow Wilson type. On the specific question of the League, he also appeared to agree with Lodge at least to the extent of declaring that the Wilson League was unacceptable. However, Harding asserted that he did not want to hold aloof from world affairs. As a sop to those who believed in the League idea, he added: "I can speak unreservedly of the American aspiration and the Republican committal for an association of nations, cooperating in sublime accord, to attain and preserve peace through justice rather than force, determined to add to security through international law, so clarified that no misconstruction can be possible without affronting world honor."[4]

The reaction of the press was highly favorable. The *Chicago Tribune* applauded the "reasonableness and mildness" of the speech; the *Milwaukee Sentinel* thought it a "powerful address"; the *San Francisco Chronicle* claimed it marked Harding as "a practical man with a thorough grasp upon the problems the country is called upon to solve." On the League question, there was considerable disagreement about Harding's meaning. But on balance Harding's words were considered by party leaders to be more anti-League than anything else. Senator Johnson, for example, approved Harding's position while it was rumored that Herbert Hoover, who was pro-League, might repudiate Harding for his League remarks.[5]

Two weeks later, on August 7, a similar gathering met in the Dayton fairgrounds eighty-five miles away. Governor Cox was officially notified of his nomination before a crowd of 100,000 and responded with a blustery address that immediately set him apart from his Marion opponent. No newspaperman accused Cox of creating a churchlike atmosphere and his aggressiveness was more jarring than inspiring. He indicated that he would fight the Republicans for every vote in every area of the country and carry the battle to them on any issue they might name. But, he admitted, one issue would probably outweigh all others—the League—and he now left no doubt where he stood. Under great pressure from Wilson, he fatalistically accepted the challenge of a "great and solemn referendum": "The question is whether we shall or shall not join in this practical and humane movement. . . . Senator Harding, as the Republican candidate for the presidency, proposes in plain words that we remain out of it. As the Democratic candidate, I favor going in."[6]

The preliminaries were over. The campaign could begin.

⌈ 2

HARDING had prepared the ground well. Immediately after his nomination in mid-June, he had attempted to gather around his banner all those splintered and dissident Republican groups left in the wake of the Chicago convention. He indicated that he would welcome them all and would

45

follow a path of harmony and reconciliation. Such efforts paid rich dividends. Harding's direct appeals to Senator Johnson and Charles Evans Hughes brought promises of help from both. William Howard Taft also indicated that he would work for the ticket. After breakfasting with Harding on June 18, Herbert Hoover announced that he intended to support the Republican nominee. Other stragglers joined the Harding camp. Fiorello LaGuardia, the New York Republican maverick, declared his intention to stump his state for Harding. Much more reluctantly, "Fighting Bob" LaFollette dropped his tentative plans to be a third-party candidate and remained in the Republican ranks. William Allen White, who alone of the Kansas delegation had refused to vote for Harding on the successful tenth ballot, ultimately succumbed to the senator's quiet charm. Warning Harding that progressives of his type did not like this "back to normal" business, White nevertheless decided to support the ticket.[7]

By all odds the biggest Harding coup was the acquisition of the support of the Wood element and the Roosevelt progressives. At a dinner at the Harvard Club in New York on July 1, former Bull Moosers such as Henry L. Stoddard, Hermann Hagedorn, William H. Childs, and Lawrence F. Abbott pledged their allegiance to the Ohio senator. Shortly thereafter General Wood visited Marion and by his presence emphasized party solidarity. Even Raymond Robins, chairman of the Progressive National Committee of 1916, announced for Harding and vowed that he would swing as many progressive judges, lawyers, religious leaders, and businessmen to the Republican candidate as he could.[8]

Besides healing wounds and building party unity, the other priority for the Republican candidate was the careful organization of the campaign machinery. Immediately after his nomination, Harding requested that Will Hays continue as chairman of the Republican National Committee. Originally appointed in 1918, Hays thus became the first chairman in the party's history to continue in office after the close of a national convention. Hays was a perfect choice for Harding because he, too, had a reputation for promoting party harmony and encouraging conciliation. An elder in the Presbyterian church, Hays had introduced something novel into politics by opening sessions of the National Committee with prayer. Although puritanical and deeply religious, Hays was still sufficiently worldly wise to understand American politics thoroughly. Nominally in charge of all campaign activities, Hays concentrated mainly on publicity,

46

finances, and party organizational matters. He was not a top campaign strategist.[9]

For the latter role, Harding relied on Harry Daugherty. This decision caused critical comment even among Harding's closest friends. But Daugherty had proven his value and his loyalty too well to be abandoned at this juncture. Harding retained confidence in Daugherty throughout the 1920 struggle, and Daugherty never gave the senator any reason to doubt the feelings that he expressed in a letter written to Harding early in the campaign: "I have only one desire and one ambition—your success now and in the great days to come. You keep constantly in mind the fact that it is your cause and yours alone I serve, even to the point of disagreeing with you when I think you are mistaken."[10]

There was always some friction between Hays and Daugherty over matters of campaign jurisdiction. Daugherty was very zealous to keep all the "practical" aspects of the campaign in his own hands. Constantly smelling intrigue and looking for the double-cross, Daugherty was suspicious of Hays because of the latter's control over publicity. He feared that Hays was more interested in his own future than in Harding's election. Whenever he could, Daugherty by-passed Hays in dealing with disgruntled elements in the party, and shot letters here and there, making alliances, arranging for speakers, and offering unlimited suggestions. Daugherty personally took charge of securing Negro support and endeavored to keep Hays away from "the bread and butter operation" that paid off in votes.[11]

All things considered, however, the Republican staff worked well together, especially as the campaign progressed. Hays maintained his headquarters in New York and kept a careful eye on eastern developments. Frederic W. Upham, national Republican party treasurer, operated out of his offices in Chicago. Harry New, placed in charge of the National Speakers Bureau, also had his main headquarters in Chicago. Working out of both Chicago and New York was Albert D. Lasker, the famous advertising executive, whom Hays recommended, and Harding accepted, as the primary "idea man" for all campaign publicity.

But the nerve center of the entire operation remained in Marion. Here a core of advisers, speech writers, and secretaries surrounded the candidate and gave substance to the campaign. George Christian, Jr., Charles Hard, Judson C. Welliver, and Kathleen Lawler handled the correspondence, made traveling arrangements, organized the press corps, provided

47

accommodations for visiting dignitaries, and otherwise attended to those myriad details upon which a political campaign rests. Primarily responsible for helping Harding with his speeches were former Senator George Sutherland of Utah and Richard Washburn Child, an editor of *Collier's Weekly*. Sutherland, an early Harding supporter and friend, was later appointed an associate justice of the Supreme Court while Child was named ambassador to Italy. In the campaign of 1920, speech writing paid high dividends politically.

Besides the ubiquitous Daugherty, other trusted advisers at Marion were John Weeks, former senator from Massachusetts, and Henry C. Wallace, farm-journal editor from Iowa. Weeks did not remain in Marion all the time, nor did Wallace. They drifted in and out, helping to set policy on specific issues or aiding in the framing of particular speeches. Through Weeks, Harding had immediate access to the business and financial world. In Wallace he possessed a valuable contact with important farm organizations, especially the American Farm Bureau Federation and its president, James R. Howard. Not known to Harding before the campaign, Wallace had been recommended as an adviser by Senator Arthur Capper of Kansas, who considered Wallace the most knowledgeable man in the country on the farm situation.[12]

Conspicuously absent from Marion during the campaign were the leaders of the alleged Senate cabal and chief occupants of the smoke-filled room. Sensitive to the criticism that he was merely a tool of the cabal and that he could not make an utterance without the approval of its members, Harding wisely discouraged their visits. Of course, they corresponded with him and made numerous suggestions, but this was not the same as being in Marion and having Harding's ear. Both Lodge and Harvey chafed under this restriction; still, they recognized its logic and, so far as the public knew, they maintained a discreet distance throughout the campaign. Harvey did go to Marion for a short time in August 1920, but contrary to his later exaggerated assertions wielded no decisive influence. Coolidge also was used sparingly by the Harding high command. More as a result of personal incompatibility than design, Harding did not rely on him for either advice or many public appearances. Coolidge was not an effective stump speaker anyway and shunned such performances. In October, accompanied by Lowden, he made an eight-day tour of the South which was mildly successful, and he led a parade down Fifth Avenue at the close of the campaign. Otherwise he was counted on to carry Massachusetts, Maine, Vermont, and New Hampshire on election day—which he did.

A far greater campaign asset was Mrs. Harding. She appealed to women voters and was well liked by the working press. She loved the crowds, the full days, the excitement, the speeches, and the parades. Delegations coming to Marion were enthusiastic about her and greeted the mention of her name with resounding applause. Carefully groomed, she always acted the perfect hostess, even while thousands of feet tramped down her shrubs and flowers. During the campaign she maintained a wide correspondence with friends, especially Evalyn Walsh McLean, and mingled chitchat with wonderment at the political events surrounding her. Toward the end of the campaign, she wrote to Mrs. McLean: "No matter what comes into my life I shall always regard this summer as one of the greatest epochs."[13]

Throughout the campaign, Warren Harding remained the dominant figure. A distorted image has been created of a weak and vacillating Harding being led about by various advisers who put words in his mouth. But his voluminous campaign correspondence shows him completely in charge.[14] He maintained close contact with party leaders in every state and knew the particular political problems they faced. He was sensitive to the subtleties of political life in local areas and wisely shunned items of potential offense. Except on the League where genuine confusion existed, he made up his own mind and fashioned his own pronouncements. Influenced by such close advisers as Weeks and Wallace, he was not overwhelmed by them nor was he controlled by them. They were not watchdogs sent out by the National Committee to monitor his actions or screen his utterances.[15] Above all, the whole tone of the Republican campaign was distinctly Harding's. The emphasis on pacification, on conciliation, on restoration, and on harmony was certainly not characteristic either of the Lodge-style politician or of the Johnson-type irreconcilable. This was uniquely Harding and he maintained it as the *primary* thrust of the campaign.

On matters of timing and procedural strategy Harding was relatively pliable. From the outset his advisers were inclined to recommend that he not stump the country but remain in Marion as much as possible. Senator Walter Edge took credit for the "front-porch" idea, writing Harding only two days after his nomination that he should ". . . go home to

49

Ohio, remain for a week or two receiving the formal and informal visits that would naturally follow your return, and divide the holiday period of the summer from approximately the first of July to early September in two resort sections of the country, still maintaining the same policy of gladly welcoming delegations and visitors, but having them come to you rather than you going to them."[16] Actually, others besides Edge made similar proposals. On the same day that the Edge letter was written, Chairman Will Hays told the press that he believed Harding should not make more than a dozen speeches throughout the country and should remain at home, conducting mainly a "porch campaign."[17] Harding had already been thinking along these lines himself and quickly adopted portions of the various suggestions. He rejected Edge's idea of using a resort as the base of his activity because of the "unseemly" appearance of being "on vacation" during a presidential campaign. However, to remain on his own front porch and have delegations come to him had an appealing quality, especially since it would enable him to emulate his fellow Ohioan William McKinley. Close advisers like Daugherty and Sutherland quickly accepted the front-porch idea and it was announced to the press as campaign policy on July 10. Harding's home certainly possessed a porch suited to the purpose. Built at the turn of the century to replace an old one which had collapsed under the weight of numerous well-wishers after Harding's successful state senatorial campaign in 1899, it ran the entire length of the house and ended in a large protuberance resembling a bandstand. Meanwhile, the flagpole which had stood on McKinley's lawn in Canton during the porch campaign of 1896 was removed to the Harding yard in Marion as a good luck symbol.[18]

Campaign publicity now shifted into high gear. As soon as the basic campaign strategy was agreed upon, Hays unleashed Lasker, who inundated the country with Harding material. He extracted every potential for publicity from the front-porch tactic, supplying bands, streamers, and huge Harding portraits, and securing movie and still photographic coverage of each arriving delegation. Lasker even arranged for William L. Veeck to bring his Chicago Cubs to Marion on September 2 to play a local team for the benefit of baseball fan Warren Harding. After Harding pitched the first three balls, the great Grover Cleveland Alexander went on to win the game for the Cubs, 3–1.

By the close of the campaign, through Lasker's efforts the faces of the

Hardings, especially the photogenic Warren Harding, peered at Americans from the pages of innumerable farm journals and popular magazines, or smiled at them from billboards, posters, and the movie screen. By November, the National Committee was sending out 8000 "photographic bulletins" twice each week, most of which contained photographs of either Harding or Harding and his wife. Moreover, under Lasker's direction, a "Harding and Coolidge Theatrical League" was organized whose president was Al Jolson and whose membership included well-known movie actors and actresses. In late August a contingent of such stars, about seventy strong, made a pilgrimage from New York to Marion, entertaining on an impromptu basis all the way there and back. The nation ogled in fascination as Jolson, Eddie Foy, Ethel Barrymore, Mae Marsh, Pearl White, Lillian Gish, and Anita Stewart descended on the small Ohio town to shake hands with the Republican candidate and hear him speak. Jolson even wrote a song to commemorate the event: "Harding, You're the Man for Us."[19]

Inventing such slogans as "Let's be done with wiggle and wobble," and popularizing others such as "Back to Normalcy," Lasker and his publicity department also disseminated widely the more serious campaign literature. To Negro groups went brochures on "Why the Negro Is a Republican," "Henry Lincoln Johnson Tells Why the Negro Should Vote for a Republican President," "Even Justice and a Square Deal for All," and "Lynching." For farmers and wage earners were "Protection and Prosperity," "American Farm Problem," and "A Billion a Month—Twenty Billion in All" (on Democratic waste and inefficiency). Of special interest to women and naturalized citizens were "Why Women Should Vote for Harding and Coolidge" and "A New Voters Leaflet." For unconvinced dissident liberal elements was "Why Progressives Support Harding" (written by Raymond Robins and geared especially to appeal to old Bull Moosers).

In the final analysis, what made all this publicity effective was the candidate himself. Too often this fact has been overlooked. The publicity was believable because Harding was believable. The publicity did not create a mirage, as some writers later claimed; the "mirage" was actually there to see, touch, and hear. Harding never pretended to be other than what he was, and if Republican publicity committed any crime in 1920, it was not the crime of distortion but of making a virtue out of the reality.

In Republican presidential propaganda, the highest accolade was now reserved for the "average" and the commonplace. Obviously, this approach appealed to the "average" voter who identified with the Republican candidate. Then, too, the constant use of such terms as "humble," "sincere," and "gentle" in describing the Republican standard-bearer had a quieting effect on a public mind overwrought by the passions of war and interparty strife.

Within this framework Harding was a superb campaigner. He avoided personalities, referred respectfully to Cox and Roosevelt, and called Wilson "one of the most intellectual figures of a century and a half." At the first strategy meeting after his nomination when it was suggested that the sick Wilson be the primary target of his campaign, Harding said, "I guess you have nominated the wrong candidate, if this is the plan, for I will never go to the White House over the broken body of Woodrow Wilson." [20] Harding never appeared to be either contentious or pretentious, as Cox often did, and wisely stuck to the high road of dignity rather than risk becoming mired in the low road of mudslinging. On his own front porch he was the picture of American respectability, greeting delegations in his white trousers, blue coat, and sawtooth straw hat. His friendly house, painted dark green with white trim, its front porch handsomely tiled, appeared solid and inviting to many in the various delegations who had left similar small-town homes to make the journey to Marion. As one observer noted, while Cox "was campaigning all over the lot, in a sweat, in his mental shirt sleeves, with his coat off, ringing fire alarms," Harding appeared as "a quiet gentleman who had no beads on his forehead, no dust on his shoes, no red in his eye." [21] This contrast, alone, gave Harding such a favorable image that even the lukewarm could not fail to be influenced. Wrote William Allen White to Harding in early October: "Just a word to let you know that you are making a great impression on the American people. You have grown every moment since the day of the nomination. It seems to me that your sincerity, your sense of dignity and your steady thoughts have made themselves felt in the American heart." [22]

Harding opened his front-porch campaign on Saturday, July 31, with a homey talk to 2000 factory workers, businessmen, and farmers from Ohio's Richland County. Between then and the end of September some 600,000 persons flocked to Marion to listen to the Republican candidate. Briefed beforehand about the exact composition of each arriving delega-

Warren Harding and sisters Charity (left) and Mary
(right). He was about nine years old.

Harding as a young man.

The Harding home on Mount Vernon
Avenue in Marion, with the
McKinley flagpole.

Harding in the composing room of the *Marion Star*.

The Hardings with Dr. George Tryon Harding.

In the library of the Harding home at Marion.

Campaign managers Will Hays (left)
and Harry Daugherty.

The front-porch campaign at Marion in August 1920.

Florence Harding puts a flower in her husband's lapel.

Woodrow Wilson and Harding on inauguration day, with Representative Cannon and Senator Knox seated in front.

The cabinet: first row, left to right, Weeks, Mellon, Hughes, Harding, Coolidge, Denby; second row, Fall, Hays, Daugherty, Wallace, Hoover, Davis.

The president arrives at the DAR Hall with George Christian, Jr. (at right) to close the Washington Disarmament Conference.

Charles Evans Hughes, Harding, and George Harvey.

Harding signing the Capper-Volstead Act in February 1922. Senator Volstead
is on the far left, Senator Capper third from the left.

Secretary Mellon selling Mrs. Harding the first of the new
treasury certificates. Jess Smith is at the right.

The president relaxing with members of his entourage on a trip.

The Hardings leaving "Friendship" with Evalyn Walsh McLean.

The avid golfer at the Washington Country Club.

At the old baseball park in Fort Benning, Georgia. To Harding's left are Major General Gordon, Secretary Weeks, and Secretary Fall. Behind Fall is Dr. Sawyer.

Returning to the White House from a Sunday ride, the president and George Christian, Jr.

Harding with Thomas Edison.

Harding with Secretary Work, Director Mather, and Superintendent
Albright in Yellowstone National Park, July 1923.

The Hardings with parka-clad Gov. Scott Bone of Alaska.

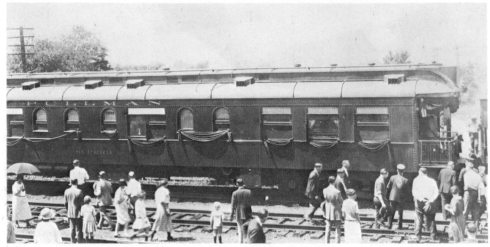

The president's private car, *Superb*, draped in black for the trip back to Washington.

The Harding memorial at Marion.

tion, Harding tailored his remarks accordingly. He never committed himself to controversial actions, was always polite, never became ruffled, and spoke from a script. While politically wise, this use of prepared speeches put a damper on Harding's normal freewheeling oratory and prevented him from engaging in the kind of "bloviation" which he enjoyed. As he once complained: "I could make better speeches than these, but I have to be so careful."[23]

There were those among Harding's advisers who entertained serious doubts about whether the front-porch tactic should be followed to the end. Senator Lodge, in particular, warned that greater exposure of the candidate was necessary. Harding at first demurred. Despite its restrictions, he liked the front-porch procedure because it permitted him to "avoid the mistakes which are sometimes fatal in national campaigns."[24] Regional campaign managers, such as Elmer Dover in San Francisco and Charles R. Forbes in Seattle, also put pressure on Harding to leave the porch, at least for a few speeches elsewhere. But Harding remained unconvinced and on August 6 wrote to Dover, "I still cling to the hunch . . . that the best course is to speak deliberately and avoid entanglements [by remaining] here at home."[25] George Sutherland strongly agreed with him and helped him fend off such suggestions. Sutherland believed that much more was to be gained through the front-porch campaign than through "a spectacular tour of the country." His clinching argument was: "Everything indicates that today [July 29] the country is with us, that we have only to sit tight to be sure of winning."[26]

Discussions continued, however, on how Harding could best use his time, and by late August, as Cox conducted whirlwind assaults on large portions of the country, the demand for Harding to take to the stump grew irresistible. Hence, on September 11, Harding announced that he would leave the porch and make a few speaking tours during the campaign's closing days. Concluding the front-porch phase with a speech to a delegation of traveling salesmen on September 25, Harding thereafter became his own traveling salesman for a Republican victory in November. In late September he campaigned through Pennsylvania, Maryland, and West Virginia, making formal speeches at Baltimore and Wheeling. Then to the delight of E. Mont Reily and Ed Scobey (campaign managers for the southwestern area), Harding journeyed in early October to Omaha, Des Moines, Kansas City, and Oklahoma City. Mid-October found him in Indiana, Kentucky, and Tennessee. A final trip in the third week of October carried him into New York to Buffalo. He closed his campaign on October 30 where his own political career had started almost twenty-one years before—Columbus, Ohio.

[3

HARDING'S front-porch speeches and his utterances on the stump revealed that the Ohio senator had clear-cut ideas on a variety of subjects and already knew what he would do if elected president. He was for an emergency tariff which would immediately protect the farmer until a new, high permanent tariff could be enacted to replace the low Underwood-Simmons Tariff of 1913. He wanted tighter immigration restriction. He advocated a big navy and an expanded merchant marine. He favored an antilynching law, the protection of constitutional rights for the Negro, and the appointment of more Negroes to federal office. He supported trade unionism and collective bargaining, but opposed any union dictation to business or government. He believed in the elimination of excess-profits taxes and the lowering of high surtaxes on private incomes. He stood for increased credit for the farmer and the implementation of a "wise" conservation policy. He was heartily in favor of economy in government and the creation of a budget system for controlling federal expenditures. Most of all he advocated allowing the nation to experience a period of tranquillity in which it could restore itself and return to "normalcy."

The traditional image of Harding as being vapid and imprecise in the campaign of 1920 rests almost exclusively on his handling of the League question. From the beginning, Harding's position was ambivalent. This represented both an asset and a liability. While he was seeking the nomination, such ambivalence was an asset because it made him acceptable to all ranges of opinion within the party. After his selection, it became a disadvantage because it prevented him from inducing the party to unite on a common position. Harding first leaned this way and then that on the League question, finally assuming the position of an embarrassing but expedient straddle. In that sense, he was the perfect candidate for the Root plank in the platform.

Harding's acceptance speech of July 22 signaled the start of a series of complicated intraparty maneuverings on the League issue. Generally

54

acceptable to anti-League elements, that speech aroused suspicions in the minds of pro-Leaguers despite Harding's allusions to some kind of an association of nations. When Senator Johnson proclaimed that the speech meant the League was dead, Hoover fired off a lengthy telegram to Harding on August 2 complaining of the "uncorrected interpretation" Johnson placed on Harding's words and requested clarification. Replying to Hoover, Harding claimed that he was valiantly attempting to avoid a party split on the issue and added: "Personally, I am confident we can eliminate all doubts and distresses about this difficult matter as the compaign progresses."[27]

But both the doubts and distresses increased as a bitter tug-of-war for Harding's loyalty ensued between the pros and the antis. The Ohioan's natural inclination was to seek advice on this matter from those whom he had known during the League fight in the Senate, especially Lodge. Lodge was myopic on the League question and believed that this issue would prove to be "the winning card." Lodge continually harped on the dangers of the League and coached Harding to "bear down" on Article X as a license for killing American boys. This, reasoned Lodge, would scare women voters into the Republican fold. Also, Lodge counseled Harding to tie Cox to Wilson as often as possible and visit the sins of the one upon the other. Neither tactic especially appealed to Harding, although he basically shared Lodge's antipathy toward the Wilson League.[28]

Other League opponents, who were either strict reservationists or irreconcilables, also bombarded Harding with appeals to "stand firm." The three most important were Knox, Harvey, and Johnson. Harding's personal friendship with Senator Knox caused him to incline an attentive ear to Knox's anti-League sentiments but he managed to resist issuing the bellicose anti-League pronouncements which Knox advocated. Harvey, in turn, warned Harding continually of the dangers of capitulation to the pro-Leaguers. Harvey's militant *Weekly* rode shotgun on the League question all along the Republican campaign trail, blasting away at Wilson and the Democratic candidates. Hiram Johnson likewise urged Harding to make the death of the Wilson League the cornerstone of his campaign and never to discuss in detail any plans he might have for international cooperation. Said the California senator, "You are on safe and high ground when you say you will first declare a state of peace to exist, and then leisurely and reflectively take up with the nations of the world, the ques-

tions of disarmament and prevention of war through international cooperation."[29]

There is little question that Harding was far more influenced in the
early days of the campaign by these men than by pro-Leaguers. Only
practical politics kept him from siding with them openly. At the moment,
his tactics were merely designed not to drive the ratificationists out of the
party. When his efforts in this direction caused some disturbance among
the anti-League group, he wrote to his friend Frank Brandegee to tell
them to keep cool: "The time will come before long," Harding said, "when
we can becomingly stress the views which you know me to hold on this
subject."[30]

But neither Harding nor the anti-League forces reckoned with the persuasive power and influence of certain pro-League men. Hoover was the
nominal captain of the pro-League group. His telegram of August 2 demanding a clarification of Harding's views was only the first of many
designed to prevent Harding from capitulating completely to the anti-
League side. Long and sometimes contentious, these missiles struck home,
proving to Harding that the pro-League element was prepared to shatter party harmony if its opinions were ignored.[31] Elder statesman Root,
who was partially to blame for the confusion because of his "miracle"
plank, flatly warned Harding not to play into the hands of irreconcilables
like Johnson and Borah, and predicted an election disaster if he did so.[32]
Charles Evans Hughes, a mild reservationist like Root, urged Harding to
keep an open mind and not to close the door on some form of League
participation. Similarly, William Howard Taft kept up a drumfire of letters and telegrams to Harding calling for a policy of "Americanizing the
League" rather than abandoning it.[33]

These entreaties unquestionably had an effect. Although they did not
change Harding's basic inclinations, they made him more sensitive to pro-
League attitudes. The proof occurred on August 28 when, from his front
porch, he devoted an entire speech to the League issue. Indicating again
that he was not in favor of joining the League sponsored by Wilson, he
advanced in greater detail his own ideas for American participation in
the maintenance of world peace. What he desired, he said, was not ". . .
an offensive and defensive alliance of great powers, like that created at
Versailles [but] an association of free nations, or a league of free nations,
animated by considerations of right and justice, instead of might and self-

interest. . . . Such an association I favor with all my heart, and I would make no fine distinction as to whom credit is due. One need not care what it is called. Let it be an association, a society, or a league, or what not, our concern is solely with substance, not the form thereof." Harding went on to suggest that the old Hague Tribunal was an example of what might become the nucleus of such an international arrangement. Joining the historical precedence of this court with his own "association" idea, he concluded: "I believe humanity would welcome the creation of an international association for conference and a world court whose verdicts upon justiciable questions, this country in common with all nations would be both willing and able to uphold. The decisions of such a court or the recommendations of such a conference could be accepted without sacrificing on our part or asking any other power to sacrifice one iota of its nationality." [34]

To the irreconcilables the August 28 speech was a shock. While Harding again declared against the Wilson League, it now appeared that he might accept "a" league tied to a world court. This was anathema to Borah and to Johnson. The former announced that as a result of this new pronouncement he would not be able to speak for Harding during the rest of the campaign, while the latter dropped all pro-Harding activity for the time being. Yet both Lodge reservationists and pro-Leaguers seemed delighted. Lodge sent Harding a telegram which read: "Congratulations. Absolutely with you." Reservationist John Weeks wired him: "Your speech yesterday was great. It suits me." From Emporia, Kansas, came a message from pro-Leaguer William Allen White: "I want to tell you how pleased I am at your recent utterances about the League of Nations." Hoover quickly wired a friend who was thinking of dumping Harding: "I would urge you to delay any decision until the Republican supporters of the League here have had further opportunity to clear the situation which looks more hopeful." [35]

As for the motive behind the August 28 speech, Harding wrote Frederick H. Gillett, pro-League Republican congressman from Massachusetts: "You have probably observed my recent utterance on the international situation. I really felt that the knot had to be cut and I cut it in the way that my speech revealed. I was particularly cautious to make such utterance as will permit anyone who wants a league to understand that I am in favor of such an association [that will] enable us to do our part in stabilizing the world."[36] In response to growls from Johnson about this same August 28 statement, Harding expressed amusement at "the varied constructions which prominent men place upon my speeches," and declared that his sole purpose was "to make it reasonably possible for our party to unite in opposition to the surrender which threatened in the course pursued by the President."[37]

Perhaps it would be too much to claim that the duplicity revealed by these two Harding letters, one to a pro-Leaguer and one to an irreconcilable, was a carefully calculated plan of obfuscation. However, Harding's desire for party unity was strong. If in achieving it he had to trim toward the pro-League side, he would do so. If, on the other hand, he needed to skirt close to the anti-League shore, this, too, he was prepared to do. His ultimate destination was an election victory and he steered his course accordingly. His compass was not his own personal convictions on the League, but merely what the diverse elements in his party would tolerate.

Except for the irreconcilables, the leaders of the contending groups sensed the importance of at least some harmony on this issue if victory was to be achieved and throughout September urged Harding to remain as noncommittal as possible. Albert Fall, a strict reservationist, encouraged him to refrain from making "any definite expressions, pro or con" on the League matter, thus steering clear of any embarrassing statements.[38] Herbert Hoover also advised Harding against being forced into intemperate pronouncements, and cautioned him to remain especially wary of such die-hard partisans as Johnson and Borah.[39]

The irreconcilables remained the major problem. After sulking for a time because of the August 28 speech, Johnson and Borah unexpectedly hit the campaign trail for Harding in late September and henceforth proclaimed that the election of the Ohio senator meant the rejection of the League, amended or not. By this brazen approach they hoped to engineer a decision in their favor. In a personal interview in San Francisco on September 20, Johnson flatly remarked: "Harding has already scrapped [the League] and the rest of us will beat it at the election beyond redemption." When a reporter asked about the obvious difference between Johnson's and Harding's views on American adherence to an "association of nations" or a world court, Johnson quipped: "Sufficient unto the day is the evil thereof."[40]

The press immediately interpreted Johnson's statements and his belated decision to campaign for Harding to mean that the Ohio senator had secretly capitulated to the irreconcilables. Pro-Leaguers now angrily broke their silence by maintaining that although Harding was not in favor of "the" League, he was not opposed to "a" league. Confusion and squabbling again reigned in late September and early October as the various forces matched claim with counterclaim. The irreconcilables continued arbitrarily to maintain that Harding was opposed to any league and viewed his words about "an association of nations" as mere window dressing.

They had some reason for this belief. Harding repeatedly attempted to mollify them and professed great distress when, in their letters to him, they charged him with betraying the anti-League position. Meanwhile, as it became increasingly apparent that public opinion had definitely turned against the League, the Lodge reservationists, a group to which Harding nominally belonged, shifted closer to the irreconcilables. While the Lodge group tolerated the fiction of talking about "a" league, by the close of the campaign they were not really interested in any league either. In Marion, both of Harding's speech writers, Sutherland and Child, belonged in this latter category and in the waning days of the campaign worked, with the connivance of Albert Lasker, to keep Harding's statements on the anti-League side.[41]

Still Harding attempted to hold to middle ground. On October 7, in a foreign policy speech at Des Moines, he again clearly rejected the Wilson League. But when Borah immediately thereafter announced that he was in complete accord with Harding's views, Harding warned the press that he was "not in complete accord with Senator Borah."[42] Four days later Harding complained that his stand on the League was being misunderstood by some of his followers and issued a clarifying statement to the press: (1) he was opposed to the League as made at Paris; and (2) he was definitely in favor of "a world association—call it what you will, the name is of slight consequence—that will discourage or tend to prevent war." To create the latter, he promised that after the election he would "call into conference with me the best minds, the clearest minds, that America affords."[43] Together they would then solve the problem.

While Harding strove to achieve unity through ambiguity, and the irreconcilables daily proclaimed his capture, the pro-League forces now adopted an unrealistic Alice-in-Wonderland position. They chose to believe that Harding, even at the expense of losing a few "highbrow" votes,

59

was simply stringing the irreconcilables along in order to keep them from bolting. But after the election, so their theory ran, Harding would act on his world court and "association of nations" idea and follow a pro-League line. Hoover told Will Hays in October that Harding criticized the League only to "hold harmony in the Republican party." [44] At about the same time Taft wrote to pro-League Theodore Burton, "I think Harding has it distinctly in mind to make Root his secretary of state . . . and there will be the chance to secure what you and I desire [the League Covenant and a world court properly amended]." [45]

As an indication of this sentiment, there appeared in the press on October 15 a full-page endorsement of Harding by thirty-one famous pro-League Republicans who claimed that voting for Harding was the surest way to bring the United States into a world organization and "advance the cause of international cooperation to promote peace." Choosing the August 28 speech as the only correct expression of Harding's views, the endorsement concluded: "The question between the candidates is not whether our country shall join in such an association. It is whether we shall join under an agreement containing the exact provisions negotiated by President Wilson at Paris or under an agreement which omits or modifies some of those provisions. . . ." Prepared by Root, this endorsement was signed by such men as Nicholas Murray Butler (president of Columbia), A. Lawrence Lowell (president of Harvard University), Ray Lyman Wilbur (president of Stanford University), Henry W. Taft (brother of William H. Taft), Herbert Hoover, Charles Evans Hughes, Elihu Root, and William Allen White.[46] Later, some of these signers would claim that Harding betrayed them. They were betrayed all right, but by their own imaginations and wishful thinking—not by Harding.

So to the very end of the campaign the Republicans were racked with confusion and strife over the League issue. Their primary target was their own candidate, whose nebulous convictions on the League were similar to those held by the reservationists but whose public position on the issue was dictated by political expediency and a desire to win. Alarmed by the wrangling, Harding attempted to harmonize all elements behind a vague plan of action which would include an association of nations and a world court. Hazy as this proposal was, he believed it was adequate and he failed to comprehend the continuing turmoil. At the close of the campaign he wrote to George Harvey: "Probably I do not understand myself, but in my mind they [his League statements] have been consistent throughout. I have at all times spoken in complete opposition to the Wilson League, and I do not know of a single speech in which I have failed to speak kindly of an association of nations based upon the rule of justice. Perhaps I have not been able to make the country understand me, but I have done the best I could, and I am willing to let it go at that."[47] To another friend he simply said: "It was impossible to harmonize my advisers on this subject and ultimately I took the course which seemed to me to be best."[48] One might fault Harding on various points—his trimming, his vacillation, his lack of specificity, his ambiguity. But his amazing success in keeping such diametrically opposite groups campaigning together at all was no mean tribute to his political talent.

The Democrats, of course, reveled in the disorder displayed in the Republican camp. Cox claimed that all he had to do to obtain new ammunition for a day of campaigning was to "look at the morning papers to find some new contradiction in speech or statement from Harding or one of the bitter-enders against the League."[49] But Cox's sallies against the Republicans did not impress the public and it retained far greater interest in Harding's vague and misty views on an association of nations than in Cox's pro-League commitment. Indeed, by settling on the League as *the* issue, the Democratic candidate played into Republican hands. Despite the Republican difficulty in securing harmony in their own ranks, all Republicans could attack what was known—and the Wilson League was known. By identifying completely with the Wilson League, Cox became the automatic recipient of all the animosity formerly reserved for Wilson. Although toward the end of the campaign, Cox became aware of this fact and realized that his strong pro-Wilson position was losing him votes, it was too late to alter the image. He and the Wilson League were inseparable. If defeated, the two would go down together.

[4

DEMOCRATIC enthusiasm was high at the beginning of the campaign. The Democrats knew that they had a handicap in the various postwar problems which remained unsolved. But they believed that the country would respond to Wilson's "great and solemn referendum"; and they possessed a general contempt for their opponent, Warren G. Harding. Colo-

61

nel Edward M. House expressed a widely held Democratic opinion when he wrote to Brand Whitlock a short time after the Chicago Republican convention: "If we can beat anyone we should be able to beat Harding."[50]

Early progressive Republican doubts about the strength of their party's candidate caused many Democrats to adopt a more optimistic view than was warranted. William Allen White, surveying the immediate post-convention political scene, tartly wrote to one of his Democratic friends, "What a God-damned world this is!" Other liberal Republicans sadly agreed that Harding was "mediocre," a "fool," "no leader," "pliable," "a third-rater," and so forth. Senator William S. Kenyon of Iowa displayed the feelings of such Republicans when he told William Jennings Bryan: "I shall support Harding but not work very hard at it." Shrewder heads, however, sized up the situation differently. Whitlock, who certainly was not enamoured of the Ohio senator, cautioned Newton D. Baker that under prevailing conditions Harding's conservatism would be an asset not a liability, and that as the campaign progressed he would develop strength that a candidate of a more original bent could not generate.[51]

Such was the case. As dissident Republicans, one after another, declared allegiance to the Harding cause, Republican hopes soared. By mid-September there was talk of victory and reports from the field indicated a surge to Harding in all parts of the country. No indication was more definite than the election on September 13 in Maine where the presidential contest was held early. Because Maine normally went Republican, the Democrats claimed a Republican victory margin of less than 20,000 votes would constitute a moral defeat. Harding won by 66,000. Coolidge, in typically laconic fashion, wired Harding on September 14: "Judge nothing can prevent your election."[52]

Confidence snowballed. By late September Reily wrote that "Everything in the West is looking the very finest." Dover, who believed that Harding's leaving the front porch drove a final nail in Cox's coffin, reported from San Francisco in early October: "We will carry all of [the West]. . . . I have never participated in a campaign in which there has been as little opposition to the head of the ticket." At the same time, Penrose wrote to Harding that in Pennsylvania "the result is certain." On Columbus Day, Charles Forbes wired Harding from the Pacific Northwest: "you will make a sweeping victory." "Looks mighty good" was Chairman Will Hays's general assessment.[53] Indeed by mid-October even die-hard Democrats were privately conceding defeat. Although Cox and Roosevelt continued to issue ringing pronouncements of ultimate victory, the politically wise knew better. Wrote Mark Sullivan to Senator Thomas J. Walsh: "Quite candidly speaking to you as a Democrat my judgment at this moment is strongly to the effect that Cox is going to fail in such a degree as to be almost unique in recent elections."[54]

Among politicians there is always the haunting fear that some totally unexpected cause célèbre may occur at the last minute, reversing trends and throwing an election to one's opponents. Harry Daugherty constantly worried about this and his fears materialized in mid-October when a situation arose which might have cost the Republicans the election. Suddenly, rumors circulated that Harding possessed Negro blood and circulars appeared purportedly proving that the charge was true.[55]

The work of William E. Chancellor, professor of economics, politics, and social sciences at Wooster College, Wooster, Ohio, these circulars spread rapidly and left in their wake consternation and suspicion. A former superintendent of schools in Washington, D.C., and an admirer of Wilson and the League, Chancellor was irrational on the subject of race, favoring both Negro disfranchisement and segregation. Somehow acquiring the idea that Harding's nomination was a plot to foist Negro domination on the country, he decided to expose it. In so doing, Chancellor simply elevated old Marion gossip to a new sensation. By means of a fake family tree and a number of worthless affidavits, Chancellor's circulars showed that no fewer than four separate and converging lines of Harding ancestors possessed Negro blood.

A few of these circulars had appeared at the Chicago convention at the beginning of the summer, but they had been either confiscated or ignored. Now, just three weeks before the election, they emerged again. Louis Seibold, a journalist assigned to Marion, was the first to call attention to them and thereafter correspondents filed reams of material on the rumor and the content of the circulars. But editors refused to print it. Democratic party leaders also decided against use of the information. Tongues wagged nevertheless and Harding supporters experienced temporary panic. There were fears that the charge would affect the vote of women and would wipe out any possibility of Republican gains in the South. Some feared that it marked the beginning of a "foul eleventh-hour attack" by Democrats to snatch victory from certain defeat. As an antidote Will Hays immediately released an authentic Harding family tree, compiled by the Historical Society of Wyoming, Pennsylvania, while Daugherty issued a statement that the Hardings were "a blue-eyed stock from New England and Pennsylvania" and possessed "the finest pioneer blood, Anglo-Saxon, German, Scotch-Irish, and Dutch." [56]

There were some tense moments in Marion. Evalyn Walsh McLean later remembered that Mrs. Harding "was red-eyed from weeping." [57] Charles Hard recalled that Harding was so upset he "wanted to go over to Wooster and beat Chancellor up." [58] But once the anger passed, Harding and his wife agreed that the best policy was inaction and silence. Typically, Daugherty prepared to fight and gathered reporters together to have Harding issue a direct refutation in the form of a press release. Instead, Mrs. Harding suddenly appeared and, glaring at Daugherty, said: "I'm telling all you people that Warren Harding is not going to make any statement." [59] Thereafter the two Hardings remained imperturbable and by their own stability set a pattern for others. Wrote Mrs. Harding to a friend who touched gingerly on the subject: "I want you to know I have known about these miserable attacks, but more than that, I want you to be assured, and absolutely certain that I am not in the least disturbed by them. . . . These wild tales have been circulated before, but never so bad as in this campaign. . . . We are unafraid, undismayed, and undisturbed." [60]

The Negro-blood story had indeed appeared in every election in which Harding had participated. Actually there was little to it. The story got its start when the first Hardings migrated from Pennsylvania to Ohio. For a brief time they lived in the same area with some Negroes, and it was rumored that the two groups were more than just neighborly. Later the enemies of Harding's father expanded this tale by claiming that his grandmother was "black as ink." In reality, she was blonde. In any event, neighborhood fights between the Harding children and their fellows thereafter produced the epithets of "nigger" and "coon" and so the rumors lived on. Throughout his life Harding had borne these accusations, for the most part, silently. Frankly, he did not know if there was any truth in them or not. Once he told his friend James Faulkner of the *Cincinnati Enquirer*: "How do I know, Jim? One of my ancestors may have jumped the fence." [61]

True or not, the charge did not affect the outcome of the campaign of 1920. Inaction and silence were the proper antidotes. Chancellor, meanwhile, was dismissed from his position at Wooster and later migrated to Canada but not before he published a ridiculous book in 1921 which elaborated on his charges. Distributed surreptitiously and sold from door to door by salesmen of the so-called Sentinel Press, all but a few of these volumes were ultimately confiscated by agents of Harry Daugherty who by that time was attorney general.[62]

So, with a momentary scare, the Harding drive surged on. The odds, which in July had been two to one, in October soared to seven to one. By election day no Cox money could be found: the odds stood at a phenomenal ten to one, the highest for any election on record. In the Harding camp there was an air of excitement and anticipation. Mrs. Harding wrote enthusiastically to George Harvey a few days before the voters went to the polls: "Such crowds—perfect throngs everywhere—such enthusiasm. . . ." To another friend she exclaimed: "We are going to win, and win BIG. . . ."[63]

[5

ON ELECTION day, November 2, Harding and Daugherty played a round of golf at the Scioto Country Club in Columbus and then left in mid-afternoon for Marion. They arrived as preparations were being completed for the evening's activities. Telephone and telegraph wires had just been installed in the kitchen of Christian's house, next door to the Hardings, where the election returns were to be tabulated and assessed. A direct wire also connected Will Hays's office in New York with the Christian home.

The usual evening meal at the Hardings was displaced by an impromptu birthday party. A cake with candles and pink icing was presented to the candidate who, with napkin tucked in his pants, happily entered the spirit of the occasion by devouring a huge piece. It was his fifty-fifth birthday. After the celebration, the Republican candidate, his father, his wife, and Harry Daugherty hurried next door to receive the early election news. Dr. Harding remained until about 10 P.M. by which time it was obvious that Warren was going to win. Happy, he slipped home to bed. Daugherty, satisfied with the manner in which he had conducted the campaign, left about 10:30 P.M. to sleep at the White Oaks home of Mrs. Harding's physician, Dr. Charles E. Sawyer. Warren and Florence Harding stayed on to savor the victory and did not turn in until 5 A.M. Two hours later Dr. Harding, awake and refreshed, showed up on the president-elect's lawn, wearing his Grand Army uniform, with a gold-corded hat, and swinging a stout hickory walking stick, graciously receiving the congratulations of early morning callers. His son slept late.

It was a fantastic victory. Newspaper headlines groped for superlatives: "Indiana Swept by Republicans"; "Illinois Trebles Republican Vote"; "New Jersey by 200,000"; "Gigantic Republican Majorities"; and so on. Politicians were momentarily stunned. George Sutherland said it was "the most joyous thing that ever happened." On the Democratic side, Joseph Tumulty moaned: "It was a landslide, it was an earthquake." Franklin Roosevelt wrote at the head of a letter to a friend: "Franklin D. Roosevelt, Ex V.P., Canned. (Erroneously reported dead)." [64]

The vote, as recorded by the *New York Times*, was 16,181,289 for Harding; 9,141,750 for Cox; and 941,827 for Eugene V. Debs, the Socialist candidate who was currently incarcerated in Atlanta Penitentiary for his antiwar activities. The Republican candidate carried thirty-seven of the forty-eight states and collected 404 electoral votes to Cox's 127. Harding won by the largest popular majority (60.2 percent) yet recorded in the nation's history. The Republicans seized the House 303 to 131; this majority of 172 was the largest in the party's annals. The Republicans also retained every seat they held in the Senate and gained ten from the Democrats, making a majority of twenty-two. Harding carried every state in which he had campaigned, except Kentucky. In every section of the country, except the South, his popular vote exceeded 60 percent; he carried both the Midwest and New England by over 65 percent. In these same two areas Cox received less than 30 percent of the votes cast.

It was later claimed that there was a poor voter turnout in 1920 (only 49.3 percent of those eligible voted), and therefore Harding's endorsement was more negative than positive. This was incorrect. Recent passage of the Nineteenth Amendment had increased the electorate by 9,500,-000 women and thus there was a greater number of persons eligible to vote than in any previous presidential election.[65] However, many women voters did not yet choose to exercise their franchise and therefore they made it appear, in terms of the percentage voting to the total voters eligible, that the election was an apathetic one. Actually, the women who did vote showed a decided preference for Harding, and there is no reason to believe that had more gone to the polls this trend would have been altered. Furthermore, the late campaign surge toward the Republicans, as well as the Maine vote in September, encouraged many voters, men and women alike, to stay home in the belief that a Republican victory was a foregone conclusion. Again, there is no reason to assume that more Democrats stayed away from the polls than Republicans. Normal voting behavior would indicate the opposite. Voter apathy usually hurts most the party which allegedly is ahead.

It was also subsequently claimed that the Republicans "bought" the election through a huge expenditure of money. According to Senator Kenyon the entire cost of the 1920 campaign (local, state, and national) was $8,100,739 for the Republicans and $2,237,770 for the Democrats. One study placed the national expenditures at $4,022,580 for the Republicans and $1,318,274 for the Democrats. Fred Upham, treasurer of the Republican National Committee, stated shortly after the election that the Republican national campaign expenses were $3,416,000.[66] Regardless of the precise figures, a considerable amount of money had been spent, with the Republicans using three dollars to every one for the Democrats. With the Senate cabal myth already in circulation, as well as rumors of the monied and oil interests controlling the Chicago convention, it was easily assumed that rich, predatory elements had bankrolled the Republican victory.

Actually, in early 1919 the Republicans had attempted to reorganize campaign financing through a system of "decentralized giving" which encouraged the "little contribution" as opposed to the big one. Will Hays was the originator of the idea and he declared that no one should contribute more than $1000 to the 1920 campaign. Heralded as a means of preventing corruption, the Hays system created greater political interest among a larger number of party members, but it did not increase party income. Hence before the conclusion of the 1920 campaign, a limited number of large contributions were solicited. In the final accounting, 56,000 persons subscribed to the Republican war chest in 1920, and with a few exceptions their gifts were less than $1000. All contributions totaled a little over $2,000,000, leaving the party with a campaign deficit of approximately $1,350,000.[67]

Significantly, because of Hays's decentralized program there were fewer large contributions to the Republican party in 1920 than in either

1916 or 1924, and there is no indication that the funding of the 1920 campaign itself (not the deficit afterwards) was in any way underwritten by predatory interests. Those few large contributions which were secured in the late stages of the 1920 campaign did not differentiate Republicans from Democrats. Both parties received sizable sums from wealthy men and corporations throughout the period 1916–24. In fact, the Democrats, not the Republicans, acquired the largest contributions. In 1916, Cleveland E. Dodge gave $79,000 to the Democratic party while Bernard M. Baruch and Edward L. Doheny gave $35,000 and $50,000 respectively. In 1920, Alan A. Ryan donated $45,000 and four years later Baruch gave another $25,000. On the Republican side, in 1916 Henry C. Frick, H. Payne Whitney, and Daniel G. Reid gave $25,000 each. Neither in 1920 nor in 1924 did any Republican campaign contribution exceed $25,000.[68]

In assessing the final victory there was also the claim that the League issue had been the primary downfall of the Democrats. This was a favorite Republican refrain. Lodge, Borah, and Johnson, in particular, spoke of the outcome in mock Wilsonian terms as being a "great and solemn referendum" in which the League was utterly defeated. Historians have disagreed ever since on precisely how important the issue was in the campaign. Unfortunately, it is impossible to determine how many voted for the Republicans believing that this choice was the quickest way to gain acceptance of a League, and how many voted for the same party equally convinced it would prevent acceptance altogether. There is virtually no way of knowing whether a vote for the Republicans was a vote for Root, Lodge, or Borah. But one fact is certain. A vote for the Republicans was a vote against the Democrats, and the Democrats represented the party of Wilson. Whatever the vote meant in positive terms, it was clearly a vote *against* Wilson. This fact, whether related to the League or to other factors, was unquestionably of critical importance in the election's outcome.

Perhaps too much emphasis for this anti-Wilson vote has been placed on the League issue and not enough on other aspects of the contemporary situation. In writing to a friend during the campaign, Hoover put his finger on a crucial point: "Since the armistice, the present administration has made a failure by all the tests that we can apply. It has obstinately held up the peace of the world for eighteen months, with a fearful cost to ourselves and to the world. It has woefully neglected and failed upon great reconstruction and administrative measures that are critically necessary as the aftermath of the war. . . . The responsibilities of government should now, therefore, be transferred." [69] In view of the Republican election victory it was obvious that a considerable portion of the voters shared Hoover's feelings. There was a massive vote against Wilsonism quite apart from the League issue itself. Cox admitted it; so did William Jennings Bryan; so did Franklin Roosevelt. The *New York Post* expressed it this way: "The colossal protest was against Woodrow Wilson and everything that from every conceivable angle might be attached to his name." Said the *New York Tribune*, "The country was weary of Wilsonism in all its manifestations." [70]

The conclusion often drawn, of course, is that Harding was simply the lucky recipient of this anti-Wilson sentiment. Any Republican could have won. Perhaps so. But the nature of the 1920 campaign, the personalities of the candidates, and the variety of issues involved show this conclusion to be overdrawn. Harding conducted a masterful campaign, displayed no vindictiveness, engendered no animosities. He made no rasping sounds or impolite thrusts at his adversaries. They, in turn, could not bring themselves to dislike him. This augured well for a future in which the hatreds and political schisms of wartime had to be healed. Harding represented solid ground, stability, a return to national tranquillity. He preached conciliation, cooperation, and respectability. While liberals scoffed at his conservative attitudes on such matters as the tariff and finance, to a nation in the midst of an economic postwar depression such attitudes did not seem illogical. He struck a positive and popular note in his call for government economy. His rather naive appeals for better labor-management relations seemed particularly timely to a society racked by labor turmoil and postwar strikes. His attention to the Negro vote was flattering to a group which was migrating in increasing numbers from the South and beginning to exercise political power in northern metropolitan communities. Harding successfully trapped the dry vote and with it many progressives who could not mark their ballot for Cox because he was a wet. And he captured the farmer who, fed up with Wilson and attracted to Harding through such men as Wallace, voted in droves for the Ohio senator.

Far from being a negative factor, Harding not only was a strong candidate, but, under the circumstances, the strongest possible candidate. His election success was not merely endorsement by default. Clearly sensing

69

political trends, he early identified with the nation's longing for peace and prosperity. In May 1920, he had told the Home Market Club in Boston exactly what the country wanted to hear: "America's present need is not heroics, but healing; not nostrums but normalcy; not revolution but restoration . . . not surgery but serenity." William G. McAdoo caustically observed that such Harding utterances "left the impression of an army of pompous phrases moving over the landscape in search of an idea. Sometimes these meandering words would actually capture a straggling thought and bear it triumphantly, a prisoner in their midst, until it died of servitude and overwork."[71] What McAdoo and many others failed to recognize was that one such "straggling thought," because of its universal appeal, was worth more in the currency of practical American politics than innumerable gems of wisdom spun off in haughty intellectual isolation. The term "normalcy," especially, caught immediate and lasting public attention. During the campaign Harding defined it as follows: "By 'normalcy' I don't mean the old order, but a regular steady order of things. I mean normal procedure, the natural way, without excess. I don't believe the old order can or should come back, but we must have normal order or, as I have said, 'normalcy.' "[72]

Hardly any American citizen could protest against such sentiment. It reflected a universal desire and a universal view. When, through his political skill and with the aid of circumstances, Harding managed to convert his "normalcy" into an antonym for Wilsonism, he became invincible.

III

The Wilson Legacy

[1

"PRESIDENT WILSON'S legacy to Mr. Harding," said the *Nation*
two weeks before the inauguration, "will be one of debts rather than assets. With the single exception of Lincoln, probably no President in our
national history has taken office with as pressing a burden of unsolved
questions as will fall to the lot of our next Executive."[1]

From the vantage point of February 1921, this was no overstatement.
The twenty-eight months between the armistice and inauguration day had
been marked by extreme confusion and turmoil. The nation had been confronted by a complex set of circumstances for which it was unprepared
and which it only dimly understood. As the country reeled through these
postwar months, one problem after another surfaced, each one seemingly
less amenable to solution than the last. Fear and despair rapidly replaced
the satisfaction which victory had brought and the United States entered
the decade of the twenties with apprehension rather than confidence. As
Frank Lowden wrote to former Congressman Edwin L. Denby: "I felt
that when peace came we'd all be so joyful that nothing could weigh upon
us again. I find, however, the problems of reconstruction loom so large
that we are as much occupied with them as we had been with the problems
of war."[2]

The most immediate post-armistice problem was that of demobilization, and its first manifestation was the disbanding of the army. Millions
of families demanded their men immediately regardless of the consequences or the cost, and no administration could afford to stand in the

way. Six hundred thousand servicemen were discharged almost at once. By April 1919, a total of two million were released. By November 1919, only a year after the armistice, the American wartime military establishment of four million men was virtually liquidated. Only some troops of the Third Army, stationed at the Coblenz bridgehead for occupation duty, remained in Europe as lonely reminders of the American contribution which had helped the Allies contain the German juggernaut.

This rapid reduction of military manpower was but one aspect of demobilization. Tremendous quantities of property, supplies, armaments, and ships likewise required attention. The disposal of surplus property often involved intricate real-estate transactions both in the United States and abroad. The completion of such arrangements required delicate diplomacy and the mutual presentation of claims, which were not fully liquidated until years later. Suffused through all this was a colossal amount of waste and inefficiency, as well as some black-market activity and corruption.[3]

The Wilson administration was woefully ill prepared to handle these normal stresses of demobilization, let alone the much more complicated economic and social readjustments necessitated by the end of the war. Wilson had no one to blame but himself. As early as October 1917, he had been urged to create a reconstruction commission to study postwar problems, but he considered the time not yet ripe for such a move. Interested persons, such as Samuel Gompers (hoping to protect labor's favorable wartime position), Federal Reserve Commissioner Paul M. Warburg (concerned over postwar capital dislocations), and New York banker Frank Vanderlip (worrying about postwar reinvestments), continued to prod the president to make a serious study of peace problems, but Wilson remained unresponsive. Like the majority of business, labor, and political leaders, he talked about the advisability of postwar planning but did nothing to initiate it.

Just before the armistice the administration did attempt to make amends. It had discovered, belatedly, that many government agencies had only nebulous ideas concerning their postwar role and that there was no central coordination or direction. The old Council of National Defense, originally created during the preparedness crusade of 1916, offered its services as coordinator and Wilson agreed. The council immediately appointed one economist and one sociologist to study reconversion problems, but the war ended before they could make a report. It was a frustrating exercise in futility anyway. Duplication, cross-purposes, apathy, and ignorance so permeated the thinking on postwar needs that no intelligent plan could have emerged. Some agencies, such as the Department of Agriculture, would not even admit that there was a reconstruction problem. It merely concluded that postwar agriculture "could not be very different from that which [preceded] the war."[4]

By December 1918 President Wilson accepted the fact that his administration had no postwar plans. He even justified that condition. In his December message to Congress, just before departing for Versailles to make postwar plans for the entire world, he remarked that as far as the domestic American scene was concerned the American people would make their own reconstruction plans and "any leading strings we might seek to put them in would speedily become hopelessly tangled because they would pay no attention to them and go their own way."[5]

In the absence of any postwar blueprint the whole wartime regulatory structure quickly collapsed. Interviewed during the war, Bernard Baruch, head of the War Industries Board, once said, "We have only one object— to place the industries of the country on a war basis. In order to do that we have had to scramble a good many eggs. After the war, I suppose, we shall be expected to unscramble them."[6] Yet eight days after the armistice Baruch submitted his resignation to Wilson and a month later the activities of the War Industries Board ceased. The Food Administration folded with Herbert Hoover's resignation on July 1, 1919. Harry A. Garfield's Fuel Administration disappeared by the close of 1919. The War Trade Board ceased to function after it was absorbed by the State Department in June 1919. McAdoo's Railroad Administration concluded its activities on March 1, 1920, when the railroads were returned to their private owners. Only the United States Shipping Board remained in existence with the arrival of the Harding administration, but even it was under mandate by the Jones Merchant Marine Act of 1920 to liquidate its holdings and disappear as soon as possible.

If executive leadership was missing in all this, sane congressional action was equally absent. Although resolutions to create postwar study commissions were introduced in Congress as early as September 1918, none were passed as wrangling between Democrats and Republicans prevented any action. What minimal political cooperation existed between the parties during the war was totally shattered by the armistice.[7] Moreover, the November elections of 1918 changed the political scene drastically. The first postwar (66th) Congress which President Wilson called into special session in May 1919 was Republican-dominated, with both houses controlled by that party for the first time since 1911. Exclusively occupied with the struggle over the Treaty of Versailles, this Congress contributed as little to a sensible postwar readjustment as had the wartime Congress which preceded it. A dozen urgent problems involving foreign trade, tariff, taxes, veterans' welfare, appropriations, and immigration begged for solution while Wilson and Lodge engaged in their dance of death over the League.

Under such circumstances the only significant postwar planning that existed was done by state and local authorities or by individual businesses, unions, industrial combines, and farm organizations. Federal government inaction by the spring of 1919 encouraged the growth of a maze of haphazard and often conflicting plans to soften the blow of economic and social reconversion. In many areas relief and employment committees were created to place men in new peacetime employment or help returning soldiers find jobs. Some emergency state agencies were established to put men to work temporarily until permanent employment could be found. Simultaneously, scores of proposals were circulated by various pressure groups on how best to effect a successful peacetime reconversion. Labor organizations, especially the American Federation of Labor, called for immigration restriction, retention of excess-profits and inheritance taxes, a forty-hour week, transition income for displaced laborers, municipal control of public utilities, and continued government control of the railroads. Business organizations clamored for the return of the railroads to their private owners, immediate abolition of excess-profits and wartime taxes, protection of American industry, and the elimination of all wartime controls. Farm organizations desired increased farm credit, better rural education, a uniform system of crop reporting, abolition of farm tenancy, and greater conservation of natural resources. Obviously each group championed what it believed would benefit it most. Without either congressional or executive direction, the result was not the harmonious blending of different interests but the cacophony of conflict.

This postwar confusion was accompanied by economic dislocations which underscored the tragedy of not having centrally coordinated postwar plans. At the armistice, American industry was still in the process of tooling up for full wartime production. The sudden liquidation of war contracts, whose long-range commitments had reached $35 billion, represented a staggering blow to the industrial community. Some short-term relief for certain industries was allowed by the government, but most of them were left to shift for themselves. Those which had not yet converted to wartime production were the least affected; but those whose production had been geared to wartime demands were disastrously hit. Production quickly declined in the iron, steel, copper, textile, and chemical industries. Many "war babies" simply folded although a few made the successful transition to peace after painful and sometimes protracted reorganizations.

The immediate effect on labor was likewise harmful. Despite the rosy Armistice Day prophecy of Secretary of War Baker that "there is work enough in the United States for all the labor in the country," the employment figure of forty million dropped sharply. About eight million of these were in war work and after November 11 faced the prospect of long layoffs or dismissal. Fortunately, some two million were women who simply returned home. But offsetting this attrition of female workers were millions of returning war veterans who arrived on the labor market just in time to experience the declining labor demand. By February 1919 an estimated three million persons were unemployed and this condition remained to the summer of 1919. Until that time, when business took an upswing, the country reaped a bitter harvest from the seeds of apathy and inaction sown by President Wilson and Congress months before.[8]

[2

EVEN before his sudden illness in late September 1919, Woodrow Wilson had ceased to be an effective president.[9] His mind was so preoccupied with League matters that the government drifted aimlessly before the sea of postwar problems that threatened to engulf it. Only intermittently did Wilson turn his attention to domestic issues and then he dealt with them hurriedly before plunging back into the League struggle. His western speaking tour in the early fall of 1919 was symbolic of his concentration on the League and his determination to achieve a victory over Lodge and a recalcitrant Senate at all costs. Flaying irreconcilables and reservationists alike, Wilson sought to rally the nation behind him in his battle. However, in those few tense hours on the train between Pueblo, Colorado, and Wichita, Kansas, when he became desperately ill, not only was the League fight lost but also any possibility that the nation might regain effective presidential leadership. From this moment until March 4, 1921, the nation was without a properly functioning chief executive.

It was possible that Wilson's first thrombosis may have occurred at Paris in April 1919, when a nasty siege of illness was diagnosed as influenza. But the attack after his speech at Pueblo was unmistakably what laymen would call a stroke as one-half of his face fell and his arm and leg became temporarily paralyzed. On the morning of October 2, back in Washington and making a slow recovery, he suffered another, and more severe, thrombosis while in his bathroom, leaving his left side permanently paralyzed. For weeks thereafter he was in critical condition, lying in bed, not only unable to carry out the functions of his office but even unaware that there were any.

Wilson's illness sent shock waves through his administration. His cabinet members were bewildered. Secretary of War Baker greeted the first news of this sickness with "I am scared literally to death."[10] When no official word filtered to them from the president's bedroom, they became perplexed. Some cabinet officers, such as Secretary of Agriculture David F. Houston, Secretary of the Navy Josephus Daniels, and Secretary of State Robert Lansing, finally guessed the extent of the president's helplessness, and considered alternate courses of action. Secretary Lansing believed that Vice-President Thomas R. Marshall should take over; but Marshall was horrified at the thought and neither Wilson's personal physician, Admiral Cary T. Grayson, nor his private secretary, Joseph P. Tumulty, would consider declaring Wilson incompetent. Hence, under Lansing's direction the cabinet continued to meet once each week in an endeavor to keep the government running, but without any presidential guidance. Wilson, meanwhile, was kept in complete isolation by Admiral Grayson and Mrs. Wilson.

Deliberate lies were told the country about the true nature of the president's condition. It was first stated that he simply had a nervous breakdown. It was even said that he was on the road to a full recovery. But Dr. Grayson knew better and several months after the October seizure

76

told Robert W. Woolley, the Democratic publicist, that Wilson "is permanently ill physically, is gradually weakening mentally and can't recover."[11] Still, the pretense was maintained. Just twenty days after his last thrombosis and while he was only half-alive, Wilson scrawled an unnatural signature on four bills sent to him by Congress as Mrs. Wilson steadied his hand. A few days later the same distorted scrawl appeared on a veto of the Volstead Act. Some senators immediately claimed that either Mrs. Wilson or Tumulty forged these signatures. At one meeting of the Senate Foreign Relations Committee, Albert Fall charged that Wilson was no longer able to act as president and, pounding his fist on the table, exclaimed: "We have petticoat Government! Mrs. Wilson is President!"[12]

For seventeen months the second Mrs. Wilson (Edith Bolling), a woman who had very little interest in statecraft, was the closest thing the United States had to a president. Throughout Wilson's illness she screened all presidential visitors and even messages. No one could see him without her approval. Even members of the cabinet were kept away. When they attempted to see Wilson, they were received in a small sitting room off the president's bedroom by Mrs. Wilson who then acted as courier, carrying notes back and forth between them and the president. The unintelligible scrawls they received were all they got for their pains. Interestingly, during this period two cabinet officers were appointed in this "middle-woman" way and never saw Wilson at all.

A few persons were allowed in. In early November, Senator Gilbert M. Hitchcock, the Democratic floor leader, was ushered into the president's bedroom to urge him to compromise with Lodge on the League. He was shocked by Wilson's gaunt visage and white beard (the president had not shaved for weeks). Hotly denying that there could be any compromise, Wilson displayed the reactions of a man whose mind and personality were in the process of disintegration and who now sought martyrdom rather than the resolution of a difficult situation. A month later, as rumors swept Congress that Wilson had lost his reason, Senator Fall was permitted to see the president, ostensibly on Mexican matters, but actually to gain information for his Republican colleagues on the condition of the president. Before Fall arrived there were elaborate preparations. The Senate's recent report on Mexico was placed so that the president could grab it with his good right hand. His paralyzed left arm was buried under the blankets.

Mrs. Wilson stationed herself so she could monitor every word and clutched paper and pencil with which to record the proceedings.

Wilson was marvelous. He shook Fall's hand vigorously and quipped about the senator's Mexican investments. Once during the brief conversation Wilson waved the Senate's Mexican report under Fall's nose to emphasize a point. When Fall prepared to leave and remarked he was praying for him, Wilson shot back: "Which way, Senator?" Surprised and flustered, Fall rapidly retired while Mrs. Wilson continued recording every word. The Wilson "bedroom circle" was ecstatic. The Fall visit doomed any incipient Republican attempt to oust Wilson and assured his continuance in office fifteen months more.[13] In the momentary joy it was overlooked that Wilson was completely drained by the experience, lapsing again into almost complete physical and mental inactivity.

By Christmas 1919 Wilson could work or concentrate for about five to ten minutes at a time and then would lose the thread of what was going on. Thus, the government remained on dead center as a sick president and a protective wife strove to maintain the appearance of effectiveness. But requests were ignored, cabinet officers could get no answers to their problems, even the State Department's work ground to a halt. Lansing received only one presidential reply out of a dozen inquiries and that one contained "answers communicated through Mrs. Wilson so confused that no one could interpret them."[14] At the time, diplomatic appointments were needed in twelve countries; United States wartime interventions in Latin America were crying for attention as were relations with Mexico; and European policies were in a shambles. As Ray Stannard Baker confided to his diary in late December 1919, it appeared "as though our Government has gone out of business."[15]

Throughout the winter of 1920, Mrs. Wilson and Admiral Grayson devoted their energies to helping Wilson recover while he, in turn, expended his meager energy on brooding about the League. Despite the Senate's adverse vote in November, Wilson remained obdurate and refused to compromise. Instead of seeking a solution he sought scapegoats. On February 7, 1920, he summarily asked Secretary of State Lansing to resign. Piqued at Lansing for calling cabinet meetings in his absence, Wilson also believed Lansing had not adequately pressed the League fight. Tumulty advised against firing Lansing, but Mrs. Wilson canceled his influence by flatly stating: "I hate Lansing."[16]

To succeed Lansing, Wilson picked a man almost totally inexperienced in foreign affairs, a New York lawyer on the Shipping Board, Bainbridge Colby. Colby could scarcely believe his ears when the president made the offer and he accepted only reluctantly. This appointment caused rumors again to circulate that Wilson had lost his mind. Indeed, in a pattern normal to victims of thrombosis, while physical recovery had shown some progress, emotional and mental recovery had lagged behind. Wilson's reactions in the late winter and spring of 1920 were quixotic and vengeful, sometimes accompanied by temper tantrums and tears. Meanwhile, his fixation on the League increased. When, on March 19, 1920, the Senate again rejected the treaty his despair became impenetrable. George Creel, who was one of the favored few to see the president, reported that after this second defeat Wilson was consumed by a vast inner loneliness. Wilson later admitted that after the March 19 vote he would have gone mad "if I were not a Christian." In utter desolation of spirit, he once remarked to those around him that it would have been better for the nation and for himself if he had died on the train while it carried him from Wichita to Washington.

Still, the shell of the man lived on. April 14 marked the first time in over eight months that he attended a cabinet meeting. It was a trial for the cabinet. Wilson repeated himself, spent much time rehashing the League defeat, and quickly closed off debate on matters that had occurred during his illness about which he knew little. Later cabinet meetings went no better and mercifully were held only infrequently after April. Meanwhile, each officer continued to run his department as best he could without presidential guidelines or a unified policy.

Unfortunately, Wilson's cabinet at this time was not strong. Only four of his original appointees remained, and such recent additions as Colby (secretary of state), A. Mitchell Palmer (attorney general), John Barton Payne (secretary of the interior), and Edwin T. Meredith (secretary of agriculture) augured a conservative trend which foreshadowed a "return to normalcy" long before Harding arrived on the scene. New to one another, and not closely acquainted with the president, these men failed to produce satisfactory results.[17]

By the summer of 1920 Wilson was somewhat better. Now and then he would watch a movie or take an automobile ride. He attended to some

79

government business, but the topics were always screened by Mrs. Wilson and none were admitted that might excite him. Gradually he even showed some interest in politics, but in an egocentric way. As the time for the Democratic convention approached he began thinking of himself as a candidate. As a result he withheld crucial support from his own son-in-law, McAdoo, a fact which helped prevent the latter's nomination. Wilson refused to sponsor any candidate, foolishly waiting for the lightning to strike. Once when Senator Carter Glass mentioned Cox as a possibility, Wilson exclaimed from his wheelchair: "Oh, you know Cox's nomination would be a joke."[18]

Wilson's friends at San Francisco blocked any attempt to present his name because they agreed that his selection would be "unthinkable." But back in the White House rage and a stream of profanities met the announcement of Cox's nomination as the president childishly felt himself rejected. Ultimately he accepted the decision, had a brief and tearful meeting with the Democratic candidates during which he secured their pledge to campaign on the League issue, and persisted in believing that the voters would vindicate him through Cox on election day. Wilson stayed up two hours past his nine o'clock bedtime on November 2 in order to hear the results, but retired when it was obvious Harding would win. He issued no public statements and seemingly ignored the outcome, but the staggering Republican victory drove him even farther into a desperate depression.

For the next four months this depression remained although he tried to pull himself together. Even his winning the Nobel Peace Prize in December 1920 failed to restore his spirits. And as his administration drew to a close a funereal pall descended over everything. As one observer remarked in mid-February 1921, "I went to the White House offices one day this week. It is a place of quiet and stillness. Some two or three odd persons of no consequence sat on the leather covered benches in the anteroom. . . . The whole thing was like a scene preserved. It just stands there all unmarked and unadorned waiting what may come."[19] Certainly no one sensed this purposelessness more keenly than Wilson himself. To one supporter who proclaimed that he would follow Wilson after he left the White House no matter where he might go, the crippled president sadly replied, "There is nowhere now to go."[20]

[3

"THE disability of President Wilson was one of the most important events of the age, when consequences are considered." So spoke the *Washington Post* eighteen months after Wilson's first attack.[21] The collapse of Wilson was indeed significant because it meant far more than the fate of one man—it signaled the temporary collapse of government itself. Under normal circumstances, this condition would have been serious enough. But in a turbulent postwar era of economic boom and bust, the results were especially tragic.

As already noted, the immediate postwar period of reconversion and dislocation came to an end by mid-summer 1919. Thereafter the industrial index quickly recovered to a point 19 percent higher than the last prewar year of 1914 and slightly above the wartime level of 1918. Accompanied by an upsurge in employment, the economy demonstrated increasing strength until the late spring of 1920. Some analysts claimed the primary reason was the release of pent-up demands of consumers, who during the war had been unable to purchase durable items. Later studies rejected this "deferred demand" thesis, claiming that the basic reasons were the continuation of government spending at a high rate, the granting of reconstruction loans to Europe, subsidization of heavy exports through overseas credits, the emergence of a domestic building boom, and an "easy credit" Federal Reserve policy.[22]

Whatever the reasons, this upturn in the economic cycle would have been more beneficial had it not been accompanied by a ruinous inflation. An ominous rise in prices began in April 1919 and rapidly accelerated, reaching a hectic climax in May 1920. The contemporary explanation was that the increase in production did not keep pace with the expansion of purchasing power. The real culprits, however, were dealers who were piling up excess inventories in the face of suspected (but nonexistent) shortages and speculators who wanted to take advantage of the emergent price rise by bidding up prospects of the future. Moreover, the Federal Reserve Board did not top off the price surge by tightening credit restrictions. The Treasury Department's use of bank credit to help float the final Victory Loan did not help matters. Between June 1919 and June 1920 loans and investments of Federal Reserve banks increased by $2 billion and Federal Reserve notes in circulation rose by 20 percent while the reserve ratio fell to 41 percent.

The effect on the cost of living was disastrous. By November 1919 the cost of living was 82.2 percent above the 1914 level and rising rapidly. By July 1920 it stood at 104.5 percent. The biggest jumps were in clothing and food—clothing increased to 177 percent and food to 119 percent. Since wages and salaries did not keep pace with this runaway inflation, grumbling occurred everywhere. Housewives went on buying strikes. Unions put their men on the picket lines. Congressmen hotly debated remedial legislation or futilely called upon the White House to do something. The press angrily condemned Wilson for worrying about the plight of Europe while the high cost of living (simply called "HCL") was killing the United States. Wilson, of course, was ill during the worst of this inflationary period and did nothing.[23]

Suddenly in the spring of 1920 the collapse came. The first sign was a break in agricultural prices in May. Then other wholesale prices began to fall, sometimes at a rate of 3 percent per month. From 104.5 percent above the 1914 level in July 1920 the cost of living fell to 93.1 percent in November, then to 68.7 percent in March 1921, and a year later, in March 1922, reached its low point of 54.7 percent. This was the sharpest slide for any comparable period in American history. In terms of a ratio in which 100 percent represented the cost of living in July 1920, the decline to March 1922 was 24.4 percent. The major decrease came in food (36.5 percent) and clothing (42.0).[24]

The economic effect of this sudden deflation was staggering. Hardest hit was the farmer. Benefiting from good times during the period 1914–20, the farmer had begun to take prosperity for granted. Spurred by the slogan "Food will win the war," the farmer not only had increased his production but also had enjoyed a consistent rise in income. Wheat acreage grew during the war years from forty-seven million acres to seventy-four million acres. Gross farm income rose to a peak in 1919 of $16,953,000,-000, which was 152 percent above the prewar annual average. By 1919 agricultural prices in livestock and meats were 83 percent above the 1914 level. Throughout the immediate postwar months, while industry experienced the temporary shock of dislocation and reconversion, agriculture remained remarkably stable. Hence the farmer was not prepared for the severe price collapse in the spring of 1920.[25]

82

It was the most serious price crisis that American agriculture had ever experienced. Between July and December 1920 the average price of the ten leading crops fell 57 percent; by May 1921 these prices were only one-third what they had been in June 1920. Although this downward trend was part of a worldwide break in agricultural prices, the American decline was far more precipitous. From the beginning of 1920 to the summer of 1921 the average drop for farm prices in the United States was 54 percent; in the United Kingdom the decline was only 31 percent. United States corn, which had sold for $1.88 a bushel in August 1919, brought only 42 cents by the fall of 1921. During that same period wheat fell from $2.50 a bushel to $1.00. This decline in farm prices far surpassed that in industrial prices during the same period. For example, in 1919 a bushel of corn would buy five gallons of gasoline; in 1921 the same bushel would buy little more than one gallon.[26]

This price debacle was immediately reflected in declining farm incomes. On a 1914 base of 100, net farm income in 1919 was 219. In 1920 it was 185; in 1921 it fell to 84. To put it another way, between 1919 and 1921 farm income dropped more than 50 percent. At the same time farm bankruptcies, which had averaged 1.5 per 10,000 farms during the years 1905–14, in 1920 stood at 20. By 1922 the average was 21.5 and still climbing. Simultaneously there was a collapse of agricultural land values. Caught with overextended credits in machinery and farm land, many rural banks went under, thereby further increasing farm distress.[27]

Although less disastrously affected, both industry and labor also suffered from the deflation of 1920. From July 1920 to December 1921 labor's earnings declined 20 percent. On a July 1914 base of 100, hourly earnings of factory laborers fell from 261 in 1920 to 198 in 1922. However, because wage declines between 1920 and 1921 averaged slightly less than the drop in both agricultural and manufacturing prices, the adverse effect on workers was more apparent than real. Interestingly, professional groups on fixed salaries—ministers, schoolteachers, and so on—actually benefited from the price deflation. Declining prices brought them relief. Even so, by late 1921 they were only just reaching their 1914 salary levels in relative purchasing power.[28]

Mounting unemployment and a decrease in business activity inevitably followed the price collapse. Having just recovered from the dislocations of the immediate postwar period, the labor market again became oversubscribed. The problem involved not only the renewed necessity of layoffs but the inability of industry, under existing circumstances, to absorb new workers coming onto the labor market. It was estimated that in 1920 there were approximately thirty million persons (excluding farmers) gainfully employed. Of these, an estimated 16,969,000 were industrial wage earners. A survey indicated that in January 1921 there were 3,473,446 fewer persons in industrial employment than in January 1920. This would represent an unemployment rate of about 20 percent. Total unemployment for the winter of 1920–21 was estimated at 4,754,000. In August 1921 the Labor Department gloomily admitted to a figure of 5,753,000. Not until the depths of the Hoover depression in 1931–32 would unemployment figures surpass these peaks.[29]

The causes for the depression of 1920–21 were loudly debated at the time and have been analyzed and reassessed by economists ever since. Some contemporary observers were convinced that the deflation was deliberately planned by banking authorities, with the Federal Reserve Board playing a leading role. Farmers, especially, charged that the price panic in agriculture was brought about by a Federal Reserve "conspiracy" to restrict credit after December 1919. The fact that the prices of other commodities did not fall as low as those in agriculture gave farmers an emotional issue. It was the "Crime of 1920"—agriculture had been singled out for deflation. To the farmer, Governor W. P. G. Harding of the Federal Reserve Board and David Houston, secretary of the treasury, were the "Deflation Twins." Moreover, the farmer firmly believed that an increase of approximately 33 percent in freight rates, ordered by the Interstate Commerce Commission when the railroads were returned to their private owners and made effective August 1920, was specifically directed against them and was another cause of the price decline. Coinciding with the harvest season, these higher rates weighed heavily on farmers at the precise moment of falling income. The connection seemed obvious to them—freight rates went up, prices went down. Plainly, it was a plot of business and Wall Street.

Contrary to popular farm opinion, the tightening of credit by the Federal Reserve Board came too late rather than too soon. Discount rates should have been raised in early 1919. But it was not until early 1920 that Federal Reserve officers raised them from 4.75 to 5.5 percent. When this seemed to have little effect, the Federal Reserve Board announced in May 1920 that the rediscount rate on commercial paper in Chicago and New York would jump to 7 percent, effective June 1. The fact that this action coincided so neatly with the break in agricultural prices was too striking for farmers to miss. Yet the connection existed in the mind of the farmer and not in reality.

As with any depression, the real causes were many and inextricably bound together. First of all, the decline was not merely a local phenomenon but part of a worldwide economic dislocation resulting from the war. Furthermore, in the United States the downturn was not the periodic manifestation of a mere business cycle but reflected a fundamental reshuffling of economic resources. Perhaps the most significant factor was the drying up of huge governmental expenditures. No longer was this largess available for either industrial or agricultural purposes. By mid-1920 government spending was cut drastically and treasury receipts were beginning to surpass expenditures. This increase in revenue resulted largely from a sharp rise in taxes occasioned by the Revenue Act of 1918, and its amendment of February 1919, which raised income taxes to a maximum of 8 percent, surtaxes to 65 percent, and the corporation tax to 10 percent. Inflation, meanwhile, meant that incomes after taxes could purchase fewer goods. The rate of purchasing fell off in 1920–21, not because of buyers' strikes, but because incomes would buy less.

Thus, while consumer demand remained relatively high, the physical consumption and acquisition of goods declined. Businesses, with heavy inventories, hoping to cash in on the anticipated pent-up wartime demand, suddenly panicked and released their goods at reduced prices as bank credit needed to hold these inventories became scarce. The Federal Reserve Board's actions in restricting credit in the early months of 1920 made business all the more uneasy. Cancellations of new orders as well as the liquidation of existing inventories became the norm as confidence in the future waned. Meanwhile, the vast overproduction in agriculture became glaringly apparent. Rural credit quickly contracted in the face of expected surpluses. With domestic needs being more than met, the need to export American goods became especially critical. Yet there was a decline in both manufacturing and agricultural exports in 1920–21. This decline in exportation resulted largely from the curtailment of European credits in the United States rather than the sudden recovery of European business or agriculture. In short, the tapering off of American wartime and reconstruction loans to Europe was immediately reflected in diminishing American exports.

One additional fact about the depression of 1920–21 was obvious—at least by hindsight. There were as yet no refined theories of economic behavior upon which either the business or the agricultural community could rely to adjust to the rapidly changing postwar circumstances. Moreover, the full implications of national fiscal policy or of the expansion or contraction of governmental spending were not yet fully understood. While the postwar period encouraged a more careful analysis of economic trends, the results of such labors were not yet sufficiently appreciated. In 1920–21 there also was too little quantitative information available on purchasing power and the course of industrial production. The art of economic prognostication and statistical evaluation was still in its infancy.

Even if there had been greater sophistication of data gathering or economic theorizing, the Wilson administration was in no position to benefit from it. Ill during the period of rampant inflation and still not in full control of affairs after the depression's onset, President Wilson largely ignored the declining economic situation. What few suggestions he did make were shunted aside by a hostile Republican Congress. His cabinet officers, demoralized and leaderless, were helpless to take any effective action. Consequently, for many in the general public election day 1920 offered an opportunity for them to vote not so much on the League as on the administration's ineffective reaction to the nation's postwar economic problems.

[4

ONE factor often deemphasized or totally ignored in most analyses of the 1920–21 depression was the public attitude toward political and social events which created a psychic milieu that exacerbated the emerging economic distress. In the eighteen months immediately preceding the price collapse, the nation suffered political and social disruptions of great magnitude. With a sick president in the White House and an ineffective administration floundering in confusion, political instability was an obvious fact. But social instability was equally apparent.

Naively, many persons had believed that the return of peace would usher in the millennium. Wilson himself had proclaimed peace would bring a new day "of greater opportunity and greater prosperity for the average mass of struggling men and women." Some were even more sanguine. The head of the Psychology Department at Columbia University greeted the armistice with the statement that returning peace would make Americans "less selfish, more social, less timid, more devoted. . . . Personal loves, personal jealousies, and the pursuit of personal gain will not function as they customarily did." [30]

Instead, the end of the war unleashed a wave of hatreds and hysteria unmatched in modern American history. Shocked by the excesses of the current Bolshevik upheaval in Russia, the American public shivered in fear that a Soviet-style revolution was about to be repeated here. Throughout 1919 the press filled its pages with largely erroneous, but highly sensational, accounts of domestic radical activity and issued paranoid warnings of impending crisis. By the summer of 1919, after some radical riots had occurred and a number of bombs were discovered in the mails, public alarm reached a crescendo.

Meanwhile, labor struggles lost their economic significance as citizens chose to view them as a prelude to political revolution. Disastrous strikes in the coal and steel industries immeasurably heightened public fear of the success of domestic radical activity while other walkouts, such as the Seattle general strike and the Boston police strike, had already prepared the public to believe that a "Red revolution" was actually in progress. Governor Calvin Coolidge became an overnight national hero solely because of his forthright stand in telling the Boston police: "There is no right to strike against the public safety by anybody, anywhere, any time." Likewise, Attorney General A. Mitchell Palmer became a savior in the eyes of many frightened citizens because of his rigorous action in securing an injunction against the striking coal miners in October 1919.

Employers naturally seized upon this public fear and antilabor sentiment to resist such traditional labor demands as higher wages, shorter hours, and union recognition. Combining forces to "fight the foe" were powerful employer organizations such as the United States Chamber of Commerce, the National Metal Trades Association, and the National Founders Association. The end result was a general defeat for the unions, with the Wilson administration lining up solidly behind employers.

The public reacted in various ways to this supposed threat to the American way of life. Some joined, or at least morally supported, various superpatriotic organizations like the National Security League, the American Defense Society, and the National Civic Federation. Attracting to their memberships those who wished to "keep America safe," they circulated throughout the country pamphlets, flags, copies of the Constitution, and speakers to encourage a "healthy patriotism." The most famous such organization was the American Legion, which held its first convention in St. Louis in 1919, and claimed it was specifically dedicated "to foster and perpetuate a one hundred percent Americanism." Returning soldiers joined this organization in droves, transferring their army-instilled patriotism to the civilian scene.

But mere talk, flag-waving, and parading were not always the only activities of these superpatriots. They kept schoolteachers and ministers under surveillance for breaches of a proper love of country. Sometimes they banded together to tar and feather suspected radicals and run them out of town. In southern areas, the revived Ku Klux Klan performed such chores willingly in an endeavor to keep the countryside "pure." The most vicious and spectacular eruption of violence occurred in the little town of Centralia, Washington, on November 11, 1919, when an altercation between local Legionnaires and members of the radical IWW resulted in the death of four ex-servicemen and the brutal lynching of one Wobbly. The latter was emasculated by the local populace before being hung from a railroad bridge; his body was then pumped full of bullets and left dangling for two days. The coroner's verdict was suicide.

Mounting public fear ultimately spawned repressive government action. State governments passed syndicalist, loyalty-oath, and Red-flag legislation as a means of combating what was erroneously thought to be wholesale sedition and insurrection. At the national level Attorney General Palmer undertook a series of raids in November 1919 and January 1920, which netted several thousand suspected radicals and adherents to the newly formed Communist party. Several hundred of these were later deported to Russia. Meanwhile, in January 1920, five duly elected Socialists were refused their seats in the New York Assembly. In 1919 the United States House of Representatives twice refused to seat Victor L. Berger, a properly elected Socialist from Milwaukee.

Fortunately the worst aspects of this hysteria passed by the summer of 1920. But the deleterious effects of the Red Scare lingered on. Obviously, this public fear with its accompanying turmoil was not conducive to business confidence or economic stability. Moreover, this fear of radicalism placed a high premium on conservatism and thereafter both economic and social innovations were viewed with suspicion. The union movement emerged from the Red Scare era seriously weakened while the influence of the businessman was on the rise. The American plan, as opposed to the closed shop, was rapidly enthroned. The clamor for tighter immigration restriction to keep out radical undesirables markedly increased. Also embedded in the Red Scare experience was a continuing American antipathy to Soviet Russia and a justification for the policy of nonrecognition.

Again, the Wilson administration proved powerless to alter the trend of events. Despite Wilson's warning to Palmer in the late summer of 1919 not to let the country "see Red," Wilson himself often ran with the pack, baying at the scent of radicals. By the time of his breakdown in September, he had come to think of bolshevists and radicals as being one of the most insidious pressure groups working against his ideas on world peace and condemned them as enemies not merely of the United States but of all mankind. Still, he remained insightful enough to recognize that "the seed of revolution is repression" and that restrictions on individual liberty had to be exercised with the utmost care. Unfortunately, the blood clot that walled off part of Wilson's brain in the fall of 1919 also opened the door for his attorney general to act without restraint, and Palmer transformed the Wilson administration into an agent for repression throughout the remainder of 1919–20. When the break in public hysteria finally occurred by the summer of 1920, Warren Harding's quiet promises of serenity were far more appealing than the continued frenzy of Attorney General Palmer.[31]

[5

IN MARCH 1921 the Wilson legacy was a potpourri of unsolved problems and mounting tribulations. Business, once healthy and profitable, had suffered through a recession and inadequate postwar planning only to experience the wrench of a shaky boom followed by a tragic bust. Businessmen were fed up with Wilsonian idealism and wanted a straight business approach to the nation's problems. They wanted to rid themselves of wartime and excess-profits taxes—all of which seemed perfectly logical in view of the depression of 1920–21. Even former Secretary of the

Treasury McAdoo agreed in 1921 that such taxes were "having an injurious effect on business" and should be reduced by at least one billion dollars annually. Moreover, business wanted no more loans made to Europe but believed that repayment should begin immediately. At the same time, it expected continued aid from the government in the form of high protective tariffs, subsidies for American shipping, aid to commercial aviation, guaranteed profits for the railroads, help in disciplining labor, and greater efficiency and frugality in government operation. Anxiously business awaited the demise of the Wilson regime and the return of Republican rule to the White House.

For the laborer and the farmer, the Wilson legacy was a deteriorating economic condition. By March 1921 over four million laborers were unemployed with few prospects for jobs in the near future. Those who were employed found that their rights were being eroded by the militancy of employers. The farmer, meanwhile, had rapidly been demoted to a junior partnership in the nation's economic life. No crisis, except in the 1890's, had so altered the position of agriculture in relation to the rest of the economy. As a result, by the close of the Wilson administration the farmer was in a rebellious state. He became more aggressive and radical in politics as moribund organizations such as the Grange, the Farmers' Union, and especially the American Farm Bureau Federation flared into life. He called for increased aid from the federal government in the form of high protective tariffs, extension of rural credits, continued loans to foreign purchasers of agricultural products, and a better system of domestic marketing. To achieve these goals, a group of Iowa congressmen, including Senator William Kenyon, banded together in the closing days of the 66th Congress to form a nucleus for concerted farm action. Although they sponsored a protective tariff measure and a host of farm relief bills, these either failed of passage or ran afoul of Wilson's last-minute vetoes. This organizational development nevertheless presaged continued political action by farmers. Hence, while Warren Harding reaped the farm vote on election day, he also inherited from Wilson a disaffected farm population and an emergent and fractious congressional farm bloc.

The Wilson legacy included other important although not so obvious bequests. There was a postwar relaxation of conventional morals and a general looseness of public morality. Simultaneously there existed a mounting note of cynicism and disillusionment stemming not only from the war but from the failure of Wilsonism. Finally, there was the problem of enforcing prohibition which was simply passed along for Harding to handle.

The Wilson legacy also contained some undesirable gifts for the progressive movement and for Wilson himself. Although it was later fashionable to say that the election of 1920 marked the defeat of progressivism, the claim was untrue. There was no progressive candidate in 1920 and no progressive program. Both the war and the events of Wilson's last years had eliminated progressivism as an ideological entity. Certainly the "old" progressivism of the New Freedom variety was gone. No longer could liberals coalesce on principle or unite behind a single personality. The League issue proved unsatisfactory as a catalyst because liberals were divided on it. Wilson was no longer a rallying point; he was ill. Thus, by 1920 the progressive movement, as such, was dead. The liberal coalition which had centered on Wilson had already begun to disintegrate with the war and collapsed completely in the postwar turbulence.[32]

Ironically, and tragically, in the months from the convention to the election in 1920 Wilson was mentioned only peripherally by the press, and thereafter he was soon forgotten. A survey of publications from July 1920 to March 1921 reveals a striking lack of public interest in Wilson, except for certain eastern journals. It was as if he were dead along with his League and his progressivism. Eugene Debs, writing from Atlanta Penitentiary where Wilson had placed him and from which Wilson had refused to release him, issued this epitaph on the fallen leader shortly after the 1920 election: "Woodrow Wilson is an exile from the hearts of his people . . . the most pathetic figure in the world. No man in public life in American history ever retired so thoroughly discredited, so scathingly rebuked, so overwhelmingly impeached and repudiated as Woodrow Wilson."[33] Such was the disastrous legacy of the last years of Wilson's administration to the contemporary reputation of its own leader.

As for the Ohioan who now moved into the White House, his portion of the legacy was anything but welcome. From Wilson he received a disintegrating presidency, a confused and rebellious Congress, a foreign policy in chaos, a domestic economy in shambles, a society sundered with hatreds and turmoil. The *Nation*, which was certainly no admirer of Harding, admitted that "all this seems like an overwhelming task for our next President." Newton Baker, who knew from the inside the failures of the

Wilson administration, confided to Brand Whitlock: "Senator Harding's problems of course [will be] immensely difficult. . . ." Writing a quarter of a century later, Colonel Edmund W. Starling, chief of the White House secret service and an admirer of Wilson, summed it up best: "the country was in a mess." [34]

IV

The New Administration Begins

WITH the taste of a stunning election victory still in his mouth, President-elect Warren Harding announced on November 5, 1920, that he intended to leave Marion the next day for a month's vacation in Texas and Panama, but that upon his return he would consult the "best minds" of the country about his cabinet and his future course of action. He warned that all speculation in the interim about cabinet selections would be fruitless because he did not intend to name anyone until he returned to Marion.[1]

No sooner had Harding's special train turned southward than the press was filled with intense speculation. Each issue brought forth new cabinet names "on the highest authority" or eliminated old ones on the basis of information from "someone close to Harding during the campaign." On the day Harding left, the *New York Times* claimed that General Wood and Frank Lowden would certainly be in the cabinet. Others picked Senators Lodge and New as sure bets. The guessing for secretary of state centered on Root or Senator Knox, with an occasional mention of Charles Evans Hughes.

While the speculation continued, Harding's special train carried him first to Point Isabel, Texas, where he remained for several days as a guest of Ed Scobey. After some fishing, poker playing, and golf, he journeyed by auto to Brownsville where he visited with his Senate partner Albert Fall. Three days later he was in New Orleans boarding a boat for Panama, arriving at Cristobal on November 23. For several days he conferred with American naval and military officers there and returned to the United States via Jamaica, arriving at Norfolk on December 4. The following day he was in Washington, D.C., relaxed and fit after a month in the sun.

When the Senate convened on December 6 for the opening of the third session of the 66th Congress, Harding was present to bid farewell to his former colleagues. He entered the chamber from the Republican cloakroom at two minutes to noon and was greeted by a standing ovation from the packed galleries and members on the floor. As the applause mounted, he walked to his desk in the third row on the Republican side. After the prayer and the swearing in of two new senators, Lodge addressed Vice-President Marshall, calling attention to the fact that for the first time in history an active senator had been elected president, and requested permission for Harding to speak. Cheering and applause again filled the room as Marshall left the rostrum to escort the president-elect to the platform. There, with a wave of the hand, Marshall formally presented him to the galleries. Mrs. Harding, accompanied by Evalyn Walsh McLean, was a tense spectator.

Harding spoke for ten minutes, expressing with great emotion his regret at leaving the Senate. But his speech was not all sentiment. Aware of press inferences that his cabinet would be packed with senators and that a "Senate oligarchy" would dictate administration policy, he inserted these comments which were met with silence on the floor: "When my responsibilities begin in the executive capacity I shall be as mindful of the Senate's responsibilities as I have been jealous for them as a Member, but I mean at the same time to be just as insistent about the responsibilities of the Executive. Our governmental good fortune does not lie in any surrender at either end of the Avenue. . . . Something has been said about the senatorial oligarchy. Of course, everyone here knows that to be a bit of highly imaginative and harmless fiction."[2]

Tumultuous applause followed his concluding hope that he and the senators would remain good friends and much handshaking and back-slapping ensued as the Senate adjourned for the day. Senators on both sides of the aisle detained him for one-half hour, offering him their personal cooperation and best wishes. But Harding was a smart enough politician to know that these displays of affection were as much for show as for anything else. Patting Bob LaFollette on the shoulder, Harding said,

"Now, Bob, be good." Momentarily dropping his guard, LaFollette shot back, "I'll be busy making you be good." It was prophetic.[3]

Back in Marion on December 10, Harding turned to the task of selecting a cabinet. He was in a fortunate position. He had come into the presidential office under obligation to no one. Although he owed his Ohio supporters and a few close friends, such as Daugherty, a deep debt of gratitude, he had received the nomination and achieved final victory without promises or deals. This gave him a freer hand in selecting his official family than most presidents had enjoyed.

He was determined to acquire an independent-minded, first-class cabinet. His hope was to attract equals and not rubber stamps. He desired to follow in the tradition of Washington and Lincoln in this respect, and not Wilson. But Harding recognized there were, necessarily, some restraints on his freedom of choice. Once he said to reporters when lecturing them on the problems of cabinet making: "Three things are to be considered in the selection of a cabinet. First, there is the man's qualification for public service. That is the most important consideration of all. Second, there is the attitude of the public concerning the man under consideration. Third, there is the political consideration. As to that—well, this is going to be a Republican cabinet."[4] This was the framework within which Harding operated, but arbitrary action was not his way. A master at adjudicating differences and a firm believer in collective party wisdom, Harding now sought broad agreement on his cabinet and elected to consult widely— the "best minds"—before making final decisions.

[2

NEVER before had there been such a pilgrimage of political leaders to a president-elect as occurred after December 10 at Marion, now dubbed "the Great Listening Post." For the next month as many as six or seven invited guests funneled through Harding's makeshift office each day, being asked advice on a variety of matters, especially cabinet selections. No shade of opinion was excluded nor were favorites played. Once, when it came to Harding's attention that Republican House members were disgruntled because of the preponderance of senatorial visitors, he ordered Will Hays, who was in charge of the invitations, to include more representatives. Even leading Democrats were requested by Harding to appear at Marion.[5]

Harding rapidly became discouraged by the lack of advisory unity among the "best minds." Worse, he found himself the vortex of subtle intrigues designed to sway him one way or another. He soon learned that the "big men" he wanted for his cabinet also possessed "big enemies" and that political considerations were often used to cancel out superior qualifications. Once, in the midst of discouragement, he wrote to his Ohio friend Malcolm Jennings: ". . . what a job I have taken over. The man who has a Cabinet to create has one tremendous task." To another friend he confided, "My cup is full." Yet, despite his inner turmoil, Harding weathered it well. Insiders were amazed at his patience and tact, his cordiality and sincerity. William Howard Taft came away from Marion convinced that Harding was trying to "do the right thing." Nicholas Murray Butler left with a solid impression of Harding's "good judgement and sound common sense" and was satisfied that the Ohioan possessed a "perfect familiarity with the various troublesome elements in his political party."[6]

The marathon discussions soon convinced Harding of several things: the secretary of state had to be a man universally respected by the country yet able to work with all elements in Congress; the secretary of agriculture ought to be a practical farmer and not merely a professor of farming or an agricultural lobbyist; the Labor post should go to someone identified with labor, but not of the "Gomper element"; and the Treasury position should be filled from the Midwest, not from New York or New England. Harding was also convinced that one, if not two, positions on the cabinet should be reserved for his own friends—men upon whom he could rely for personal advice and whose loyalty he could absolutely trust.[7]

These convictions provided at least a partial basis for decision making and were reflected in his action in filling the first position—secretary of state. Much nonsense has been written about this appointment. Some later writers contended that Harding really wanted to give the post to his friend Albert Fall but that visitors to Marion shook him out of this notion with their sharp opposition. It was also claimed that he considered George Harvey and then Root before deciding on Hughes.[8] Actually, Harding offered the position to Hughes on December 10, when the New Yorker appeared in Marion as one of Harding's first visitors. Three days later Hughes wrote Harding that he had talked the matter over with his law partners and "was glad to say that I have arranged to be free to assume the responsibilities of which you spoke."[9] On December 22, Harding replied that he was delighted with Hughes's decision and that the matter was closed. They both agreed, however, that no public announcement would be made until later. Such an announcement—the first regarding a cabinet position—was made on February 19, 1921.

In the meantime, ignorant of this decision, the press continued its speculation and politicians argued. Anti-League Republicans, such as Senator Borah, championed the cause of Senator Knox. Senator Brandegee, another bitter-ender, contended that if Harding could not appoint Knox, he should at least name Lodge. A few, such as Senator Wadsworth and Charles Hilles of New York, clamored for the selection of Root; and when Harding invited Root to come to Marion in mid-December, speculation soared that he was about to be chosen. When no offer to Root was apparently forthcoming, press interest shifted back again to Hughes. At the same time, the Old Guard, frightened by increasing rumors of Hughes's appointment, ultimately closed ranks behind Root even though they still wanted Knox. Senator Penrose made an eleventh-hour fight in late January to block Hughes's selection by dangling Root before Harding's eyes. But Harding had already made his decision and stuck with it. Moreover, it was *his* decision and Hughes was *his* choice—his *first* choice. It was a fearless act of cabinet-making statesmanship.[10]

A second decision which reflected a strong Harding preference was the selection of Henry Wallace as secretary of agriculture. Born into a farming family in Iowa's Adair County, Wallace, after attempting farming for five years, developed more interest in teaching (for a time he was an assistant professor at Iowa State) and in farm journalism than in plowing. One of the best known agriculturalists in the United States because of his editorship of *Wallace's Farmer*, he had helped write the 1920 Republican farm plank and had, of course, aided Harding during the campaign. By a curious twisting of definitions, Harding classified Wallace as a "dirt farmer" and thus eminently qualified to head the Agriculture Department. Even before the election, Harding had his eye on Wallace as a potential secretary. On November 1, 1920, Harding wrote him: ". . . if the verdict on Tuesday is what we are expecting it to be I shall very much want your assistance in making good the promises which we have made to the American people."[11] After the election, when others were brought forward as candidates, such as Senator Arthur Capper and Marion Butler, Harding barely gave them consideration. Wallace was Harding's man from the beginning even though press speculation did not center on him until late December.[12]

By that time, Harding was being subjected to extreme pressure regarding the Wallace selection. Conservative leaders strongly objected. Wallace's liberal tendencies scared Old Guard members while his editorial assaults against the malpractices of the packing and food-processing industries had earned him the hatred of these powerful elements. A delegation headed by Everett C. Brown (president of the Chicago Live Stock Exchange) hastened to Marion to protest his nomination. The packers and millers also had their spokesmen present. But Harding did not waver, and Wallace joined Hughes on the cabinet list.

If Hughes and Wallace were not to the liking of the president-elect's Senate cronies or close political friends, this was also true of a third selection—Herbert Hoover. From the outset Harding was attracted to Hoover as a cabinet candidate for Interior or Commerce even though certain elements in the party lived in constant fear of his being selected for either. No sooner did Hoover arrive in Marion (December 12) to confer with Harding than a bitter campaign was begun to keep him out of the cabinet. The opposition was both impressive and articulate. Frank Brandegee stated the anti-Hoover position succinctly: "Hoover gives most of us gooseflesh."[13] Too liberal, too internationally minded, too popular, and too ambitious for the Old Guard, Hoover was not opposed for a particular cabinet post, but for any. Senators Knox, Curtis, and Smoot voiced strong opposition and warned Harding that Hoover would not "get along well" with other cabinet officers. Not only the Old Guard, but even insurgent senators, such as Hiram Johnson, were antagonistic. Harry New, one of Harding's troubleshooters on cabinet appointments, wrote to Marion shortly before Christmas: "Many senators have expressed the hope that Hoover may be omitted." Daugherty reported essentially the same information.[14]

Harding's attitude toward Hoover remained unshaken. On January 12, 1921, in reply to a letter from Hoover in which the latter had endorsed Wallace's appointment as secretary of agriculture, Harding wrote: "Your opinion concerning [Wallace] is important to me. Indeed, I hold you in such esteem that your opinion on any matter is of real importance."[15] Under the fierce attacks this esteem grew stronger. On February 9, Harding wrote Daugherty: "The more I consider him [Hoover] the more do I come to think well of him. Of course, I have no quarrel with those who do not think as I do, but inasmuch as I have the responsibility to assume, I think my judgment must be trusted in the matter."[16]

Several days later, on February 12, Harding formally offered Hoover the post of secretary of commerce which he understood Hoover preferred. The precise position was immaterial to Harding. Hoover, on the other hand, was not anxious to accept. Indeed, considerable persuasion was necessary. At one point Harding asked Hughes and Will Hays to intercede and convince Hoover he should enter the cabinet. Then, on February 22, in a phone call from St. Augustine where he was relaxing before his inauguration, Harding restated to Hoover his deep desire to have him join his official family. In the face of such pressure Hoover wavered and the next day wired Harding that although he much preferred to remain out of public life, "I have no right to refuse your wish and I will accept the Secretaryship of Commerce."[17] Formal announcement was made to the press on February 24.

Hoover's selection as secretary of commerce was closely connected with that of Andrew W. Mellon as secretary of the treasury. Contrary to later assertions, Harding displayed not only his independence in this instance but also his shrewdness. Mellon was not Harding's first choice for the Treasury post. Mellon's name was not even among the early candidates—John Weeks (Massachusetts), Charles G. Dawes (Illinois), and Charles Hilles (New York). Of these men, Dawes was Harding's favorite. During his visit to Marion in mid-December, the Chicago banker was asked by Harding if he could be enticed into the cabinet, and Dawes replied "probably not," but no final decision was reached one way or the other.[18]

Dawes possessed some attractive advantages: Chicago and the midwestern banking fraternity strongly endorsed him; he was renowned for his ability to effect efficiency and economy; and he was fearless, frank, and unpledged to any particular faction in the party. But many in the East did not like Dawes, considering him too erratic. Temporarily these elements united behind Weeks as their candidate and urged his selection. However, Harding was not impressed by eastern arguments against Dawes; besides, he did not wish the post to go to a New Englander or a New

Yorker because of "Wall Street" connotations. As late as Christmas, Harding still inclined toward Dawes.

The first mention of Mellon was made by Senator Knox. Once, while Harding was wrestling with the Treasury problem and weighing the pros and cons of the Midwest versus the East, Knox remarked that if a neat geographic solution was wanted, as well as experience and competency in the job, Pennsylvania could provide the Pittsburgh multimillionaire. A short time later Mellon was invited to Marion, had lunch with Harding, and chatted for about an hour. Harding briefly mentioned the Treasury position and inquired if Mellon was interested. The financier did not give a flat "no," but he reminded Harding of his vast holdings and the impropriety of making such a wealthy man secretary of the treasury. Harding asked him to keep the matter open.[19]

The president-elect still wanted Dawes but was forced to recognize the logic of a Mellon appointment. Besides, this turn of events presented Harding with an unexpected opportunity. He needed something to assure Hoover's confirmation if that selection was made. At the same time, he was juggling his preference for Dawes with his desire to placate certain members of the Old Guard, especially the eastern money "establishment." In late January, Harding met with Dawes a second time and explained this complex situation to him. Dawes indicated that he really did not want the Treasury post and personally would support Mellon. Harding then requested Dawes not to let it be known that his name was being withdrawn until the president-elect could outflank Penrose, Knox, and other Old Guard members who were bitterly opposed to Hoover. Harding confided to Dawes that he intended to trade Mellon as secretary of the treasury for Hoover as secretary of commerce. Shortly thereafter, Harding sent Daugherty to Washington to indicate to Senators Knox and Penrose that Mellon was a possibility, but only if their attacks on Hoover ceased. Reluctantly, they agreed—and Mellon was chosen.[20]

The selection of the financier was a curious blend of politics, chance, shrewdness, and cold calculation. It was cabinet making at its best. In the end, everyone won—the Old Guard, both midwestern and eastern banking interests, Hoover supporters, and most of all Harding. Not every president could boast that one of the wealthiest men in the world was in his cabinet. At the same time Harding realized that Mellon's appointment was a two-edged sword. In his talk with Dawes, Harding had admitted: "Mellon probably has too much money for a Secretary. I may get as much criticism over his appointment as I would if I put J. P. Morgan in that place."[21] Harding almost did, but he was prepared to accept it. Mellon was not so sure about himself. He did not relish the personal sacrifices he would have to make or the criticism he would have to endure. Yet, encouraged by Senator Knox, Mellon was intrigued by the thought of entering the world of politics. As Mellon later described his ambivalent feelings: "I really didn't want to come to Washington but I did not want absolutely to refuse."[22] He finally capitulated and an announcement was made to the press the last week in February.

While these four selections—Hughes, Wallace, Hoover, and Mellon—were based to a large extent on Harding's own desires, four other appointments represented the normal surrender to sheer political expediency. In these cases, the president-elect merely followed the advice of his political advisers or the dictates of party necessity. Although the results of the election demonstrated that there was no great need to sacrifice cabinet positions to the Wood faction, Harding and his advisers were nevertheless aware of the general's personal popularity. The "Great Listening Post," for example, was bombarded with requests that Wood be made secretary of war in order to "salve his disappointment" over losing the nomination. In a *Literary Digest* poll, 242 of 300 Republican editors endorsed him for this position.

In Harding's advisory circle there was considerable opposition to Wood. It was claimed that his appointment to the War Department would cause internal friction in the army because he would have to pass on the promotions of officers under whom he had served or with whom he had been in school. Some of Harding's advisers were opposed to Wood for any cabinet position because of his popular appeal and his obvious political ambitions. Besides, old wounds still remained from the preconvention campaign fight against Harding in Ohio. Harding agreed that these various reasons precluded Wood's appointment to the cabinet, but he expressed hope of using Wood's talents elsewhere.[23]

Political and geographic requirements pointed ultimately to John Weeks of Massachusetts as secretary of war. An early contender for the post of secretary of the treasury, he had been vigorously supported by Senator Lodge who acquiesced in the selection of Mellon only after receiving assurances from Harding that Weeks would be put "somewhere" in the cabinet.[24] At one time or other, Weeks was considered for post-master general and secretary of the navy.

His credentials for both of these latter positions were rather impressive. Weeks had been a member of the House from 1905 to 1913 and then had served six years in the Senate. While in the House, he had been chairman of the Committee on Post Office and Post Roads; in the Senate, he had been a member of the Military Affairs Committee. In addition, Weeks possessed a naval record. In 1877, at age seventeen, he had enlisted as a cadet midshipman and, four years later, graduated from the Naval Academy. He served in the regular navy for two years and was honorably discharged. During the Spanish-American War he again donned his naval uniform, signing on as a lieutenant for the duration. Thereafter, he returned to his Boston banking business, which expanded so rapidly that it made him one of the major New England bankers by World War I. His defeat for reelection to the Senate in November 1918 was a surprise, especially to some of his close Senate friends such as Harding and Lodge.

Weeks had been a valuable adviser during the campaign and Harding was more than willing to have him represent the Northeast in the cabinet. The logical post seemed to be secretary of the navy. But Weeks shunned this position for the same reason that made Wood unsuitable for secretary of war: it would not be wise for him to pass on the qualifications and promotions of those with whom he had served or attended school. Just before Christmas, therefore, feelers were sent out from Marion to determine whether Weeks would accept appointment as secretary of war. The Boston banker indicated through his Senate friend Harry New that he would.[25]

On January 15, 1921, Weeks was summoned to Marion to talk with Harding, and his selection was made final. Yet more than a month elapsed before Harding issued an official announcement. The reason for the delay was not any latent opposition to Weeks, but a desire on Harding's part to wait until announcements could be made about other cabinet choices as well. Actually, Weeks's selection was a popular one with the party and with the military. Senator Wadsworth, chairman of the Senate Military Affairs Committee, wrote to Harding after the decision was made public: "I would like a dollar for every Army officer and every member of Congress who during the last two months has expressed the hope that Weeks could put his hand to this great big task." [26]

The job of secretary of labor posed a particularly thorny problem. Continuing labor disturbances in the postwar period focused unusual attention on government-labor relations, and the Republicans were anxious to appease the rank and file of labor if possible. Among the persons most often mentioned for the position of secretary of labor were James Duncan, William L. Hutcheson, Thomas V. O'Connor, and James J. Davis. Head of the Granite Cutters' Union and a vice-president in the AFL, James Duncan was the personal choice of Samuel Gompers and, interestingly enough, was also supported by Lodge—Duncan was from Massachusetts. Despite Lodge's blessing, Gompers's support proved the kiss of death. Hutcheson, as general president of the Brotherhood of Carpenters and Joiners, possessed considerable rank-and-file labor support but had no one in the Republican party leadership strongly pushing him. O'Connor, president of the International Longshoremen's Association, was also championed by strong elements in organized labor, but his earlier advocacy of the closed shop and low tariffs created suspicion.

The most palatable candidate was James Davis. While Davis claimed to be a laboring man and at one time had been an iron "puddler" and active union member, he had long since become better known for his lodge work. Director-general of the Loyal Order of Moose and one of the founders of Mooseheart (a city of fatherless children in the Fox River Valley west of Chicago), he was sometimes called "The Napoleon of Fraternity" because he supposedly could call thousands of men by their first names. This proved to be a decided political asset, for hundreds of Moose lodges sent endorsements of "Puddler Jim" Davis to Marion. When support also came from such diverse labor organizations as the Street Carmen's Union and the Iron Moulders' Union, Davis appeared unbeatable. Besides, he was anti-Gompers, was a hard-working Republican party member, and had been a staunch backer of Harding during the campaign.[27]

The decision regarding the Labor post was allowed to simmer until after Christmas while more pressing cabinet business was settled. Then on January 7, Harding telegraphed Davis to come to Marion and discuss the labor policy of the new administration. Three days later he offered Davis the cabinet position and Davis accepted.[28] No announcement was made, however, and press and labor speculation continued regarding the selection. In the ensuing weeks many labor leaders voiced concern over the possible appointment of Davis and hurriedly joined forces to oppose him. They did not regard Davis as sufficiently labor-oriented and feared that his interest lay more in Mooseheart than in the shops and mines. In a last-minute effort to forestall his appointment, Gompers sent a lengthy telegram to Harding on February 7 stating that "no man is fully capable to fill the position of Secretary of Labor who lacks the sympathy, respect and confidence of the wage workers of our country."[29] If Harding needed a reason to reinforce his earlier decision to appoint Davis, Gompers's telegram supplied it. Still, Gompers was right; the appointment was not a particularly strong one.[30]

On the other two political appointments, the selection of the postmaster general was the easier. While a number of candidates existed, there was never any doubt that Will Hays, as chairman of the Republican National Committee, could claim the post if he wished. Strangely enough, Hays did not relish the thought of supervising the nation's mails and preferred the Commerce job. However, Harding had already reserved that position for Hoover and on January 17 gave Hays his choice of either postmaster general or chairman of the proposed Commission to Reorganize the Government. Three weeks later, after weighing the alternatives, Hays told Harding that he would accept the cabinet post.[31]

The selection of secretary of the navy was almost an afterthought and came at the very end of the wearisome process of cabinet making. After former Senator Weeks dropped out of contention in late December, it was decided to offer the position to Frank Lowden. In this way the Lowden faction would be rewarded for its support of Harding at the convention and during the campaign. When Lowden received the offer on January 17 he was surprised. He had nursed the hope of being secretary of the treasury or secretary of agriculture and felt qualified for either. But he hardly knew the bow of a battleship from the stern. Hence, after some soul searching, he telegraphed Harding his refusal. Harding persisted and reaffirmed the offer not simply as a courtesy, but as a genuine desire for him to enter the cabinet. When Lowden again demurred, Harding attempted still a third time to get him to reconsider. Harding's last telegram of February 14 read: "I think a great public approval awaits your acceptance. If you insist once more on the impossibility, I will accept its finality."[32] Lowden insisted.

Edwin Denby's name had first been mentioned to Harding by Weeks at the time that he had indicated his preference for War rather than Navy. Lowden had also mentioned Denby during his series of refusals of the Navy position. Almost in desperation, Harding now turned to this quarter. On the basis of qualifications and availability, Denby made an excellent candidate. He had served as a gunner's mate in the Spanish-American War and in 1917, although forty-seven years old, had enlisted as a private in the marines, rising to the rank of major before his discharge. In between his military experiences, he served for six years in Congress where, among other assignments, he was a member of the House Naval Affairs Committee. Losing his seat in the insurgent revolt of 1910, he became involved in the budding automobile industry and by World War I had made a fortune manufacturing automobiles. In the preconvention days of 1920, he was a Lowden man, but he had worked diligently for Harding in the election campaign. On February 22, Harding offered him the Navy post. Denby was amazed. Said he: "The invitation took me off my feet. I was overwhelmed." He was not as surprised as the press. Reporters greeted the announcement of the appointment with "Denby, Denby —who is Denby?" [33]

Much drama has been written into the relatively simple story of Harding's selection of two of his personal friends for the remaining cabinet positions. His friendship for Albert Fall and his gratitude to Harry Daugherty gave them both a high priority on his list of available candidates.

In the case of Fall, Harding simply liked him. Fall had an attractive and colorful personality. Born in Frankfort, Kentucky, in 1861, Fall had worked in a cotton mill in Nashville when he was only eleven years old; at eighteen he had studied enough law to become a lawyer. Shortly thereafter he set out for the Red River country and for three years was a United States marshal in the Panhandle area. Turning next to prospecting in Mexico, he worked the region around Zacatecas as a mucker, ore sorter, and drill sharpener. The year 1885 found him back in the United States digging for riches in the mountains of New Mexico. During the Spanish-American War he rode with Roosevelt and the Rough Riders, later settled down in Las Cruces, served in the legislature of the New Mexico territory, and was elected to the United States Senate in 1912. There, wearing a broad-brimmed Stetson, flowing black cape, and handlebar mustaches, he occupied a seat close to Senator Harding and became a poker-playing crony of the future president of the United States.

But friendship was not the sole factor in Fall's selection. Harding had deep respect for his ability. So did others. Fall was considered an expert on western matters and on Mexican and South American affairs. He wrote the Mexican plank in the 1920 Republican platform. Also, he had served on the Senate Foreign Relations Committee with Harding and had been a strong opponent of Wilson's League. A ruthless in-fighter, Fall was at his best in the kind of give-and-take political debate which endears a politician to party stalwarts.

Harding mentioned Fall casually in connection with a number of positions. However, he considered him seriously only for secretary of the interior, and then only after it became clear that Hoover wanted Commerce and not the Interior post. Fall's appointment represented a convenient marriage of certain geographic considerations and Harding's desire to reward a friend. Fall was from the West and the Interior appointment usually went to a westerner. That Fall was basically anti-conservation in his views did not play a part in Harding's calculations. Fall, in turn, did not know definitely until February 4 that he was to become secretary of the interior. Hence, later talk of his appointment being the consummation of secret deals made with oil interests at the 1920 nominating convention was complete nonsense. His selection was the last to be announced—on March 1.[34]

At no time was there opposition to Fall on ethical grounds. He was regarded as above suspicion by friend and foe alike. The only opposition to him came from those who opposed his conservation views, not his morals. A few rabid conservationists, such as Gifford Pinchot, maintained a drumfire of criticism against the Fall appointment, but they were only a small minority. From everybody else's point of view, the appointment was perfectly logical. As Albert Shaw, editor of the *Review of Reviews,* later commented, "The Senator from New Mexico was recommended for a cabinet place by almost every public man in Washington. . . . His appointment was made by Mr. Harding in entire good faith."[35]

The selection of Harry Daugherty as attorney general was without doubt the most controversial appointment made by Harding. Daugherty's questionable Ohio past, together with the host of high-placed enemies he had acquired during his lifetime, made protests inevitable. From the stream of callers who visited Marion, there was barely a kind word heard for Daugherty. But Harding would not be swayed. In mid-December, to a disapproving Senator Wadsworth, he exclaimed: "I have told him that he can have any place in my Cabinet he wants, outside of Secretary of State. He tells me that he wants to be Attorney-General and by God he will be Attorney-General!" [36]

Daugherty later claimed that he did not really want to be attorney general and urged Harding to name George Sutherland instead. However, there is little doubt that Daugherty realized the appointment would give him increased prestige in the legal profession and help wipe out the curse of dubiety on his past career. To Ohio friends he confided that one of the main reasons he might take the post was so he could walk down Broad Street in Columbus, Ohio, and tell his arch-enemy, newspaperman Bob Wolfe, "to go to hell." [37] But whether he wanted it or not (and secretly he did), the initiation of the offer certainly rested with Harding and not with his campaign manager. Finley Peter Dunne, writing much later, correctly gauged the relationship: "I believe that if Harding had refused him the appointment he would have gone into a corner and cried. But then he would have wiped away the tears and come back and served as faithfully as ever." [38]

Up to the moment of the formal announcement, certain elements of the press maintained bitter opposition to Daugherty. This was especially true of Louis Seibold of the *New York World* who was covering the political scene at St. Augustine while Harding was vacationing there just before the inauguration. His assaults on Daugherty stung Harding and on February 21, seeing Seibold in the crowd of reporters, the president-elect angrily stated: "I am ready to-day to invite Mr. Daugherty into the cabinet as my Attorney-General; when he is ready there will be an announcement, if he can persuade himself to make the sacrifice." [39] Later that day, Daugherty issued the statement: "No man could refuse to serve a friend and his country under the circumstances." [40] Seeing Daugherty a short time later, Mark Sullivan, another reporter who had questioned his qualifications, extended his hand in congratulations: "Well, you're going to be Attorney-General!" Daugherty growled good-naturedly: "Yes, no thanks to you, goddam you." [41]

In the midst of all this sparring the merits of the appointment were lost to sight. Daugherty was a lawyer and, contrary to opposition propa-

107

ganda, a shrewd lawyer. True, he had spent more of his time being a lobbyist than a practicing attorney; yet even that had some advantages. He
understood lobbying tactics and was in a position to use such knowledge,
if he desired, for the protection of the common good. As he once told
Sullivan: "I know who the crooks are and I want to stand between Harding and them."[42] Also he was an ace political troubleshooter. His potential
value to Harding in handling matters of patronage was incalculable. More
important, he was a proven and loyal friend on whom the president-elect
could absolutely rely.

Subsequent events cast doubt on Daugherty's performance in this latter regard. But even some of Daugherty's most violent contemporary detractors ultimately adopted a positive view. In 1935, in his book *Our
Times*, Sullivan claimed that Daugherty was really high-minded about his
fellow Ohioan and "would not himself deliberately do anything that might
reflect on Harding."[43] In that same year, Louis Seibold wrote: "I have
always believed that Daugherty really wanted to protect Harding."[44] Writing in 1932, Daugherty's own assessment of his appointment was far less
charitable: ". . . in a moment of mental aberration I accepted the post
of Attorney-General in the Harding Cabinet and made the tragic blunder
of my life."[45]

This, then, was Harding's cabinet: two Pennsylvanians, and one each
from California, New York, Massachusetts, Ohio, Michigan, Iowa, Indiana, and New Mexico. There were two bankers, an automobile manufacturer, a lodge director, a humanitarian-engineer, a rancher, a farm-journal
editor, an international lawyer, and two professional politicians. The cabinet was relatively young: Hays 41, Hoover 46, Davis 47, Denby 51, Wallace 54, Hughes 58, Fall 59, Weeks 60, Daugherty 61, and Mellon 65.
There was even a spread of religious affiliations: Mellon and Hays were
Presbyterians; Hughes and Davis were Baptist; Weeks was Unitarian;
Daugherty was Methodist; Hoover was Quaker; Wallace was United Presbyterian; Denby was Episcopalian; and Fall was unaffiliated.

Later, during the period of the oil scandals, it was the vogue to depre-
cate these selections. Journals such as the *New Republic* and the *Nation*
would speak of Hughes and Hoover as mere "deodorizers" for Daugherty and Fall. Actually, the vast majority of the nation's press and of its
political observers greeted the final cabinet with approval in 1921. Their
only reservation was Daugherty. As the *New York Times* put it: "From

Hughes to Daugherty is a pretty long step." But aside from this, they appeared content. Mark Sullivan, writing in May 1921, called it "one of the strongest groups of presidential advisors and department heads in a generation."[46] In an article for the *Atlantic Monthly* in March 1923, two years after the cabinet was selected, William B. Munro still reflected a widely held belief when he stated: "No presidential cabinet during the past half-century has been better balanced, or has included within its membership a wider range of political experience."[47]

[3

THE inauguration was intended to be a spectacular affair. Ned Mc-Lean, the dapper millionaire friend of the president-elect, was named chairman of the inaugural committee and laid plans for "the most dazzling celebration within the memory of the present generation." Immediately there were cries of protest in Congress about the propriety of such action in view of the economic depression and Republican promises of government economy. Harding, who had not been consulted on the plans for the inaugural, immediately agreed with the protesters and on January 2 wired McLean that he wanted only a simple ceremony. "There is such a widespread desire for economy," he stated, "that I believe most heartily in a practical keeping of faith in the very beginning."[48]

Reluctantly plans for an inauguration spectacular were set aside. McLean notified Harding that the committee would respect his wishes and keep it simple. There was to be a small parade, but no public-sponsored inaugural ball. A private dance would be held at McLean's Washington estate, "Friendship," which would be paid for by McLean and to which officials of the new administration and visiting dignitaries would be invited. Congressmen, the general public, and the press applauded this decision and considered it a good start for the incoming administration. It indicated the new president's sincerity in carrying out his campaign promises.

March 4 was a crisp but clear spring day. At 10:30 A.M. the Hardings appeared at the White House where President and Mrs. Wilson met them. Although it was a laborious process, Wilson walked that day, leaning on a cane with his good arm and resting the other in Harding's vise-like grip until they arrived at the front door of the White House, at which point Wilson's valet and secret-service men took over. Lifted bodily into

109

a waiting Pierce-Arrow, Wilson looked especially gaunt and haggard beside the rugged Ohioan who now seated himself on the president's left for the drive to the Capitol. No one in the crowds which lined the route knew then that the sick Wilson would outlive the robust man who was taking his place.

Although it was traditional for the president and the president-elect to mount the long Capitol steps together, President Wilson did not attempt it. Harding strode up alone while Wilson was driven to a side entrance where a platform had been constructed to receive his wheelchair. Wilson was then taken through the Capitol corridors to a private elevator and finally to the President's Room in the Senate wing. There he met with members of his cabinet for the last time and signed those bills which were passed on this last day of the 66th Congress. Suddenly Senator Lodge, chairman of the Senate Notification Committee, entered the room and indicated to Wilson that the Congress was ready to adjourn unless he had further use for it. A hushed silence fell as these two foes faced each other for the last time. Controlling his emotions, Wilson quietly said, "I have no further recommendations to make."[49]

Wilson wanted to attend the inaugural ceremonies, but Harding, who now briefly joined him in the President's Room, urged him not to do so. "I guess I had better not try it," Wilson said. "I understand," Harding replied. Despite his own bitterness, Wilson suddenly felt a kinship with this affable man who was about to shoulder the awesome responsibilities of the presidential office. He later admitted to a close friend that there was something about Harding that appealed to him. "I really like him," he exclaimed. But at the moment the only feeling Wilson betrayed was a murmured "All the luck in the world" as Harding departed to take the oath of office. Wilson, in turn, left the Capitol by the same route he had come. As he moved slowly through the corridors he heard the marine band strike up "Hail to the Chief" for the new leader, and by the time he reached the side entrance he was no longer president. Tired and his emotions near the breaking point, he entered a White House limousine and, accompanied by Mrs. Wilson, Admiral Grayson, Joseph Tumulty, secret-service man Edmund Starling, and his valet, Arthur Brooks, was driven directly to his new home on S Street. After farewells all around, Starling quickly returned to the Capitol to guard the new president.[50] The Wilson years were over.

At 1:18 P.M. Chief Justice Edward D. White began: "I, Warren Gamaliel Harding, do solemnly swear . . ." The Bible was opened to Harding's favorite passage in Micah: "What doth the Lord require of thee but to do justly and to love mercy and to walk humbly with thy God." Clad in conventional morning attire and wearing a dark overcoat with a velvet collar, Harding remained bareheaded throughout, his chiseled features, dark eyebrows, and silvering hair presenting a most distinguished appearance. Cheers greeted the conclusion of the oath taking and the band struck up "The Star-Spangled Banner." Then Harding put on black-rimmed nose glasses, drew his inaugural address from his pocket, and delivered it almost from memory, making little reference to the manuscript.

The speech was short, lasting only thirty-seven minutes. But it outlined what the new administration stood for. After opening with a few patriotic remarks typical of inaugural addresses in general, Harding stated that he did not favor "entangling alliances" and that the United States could not be a party to political or economic commitments "which will subject our decisions to any other than our own authority." Yet, he declared, the people of the United States should be willing "to associate ourselves with the nations of the world, great and small, for conference, for counsel" in order to maintain peace and achieve disarmament. At this point he looked toward a little knot of fifty or so wounded veterans who had been wheeled near him to hear the address and assured them that so long as he was president their wartime sacrifices would not be forgotten.

Turning to the domestic front, Harding declared that the primary necessity was to resume "our onward, normal way." This meant reducing expenditures, establishing economy in government, and repealing excessive taxes. "Our best assurance," he said, "lies in efficient administration of our proven system." To this end he promised to encourage prosperity and to work for "the omission of unnecessary interference of Government with business." He concluded by pledging his administration to seek industrial peace, to reestablish protection for American industry and agriculture, and to achieve full employment.[51]

The first inaugural address in history to be carried by amplifier, it was heard distinctly all over the Capitol grounds and was well received. While some listeners wished for a return to the days of crisp Wilsonian prose, by inaugural address standards Harding's effort was not inferior. Its syntax, its general word choice, and its content marked it as average, if somewhat old-fashioned. Not surprisingly, William Jennings Bryan thought it a great address. The *New York Times* was somewhat more temperate, claiming the speech "did not fall below the general expectation," and "will confirm the popular impression of [Harding] as a man who makes no pretense of uncommon wisdom or force, but whose intentions are of the best, and who is sincerely anxious to make his Presidency useful and safe rather than brilliant."[52]

To the man on the street, the speech was precisely what he wanted to hear. It not only captured his mood but also attracted his allegiance. It was something he could support easily and intelligibly. As one woman was heard to exclaim while listening to the speech in front of the Capitol: "We have had Wilson eight years, and I have not understood him. I understand Harding already."[53]

To the strains of "America," Harding left the inaugural platform to revive a custom last used by Thomas Jefferson. He strode to the Senate chamber where he presented his cabinet slate in person. While both La-Follette and Borah later claimed that they were uneasy about this procedure, they did not indicate so at the time and applauded along with the rest as Harding read his list of ten names. Borah and LaFollette also acquiesced, along with every other senator, when Lodge suddenly moved "that Senator A. B. Fall be immediately confirmed by the Senate as Secretary of Interior without the usual formality of a reference to a committee." The New Mexican thus became the only cabinet officer in history to be accorded such a vote of confidence. Spontaneous applause greeted this decision as Fall submitted his resignation as senator to Vice-President Coolidge on the spot.[54]

About 2:30 P.M. President and Mrs. Harding entered a White House car and drove amid cheering crowds to their new home at 1600 Pennsylvania Avenue. Later that afternoon Harding reviewed a brief inaugural parade with enthusiasm, once sending a secret-service man to recall to the reviewing platform a Negro drum major, dressed in white and gold, whose skill at handling a twirling baton amazed him. That evening the Hardings were the honored guests at the McLean-sponsored inaugural ball at "Friendship." Dancing continued until the small hours of the morning when the simplest inauguration in modern history ended. The Harding years had begun.

[4

THE change in atmosphere was immediate. For two years the White House with its barred gates and its funereal quality had symbolized all of Washington, D.C. Now, less than two hours after returning from the inauguration, the new president issued his first order—throw open the White House gates, closed since the declaration of war in 1917. This action was immediately interpreted as a step toward normalcy, and eager citizens came to stand outside the north portico or the main entrance and peer at all those who entered the White House or left. That night Mrs. Harding ordered all the blinds opened so the crowd, standing on tiptoe, could see inside. "It's their White House," she said, "let them look in if they want to."[55] The next day, when portions of the White House itself were opened to the public, thousands flooded through the east portico and down the corridors to the East, Red, Blue, and Green rooms. This little historic journey thereafter became a "must" on everybody's Washington trip.

Mrs. Harding immediately endeavored to introduce some gaiety into the somber presidential mansion. Brighter colors were added and flowers suddenly appeared everywhere. Thousands of bulbs were planted in the lawns, and birdhouses were installed in the trees. Mrs. Harding reinstituted White House teas and during that first summer gave three garden parties. During the first Christmas the customary White House holiday receptions were resumed. Laughter and cheerfulness replaced the hushed tones and smell of the sickroom.

It was said that the Hardings represented Main Street come to Washington. Sinclair Lewis had just published his famous novel and the connection was easily made. The Hardings did move into the White House with their small-town background intact. They did not hesitate to admit being "just folks" or to practice small-town ways. To a caustic critic like H. L. Mencken, this seemed hopelessly gauche; but to the majority of citizens it was welcomed as a breath of fresh air. As one journalist described it, "The Washington atmosphere today is that of old Home Week or a college class reunion. The change is amazing. The populace is on the broad grin. . . . Distinctly the sunny side is up."[56]

Nowhere was this change more manifest than in the relations between the White House and the working press. Newsmen liked the new presi-

dent. The affinity arose partially from the fact that he, too, was a newspaperman. But it went beyond that. Reporters liked his frankness in con-
fessing his limitations and his refreshing candor about presidential problems. The press was taken behind the scenes and shown the inner workings of the presidency to an extent never allowed before. Harding restored
the regular White House press conferences, which Wilson had abandoned,
on a free give-and-take basis and, where Wilson had loathed them, Harding enjoyed them immensely.

Harding's skill in handling the press was evident from the first news
conference. Harding met the incoming throng of reporters at the door,
shaking hands with each one. For many he had an individual word of
greeting. Then, in the center of a triple ring of reporters, he leaned or
half-sat on a flat-topped desk and, without waiting for specific questions,
began to talk. Harding knew their professional interests, what "story"
was in it for them, and he gave it to them. He talked frankly but not in-
discreetly. Naturally, the reporters reacted with sympathy. As one veteran
expressed it: "All but a few chronic kickers are hailing him. The great
majority of the correspondents have laid aside their axes and fine tooth
combs."[57]

Unquestionably Harding had the best relationship with the press of
any president in history. Some of the men who covered the White House
he knew personally and he called them by their first names. To the Hardings they were "our newspaper family." Never did he treat reporters in
a high-handed fashion or ignore them. On a few occasions he subjected
them to lectures about greater press responsibility and once or twice, especially in late 1922, expressed his displeasure at their criticism of Daugherty and of several administration measures. But in general their good
relationship held to the end.[58]

Certainly there was no greater contrast between the Wilson years and
the Harding period than the personality of Warren Harding himself. Any
description always begins with his remarkable physical features. Harding
was indeed distinguished looking. In the parlance of his own time: "He
looked like a president." Large in frame and features, Harding stood a
little over six feet and weighed 210 pounds. He had a high forehead, heavy
square jaws, and sympathetic, calm gray eyes. His mouth was generous
and sensuous, strikingly expressive when he spoke. His nose was large
but in keeping with the proportions of the rest of his face. He had a "high

114

stomach" which gave him a little paunch that crowded his breastbone, but there was no hint of obesity. He was vain about his person: his straight silver hair was always well brushed, his heavy dark eyebrows were neatly trimmed. His suits were immaculate and well pressed. His neckties were rarely loud or conspicuous. Partial to jewelry, he customarily wore a diamond ring, stickpin, and large watch chain. He varied his dress considerably, more so than most presidents, to fit the occasion. Sometimes he dressed rather more "sporty" than Mrs. Harding liked.

Harding had a magnetic quality that made both men and women like him. He possessed not so much the charisma of a leader as the simple attractiveness of a friendly and engaging individual. Ike Hoover, who served as chief usher at the White House for many years, listed Harding as second only to Teddy Roosevelt in human interest and personality. Yet, unlike Roosevelt, Harding displayed little egotism.

Next to Lincoln, Harding was probably the most human man to occupy the presidential office. As one close friend put it: "W. G. always wore the human side of him out." He had a temper and displayed it occasionally. These outbursts were accompanied by a symphony of profanity, an art he had acquired as a young newspaperman. But he always quickly repented and then suffered a degree of shame afterward. In his own words, such outbursts were not "becoming."

Harding was primarily remembered, however, not for these occasional fits of temper, but for his fantastic capacity for kindliness and friendliness. These two traits were merely extensions of his gregarious nature. He liked people, and he wanted to be liked by people. Wherever he went he was accompanied by a veritable crowd. On his trips as president it sometimes required ten cars to transport his party. These traveling companions were not just "cronies" but persons whom Harding invited on the spur of the moment. His desire to be liked and to please made him extend invitations even though it was unnecessary. He went out of his way to be generous to friend and foe alike.

Part of Harding's penchant for generosity was naturally rooted in his dislike of disharmony and contention. But it also grew out of his compulsive need for friends. To Harding, friends were as important as life itself. Later writers variously attributed this to his small-town background, to a defect in his character, to an attempt to compensate for his alleged Negro blood, to an abnormal craving for recognition and acceptance, to

115

a basic insecurity, and to a disbelief in his own capabilities. Whatever the cause, to be wanted and to enjoy good fellowship had always been important to him whether he was in Marion in the Elks Club, in Columbus in the state legislature, or in Washington in the Senate. One of the aspects of the presidency Harding liked least was the distance the office inevitably placed between himself and his friends. Throughout his term he attempted to compensate for this fact by holding on too tightly to former friendships and trying too desperately to bridge the gap between being a good fellow and being a good president.

In this mixture of modesty, kindness, generosity, and friendliness, loyalty played an extremely important role. An acquaintance once said: "He liked politicians for the reason that he loved dogs, because they were usually loyal to their friends."[59] To Harding loyalty was a paramount virtue. For this reason he had boosted Marion, supported Taft and opposed Roosevelt in 1912, and retained Daugherty despite intense opposition. Loyalty was a pledge, a mark of honor. Not only was it necessary for political self-preservation, it was a way of life.

When combined with kindliness and generosity, loyalty became a dangerous trait because it caused Harding to commit some egregious errors while president of the United States. Under its mandate, he too easily overlooked ethical or moral defects in others and remained too indiscriminate in his own personal contacts. His fear of offending anyone, especially his friends, prompted him too readily to grant their requests, while his emphasis on loyalty forced him to stand firmly by them regardless of what they had done. Harding recognized the perils involved in this condition but seemed powerless to avoid them. In an off-the-record speech at the National Press Club in 1922, Harding recalled that his father had once claimed that it was fortunate he was not a girl; he would have been in a family way all the time because he could not say no.

After his death and in later years much adverse comment was made about certain of Harding's personal habits although at the time of his election to the presidency they did not cause undue alarm. Harding liked to play poker. Sometimes he watched movies or attended theater productions such as George M. Cohan's *Mary* where he was observed putting his program to his mouth and calling in a stage whisper to a congressman friend in the audience: "Hey, John, how do you like the girls?"[60] But poker remained his primary form of entertainment. As a senator he had had a group in every Saturday night for "food and action" and, after becoming president, he continued playing poker approximately twice a week, usually at the White House, but occasionally at a friend's home. Beginning sometime after dinner, these games rarely lasted beyond midnight and were primarily for relaxation, not profit. Harding sought not only escape from the cares of office during these sessions but also the camaraderie of other men. By his own admission his most enjoyable evenings were spent dealing cards, swapping stories, and making small talk with his poker-playing friends.[61]

The White House poker group, limited to eight at one sitting, had a highly fluid membership. The most frequent participants were Daugherty, Weeks, Fall, McLean, Hale, Frelinghuysen, George Christian, Jess Smith, "Doc" Sawyer, and Albert Lasker. But others constantly moved in and out and attended more or less regularly: Charles Curtis, Charles Forbes, Hays, Wallace, Brandegee, Dawes, Knox, Nicholas Longworth, Gillett, and Mellon. Visiting out-of-town members were George Harvey, Harry Sinclair, Ed Scobey, and Charles M. Schwab, the steel magnate. This by no means exhausts the list but simply indicates the catholicity of Harding's poker sessions. Even Hoover and Hughes were invited to play and did so—but only once. Hughes did not like poker and Hoover, although admitting that it was fun and the stakes low, ceased attending because "it irked me to see it in the White House."[62]

Later charges that the poker crowd "ran" the government or exercised a hypnotic influence on Harding were untrue. Inevitably, some government business was discussed. But these men were Harding's playmates, not his mentors. These card sessions were not bacchanalian orgies nor did they mask dark plots to plunder the government. Perhaps they indicated the relatively low cultural level of Harding's background, but there was nothing sinister or sinful about them. Harding was not the first or the last president to gamble or play poker.

Harding's love of cards was matched by his love for golf. He liked certain other sports, too, especially baseball which he had played as a boy and a young man; but his attachment to golf was a passion. His clubs accompanied him everywhere. Delighted at breaking a hundred, and in ecstasy on those few occasions when he shot in the low nineties, Harding worked hard at the sport. While he said he relaxed, his companions claimed differently. Albert Lasker, who was much younger than Harding,

117

once accompanied him on a trip to Florida which included stopping at virtually every golf course along the way. At the conclusion of one particularly strenuous day of playing, Lasker dropped into bed sighing, "I'm glad Harding doesn't skip rope!"[63]

Every hack golfer who turned up at the White House was invited to a match. Every professional golfer who came to Washington faced a command performance. When winter drove Harding inside, he fretted about not being able to play and the first hint of spring found him out on the south grounds practicing tee shots. There he was able to combine golf with his lifelong attachment to dogs. Laddie Boy, a homely Airedale whose affection for Harding caused much comment in the press, had been trained by the president to chase and retrieve his practice balls. On the golf course the dog was often at his side.

Harding's human golfing companions were usually Frank B. Kellogg, Secretary Wallace, Hale, Frelinghuysen, Gillett, or Christian. As with the poker group, others joined him from time to time. Harding made an affable golfing partner and remained pleasant whether he won or lost. Yet he was a vigorous competitor. To add an edge to the competition he would bet six dollars Nassau (six dollars out, six in, and six total) on each eighteen holes. Sometimes, if it was a close match, he would bet on individual holes and even on individual shots. And he played without regard to his office. No matter how bad his lie he played it, even though his opponents asked him to pick it up. "Forget that I am President of the United States," he would say; "I'm Warren Harding, playing with some friends, and I'm going to beat hell out of them."[64]

The demands of the presidency prevented him from enjoying the game as much as he had while a senator. During good weather he got to the course about two times a week, except toward the end of his tenure. But he was unable to get away from the White House much before 3 P.M. which concentrated his playing into the dinner hour. Only on vacations and trips to the South was he able to play as much golf as he wanted. Such golfing expeditions made it appear as if he spent all his time on the golf course and occasioned later comments that he was rarely in his office. This was not so. Sometimes days and weeks went by, especially during the turbulent summer of 1922, when he did not see a golf ball. While in the White House, Harding wasted no more time on the golf course than did Wilson before his stroke and devoted no more hours to it than

118

other presidents did to their swimming, walking, sailing, or medicine-ball throwing.

Subject to some contemporary criticism were Harding's twin habits of smoking and drinking. Although he was careful not to be photographed doing either, it was well known that he did both. He used tobacco in all forms. He normally smoked two cigars a day, interspersed with a pipe and an occasional cigarette. Because of this, such organizations as the Boys Anti-Cigarette League constantly badgered him. Indeed, he received numerous letters chastising him, especially for his cigarette smoking. One broken-hearted Sunday School teacher in Vermont begged him to stop because her backsliding pupils were using him as their example.[65] Harding also chewed—a habit which dated back to his early Marion days. Although he had tapered off somewhat by the time he became president because of the Duchess's nagging, when nervous he would still split open a cigarette and pop the tobacco shreds in his mouth. To many, chewing was a filthy habit and Harding drew inevitable censure. But not from Thomas Edison. Harding once shared a plug of tobacco with the inventor, causing Edison to remark: "Harding is all right. Any man who chews tobacco is all right."[66]

More controversial was Harding's use of liquor, and his drinking habits were later somewhat exaggerated. Throughout his adult life Harding drank and saw nothing wrong in it. He had voted for prohibition and the Volstead Act purely on political grounds and, like many other Americans, pretended neither applied to him. It was claimed by some that Harding was a heavy drinker. Yet not one close friend or confidant ever went on record as seeing Harding drunk. Daugherty said that he knew Harding for thirty years and in all that time never saw him drink to excess or at the wrong time. Edmund Starling declared in his memoirs that Harding was only a "one drink man." It was freely admitted that Harding served liquor in the private rooms of the White House, although not at public gatherings or in the social rooms on the first floor. Mark Sullivan once received a drink in Harding's private bedroom, having been invited upstairs by the president for that specific purpose.[67] Harding believed that what he did in his own living quarters was his own business. Still, such "sneaking around" by the president to break the law was a fit subject for gossip and, when added to smoking, poker playing, and gambling, raised in some minds the specter of low-life carousals.

Harding wore religion lightly. Although his mother had exposed him as a boy to the old-time fundamentalist faith, in college he had roomed with an agnostic friend who superficially introduced him to the higher criticism. For a period thereafter he shunned religion altogether, but finally adjusted to a comfortable compromise conformity. What attachment he had to any specific creed came mainly from his childhood. Micah 6:8, his favorite scripture, he had learned at his mother's knee. "Lead Kindly Light," his favorite hymn, he had sung as a boy.

When the Hardings moved to Washington in 1915 they joined the Calvary Baptist Church. In deference to public tastes, Harding refused to play cards or golf on Sunday, and for relaxation went horseback riding instead. He believed in regular church attendance for others, but did not care to go himself. Mrs. Harding, however, forced him to attend rather frequently. This caused him some pain because he disliked the sham of it. During the campaign when his advisers wanted to picture him as a devout worshiper, Harding vetoed the idea. He claimed that such publicity would indicate he was more religious than he actually was. Mrs. Harding had a particularly difficult time dragging him to church on Communion Sundays. He begged off by claiming that he was too much of a sinner to participate.[68]

There is some doubt that Harding believed in the usual Christian tenets of Christ as Saviour, the Virgin Birth, the Holy Ghost, the Resurrection, justification by faith, the authority of the Bible, and so on. Indeed there is no indication that he spent much time thinking about such matters. But he often affirmed a belief in God, in the value of prayer, and in the power of an unselfish Christian life. His frequent references to the Deity were later viewed by some critics as sheer hypocrisy. But they were no more hypocritical than his belief in the progress of Marion or in the necessity of loyalty between friends. He merely took such things for granted.

In the end, it was the quality of Harding's mind, as much as any personal habits or character traits, which limited his effectiveness as president. Wilson claimed that Harding had a "bungalow mind." It was true that Harding tended to accept the pat answer rather than reason through to a more sophisticated position. Actually, Harding had a good mind but he simply made little use of it. His mentality was undisciplined by hard effort. He had never experienced intellectual sweat and lived his life in

120

the realm of clichés, maxims, and emotionally held opinions. As a small-town editor, he had not faced sharp intellectual competition. No strong intelligence had ever challenged him directly. He had never been required to study hard and one of the reasons he had decided against the law was the unappetizing prospect of a stiff mental regimen.

Significantly, Harding's closest Senate colleagues were not noted for their intellectual prowess. He selected his companions for other reasons. Personality counted more with him than ideas. In Harding's small-town world one dealt mainly in personalities. Philosophical ideas or discussions, or impersonal technical matters like economic theory, simply did not appeal to him. Indeed these things were frightening in their very abstraction. In this respect Harding was the exact opposite of Wilson, who could handle abstruse intellectual problems, but failed miserably in personal relationships.

Harding was typical of that America whose tastes were the movies and popular magazines, who knew only what appeared in the paper, and who after work desired to go home and be entertained by the inanities of the radio. There is no indication that Harding ever spent a great amount of time reading although his personal library was fairly well stocked. When he did read, he concentrated on Mark Twain and Zane Grey, or magazines like the *Saturday Evening Post* and *Literary Digest*. As long as he was president, he read the *Washington Post* and the *Chicago Tribune*, and for the home touch, the *Columbus Dispatch*. Invariably he checked the stock market—something Wilson never did—and he devoured the "funnies." [69]

Harding did not possess a deep knowledge of public questions or of their foundations in history, economics, or law. As a senator he had managed well without such knowledge. But as president, this limitation was constricting. One major difficulty during the Harding years was that the cabinet had to funnel its collective intelligence through this relatively untrained and undisciplined mind. Occasionally Harding did not understand, other times he was too cautious, sometimes he was too fearful. Often he simply endorsed a solution worked out by others.

Yet he was surprisingly accurate in his basic observations and had a superb feel for the right political action at the right time. His intuitive responses were often more sound than those of his cabinet officers who reasoned their way to their conclusions. His understanding of human motivation and of personal relationships was uncanny and proved invaluable to the success of his political program. And his rapport with the aspirations of the general public was amazing. As Senator Wadsworth phrased it: "He had a very good grasp of the whole nature of America."[70]

Some critics, at the time and since, have equated the quality of Harding's mind with the style of his speeches. Mencken, the Baltimore sage, compared Harding's style to a "string of wet sponges." It was so bad, said Mencken, that a kind of grandeur crept into it. President Wilson, in passing pleasantries with his cabinet for the last time just before Harding's inauguration, commented that while he was looking forward to his retirement, "there will be one very difficult thing for me . . . to stand, and that is Mr. Harding's English."[71] Harding did make verbs and adjectives out of nouns, disregarded proper syntax, and often ignored the difference between active and passive voice. His two pet words, "becoming" and "seemly," especially grated on sensitive ears. But this did not betray an ignorant or fuzzy mind as much as an outmoded, old-fashioned oratorical method of expression. It was the idiom of a July Fourth political gathering in turn-of-the-century Ohio where strings of words were constructed not so much to convey meaning as to evoke comforting memories and inspiring symbols in the minds of the listener.

Surprisingly, few contemporaries agreed with Mencken's or Wilson's views. Reporters covering the administration often marveled at Harding's vocabulary and while they quibbled from time to time with his syntax, they thought his choice of words was superb. Calvin Coolidge described Harding's oratorical style as impressive and claimed he "never failed to interest and hold his audience." In a direct refutation of Mencken, the *New York Times* said: "Mr. Harding's official style is excellent. It carries where finer writing would not go. . . . Mr. Harding is not writing for the super-fine weighers of verbs and adjectives, but for the men and women who see in his expressions their own ideas, and are truly happy to meet them. . . . [It] is a good style, let the pundits rage about it as they will."[72]

In any event, Harding never took his speechmaking lightly and prepared his addresses with great care. The drafts of minor speeches were written by Judson Welliver, who was retained by Harding after the election as a speech writer. Harding would indicate to Welliver what he wanted to say and then supply him with some of the key phrases or ideas. It was

Welliver's job to do the rest. The most important speeches, however, were written by Harding himself. He would first gather data, occasionally using the services of the Library of Congress. Sometimes he would consult individual cabinet members about specific content or information. Then he would seclude himself with a large pad and a supply of lead pencils and, where Wilson had typed and Roosevelt dictated, Harding would write his out in longhand. The draft was then sent to a typist who triple-spaced it, after which the president would revise, scratch out, and insert. Finally it was sent to the public printer. In the final product, while the style was always Harding's, the ideas were a composite of political intuition, factual information, some compromise, and a basic conservatism.

Whatever his intellectual limitations, Harding was a hard-working president. And as the months passed, he took his job increasingly seriously. He rarely retired before midnight and was at his office at 8 A.M. The contemporary press often commented on his ability to do huge quantities of work. Mark Sullivan wrote in 1922: "In the mere prosaic quality of capacity for hard work, Harding is extraordinary."[73] Especially was Harding's private letter writing prodigious as the hundreds of manuscript boxes in the Ohio Historical Society Library demonstrate. Harding may have "daily shrank from [the presidency's] exacting and gruelling toil," as one of his close friends later claimed, but this was only a state of mind since there is no indication that Harding ever physically shirked his presidential duties.[74]

According to contemporary White House observers Harding worked harder as president than either Wilson or Roosevelt and twice as hard as Taft. Ike Hoover listed him as one of the hardest working presidents he had known. Harding may have had to work so hard because of his relatively limited capabilities. Certainly more than most men he knew his weaknesses. He knew he was no match for Wilson's intellect or for Roosevelt's drive. His mark would have to be made another way. With considerable insight, he once remarked to Charles Michelson of the *New York World*: "I cannot hope to be one of the great presidents, but perhaps I may be remembered as one of the best loved."[75]

[5

INASMUCH as the Harding administration offered a contrast with the late Wilson years in the personality of its chief executive, there was hope that it would provide some quick solutions to those many unsolved problems which Wilson had left as its legacy. The new administration, however, had difficulty in getting under way. On March 7, three days after the inauguration, a group of congressional leaders met with the new president and for four hours reviewed with him the most critical matters facing the nation. There was a general consensus that a special session of Congress should be called, but there was marked disagreement about what problems should be attacked first. Senator Penrose, chairman of the Senate Finance Committee, argued for immediate tax revision. Representative Joseph W. Fordney, chairman of the House Ways and Means Committee, pushed for an emergency tariff. Each of the other current problems had at least one congressional champion. Hence, the conference adjourned without any specific decision, but with a feeling that tax and tariff reforms were the most pressing.

The following day the first cabinet meeting was held with the innovation of having the vice-president in attendance. Since some of the cabinet members barely knew each other, this meeting was largely devoted to getting acquainted. But some brief discussion was held on the awesome tasks confronting the administration, especially the tariff and tax problems. No decisions were reached, however, and Harding adjourned the group by announcing that they would meet thereafter every Tuesday and Friday at 10 A.M.

The pattern for subsequent cabinet sessions was as follows: Harding always began by recounting those matters which seemed most important to him at the moment. Each secretary then made a brief report on the activities of his department. The order of reporting was according to seniority with Hughes first and Hoover last. Finally, there was a general discussion touching on matters of mutual concern, usually led by Harding. No stenographers were present and no debates or votes were recorded. There was an unwritten agreement among the cabinet members that all discussions were to be kept confidential and that only the president was authorized to divulge, if he chose, what was said.[76]

At its first several meetings, the cabinet was unable to reach agreement on administration priorities and confusion continued to reign as contending congressional forces urged upon the president different courses of action. Harding, meanwhile, was so swamped with the demands of office seekers that he had little time to think of anything else. On March 14, however, after a conference with Senators Lodge, Smoot, and Underwood, he issued a call for a special session of Congress for April 11. He still had not settled on administration priorities.

Harding's vacillation at this early stage was prophetic and underscored his lack of decisiveness when confronted with a dilemma, especially when it involved power blocs in Congress. On the question of tariff versus tax reform, he realized that the farm bloc, supported in the cabinet by Secretary Wallace, wanted an emergency tariff measure; business interests, championed by Secretary Mellon and such conservative senators as Penrose, wanted immediate tax relief. On March 17 the word was circulated that Harding basically agreed with Mellon and Penrose and favored tax revision first. This prompted Representative Fordney to exclaim: "The West will raise hell!" Then, two days later, on March 19, Harding told a visiting group of farm delegates that he expected Congress to pass as soon as possible, and preferably "within forty-eight hours," an emergency tariff law designed to protect farm products.[77]

This action was typical of Harding. He attempted to mollify both sides by appearing to support each, thus remaining friends with everybody and relying on time to rescue him. In this case it worked. On March 21, the members of the House Ways and Means Committee and of the Senate Finance Committee agreed to a loose formula by which hearings and congressional action would begin immediately on both tax reform and tariff revision, with the House taking up the tariff issue and the Senate new tax legislation.[78]

The Republican-dominated 67th Congress opened as scheduled at noon on April 11. The next day Harding delivered a special message which indicated the scope and magnitude of the challenge confronting his administration. Declaring that Congress should first turn to domestic problems and put "our own house in order," he mentioned not only increased tariff protection and lower taxes as prime issues, but the necessity for "the utmost economy in administration," federal government reorganization, legislation "providing for the national budget system," reduction of railway rates, construction of "a great merchant marine," creation of a system of national highways, encouragement of aviation for civil and military purposes, further development of radio and its "effective regulation," expansion of hospital facilities, enactment of a maternity bill, passage of an antilynching law, establishment of a Veterans' Bureau, and creation of a Department of Public Welfare. With respect to foreign affairs he expressed hope for an association of nations "binding us in conference and cooperation for the prevention of war," but flatly declared that the United States should not enter the League. He further declared that peace should be established with all former enemies, that an orderly funding and liquidation of war debts should be undertaken, and that the United States should aid in the economic recovery of Europe.[79]

This speech was unquestionably one of the best of Harding's presidential career. It showed that he possessed an awareness of every major problem confronting the nation even though he did not have a solution for each one. A significant and surprising portion of his address was devoted to social welfare and internal improvements. In relation to these matters he indicated that he was by no means an economic antediluvian. His suggestion for a Department of Public Welfare to coordinate expanding federal government activity in education, public health, and sanitation was far ahead of its time, and his recommendations for increased federal participation in the development of radio, aviation, and highways had a prophetic ring. By this speech Harding demonstrated that he was more advanced in his thinking about the total range of domestic problems than were those congressmen who were currently quibbling over which should come first, tax revision or tariff legislation. Not unexpectedly, the weakest part of his speech was that devoted to foreign affairs. He was still caught in the ambivalence of his own position on the League. Yet at the same time he evidenced a liberal view of America's role in the recovery of Europe and in the restoration of normal trade relations and economic ties.

Congress received the speech with some surprise. Because of its breadth, there was something in it that appealed to almost everyone. But there was also something in it that offended almost everyone. Liberals and progressives were antagonized by Harding's conservative tax and tariff suggestions; conservatives were edgy about his references to lower railroad rates and new social and regulatory legislation. Pro-Leaguers were saddened by his reiteration of nonparticipation in the League; anti-League stalwarts were wary of his repeated talk about an association of nations. Bureaucrats were frightened by his insistence on government reorganization. Hence, although it was hailed as a "solid effort" and "a fresh approach to national problems," this address, because of both its content and its quality of independence, raised an immediate question about Harding's relations with Congress.

Ironically, one of the changes from the Wilson years which most observers expected to see was a closer relationship between the Congress and the executive. After all, Harding knew intimately the workings of the Congress and was equipped temperamentally to soothe congressional sensibilities. The "Senate oligarchy" myth supported the assumption that Harding would mainly be a "kept" president. Walter Lippmann had prophesied at the time of the inauguration that the Harding years would be known "as the Regency of the Senate."[80]

Harding had fully expected to get along well with Congress. After his election he had indicated that he would consult with party leaders on required legislation and remain on good terms with all factions. Frankly, he hoped others would assume the burden of guiding the administration's programs through Congress while he remained above the strife. He viewed the presidency as primarily a ceremonial office and he conceived of his political role as that of counselor rather than partisan fighter. In short, he believed in government through the sponsorship of political parties rather than personal domination.

From the beginning, however, Harding enjoyed no real honeymoon with Congress. His early difficulty with congressional leaders over priorities, the continued rumblings concerning the League question, and persistent allegations that he would be merely a tool of the Senate caused him to be cautious and defensive. He early sensed that certain congressional leaders hoped to reduce him to a cipher and hold the presidency as hostage. Hence in his special message in April he included another reference to executive privilege like the one he had inserted in his farewell speech to the Senate on December 6. Stating that it would be objectionable if the legislative branch should attempt to assume the functions of the presidency, Harding again cautioned that "Our highest duty is the preservation of the constituted powers of each, and the promotion of the spirit of cooperation so essential to our common welfare."[81]

Such a warning indicated that despite his desire for good relations, Harding did not intend to surrender presidential prerogatives without a fight. Shortly after the special session opened, the press commented on this unexpected independence and expressed surprise that he gave "no evidence of being putty in the hands of politicians." Indeed, Harding found

127

it increasingly difficult to play the role simply of honest broker and in some anguish wrote to Malcolm Jennings in July, "I find I can not carry out my pre-election ideals of an Executive keeping himself aloof from Congress." [82] Not long afterwards he again commented to Jennings: "One gets a very different view of Congress from the Executive office than I have ever entertained heretofore. Indeed, one gets a very different view of all problems of government. Responsibility has a strange effect. [One is] imbued with the desire to serve above and beyond most selfish aims. I find even myself growing less a partisan than I once was." [83]

Unfortunately Harding was not able to couple this early show of independence with dynamic leadership. If he did not bow down to Congress, he possessed neither the desire nor the ability to lead Congress. His proclivity for consultation and consensus, which had been so important to his nomination and election, now hampered his effectiveness as president, especially in the face of congressional deadlock and confusion.

And Congress was confused. Despite the tax-tariff priority formula and the best of intentions, the special session of the 67th Congress quickly became snarled in wrangling over what emergency action to take, and for the first several months it made little headway in implementing any of the president's recommendations. Thus, the Harding years got off to a slow start. Harding retained wide popular acclaim because of his cabinet selections, his curtailment of inaugural expenses, his opening of the White House to the public, and his excellent April 12 message. But congressional anarchy and lack of decisive presidential direction raised storm signals for the future.

V

Liquidating the War

[1

CONTRARY to the expectation of either Harding, the Congress, or the public, the administration's first successful action came in foreign affairs. Although the plan was for domestic issues to take precedence, dissension within the Republican congressional leadership produced a vacuum which the State Department and the pressure of international problems rapidly filled.

From the outset the administration found itself in the difficult position of having to deal with the same foreign policy questions that had wrecked the Wilson administration. Final settlement of the peace simply could not wait on tax or tariff matters, and with much apprehension Harding, prodded by Secretary of State Hughes, moved gingerly in this direction. Harding's apprehension was well founded. Nowhere were congressional attitudes more rigidly held than in the field of foreign policy. Indeed, so wary was Congress, especially the Senate, of presidential action in foreign affairs and so zealous of its own powers that the administration operated under an almost impossible handicap.

In January 1921 Senator Penrose had uttered what most senators regarded as a truism: "It makes no difference who is Secretary of State, the Senate will make the foreign policy."[1] Fresh from its victory over Woodrow Wilson, that body was experiencing a sense of power—power which Harding himself had helped it acquire. The Foreign Relations Committee, headed by Lodge, was packed with strict reservationists and irreconcilables who were prepared to keep the League issue buried and also to maintain supremacy over the executive in all areas of foreign affairs. Such committee members as Borah, Brandegee, Johnson, New, and Wadsworth interpreted "advice and consent" in the broadest possible terms and had already served notice that *any* administration would ignore their views at its peril.

Harding recognized this condition and from the beginning was solicitous of the Senate's views on foreign matters. He sought senators' opinions and listened carefully to their suggestions. He even asked advice from the Democratic side of the aisle. He constantly attempted to soothe senatorial feelings and steered clear of potential trouble areas. Still, Harding feared an ultimate clash between executive and legislative authority on foreign policy, a clash which he hoped to forestall if possible.

If Harding was circumspect in handling the Senate, he was matched by his secretary of state. On those occasions when Hughes testified before Senate committees, he was punctual, straightforward, and clear. He neither engaged in semantics nor sparred for verbal advantage. Anxious not to give offense, he was nonetheless firm and articulate in expressing his convictions. Hughes's personal dignity and stature permitted him a latitude with the senators which those of lesser prestige, like Lansing or Colby, did not enjoy. Even so, Hughes never traded on his status and sought only limited and obtainable objectives with the Senate.

Hughes once said that the primary lesson taught by Wilson's experience was to avoid a fight with the Senate unless public opinion firmly backed you.[2] Consequently Hughes paid more attention to good public relations than had any previous secretary of state. From the moment Harding announced Hughes's selection the New Yorker undertook a vigorous campaign of propaganda and public education. He attempted to make foreign affairs seem as important as the murder trials and other ballyhoo which were beginning to infiltrate the nation's newspapers. Despite his aloof personality, he became a bubbling fountain of information in the early months of the administration as he underscored his belief in "open diplomacy." Popularizing the State Department as the "Department of Peace," he sought specifically to allay the suspicions of those who remembered the secrecy of Wilson.

Hughes was well aware that this course of action had its dangers and that closed diplomacy could sometimes achieve more salutary results. But for the moment he desired to create an image of openness, and he was successful. The State Department held two press conferences each day, one handled by an undersecretary and the other by Hughes himself. While reporters were asked not to quote him directly, the secretary permitted them to question him freely. In return, the press treated Hughes with respect and did not break his confidences. Newsmen appreciated his frankness and his willingness to give them accessibility to State Department information.[3] This certainly marked a contrast with the Wilson years.

As secretary of state, Hughes was master of the art of the possible. He was intensely practical and realistic. He was a lawyer and possessed a legalistic mind which was not too inclined to innovation or imagination. Justice Brandeis once claimed, "His is the most enlightened mind of the eighteenth century," to which one Washington correspondent rapidly rejoined, "At least he always has it with him."[4] Therein lay both Hughes's strength and his weakness. In any event, it was probably fortunate that the United States had a practical lawyer for secretary of state at this time in view of the legal entanglements stemming from World War I. Hughes liked diplomacy well enough, but he was happiest when involved in legal controversy with foreign states where he could be less the diplomat and more the lawyer. As might be expected, justice, more than morality, was the key factor in his philosophical orientation.

Hughes was an indefatigable worker and kept his finger on every phase of State Department activity. He demanded daily reports from his subordinates and froze the blood of young staffers by shredding their position papers. Unfortunately, such brusqueness encouraged those under him to submit ideas which they knew he would approve rather than their own independent judgments. In the end, Hughes made all final decisions. The strain of such personal direction would have broken other men, but Hughes actually enjoyed it. He was happy with his position and he admitted it. As one reporter phrased it: "He will tell the world that he likes his job. He fairly revels in it, and is as enthusiastic as the little boys before Christmas who believe in Santa Claus."[5] What many people did not know was that a chief reason for this happiness was Hughes's boss, Warren Harding.

The relationship between Hughes and Harding was significant. Where Wilson had reduced his secretaries of state to mere experts in international law, Harding permitted Hughes free rein. Many critics later claimed that this was necessary because of Harding's abysmal ignorance in foreign affairs. This was untrue. Harding gave Hughes autonomy by choice and not by default. Hughes was his most important cabinet selection and Harding never doubted that Hughes was the biggest man in it. From the beginning, Hughes's appointment had carried two clear messages: Harding did not intend to be his own secretary of state, and control of foreign policy would not be abdicated to the Senate.

Because the two men possessed such contrasting personalities there were constant rumors of differences between them. Since Hughes carefully monitored the president's utterances on foreign policy and even assigned a State Department representative to presidential news conferences, many jumped to the conclusion that Hughes did not like or trust the president. From time to time there were reports that Hughes was about to resign over some slip of the presidential tongue. But these assumptions were also false. Harding's off-the-cuff interviews with reporters did present problems for Hughes; however, the department's representative was present at such gatherings to provide the president with up-to-date information rather than to spy.

As for their personal relationship, it was never close like that of Harding and Daugherty. Hughes did not permit such warm personal attachments. On the other hand, their relations were not perfunctory or mechanical. Hughes retained a peculiar affection for Harding; Harding treated Hughes with respect and some awe. Hoover later claimed that Harding was afraid of Hughes.[6] If so, it was not evident in either their correspondence or their personal contacts. More accurately, the two men regarded themselves as co-workers in an enterprise that required the help of both and the special talents of each. Hughes relied on Harding for his political sagacity and knowledge of the Senate. Harding left to Hughes the job of running the State Department and formulating the administration's foreign policy. Toward the end, Harding began to lean on Hughes for general advice not touching on foreign affairs, but Hughes never felt comfortable in that position. By the time of his death, Harding regarded Hughes, along with Hoover, as his most important adviser.[7]

There is no doubt that Hughes took the initiative with respect to foreign affairs, but he kept Harding informed of every step along the way. On serious matters Hughes talked with Harding first and never acted without the president's specific approval. Hughes either went to the White House or had other contact with Harding almost every day. The secretary reported *everything* to the president, even his absences from the office—a procedure which Harding found amusing. All major diplomatic dispatches were sent verbatim to the White House immediately. No ambassador returned to the United States without giving a firsthand report both to Hughes and to Harding. Hughes provided Harding with lengthy position papers on all major policy questions and Harding read them carefully as his replies indicated. Harding, in turn, gave Hughes advice on how to circumvent the sensibilities of senators or to mesh foreign policy with what he felt was the mood of the general public.[8] Together they slowly rebuilt the working relationship in foreign affairs between the executive and Congress which had broken down in the Wilson years, and their smooth efforts did much to stabilize the American governmental system in the postwar era.

[2

FOLLOWING the oath which was administered to him on March 5, 1921, Charles Evans Hughes settled himself in the large rectangular room on the second floor of the State, War, and Navy Building, with its south windows looking across to Washington's monument. In this same room John Hay had worked as secretary of state—and in an earlier day so had John Quincy Adams, Jefferson, Madison, and Monroe. Hughes was not out of place there.

Hughes immediately surrounded himself with topflight personnel. His undersecretary until 1922 was Henry P. Fletcher, a man of broad diplomatic experience. Fletcher had been ambassador to Chile and Mexico, and in 1922 was named ambassador to Belgium. To replace Fletcher, Hughes selected William Phillips, another career man who had been minister to the Netherlands. To head the various divisions, Hughes appointed Sumner Welles for the Latin American Affairs Division (he was succeeded in 1922 by Francis White); William R. Castle, Jr., for Western European Affairs (he was later undersecretary during Hoover's administration); Allen W. Dulles for Near Eastern Affairs; DeWitt C. Poole for Russian Affairs; and John V. A. MacMurray for Far Eastern Affairs. Hughes's habit of bringing in career men from the field to fill these various slots gave a professionalism to the State Department which rarely had been imparted before.

133

If Hughes was careful in making staff appointments, he was no less meticulous in filling diplomatic posts. In this regard, Harding was a key factor. Despite extreme pressure, the president protected diplomatic assignments from the ravages of party patronage as best he could. As early as January 1921, he had agreed to consult Hughes on all such appointments and to satisfy Hughes's desire to name only "men of first-rate ability."[9] But Harding had no idea at the time of the difficulty involved in keeping this promise. Even before the inauguration he was hounded by office seekers who wanted overseas assignments. He succumbed to a few, the most notable being George Harvey. Over Hughes's opposition, Harding personally selected Harvey for ambassador to the Court of St. James. It was not a popular appointment. Harvey's reputation as a turncoat foe of Wilson followed him to England where, more than once, he put his foot in his mouth with his intemperate comments.[10]

But, in general, when Harding and Hughes had differences over selections, they managed to work them out agreeably. Hughes recognized that the top diplomatic positions were political plums and that his burden in this respect "was the common lot of all secretaries since John Quincy Adams." In several instances where Harding had a strong preference, Hughes proved amenable. Such was the case with Harding's old Ohio friend Myron Herrick, who was selected as ambassador to France. Herrick had already served in this position during Taft's administration and Harding wished to send him back. Herrick had been popular with the French and Hughes quickly agreed.[11] A similar case involved Richard Washburn Child, Harding's campaign adviser and speech writer. With somewhat less enthusiasm Hughes agreed to his appointment as ambassador to Italy, but quickly found him to be extremely able and acquired a deep respect for him.[12]

In other diplomatic posts, career personnel were given primary recognition and the patronage line was rigidly held. Joseph Grew was named minister to Switzerland; Hugh Gibson, minister to Poland; Peter Augustus Jay, minister to Rumania; John W. Riddle, ambassador to Argentina; Edwin V. Morgan, ambassador to Brazil; William M. Collier, ambassador to Chile; Lewis Einstein, minister to Czechoslovakia; Charles S. Wilson, minister to Bulgaria; and so on. These appointments of career men were important morale builders and acted as a stimulus to the whole diplomatic corps. Even those few posts which were given to political appointees were filled with above-average talent. Jacob G. Schurman, president of Cornell University, was made minister to China. Charles Beecher Warren, a Michigan lawyer with international judicial experience, was named ambassador to Japan. Alanson B. Houghton, an able congressman from New York, became the new ambassador to Germany. Cyrus E. Wood, who had been minister to Portugal under Taft, was returned to the Iberian Peninsula, this time as ambassador to Spain.

By any comparison, the Harding administration compiled an enviable record in its diplomatic and consular appointments. In the fall of 1922 a special committee of the National Civil Service Reform League offered high praise to both Hughes and Harding for reducing the hold of politics on the State Department. The committee noted that in the first fifteen months of the Harding administration not a single appointment was made to the consular service except through civil service channels and that of 102 appointments, 87 involved promotions of men with an average of ten years' experience. This represented "an unequaled record of adherence to the merit system." In the diplomatic area, of the nine ambassadors selected, six had previous experience in the foreign service. Of thirty ministers, eight were carried over from the Wilson years and six others had engaged in previous diplomatic activity. With no fear of contradiction, the State Department historian Graham H. Stuart wrote: "The Harding-Hughes regime made a far better record in diplomatic appointments than the Wilson-Bryan administration which preceded it." [13]

[3

WITH the possible exception of Jefferson, no secretary of state inherited a worse situation than Hughes. In the last days of Wilson's administration the State Department was "in a condition of virtual coma." [14] There was hardly a phase of American foreign policy that was not hanging in midair. Of all these problems none was more serious than the final disposition of the League question.

Harding's stunning victory played directly into the hands of the strict reservationists and the irreconcilables. They assumed that the "solemn referendum" of 1920 indicated the general public wanted no part of the League. Borah and Johnson were elated by the results while Lodge declared, "We have torn up Wilsonism by the roots." [15] Anti-Leaguers of all stripes immediately indicated to Harding that they would tolerate no back-sliding. George Sutherland, who throughout the campaign had struggled to keep Harding in line on the League question, wrote him soon after the election: "We must proceed with the utmost caution in the work of insti-tuting any new world relationship. . . . We should never allow ourselves to be beguiled into any arrangement which will permit Europe to med-dle in the affairs of this continent or compel us to meddle in the affairs of Europe."[16]

Although his appointment of Hughes and Hoover to the cabinet caused some pro-Leaguers to assume that he wished to adopt a flexible approach, there was never any doubt in Harding's mind that the Wilson League was dead.[17] He accepted the view that it could not function "in a great emer-gency" and would experience an "utter inability" to preserve peace. In his April special message he stated his views clearly: "In the existing League of Nations, world governing with its super-powers, this Republic will have no part. There can be no misinterpretation, and there will be no betrayal of the deliberate expression of the American people in the recent election. . . . the League Covenant can have no sanction by us."[18] Harding believed that this conclusion was not only mandated by the mil-lions of votes cast for him, but also by the fact that it represented a return to the ancient and time-tested rule: friendly relations with all nations, en-tangling alliances with none.

As one of the thirty-one pro-League Republicans who had endorsed Harding during the campaign, Secretary Hughes seemingly occupied an untenable position. In reality, however, his specific attachment to the League was marginal. Hughes favored the general idea but not necessarily the arrangement worked out by Wilson. Not only was Article X a stum-bling block for him, but he doubted that any of the Great Powers would, if it came to a test, permit their vital interests to be "decided upon in any large group." Still, Hughes did not believe that it was necessary to begin all over again and he was willing to consider the Wilson League as a starting point.[19]

Harding never objected to Hughes's moderate pro-League views after he became secretary of state, nor were Hughes's opinions on the League of any real concern to Harding in appointing him. Harding's only condition was that whatever Hughes chose to do about it, he had to act with the assurance of Senate acceptance. Harding most emphatically did not want a repeat of 1919. Hughes understood this and used it as his frame of reference in dealing with the League problem.[20]

Hughes, no less than Harding, was trapped by what was referred to as "the mandate of 1920," and the constant surveillance by a Senate dominated by strict reservationists and irreconcilables. The outlook for any favorable action on the League was frankly dark. As a consequence Hughes did not resume the League debate or ask for congressional reconsideration. Hughes later confided that he took no action because he did not feel that he should risk wrecking the administration in order to have the United States enter the League. As he put it: "To revive the old controversy in any phase would have been easy but disastrous."[21] Instead, Hughes played along with the Senate and was careful not to offend it on matters relating to the League.

Precisely what kind of official contact to maintain with the League was naturally a troublesome problem. When the Harding administration took over there were eighteen communications from the League requiring answers. But the State Department under Hughes made no reply for almost four months; then it merely acknowledged the communications had been received. So clipped were Hughes's early dealings with the League that many former pro-Leaguers could only shake their heads at his behavior. Later they charged both Harding and Hughes with perfidy and claimed that they had betrayed the Thirty-One. Hughes, however, was firm in his defense of the administration. To one protesting friend he wrote: "The plain fact is that President Harding, if he had undertaken to bring about our entry into the League, even upon the basis of reservations or a modified agreement, would have precipitated a controversy of the most serious character, but he could not have achieved the result. The opposition was too determined and resourceful. They had decided that there should be no participation in the League on any terms. No matter what Mr. Harding had said as a candidate, or the Thirty-One had said, the President was required as a statesman to take account of this condition."[22]

Actually, it was not Harding, or Hughes, or even the Senate that abandoned the Wilson League. The country did. By the summer of 1921, the public was no longer interested in the League question. No responsible politician could use the League as a voter issue any longer and few even bothered to discuss it. By the late spring not thirty senators would have

137

voted even for reservations. The tide had simply swung against it and both Harding and Hughes realized this. Even the broken and ill Woodrow Wilson, isolated in his house on S Street, perceived the shift in attitudes. To one of his daughters he remarked that it was perhaps best that the United States had not joined the League after all because it would have represented only a personal victory for him, not a real national commitment.[23]

[4

THE immediate result of American nonadherence to the Versailles Treaty was the necessity of finding some alternate means for concluding the state of war still existing between the United States and the Central Powers. The old 66th Congress had attempted to terminate the conflict through a simple resolution introduced by Senator Knox, but this had been vetoed in May 1920 by Wilson who still hoped for American acceptance of the Versailles Treaty. Unable to muster the necessary two-thirds to override the veto, Republicans in Congress had dropped the matter until after Harding's inauguration.

Since Harding had voted for the Knox resolution, it was assumed that he was in favor of its resurrection. In his April special message to Congress he indicated that he would accept such a proposal to end the state of war. Senator Knox reintroduced his resolution and on April 30 the Senate quickly passed it. Surprisingly, the Knox Resolution was opposed in the House because it terminated the conflict by repealing the war declaration of April 6, 1917. The House thought such a repeal might cast a reflection on the judgment of Congress, and it preferred merely a simple statement that the war was at an end. On June 13 the House adopted the Porter Resolution which embodied this view. Shortly thereafter a conference committee decided to accept the Porter declaration but to add to it a clause which the Knox Resolution had included, namely reserving to the United States all those rights which were contained in the Versailles Treaty even though the Senate had not ratified it. On June 30, the House endorsed the work of this committee and on the following day so did the Senate. On July 2, 1921, President Harding signed the Knox-Porter Resolution which brought the war to an end.[24]

Reserving rights did not create them and the State Department now

138

had the task of reaching detailed agreements with each of the defeated nations. Hughes's problem was threefold: (1) to devise peace treaties which would not commit the United States to anything which the Senate would reject, (2) to secure for the United States all those prerogatives to which the victorious countries were entitled under the Treaty of Versailles, and (3) to construct these agreements in such a way that the Central Powers would accept. Hughes was superb in handling this delicate situation. In the case of Germany he decided simply to append to the July 2 Knox-Porter Resolution those parts of the Versailles Treaty which were applicable and insert a disclaimer regarding the United States and the operation of the Covenant of the League. Germany could not refuse the United States the same rights she had given to other powers in the Versailles Treaty, and therefore would probably accept; the Senate in turn would agree to anything to which the Joint Resolution of July 2 was attached. On this basis, the so-called Berlin Treaty was negotiated and signed at the German Foreign Office on August 25, 1921. Similar treaties were arranged with Austria and Hungary. The treaty with Austria was signed at Vienna on August 24, 1921, and contained the necessary portions of the Austrian peace treaty signed at Saint-Germain-en-Laye on September 10, 1919. Similarly, a treaty was negotiated with Hungary and signed at Budapest on August 29, 1921, to which were added the requisite portions of the Allied peace treaty concluded at Trianon on June 4, 1920.[25]

Despite his careful and circumspect action, Hughes submitted these treaties to the Senate with some apprehension. As he feared, the Senate Foreign Relations Committee was not fully satisfied and refused to support the Berlin Treaty until a further reservation was attached. This caveat specified that the United States government could not be represented or participate in any body, agency, or commission authorized by the Versailles Treaty "unless and until an act of the Congress of the United States shall provide for such representation or participation."[26] With this safeguard against *any* League participation, the Foreign Relations Committee voted 9–1 for ratification and sent it along with the other treaties to the floor on September 24.

Lodge now became chief spokesman for the treaties and urged their passage by claiming, "We receive all that is desirable for the United States and we are not called upon to make any embarrassing concessions."[27]

The ensuing debate was frequently acrimonious. Some Democratic senators attempted to needle the administration by discussing those portions of the Treaty of Versailles embodied in the United States–German peace treaty and threatened to add a series of reservations. It was rumored that these troublemakers were getting advice from former President Wilson. But Senator Underwood, Democratic floor leader, refused to support these harassing tactics and indicated his intention to vote for all the peace treaties.[28]

Not Wilson Democrats, but Republican irreconcilables provided most of the fireworks. Senator Borah warned of involvement in Europe's affairs and claimed the proposed treaties were "first steps" toward League membership. Another irreconcilable, LaFollette, fumed over the alleged chicanery being perpetrated by Hughes and the State Department. But Lodge skillfully parried the attacks, denied that the treaties meant assuming any League obligations whatsoever, and complimented the State Department on the excellent manner in which the treaties had been constructed. As a final argument, Lodge read to the Senate a letter from President Harding urging passage of the treaties "so that we may put aside the last remnant of war relationship and hasten our return to the fortunate relations of peace."[29]

On October 18 fourteen Democratic senators, including Hitchcock and Underwood, voted with Lodge and fifty-one other Republicans to ratify the German treaty 66–20. The minority was composed of eighteen Democrats plus two Republican irreconcilables—Borah and LaFollette. In rapid succession the Senate then ratified the Austrian treaty 66–20 and the Hungarian treaty 66–17. Three weeks later the president issued a proclamation declaring World War I to have officially ended on the preceding July 2 when the Knox-Porter Resolution had been signed.[30]

[5

SINCE the beginning of World War I the major powers had been engaged in a naval race. In prewar days, the United States normally had constructed two capital ships a year. However, in August 1916 Congress passed a Naval Appropriations Act which called for ten first-class battleships, six battle cruisers, and 140 smaller vessels to be built in three years' time. Upon American entrance into World War I the United States sus-

pended this program to concentrate on building merchant ships and submarines, with the intention of resuming the original schedule as soon as
hostilities ceased. The long-range goal was to create "incomparably the
most adequate navy in the world" and to replace Great Britain as mistress
of the seas.

The resumption of the American naval program following the war was
matched by similar developments in England and Japan. In July 1920,
the Japanese Diet adopted the so-called eight-eight program whereby Japan would ultimately possess a two-squadron fleet of eight battleships, each
of which was to be replaced every eight years. England, in turn, announced
in March 1921 her intention to initiate a naval construction program which
would make sure that Britannia continued to rule the waves. The American press greeted these developments with some alarm, especially in view
of the existing Anglo-Japanese Alliance. However, the press assured the
American people that as long as the United States stuck to its own building plans the American battle fleet would be superior to anything on the
high seas by 1924.

Buried in the Naval Appropriations Act of 1916 was a provision that
the rebuilding program could be altered at any time by presidential order
if international action found solutions to the world's problems. The Wilson administration had hoped that American acceptance of the Treaty of
Versailles would obviate the necessity of pursuing naval rearmament and
in anticipation had quietly halted most naval building in 1919–20. When
it became obvious that the United States would not accept the Versailles
Treaty, the Wilson administration, mainly through the person of Secretary of the Navy Josephus Daniels, renewed its support for naval rearmament. The administration also requested increased congressional appropriations and opposed any reductions in the strength of the army and navy
as long as there was no final settlement of the war.

Congress was in a dilemma. Apparently the only alternative to the
League was the continued pursuit of naval supremacy. Yet this was ex-
pensive and ran counter to a developing drive for peace and for economy.
Congressional action was therefore ambivalent. While there was much
congressional talk of the need for a first-class navy, the necessary funds
were not forthcoming. Throughout the last months of Wilson's administration, appropriation requests were either cut—the navy request for 1921,
alone, was slashed almost 50 percent—or ignored as disarmament advo-

cates, such as Senator Borah, filibustered appropriation measures to death.[31]

Harding was a "big navy" man. He had supported the 1916 program and all subsequent appropriation bills. After his election as president, he indicated that he intended to see the 1916 plans through to completion. His interest in economy did not extend to crippling the military and, as he wrote to Lodge in February 1921, "I cordially favor . . . disarmament, but when that day comes I want America to have the best that there is for the advance of our commerce and I know that we shall not have it unless we complete the present [naval building] program."[32]

Senator Borah had different ideas. A magnificent orator and superb actor, Borah had seized upon disarmament as a popular issue and unconscionably exploited it through fervent speeches and public appearances. Actually he had no integrated peace program except that of renouncing military preparedness and slashing military expenditures. Borah's concept of world peace was naive in the extreme, especially in his insistence that it be achieved without regard for such international realities as the Anglo-Japanese Alliance. In a curious way, his interest in disarmament was compatible with his general insular outlook. In his thinking, naval races invariably produced international contacts and friction; disarmament would therefore create the reverse situation. The more completely the military could be debased, the greater the degree of isolationism that could be achieved.

On the specific question of naval appropriations, Borah was determined to have his way. He consistently used his opposition to additional naval expenditures as a weapon to force the executive to initiate disarmament discussions with other powers. On December 14, 1920, he sponsored a joint resolution requesting President Wilson to negotiate with Great Britain and Japan to reduce naval expenses. Similarly, he attached an amendment to the naval appropriations bill on February 15, 1921, calling on the president to invite Great Britain and Japan to a naval disarmament conference to effect reduced naval expenditures. Neither the appropriations bill nor the Borah amendment was voted on before the end of the Wilson administration.[33]

If there was any hope that Borah would prove less obstreperous under the Harding administration, it was dashed by his own statement near the close of the 66th Congress: "Let me say here, and I say it with the utmost respect, that I shall not abdicate my judgment in the Chamber in the next four years any more than I did in the last eight."[34] Indeed, no sooner was a new naval appropriations bill introduced on the day following Harding's special message in April than Borah reintroduced his amendment. Borah reiterated that his sole purpose was to bring about changes in proposed naval programs by a conference of the three major naval powers.

The Borah resolution had tremendous popular appeal. The nation's press, in particular, supported the Borah approach. A few "big navy" papers, such as the *Washington Post*, the *New York Tribune*, and the *Boston Transcript*, urged caution, but even they had to admit that a conference might be a significant step away from an intensified international naval rivalry. Borah, of course, actively cultivated this sentiment and obviously relished being hailed as a champion of peace when but a short time before he had been condemned as a betrayer of humanity for his stubborn position on the League.[35]

Harding was by no means oblivious to this disarmament sentiment, nor had he ignored the possibility of calling a conference such as the Borah amendment requested. As early as the Marion talks following his election, Harding had discussed the conference idea with several persons, among them Nicholas Murray Butler and William Jennings Bryan. He had indicated at that time that he was not opposed to such a conference, but did not intend to delay the 1916 naval program in anticipation of one. In his inaugural address he again stated the new administration's willingness to consider a disarmament conference: "We are ready to associate ourselves with the nations of the world . . . to recommend a way to approximate disarmament and relieve the crushing burdens of military and naval establishments." However, in his special message on April 12 he reiterated his contention that adequate defense had to come first: "We shall not entirely discard our agencies for defense until there is removed the need to defend. We are ready to cooperate with other nations to approximate disarmament, but merest prudence forbids that we disarm alone."[36]

The president's position did little to satisfy the mounting clamor and the disarmament question remained in the foreground throughout the spring of 1921. At a cabinet meeting in May, Harding asked for a brief list of the greatest problems facing the nation from each of his secretaries, and several included "disarmament." Hoover put it at the top of his list, which prompted a reply from Harding on May 14: "I hope I need not assure you that a step in this direction will be taken very earnestly at the earliest day in which the European situation makes it seem advisable." [37] Nine days later Harding again commented on disarmament—this time publicly—when he stood on a pier at Hoboken, New Jersey, as the bodies of 5212 soldiers, sailors, and marines killed in the war arrived aboard the freighter *Wheaton* for burial. In a short, moving speech, which brought tears to his eyes and to those of his listeners, he pledged every effort to establish a lasting peace and reduce the danger of war: "I find a hundred thousand sorrows touching my heart, and there is a ringing in my ears, like an admonition eternal, an insistent call, 'It must not be again! It must not be again!' " [38]

Despite the tears and flowery language, Senator Borah was neither convinced of the new administration's sincerity nor satisfied with its speed, and he continued to push for the acceptance of his amendment. Congress, in turn, was embarrassed, torn between its desire to satisfy popular sentiment and its wish not to undermine the new president. Harding, as well as most congressmen, knew that one purpose of the Borah amendment was to tie the president's hands and it thus represented an extension of the executive-legislative struggle which dated back to the League fight. Yet Harding was also aware of the popular support behind the Borah resolution, and he was fearful of the public misunderstanding which might result if he opposed it too vigorously.

In early May, as the Senate turned to debate the naval appropriations bill with its appended Borah amendment, Harding let the word circulate that he would not relinquish his presidential prerogatives in any way, nor would he be hurried into a conference at the Senate's direction. But he further indicated that as long as the executive's prerogatives were not compromised and no directive was issued for unilateral disarmament, he had no objection to the Senate expressing itself in general on the subject of a disarmament conference. [39] With a sigh of relief senators of all persuasions interpreted Harding's words as a conciliatory gesture and jumped on the bandwagon in order to reap benefit from the popular appeal of the Borah amendment. The Senate vote on May 25 was 74–0. Many pro-Harding senators voted for the measure on the assumption that the House would modify the language to suit the president anyway.

Throughout his administration Harding did indeed use the House as a counterforce to the Senate in bending legislation more toward his views.

In this instance he sought help from Stephen G. Porter, chairman of the House Foreign Affairs Committee, who agreed to sponsor a substitute resolution for the Borah amendment which would merely endorse Harding's April 12 statement on disarmament and concur in his desire to call "an international conference to consider the limitation of armaments as soon as feasible."[40]

This substitute resolution, however, ran into immediate difficulty in the House-Senate conference committee where sentiment for the original Borah amendment remained strong. A deadlock ensued. Finally, on June 25, in the realization that further squabbling over the precise wording would delay badly needed naval appropriations, and believing that he had sufficiently protected the prerogatives of his office by carrying the fight this far, Harding issued a face-saving letter to Frank W. Mondell, the Republican floor leader, which stated: ". . . it is not a particular concern to the administration what form the expression of Congress [on a possible disarmament conference] shall take. . . . I am vastly more concerned with the favorable attitude of the Congress on this question than I am as to the form of expressing that attitude."[41] Following this statement, the Borah version—specifically calling for a conference among the United States, England, and Japan—was quickly adopted and was passed four days later by the House, 330–4.

It was later claimed that the Borah amendment forced a reluctant Harding to call the subsequent Washington Conference. Unquestionably the Borah amendment kept the pressure on the administration to "do something." However, while the debate on the amendment was still in progress, the Harding administration was already moving in the direction of calling a disarmament conference. On May 19, six days before the Senate voted on the amendment, Harding wrote to disarmament champion Raymond Robins: "There has not been very much said about it, and the present administration is not disposed to do over much boasting in advance [but] I am glad to have you know personally that some of our diplomatic spokesmen abroad are already making inquiries on this important subject."[42] A month later in his letter to Mondell agreeing to the wording of the Borah amendment, Harding again stated that the administration was currently involved in "inquiries and negotiations" with foreign governments over disarmament matters.[43]

Nowhere do any official papers indicate a formal exchange of ideas on

145

a disarmament conference between the United States and other governments before July 1921.[44] But numerous contacts of an informal nature had already been made. In early June Ambassador Harvey put out "informal feelers" to the British government. At about the same time Admiral William S. Sims, who was in England to receive an honorary degree from Cambridge, sounded out the British Admiralty on the subject of a joint naval conference. When Nicholas Murray Butler traveled to Europe in that same month, he had Harding's approval to ascertain the attitude of key European governments toward the convening of an international disarmament conference. During both May and June, other private citizens, military liaison officers, and visiting foreign dignitaries exchanged information and views with Harding concerning disarmament and American strategy in the face of the existing Anglo-Japanese Alliance.[45]

It was this alliance and its pending renewal which actually provided the immediate impetus for the Washington Conference. According to the terms of the alliance, it would automatically remain in force beyond its July 13, 1921, renewal date if no objection was raised by either party. Before June 1921 neither England nor Japan had formally recorded any dissatisfaction and therefore, by their silence, had indicated a willingness to continue it. The Japanese wanted to retain the alliance because it offered a counterbalance to the Americans in the Pacific and forestalled a much-feared British-American rapprochement. For the British, the alliance provided a measure of safety in view of the impending naval race between herself and the United States.

But it was almost inconceivable that the United States and England should go to war; the alliance, therefore, represented something of an embarrassment for British policy makers. In late June when the Imperial Council convened in London to discuss the renewal of the alliance, differences immediately arose among the various Commonwealth members about its real value. There the matter stood until July 7 when Prime Minister Lloyd George, in reply to a question in Commons about the possibility of Britain convening a conference of the United States and Japan to discuss Far Eastern problems, stated that at the moment feelers on this very subject were being extended to foreign governments.[46]

Already, on July 5, the George government through Lord Curzon had broached the subject to Harvey, but the American ambassador had not informed the State Department immediately and it was not until Friday,

July 8, at 8 P.M. London time, that Harvey dispatched a cable to Hughes relaying the Curzon suggestion. In this same dispatch Harvey recommended that the United States ought to seize the initiative for such a conference. Ironically, having already received intimations of the British move from other sources, Hughes, after hurriedly discussing the matter with Harding, had cabled American ambassadors in Great Britain, Japan, France, and Italy on Friday afternoon, at 4 P.M. Washington time, to ascertain whether a proposal for a conference on the limitation of armaments would be favorably received. Thus, the Harvey and Hughes cables crossed in transmission. Upon reading Harvey's message several hours later on Friday evening, Hughes immediately cabled him to inquire if the British would agree to an expansion of the American suggestion on disarmament to include problems relating to the Far East. On Saturday, while waiting for a reply from Harvey, Hughes drew up a draft for informal invitations and a press release which he submitted to Harding who approved them before leaving on a weekend cruise down the Potomac. When, on Sunday, July 10, Hughes received word from Harvey that the British were agreeable to the plan, Hughes sent out the invitations and gave reporters the press statement for release on Monday morning.[47]

This action in calling an international disarmament conference went far beyond the Borah amendment. Borah had not contemplated a discussion of Pacific problems at all and desired disentanglement, not further involvement in the world's affairs. Moreover, his amendment had referred only to naval armaments while the Hughes proposal left open the possibility of discussing *all* forms of armaments. As Borah later said, ". . . it was not the disarmament conference for which the resolution provided. It included subject matters which the resolution did not cover. It included countries which the resolution did not cover, and it included subject matters which even disarmament did not cover." Clearly, the administration's action in calling the conference was the product of many forces and not just the Borah amendment. The timing was obviously related to British developments concerning the renewal of the Anglo-Japanese Alliance. The conference idea was in response to a desire for government economy, fear of a naval race, and popular opinion.[48]

The press, which had received little hint of the feverish diplomatic activity going on, splashed the news of the conference invitations across its front pages on Monday, July 11. Everywhere there was commendation.

147

It was "inspiring news" and offered "great promise for the future." Said the *New York Times*: "The President is truly responding to the desire of all nations. He has given to [this country] the high distinction of leading in a noble work for civilization."[49] Enthusiasm for the American proposal was not confined to the United States. From around the world came acclaim. Writing to Mrs. Harding from London, Ambassador Harvey remarked: "The President's call for a conference made the greatest hit that I have any recollection of."[50]

By early August, the four powers had indicated a willingness to attend and November 12 was set as the conference's opening date. After consultation with the other participants, President Harding also invited China, Belgium, the Netherlands, and Portugal to attend sessions relating to Far Eastern questions because of their interests in that part of the world. The president, meanwhile, announced a blue-ribbon delegation to represent the United States. These appointments amply demonstrated Harding's political sagacity. Unlike Wilson, he calculated his selections so that they would be weapons in his arsenal in the event of subsequent trouble with the Senate. As expected, his choice for chairman was Hughes. But beyond that he carefully weighed the possibilities. He eliminated Borah because he had no desire to boost Borah's prestige and correctly assumed him to be an enemy. He also eliminated other former irreconcilables such as Johnson. Hoover was considered, but Harding rightly concluded that his appointment would unnecessarily antagonize the bitter-enders.

Harding finally settled on Root and Lodge as the perfect combination to represent the majority party. Root was championed by Hughes, had an impeccable reputation, and was acceptable to almost all elements in the Republican party. Lodge, as chairman of the Senate Foreign Relations Committee, was regarded by Harding as a key to securing Senate ratification of any treaties. Then, in a master stroke, Harding gave the Democratic party representation by selecting Senator Underwood, the Democratic minority leader and ranking Democratic member of the Foreign Relations Committee, as the fourth and final member of the delegation.

To assist this four-man team Harding appointed an Advisory Committee. Its published function was to act as a sounding board for public opinion. In reality, it afforded the president an opportunity to satisfy the personal vanity of numerous influential individuals and recognize certain vested-interest groups and pressure blocs. Its twenty-one members sym-

148

bolized finance, labor, commerce, agriculture, the three major faiths (Protestant, Roman Catholic, and Jewish), and each geographic section. Again, Harding showed himself a master politician by tying important national figures and groups to the success of the conference and building up a reservoir of favorable public opinion which could be drawn upon if necessary. Even the emerging influence of female voters was recognized by the appointment of four women to the Advisory Committee.[51]

If the political and public relations aspects of the conference were well handled, the staging for it was perfect. Coincidentally, but fortuitously, Armistice Day, Friday, November 11, had been selected as the time for the dedication of the grave of the Unknown Soldier. Some weeks before, this unidentified serviceman had been chosen from among four in a musty little chapel in the French village of Châlons-sur-Marne. The plain pine box was then placed on the battleship *Olympia* and brought to Washington. There on November 9, it lay in state under the shadowy dome of the Capitol rotunda where only Lincoln, Garfield, and McKinley had slept in death before. On November 10, 90,000 persons streamed by to pay homage as innumerable wreaths and decorations were placed on the bier.

On November 11 a ceremonial procession began at the Capitol and ended at Arlington Cemetery. President Harding walked part of the way; former President Wilson rode as far as the White House. At the graveside a bugle sounded for two minutes. Rosa Ponselle sang "I Know That My Redeemer Liveth," and the marine band played "America." Then Secretary of War Weeks introduced the president. To a crowd of some 100,000, including the recently arrived foreign delegations to the Washington Conference, Harding spoke emphatically and earnestly:

Standing today on hallowed ground, conscious that all America has halted to share in the tribute of heart and mind and soul to this fellow American . . . it is fitting to say that his sacrifice, and that of the millions of dead, shall not be in vain. There must, there shall be, the commanding voice of a conscious civilization against armed warfare.

As we return this poor clay to its mother soil, garlanded by love and covered with the decorations that only nations can bestow, I can sense the prayers of our people, of all peoples, that this Armistice Day shall mark the beginning of a new and lasting era of peace on earth, good will among men.[52]

As his words came through the loudspeakers on the cemetery grounds and were also carried by wire to 35,000 in Madison Square Garden and to 20,000 in the Plaza in San Francisco, a nation responded with an

149

outpouring of feeling and reverence. But the highlight came at the conclusion of Harding's address when he asked the throngs to join him in repeating the Lord's Prayer. Harding's voice stood out above all the others as the Unknown Soldier was reverently laid to rest. Statesmen from foreign lands as well as common American citizens silently walked away, too moved to hide their emotions. Wrote Kirke L. Simpson of the Associated Press, who won a Pulitzer Prize for his story that day: "Under the wide and starry skies of his homeland, America's unknown dead from France sleeps tonight, a soldier home from the wars." [53]

It was a stirring and apt prologue to the Washington Disarmament Conference.

[6

ON SATURDAY, November 12, the Washington Conference convened in the Pan-American Building. The main conference room with its white-paneled walls and American simplicity offered a marked contrast to the glaring red and gold of the room at Paris where the Versailles Conference had been held. On this day the entire cabinet was present. Mrs. Harding sat erect in her box. Calvin Coolidge austerely occupied the place beside her. Directly across in the gallery was a phalanx of senators. In the section reserved for the Supreme Court sat the venerable Oliver W. Holmes, Jr., and close beside him was Justice Louis D. Brandeis. On the floor were milling newspapermen, each attempting to buttonhole entering delegates.

Suddenly there was a ripple of applause. Hughes entered with every whisker, according to Mark Sullivan, "at a satisfactory angle." Then a much larger wave of applause swept the room as Harding appeared. Hughes spoke the first words of the conference—it was to announce the prayer—and when it was over he said simply: "The President of the United States."

To Harding, as to the others there, the burial of the Unknown Soldier and the opening of the conference represented a symbolic union. Harding called attention to this fact in a brief speech which welcomed the delegates to Washington and concluded: "A world staggering with debt needs its burdens lifted. Humanity which has been shocked by wanton destruction would minimize the agencies of that destruction. . . . I can

150

speak officially only for our United States. Our hundred millions frankly want less of armament and none of war. Wholly free from guile, sure in our own minds that we harbor no unworthy designs, we accredit the world with the same good intent. So I welcome you, not alone in good will and high purpose, but with high faith."[54] Prolonged applause ensued. William Jennings Bryan, who was covering the conference as a reporter, dropped his paper and pencil and leaped to his feet to lead the clapping. It was a good speech, not brilliant, but brief and sincere. Hughes shook Harding's hand; Arthur Balfour, the chief British delegate, also grasped his hand as did Aristide Briand, head of the French delegation. Others attempted to congratulate him as he slowly made his way toward the door amid the continuing applause. Then he was gone.

Not by accident did the president quickly leave the center of the stage. Secretary Hughes was the first of the official delegates scheduled to speak, and he now delivered a fateful address. Where Harding's speech had inspired, Hughes's shocked. The first part was "old stuff," a lawyer's brief and somewhat boring. Then he moved into the American proposal for disarmament, indicating that the United States was prepared to scrap thirty capital ships with an aggregate tonnage of 845,740. This was astounding enough but just as everyone thought the speech was over and had begun to applaud Hughes suddenly turned toward the British delegation and continued: "It is proposed that Great Britain: (1) Shall stop further construction of the four new *Hoods*. . . ." All eyes shifted to Lord David Beatty, First Lord of the Admiralty, who lurched forward in his chair like "a bulldog, sleeping on a sunny doorstep, who has been poked in the stomach by the impudent foot of an itinerant soap-canvasser."[55] After disposing of 583,375 aggregate tons of British warships, Hughes next turned to Japan which he proposed should forfeit 448,928 tons. All in all, Hughes's speech laid waste to 1,878,043 tons of the three finest navies in the world and left the United States with 500,650 tons, Great Britain with 604,450, and Japan with 299,700. Moreover, Hughes proposed a ten-year construction holiday before any new keels could be laid down and suggested that replacement tonnage remain within a fixed final limit of 500,000 for the Americans, 500,000 for the British, 300,000 for the Japanese, 175,000 for the French, and 175,000 for the Italians (5:5:3:1.75:1.75). Furthermore, capital ships could be replaced only after they were twenty years old and no capital ship could displace more than 35,000 tons. Hughes also expressed hope that similar agreements could be worked out for auxiliary craft such as destroyers, cruisers, submarines, and aircraft carriers.[56]

At the conclusion of Hughes's speech the cheering lasted for ten minutes. Hats waved, handkerchiefs fluttered, men slapped, hugged, and embraced one another. In the midst of the excitement and upon a motion by the American delegation, the conference adjourned until Monday, November 14, giving the delegates an opportunity to catch their breath. All Sunday papers carried the Hughes "surprise" and descriptions of the opening session taxed the verbal limits of reporters. Words like "dramatic," "unique," "inspired" accompanied such phrases as "a brilliant coup," "masterful timing," "consummate statesmanship," and "a great diplomatic adventure." Even as late as 1946 William Allen White claimed Hughes's address was "the most intensely dramatic moment I have ever witnessed."[57] Indeed, imaginations were gripped everywhere—Hughes's proposal was the talk of the globe. But nowhere was it more talked about than in the Franklin Square Hotel where the British naval experts were housed and in the old-fashioned mansion on Dupont Circle where the Japanese delegates were living. At both places the lights burned brightly throughout Saturday and Sunday nights.

Most sensations occur accidentally, but this one had been carefully planned and timed. The credit belonged mainly to Hughes, but it was shared by Harding. From the beginning, the secretary of state feared that the conference might not accomplish anything if it followed the pattern of most international gatherings. He was determined to get action even if it required extraordinary measures, and he developed his disarmament proposal with that goal in mind. Meanwhile, he relied on Harding to hold in line the United States navy, which wanted parity with Great Britain and a two-to-one edge over Japan. Hughes convinced Harding that while the British might accept parity, the Japanese would settle for no less than a tonnage ratio of 60 percent and any other course would wreck the conference. As Hughes hoped, Harding forced the navy to acquiesce. Work on the American plan was not completed until forty-eight hours before the opening of the conference, and Hughes's speech remained top secret until the moment of its delivery.

It was Hughes's idea to spring the American proposal as a surprise. Originally, he had not planned to unveil it on the opening day, but as he told Harding, "I am so afraid that a leak or some other development might spoil its effect that I think it should get off right away." Harding agreed and decided to keep his own speech simple in order to focus attention on Hughes. The secretary of state counted on the shock effect of his proposal to throw the conference into consternation, and the American delegation had been forewarned to seek an immediate adjournment. Both Hughes and Harding wanted the weekend to intervene in order to reserve for the American plan prime newspaper space and editorial comment.[58]

After reconvening on Monday, November 14, the conference proceeded to debate the American proposal on naval disarmament and also to discuss other pertinent questions. It deliberated twelve weeks. In reality, the gathering was two distinct conferences, each with a special task: (1) to effect a limitation of armaments on the part of the five major Allied powers, and (2) to solve Pacific and Far Eastern problems by a concerted effort on the part of all nine nations. This latter phase of the conference was important, but of less interest to the general public than the disarmament discussions.

While the working sessions of the conference were restricted to delegates, there were seven plenary sessions which were open to the public and at which the decisions of the working sessions were announced. This style of "open diplomacy" was Harding's idea and was calculated to offset anticipated Senate criticism and offer a contrast to the "secret diplomacy" of Woodrow Wilson. The press, in particular, was given free access to the delegates, who held regularly scheduled briefings and permitted themselves to be questioned on any subject. Secretary of State Hughes later commented: "There never was an international gathering in which candor and fairness more fully dominated the intercourse of great Powers and where intrigue had less play."[59]

The deliberations on disarmament ultimately led to the formulation of three treaties—one on the abolition of poisonous gas and the use of submarines, one on the status quo in the Pacific, and one on naval tonnage. The first was of little moment; the second, the Four-Power Treaty, was a complete surprise; and the third, the famous Five-Power Naval Treaty, was a major result of the conference and a direct outgrowth of the Hughes proposal.

By the Naval Treaty, which was to run for fifteen years, capital ship tonnages were pegged at 525,850 for the United States, 558,950 for Britain, 303,320 for Japan, 221,170 for France, and 182,800 for Italy. Replacement ratios were fixed at 5:5:3:1.75:1.75. According to the treaty, the United States had to scrap 845,740 tons, Britain 583,000 tons, and Japan 435,328 tons. Under the existing limits neither France nor Italy was required to scrap any. There was to be a ten-year holiday on capital-ship building and thereafter no capital ship was to exceed 35,000 tons. Guns on capital ships were limited to sixteen-inch caliber; guns on light cruisers were limited to eight inches. No light cruisers of more than 10,000 tons were to be built. No aircraft carrier could exceed 27,000 tons nor its gun caliber eight inches. Total tonnage of aircraft carriers was limited to 135,000 for the United States, 135,000 for Great Britain, 81,000 for Japan, 60,000 for France, and 60,000 for Italy. The status quo in naval fortifications was to be maintained by the United States in the Aleutians and all American island possessions west of Hawaii; by Britain in all islands east of Singapore excepting those adjacent to Australia and New Zealand; and by Japan in all her insular possessions outside of Japan proper.[60]

While this naval agreement was being negotiated, private talks were held outside the confines of the conference, first between the United States and Britain, and then including Japan and France, which eventually led to the Four-Power Treaty. A direct result of Britain's desire to bind the United States to a general arrangement which would make the Anglo-Japanese Treaty obsolete, the Four-Power Treaty was relatively short and somewhat ambiguous.[61] By it, the four major Pacific powers agreed to respect each other's rights "in relation to their insular possessions and insular dominions in the region of the Pacific Ocean," and in case of controversy would hold a joint conference to adjust any differences. If those rights should be endangered by any outside power, they agreed to communicate on the joint, or separate, action to be taken "to meet the exigencies of the particular situation." This treaty, which now superseded the Anglo-Japanese Alliance, was to remain in force ten years and required a twelve-month termination notice.[62]

Negotiated in secret, the Four-Power Treaty certainly was at variance with the publicized openness of the conference. No official documents or records were kept of the meetings leading to the agreement, nor were such meetings listed on the conference agenda. Although three days before the treaty's announcement the press had carried rumors about some "private conversations" and surmised that they probably involved an abrogation of the Anglo-Japanese Alliance, reporters could get no concrete information. The whole affair had a cloak of mystery about it and smacked of old-style secret diplomacy.[63]

Hence, when the agreement was made public, the press and especially certain senators became "comma hounds" dissecting the text for hidden and dangerous meanings. Matters were not improved when Harding, asked by reporters on December 20 why the Japanese home islands were construed to be covered by the Four-Power Treaty, replied that they were not—only to be corrected by Hughes who stated that the provisions of the treaty did embrace the Japanese homeland. Such apparent confusion fed the myth that Harding was totally ignorant of the nature of the Four-Power Treaty and had not been briefed by Hughes.

Harding's *faux pas* was understandable. The Japanese changed sides on the homeland issue at least once and Harding became momentarily confused about their latest position. Hughes had told Harding in his daily presidential review of the progress of the Four-Power talks that Baron Tomosaburo Kato, chief of the Japanese delegation, had asked first that the main islands *not* be included, but had finally dropped this request. When asked by reporters about it, Harding was caught short on the final situation and picked the wrong answer. Explained Harding to Hughes later: "Hughes, I didn't want to appear to be a dub."[64] They both laughed over it, but the press and senators such as Reed and Borah blew the incident up out of proportion. Recalling the matter some ten years later, Hughes claimed that the president's mind had been so crowded with details about all aspects of the conference that he had not been able to assimilate them entirely and that he had been unjustly maligned in this instance. An interesting corollary to the Harding mistake was the fact that before the conference closed the Japanese changed their minds once again and asked that the Japanese homeland not be included in the coverage of the Four-Power Treaty. This had been their original position and the one Harding had reported them to possess.[65]

On Pacific and Far Eastern questions the American delegation did not take the same kind of initiative as it had on naval disarmament. In general it relied on the Chinese delegation, headed by thirty-five-year-old Dr. Wellington Koo, Chinese minister to London, to advance the principle of the "open door." Since China's "rights" served as the basis for most of the discussions relating to Far Eastern problems, success hinged largely on the willingness of the Japanese to cooperate. Japan's decision to negotiate the return of the Shantung peninsula to China and to begin the withdrawal of Japanese troops from Eastern Siberia was taken as evidence of her good faith. Both these actions were consummated after the conference was over. Meanwhile a treaty and ten resolutions directly affecting China came out of the discussions. The resolutions concerned postal agencies, customs, the presence of foreign troops, railways, radio stations, private contracts with Chinese authorities, and so forth. The lone treaty involved Chinese customs regulations.[66]

Also growing out of the Far Eastern discussions were two treaties which involved the United States. The first was a bilateral agreement with Japan over the island of Yap. The second was the Nine-Power Open Door Pact. By the Yap Treaty the United States formally recognized the League of Nations' grant of all former German possessions north of the Equator to Japan as mandates, but American citizens were to have free access to the island of Yap "in all that relates to the landing and operation of the existing Yap-Guam cable, or of any cable which may hereafter be laid or operated by the United States or by its nationals connecting with the Island of Yap." The Nine-Power Treaty, which was written mainly by Elihu Root, attempted to elevate the "open door" concept to international law. By it, the contracting powers agreed to respect the sovereignty and territorial integrity of China, to maintain the principle of equal commercial opportunity, and to refrain from seeking special rights or privileges in China. China, in turn, agreed not to discriminate against the legitimate activities of the nationals of foreign powers. Hailed by Hughes as a "Magna Carta" for China, it was largely a pious restatement of traditional American policy toward the Asian mainland.[67]

The Washington Conference met for the last time on February 6, 1922. After three months' work the delegates were generally satisfied, believing no one country was walking off with a major advantage. The American press, except for the Hearst papers which were bitterly anti-British and anti-Japanese, greeted the conference's conclusion by calling it "a turning point in history." Secretary Hughes expressed his belief that the work of the conference ended the naval race and that the world was "taking perhaps the greatest forward step in history to establish the reign of peace."

Baron Kato claimed the conference had succeeded "beyond the hopes of those who called it into being." [68]

The man who had called it into being—President Harding—had ample reason to be gratified. He had regarded this conference as being crucially important. Contrary to later claims, he had kept in constant touch with its progress. Hughes had seen him every day and had reported to him all discussions and secured his approval for all decisions.[69] By choice, however, Harding had remained in the background and, except for the occasion on which he made the slip about the Japanese homeland, had refused to be dragged by reporters into commenting on the conference's work. Harding had relied heavily on Hughes during these months and had retained absolute confidence in the wisdom of his secretary of state. Rarely had the president found it necessary to alter any of Hughes's suggestions and Harding backed him with all the power of the presidential office, a fact which enhanced Hughes's position as spokesman for the United States. More important, Harding himself had provided the conference with a sense of stability and trust. If Hughes had been its brains, Harding had been its heart. "The tranquilizing spirit of President Harding permeated the endeavors of the Conference," said Secretary Hughes several years later, while at the time Mark Sullivan wrote: "His unruffled serenity is one of the most striking things that appeal to those of us who make the daily rounds of events here. . . . There can be no doubt of the fact that his equanimity and his personal armor against the infection of excitement have much to do with the success of the Conference, and especially with the creation of the spirit and atmosphere of it. . . . These serene, unhurried, and unexcited qualities of Harding's personality are most certainly a highly important part of the Conference." [70]

But Harding took no credit whatever for the success of the conference when he addressed the delegates for the last time on the closing day, February 6. It was their triumph. The world, he said, had hungered for a new assurance of peace in which there would be no victors and no vanquished. This conference had provided it. Setting aside national advantage, he continued, the delegates had kept faith with the desires of mankind and had pointed the way to a new and better epoch in human progress. "This conference," he concluded, "has wrought a truly great achievement. It is hazardous sometimes to speak in superlatives [but the result is] so fine, so gratifying, so reassuring, so full of promise, that above

157

the murmurings of a world sorrow not yet silenced; above the groans which come of excessive burdens not yet lifted but soon to be lightened; above the discouragements of a world struggling to find itself after surpassing upheaval, there is the note of rejoicing which is not alone ours or yours, or all of us, but comes from the hearts of men of all the world." [71]

The conference was over. Now the struggle with the Senate could begin.

[7

ON FEBRUARY 10 President Harding appeared before the Senate and asked for the ratification of the conference treaties. His message was couched in soothing terms as he urged the senators not to be swayed by narrow suspicions and fears. He assured them that the various treaties, even the Four-Power Treaty, were open covenants which concealed no "alliance, entanglement or involvement" and had been constructed "in accordance with our constitutional methods." After giving such assurances, he reminded them that as a former member of the Senate he was well aware of the senatorial desire to exercise the Senate's prerogatives. But he pointedly added: "Since [my Senate] experience I have come to know the viewpoint and inescapable responsibility of the Executive. To the Executive comes the closer view of world relationship and a more impressive realization of the menaces, the anxieties, and the apprehensions to be met." Pass these treaties, he said, not merely because it is right to do so, but because the president feels that they are absolutely essential to the welfare of the United States. [72]

Five minutes after Harding left, Senator Lodge moved that the treaties be referred to his own Committee on Foreign Relations. Lodge had been "pleased as punch" to serve on the American delegation and, as expected, now became the chief spokesman for the treaties. He bluntly warned his Senate colleagues in words reminiscent of his pro-League adversaries in 1919 that to defeat the treaties would shock and disillusion the entire world. Senator Underwood, the other senatorial representative on the American delegation, supplemented Lodge's efforts, emphasizing that the public approved of these treaties and the Senate should pass them. Public opinion did strongly support favorable Senate action. A *Literary Digest* poll showed that of 803 newspapers, 723 were for ratification, 66 against, and 14 noncommittal. The *Washington Post*, executing a radical switch from its anti-League days, reflected an almost universal sentiment when it cautioned the Senate that "rejection of these treaties would plunge the international situation into chaos." [73]

Such arguments did not impress men like Borah, Johnson, and Reed. Senator Reed, the Democratic *enfant terrible*, had taken pot shots at the Washington treaties even before they were submitted to the Senate. As soon as the existence of the Four-Power Treaty became known in mid-December, Reed sarcastically denounced it as "diplomatic chicanery." Reed also pounced on Harding's slip concerning the Japanese homeland and used it as an excuse for a scathing attack on the whole Washington Conference. A former irreconcilable, Reed vowed at that time that he would never permit the United States to become entangled in the world's affairs by this "backdoor manner." [74] Hiram Johnson also began to express his opposition early. A month before the treaties were submitted Johnson told a California audience that the Four-Power Treaty was especially dangerous and that the Senate would have to "study every word and phrase before we commit our country to this unexpected and extraordinary contract." [75]

But Borah was the star of the opposition show. The calling of the conference seemed to have enraged him and rather than cooperating for its success, he threw every possible obstacle in its path. No sooner had it convened than he warned the country against betrayal, against an "association of nations," against giving away American sovereignty. He did not like Far Eastern questions being discussed; he did not like the Four-Power Treaty. Most of all he did not like the fact that Harding had "stolen" the disarmament issue and appropriated it as his own. [76]

Because of a concentration of anti-treaty sentiment among its members, the Foreign Relations Committee provided the arena where the most crucial debates occurred. The Four-Power Treaty and the Five-Power Naval Treaty drew the most fire. Even Lodge could not prevent recalcitrant committee members from attaching a reservation to the Four-Power Treaty as a price for favorable recommendation to the floor. Sponsored by Senator Brandegee, this amendment declared: "The United States understands that under the statement in the preamble or under the terms of this treaty there is no commitment to armed force, no alliance, no obligation to join in any defense." [77]

The Brandegee reservation was unnecessary and was added more in the desire to reaffirm the Senate's power vis-à-vis the executive than to improve foreign policy. Lodge realized this and wrote to London asking George Harvey, one of Brandegee's closest friends, to urge Brandegee to withdraw it. Complained Lodge, "there is not a word in [the Four-Power Treaty] which justifies calling it an alliance or which binds us to do anything whatever." [78] But Brandegee remained obdurate and the Four-Power Treaty went to the floor with his amendment attached.

The floor debate, especially on the Four-Power Treaty, was spirited and acrimonious. Democrats, in general, relished the discomfort of the Republicans and sought to embarrass the administration by asking for the full record of all negotiations relating to the four-power pact. Lodge was forced to admit there was none. Senator Joseph T. Robinson, a former supporter of the League, called it a "sell out" to Japan and attempted to add crippling amendments which were invariably supported by former irreconcilables, but which were defeated by pro-administration Republicans and a number of pro-conference Democrats. As expected, in the floor debate Senators Reed, Borah, and Johnson bitterly condemned the Four-Power Treaty. Borah cried, "I am for peace. God knows I want to serve that cause," but added that voting for this treaty was no way to do so. Johnson charged that the country faced the prospect of being saddled with obligations much worse than those envisioned by the League. But the rapier thrusts of Reed drew the most blood. Speaking directly to Lodge, he once sarcastically said: "I remember that another President had a plan and insisted that it was America's plan and he, too, I suppose, thought it ought not to fail. Yet with all the sagacity he possessed, the Senator from Massachusetts sought to bring that to failure because it was wrong." [79]

The debate in the Senate on the Four-Power Treaty ultimately filled over 200 pages of the *Congressional Record*, involved some fifty roll calls, thirty-three on the final day alone. Thirty reservations were offered at one time or another, mostly for destructive purposes, but in the end only one—the Brandegee amendment—survived. The final vote came on March 24. After accepting the Brandegee amendment 90–2, sixty-seven senators (fifty-five Republicans and twelve Democrats) voted for ratification and twenty-seven (twenty-three Democrats and four Republicans) against. The four dissenting Republicans were Borah, Johnson, LaFollette, and Joseph I. France of Maryland, causing Johnson to snort, "If this treaty had been sent to the Senate by President Wilson, there would have been forty Republican votes against it instead of four."[80] The margin of victory on the ratification was only four votes, indicating the importance of the twelve Democrats, including Senator Underwood, who voted for the treaty. It was a clear vindication of Harding's bipartisan policy and Hughes's maxim that to win ratification in the Senate public opinion must be secured first.

Although both Harding and Hughes had been fairly confident of victory, the debates on the Four-Power Treaty made them nervous. When the final count was in, the press reported that Harding was "feeling like a boy" and that Secretary Hughes displayed "a buoyant spirit when he received newspaper men." Harding, in particular, could afford to feel pleased because he had been a vital factor in the successful outcome. He would have preferred the treaty without the Brandegee amendment and early had to make the critical decision whether to oppose it. On March 20, Lodge told him that there were "four or five" senators who would vote for the treaty with the amendment but might vote against it without. Harding wisely decided to accept the amendment rather than jeopardize ratification and endanger all the remaining treaties yet to be considered. Two days before the vote, he wrote to Ambassador Harvey that "it is necessary for me to help the Brandegee forces secure the adoption of the reservation" in order to safeguard final ratification. Indicating a realistic appraisal of the situation, he added, "I think [the amendment] to be perfectly needless and almost childish, but we have gotten to a point where there must be a manifestation of [Senate] influence, and this is the way to give expression to that ambition."[81]

The ratification of the Four-Power Treaty was the key action and thereafter the other treaties, including the Five-Power Naval Treaty, were rapidly endorsed. By April Fool's Day the Senate had cleared its calendar of all Washington Conference matters. This was only eleven days later than Harding had set in his timetable more than six weeks before in submitting the treaties to the Senate. At that time he had written George Harvey that he hoped the Senate would pass the treaties by March 20 and "free us from many of the anxieties we have felt for several weeks." Offering an interesting insight into his own thinking, Harding added: "I am hopeful that we will establish the conviction in the minds of the world that it is possible for the American government to enter into international agreements and be able to secure the approval of the Senate." [82]

With the final acceptance of the conference treaties, Harding succeeded where Wilson had failed, and this action did much to restore the confidence of the world in American international policies. The nation was at last emerging from under the cloud of political strife and party warfare that had wrecked Wilson's plan and had reduced American foreign policy to a shambles. The acceptance of the Washington treaties did not, of course, place the United States on the high road of enthusiastic international cooperation. But along with the peace treaties, this action provided a significant landmark in reestablishing normal postwar relationships. And to Warren Harding must go much of the credit. Wrote William Allen White in an editorial entitled "Hats Off to Warren G." in his *Emporia Gazette* shortly after the ratifications: "The treaties establishing the work of the Washington conference for the limitation of armament have all been passed, and practically without opposition. And the passage of these treaties is due largely to the good sense and tact of President Harding. . . . Mr. Harding is not an intellectual giant. He may not be a moral heavy weight. That is as it may be. But he is a courteous, sensible American gentleman, and he does bring home the bacon." [83]

If, at the time, Harding's role in the successful outcome of the Washington Conference was widely appreciated, the significance of the conference was the subject of some controversy. Both then and later, the value, especially of the Four- and Five-Power treaties, was debated. Some newspapers claimed Japan was the real winner, but others thought the United States emerged victorious. The Japanese claimed it was an American victory by pointing to the fact that Japan lost the security of the old Anglo-Japanese Alliance without really receiving anything in return. The British also believed it was an American victory but one in which they were well pleased. Mark Sullivan, writing in 1922, listed the British acceptance of naval parity with the United States "without battle, without strife, and without envy or covetousness" as the most significant event of the conference. Secretary of State Hughes also regarded this as a coup for the Americans. [84]

The general consensus was that regardless of who "won," the conference had achieved substantial results. War between the United States and Britain had been made almost impossible. War between the United

States and Japan had been indefinitely postponed. Britain had been transferred from the Japanese side to the American side of any potential Pacific dispute. The open-door policy had been given a new lease on life and the Japanese promises about Shantung and removal of troops from Siberia were portents of a restoration of a workable balance of power in the Far East. Finally, the conference presaged the saving of billions of dollars for the taxpayers not only of the United States but of the world.

In later years, especially with the approach of World War II, the Washington Conference was downgraded. One writer in 1943 described the conference as "one of the costliest bits of diplomatic blundering that ever befell the United States."[85] Japan came to be regarded as the real conference winner. It was claimed that Japan had outwitted the United States and had given only worthless paper promises concerning the open door in the Far East. The pledge of "no fortifications" in the Pacific area was viewed as a calculated move to prepare the road for later Japanese expansion. The Washington Conference, according to the criticism, provided only a "parchment peace" which did not bind the United States to any military obligation while at the same time restricting freedom of American diplomatic action.

These subsequent developments, however, were not the fault of the Washington Conference itself, but of the later intent of those who had attended it. Even in 1922, Secretary Hughes and President Harding realized the success of the conference would ultimately rest on the various nations' "will to peace." If the agreements were to prove lasting, they would become so "not through force," but through good will and a "feeling of respect and friendship." As Elihu Root later observed, it was wrong to assume that the Washington treaties were failures simply because bad faith finally replaced the mutual trust and confidence upon which they had originally been erected.[86]

On the other hand, it is true that by later standards, American policy at Washington in 1921–22 was naive both in its inattention to enforcement procedures and in its motives. As to the former, it was unlikely that the Senate would have accepted any rigid enforcement provisions if they had been negotiated. As for the latter, American officials saw armaments as the evil cause rather than the inescapable result of international tension. Moreover, most Americans in the early twenties, including Harding and Hughes, failed to grasp the fact that any effort to reduce arms demanded more than a one-shot conference situation, requiring instead an active and sustained participation by the United States in the psychological, political, and economic reconstruction of the postwar world.

Whatever the long-range significance of the conference, there were some interesting instantaneous results in 1922–23. The apparent success of the conference encouraged both peace advocates and supporters of government economy to strive immediately for drastic slashes in military appropriations. Along with the Navy League, the American Legion, and the National Civic Federation, President Harding firmly resisted such cuts. He supported Secretary Denby and Secretary Weeks in their attempts to maintain an adequate military posture. Harding particularly believed in keeping the navy up to treaty strength and would permit no reductions below 86,000 men. This struggle between the "silly pacifists," as Secretary Weeks called them, and the Harding administration lasted to the moment of Harding's death.[87]

In one matter Harding was surprisingly farsighted. As a result of the Washington treaties, he encouraged the military to plan new strategy and move into new weapons development. In particular, he became a strong advocate of air power and was intrigued by General Billy Mitchell's ideas. He agreed with Senator Miles Poindexter, chairman of the Senate Naval Affairs Committee, and Representative Frederick C. Hicks, another champion of naval air power, both of whom constantly preached the importance of the aircraft carrier. By 1923 Harding was so convinced that the nation needed more vessels like the experimental *Langley* that he advocated converting a number of battle cruisers into carriers. Before his final trip west, he asked Secretary Denby to prepare such a recommendation for an appropriations request to the 68th Congress.[88]

Still fearing Japan as a potential aggressor in spite of the Washington Conference, Harding also supported the rapid conversion of the navy to the fast, oil-burning heavy cruiser for increased range and mobility. Furthermore, he endorsed the creation of the United States Fleet in late 1922, with its most powerful subdivision, the Battle Fleet, based on the Pacific Coast. This reorganization was recommended by Secretary Denby, who, despite the reputation he later acquired during the Teapot Dome affair, well understood the sea-power requirements of the future. The Battle Fleet, stationed on permanent duty in the Pacific by Harding, represented American strength in that area down to 1939. With the encouragement

164

of Denby and Assistant Secretary Theodore Roosevelt, Jr., naval planners immediately sought to create an adequate backup for this fleet in shore installations and oil storage depots, and selected Hawaii as the focus of all American naval power in the Pacific. Beginning with the Harding administration, the naval base at Pearl Harbor became critically important.[89]

One further outgrowth of the Washington Conference, and this in most aspects was embarrassing for the Harding administration, was renewed speculation about "an association of nations." Old pro-Leaguers, in particular, talked themselves into believing that the Washington gathering was a first step in that direction and that such conferences might metamorphose into the basis for a world concert of peace-loving powers. Harding himself was at first intrigued with the idea. Very subtly he began to hint that the Washington Conference might be a prelude to an "association of nations" and in late November suggested the possibility of "annual meetings" of nations for solving the world's problems. Anti-League senators were furious. Borah and Johnson threatened to re-form the Battalion of Death which had killed Wilson's League and warned that any extension of the Washington Conference into an "association of nations" was doomed to failure.

Thereafter there was little further talk of "an association" and it was claimed that President Harding gave Senator Johnson "positive assurances . . . that no further steps towards a definite organization of an association of nations were to be taken for the present." Harding did let the matter die. But Hughes, not Johnson, was responsible. Hughes had not encouraged Harding to revive the association idea because he feared it would unnecessarily complicate the prospects for Senate approval of the conference's work. The secretary curtly turned aside all questions by reporters on the subject and was relieved when Harding finally took the hint.[90]

In the long run Harding assumed the position that through the Washington Conference his administration had actually fulfilled the hopes held for an association of nations anyway. What difference did the form make, if the substance of world peace was achieved? The criterion was performance. On this score Senate ratification of the treaties, in view of the earlier League fiasco, represented a tremendous endorsement of Harding's brand of international cooperation, whatever one chose to call it. Harding looked at it this way: every administration's reputation in foreign policy rests on one or two main acts; through the Washington Conference, he believed, his administration's name was secure in history.[91]

[8

IT WAS ironical that the Harding administration's success in liquidating the war and achieving a return to peace rested almost as much on a sixty-five-year-old inmate in Atlanta Penitentiary as on an august gathering of foreign dignitaries in Washington. Eugene Victor Debs, the grand old man of the Socialist party and perennial candidate for the presidency, had been arrested in the summer of 1918 for seditious antiwar activity. The Supreme Court had upheld his conviction and President Wilson had concurred in its action. Still, there were many who believed that Debs's arrest and incarceration were unnecessary and hoped for his early release. Indeed, a pardon was recommended for him in 1921 by no less than A. Mitchell Palmer, Wilson's Red-baiting attorney general, who perceived that Debs represented no danger to the United States. Yet Wilson vented on Debs some of his own postwar frustration by scrawling across Palmer's recommendation the single word: "Denied."[92]

No sooner was Warren Harding inaugurated than a parade of letters began to reach the White House requesting the release of all wartime political prisoners, especially Eugene Debs. Such prominent men as Sidney Hillman and Morris Hillquit beseeched the White House to take immediate action while Socialist Norman Thomas, who as a youngster had been a newsboy for the *Marion Star*, begged his former employer to release Debs, claiming that "in prison [he] speaks far louder than he could were he free." Jacob Coxey, remembered for his famous march in the 1890's, wrote to Harding from Massillon, Ohio, that he would be delighted to serve as the government's personal messenger to carry a presidential pardon to Debs in Atlanta.[93]

Harding's involvement in the Debs case was not new. While a senator he had been urged by Clyde R. Miller, a reporter for the *Cleveland Plain Dealer*, to use his personal influence to secure Debs's freedom. Ironically, it was Miller's testimony about one of Debs's wartime speeches that had helped put the Socialist behind bars. Miller had come to doubt the wisdom of his action and through Harding hoped to rectify it. The Ohio

166

senator had promised Miller he would do what he could and, if elected president, might pardon Debs. During the 1920 campaign, Harding referred to political prisoners on several occasions and indicated a willingness to review their cases.[94]

Two weeks before the inauguration, Harding told Daugherty that he wished to free Debs if possible and asked him to investigate the matter. Shortly thereafter, Daugherty requested Debs to visit him in Washington, and alone, and unguarded, Debs arrived at Union Station on March 25 and was escorted by Jess Smith to Daugherty's office. According to Daugherty, they "talked freely for several hours. . . . I found him a charming personality with a deep love for his fellow man." At the conclusion of the interview, the Socialist was returned to the train by Smith who, before seeing him off, purchased for him a huge bundle of quill toothpicks because Debs had complained that he was unable to find any in Atlanta. Daugherty advised Harding that at some risk Debs might be set free as soon as feasible.[95]

But a flurry of opposition arose to Debs's quick release. War-engendered passions still ran high and considerable sentiment existed to keep Debs in jail until the end of his sentence in December 1925. Said the *New York Times* curtly: "He is where he belongs. He should stay there." Other newspapers picked up the chant while many Republican politicians expressed fear that a backlash would follow his release. The issue was particularly explosive since the United States was still technically at war in the spring of 1921 and the Sedition Law under which Debs had been tried and convicted was still in effect. Always sensitive to public opinion, Harding at last decided to postpone releasing Debs at least until the treaties of peace were signed with the Central Powers officially ending the war.[96]

When the ratifications for the German peace treaty were exchanged in November 1921, the last barrier to Debs's release seemed removed. Visitors to his cell in Atlanta told the prisoner that they felt certain the president would act soon. But Harding was still having his troubles. Only a few in his official family were eager to take the action. Daugherty continued to have some misgivings and other cabinet officers, notably Hoover and Davis, regarded it a mistake. Mrs. Harding was flatly opposed to releasing Debs.

When Harding persisted in his own belief that the Socialist should be

167

freed, Daugherty drew up a commutation for Debs and twenty-three other political prisoners in mid-December. Included with each commutation was an oath which the attorney general believed all political prisoners, if released, should sign. By it, they would agree to "lead an upright life and obey and respect all of the laws of the United States." However, in the case of Debs, Daugherty wrote Harding, "I would not advise that an oath of the character enclosed be required. . . . he might go upon his honor, if he has any."[97] Lincoln Steffens later claimed that he (Steffens) convinced Harding that Debs ought not be forced to sign anything upon his release. But Daugherty, not Steffens, was responsible. Anyway, Harding did not like the idea of the oath being required of any prisoner, and two days after receiving Daugherty's suggestion wrote back: "It is my judgment that this sort of a pledge would be of little avail. It would have the savor of bargaining for amnesty and I doubt if that would meet with any marked degree of approval."[98]

Daugherty originally set the date of December 31, 1921, for Debs's release. But Harding changed it to December 24 saying, "I want him to eat his Christmas dinner with his wife." News of Harding's action did not reach Debs in Atlanta until the day of his release at which time 2300 convicts gathered to cheer him as he left. With tears streaming down his cheeks, he waved farewell and left by train for Washington. He would have preferred to go directly to his home in Terre Haute, Indiana, but President Harding had asked him to stop by the White House en route and Debs could not refuse. On the morning of December 26, Debs was ushered into the president's office. Bounding out of his chair, Harding exclaimed: "Well, I have heard so damned much about you, Mr. Debs, that I am now very glad to meet you personally." A flood of reporters met Debs when he came out of the White House, asking him what he thought of President Harding and the presidential mansion. Said Debs: "Mr. Harding appears to me to be a kind gentleman, one whom I believe possesses humane impulses. . . . As for the White House—well, gentlemen, my personal preference is to live privately as an humble citizen in my cottage at Terre Haute." With that statement America's most famous wartime prisoner returned home. His Christmas dinner with Mrs. Debs was two days late.[99]

Lost in the furor over Debs's release was the fact that Harding also freed twenty-three other political prisoners on December 24. Throughout

1922 and 1923, he released many more. A firm believer in judging each case on its merits rather than granting a general amnesty, Harding attempted to free every prisoner who was eligible. In each instance, his sole criterion was whether the person had committed any criminal or destructive act in connection with his antiwar activities. While deeply antagonized by their political ideology, Harding even commuted the sentences of IWW's as long as they met his criterion. Indeed, the very day before he left on his Alaska trip in June 1923, he commuted the sentences of twenty-seven Wobblies seized in various wartime raids. Before his death, he had virtually emptied the nation's jails of all wartime prisoners.

These numerous commutations were acts of moral courage, but none required as much fortitude or was as significant as the release of Eugene Debs. Harding received some bitter criticism but he stuck to his guns. Regarding the Debs case the *New York Times*, for example, warned that "the majority of the American people will not approve this commutation," while Harding's close friend, Malcolm Jennings, wailed in a letter: "I don't know what led you to it." But to Harding the answer was plain. In reply to Jennings, he wrote: "I was persuaded in my own mind that it was the right thing to do. . . . I thought the spirit of clemency was quite in harmony with the things we were trying to do here in Washington."[100]

This was the crux of the matter. Harding had been elected to restore peace and return the nation to tranquillity. The release of Debs was symbolic of Harding's sincere pursuit of that goal. It was perfectly in keeping with the burial of the Unknown Soldier, the passage of the Central Power peace treaties, and the convening of the Washington Conference. Aside from his natural instinct to help a fellow human being, Harding correctly sensed the attitude of the nation in the Debs case and acted on it. Better than the *New York Times*, the president knew that the public mood was one of peace and Debs's release would be accepted as a signal that the war and everything connected with it had finally terminated. More in relief than in anger the nation saw Debs and other political prisoners return home. For them, too, the war was over.

VI

Restoring Prosperity

[1

IF THE early wrangling over legislative priorities had caused a lag in congressional action on the domestic front, it did not delay the Harding administration in creating almost immediately a more favorable economic atmosphere or effecting reductions in the cost of government. These twin goals had occupied a prominent place in Harding's campaign oratory in 1920, and certainly few aspects of his "return to normalcy" were more eagerly anticipated or widely supported.

Inevitably, the avid pursuit of these goals produced a conviction on the part of many critics that all decision making during the Harding years was subject to business domination. But such charges were exaggerated. The depressed economic scene from 1921 to 1923 was inhabited by a congeries of economic interests, each one struggling for advantage. The laborer, the businessman, and the farmer were constantly jockeying for preferential governmental treatment and no clear-cut priority was established among them until after 1923. The Harding era was more a time of conflict and testing than a time of one-sided victory for any economic group.

Still, there is no question that business thinking of the type identified with the middle class permeated the Harding administration. To Harding, a profession, a newspaper, a grocery store, even a farm, was as much a "business" as was a steel corporation. In a typical small-town manner Harding used the term "business" to indicate a state of independence rather than to delimit a specific enterprise. This is quite different from saying that Harding was oriented toward big business and Wall Street as was sometimes charged. Indeed, Wall Street frequently found Harding exasperating. He was too prone to listen to all sides of an economic conflict. His decisions were too much a product of compromise. And he talked too freely about the "rights of the community" while being too swayed by humanitarian impulses. As William Allen White stated in 1922, "Harding is not a tool of Wall Street. Wall Street has little standing in the President's cosmos. . . . the President is a country town man with a country town's distrust of Wall Street." On another occasion, White claimed that Harding was "a puzzle to a plutocracy that was used to dealing with messenger boys. They never quite got him." [1]

If not dominated by big-business interests, Harding's basic economic views were compatible with theirs. Significantly, in his pre-presidential years his favorite stock speech while touring the summer Chautauqua circuit had been on Alexander Hamilton and his contributions to American economic stability ("Hamilton, Prophet of American Destiny"). Harding was a confirmed conservative on the matter of taxation, government economy, and the relationship between government and business. He had always decried high taxes, government waste, and excessive governmental interference in the private sector of the economy. In February 1920, shortly after announcing his candidacy, he advocated a cut in government expenditures and stated that government ought to "strike the shackles from industry." "We need vastly more freedom than we do regulation," he said.[2] Surprisingly, big business took very little notice of him at the time and did not begin to sing his praises until after his election in November. Harding, meanwhile, wrote an article for *World's Work* entitled "Less Government in Business and More Business in Government" which appeared just at the time of his election and which quickened the pulse of the business community. Among other things, it called for a national budget system and "a closer understanding between American government and American business."[3]

During the interim between his election and inauguration, Harding discussed general economic conditions with a variety of top business leaders, and it soon became evident that Harding was acceptable to business, big and little alike. His inaugural address was lauded not only by such big-business spokesmen as Elbert H. Gary and Thomas W. Lamont but

171

by small-business men as well. His special message to Congress in April also cheered the business world and it responded favorably to his statement: "I have said to the people we meant to have less of Government in business as well as more business in Government. It is well to have it understood that business has a right to pursue its normal, legitimate, and righteous way unimpeded."[4]

From the beginning, therefore, the Harding administration possessed a large reservoir of business good will because of three factors: the administration's desire to initiate greater cooperation and trust between government and business; its promise to revamp existing tax laws; and its pledge to install a budget system and effect decreased expenditures. Clearly, Harding had expounded these ideas before he became president and before it was claimed that business had a dominant voice in his regime. Business joined in support of Harding because he held such views; business did not force him to accept them. Indeed, it is highly unlikely that any candidate who did not hold such views could have been elected in 1920. Public opinion after World War I would have regarded an antibusiness administration as dangerous to the country's welfare — especially in view of the Red Scare and the 1920–21 depression.

[2

BY 1920 the cost of government had reached staggering proportions. Federal expenditures had risen from less than $1 billion in 1914 to $18.5 billion in 1919. While the latter figure was due to wartime circumstances, government expenses in the first postwar year of 1920 remained relatively high —$6,139,000,000. Similarly, although the number of federal employees dropped from a wartime peak of 918,000 in 1919 to 691,116 by the close of Wilson's administration in 1921, this was still far above the prewar number of 435,000. Even more disconcerting was the status of the national debt. In 1914 it had been $1,188,000,000, or slightly under $12 per capita. By 1919 it had soared to $25,484,000,000, or $242 per capita.[5]

Conditions were ripe for an economy drive. For some time it had been clear that the opening attack should involve the creation of a national budget system. Current procedures for government spending were sloppy and haphazard. Each December the Treasury Department submitted to Congress the estimates of expenses for all departments for the succeeding fiscal year. But the Treasury Department acted merely as an agent of transmittal, not as a "watchdog." The president, too, played no decisive role; he had no way of knowing whether the requests made by the various departments were valid or not. Departments simply made their requests without reference to any over-all plan. As a result, no fewer than fourteen separate appropriation bills usually came before the House, each being enacted on its own merit. Under such circumstances there was little incentive to reduce expenditures.

In his annual message to Congress in December 1919, President Wilson had called for the creation of a national budget system, but Congress had anticipated him and was already at work on such a plan. The result was the passage of two measures, one by the House and one by the Senate: the Good bill, named for James W. Good, chairman of the House Appropriations Committee, and the McCormick bill, sponsored by Senator Medill McCormick. Sent to a conference committee in May 1920, these two measures differed on one crucial point. The House bill gave the president direct responsibility for the budget and created a budget bureau in the executive office. The Senate bill gave responsibility to the secretary of the treasury and placed a budget bureau in his office. The conference committee finally agreed on a compromise measure which did not satisfy anyone, holding the president basically responsible for budget matters but placing the bureau under the secretary of the treasury. On June 4, 1920, President Wilson vetoed the conference measure and no further action was taken during his administration.

In advocating a national budget system Harding obviously was a follower rather than a leader. Still, he was able to do what Wilson could not do—secure from Congress a measure which would give the president *complete* authority over all budget matters. Shortly after the special session opened in April 1921, the Senate, wary as usual of the expansion of presidential authority, repassed the McCormick bill. Sent to the House, this measure was immediately rejected by the Good bill advocates who substituted the earlier House version by an overwhelming vote of 344–9. Just as the year before, the matter went to a conference committee which on May 25, 1921, reached agreement on a compromise substantially like the Good measure—the only concession to the Senate being the physical placing of the Budget Bureau "in the Treasury Department." However, this concession was not significant since the secretary of the treasury was given no control whatever over the Budget Bureau. The director and assistant director of the bureau were to be appointed by the president and report only to him. As Congressman Good stated in commenting on the final wording: "it would have been better not to have put in the words 'in the Treasury Department' but . . . it is an idle phrase."[6]

Signed by Harding on June 10, the Budget and Accounting Act of 1921 required the president, with the aid of the Budget Bureau, to prepare an annual budget giving to Congress complete information regarding revenues, expenditures, and the condition of the treasury, together with a forecast of administration plans for the future. Harding immediately thought of Charles Dawes as the bureau's first director. Indeed, the day before he signed the act, Harding wrote to the man whom he had earlier wanted for the secretary of the treasury: "I am soon to make probably the most important appointment I am to be called upon to make. I refer to that of Commissioner of the Budget. . . . Nothing would please me more than to call a man of your outstanding prominence and eminent qualifications to such a service."[7]

Dawes had a reputation for efficiency and outspoken bluntness. In 1897 he had organized what later developed into Chicago's fifth largest bank. While yet a young man, he had been appointed by President McKinley as comptroller of the treasury. At the outbreak of World War I he became a major in the 17th Engineers and was among the first 20,000 troops to follow Pershing to France. There he soon became General Dawes, a firm apostle of the "we're-on-our-way" and "let's go" philosophy. During the war, he was one of the key officers on Pershing's staff and was responsible for matériel procurement and supplies. After the war he made quite a splurge through his summary treatment of the House Committee on War Expenditures which was investigating war frauds. Called upon to testify, he attacked the committee for its picayune attitude, told the members they were wasting their time, and finally, in reply to a question whether he had paid excessive prices for army mules, yelled, "Hell and Maria, we weren't trying to keep a set of books, we were trying to win the war!"[8] A man's man who could be charming one minute and behave like a boor the next, Dawes was a colorful figure who commanded public attention. He was a lover of classics and an excellent amateur violinist, but possessed a stevedore's vocabulary which he unleashed at the slightest provocation. Smoking incessantly either a pipe or a cigar, he loved to talk and fancied himself a great speaker. He feared no audience, speaking with strident voice and jerky gestures, often lecturing his listeners unmercifully while peering through black-rimmed glasses. Not everyone liked Dawes's curt manner, his profanity, or his habit of breaking into flattering introductions with "Cut out all the flub dubs." But Harding was not selecting him for the social register. Even his defects made Dawes the right man for the budget job.[9]

In June 1921 Dawes had just booked passage for Europe when he received Harding's invitation to be director of the budget. Dawes accepted on the condition that he would have Harding's complete support and that "the Bureau of the Budget shall be impersonal, impartial, and non-political." Prophetically, Dawes warned, "You must realize that you are the first President to tackle the job of a coordinated business control over the departments. I doubt if you recognize the strength of the 150 years of archaisms which you must fight. 'Delay, linger, and wait' is the watchword of bureaucracy." The task, said Dawes, was like having a "toothpick with which to tunnel Pike's Peak."[10]

Dawes arrived in Washington on June 23 and immediately began the preparation of the budget for the year ending June 30, 1923, as well as initiating steps to cut expenditures for the year ending June 30, 1922. With Harding's approval Dawes met with the cabinet on June 28, where he compared his function to that of the ship's engineer who stands in the stokehole to see that the coal is not wasted while the captain is on the bridge guiding the vessel. He indicated that he would "not be timid" in exercising the powers of the budget director and, with the president's backing, fully intended to trim expenses drastically.[11]

The next day, at Dawes's request, the first meeting of the so-called Business Organization of the Government was held in the auditorium of the Interior Department building. Present were the members of the cabinet and 1200 bureau and division chiefs. Harding opened the meeting by telling them, "The present administration is committed to a period of economy in government. . . . There is not a menace in the world today like that of growing public indebtedness and mounting public expenditures. . . . We want to reverse things." Dawes then took over for an hour, explaining the function of the Budget Bureau and indicating that his specific goal was to remove "fat" from requests and eliminate extravagance

175

in expenditures. With evangelistic fervor Dawes concluded by requesting all those upon whom he could depend to rise. The entire audience rose.[12]

Dawes knew that his most critical problem would be the cabinet itself. He recognized cabinet members' sensitivity to his new position and their resentment of his authority. Of course, all cabinet officers pledged their full support to Dawes, but when the axe began to fall on their own departments, their real feelings began to show. Mellon was the key as far as Dawes was concerned, and when it became evident that he intended to cooperate, Dawes's task was made easier. Hoover frequently squirmed under Dawes's restrictions because he had a tendency to "ask for the moon." But once a budget decision was reached, Hoover tried to live by it. Fall and Daugherty both claimed preferential treatment for their departments, but Dawes sought and got Harding's help in resisting them. Hughes and Hays were generally cooperative, but Secretary Weeks often found himself in violent disagreement with Dawes. He frequently complained to Harding that the budget director unconscionably slashed his military requests. From time to time disputes between Dawes and cabinet officials spilled over into public print. These occasions brought stern warnings from Harding that departments were not "to carry their disappointments and argue their cases in the public press."[13]

As a result of diligent effort and hard-nosed bargaining, Dawes not only presented to Harding on August 1 a tentative schedule of savings for the year ending June 30, 1922, but by October 12 gave him a final budget request for submission to Congress for the year ending June 30, 1923. Dawes estimated government expenditures for 1922 at $3,967,-922,366, providing rigid economies were enforced. The figure for 1923 he set at $3,505,754,727. This latter sum was over $1.5 billion less than the actual expenditures for the year 1921.[14]

On December 5, 1921, Harding presented to Congress the first coordinated budget in history, thus fulfilling his obligation under the Budget and Accounting Act. Before doing so, he wrote to Dawes: "We are going to come to a test of the Budget system when we see what action Congress takes. . . . I look forward to that test with some anxiety."[15] Fortunately, the president's fears proved groundless. While the normal congressional penchant for pork-barreling altered individual department requests slightly, the over-all result was salutary. The reaction of both the congressmen and the country was one of satisfaction. Said the *Commercial and Financial Chronicle* shortly after the first budget was passed: "The Government is now on the way to an orderly and healthy system of business management, thanks to the courage and ability of General Dawes, and the prompt and unqualified cooperation of the President."[16]

Despite this early success, Dawes had no intention of resting on his laurels and, shortly after the budget submission to Congress, requested Harding to call a second meeting of the Business Organization of the Government. (Dawes believed that these meetings should be held every six months in order to maintain adequate communication and to build an *esprit de corps*.) Held on February 3, 1922, in Continental Memorial Hall, this gathering watched Dawes give a stellar performance. After a few opening remarks by Harding in which the president reiterated his support for the director, Dawes delivered a rousing address designed to wipe out any small pockets of anti-economy resistance left in some bureaus and jolt into line those few officials who were still recalcitrant.[17] Harding later commented that Dawes was the only man he had ever seen who when he talked could keep "both feet and both arms in the air at once." The *New York Times* described the director as "waving his arms, stamping the floor, and pounding the table." Continued the *Times*: "Mr. Dawes roamed back and forth, pouring out denunciations upon the sinners on the floor and in the galleries. . . . The conventional sin of governmental extravagance was pictured by Dawes with all the fervor with which 'Billy' Sunday and similar revivalists assail a personal devil. He waved two energetic arms. He loosened his collar, pointed his finger at Cabinet members, and shook his fist at galleries filled with bureau chiefs."[18]

It was Dawes's swan song. Upon accepting the appointment in June 1921, he had told Harding that he would remain only one year. His reasons were personal but also realistic. He knew that no one who had to break so many eggs to get a budget system started could continue long in the director's position. On the other hand, he was convinced that in one year's time he could create regulations and establish precedents which would permit a successor to continue with confidence. His own choice for his replacement was General Herbert M. Lord, chief finance officer of the United States army. By December he had convinced Harding that Lord was the man, and for the last six months of his tenure Dawes worked with Lord to effect a smooth transition. Lord inherited from Dawes an efficient bureau staffed largely with army men whom Dawes had known in World War I and whose experience in supply, procurement, finance, and budgeting was extensive. More important, Lord also inherited an effective bureau, one which had already achieved success.

With less bombast and flair, Lord continued to popularize economy while receiving the same dogged support from the president which Dawes had enjoyed. With Harding's approval the Budget Bureau under Lord continued the semiannual meetings of the Business Organization of the Government and, although the thumping and shouting of Dawes was missed, the message of economy was gotten across. The last such meeting was held on June 18, 1923, just two days before Harding left for Alaska.

By that time there was no longer any doubt about the success of the drive for government economy. The final expenditures for the year ending June 30, 1922, were $3,795,000,000, which represented a reduction over the previous year of almost $1.4 billion. By the end of the next fiscal year, June 30, 1923, federal expenditures had been cut still further to $3,294,000,000. This last figure represented almost a $2 billion savings over the final Wilson year of 1921.[19]

Three factors are usually mentioned as being responsible for this spectacular result: (1) the passage of the Budget and Accounting Act of 1921, (2) the appointment of Dawes as first director of the budget, and (3) the firm support of Harding. Too little credit is often given to this last factor, which was particularly crucial. Harding clearly understood how important his support was, for he told Dawes upon his retirement in June 1922: "I mean to give [the bureau] such influence as I have in order to retain its influence and high standing."[20] Shortly thereafter Dawes confided to his journal: ". . . my mind keeps reverting to the President. . . . In all my life I have had no more satisfying an experience than I have had under President Harding. This work could not have been done under a weak, vacillating or irresolute man." Earlier in this same journal, he had written that on fiscal matters Harding's mind was "quick as lightning" and "His ideas of business are exact. His knowledge of business principles and what must be done to establish them is as profound as that of any great business man. This being so, his larger knowledge of government, political conditions and the state of public opinion, make him the hope, and the only hope, for a permanent improvement in the government business system. Without him a mere budget law would mean little or nothing."[21]

Harding thus kept faith on his promise to effect economy in government and establish a sound budget system. Somewhat out of character, he remained firm and unyielding even with his friends on the matter of cost reductions. More than once he turned down pleas by dissatisfied cabinet members for deficiency appropriations, among them Harry Daugherty to whom he once wrote, "the Executive will frown on any future requests of similar character."[22] To congressmen he presented stern resistance against altering budget submissions and held the line on pork-barrel requests. As Dawes summed it up in a colorful after-dinner speech in 1922 at the Waldorf: Before Harding "everybody did as they damn pleased"; when it came to spending money, cabinet officers were "Comanches" while the Congress was simply a "nest of cowards"; but Harding "waved the axe and said that anybody who didn't cooperate, his head would come off." The result, said Dawes, was "so much velvet for the taxpayer."[23]

⌈ 3

ANDREW MELLON was one of the three richest men in the nation. Son of a wealthy Pittsburgh banker, Mellon at age twenty-five had assumed charge of his father's business and had proceeded to pyramid the existing family wealth into a stupendous fortune. Acting as backer and financier for aggressive entrepreneurs such as Henry Clay Frick, Mellon had expanded his influence markedly during the age of the robber barons, and by 1920 had developed the Mellon Bank into one of the top financial institutions in the country. By that time his fortune was surpassed only by those of Rockefeller and Ford. But unlike theirs, Mellon's riches did not rest on a single product or activity. From his thronelike swivel chair on the second floor of the imposing Mellon Building, he channeled Mellon money into steel, railroads, public utilities, water power, distilleries, insurance companies, coal, aluminum, and oil. Mellon was the archetype of the modern finance capitalist.

When appointed secretary of the treasury at age sixty-five, Mellon began a new career. His only brush with politics up to that point was his attendance at the Republican National Convention of 1920 as a delegate-at-large. He had been trapped into going and was sufficiently unimpressed with the experience that he left no record of either his views on

179

the convention or his preference among the candidates. Before his Marion visit with Harding in late December 1920, he had shown no inclination whatever for public office nor a desire to shoulder any type of political responsibility.[24]

Mellon's appointment was immediately regarded as bold evidence that Harding meant what he said about more business in government. With a man of Mellon's influence and experience in charge of the nation's finances, the business world breathed easier. His appointment buoyed spirits in a time of economic depression and, as one important banker said, was "a tremendous uplift for the Country's business future."[25] It mattered not that by his own admission Mellon knew little about the Treasury Department or its history; nor did it matter that he lacked sophisticated theories on treasury finance or international loans and trade. What was important was that he brought to the office of secretary of the treasury the most highly prized qualifications the business community recognized: intuitive business skills, practical experience in high finance, and a record of fantastic success.

As Harding realized in appointing him, Mellon's immense wealth was both an asset and a liability. His financial interest in Overholt Distilleries, for example, was often used as a weapon against him. His large contributions to the Republican party were seized upon by some critics as originating from malevolent motives. Some opponents later claimed that he did not pay his proper income taxes. And hardly a financial deal was announced to which the United States was a party but that some critic charged Mellon with making a secret profit for himself or his corporations. No person so wealthy could be thought of as committing a wholly disinterested act. Yet according to Herbert Hoover: "I knew that in the years he was supposed to be robbing the government he was spending several times the amount charged against him in support of public institutions and upon the unemployed in his state."[26] Whatever the truth of the matter, this Croesus, by his very touch, made it appear to friend and foe alike that the Harding administration was influenced not just by business ideas, but by "big-business" ideas.

Unlike Dawes, who was also a wealthy man, Mellon was never really popular with the general public. His personality traits and his class ideas tended to support his critics' charges of malevolency rather than his friends' claims of magnanimity. Said one reporter: "If [Mr. Mellon] were unjustly accused of a crime he would hang himself by appearing in his own defense."[27] Mellon was not a prepossessing figure. He was slight and frail, usually appearing in dark clothes with a black tie, drooping black cotton socks, and a buttoned coat. He smoked small black-paper cigarettes, relighting them when they went out, and wasting not so much as an eighth of an inch. There was nothing careless or frivolous about Mellon. He was always serious. A smile rarely crossed his face. He had an odd little hesitation in his speech, and usually was so quiet as to appear inarticulate. His manner was strangely diffident and he shook hands only with the tips of his fingers. Considering his great wealth, the total effect was somewhat disconcerting. One shocked reporter claimed that he looked like "a tired double-entry bookkeeper who is afraid of losing his job." Another said Mellon reminded him of "a dried up dollar bill that any wind might whisk away."[28]

It was not strange that Mellon was never a close friend of the president. Their interests and personalities simply did not mesh. Mellon was no confidential adviser either. One well-preserved myth was that the financier had some great influence over Harding. Certainly Harding was never Mellon's puppet as some writers later claimed. The personal correspondence between Mellon and Harding was crisp and businesslike with no condescension shown by Mellon and no fawning by Harding. Compared with other cabinet officers, Mellon's contact with the president was minimal.[29]

On almost all important economic questions, Mellon found Harding sound and perhaps he never felt a need to be obtrusive. In cabinet meetings he said almost nothing, and never spoke on nonfinancial matters. He pretended no expertise in any field other than finance. Once, after all the other cabinet members had commented on a particular nonfinancial problem, Harding turned to Mellon and said: "What has the Sphinx here got to say on the subject?" Replied the nonplused Mellon: "Well, Mr. President, I think there is a good deal to be said on both sides."[30] On those rare occasions when the financier chose to speak, especially on taxation or the tariff, everyone, including the president, listened carefully. That the president and the cabinet often deferred to Mellon on these matters was not because of his arguments or his great wealth, but because of a common economic philosophy which they all shared. On these occasions Mellon was their spokesman, not their persuader.

REDUCING taxes was obviously one of the most pressing domestic problems confronting the administration in the spring of 1921. Tax revision had been a popular topic of discussion since the end of World War I. Not only businessmen who clamored for an immediate elimination of excess-profits taxes, but all taxpayers looked forward to a reduction in wartime rates. Wilson's secretary of the treasury, Carter Glass, had urged in late 1919 a reduction both in the excess-profits tax and in the surtax rates on incomes. At that time he had claimed that "the upmost brackets of the surtax have already passed the point of productivity." Secretary Houston, who succeeded Glass in early 1920, also urged an immediate revision of the tax structure, advocating total repeal of the excess-profits tax and a drastic reduction in the surtax rate. As a result, President Wilson in his final message to Congress in December 1920 requested that body to examine the tax laws and revise them where necessary. Rural sentiment, however, in its drive to bring about immediate tariff revision, proved strong enough to prevent a consideration of tax matters during the last months of Wilson's term.

As already noted, the Harding administration not only inherited the tax problem but was also confronted by renewed rural demands for tariff revision. By agreeing that the House should push ahead on the tariff while the Senate Finance Committee began tax hearings, Harding had attempted to placate all sides. However, the president's indication that he would accept an emergency tariff as soon as one could be passed was regarded in business circles as a defeat. They had hoped that Harding would first summon the leaders of Congress and the business world together and formulate a broad tax program for industrial relief. Instead, the president seemed as sensitive to the plight of the farmers as to the demands of the business community.

If business leaders doubted Harding's commitment to immediate tax revision, they could not doubt Mellon's. The millionaire's study of the economic situation had convinced him that an immediate alteration in the tax structure was imperative. Mellon's reasoning was as follows: Through the use of the income tax and the pressures of war financing, the federal government had shifted the tax burden increasingly onto the upper middle class and the wealthy, the two groups which normally supplied

182

most of the risk capital for economic expansion. Corporations, too, because of excess-profits taxes and corporation income taxes, had been asked to carry an unfair proportion of the tax load. Hence, if economic prosperity was to return, quick relief had to be given to these groups.

In his economic philosophy, Mellon displayed the biases of an extremely wealthy man. He expressed little sympathy for the poor and was exceedingly narrow in his social awareness. He certainly did not view taxes as a means of combating society's ills or redistributing wealth, but only as a means of government revenue. The goal of taxation was to "bring in a maximum amount of revenue to the Treasury and at the same time bear not too heavily on the taxpayer or on business enterprises." To Mellon there were three primary factors in a proper tax program: (1) it must produce sufficient revenue for the government to meet expenses and make payments on its debt, (2) it must rest as lightly as possible on those least able to pay, but (3) it must not provide obstacles which would retard the steady development of business and industry. Mellon believed that excessively high taxation, even if levied on an equitable basis, injured the economy because such taxes were ultimately borne by the consumer, not just those on whom the high taxes fell. Moreover, he was convinced that high taxes meant neither more revenue nor the greater sharing of the wealthy in the total tax burden. He believed such persons simply diverted their wealth into nontaxable areas, such as tax-exempt securities, with a resultant loss of revenue to the government. By decreasing tax rates at the upper levels, according to Mellon, the government possessed a better chance not only to collect more taxes, but also to spur the expansion of business and industry.

As far as debt reduction was concerned, Mellon used Alexander Hamilton as his guide. It was simply "common sense" to pay the debt; the liquidation of the debt would obviate the necessity of supporting bondholders through the payment of interest collected as taxes from the nation at large. Furthermore, payments on the debt principal would find their way back into the economy through capital investments, whereas if no payments were made this amount would probably be dissipated by the government "in useless expenditures." According to Mellon, the three keys to restoring prosperity and business health were decreasing taxes, reducing the national debt, and maintaining rigid economy in government operation.[31]

183

For the first two Mellon himself would fight; to achieve the last he would back Dawes to the hilt.

While the Senate Finance Committee was conducting its tax hearings in April and May, the House finally agreed on an emergency tariff which was rapidly endorsed by the Senate and sent to the president. When Harding affixed his signature to this measure on May 27, one of the major obstacles to early House consideration of tax revision appeared removed. But discussions on the Budget and Accounting Act and disagreements on a soldier's bonus bill intervened, and it was not until July that the House Ways and Means Committee finally began its own hearings on a new tax structure.

At that time the House committee asked Mellon for his recommendations on revisions in the existing revenue law. That law, the Revenue Act of 1918, as amended in 1919, provided for a 4 percent tax on the first $4000 of income and 8 percent on the remainder. Surtax rates ran from 1 percent on incomes in excess of $5000 to a maximum of 65 percent on incomes over $1 million. The tax rate for corporations was 10 percent and an excess-profits tax was also charged. Appearing before the committee in person on August 4, Mellon recommended, among other things, that the excess-profits tax be repealed as of January 1, 1921, that the maximum surtax rate be reduced from 65 percent to 32 percent as of January 1, 1921, and that the general income tax rates of 4 and 8 percent remain the same.[32]

The House Ways and Means Committee, composed of seventeen Republicans and eight Democrats, was headed by Joseph Fordney of Michigan, a wealthy, relatively uneducated, conservative, self-made man. He was strongly in favor of Mellon's tax position and marshaled his forces against determined opposition from southern and western committee members such as James A. Frear of Wisconsin, Claude Kitchin of North Carolina, and John N. Garner of Texas. Vigorous though they were, these dissidents could not prevent the majority of the committee from agreeing with Fordney that the excess-profits tax should be repealed as of January 1, 1921, and a new surtax rate be set at 32 percent as Mellon had recommended. The southern-western coalition did force the committee to raise the corporation tax to 12½ percent in order to offset the repeal of the excess-profits tax and to give some relief to low-income groups by raising the 1918 tax exemptions of $1000 and $2000 to $1500 and $2500. The

184

allowance for dependents was increased from $200 to $400 and the exemption for the head of a family was raised to $500.[33]

This Ways and Means bill raised an immediate furor. Opponents, in general, condemned it as a rich man's measure. Soldiers, who were clamoring for a bonus and had been fed on a diet of war-profit stories, saw the proposal as a gift to those who had already plundered the country. The farm element, always sensitive about "eastern business," claimed that the bill would further enhance corporation control over the economy. Labor, especially the unemployed, certainly had no stomach for easing the tax burdens of the wealthy. Meanwhile, insurgent Republicans, like Fiorello LaGuardia, joined Democrats in making dire prophecies about the future if the bill were passed. Said the Little Flower in a typically ungrammatical but pointed blast: "To he that hath, to him shall be given; and he that hath not, from him shall be taken even that which he hath."[34]

Obviously the major defect in the measure was the absence of relief for those in the lower income groups. Still, as a revenue *and* a recovery measure, the bill had much to commend it. Statistics showed, although critics were not willing to believe them, that the rich were currently diverting income into tax-free securities and the number of individuals paying the highest surtax rates was declining. Moreover, revenue collections had been decreasing for some time despite the continuance of high rates. In addition, despite the furor in Congress about the "poor" taxpayer, fewer than 28 percent of the eligible voters of the nation, and fewer than 18 percent of those gainfully employed, were required to file a return in the year 1920. Not all of these paid a tax. Corporations, meanwhile, were supplying over one-third of all the direct taxes collected by the federal government. As for the farmer, he was contributing a declining proportion of taxes even taking his falling income into account. While nonfarm elements in the population increased their contributions to taxes of all types by $4,055,000,000 between 1913 and 1920, the farmers' tax burden rose only $812,000,000. The numerical increase in the nonfarm population during this time was only threefold, but the taxes it paid increased fivefold.[35]

President Harding did not understand all the intricacies of the tax problem. He was frankly confused by the conflicting opinions. He once confided to Judson Welliver: "I can't make a damn thing out of this tax problem. I listen to one side and they seem right, and then—God!—I talk to the other side, and they seem just as right."[36] Under such circumstances, Harding's natural inclination was to seek a compromise and adjust differences. But Mellon was so confident in his views, and Harding possessed such faith in Mellon's financial wisdom, that in this case he backed the secretary without always knowing why. To the House he indicated that he supported the repeal of the excess-profits tax and the reduction in the surtax rate proposed by Mellon. As for the repeal date of January 1, 1921, he indicated that he was willing to accept January 1, 1922, as a compromise if that would facilitate the bill's passage. But beyond that he refused to go. On this basis then, administration supporters in the House closed ranks, protected the bill from emasculation, and, under a special parliamentary maneuver, rushed the final product through in four days. The vote on August 20 was 274–125. Only three Democrats voted for the measure and nine Republicans voted against. All nine Republicans were from Michigan or farther west.

In the Senate the story was different. Here attitudes regarding a change in the tax structure were markedly affected by demands for farm relief and a soldier's bonus. Since the passage of the emergency tariff in May, a group of senators from the agricultural states had agitated for *immediate* consideration of other farm-relief measures and had threatened reprisals on plans for tax revision if their desires were not met. Simultaneously there was considerable sentiment in the Senate to act on a soldier's bonus of some kind. Although the Republican party had remained silent on the bonus issue in its 1920 platform, the idea possessed great popular appeal and by mid-1921 it was a dense Republican politician who did not perceive the issue's value as a vote-getter.

To the administration's dismay, the Senate proved utterly incapable of resolving its difficulties and for over a month wallowed in controversy. Finally, in early July, by a vote of 46–4 the Senate decided to take up a soldier's bonus bill simply because it was the only item on which bipartisan agreement could be achieved.[37] Of course, this was bad news for all advocates of tax and debt reduction. Obviously the passage of a multibillion-dollar bonus would render ineffective Dawes's herculean efforts to cut government expenditures as well as dash Mellon's hopes to reduce taxes and lower the national debt.

Because of the danger, the administration decided to intervene. On July 6 Secretary Mellon directed a letter to the Senate urging it not to

186

take action on the bonus bill, at least until the matter of tax revision was settled. The next day, while lunching with old senatorial friends at the Capitol, President Harding personally urged them to defer consideration of the bonus measure. He warned that its passage would ruin economy programs and indicated that he would shortly send a message to the Senate formally requesting a delay. On July 12, to the surprise of many, Harding delivered it in person. He first chided the Senate for being slow on tax revision. Then he indicated that he wanted the passage of a new tax law immediately, after which the Senate could take up other matters. As for the bonus bill, Harding expressed great sympathy with the principle and devoutly wished such a measure could be passed. But he admitted to a fear of "disaster to the Nation's finances" if it was enacted without proper funding. He bluntly concluded that under current circumstances "no thoughtful person, possessed with all the facts," could recommend passage of the bonus.[38]

His warning was clear, forceful, and to the point. Delivered the day after the press had announced his calling of the Washington Conference, it came when Harding's stock was high and the public supported him. They liked this sudden demonstration of executive authority and this "no nonsense" approach to the Senate. Some senators, such as Borah and LaFollette, were incensed that the president should have personally intervened in Senate affairs, but discovered that they had to hold their tongues because of the popular acclaim. The press spoke of Harding's "outstanding courage" and his "intelligent patriotism." Some thought his action was reminiscent of Cleveland. The *New York Times* said he showed himself to be "President of the whole people, not an opportunist politician." Concluded the *Times*: "The people are with him. There is nothing for the Senate to do but to recommit the Bonus bill."[39]

It was later claimed that the real power behind Harding's action was Mellon who put the words in the president's mouth and sent him to the Senate to say them. This was untrue. It was Harding's idea to deliver the address and he relied on Mellon only for technical information. The views expressed were his own and were no different from those which he had held long before Mellon arrived on the scene. As early as September 1920, Harding had told the *Stars and Stripes* (a weekly publication of interest to former servicemen) that if he became president he would do all he could for the wounded and disabled veteran, but the financial stability of the country took precedence over any general postwar compensation for those who had served in the armed forces. Any monetary outlay for that purpose, he said, would have to be adequately funded; otherwise it could not be justified.[40]

Despite a minority chorus of complaints from veterans' organizations and bonus lobbyists, the Senate did precisely as the *New York Times* prophesied. On a motion by Senator Penrose on July 15, the bonus bill was sent back to committee. However, those who had any thoughts that the soldier's bonus was dead were indulging in wishful thinking. With grim determination bonus advocates, especially the American Legion, prepared for a long struggle. In similar warnings to Harding and Mellon, that organization stated that the bonus question "cannot be downed." It was prophetic. Before the end of the year, the bonus issue was very much alive.

This episode did not put the Senate, especially pro-bonus and farm-bloc senators, in a happy frame of mind for considering the House tax bill. That measure had first gone to the Senate Finance Committee, which was composed of nine Republicans and six Democrats, and headed by Boies Penrose. At the time Penrose was a dying man; he once had weighed as much as Taft but now had shriveled from the ravages of cancer until even his friends hardly knew him. Penrose undertook this tax struggle as his last great legislative battle; he would be in his grave before the end of December.

Throughout, Penrose acted as the administration's spokesman. He provided Mellon with information about the Finance Committee's deliberations, and through him Mellon secured an effective airing of his own tax views. Mellon had not been pleased by Harding's willingness to accept from the House a repeal date of January 1, 1922, for the excess-profits tax and wanted it returned to January 1, 1921. He also desired insertion of a provision which would permit a further reduction in the surtax rates from 32 percent on January 1, 1921, to 25 percent on January 1, 1922. After vigorous debate during which LaFollette charged that Mellon "ought to be retired from his place" for his economic views, the committee finally decided to reduce the surtax rate below the House figures on individual incomes between $20,000 and $30,000, but keep the rates on incomes above $30,000 at the original House levels. The committee also agreed to retain the House date of January 1, 1922, for the repeal of the excess-profits tax.[41]

When introduced on the Senate floor, the bill faced sullen opposition. Most of it came from the agricultural states of the Midwest, but the spearhead of the attack was supplied by the Democratic party. Furnifold M. Simmons of North Carolina and David I. Walsh of Massachusetts, both minority members of the Finance Committee, opened the assault, but Republican farm-bloc members rushed forward to help. Such Republican defections made the situation dangerous. Of the sixty Republican senators, thirty-three came from states bordering on or lying west of the Mississippi. Lodge cautioned Harding that this group could not be pushed too hard, especially on surtax rates, and by the middle of October, having already compromised with the House on the date of repeal for the excess-profits tax, Harding began to make conciliatory noises about accepting higher surtax rates.

As finally passed on November 8 after fifteen hours of continuous debate, the Senate tax measure differed little from that of the House except in the matter of surtaxes. After a move by the Democrats to restore the old 65 percent rate had been defeated, the Senate, by a vote of 38–24, accepted a 50 percent surtax instead of the House-passed 32 percent. Only three Republicans voted against the bill—LaFollette, Moses, and Norris—but a considerable number did not cast a ballot. For that reason, the Republican "fallout" in the Senate was worse than it had been in the House.[42]

The bill now went to a conference committee which generally adopted the Senate changes. However, after nine days' work, the matter of the surtax rate had not been solved. The conferees appealed to the White House, and in a letter to Chairman Fordney of the House Ways and Means Committee Harding indicated presidential approval for a compromise rate of 40 percent. But when the conference bill was reported to the two houses on November 17 with the 40 percent rate included, the House voted 201–173 to accept the higher Senate rate of 50 percent rather than the presidential compromise rate. No fewer than ninety-four Republicans broke from the party leadership to reject Harding's proposal.[43]

The House vote was the crucial one. In the Senate there was quick acceptance of the conference measure as amended by the rebellious House.

One Democrat (Edwin S. Broussard of Louisiana) joined thirty-eight Republicans to outvote the twenty-nine senators who were against the bill. Six Republicans—Borah, LaFollette, Norris, Norbeck, Moses, and Ladd —joined the Democratic opposition. All but Moses (New Hampshire) were from western or farming states.[44]

The Revenue Act of 1921 was not at all what Mellon had wanted, but Harding regarded it as acceptable and as fulfilling his campaign promise of lower taxes. He signed it on the same day it was passed, November 23. That date also marked the adjournment of the special session which he had called into being some eight months before.

In the area of domestic affairs, this special session had proved to be a bitter disappointment. Torn by internal dissension and suffering from a lack of leadership, the Congress, especially the Senate, had not risen to the challenges presented by Harding's special message of April 12, 1921. An emergency tariff to protect farm products and several farm-relief measures had been enacted; the Budget and Accounting Act had been passed; and finally, on the last day, tax revision had been accomplished. But the manner in which this had been achieved did not indicate a high degree of congressional efficiency. Moreover, congressional action on the tax bill revealed a creeping disintegration of Republican unity and signaled further trouble for the administration in the upcoming regular session.

As for the Revenue Act, it was a more equitable tax than has sometimes been portrayed. It was certainly fairer than the proposal Mellon originally advanced. In essence a compromise measure, its liberalization in exemptions was of benefit to lower income taxpayers. The increase in the corporation tax from 10 to 12½ percent partially compensated for the loss in revenue resulting from the repeal of the excess-profits tax. For the extremely wealthy the reduction in the maximum surtax rate from 65 percent to 50 percent somewhat eased their tax burden. But everything considered, the 1921 act was as much a disappointment to those who wanted a thorough revision as to those who wanted no change at all. Perhaps the greatest factor in the measure's favor was that no one really liked it. Business considered it a sellout because the excess-profits tax was not repealed immediately. Men of wealth thought it a mistake to maintain a surtax rate as high as 50 percent. Those in lower income brackets took their increased exemptions willingly, but protested the lowering of the surtaxes on large incomes.[45]

190

In the first year, tax savings under the law amounted to $800 million.[46] This, after all, was the primary advantage passed along to those who filed income tax returns for 1921. Even though the measure marked no radical departure from the past and appreciably altered the status of neither the wealthy nor the poor, it did indeed fulfill Harding's earlier promise to effect tax reductions. Coupled with the current retrenchment in government expenditures, these tax savings represented a significant accomplishment and one in which the president took pride. Unquestionably these reductions aided business and encouraged economic recovery.

[5

HOOVER was a household word even before the 1920 election. Son of Iowa Quaker parents, both of whom died before he was ten, Hoover had been raised by an uncle and other relatives in the West. "On a shoestring of money and a thimbleful of preparatory education," he had entered the newly created Leland Stanford Junior University as a member of the Pioneer Class. After one year in mechanical engineering, he switched to geology and, following graduation in 1895, worked first with the U.S. Geological Survey, then as a laborer in Nevada mines, and finally as a geologist for various mining firms, traveling throughout the American West, Australia, and China. Caught in Tientsin by the Boxer Rebellion in June 1900, Hoover helped to provision the beleaguered foreign colony there and received his introduction to the problems of wartime relief.

From 1900 to 1915 Hoover made his fortune, estimated in the latter year at $4 million, by working primarily as an independent mining engineer. Thereafter he devoted his life to public service. When World War I began, he was in London, and turned his attention to the alleviation of wartime distress, ultimately assuming charge of all Belgian relief. Called home in May 1917, by President Wilson, he became head of the United States Food Administration and its price-fixing and rationing operations. "To Hooverize" meant to wartime Americans "to economize" and Hoover soon emerged as a kind of popular hero. However, by shouldering the responsibility for holding down war profits for farmers, he also became the recipient of much rural criticism. *Wallace's Farmer* often charged him with having a "mental bias" against farmers and regarded him as "a typical autocrat of big business."[47] At the close of the war, Hoover returned to Europe as head of the American Relief Administration to combat starvation and chaos on the European continent in the post-armistice period.

Hoover's name was mentioned in connection with the 1920 presidential nomination of both major parties, but he was identified more as a Republican than a Democrat, and a boomlet ultimately developed for him within the GOP. He made a surprising showing against Senator Hiram Johnson in the California primaries, even though that irreconcilable painted him as a rampant internationalist. After the Chicago convention, where he received a smattering of votes, Hoover was frequently mentioned as a cabinet possibility. As already noted, Harding's determination to appoint him to the cabinet was firm enough to transcend strong Old Guard opposition, and he even gave Hoover the choice of several cabinet slots. The fact Hoover selected Commerce was significant in revealing his basic interests.

Ironically, liberals and progressives looked to Hoover to offset the economic conservatism of Mellon in the Harding cabinet. Hoover's humanitarianism in the relief field temporarily blinded them to the realities of Hoover as an engineer and businessman. A foremost champion of "normalcy," Hoover no less than Mellon believed that a revival of business prosperity was of primary importance. If Hoover was somewhat less "tax conscious" than Mellon and less "budget conscious" than Dawes, he was as probusiness as either. To Hoover, the secret of returning prosperity was the encouragement of business expansion and greater business efficiency. He was convinced that further intensification of the business life of the country would bring advantages to all classes of citizens and eventually enhance individual freedom as well as banish economic distress.

Although Hoover exerted a formative influence on both foreign and domestic economic policies, he was neither a skilled politician nor a trained economist, but simply a shrewd mining engineer in politics. He attacked symptoms, not basic causes; he was interested in efficiency, not remedies. Even his approach to humanitarian problems betrayed the workings of an engineering mind. When asked once why he was sending corn to starving Russians instead of wheat, he replied: "Because for one dollar I can buy [more] calories."[48] Very sensitive to criticism, Hoover never fully adjusted to the world of politics even though he spent his later life immersed in it. He lacked political acumen and, unlike Harding, he had no political intuition. As one observer commented: "Give him a mining problem, give him a financial problem, give him a supply problem and he is brilliant. In politics, he is not; he is baffled."[49] As a result Hoover was usually stiff in political situations, and also defensive. He lost his temper too easily, was too prone to argue, and assumed too quickly that he was right. His tendency was to *tell* people what to do, a trait that proved abrasive.

Paradoxically, Hoover was the best known and the least known of the cabinet officers. Realizing the value of publicity, Hoover was a constant advertiser of himself, always seeking to achieve greater popular recognition. But it was his name and not his person that received the attention. Hoover's methods, Hoover's proposals, and Hoover's actions garnered the publicity, but not Hoover himself. He did not say bright and clever things; he did not have endearing personal qualities. Indeed, the public knew little about him as a man. But, then, it was difficult to popularize the essence of a personality which was basically austere. Uncharitably, a reporter once asked: Who can love an efficiency engineer? Hoover appealed to the American sense of logic and organization, but not to the American heart.

Whatever his personal characteristics, Hoover was distinctly one of the creative forces in the Harding cabinet. Unlike Mellon, who minded his own business, Hoover was secretary of commerce and "assistant secretary of everything else." He acted as the all-around expert, a fact constantly mentioned in the press. On foreign finance it was Mellon "and Hoover." On labor problems it was Davis "and Hoover." On agriculture it was Wallace "and Hoover." Yet Hoover's contacts with the members of the cabinet were neither close nor especially friendly. Too quick to insinuate himself into their respective areas, Hoover drew the suspicion of other cabinet officers even though they sometimes sought his advice. In their reaction to Hoover, resentment and admiration went hand in hand. Mellon found him to be "too much an engineer" and too officious. One slim folder in the Hoover Papers contains all the Mellon-Hoover correspondence for the years 1921–23.[50] Secretary Wallace had personal respect for Hoover, but he found no reason to change his earlier criticism of him in *Wallace's Farmer* and serious altercations quickly developed between them. Secretary Davis also admired Hoover and from time to time relied on him for help in adjudicating labor disputes. But Davis was often piqued by the manner in which Hoover publicized his own efforts while belittling Davis's role.

Hoover was probably closer to Hughes than to any other member of the cabinet, but it would be too strong to call them friends. It was always "Mr. Hoover" and "Mr. Hughes." Perhaps their personalities would permit no more intimate contact. Still, Hughes was generally open to Hoover's advice and seemed more pleased by compliments from Hoover than from anyone else in the administration except Harding. Hoover, meanwhile, believed Hughes to be the most able man in the cabinet, next to himself. The two men possessed a kind of mutual respect and understanding which, despite the formalities, bound them together.[51]

Strangely enough, the most outspoken supporter of Hoover in the cabinet was Albert Fall. At the same time Hoover was curiously drawn to the New Mexican because of the latter's progressive past and his deep interest in broadening American trade overseas. Fall's own prospecting and mining background also gave them a common point of reference. The flamboyant secretary of the interior intrigued the stolid engineer and when Fall resigned from the cabinet in 1923 Hoover was the first to praise his work.[52]

President Harding remained a consistent Hoover champion. While some cabinet members groused about Hoover's nosiness, Harding was completely captivated by him. Hoover's brand of "rugged individualism" appealed to the president, and Hoover's belief that each individual should "be given the chance and stimulation for development of the best with which he has been endowed in heart and mind" supplemented Harding's own concept of "normalcy." Moreover, Hoover's view of government as an umpire rather than a policeman in the economic sphere was fully compatible with Harding's own thinking. Harding especially agreed with Hoover's belief that the federal government should promote government-business cooperation and maintain an economic atmosphere in which industry could flourish and expand.

Harding's *official* contact with Hoover was probably greater than with any other member of the cabinet except Hughes. Harding sought out Hoover for advice on a whole range of problems and quickly discovered that, unlike Hughes and Mellon, Hoover was quite willing to give it. "I will await your frank advice on the subject" was a common sentence ending many a Harding-to-Hoover letter.[53] Hoover, in turn, like the dignified Hughes and the silent Mellon, depended on Harding to supply the human warmth and the political touch which he himself lacked.

Most important to Hoover, of course, was Harding's steadfast support. Said Hoover much later, "Harding encouraged me in everything I wanted to do. I never knew him to give a promise that he did not keep."[54] Indeed, to the time of his death, Harding retained the highest regard for his secretary of commerce and often deferred to his judgment. As he once remarked to E. Mont Reily: "Reily, do you know, taking Herbert Hoover up one side and down the other, and taking into consideration the knowledge he has of things generally, I believe he's the smartest 'gink' I know."[55]

[6

WHEN Herbert Hoover assumed the post of secretary of commerce it was next to the bottom in cabinet prestige and of little real significance. Oscar S. Straus, Hoover's predecessor, told him that he would need to work only two hours a day "putting the fish to bed at night and turning on the lights around the coast."[56] But Hoover had different ideas. Before accepting the position, Hoover made it clear to Harding that he intended to reorganize Commerce and transform it into an agency of foremost importance. No sooner was his oath of office administered than he issued a stream of pro-Commerce propaganda and by the end of fifteen days began to implement some of his reorganization ideas. He rapidly removed political hacks and raided the business world for top administrative personnel. Within the first month he enticed twenty-five distinguished business, labor, and agricultural leaders to serve as an advisory committee on the policies and programs of the Commerce Department.[57] Such whirlwind action proved to be typical.

In the ensuing years as secretary, Hoover continually broadened the Commerce Department's activities. Under his direction the number of departmental employees grew from 13,005 to 15,850 and appropriations from $24.5 million to $37.6 million. As budget director Dawes quickly discovered, Hoover sought to expand his department at every opportunity. For example, while he was secretary he raised the expenditures of the Bureau of Foreign and Domestic Commerce from $860,000 to $5 million and quintupled its personnel. Moreover, he was determinedly acquisitive. In 1921 he took over the Bureau of Custom Statistics from Treasury and

195

somewhat later acquired the Bureau of Mines and the Patent Office from Interior. When aviation and radio required some government supervision, Hoover created divisions in Commerce for them. Obviously Hoover was, and never ceased to be, an empire builder. But he justified himself on the grounds that such expansion was essential to keep pace with the needs of American business and industry. Naturally this delighted the business community and understandably the United States Chamber of Commerce hailed him as a genius.[58]

Such spectacular progress did not occur without friction. Farming interests, especially, were not pleased by Hoover's success and there were constant difficulties between the Agriculture and Commerce departments. The most bitter dispute centered around the collection and analysis of accurate marketing and production data. Hoover contended that all such information should be gathered by Commerce through its Bureau of the Census instead of by Agriculture's Bureau of Markets. Not content to offend Agriculture alone, Hoover claimed that the data-gathering functions of the Labor Department's Bureau of Labor Statistics ought to be under Commerce also. But neither Wallace nor Davis intended to surrender these functions to Hoover and they joined forces to resist him successfully.[59]

Despite such rebuffs, Hoover and Commerce blithely went their own way. By the summer of 1922, Commerce was collecting and distributing its own marketing and production data. Disclaiming any intention of usurping the functions of either the Bureau of Markets or the Bureau of Labor Statistics, Hoover created a statistical program in Commerce which was more meaningful and adaptable to the needs of the business community. Commerce data regularly made their way into 160 dailies each Saturday morning, reaching five million readers. Specific trade information was issued monthly; it covered foreign and domestic businesses and involved approximately 19,000 firms. Commerce figures were also made available to trade associations and to American exporters and importers. Such Commerce Department information was undeniably beneficial to the American businessman and by 1923 was widely regarded as an important factor in increasing his profits and reviving business prosperity.

The most significant work of the Commerce Department under Hoover, however, was concentrated in the Bureau of Foreign and Domestic Commerce. Before 1921 this agency had been generally ineffective

196

and largely worthless. Hoover now made it indispensable. He cleaned out most of President Wilson's appointees and replaced them with men who had experience in foreign languages, economics, political science, law, or geography. As head of the bureau, Hoover appointed Dr. Julius Klein, professor of Latin-American history and economics at Harvard, and a former commercial attaché at Buenos Aires. A masterful administrator, Klein was in absolute agreement with Hoover's business ideas and ultimately became his most trusted adviser. Together they made a perfect team.[60]

Their primary job was to rejuvenate American foreign trade. By reorganizing the Bureau of Foreign and Domestic Commerce along commodity lines and by creating trade offices in major American cities as well as abroad, Hoover and Klein geared the Department of Commerce for more intensive trade activity and publicized their intent to the nation as a whole. Farmers, however, remained suspicious of Hoover and resisted his attempts to make them "overseas conscious." They did not accept his contention that returning farm prosperity rested to a considerable extent on the ability of the farmer to sell his products abroad. Business, on the other hand, reacted joyously to Hoover's activities. Hoover relied on business support to help him in his empire building and in his altercations with other departments over jurisdictional matters. The reaction of business was that whatever other departments were doing for the businessman, Hoover could do better. Even the State Department was not immune from Hoover's meddling. Hoover demanded and, backed by business sentiment, secured Hughes's agreement that the Commerce Department would be consulted on such matters as foreign loans, war debts, and trade treaties. Moreover, Hoover resisted any attempts by Hughes to lessen the importance of commercial attachés overseas or to place them under the sole control of the State Department. Under Hoover, not only were their sacrosanct positions in American embassies and consulates maintained but their functions were constantly expanded.[61]

Hoover, with Harding's support, pushed business interests on other fronts. He was a strong advocate of better housing and a booster of expansion in the home-building industry. In 1922, he created a Division of Housing within the department whose function was to study major housing problems, develop interest in home ownership by the individual, encourage the development of honest credit facilities, standardize building

197

material, and secure the removal of cumbersome municipal and state building regulations. Also Hoover vigorously supported trade associations. He
knew that such organizations could work against the public interest and
he opposed the open price malpractices to which trade associations were
often an invitation. But, despite this danger, he believed that trade associations themselves were beneficial. He was primarily attracted to them because of their ability to undertake industrial research, improve the gathering of statistical information, and effect standardization and efficiency
within the industrial and commercial field. As a result, Hoover considered
any overzealous enforcement of the antitrust laws against such associations
as a "perversion of justice." [62]

Greater industrial standardization and efficiency especially appealed
to Hoover and he championed all moves in that direction. The Commerce
Department sponsored some 900 group conferences between 1921 and
1924 and had 229 committees at work on various phases of efficiency
and standardization. Simultaneously, Hoover promoted industrial and scientific economic research as a weapon against waste and inefficiency. The
National Bureau of Standards, although originally established to maintain
standards of measurement, was transformed under Hoover into an agency
to handle much scientific and industrial research. Greatly interested in
"simplified practice," Hoover hoped such activity would point the way
to an elimination of unnecessary varieties of industrial products and specifications. [63]

Of course, no one of these many probusiness activities of Hoover was
as significant as the impression that his combined efforts, based on his
optimistic and buoyant philosophy, conveyed to the business mind. While
Mellon imparted to the business community the conviction that its tax and
fiscal ideas were being heard at the highest level of government and Dawes
successfully translated into action the desire of business for government
economy, Hoover became the symbol of its aspirations for expansion and
for greater government-business cooperation. His avid pursuit of Jeffer-
sonian goals by aggressive business means became a hallmark of the
twenties and Hoover, through his position as secretary of commerce, remained its chief spokesman. As missionaries for the Harding administration's crusade to promote business confidence and to restore prosperity,
Hoover and his Commerce Department were unexcelled.

VII

Help for the Farmer

[1

HENRY WALLACE did not really want the job of secretary of agriculture. He was content to have helped Harding during the campaign of 1920 and wished to return to Des Moines and his editorship of *Wallace's Farmer*. He was satisfied that the Ohioan's election had been in the best interests of the American farmer and was prepared to support the new administration through his pen rather than direct personal involvement. Harding, however, had no intention of losing the benefit of Wallace's advice and his appointment to the Agriculture post was designed to make permanent their campaign relationship.

Wallace's selection was extremely popular with the nation's agrarian community. "A leader of farmers," he stood high in the agricultural world as a man who fully understood and identified with farm problems. Just as Mellon was considered by business to be one of their own kind, so Wallace was viewed by agriculturalists. Through Wallace, they could rightfully anticipate that agricultural sentiment would have a strong voice in the Harding government. In view of Wallace's progressive past and his generally combative personality, they had no reason to fear that agriculture would become merely an adjunct to business or be overrun by business influence.

From the moment he assumed his position, Wallace was one of the most conscientious cabinet officers. At every opportunity he put forward the views of farmers and relentlessly pushed his arguments on their behalf. No national question was ever discussed that Wallace did not view it in an agricultural context or relate it to the condition of the farmer. No piece of legislation was framed that he did not analyze it for its rural effects. The man of the soil was Wallace's sole concern while he was secretary of agriculture and he served his cause proudly.[1]

Sensitive concerning his prerogatives and volatile in temper, Wallace made a formidable adversary. Few in the Harding cabinet chose to cross him in matters on which he held vigorous views, and those who did usually had scars to show for it. Wallace was the one man in the cabinet who could fight Hoover to a draw and the only one of whom Hoover was afraid. As Pinchot once said "[Wallace was] a natural born game-cock . . . redheaded on his head and in his soul."[2]

When not aroused, Wallace—commonly called "Harry" by his friends —possessed a disarming earthy charm which was revealed by a warm smile and hearty laugh. He could make friends as quickly as he made enemies. He wore a pince-nez on a firm round face which was highly mobile and easily betrayed his emotions. His favorite pastimes were bowling, poker playing, and golf. The latter he played with some skill, shooting in the low to middle eighties. Harding, who was a much poorer golfer, liked to play with Wallace because he represented a challenge, even at a stroke-a-hole handicap. Like Harding, Wallace chewed tobacco, usually in small, almost imperceptible quids. He never spat and never moved his jaws, swallowing the juice.[3]

Wallace's relations with other members of the cabinet were never close. Surprisingly, he was most compatible with Hughes with whom he frequently played golf. His intensely partisan approach to agriculture caused most cabinet members to downgrade the value of his advice. His frequent arguments with Fall over conservation were essentially parochial and his range of vision, outside of agriculture, was narrow. In affairs impinging on the Department of Agriculture, cabinet members found him overbearing. Only when he tangled with Hoover did they show him much sympathy. In these periodic altercations, the majority preferred Wallace to win even though they thought Hoover had the better argument.

Wallace and Hoover were indeed frequent and bitter antagonists. Their conflicts over such matters as the Agriculture Department's Bureau of Markets were sharp and prolonged. While superficially involving jurisdictional questions, these squabbles betrayed a fundamental difference between the two men. Although both viewed agriculture as a business and both desired to apply scientific standards to the American farm, Hoover saw agriculture as simply *another* business, while Wallace regarded it as the *predominant* national economic enterprise. Wallace often said, "If we are to have a prosperous nation we must have a profitable and satisfying agriculture."[4] Wallace, like the constituency he represented, frequently became emotional on this point.

Wallace liked President Harding and Harding liked him. The president called him "Hank" when not in company and enjoyed his amazing repertory of Scotch jokes. An amiable companion at both golf and poker, Wallace appealed to Harding for exactly the opposite reasons which attracted the president to Hoover. Where Harding admired Hoover's precision and logic, he was drawn to Wallace's frankness and partisanship. More important, Harding's and Wallace's views regarding agriculture closely coincided. The president supported the 1920 farm plank which Wallace had written and which advocated more farm exports, scientific cost studies, national laws protecting farm cooperatives, improvement in the federal farm loan system, and increased farm representation on federal boards and commissions. Harding also agreed with Wallace's desire to make the farmer more efficient in the business operation of his farm and supported the Agriculture Department's various plans toward that end. Moreover, Harding, along with Wallace, advocated greater tariff protection for agricultural commodities.[5]

Harding differed from his secretary of agriculture in his reluctance to consider farmers as a special group to be subsidized, if necessary, by the United States treasury. Harding was willing to support any and all self-help measures but he balked at adopting any radical plans. As the agricultural depression continued, however, Harding dimly perceived that there was something desperately wrong with the whole agricultural system. He was especially puzzled by the fact that producing goods did not always result in making money. Toward the end, as Wallace moved in the direction of more direct government involvement, Harding slowly inched along behind him. One scholar of the period later wrote, "Wallace's influence [on Harding] grew with time and with the failure of the farm crisis to produce its own solution."[6]

Harding's desire for a solution to the farm problem was, of course, partially political—farmers possessed votes. But it was also personal. While he had not come from a farm family, most of his relatives were farmers and he had lived much of his own life in a rural atmosphere. Even as the prosperous owner of the *Marion Star*, he had served a clientele which was essentially agrarian in its orientation. Main Street, Marion, was much closer to the farm than to Wall Street, and Harding was spiritually more attached to the man of the soil than to the financier. If his small-town business ideas were generally acceptable to the latter, his heart remained with the former. Both as senator and as president, when he undertook barnstorming trips he usually went into the agrarian Midwest. He felt at home there. Indeed, he knew the farm states of the Midwest more intimately than almost any other modern president.

For these reasons, Gutzon Borglum, the sculptor of Mount Rushmore and an admirer of Teddy Roosevelt, early predicted that Harding, supported by such capable advisers as Wallace, would be "the best friend of the farmers who has ever risen to be head of the Federal Government of America."[7] While this proved to be an exaggeration, Harding's interest in their problems was sincere. Years later, long after the turmoil and name calling of the Harding era had died away, Senator Arthur Capper, himself a son of the Middle Border and a leader in the farm bloc, wrote: "President Harding had a very sympathetic and understanding attitude toward the American farmers. The various farm measures advocated by the Farm Bloc during his Administration received favorable consideration at his hands."[8]

[2

A FARM bloc of one sort or another had always existed. Local and geographic representation in the American governmental system had traditionally permitted rural elements to join forces on various issues and make their wishes known. But because American economic life did not become polarized between industrial and agrarian interests until the late nineteenth century, the existence of a business-rural split before that time was not always obvious. After the Industrial Revolution, however, an agrarian position emerged clearer and more unified.

Post-World War I America, with its devastating agricultural depression, was a time of fruition for this latter development. A new phase in agrarian politics was inaugurated as farmers sought through their congressmen and through national pressure groups to protect and expand their interests. Although somewhat reminiscent of farmer activity in the late nineteenth century, this modern development was less emotional and far more realistic. Despite the agitation of some radical agrarians, no effort was made to build a new party; instead, the goal was to elect to public office sympathetic members of both parties who would constitute a loose farm bloc pledged to advance agricultural causes.

The Harding administration fell an early victim to this movement and found its plans for business recovery endangered by it. Technically the bloc came into being on May 9, 1921, when Gray Silver, Washington lobbyist of the American Farm Bureau Federation, and Senator William Kenyon of Iowa, nominal leader of the Senate farm element, sponsored a meeting of midwestern and southern senators in Silver's office to discuss plans to meet the postwar needs of agriculture. Besides Silver and Kenyon, those attending were George W. Norris (Nebraska), John B. Kendrick (Wyoming), Frank R. Gooding (Idaho), Arthur Capper (Kansas), Ellison D. Smith (South Carolina), Duncan U. Fletcher (Florida), Robert M. LaFollette (Wisconsin), Morris Sheppard (Texas), Edwin F. Ladd (North Dakota), Joseph E. Ransdell (Louisiana), and J. Thomas Heflin (Alabama). These senators agreed that the Harding administration should be held to its agrarian campaign promises and that there should be a readjustment of freight rates, better commodity financing, an extension of farm credits, broader laws governing cooperatives, stricter regulations on meat packers, a higher tariff, and new amendments to the Farm Loan Act and the Federal Reserve Act. Senator Kenyon was designated as "chairman" of the group which thereafter sought to recruit other senators into the fold. Soon this original group was augmented by the inclusion of Charles L. McNary (Oregon), Peter Norbeck (South Dakota), John W. Harreld (Oklahoma), Henry F. Ashurst (Arizona), Byron P. "Pat" Harrison (Mississippi), Wesley L. Jones (Washington), Robert N. Stanfield (Oregon), Frank B. Kellogg (Minnesota), and Claude A. Swanson (Virginia).

Shortly after the May 9 meeting of senators, a House faction of rural representatives, under the leadership of Lester J. Dickinson of Iowa, organized itself into committees to study farm transportation, finance, and the tariff. The membership of this group was somewhat fluid. At its peak there were approximately 100 members, but normally the number was less. Like the Senate group, it represented a semiformal body of farm opinion and, from time to time, wielded considerable influence in the House. The contemporary press referred to both these cliques as the "farm bloc" and the name stuck.

One of the main factors in the bloc's founding was a fear that the Harding administration would concentrate on business recovery and devote less attention to agricultural distress. From the outset, the farm bloc was candid about its goal: to force an immediate consideration of agricultural problems regardless of the desires of the president or anyone else. No less arbitrary and willful in its demands than any other vested interest group, the farm bloc was concerned only with its own welfare and possessed as myopic a view of the national interest as any eastern industrialist. It was a minority faction seeking to outflank another minority which it believed to be more powerful and influential—industry.

Opposition to the farm bloc was naturally intense in commercial and financial circles. Secretary Mellon warned of its insidiousness while Hoover opposed it as disruptive and disloyal. Numerous Old Guard senators, such as Brandegee, Knox, and Watson, viewed the bloc's members as party traitors. Secretary Wallace, meanwhile, strove to interpret the bloc favorably to both the president and the cabinet and at the same time used his influence to keep the bloc temperate in its demands. Significantly, the bloc did not regard itself as "anti-administration" and did not advertise itself as anti-Harding. However, it was avowedly antibusiness, anti-Old Guard, anti-Hoover, and anti-Mellon.[9]

Under such circumstances, Harding's success in getting these various elements to work together at all in the opening months of his administration represented a feat of political diplomacy. His vacillation on the matter of legislative priorities early in his tenure might have shown poor executive leadership. But in the long run perhaps no other course could have achieved as much. To have sided openly with one group or the other might have produced worse than temporary confusion. It might have resulted in permanent legislative stalemate. Clearly Harding's malleability and unruffled reactions in the face of heavy pressure from both agrarian and industrial partisans were necessary preconditions to long-range legislative success for both business and agriculture.

Too much credit has been given to the farm bloc as a formative legislative factor during the Harding years. Actually, its most publicized victories were negative rather than positive. It prevented a tax revision before an emergency tariff was passed and it helped to prevent the Mellon-sponsored surtax reductions from being included in the Revenue Act of 1921. Aside from this, in the years 1921–23 the farm bloc did not press for a single major agricultural reform which the administration opposed. Both Harding and Wallace supported all the agricultural bills which were passed, and Harding signed them willingly. The main difference between the president and the farm bloc was one of timing and of party irregularity. Rarely did the bloc's members offend him with their agricultural beliefs.

The farm bloc and its chief supporting groups were economically almost as conservative as Harding. The most important influential element behind the bloc was the American Farm Bureau Federation. Organized in 1919, the Farm Bureau was different from and hostile to the more radical National Farmers' Union and the Nonpartisan League. Safe, sane, conservative, and stable, the Farm Bureau advocated the development of rural cooperatives, greater credit extension, scientific farm management, and tariff protection for farm commodities. James R. Howard of Iowa was its president and wielded considerable influence in Republican party circles. Gray Silver of West Virginia, nicknamed the "Silver Eel," was its $12,500-a-year lobbyist in Washington, D.C., and allegedly controlled the votes of more congressmen than did big business.[10]

By June 1921 the Farm Bureau had attracted a membership of over one million. Its chief competitor, the Grange, fell to second place. The Grange was only slightly less conservative than the Farm Bureau and only slightly less influential with the farm bloc. Both the Grange and the Farm Bureau were essentially middle-class organizations. During the Harding years, neither advocated direct government intervention in the farm situation, and both supported the Republican party's farm planks of 1920. In the eyes of both the Grange and the Farm Bureau, the farm bloc was not a radical wedge by which agricultural interests could subvert the normal governmental process or force economic innovations inimical to traditional thinking. The bloc was simply the means whereby the Republican party could be held accountable on farm policy and made to fulfill its own campaign promises.

Clearly the farm bloc advocated a restrained approach to the agricultural dilemma even though some of its actions caused the Harding administration much concern and grief. For its leadership the bloc turned only to Republican moderates such as Senator Kenyon or, later, Senator Capper. LaFollette and Norris, for example, were regarded as too radical to provide it with stable guidance. Its legislative goals differed in no significant respect from those set by the Republican platform or supported by the Harding administration. And like the Harding administration, which it oftentimes castigated, the farm bloc dealt only with the symptoms of farm depression and not the central causes. Hence, both the farm bloc's alleged victories and its failures were only vicariously experienced. Both belonged to the Harding regime.

[3

OF ALL the legislative action advocated for helping the farmer, none was considered to be so important as the passage of an emergency tariff. Because of the drop in agricultural prices in 1920 and the ensuing decline in farm income, pro-tariff sentiment swept through the rural sections of the West and South in late 1920 and early 1921. The assumption grew that foreign competition in agricultural commodities and the dumping of foreign surpluses on American shores had helped trigger the catastrophic break in farm prices. Normally only lukewarm on the matter of tariff protection, the stricken western and southern farmer became smoking hot on the issue and demanded quick action.

Abetted by postwar chauvinism, this rural sentiment forced congressional consideration of the problem in the closing days of the Wilson administration. The result was the passage of the Fordney Emergency Tariff Act. Surprisingly, President Wilson, on the last day of his administration, March 3, vetoed it with a message that was as prophetic as it was unheeded: "If we wish to have Europe settle her debts, governmental or commercial, we must be prepared to buy from her, and if we wish to assist Europe and ourselves by the export of either food, raw materials, or finished products, we must be prepared to welcome commodities which we need and which Europe will be prepared, with no little pain, to send us. Clearly, this is no time for the erection of high trade barriers."[11]

Harding made no pretense at being an expert on the tariff. His understanding of the subject was not profound. But he knew that he favored protection for both business and agriculture. All his life he had supported the Republican policy of high tariffs and he agreed with the 1920 platform that demanded tariff protection for farmers. As a result, as soon as he became president, he placed the weight of his administration behind the Fordney emergency measure and signed it as soon as it was repassed by Congress in May 1921. This law contained an anti-dumping provision as well as high duties on wheat, corn, meat, wool, and sugar.[12]

Despite the grumbling in business quarters where tax revision was regarded as more important, the administration's immediate response to the demand for an emergency tariff was hailed as a first step toward rural recovery. But, as we have noted, farm advocates, especially in the Senate, were not content to stop there. Despite administration desires, these men demanded that other farm legislation be discussed before the tax revision question was resolved. As a consequence, in early July President Harding sent for Gray Silver and leaders of the farm bloc and asked which of the many proposed pieces of farm legislation they wished to consider. In consultation with the president, five out of more than a dozen were selected and congressional debate was begun.[13] Between then and August 25, when the special session took a short recess, these five agricultural measures were passed by both houses and signed by the president.

Four of these bills were relatively noncontroversial and were adopted without much difficulty. They were the Packers and Stockyards Act, the Future Trading Act, and two amendments to the Farm Loan Act. The Packers and Stockyards Act was partially the brainchild of Secretary Wallace who supported the bill and helped shepherd it through Congress against Old Guard opposition. Growing out of farmers' distrust of packers and wartime profiteering in meats, this law prohibited interstate packers from resorting to unfair or discriminatory practices, manipulating or controlling prices, and creating a monopoly or restraining commerce. Yard dealers and all those who engaged in stockyard services were required to establish reasonable rates. The secretary of agriculture was empowered to enforce this act subject to court appeal.[14]

The Future Trading Act (Capper-Tincher bill) was the culmination of rural agitation dating back to Granger days to regulate the grain exchanges of the country. Again, Secretary Wallace was a prime mover and gave this legislation his full blessing. The measure placed a prohibitive tax of twenty cents a bushel on speculative transactions such as "puts and calls," "bids," and "offers," and on grain sold for future delivery except

207

when such transactions were conducted by the grain owners themselves through authorized contract markets. These contract markets were placed under the supervision of the secretary of agriculture who, along with the secretary of commerce and the attorney general, could revoke violators' privileges.[15]

The net effect of the two amendments to the Farm Loan Act was to make loans more easily available to the farmer and in larger amounts. Again, both actions were supported by the administration. The first amendment increased the capital of federal land banks and authorized an increase in the maximum size of rural loans. The second amendment raised the interest to the investor on farm loan bonds from 5 to 5½ percent without increasing the rate to the borrower.[16]

The fifth, and most controversial, piece of farm legislation was the Emergency Agricultural Credits Act. No other farm measure provided such an interesting insight into the relationship between the administration and the farm bloc or into the differences of opinion within the farm bloc itself. This law was actually a substitute for another proposal known as the Norris Farm Relief Bill which had been introduced by Senator Norris, chairman of the Senate Committee on Agriculture and Forestry, in the opening days of the special session. Norris was always to the left of his Republican farm colleagues in his economic beliefs. His curious blend of humanitarianism, isolationism, and agrarian populism was typical of the Minnesota-Dakota-Nebraska area in the postwar era, and not only did he reflect much of the thinking prevalent there, but he looked the part. As one observer said: "Get on any train in the corn and hog states anywhere between Chicago and Lincoln, Nebraska, and you will find a dozen men like George William Norris."[17]

The Norris Farm Relief Bill was a complicated measure. Designed to perform the dual function of giving food relief to Europe and eliminating farm surpluses at home, the bill called for the creation of a government corporation to buy farm surpluses for cash and then sell them abroad for credit over a period of five years. The secretary of commerce was designated as the ex officio chairman of a board which would be created to run the corporation. The bill further provided that the merchant marine, built during the war and now mainly idle, would be used to transport the goods free of cost.

The bill had some appeal. At first Senator Kenyon was enthusiastic about it as were other members of the farm bloc. Hoover, who would have been chairman of the proposed corporation, was mildly interested and indicated his willingness to consider it. But strong opposition appeared. Secretary Wallace approved neither of Norris's relief plan nor of Hoover's projected role in it. Harding, taking his cue from his secretary of agriculture, also opposed it. Southern farm leaders, coming under heavy pressure from the cotton industry which feared the Norris bill might aid the rehabilitation of European textile mills, announced that they could not support it. The private shipping industry, of course, was bitterly against the proposal. Finally, Hoover, carefully noting the trend of opinion, withdrew his tentative support.[18]

The administration now sought an alternative to the Norris plan. Harding believed that any new financial help for the farmer should come through the already established and functioning War Finance Corporation. Hence with the consent of both Harding and Wallace, Secretary Hoover, in concert with Eugene Meyer, chairman of the War Finance Corporation, drafted the Emergency Agricultural Credits Act. This measure was then given to Senator Kellogg of Minnesota, a moderate in the farm bloc, who agreed to present the bill at the proper time.

The moment came on the morning of July 26, 1921. Vice-President Coolidge, who should have been in the chair, arranged instead for Senator Curtis of Kansas to be there. The reason for the Coolidge-Curtis switch was that Coolidge, just the day before, had promised Norris to recognize Senator Ransdell on the morning of July 26. Ransdell wished to speak in behalf of the Norris bill. But when the Senate opened with Ransdell on his feet, Curtis calmly ignored him by saying, "The chair recognizes the Senator from Minnesota." Stunned by Ransdell's vigorous shouts for the floor, Kellogg heard his name repeated three times before he managed to leap up and present the administration measure as a substitute for the Norris bill. Immediately thereafter, Coolidge appeared and took the chair.[19]

Such maneuvering caused bitter feeling. Coolidge felt the lash of Norris's wrath, while moderate farm-bloc members, such as Kellogg, had difficulty in explaining their complicity in the matter. Numerous senators were offended by the fact that the administration measure had not first gone before the Senate Agriculture Committee. Few had even heard of the administration proposal until the moment Kellogg presented it. Nevertheless, the combined support of moderate farm-bloc senators, led by Senator Kenyon, and the strong backing of Hoover, Wallace, and Harding carried the bill through. Norris collapsed after a continuous three-day battle to save his own measure and was not able to return to the Senate until the following October. He later called this episode "the greatest single disappointment of all my public service." [20]

The Emergency Agricultural Credits Act was signed by Harding on August 24, 1921. By this act, the War Finance Corporation was authorized to advance loans not only to exporters and banks (which it could do already), but also to farmers' cooperatives and foreign purchasers. In addition it could grant loans for the breeding, raising, fattening, and marketing of livestock. Also the War Finance Corporation could purchase from rural banks paper secured by agricultural products. This latter provision was designed to save the banking system in certain badly depressed agricultural sections of the country. Within a few months after the law's passage, 7000 loans were made to rural banks, aggregating some $200 million; $84 million went to livestock companies; $64 million were placed at the disposal of farm cooperatives. By the beginning of 1923, the War Finance Corporation had loaned more than $420 million under this legislation.[21]

As with the other agricultural relief measures, the farm bloc claimed chief credit for the Emergency Act's passage and its subsequent success. The bloc never admitted that all five laws had been supported by the administration and that the last was a measure totally sponsored and conceived by the administration. As a result, in many farm areas it was assumed that all this legislation had been passed without the administration's help. In some rural areas it was believed that Congress as a whole, except for the farm bloc, was violently anti-agriculture, and only by bulldog tenacity were farm representatives able to secure favorable action. Farm journals and weeklies spread such propaganda as did the Farm Bureau Federation and the National Grange. Many farm areas became so engaged in lambasting the administration and Congress for their alleged shortcomings that they never bothered to examine what had actually been accomplished.

By late 1921 it was obvious that a real communication and credibility gap was developing between Washington and the farmer. Representative Philip P. Campbell of Kansas, chairman of the House Rules Committee, remarked to Harding after a brief return trip to his state in September that many farmers did not know of the remedial legislation or of the administration's role in securing it. He suggested that the administration immediately institute a program of educating the farmer.[22] Harding ruefully admitted that "Perhaps we have been remiss in making use of all the publicity that we ought."[23] Secretary Wallace, meanwhile, complained to Harding in a similar vein: "The fact of the matter is that people generally have not given [the administration, including Congress] the credit to which it is entitled."[24]

[4

INTEREST in agricultural relief in 1921 was not confined to legislative action. Even while the various agricultural relief bills were being considered and passed by Congress, there were many who believed that such activity might prove useless unless a study was first made of the causes for the agricultural depression and agreement reached on the correct approach. Although not willing to wait on the results of such a study, farm-bloc members certainly had no objection to it and supported all efforts in that direction.

On April 25, shortly after the opening of the special session, Senator Irvine Lenroot of Wisconsin and Representative James G. Strong of Kansas introduced a concurrent resolution calling for the creation of a commission to investigate conditions affecting the farm and to make recommendations. Passed on June 7, this resolution gave birth to the Joint Commission on Agricultural Inquiry, which included members of both houses, appointed by the president, and which was to make a report in ninety days. The commission, whose membership was drawn mainly from the farm bloc, held hearings during July and August, gathering statistics and voluminous information. Its work was so detailed and comprehensive that it was unable to finish within the allotted time and fall passed with no report forthcoming.

There were, meanwhile, other plans advanced for attacking the agricultural problem. Secretary Wallace favored calling a National Agricultural Conference. He first made this proposal to Harding during the 1920 presidential campaign, and after the election urged the idea upon him again. But Hoover and Mellon opposed such a conference at that time, claiming that it would heighten the impression that the president was more interested in agriculture than in industry. As a result, Harding said neither "yes" nor "no" to Wallace, preferring to wait for a more propitious moment.

That moment arrived in late December 1921. By that time the special session had adjourned and the Joint Commission on Agricultural Inquiry was about to make public the first portion of its findings. As the story goes, Harding and Wallace were playing golf on an unusual springlike day, and Wallace was again bombarding the president with arguments for a national farm gathering. As he holed out his last putt, Harding turned to Wallace and said: "Go ahead with your Agricultural Conference, Hank." Shortly thereafter, on December 30, the president wrote Wallace a formal letter, requesting him to call the conference. For public consumption, this letter stated: "I am convinced that a conference may be made a very helpful agency in suggesting practical ways of improvement, particularly if brought into coordination with the helpful investigation which has been begun by the Congressional Committee committed to a related work." The letter further suggested that the conference concentrate on two main goals: (1) consideration of the immediate agricultural situation and (2) examination of the agricultural future with a view to establishing general farm policies.[25]

By the time the conference convened on January 23, 1922, the first portion of the Joint Commission's report had been released together with its basic recommendations. Consisting altogether of four parts (which were submitted to Congress at intervals between late December 1921 and March 1923), the commission's report included much technical knowledge about the farm industry and provided excellent material on the background of the farm depression. Among other things it laid to rest the rural myth that the depression was a conspiracy of business against agriculture and had been caused by the willful action of bankers and the Federal Reserve Board. The report found instead that the farm depression was the result of an interplay of a host of domestic and international economic forces. The commission's recommendations, while not as specific as many farm supporters would have liked, advocated increased encouragement of farm cooperatives, additional farm credit, reduction in general freight rates, more agricultural research, more adequate wholesale terminal facilities for perishable products, and better roads from farms to markets.[26]

212

With this background the Agricultural Conference met in Washington for four days from January 23 to 27. Present were 336 delegates from 37 states, including farmers, representatives of agricultural organizations and of businesses related to agriculture, and a few economists and other scholars. President Harding was on hand to deliver the keynote address. He asked the delegates to consider not merely emergency measures, but steps calculated to aid the farmer permanently. Speaking of agriculture as the "most elemental of industries," he parroted Wallace by claiming that no part of the nation's economy could be healthy while agriculture was sick. He then briefly analyzed the salient characteristics of farming with its natural competitiveness and independency, and demonstrated a solid grasp of the economic realities of farm life. Finally, Harding emphasized that no one in the United States had a monopoly on worrying about the welfare of the farmer: "The whole country has an acute concern with the conditions and the problems which you are met to consider. It is truly a national interest and not entitled to be regarded as primarily the concern of either a class or a section," and here he looked up from his manuscript and raised his voice, "—or a bloc." [27] The point was not lost on the delegates.

It was a strong speech. Secretary Wallace claimed it was "the most thoughtful address on agriculture ever delivered by a president of the United States." The press characterized it as "wise," "constructive," "sympathetic," and "sound." Many newspapers commented on the contrast between the logic in Harding's speech and the emotion and economic nonsense often found in the utterances of farm-bloc senators. Of course, no sooner did the echoes of Harding's voice die away than some elements in the farm bloc raised their voices in anguish. They were incensed by Harding's reference to "the bloc" and claimed he was attempting to ram through his own farm views by means of a "hand-picked" conference. A few radical bloc members, such as LaFollette, adopted the strange attitude that the conference was a rival to the bloc. To these members, farm-bloc survival seemed to be more important than farm recovery. [28]

Divided into twelve working committees, the conference discussed all aspects of the agricultural problem. In the end the delegates endorsed a series of recommendations which were very similar to those of the Joint Commission on Agricultural Inquiry. Guided by moderate farm-bloc members and administration officials, notably Secretary Wallace, the conference's proposals, like those of the Joint Commission, dealt mainly with symptoms and not cures. As its critics later claimed, no drastic solutions were offered.[29] The conference applauded the recent remedial farm legislation of the special session of Congress. It advocated a new permanent tariff law supervised by a tariff board. It proposed development of a Great Lakes–St. Lawrence Seaway and further government support for the construction of farm-to-market roads. It suggested to farmers that they diversify toward subsistence crops and not export staples. It further advised them to reduce their costs of production, develop cooperative marketing, and decrease crop acreage. Among the conference's other recommendations were the following: further strengthening of the War Finance Corporation, inclusion of an agricultural representative on the Federal Reserve Board, enactment of a farm cooperative marketing measure, creation of an intermediate credits law, and a general decrease in railroad freight rates.[30]

The conference consciously steered away from recommending government production controls or price fixing. The only reference to such matters was one minor suggestion that Congress and the president examine the possibility of reestablishing a fair exchange value for all farm commodities in relation to other products. Adopted as a result of pressure from a liberal element led by Senator Norris, this insertion did not alter the pattern of moderation. Consequently the radical National Farmers' Union and the Nonpartisan League heaped scorn upon the conference. But the National Grange and the American Farm Bureau Federation hailed it. President Howard of the American Farm Bureau called it "the most far-reaching conference of farmers ever held" and, referring to Harding, claimed that "no Chief Executive of the nation has previously indicated so deep and intelligent interest in the farmer's affairs."[31]

President Harding and Secretary Wallace were both pleased with the conference's result. As reports funneled back to him from all parts of the country, Wallace wrote Harding: "It seems to me you have reason to feel abundantly satisfied with the outcome of this Conference. . . . The expressions concerning it are invariably favorable."[32] For Harding, the work and recommendations of the conference were not half so important as the propaganda advantages it afforded. It enabled him to demonstrate his personal concern for the farmer. It helped him mend his administration's fences with large segments of the farm population. It temporarily flattered farm leaders by placing them and their problems in the national limelight. And it stole some of the thunder from the farm bloc and gave the administration a badly needed breathing spell.

[5

THE aftermath of the National Agricultural Conference was marked by two important developments: first, a decline in the power and unity of the farm bloc; and second, the rapid implementation of many of the conference's recommendations.

The decline in the influence of the farm bloc was at first barely perceptible. Experiencing a real sense of power following the passage of its priority farm legislation in the special session, the bloc continued to harass the administration. Its tactics in regard to the final passage of tax revision in November 1921 was indicative of its general mood. An even better example of its militancy was its drive for farmer representation on the Federal Reserve Board.

This issue came to a head just one week before the opening of the Agricultural Conference. But it had a long background. From the onset of the depression in 1920, farmers had complained that they were not sufficiently represented on government agencies and boards, specifically on the Federal Reserve Board. Presumably, so the rural belief went, if farmers had been represented on the board, the depression might have been averted. After Harding became president, it was expected in rural circles that he would appoint some farm members to governmental boards, especially the Federal Reserve Board. The Republican platform of 1920 had promised such action. When no farm appointments were forthcoming immediately, the administration was soundly condemned in agrarian quarters.

Pressure grew within the farm bloc to force the president's hand. Shortly after the opening of the regular session in December 1921, a farm-bloc bill was proposed which would enjoin the president to name an additional, or sixth, member to the Federal Reserve Board who was "a farmer." This proposal caused some discomfort in the White House. Harding did not wish to jeopardize the chances of the upcoming Agricultural Conference by clashing head-on with the farm bloc at this time. On the other hand, while he approved of greater farm representation on all boards, not only the Federal Reserve Board, he opposed a specific directive being written into law.[33]

On January 16, 1922, the day before the Senate was to vote on the measure, Harding invited two farm-bloc senators, Kenyon and Kellogg, to the White House to seek a compromise. With his usual political finesse, Harding managed to gain agreement on a substitute proposal which would not name "a farmer" specifically but would guarantee agricultural representation. The law originally creating the Federal Reserve Board had stated that the president should have regard for "a fair representation of the different commercial, industrial and geographic divisions of the country." Under the compromise, the law would read that the president should give attention to "a fair representation of the financial, agricultural, industrial and commercial interests."[34]

Presented by Senator Kellogg on January 17, this compromise was accepted by the Senate, 63–9. Bankers and commercial interests immediately charged Harding with "giving in" to the bloc and the New York Times spoke of "the disquietude and chill" brought on by Harding's "surrender." But Harding maintained that he had got the best of the bargain. To Will Hays he wrote that all the excitement in business circles was ridiculous because "no harm [was] done." It was perfectly natural, he said, that agriculture should have wanted a parity with commercial and financial interests. But, Harding added, he had possessed "no sympathy with the congressional desire to tell me whom I must name and when I must do it."[35]

The compromise bill did not finally pass Congress until June 1922, and Harding did not make an appointment under the law until January 12, 1923, when he selected Milo D. Campbell of Coldwater, Michigan, as the first "farmer" member of the Federal Reserve Board. To the end, despite Harding's claims to the contrary, the press and the general public continued to believe that the farm bloc had forced a humiliating capitulation upon the administration. This conclusion, however, ignored the alternatives facing the president. To have fought the farm bloc might have meant legislative stalemate and complete alienation of the bloc's more moderate members. By his compromise, Harding removed a real source of rural irritation and strengthened the hand of farm-bloc moderates.

If this compromise was a farm-bloc victory, it soon proved to be pyr-

216

rhic. By its reasonableness the administration diluted the bloc's militancy. More significantly, the Federal Reserve Board issue was the prelude to a change in bloc leadership. The bloc's guiding spirit, Senator Kenyon, had long coveted a federal judgeship and had made his wishes known to the president soon after Harding had assumed office. Harding had indicated to Kenyon at that time that he would appoint him to a judgeship as soon as a vacancy occurred which the president considered suitable. Harding thus retained control over timing. On January 31, 1922, four days after the close of the Agricultural Conference and two weeks after the Federal Reserve Board compromise, Harding nominated Kenyon as circuit judge for the Eighth District. Farm-bloc members immediately charged that Harding had taken this action to "break up" the bloc by removing its leader. Against the background of Harding's reference to the bloc in his Agricultural Conference address, such a theory seemed plausible. Its credibility was further enhanced by anti-bloc congressmen who gleefully claimed that Harding had indeed taken this action to cripple the farm group.

The charge was only partially correct. The president certainly did not waste any tears over the farm bloc's misfortune, but he did not create Kenyon's desire for a judgeship or his willingness to leave the Senate. Like any good politician, the president combined coincidence with circumstance and turned both to his advantage. He naturally denied that his motives were anything but pure. Shortly after the appointment Harding wrote Kenyon that he was "more amused than irritated" by the various newspaper reports ascribing political meaning to his action, and suggested that somebody "ought to write a book on the misconstrued motives of public men." Delighted with his judgeship, Kenyon replied two days later, "I agree," and added that somebody also ought to write a book "on the malicious misrepresentations of newspapers."[36]

Whatever the presidential motives, one salient fact emerged. There was an immediate decline in the effectiveness and prestige of the farm bloc. Never again was it so tightly disciplined or closely knit. At times it would resume its vociferousness and appear to wield considerable influence. But its finest hour had been reached during the summer and fall of 1921. Senator Capper, who succeeded Kenyon as bloc chairman, was less effective as a floor manager, less aggressive, and even more conservative. Thin and sparse, with a hawklike visage, Capper remained a farm critic of Republican presidents throughout the twenties, but he displayed few of the nonconformist tendencies of Kenyon and always worked within the party. A rural radio and newspaper owner with huge holdings, Capper reflected moderate "grass-roots" agricultural thinking in the central Mississippi River basin and none of the radical Nonpartisan League variety. He did not impart to the farm bloc a crusading zeal, but a business-like, straightforward philosophy which increasingly alienated its more liberal members. Surprisingly, however, Capper's name was more frequently associated with reform farm legislation in the 1920's than any other, including Norris's.[37]

Working in cooperation with Capper, the Harding administration throughout the remainder of 1922 attempted to implement most of the recommendations of both the Joint Commission on Agricultural Inquiry and the National Agricultural Conference. Perhaps the most important action was the passage of the Capper-Volstead Act relating to farm cooperatives. President Harding had always favored protecting cooperatives and during the brief interim between the special session and the regular session (November 23, 1921, to December 5, 1921) made it clear that he wanted such a protective bill passed.[38] Secretary Wallace also urged immediate enactment of such a law. No one in the administration, however, supported such legislation more than Secretary Hoover. To him, farm cooperatives were like trade associations and offered benefits in efficiency, elimination of waste, and price stabilization. Farm cooperatives, he believed, would bring prosperity to the farm, just as trade associations would help revive business. Throughout the Harding era, the secretary of commerce emphasized this type of self-help as the real solution to the farm problem.[39]

Passed on February 18, 1922, by an overwhelming 295–49 vote in the House and a 58–1 vote in the Senate, the Capper-Volstead law went far beyond the protection for cooperatives written into the old Clayton Act. By this new measure, any farm association, corporate or otherwise, with or without capital stock, was now exempted from the operation of the antitrust laws. This legislation frankly gave farm cooperatives special privileges which no trade association or any other form of corporate enterprise possessed.[40]

The Harding administration also supported other conference proposals to aid the farmer. For example, it extended the life of the War Finance

Corporation for another year, and in March 1922 made an additional $1.5 million available to farmers for the purchase of seed grain in areas of severe crop failure. Under this latter arrangement about 12,000 loans averaging $300 were made to farmers in the Dakotas, Montana, Idaho, and Washington. In September 1922 the administration supported the passage of the Grain Futures Act, necessitated by the fact that the Supreme Court in May 1922 had invalidated the Future Trading Act of 1921 as an illegal use of the taxing power. Based on the interstate commerce clause, this new act authorized the Agriculture Department to create the Grain Futures Administration which thereafter licensed grain exchanges and boards of trade conducting futures markets, supervised future trading in grain and examined records, monitored the operations of speculators in order to prevent unfair manipulation, checked on misleading or false information, and handled complaints of market violations.[41]

While this additional remedial legislation was being passed for the farmer, Secretary Wallace throughout 1921–22 streamlined the Department of Agriculture to better meet the challenges of modern conditions. During the Wilson administration, Secretary Houston had already begun a number of administrative reorganizations in the department and Wallace now added to them. Houston had grouped the department along functional lines under three main headings: regulation, research, and extension. Wallace expanded this approach by creating a separate director of regulatory work, a director of scientific work, and a director of extension services.

Receiving Wallace's primary attention were the scientific activities of the department. Believing, at least at first, that the agricultural crisis was a temporary affair, Wallace placed major emphasis on research, and especially research in agricultural economics, as the key to returning agricultural prosperity. By his own admission, his most important step was the creation in July 1922 of the Bureau of Agricultural Economics. Combining the Office of Farm Management, the Bureau of Crop and Livestock Estimates, and the Bureau of Markets into this new agency, Wallace appointed as its head Dr. Henry C. Taylor of the University of Wisconsin. Since the turn of the century, Taylor had pioneered a more scientific approach to the collection, assembling, and interpretation of agricultural data and had trained an outstanding group of young disciples. Some of these young men he brought with him to the new bureau and rapidly made

219

it one of the foremost research agencies in the federal government. Secretary Wallace strongly backed Taylor and the Bureau of Agricultural Economics, using them as a counter-ploy in his interdepartmental feud with Hoover over the gathering of statistics.[42]

The findings of this bureau were circulated widely among farm leaders, farm organizations, legislators, and others. The bureau distributed "outlook reports" which contained information on domestic market conditions, production, and price trends. It even expanded these reports to include foreign market trends, claiming that Dr. Julius Klein's Bureau of Foreign and Domestic Trade in the Commerce Department was not doing an adequate job.

The purpose of all this activity by the Bureau of Agricultural Economics was not to regulate the action of the farmer but to enable him to make the most intelligent voluntary response to existing conditions. It encouraged farm organizations to develop a more sophisticated and informed approach to farm legislation and often provided the technical information necessary to enact farm measures. More significantly, the bureau became the primary arena where new ideas about farm policy could be tested and discussed. Wallace encouraged Taylor to pick the brains of less orthodox economists such as Richard T. Ely and John R. Commons. The result was a slow transformation in the thinking of Wallace on solutions to the farm problem, and a gradual shift of the bureau's attention away from the plight of the individual farmer to the broader problems of price fixing, production controls, and the equalization of agriculture vis-à-vis business.[43]

President Harding supported Wallace in his various reorganization plans and, to Hoover's discomfort, endorsed the work of the Bureau of Agricultural Economics. Harding did not pretend to understand the ramifications of the continuing farm depression or the bureau's numerous activities, but he had confidence that "the experts" under Wallace's direction would provide the answers. One of the few times during his administration that Harding endorsed supplemental appropriations for any department was in answer to a plea from Wallace in late 1922 that salaries be increased for scientific personnel, especially in the Bureau of Agricultural Economics.[44] President Harding was no economist, but he recognized a good investment when he saw one.

NO ISSUE relating to the farm problem and to farm recovery was so complicated as the freight-rate question. Certainly no issue so clearly demonstrated the Harding administration's willingness to help the farmer, even at considerable political cost to itself.

The rate problem dated back to the Transportation (Esch-Cummins) Act of 1920 which had returned the railroads to their private owners following the war. Under that law carriers were to receive a "fair" return on their investment, pegged at 6 percent per annum, and the Interstate Commerce Commission was directed to authorize rates which for the first two years would accomplish this. As a result, on July 29, 1920, the ICC announced rate increases of approximately 20 percent in passenger fares and a freight-rate increase of roughly 33 percent. These new rates became effective August 26, 1920.[45]

Despite these increased rates, the carriers were never able to realize a return approaching 6 percent. This was partly due to declining business conditions resulting from the depression of 1920–21. But it was also due to a decision of the Railroad Labor Board on July 20, 1920, which ordered a wage increase for railroad workers, amounting to $600 million, to offset the ruinous rise in the cost of living. The railroads reported earnings of only 3.07 percent in 1920 and 3.83 percent in 1921. From the carriers' point of view, either additional rate increases or lower wages were necessary to improve investment returns. As one irate holder of railroad securities told Harding in the spring of 1921, "it seems to me that something radical must be done to improve the net earnings of the roads."[46]

Farmers, meanwhile, convinced that the freight-rate increase was a major cause for deflation on the farm, bombarded the White House and the ICC with demands to rescind the rate increase of August 1920. In rural areas it became popular, especially in former Populist strongholds such as Kansas, Nebraska, and the Dakotas, to exaggerate wildly the effect of these increased freight charges on the farm depression. Rural speakers left the impression that it cost farmers more to ship goods to market than they received for them and that the railroads were ringing up staggering profits while the farmers starved.[47]

The farmer was not alone in his opposition. Many manufacturers, especially those in farm-related activities, such as agricultural machinery, petitioned the president to reduce freight rates, claiming they were hurting business. Steelmen also urged a change. James A. Campbell, president of Youngstown Sheet and Tube Company, wrote Harding in mid-May 1921, "We are operating our plant about one-third of its capacity. . . . I am strongly of the opinion that high freight rates is the principal reason for the cessation of business in this country."[48]

One possible solution, and one which big business favored, involved the immediate settlement of all government-railroad claims growing out of World War I. It was suggested that the claims of the railroads against the government for the wartime control period be paid to the railroads in cash, while the railroads, in turn, would fund their indebtedness to the government in long-term securities. In this way the railroads would receive approximately $400 million at once which would permit rates to be lowered, railroad workers' wages to remain the same, and the roads to regain financial health. The National Association of Manufacturers endorsed this approach at its annual meeting in 1921 and indicated its opposition to any further reduction in freight rates until this scheme, or something like it, was tried.[49] Subsequently, an Emergency Railroad Bill, written in part by Hoover, backed by Mellon, and endorsed by Harding, was introduced into the special session of Congress in mid-summer 1921 to accomplish this purpose. But the suspicious attitude of many congressmen, including the farm bloc, doomed the bill to extinction. By the fall, even the bill's most ardent backer, the *Wall Street Journal*, lost hope for a favorable result.[50]

With the collapse of the claims-funding proposal, the carriers reverted to the position that no decrease in freight rates was justifiable without a commensurate reduction in operating expenses—namely, the lowering of railroad workers' wages. Already in July 1921, the Railroad Labor Board had reduced some railroad wages as much as 12½ percent, but this reduction was quickly offset by a decline in railroad revenues caused by an ICC decision in August to decrease freight rates on livestock and another in October to decrease freight rates on grains. Then, as a further gesture to farm sentiment, the ICC, in January 1922, ordered a 16½ percent reduction in rates on a variety of other agricultural products. The operators naturally condemned this latter ICC decision. They also denounced the Joint Commission on Agricultural Inquiry and the National Agricultural Conference for recommending further rate reductions without including any plan for additional wage cuts. Farmers, meanwhile, were only partially satisfied by the rate reductions ordered by the ICC in late 1921 and early 1922, especially since these reductions did not involve an across-the-board decrease. Rates on farm machinery and other such necessary farm items, for example, remained unaffected.

The Harding administration was divided on the rate issue. Secretary Hoover believed that the farmer exaggerated the economic importance of freight rates and warned that any further rate decreases should not be forced upon the railroads by any new ICC fiat, but should be achieved voluntarily through "greater railway operational efficiency." The secretary of commerce also cautioned against loose talk about further ICC action and urged President Harding to discourage it. Said Hoover, "it always disturbs business by even contemplating rate changes." [51]

Secretary Wallace, on the other hand, campaigned openly and persistently for drastic rate reductions. He did not regard the decreases through January 1922 as being particularly significant and vigorously urged a major contraction in all rates. His aggressiveness on this matter stemmed not so much from a bias against the railroads as from a sympathy with the farmer. Wallace recognized the problem facing the carriers, but he reasoned that they were better able to stand the loss than the man on the farm. [52]

President Harding was caught in the middle and was deeply aware of the political implications involved. To lower rates and pay for them by further cutting railroad profits would alienate an important business group. To lower rates and compensate for the difference by decreasing workers' wages would antagonize organized labor. To retain rates at their current levels would further damage the administration's image in rural areas. Understandably Harding agonized over the unpalatable alternatives. In exasperation he once remarked: "Everybody says something should be done, but nobody describes *precisely* how to do it." [53]

Despite his indecision about the proper approach, Harding never really doubted that lower freight rates were basically desirable. By late summer 1921, he was complaining to close friends that he thought the ICC was reacting too slowly to public opinion on the rate matter. When individuals grumbled to him about his personal inaction in the rate situation, he passed

223

the buck to the ICC and Congress, claiming it was their responsibility, not his. To such a complaint from Senator Capper, he replied: "I have expressed myself as effectively as I know how in an informal way to the members of the Interstate Commerce Commission. You realize, of course, that this Commission is one which the Executive can not approach in a formal way. . . . [It] is the agent of Congress in dealing with railway rate making. If there is to be any directing utterances on the part of any official authority, naturally it must go from Congress." [54]

Harding was technically correct. But his statement belied the actual relationship between himself and the ICC. From the beginning he prodded members of that body to make rate reductions. As early as June 1921 he indicated to them that he wished some readjustment in rates on agricultural commodities and applauded their action in the fall of 1921 and in early 1922. But he also desired a general rate decrease and, after such a recommendation was endorsed by the National Agricultural Conference, he became even more aggressive in voicing his opinions. These came to the attention of the ICC mainly through his correspondence with Commissioner Mark W. Potter.

Harding and Potter carried on a frank exchange of letters concerning the rate problem. Through Potter not only was the commission apprised of Harding's views, but the president was kept aware of the latest thinking of the commission. In his letters Potter indicated that the ICC was in a quandary along with everyone else, and he chided the president for his "pressure" on the commission. Harding denied to Potter that he intended to apply pressure, but he made it clear that he favored lower overall rates. Such rates, Harding contended, would help the farmer and would also be a boon to commercial and industrial businesses; economic recovery would be encouraged both in the city and on the farm, said the president. [55]

Harding was not content simply to engage in letter writing over this matter. Despairing of a general rate reduction by the ICC, he appealed in the late spring of 1922 to the railroads themselves. On May 20 he invited to a White House dinner nineteen of the most important railroad executives in the country, including such men as Samuel Rea (president of the Pennsylvania Railroad), Ralph Budd (president of the Great Northern), Robert S. Lovett (chairman of the Union Pacific), A. H. Smith (president of the New York Central), and Daniel Willard (president of the Baltimore and Ohio). The only government officials present were Harding and Hoover. Arguing that business in general would be aided by an over-all decrease in rates and that rail profits would probably increase because of the resultant greater volume of trade, Hoover now urged the railroads to adopt a conciliatory view. Harding, who was more concerned about the rural situation, added to Hoover's arguments by claiming that returning prosperity to the farm would in itself increase rail business and offset any lower rates.

The railroad executives remained noncommittal, refusing to promise anything until a full study could be made of the matter. The president's goal, of course, was to secure an agreement from the railroads to reduce rates voluntarily apart from any ICC action. But the railroad men indicated that no such voluntary action could be undertaken without an accompanying decrease in workers' wages. However, they agreed to keep the issue open and expressed a hope that the ICC would not tinker further with freight rates until they had a chance to review the whole situation.[56]

To the embarrassment of the president, only three days after this meeting the ICC announced a general decrease of 10 percent in freight rates, except for those agricultural products which had already received the 16½ percent reduction ordered in January. The commission also set a new 5¾ percent rate of return for the railroads in place of the existing 6 percent, even though the new rates did not permit its realization. This new ruling marked the ICC's final answer to the freight-rate question.

The commissioners had reached this decision with great difficulty. Three thought the reduction should have been greater or objected to the across-the-board nature of the adjustment. Commissioner Ernest I. Lewis charged that not only was the 10 percent decrease too little, but the exclusion of agricultural products accorded with neither the president's desire nor the wishes of the farming public. Harding was indeed disappointed. Railroad executives, meanwhile, fretted over the 5¾ percent limit and immediately clamored for the Railroad Labor Board to order a reduction in wages; and big shippers claimed the decrease was only token and offered no real help to them at all. Neither Secretary Hoover nor Secretary Wallace was satisfied. And the farmer—the person most responsible for the agitation—was incensed. To him, this latest ICC decision was merely another example of the Harding administration's friendliness to business and lack of concern for the farmer.[57]

CONTRARY to rural opinion, by the fall of 1922 the Harding administration could regard its farm program with considerable satisfaction. Considering what had been achieved for agriculture in the period since March
4, 1921, and in view of the conflicting and competing economic forces
present, the administration deserved better handling than it received from
the agricultural community. Through the use of conferences, commissions,
and agricultural experts, the administration had attempted to uncover the
causes for the farm depression and establish guidelines for an intelligent
remedial policy. It had met all the basic demands of the farm bloc and
strove to implement many of the recommendations of the Joint Commission on Agricultural Inquiry and the National Agricultural Conference.
It had endorsed an emergency tariff, supported federal protection for farm
cooperatives, approved the further extension of farm credits and loans,
written new laws regulating the futures markets, and acquiesced on the
matter of agricultural representation on the Federal Reserve Board. In
addition, President Harding, at considerable political peril, had supported
the farmers' crusade for lower freight rates.[58]

Considering these various facts, the Harding administration by the
fall of 1922 was quite prepared to sit back and wait for its numerous farm
remedies to take hold. It had done all that had been asked of it and sincerely believed that time would now act as the magic catalyst. But the
tragedy shared by Harding, Wallace, the majority of the farm bloc, and
the farmer was that these remedies did not cure the economic and political
migraine known as the "farm problem." And as the farm depression continued, the farmer, despite all that had been done for him, became increasingly disenchanted and angry.

226

VIII

A Little Something
for Labor

[1

"JIMMIE" DAVIS was born in Tredegar, Wales, in 1873, migrated
with his parents to America when he was seven, and lived briefly in Hub-
bard, Ohio, before moving to Sharon, Pennsylvania. There at age twelve
he learned the art of iron puddling and by the time he was sixteen held
the position of master iron puddler in the Sharon mills. Thrown out of
work by the depression of 1893, he wandered about for three years before settling down in Elwood, Indiana. Here Davis quickly became head
of the local union in the tin plate industry and gained notoriety as a strong
opponent of the One Big Union concept. He got along well with local
businessmen, while at the same time winning concessions for the tin workers, and was ultimately rewarded by being elected city clerk on the Republican ticket in 1902. Next he became county recorder and in 1907
moved to Pittsburgh to engage in organizational work for the Loyal Order
of Moose. Thereafter he devoted his full time to lodge activities, finally
being elevated to the top job in the Moose organization.

When Harding invited him to become a member of his official family,
Davis jumped at the opportunity. Playing a double role as a labor man
and as a typical American of the joiner variety, Davis popularized through
his cabinet position the administration's spirit of conciliation among the
masses. Much in demand as a speaker, he customarily delivered homey
sermons on the old-time virtues and on patriotism to Elks, Moose, Le-

gionnaires, Masons, July Fourth gatherings, Flag Day celebrations, and Armistice Day commemorations. By far the most peripatetic member of the cabinet, Davis was actually more at home on the lecture platform than in his office in Washington. Similarly, he was more valuable to the Harding administration in its general public relations than in its specific labor concerns.

In his economic philosophy Davis was more the self-made man than the labor leader. Indeed, he was as much procapital as he was prolabor. He saw the nation's welfare as dependent upon both capital and labor, with capital supplying the organizational ingenuity and labor giving an "honest day's work for an honest day's pay." One of his favorite aphorisms was "When labor loafs, it injures labor first and capital last." He regarded labor-management cooperation as the normative relationship and viewed strikes only as a measure of last resort. Because of the current depression, Davis believed that labor's immediate responsibility was to help industry get back on its feet and not cause any harassment. According to Davis, a truce in labor-management conflict was an absolute requirement until prosperity returned.

As for the average laborer, Davis believed that he possessed ample opportunity for advancement if only he would apply himself. Davis offered his own career as an example, publishing in 1922 a rather embarrassing and egocentric ghostwritten autobiography entitled *The Iron Puddler: My Life in the Rolling Mills and What Came of It*. Urging workers not to covet what others had or rely on the egalitarian promises of radicals, Davis reduced complex economic relationships to simple equations which contained more eyewash than wisdom. "When all men are equal," he once claimed, "every prize fight will end in a draw, and every batter will knock as many home runs as Babe Ruth."[1]

Under Secretary Davis's guidance, the Department of Labor was not a dynamic or aggressive agency like Wallace's Agriculture or Hoover's Commerce. Its Bureau of Labor Statistics, Women's Bureau, Children's Bureau, and Immigration and Naturalization Service received minimal support and remained relatively static in personnel. Davis was no empire builder and appeared content to preside over an inherited structure with very few changes. The activity of his department in which Davis evidenced the most interest was that of labor statistics. Davis's retention of Ethelbert Stewart in the Bureau of Labor Statistics and his subsequent advancement of Stewart to commissioner of labor statistics was a wise move and extremely popular among statisticians and academic people. Stewart had been connected with the bureau since 1887 and had been its chief statistician for many years.

President Harding liked "Jimmie" Davis. He once confided to a friend: "He seldom fails to make a hit wherever he appears and speaks. He is a great favorite in Cabinet meetings and is everywhere as one of the representatives of the administration."[2] Davis, in turn, fawned on Harding. He wrote him gushing letters and his many little congratulatory notes about this or that descended on the White House like flakes of snow. Davis was his own twenty-four-hour-a-day public relations man. Every Davis utterance was mimeographed and rushed to the president as quickly as possible. Every Davis trip to the hinterland was noted and the president apprised of it. That such self-promotion paid off is undeniable. Harding reciprocated by sending Davis brief notes such as "You are handling matters in a fine way" or "You have brought to the office all that I have expected."[3] Harding awarded Davis his highest accolade when he spoke of his spirit of moderation: "I believe you have convinced the extremist on the labor side that a man does not need to be one of them to be a just public servant, and I believe you have persuaded those on the capitalistic side that one may be affiliated with labor organizations and still be utterly fair to all interests when aiming to serve the great American public."[4]

More than the personal propaganda or the flattery, this middle-of-the-road quality attracted the president to Davis. Harding saw in the former iron puddler the reflection of his own labor philosophy. As editor and owner of the *Marion Star* Harding had experienced firsthand an amiable wedding of capital (his) and labor (his employees). When the one prospered, so did the other. Harding had never had any trouble with organized labor and had always received the cooperation of the Marion Typographical Union. He had started a stock-savings-purchase plan for employees of the *Star* as early as 1907 and, as an employer, was much admired by his men.[5]

Harding obviously believed more in the benevolent paternalism of employers than in the activities of labor unions. This caused him to seek solutions to labor problems by talking to individual businessmen rather than by dealing with workers in the mass. Harding was not opposed to

229

unions as such and more than once claimed that the right of workers to organize and bargain collectively was not less absolute than the rights of management and capital. However, he deplored the use of the strike, and was opposed to unions having a veto on either governmental or business action. Such a conviction did not have its roots in the kind of vested-interest antiunion opposition shown by big business, but in the semi-ignorant fear displayed toward organized labor by the middle class in the small towns.[6]

Although during the campaign of 1920 organized labor theoretically supported Cox, many workers voted for Harding despite his lack of promises for labor per se. Samuel Gompers was not among them. He and other AFL leaders regarded the outcome of the election with distaste. Gompers had revered Wilson and from the beginning was simply not prepared to adjust to his successor. Harding, in a desire to win over all groups, invited Gompers to the White House soon after the inauguration for a chat on labor matters. Gompers went, but by his own admission missed the incisive wit and brilliant mind of the former occupant. The AFL president was unmoved by Harding's plea: "Mr. Gompers, I want your help. I want you to know that I do not believe you to be as black as you have been painted to me and I want to assure you that I am not as black as I have been painted to you." Although the White House remained open thereafter to the AFL chieftain, Gompers did not often go. When he did, Harding usually buttonholed him and complained about organized labor's shortcomings, especially about the unwillingness of labor leaders "to accept necessary reductions in wages and give an opportunity for a revival of industry." These sessions were painful for Gompers and made him even less inclined to appear at the executive mansion.[7]

Gompers later grumbled about the growing coolness of the Harding administration toward him, but in a sense he asked for it. It was certainly not a case of spurned love. Rarely did Gompers acknowledge any favorable action taken by Harding or his administration for labor. As Secretary Davis explained it: "[Gompers] is a Democrat and it is hard for him to hand a glass of milk to a Republican."[8] Gompers attacked Harding viciously in the pages of the *American Federationist* both before and after the election. He claimed that Republicans were the "unqualified defenders of the enemies of labor" and asserted that Harding's normalcy was "the crowning achievement of a political cynicism which has never lost hope of restoring industrial slavery and revoking political freedom."[9] Harding might not have had the mind of Wilson but he could read, and such statements as this one did not bring him any closer to the AFL president.

As time passed, and after repeated Gomperian rebuffs, Harding shunned contact with Gompers altogether. Letters from the labor leader were shunted to the side without being given much attention by the president. Sometimes they were intercepted by George Christian and sent to the proper underling for a reply without Harding's seeing them at all. The estrangement between the two men was ultimately so complete that Gompers once implied even Coolidge was more receptive to him than Harding. George Christian later claimed that Gompers was one of the few men Harding ever really disliked.[10]

This Gompers-Harding relationship, coupled with Davis's minimal identification with labor, was typical of the connection between the Harding administration and organized labor in general. There was little real communication and no bond of understanding. Unlike the businessman who had Mellon and Hoover, or the farmer who had Wallace, the laborer really had no one in the administration who articulated his views. Despite Harding's platitudes and Davis's aphorisms, the laborer was the Harding era's forgotten man.

[2

THE most critical labor problem immediately confronting the Harding administration was that of unemployment. Inheriting a depressed and unstable labor market from the Wilson years, the new administration faced a gloomy economic future in the spring and summer of 1921. Grappling with farm discontent and pressured by business for industrial recovery, Harding and his advisers first considered unemployment only as a part of the general economic malaise. It was not until the late summer that unemployment was viewed as a problem in its own right.

The first to worry about it was not Davis but Hoover. As the unemployment figures climbed above four million, Hoover predicted real suffering during the approaching winter unless something was done. His major suggestion was for local communities to begin public works and other building projects immediately rather than wait for spring. He further suggested that private business keep its workers employed throughout the fall and winter months and eliminate the usual seasonal layoffs. When, by late August, it became apparent that too little was being done along these lines to forestall mounting unemployment, Hoover recommended to Harding the convening of an unemployment conference. Harding, who had as one of his goals a rapprochement between capital and labor, saw in Hoover's proposal an opportunity to bring the two sides together in an assault on a mutual problem. He ordered Hoover to arrange for the conference at once.[11]

After careful preliminary planning the Unemployment Conference convened on September 26, 1921, in the Assembly Room of the Interior Department building. Secretary Hoover was in charge, but President Harding welcomed the more than 300 delegates. The president stated that this conference was not intended to be a "class parley" but a gathering to consider ways to relieve unemployment and minimize suffering during the winter months. He warned, however, that the conference should not seek unemployment subsidies from the federal government as a solution. Said Harding, "I would have little enthusiasm for any proposed relief which seeks either palliation or tonic from the Public Treasury." Immediately after the president finished, Hoover mounted the speaker's platform and encouraged quick conference action. But he, too, reiterated the admonition that only voluntary and local action, not federal intervention, could properly solve the unemployment problem.

Following these opening speeches, the conference divided into ten committees, each of which ultimately made a report to the conference as a whole. Working within the ground rules established by Harding and Hoover, these various reports were then distilled into a series of recommendations which were first submitted to the president and finally made public. In general, the recommendations closely followed the Harding-Hoover theme and called upon local businesses, employers, government officials, and others to move ahead building and construction plans in order to increase employment at once. The conference also recommended that work be spread and that as many new local public works projects be initiated as communities could afford. It further recommended that all deferred repairs be undertaken immediately and that a feeling of caution give way to an attitude of "do it now!"[12]

To implement these recommendations and provide coordination,

Harding immediately authorized the creation of a Bureau of Unemployment in the Commerce Department and appealed to all elements in the nation to support the work of the conference. The resultant propaganda effort was immense. Publications of such organizations as the National Association of Manufacturers boosted local work. The general press added its voice to the clamor. The new Bureau of Unemployment poured out a stream of information and encouragement. Almost daily during the remainder of the fall and early winter, Hoover sent out glowing reports of what was being accomplished in various parts of the country. Under such prodding, state and local committees sprang up to "match men with jobs," promote work projects, and persuade employers to hire additional help. By mid-winter Hoover could report that "states and cities, as well as private companies and individuals, have taken more comprehensive and effective measures than probably have ever been taken before in such a situation."[13]

To underscore the federal government's own sincerity, in January 1922, after discussing the matter with the cabinet, Harding ordered all departments to emulate local authorities in reexamining their construction and repair plans and undertake such work at once if possible. This order particularly affected the Navy, War, Agriculture, and Interior departments which let contracts immediately for work that had been scheduled for spring.[14] In such manner the administration used federal funds for relief and pump priming, while not technically violating Harding's requirement that the public treasury not be relied on for a direct solution to the unemployment problem.

The winter of 1921–22 passed safely. Suffering was kept at a minimum and the unemployment rate did not show its usual seasonal increase. From a high of nearly 5.5 million, unemployment figures leveled off and even slightly declined. As a result both Hoover and Harding regarded the Unemployment Conference as a colossal success. In May 1922 Hoover drafted a letter which Harding sent over his own signature to all cabinet officers and participants in the Unemployment Conference thanking them for their splendid efforts. The letter pointed to brightened prospects for spring employment and declared: "We have passed the winter of the greatest unemployment in the history of our country. Through the fine coordination and cooperation among federal and state officials, mayors and their committees of employers, relief organizations and citizens, we have come through with much less suffering than in previous years, when unemployment was very much less." [15]

Where were Davis and the Labor Department in all this? From the beginning Hoover attempted to soothe Davis's feelings by consulting him on conference matters relating to labor's role. But it was clear that Davis was always a junior partner in the enterprise, if that. The secretary of labor followed in Hoover's wake without much grumbling, although he was angered by the president's decision to place the unemployment coordinating agency in the Commerce rather than the Labor Department. To one of Davis's few complaining letters Hoover curtly replied: "My dear Davis: Don't get the notion that we are setting up any employment bureau in this Department. [It is only] a little machinery to . . . bring actual results from the Unemployment Conference by getting team work." [16] However, no amount of superficial Commerce-Labor cooperation or consultation really fooled anyone. As one observer humorously but truthfully remarked: "At the conference on unemployment, which was Mr. Hoover's, the best and only example of the unemployed present was the Secretary of Labor." [17]

[3

THE uneasy wartime truce between capital and labor broke down with the armistice, and the concluding years of the Wilson administration were riddled with labor-management conflicts. Strikes for the eight-hour day, higher wages, union recognition, and a shorter work week punctuated the postwar scene. The Harding administration inherited this chaotic situation as well as the Red Scare-inspired antilabor attitudes which such turmoil created. Faced immediately with a series of strikes in the shipping, printing, textile, and meat-packing industries, it waited nervously on the sidelines maintaining that the federal government would take no part in these disputes but would allow them to be settled by the natural process of attrition between the contending forces. Only in the case of the shipping strike did the administration become directly involved because of the effect on government-owned ships. Then it adopted a thinly disguised antilabor line. [18]

The hope of the Harding administration was to remain uncommitted in all labor disputes and work behind the scenes for conciliation. From

Harding's point of view, the primary function of the government was to exhibit a spirit of reasonableness which would be an example for both labor and management. Through such a spirit, strikes might be prevented and the return of prosperity achieved that much sooner. Said he in his inaugural address: "My most reverent prayer for America is for industrial peace. . . . I had rather submit our industrial controversies to the conference table in advance than to a settlement table after conflict and suffering. The earth is thirsting for the cup of good will; understanding is its fountain source. I would like to acclaim an era of good feeling amid dependable prosperity and all the blessings which attend." [19] Secretary Davis spent much time on the road in the first months of the administration preaching this gospel. To business and unions alike he cried: "Stop trying to crush each other's organizations now. Postpone your differences to a calmer time. This situation calls for patience. Every one knows that a tremendous prosperity lies just ahead." [20]

But while Davis was speaking, Hoover was again acting and stole the show from the secretary of labor. Hoover had become particularly concerned about conditions in the steel industry and, because of the intransigency of steel management, feared a recurrence of the steel strike of 1919. That strike had given rise to a number of investigations which had uncovered primeval working conditions in the steel mills, especially the practice of the twelve-hour day. All observers had recommended its immediate abolition, but steel management had ignored such pleas. By the spring of 1922, however, the continuance of the twelve-hour day was causing not only grave dissatisfaction among workers but some dissension among operators. Hoover, seeing a chance for a break in the situation, seized it.

On April 8, 1922, Hoover notified Harding that Elbert Gary, head of United States Steel, would probably make a statement about the twelve-hour practice at a company meeting on April 17. Hoover said that he did not know what Gary would say, but suggested that Harding send him a letter to "stir his imagination." Hoover even enclosed a proposed draft and concluded: "If he refuses no harm is done and, in any event, it would put the Administration's feeling in the matter right with the public." Harding thought Hoover's idea was a good one, but altered his draft completely, eliminating Hoover's somewhat strident language and blunt phraseology. The president simply told Gary that he personally would be delighted if the steelmen would at last banish the twelve-hour day.[21]

235

When no action or statement by Gary was forthcoming from the April 17 steel meeting, Harding applied additional pressure. With Hoover's support the president invited a group of steelmen to the White House on May 18 to discuss the matter. Forty-one top steel executives ate with the president that day, including Judge Gary of United States Steel and Charles Schwab of Bethlehem. Also present were Secretaries Mellon, Hoover, and Davis. After dinner Harding stated frankly that his object was to remove the "twelve-hour-day blight" from the steel industry and requested their cooperation. He then turned the discussion over to Hoover who presented the administration's case. In engineer fashion, Hoover offered an array of charts, graphs, and figures to show that any cost involved in the abolition of the practice would be offset by a gain in efficiency. Some of the steelmen immediately contested Hoover's statistics and a sharp debate ensued which threatened to disrupt the meeting. Harding saved the situation by pouring the oil of his good nature over the roiled sea of words and finally secured an agreement that a committee under the chairmanship of Judge Gary would study the matter further and make a recommendation.[22]

No action was taken by the Gary committee for over a year. But neither Harding nor Hoover gave up hope for a favorable decision although Hoover had far less faith in the Gary committee than did Harding. Meanwhile, both maintained pressure on the steelmen in their own way. After the White House dinner, Harding leaked to the press the purpose of the meeting and the general trend of the discussion. As he expected, the press wholeheartedly backed the administration. Numerous papers warned the steel industry to follow the president's suggestion or "other means of reform will not be lacking."[23] Hoover, stung by the steelmen's opposition to his figures, requested the Federated Engineering Societies (of which he was president) to study and report on the twelve-hour-day practice. Carried out under the direction of Horace Drury, an expert in scientific management, this study showed that the twelve-hour day could be abolished with a rise in steel costs of only 3 percent. Generally supporting Hoover's contentions, the study was published in November 1922 under the title *The Twelve-Hour Shift in Industry* with a foreword by President Harding which Hoover actually wrote. It said: "I [Warren Harding] rejoice to note the conclusions of this great body of experts are identical with those which I have reached. . . . It has seemed to me for a long time that the twelve-hour day and the type of worker it produces have outlived their usefulness and their part in American life in the interests of good citizenship, of good business, and of economic stability. The old order of the twelve-hour day must give way."[24]

On May 25, 1923, in a report to the annual meeting of the American Iron and Steel Institute, the Gary committee finally rejected the president's appeal for the elimination of the twelve-hour day. Said the committee: "Abolition of the twelve-hour day in the steel industry is not now feasible, as it would add 15 percent to the cost of making steel and would require 60,000 additional workers." Moreover, said the committee, the twelve-hour day "was not of itself an injury to the employees, physically, mentally, or morally."[25] The general press, labor leaders, the clergy, nearly everyone condemned this decision. But no one was more disappointed than Harding. Secretary Davis warned the president that his contact with the laboring element convinced him that the evil of the twelve-hour day simply had to be eliminated at once or "the question will develop into a political issue, which will stir public opinion to unknown and dangerous depths."[26] Hoover agreed with Davis, and on June 13 drafted a rebuttal to Gary which he submitted to the president for his approval. This letter took sharp issue with the Gary committee's decision and reiterated the president's desire that the steel industry abolish the twelve-hour day forthwith. This time Harding changed Hoover's draft hardly at all and sent it over his signature to Gary on June 18.[27]

Upon receipt of the president's letter, Gary replied that because of the president's intense feeling he would reopen the issue. One week later, on June 27, Gary and fourteen other steelmen telegraphed Harding: "Undoubtedly there is a strong sentiment throughout the country in favor of eliminating the twelve hour day. . . . On account of this sentiment, and especially because it is in accordance with your own expressed views, we are determined to exert every effort at our command to secure in the iron and steel industry of this country a total abolition of the twelve-hour day at the earliest time practicable."[28]

Harding was already passing through the Pacific Northwest on his way to Alaska when he was given the steelmen's decision. He decided to use a scheduled Independence Day address at Tacoma as the occasion to make a public announcement. To Hoover fell the responsibility of inserting the proper paragraphs in the already-prepared speech. But it was Harding's voice which read: "I wish to congratulate the steel industry on this important step. It will heal a sore in the American industrial life. . . . I should be proud indeed if my administration were marked by the final passing of the twelve-hour working day in American life." Harding stumbled over the Hooverian passage, but the audience comprehended its significance and burst forth with wild applause. As he sat down, smiling and nodding, he mumbled jovially to Hoover, "Damn it, Hoover, why don't you write the same English as I do."[29]

The next day Gary told reporters, "I can't say exactly when the United States Steel Corporation or any other company will get rid of the twelve-hour day entirely, but I can positively state that they will begin to act in that direction very soon and be very diligent in their efforts." Coincidentally, but symbolically, the day Harding died, August 2, Judge Gary announced that the elimination of the twelve-hour day would begin at once in all United States Steel mills. Eleven days later the Gary, Indiana, plant went on an eight-hour day and others soon followed.[30]

Had Harding lived, he would have credited this favorable result to patience, persistence, and reasonableness. It was a vindication of his belief in the power of conciliation and personal persuasion. Employers were to be encouraged to act benevolently and grant workers' rights not through force but by voluntary agreement. Such a procedure, as in the case of the twelve-hour-day episode, left no scars, no waste, no tragedy, and no hardship as strikes often did. It was incomprehensible to Harding that anyone should want it otherwise.

[4

IF THE Harding administration's relationship with labor could have rested solely on the Unemployment Conference and the abolition of the twelve-hour day, history might judge the record as satisfactory although meager. Unfortunately, Harding's efforts at personal persuasion in labor matters and his ability to elicit the cooperation of recalcitrant employers were not always so successful.

From the beginning of his term, Harding was plagued by severe problems connected with the railroads. As already noted, constant demands for freight-rate reductions along with declining railroad earnings turned a glaring spotlight on railroad wages. Almost all elements, except labor, accepted the proposition that if truly meaningful rate reductions were to be accomplished, some railroad wage cuts were necessary. Predictably, the business world maintained that rates and wages were inextricably bound together and that the one could not go down without the other. But even the farmer favored wage reductions. He wasted little love on the railroad worker whose high postwar wages he now believed were maintained at the expense of a lower farm income. To the farmer, who was suffering the agonies of a devastating deflation, the railroad worker's average annual wage of $1600 was galling. Some rural leaders claimed that the railroad worker could be cut $300 to $400 a year and still be better off than the average farmer.[31]

Harding was trapped by the issue of wage reductions. Committed to lower freight rates for the farmer, he was reluctant to tie them directly to decreases in wages. However, after numerous conferences with Robert M. Barton, chairman of the Railroad Labor Board, and Edgar C. Clark, chairman of the ICC, Harding became convinced that reducing wages was the only practical solution to the freight-rate and railroad investment problem. In the late spring of 1921, Harding voiced his opinion that whether freight rates were decreased or not, a reduction in wages was inevitable because of the continuing deflation.[32]

The president, however, had no direct control over railroad wages. That function belonged to the Railroad Labor Board. Created under the Transportation Act of 1920 as a nine-man quasi-judicial tribunal, this board was empowered to hear arguments and make awards relating to wages, work rules, and other conditions of railway employment. With three members representing the public, three labor, and three management, the board was supposed to act in the best interests of the nation. It possessed, however, no means of enforcing its decisions. Moreover, no provision was made for the coordination of its decisions with those of the ICC which, under the Transportation Act, regulated all other matters relating to railroads including the return on railroad investments and the setting of freight rates.

The first Railroad Labor Board, created in April 1920, had been immediately faced with workers' requests for wage increases because of the postwar inflation. On July 20, 1920, the board hastily ordered wage increases averaging 22 percent. Occurring at a time when the cost of living was extremely high, this decision was generally accepted although the carriers complained that the increase in freight rates permitted by the ICC in the following month (August 1920) did not offset the additional wage costs. When, shortly thereafter, deflation and depression cut drastically into railroad profits, the railroads complained even more bitterly about the situation.

The Railroad Labor Board remained a focal point of controversy. In the spring of 1921, at the insistence of the carriers, the board began a reexamination of railroad wages and in mid-May announced a reduction of 12½ percent, effective July 1, 1921. President Harding and other administration officials supported this decision as an essential ingredient in the deflationary readjustment. But neither the carriers nor the workers were satisfied. The former complained that the decrease was far too small and argued for more while the latter warned that a railway strike was a distinct possibility, especially if further wage cuts were contemplated. This strike threat brought forth cries of rage from elements in the public who clamored for strong government action to prevent it. President Harding immediately counseled moderation and offered a few words of wisdom to those who saw labor as the only culprit on the economic scene. "It is not unnatural," he said, "that the inevitable reduction in labor compensation is strongly resisted. It is very easy to advance rates of pay in the fever of war emergencies, but it is an exceedingly difficult thing to readjust."[33]

Throughout the summer and fall of 1921 there was talk of a further realignment of railroad wages while a strike threat continued to hover. Finally, to show their displeasure with the July reductions and to block any additional cuts, the railway unions on October 15 issued a strike call for October 30. Harding asked Chairman Barton of the Railroad Labor Board to meet with the heads of the five railway unions and avert the strike if possible. When no progress was made, Harding requested the board to arrange for a direct confrontation between managers and union leaders on October 26. The organs of public opinion called upon the president to "use the full power of the government to break any strike ordered in contempt of the law." Clearly, a rail strike would meet with universal public disapproval and the *New York Times* warned: "No great strike ever succeeded without the support of at least a part of public opinion."[34]

President Harding continued to remain calm. In reply to a plea from Secretary Weeks that he issue a strong public statement on the impending strike, Harding maintained "that the time has not yet arrived for a pronounced statement [and] an utterance now, when the Labor Board is functioning fully in accordance with the law, would seem to me much like an invitation to public debate." Harding believed that his function was to support the Railroad Labor Board, not to make decisions or arrive at conclusions himself. On October 24 he wrote to Hoover: "With every passing day I am more convinced than ever that the only sane course for us to pursue is to insist on the railway managers and railway employees alike recognizing the authority of the Railroad Labor Board." Hoover, possessing less faith than Harding in a satisfactory outcome, set in motion a stockpiling and disbursement plan which would concentrate strategic materials near certain industries and move foodstuffs and other commodities along prearranged routes if a strike occurred.[35]

On October 26 the Railroad Labor Board, after talking with both the carriers and the unions, announced that it would not consider any further wage cuts for at least six months despite the demands of the operators, and would turn its attention to reviewing work rules instead. Coming just four days before the strike deadline, this announcement was designed to pacify workers and allay their fears. Labor favored a revision of the work rules as much as it opposed additional wage reductions. Hence, some of labor's militancy was eroded and labor leaders decided to review the strike call. On October 27, after a four-hour session in the Hotel Morrison in Chicago, the "big five" railway unions voted unanimously to cancel the strike. The nation was naturally relieved by the unions' decision and nearly everyone agreed it was wise. At that moment Harding was on his way from Atlanta to Washington and did not get the word until his train stopped at Manassas, Virginia, on October 28. He said the result was what he had expected.[36] From Harding's viewpoint it was merely the natural end product of calmness, restraint, conciliation, and support for the decisions of the Railroad Labor Board.

In the midst of the relief over the passing of this strike threat, few bothered to take seriously Samuel Gompers's warning that the issues which had caused it were not solved and that further difficulty could be expected. Nor was the nation yet deeply enough concerned with a creeping unrest in the coal fields which boded ill for the future. As a result, the late fall and winter of 1921–22 passed without additional public or administration interest being shown in potential strike problems. With the advent

241

of spring, however, the Harding formula for maintaining industrial peace was again severely tested.

The challenge came first in the coal fields and not on the nation's rail lines. The roots of the unrest lay in events dating back to 1919. During the war the coal industry had been carefully monitored by the federal government, but with the armistice chaos swept the bituminous coal fields as miners demanded higher wages, a six-hour day, time and one-half for overtime, a five-day week, and double time for Sundays. The resultant coal strike of 1919, which ended when Attorney General Palmer obtained an injunction, created great labor bitterness and settled none of the issues. President Wilson attempted to adjust the conflict by appointing a three-man investigating commission which in March 1920 awarded an average 17 percent wage increase to miners but allowed no other concessions. This award was accepted reluctantly by the miners and was to run until April 1, 1922.

While the anthracite fields were not struck in 1919, anthracite miners warned that unless they received wage increases similar to those of their bituminous brethren they would not renew their contract with the operators on April 1, 1920. Fearful of such action, President Wilson immediately appointed an Anthracite Commission which succeeded in forestalling a strike by awarding comparable wage increases to anthracite miners as well as granting recognition of the United Mine Workers union. This agreement, too, was to run until April 1, 1922.

Between 1920 and 1922, severe depression hit the coal fields, especially the bituminous areas, and many operators sought to scrap the wage increases provided in the 1920 awards by forcing separate wage contracts on the miners. Since the 1920 bituminous award did not cover nonunion miners, bituminous operators immediately cut wages in the nonunion fields (mainly West Virginia, Kansas, Kentucky, and Alabama) and then proceeded to undersell the operators in the unionized Central Competitive Field (Illinois, Indiana, Ohio, and western Pennsylvania). This caused extreme confusion in the coal areas and in a short time the bituminous miner's average wage fell from $1386 to $1013. The United Mine Workers quickly attempted to organize the nonunion fields in order to save the union wage levels—an action which added to the confusion and invited employer retaliation. At the same time, the union applied strong-arm pressure on many of its own locals which were showing a willingness

242

to accept separate wage agreements. But operators successfully continued to make district and regional contracts thereby undercutting union wage scales and simultaneously reducing the power of the United Mine Workers.[37]

By the early spring of 1922 the union was losing almost everywhere in the bituminous fields and the operators saw no reason to renegotiate a general agreement at the expiration of the 1920 award on April 1, 1922. As a result, John L. Lewis, president of the United Mine Workers, ordered both bituminous and anthracite miners out on strike. Lewis hoped to use the tightly knit and unionized anthracite fields as a weapon in his fight to subdue obdurate bituminous operators. April 1, therefore, found more coal miners on the picket lines, approximately 600,000, than at any previous time in American history. Only the nonunion bituminous fields kept working. Weekly production in soft coal dropped precipitously from 10½ million tons to 3½ million. In the anthracite fields no coal was mined at all.[38]

The Harding administration failed to evidence much concern over the turmoil in the coal fields until the contract termination deadline approached, at which time Secretary Davis, with Harding's approval, attempted to bring the bituminous operators and union leaders together. The operators absolutely refused to negotiate; hence, on the eve of the strike, the administration simply retired to the sidelines to wait. Secretary Davis announced that the government's job was to guard workers, protect property, and remain neutral.[39]

During the first weeks of the conflict, the administration allowed matters to run their course. Davis reported on the strike situation at each cabinet meeting and provided Harding with summary estimates of the amount of coal on hand. He also passed along to Harding intelligence reports on the thinking of the miners which he regularly received from the coal fields. In early May, Davis arranged for a meeting at the White House between Lewis and Harding at which the president indicated to the union leader his concern not only about the strike but about the future of the coal industry. Secretary Hoover, meanwhile, reached a formal agreement with some fifty nonunion mine owners on a voluntary plan to prevent profiteering while the union fields remained struck. But beyond these activities the government did not go. The hope of the administration was that the miners and operators would soon tire of the struggle and that the operators would at last indicate a willingness to negotiate.

Before the administration could react fully to the coal strike, a more immediate challenge appeared in the railroad situation. Gompers's earlier warning suddenly came true. In late May the Railroad Labor Board concluded its review of work rules and simultaneously announced a surprise decision for further wage cuts. Action on the latter had been forced by the 16½ percent freight-rate reductions on agricultural commodities ordered by the ICC in January 1922. Naturally the carriers had demanded a new round of railroad wage decreases and the Railroad Labor Board felt powerless to refuse them. So, on May 28, while announcing certain changes in the work rules favorable to labor, the board ordered a $48 million wage cut for 400,000 maintenance-of-way employees.[40] This decrease averaged approximately 13 percent and, added to the wage reductions of July 1, 1921, returned these workers' wages to what they had been before the increases granted by the board in July 1920. Eight days later, on June 6, the board also ordered a $60 million cut in the pay of some 400,000 railway shopmen, and on June 16 followed with an announcement of a wage decrease of $26.5 million for 325,000 clerks, signalmen, and stationary engine forces. In each of these decisions the vote on the board was 6–3 with the three labor members voting against the representatives of the public and management.

Scheduled to take effect on July 1, 1922, these wage reductions prompted angry reactions on the part of the railroad unions. On June 27 Bert M. Jewell, head of the Railway Shopmen, notified DeWitt Cuyler, chairman of the Association of Railway Executives, that 400,000 shopmen would walk off the job on July 1. The other affected unions threatened to follow suit and it was estimated that as many as one million railroad workers would ultimately strike. On June 29 the Railroad Labor Board made an eleventh-hour attempt to avert the walkout by summoning labor leaders and railroad executives before it. But both sides remained adamant and were obviously spoiling for a fight. Even a direct warning by Ben W. Hooper, successor to Barton as chairman of the board, that a strike would be against the government failed to move either side.

On July 1 the Railway Shopmen struck.[41] About 90 percent effective, this walkout was not immediately joined by others. Walter L. Mc-Menimen, who was a Harding labor-appointee on the board and a former deputy president of the Brotherhood of Railroad Trainmen, quickly put pressure on Edward F. Grable, president of Maintenance of Way Men, to delay their proposed strike. McMenimen also secured a postponement from D. W. Holt, chief of the signalmen's brotherhood and E. H. Fitzgerald, head of the Railway Clerks and Freight Handlers. On July 3, the Railroad Labor Board issued a warning that if the shopmen did not return to work by July 10 they would lose all rights of seniority and their union would be declared "outlaw." This meant that after July 10 the carriers would be free to recruit new men for their jobs and drop strikers' names from their payrolls.[42]

Despite the failure of the other brotherhoods to go on strike and the Railroad Labor Board's July 3 warning the shopmen continued their walkout. No amount of threats or cajolery moved them from their intention to force the Railroad Labor Board to rescind the wage reductions. In this case, as in the existing coal strike, the Harding administration's approach of watchful waiting, coupled with an occasional attempt at conciliation, had failed to pay off. With coal supplies dwindling and rail transportation disrupted, the spirit of reasonableness and moderation upon which Harding had so relied to keep industrial peace now rapidly crumbled and the administration experienced a growing feeling of frustration and futility.

[5

THE mounting seriousness of this twin strike situation ultimately forced the administration from its general inactivity into a more aggressive role. Its first move came in the coal strike because it believed that its chances for success were greater there. Moreover, violence in the coal fields, especially at Herrin, Illinois, where in late June 1922 nineteen strikebreakers and two strikers were killed, lent a certain urgency to a solution.[43] With Harding's approval, Secretary Davis and Secretary Hoover now undertook to bring the miners and the operators together under the auspices of the presidential office. The two secretaries laid their plans carefully. Through Davis, Lewis was invited to the White House to lunch with President Harding on June 26 and the coal situation was discussed for almost two hours. Hoover got in touch with the operators, seeking an agreement on a "preliminary meeting" to examine wage negotiation problems. Two days later, on June 28, President Harding formally issued an invitation to miners and operators for a White House conference on July 1 to "devise methods for negotiations." Lewis immediately accepted, but only grudgingly did A. M. Ogle, president of the National Coal Association, announce that some representatives of the operators would be present.[44]

When Harding opened this meeting, he warned of an inevitable escalation in government action if a settlement was not reached and requested the two sides to bargain in good faith. He then assigned Hoover and Davis to meet with the bituminous operators and miners in separate discussions while Secretary of Interior Albert Fall was authorized to supervise negotiations between the anthracite miners and operators. For more than a week these various talks produced no progress, the basic stumbling block being the insistence by the United Mine Workers that any settlement involve a national wage agreement as opposed to the district arrangements which the operators advocated. By July 8 it was clear that neither side would budge. But Harding was reluctant to admit failure and, as a last resort, on July 10, ordered Secretary Davis to lay before the operators and miners a presidential proposal that (1) work be resumed on the basis of the wage scale of March 31, 1922, (2) the maximum selling price for coal be maintained at the level arranged by Secretary Hoover with the non-union fields in May, and (3) a coal commission be appointed by the president to investigate the ills of the industry and make recommendations on future methods of wage negotiations.[45]

Observers were surprised at Harding's tenacity in this matter and professed to see a hardening of the government's attitude. Some commented on the similarity between the Harding proposal and Theodore Roosevelt's coal strike plan of 1902. But the public was more impressed than the combatants. On July 15 the Policy Committee of the United Mine Workers voted to accept the appointment of a presidential fact-finding commission but rejected the rest of the presidential proposal. To do otherwise, said the union, was to abandon strikers to district wage agreements. The anthracite operators announced their "agreement in principle" with the Harding plan although they expressed fears that it subjected the country "to the rapacity of a strengthened domineering labor monopoly." The bituminous operators were in a quandary. Unable to decide immediately on the Harding proposal, they conducted a poll of all operators to determine sentiment. Finally, on July 17, they announced that a majority of the bituminous operators also "agreed in principle" with the Harding plan.[46]

After the United Mine Workers rejected the bulk of the July 10 proposal, President Harding believed that it was useless for his office to do more and asked the operators to resume work at their mines to the best of their ability. At the same time, on July 18, he sent a telegram to the governors of twenty-eight coal states apprising them of the situation and requesting them to provide adequate protection for the operators and any returning miners. "I want to convey to you in this message," he said, "the assurance of the prompt and full support of the federal government whenever and wherever you find your own agencies of law and order inadequate to meet the situation." According to the president, state and federal governments were "jointly responsible" for the production of ample coal, for ensuring conditions under which men could work in safety, and for maintaining security in all "lawful operations."[47]

All the governors except two immediately pledged their law-enforcement agencies to maintain security at the coal mines. From all over the country came congratulatory messages to the president for this "decisive" stand. But many read into Harding's telegram more than was actually there. In many areas, operators determinedly reopened their mines in the belief that not only state but federal power would *automatically* back them. Organized labor also assumed that the government had finally come down on management's side. Harding certainly had no such intention. To one irate operator who wanted federal troops sent immediately, Harding wrote, "You make a rather peremptory demand that the government send federal troops to the protection of your mine at New Straitsville, Ohio. . . . the federal government cannot adjust its policy to the call of the operators of an individual mine. . . . the use of federal troops is neither authorized nor justified until there is certification of the state's inability to maintain law and order and cut down violence."[48] To another correspondent who urged the president to take over the mines and force the men to return, Harding had Christian reply: "The President does not share your views about government ownership. He does believe that every man in America has the unquestioned right to work or to decline to work as he himself believes. The man who declines to work is entitled to protection from lawless oppression, and the man who chooses to work has the right to be protected in his lawful employment. On these definite policies the government is willing to risk the solution of the pending dispute."[49]

Harding obviously did not look upon his position in the coal strike as either probusiness or prolabor, but simply necessary to maintain individual freedom and protect public welfare. As he saw it, the need was for coal mined by anyone who desired to work. To this end he was willing to commit the power of the federal government if necessary. For the moment Harding was not overly concerned with either the mine owners' feelings or the operators' profits. Nor was his July 18 telegram antiunion in the sense that he consciously sought to undercut the union's power. However, pilloried on the one hand by operators for not *forcing* the striking miners to return, and on the other by the United Mine Workers for extending *protection* to any who did, the Harding administration was soundly condemned by both sides.

If a nonaligned mediation posture was sought by the administration in the continuing coal strike, the same was true of its action in the worsening rail situation. Abandoning all hope that the carriers and the shopmen would come to terms by themselves, the administration in late July began to play a catalytic role. The government's primary goal was to secure employer-employee compliance with the decisions of the Railroad Labor Board.

This was especially difficult since labor had lost all faith in the board. Before the rail strike, the carriers on many occasions had ignored the edicts of the board and had gone unpunished. For example, the railroads had not always followed the work rules relating to holidays and overtime pay, and had often farmed out their shopwork to nonunion agencies in order to circumvent paying union wage scales. Little wonder that labor treated the board with scorn after the wage decisions were made. Labor had come to the conclusion that the board was not only powerless to enforce its decisions but basically pro-management. President Harding sympathized to some extent with this feeling, writing to his antilabor friends that "if the railway executives had fully recognized the decisions of the Labor Board in the past and had complied with these decisions, I very much doubt if we should have the present strike situation."[50] However, Harding believed that in seeking to readjust wage levels following the deflation the Labor Board was only doing its proper duty and that once the wage decisions were made they were binding on all sides.

From the outset Harding insisted that the basic condition for any government-sponsored settlement in the rail strike was complete compliance with *all* the board's decisions. On this basis, in consultation with Hooper,

Hoover, and Davis, Harding hammered out a three-point mediation proposal which provided that (1) railway managers and workmen were to agree to recognize the validity of all decisions of the Railroad Labor Board and execute them faithfully, (2) the carriers were to drop all lawsuits growing out of the strike, and those Labor Board decisions which were involved in the strike could be resubmitted by either side to the board for a rehearing, and (3) all employees currently on strike were to be returned to their former positions with seniority and other rights unimpaired.[51]

This proposal was submitted to both sides on July 31. The railroad executives agreed to the first and second provisions but absolutely rejected the third as "wholly unthinkable." On the basis of the Railroad Labor Board's "outlaw" decision of July 3, the carriers had already hired new men and had ignored the seniority privileges of striking workmen. The executives were therefore especially incensed by this provision and unanimously opposed it.[52]

The rejection of the president's plan by the railway executives on August 1 was followed the next day by the union acceptance of the entire proposal. Frankly, the union was worried. The shopmen were facing increasing difficulty in maintaining strike discipline in view of the solid opposition of the carriers and the inaction of the other brotherhoods. When the railway executives rejected the presidential plan, union leaders feared it was the first step in a management plot to smash railway unionism altogether and they turned to the administration for help. For several days labor chiefs sought conferences with Harding to warn him that a total defeat for the shopmen would not be in the national interest. It was clear from these reactions that wages were no longer a critical factor. The goal now was simply union survival and the protection of seniority rights for striking members.[53]

Throughout, Harding clung to a position of impartiality. To a protest from New York banker Joseph W. Harriman about his "unfortunate" July 31 suggestion on the seniority matter, Harding wrote: "I have a strong suspicion that we both view the rail [strike] from differing viewpoints. . . . It is a very great pity that the railroad strike was not settled on the terms which I proposed." Conversely, in reply to a letter from one union leader that the carriers were immoral in rejecting the July 31 proposal, Harding snapped: "I do not agree with you that the blame is entirely one-sided.

I believe the strike of the shopcraft men to be wholly unexcusable." This pox-on-both-your-houses attitude was clearly reflected in a telegram of August 4 which Harding sent to all carriers and all union leaders: ". . . the government expects both employers and employees to accept and abide by the decisions of the United States Railroad Labor Board, and I now call upon you for that transportation which is requisite to the needs of the American people. This notice relates to all decisions heretofore made and ignored, and to those which may follow, so long as the United States Railroad Labor Board remains the agency of the government in deciding disputed questions between carriers and their employees."[54]

After sending this telegram, Harding made one final attempt to bring the carriers and the men together. In consultation with Hoover and Davis, the president hit upon the idea of submitting the seniority question to the Railroad Labor Board for adjudication after all workers returned to work. This suggestion was formally submitted to the carriers and the shopmen on August 7. Four days later, on August 11, the railway executives indicated their acceptance but on that same day Jewell notified Harding of the union's rejection. Mindful of the various 6–3 decisions against labor during the board's wage discussions, union leaders were fearful that the same division would hold on matters relating to seniority.[55]

As in the case of the continuing coal strike, all attempts by the president's office to mediate the rail dispute finally ended in failure. In both strikes, Harding had striven to maintain a posture of objectivity by adopting a legalistic stance. The right of the individual to work or not to work was to be maintained and the decisions of governmental boards were to be obeyed. Yet his vaunted ability at compromise had not produced desirable results and this troubled him. He was not accustomed to the intransigency which he found in the labor-management field or to the kind of problems which could not be settled by persuasive heart-to-heart talks. He became frustrated and waspish, feeling himself betrayed first by one side and then the other. As the crisis in both strikes deepened, the pressure mounted for him to take summary action against the strikers. However, before mid-August, Harding resisted such pressure. On August 10, at the moment his last mediation offer concerning seniority was being spurned by the shopmen, Harding told a Marion friend, who advocated "cracking down" on labor, that the president's function was not to take sides but to bring peace and eradicate industrial turmoil. He was determined, he said, to "go a long ways to avoid civil conflict" and concluded: "Perhaps the battle between capital and labor must be fought again [but] I would rather seek [a solution] by . . . peaceful methods."[56]

[6

DESPITE President Harding's hope for a peaceful solution to the coal and rail strikes, the increasing seriousness of the situation by August 1922 now moved the administration toward unilateral intervention. A potential coal shortage with winter approaching was of foremost concern.

Already the Commerce and Interior departments had laid elaborate plans to handle the crisis. A temporary fuel distribution committee had been created under the chairmanship of Hoover and by August 1 the Interior Department had completed preparations through its Bureau of Mines to extract from a skeletal group of the struck pits sufficient coal to meet any public emergency. By the time of the rejection of the final presidential coal proposal of August 10, all that was required to set this machinery in motion was an order from Harding. Certainly there was enough public support. As the *Boston Herald* editorially cried: "Democracy is on trial! Warren G. Harding is on trial! The government is on trial!" Significantly, Harry Daugherty, one of the most outspoken advocates of direct action, sent this editorial to the president on August 16 with these sentences underlined and an appended note saying "For your information."[57]

But Harding, exercising far more patience and restraint than many of his advisers, remained reluctant to commit the administration to either seizure or other arbitrary action without a final appeal — this time to Congress. Harding knew the political dynamite in any summary executive moves against either the coal or rail strikers, and believed that Congress had to be involved. On August 18, he therefore appeared before a joint session and presented it with the twin strike problem. First, he traced the major events of the coal strike, placing some blame on the operators for originally refusing to meet with the miners, but putting major blame on the United Mine Workers for rejecting his July 10 mediation offer. He then urged Congress to authorize him to create a coal commission to examine the whole coal industry. He also requested congressional action to legalize the administration's plans for the mining, purchasing, selling, and distribution of coal if the strike continued into winter. Moving to the rail strike, Harding briefly traced its main outline, discussed the problem of seniority in which he sympathized with the shopmen, and mildly rebuked the obstinacy of the carriers. But he emphasized the growing violence on the nation's rail lines and reminded union labor that "there are statutes forbidding conspiracy to hinder interstate commerce." Simultaneously he made a significant reference to management:

I have come to appraise another element in the engrossing industrial dispute of which it is only fair to take cognizance. It is in some degree responsible for the strikes and has hindered attempts at adjustment. I refer to the warfare on the unions of labor. The Government has no sympathy or approval for this element of discord in the ranks of industry. Any legislation in the future must be as free from this element of trouble-making as it is from labor extremists who strive for class domination. We recognize these organizations [unions] in the law, and we must accredit them with incalculable contribution to labor's uplift. It is of public interest to preserve them.[58]

Most members of Congress welcomed the Harding address. The major criticism was that he should have made it sooner. A few newspapers thought it contributed nothing to a strike settlement, but the majority applauded Harding's effort. While labor elements described the speech as "ill-timed" and ignored the president's harsh words for business, businessmen grumbled about the president being too prolabor. This caused the *New Republic*, usually a Harding critic, to comment that the speech was superior since both labor and management disliked it. What the president did, said this journal, was to "think aloud" for every disinterested American. Harding's mail seemed to bear out the *New Republic*'s contention. Wrote one Cleveland citizen to the president: "For years I have been hoping that some Government Executive would come out in an open manner and in plain American language tell the capitalist as well as the unions of labor what their duty is to their country. . . . I wish to offer my humble congratulations."[59]

On August 21 a Coal Inquiry Bill was introduced in Congress in keeping with the president's recommendation, quickly cleared both houses, and authorized the president to appoint a commission of impartial public representatives to study the coal industry and make a report. Then, on August 30, the House passed by a vote of 214–61 an administration-backed Coal Distribution and Control Bill which was slightly modified by the

Senate and was subsequently signed by the president as the Cummins-Winslow Act. This measure created the necessary agency—the Fuel Administration—to execute and formalize the administration's plans for the pricing, control, and distribution of coal during the strike emergency.[60]

Aside from these actions, which Harding had specifically requested, Congress took no further steps. Within three days after the president's message it was clear that few congressmen had any intention of initiating more drastic strike legislation. The approaching November elections made them cautious. Naturally, Democrats, who daily were becoming more aggressive in their condemnation of the administration's handling of the strikes, were secretly delighted by the Republicans' discomfiture and offered no solutions. But even those Republicans who were the most critical of Harding's strike approach sat on their hands. Indeed, throughout the entire summer crisis not one congressman came forward with any feasible solution to the strike problem. Such normally loquacious senators as Borah and LaFollette remained strangely silent. Thus the administration, which had hoped to transfer responsibility to the Congress and place the onus for any disagreeable action on that body, discovered that the strike problem was still in its own lap.

Under such circumstances Harding now found that his moderate nonaligned position was untenable. Public opinion was the decisive factor. From the beginning of both strikes public opposition was manifestly evident. Having not yet fully recovered from the Red Scare, the public reacted with mounting vehemence as the conflicts lengthened, and by August antistrike opinion had become ugly and demanding. Each new disclosure of violence at the mines or on the rail lines was taken as an example of labor's irresponsibility. The stopping of trains and the occasional vandalism that occurred were sensationally reported in the press with a consequent antilabor impact. The abandonment by crewmen of one passenger train in the Arizona desert in mid-August became a cause célèbre and was portrayed as the epitome of labor recklessness. As the *Philadelphia Bulletin* warned in late August, "Whom the gods would destroy, they first make mad. . . . These acts are bringing down upon the unions the crushing weight of an indignant public opinion."[61]

The public greeted each new presidential attempt at mediation with applause and each union rejection with vituperation. However, when the carriers or the coal operators refused to agree on a specific point, public

253

opinion was lenient. By August general opinion had gradually shifted from being merely antilabor to being pro-management. This fact was not lost on the business community, especially the railroad operators, who believed that such strong public support would enable them to destroy the railway unions. For this reason, Harding with his middle-of-the-road attitude was regarded by business not as an ally, but as an enemy—a fact which the *Wall Street Journal* implied on several occasions.[62]

Farmer groups, meanwhile, which no less than labor unions or management were busily engaged in protecting their own economic interests, adopted an increasingly pious attitude and threw brickbats in all directions—at the unions, at management, and at the administration. One of the farmer's chief spokesmen, Senator Norbeck, remarked that "if the farmer threatened to go on a strike for a living wage, he would have little sympathy from organized labor" and added that railroad workers simply *had* to accept their share of deflationary woes. Secretary Wallace voiced a universal farm opinion when in a speech in mid-August he exclaimed: "The farmer is sick and tired of this sort of business. He is disgusted with these recurring disputes between capital and labor."[63]

Never one to adjust easily to crises or unresolved conflicts, Harding by late August was totally frustrated. During the preceding months he had encouraged the two sides in each of the strikes to settle the matter themselves with the government keeping "hands off." That had failed. He had then attempted government mediation. This, too, had failed. Finally he had laid the problem before Congress, but it had avoided the issue. This was the situation when he left Washington on August 26 for a three-day weekend cruise on the Potomac aboard the *Mayflower* with Daugherty, Hoover, Fall, Albert Lasker, Senator Kellogg, Senator Cummins, Senator Watson, and Representative Winslow as guests.

There are no reliable records on what happened during this voyage. From subsequent events, however, it was obvious that Attorney General Daugherty suddenly emerged as the dominant figure in the strike picture. From the outset Daugherty had possessed definite views on the strikes. He did not agree with Harding's mediation policy or with his moderate position. In cabinet meetings Daugherty always pressed for a hard line and often tangled with Hoover and Davis who supported a mild approach. From mid-August on, Daugherty openly championed stringent legal action against the strikers. However, at the one cabinet meeting where Daugherty broached this subject, Harding joined Fall, Hoover, and Davis in opposing such action and the matter was dropped.[64]

To Daugherty the rail strike, especially, was a "civil war" and as time passed and violence increased he professed to see radicalism at the root of it. Like his predecessor, Attorney General Palmer, Daugherty began to talk of "Reds," of "bolshevism," and of "revolution." According to him, "the IWW's" were active in the rail strike and most incidents of violence were caused by them. Surprisingly, Daugherty was the only administration official who "saw Red" in the strike—Harding, for example, never mentioned it—and the attorney general's warnings of impending revolution were discounted even by Mellon and Weeks who also championed a strong antilabor, antistrike line but for economic reasons.[65]

Immediately after the *Mayflower*'s return, Daugherty suddenly disappeared and his office announced only that he had gone to Columbus on personal business. However, two days later (September 1) he turned up in Chicago before Judge James H. Wilkerson of the Northern Illinois District and petitioned for a sweeping restraining order against the rail strikers. Judge Wilkerson had been appointed to his post by Daugherty and much was subsequently made of this connection. But the judge was not known to Daugherty personally and the basic reason for the attorney general's selection of Chicago was not Wilkerson but the fact that the headquarters of the shopmen's union was located there.

Daugherty later claimed that this action was taken with Harding's full support, presumably as a result of a decision reached by the two men on the *Mayflower* trip. Daugherty further claimed that they decided not to tell other cabinet members of their decision until after the injunction was secured. From telegrams in the Harding Papers there is little doubt that the president knew where Daugherty was and what he intended to do. Furthermore, Harding met with the cabinet at its regularly scheduled meeting on the morning of September 1 and made no mention of Daugherty's pending mission. Cabinet members were not informed of the move until it was announced in the press.[66]

The Wilkerson action represented the most sweeping injunction in American labor history. Covering the entire territory of the United States, it enjoined rail workers from tampering in any manner with the operation of the railroads. The striking shopmen and their union officials were enjoined from interfering with any person employed by the roads or desiring to seek employment with the roads. The strikers, their associates, attorneys, and leaders were forbidden to encourage continuance of the strike by letters, telegrams, telephones, or word of mouth; they could not picket, issue strike directions, or use union funds to continue the conflict.[67]

A complete surprise, this injunction had an electrifying effect on carriers and shopmen alike. It also stunned the cabinet. According to Hoover, at the first meeting after Daugherty's return from Chicago he (Hoover) opened with a slashing attack on the injunction and was vigorously supported by Hughes. Hoover further claimed that Harding was unaware of the full implications of the sweeping nature of the injunction, particularly those sections which virtually eliminated civil liberties, and when apprised of them turned on Daugherty with such vehemence that "Daugherty was obviously flabbergasted." Harding, said Hoover, "abruptly instructed him to withdraw those sections of the injunction at once." Secretary Fall and Assistant Secretary Theodore Roosevelt, Jr. (who was sitting in for Secretary Denby) also lambasted the Daugherty action, pointing out that the injunction was too broad and, further, was politically unwise in view of the upcoming congressional elections.[68] Daugherty, in turn, later recalled that this cabinet meeting was actually milder than he had expected, with neither Hughes nor Hoover objecting too strenuously, and only short outbursts coming from Fall and Roosevelt before Harding shut off debate by announcing firm support for Daugherty's action.[69]

Whatever the true nature of the cabinet discussion, management was ecstatic. This was precisely the solution they wanted. Exclaimed Charles Dawes, who was one of the most outspoken strike critics: "The Daugherty injunction in my judgment future generations will regard as the beginning of a new era of law and order in this country." Labor, on the other hand, met the injunction with shocked incredulity. Labor leaders labeled the action "outrageous" and condemned both Harding and Daugherty, reserving for the attorney general special censure. One union after another sent resolutions to the White House demanding Daugherty's removal or impeachment. Most congressmen, having been too timid to provide any solution themselves, now angrily debated the wisdom of the injunction. Republicans, in particular, wrung their hands fearing that the administration had irreparably hurt their chances at the polls. Congressmen were especially sensitive to the fact that the action had been taken by Daugherty—a man with an unsavory reputation and hardly known for his conciliatory qualities.[70]

In view of its virulent antistrike bias, the general public, judging from editorials and newspaper comment, was surprisingly ambivalent in its opinion. Of course, it was relieved that the government had at last moved, but there was some sympathy for the strikers. The *Washington Evening Post*, although opposed to the strike, called the sweeping nature of the injunction "a blow below the belt," while the *New York World* claimed that it was a "clumsy step." On balance, however, the majority believed that some such move was necessary "to maintain the paramountcy of the 'common good' and to uphold law and order." Still, most journals hoped that the government would not press the enforcement of the Wilkerson injunction to the limit.[71]

On this latter point Harding agreed. As Hoover claimed, Harding believed the Wilkerson injunction was much too broad and quickly announced that the administration's purpose was not to abridge civil liberties, but simply to prevent interference with interstate commerce and protect the safety of the traveling public. The president immediately ordered Daugherty to soften the impact of the injunction and the attorney general requested the elimination of its most objectionable parts when he appeared in federal court on September 11 to have the temporary restraining order made permanent. But aside from this retreat ordered by Harding personally, Daugherty remained adamant in his own position and undaunted by the criticism. He did not object to being a lightning rod for the administration on this issue and displayed a flinty "go to hell" attitude.[72]

As for Harding, his name thereafter was permanently tied to the Wilkerson injunction. By allowing the rail strike to be handled in this abrupt manner, he brought upon himself the unrelenting hatred of labor in general and the railway worker in particular. More especially, by this action his own true feelings toward labor were forever obscured. His patience, tact, and moderate views were obliterated by this one explosive action which, in itself, was quite contrary to his previous behavior. But, badgered by public opinion and fearful of the economic and political consequences if he procrastinated any longer, the president finally turned to a trusted friend who offered him a quick and legal solution.

While not fully prepared for the sweeping nature of the injunction, Harding was aware of its probable consequences. To Dawes he wrote that

257

as a result of the injunction he expected to hear "a great deal of grief uttered by Mr. Gompers and many of his shouting associates." But Harding consoled himself that some action *had* to be taken and, in view of Congress's lethargy, an appeal to the courts was the only means left of maintaining "a state of freedom and security in which men may work as they choose to do." The president fatalistically adopted the position "that the maintenance of transportation is of vastly greater importance to the American people than the contentions of either the executives or the shopmen," and that if in maintaining that service he appeared to be a partisan of one side or the other, then so be it.[73] At least the agony of indecision was over.

[7

THE Wilkerson injunction is usually regarded as the climax of the labor unrest during the Harding era. Actually it represented more of a denouement. Ironically, both the coal and rail strikes were in the process of being settled at the time the injunction was issued. Ironically, too, settlements were emerging along the lines originally desired by Harding—between the participants themselves without government interference or involvement.

Prospects of an agreement appeared first in coal. Two weeks before the Wilkerson injunction, negotiations were held between certain soft-coal operators and the United Mine Workers. The primary cause for the about-face on the part of these operators was the failure of any appreciable number of miners to return to work in response to Harding's July 18 call. When only a corporal's guard reported back to work, the operators realized their position was precarious and began to drift into negotiations with the union. Secretary Davis encouraged this trend and through President Harding sought help from Secretary Mellon. Because of his fifteen-year business connection with the Pittsburgh Coal Company, Mellon was able to put some pressure on Pennsylvania operators to settle with the miners.[74] An additional factor in enticing the operators to the negotiating table was the increasing shortage of coal which meant large sales and huge profits if they could resume production.

On August 15 the union and representatives from about 20 percent of the coal fields met in Cleveland and agreed to a formula whereby the status quo of March 31, 1922, in wages and working conditions would be maintained until April 1, 1923. At the same time the president was asked to appoint a commission to investigate the best way of conducting future wage negotiations. Significantly, this breakthrough was engineered by Thomas H. Watkins of the Central Pennsylvania field, a leader in Pennsylvania coal mining and a close friend of Andrew Mellon.

The Cleveland formula immediately set the pattern for other negotiations and for settlements along similar lines. For example, on August 22, operators and miners in Indiana and Illinois reached an agreement on the basis of the Cleveland formula. By early September the strike in the Central Competitive Field was largely liquidated as a result of agreements following the Cleveland pattern. This outcome was a victory for the United Mine Workers since these various agreements, while negotiated on a piecemeal basis, all followed the Cleveland formula and therefore represented a general settlement rather than regional or district ones.[75]

The break in the soft-coal strike created favorable conditions for a rapid settlement of the anthracite struggle. On August 16, the day after the Cleveland soft-coal agreement was reached, anthracite operators met in Philadelphia with representatives of the union. For five days discussions continued but finally collapsed as the two sides were unable to agree on whether arbitration should be used in future wage disputes and whether the wage contract should be extended to March 31, 1923, or to March 31, 1924. At this point Governor Sproul of Pennsylvania, along with that state's two senators, David A. Reed and George W. Pepper, urged the two groups to try once more to reconcile their differences and even presented them with a compromise solution.

The two sides met again in Washington, D.C., on August 29. Fearing government seizure of the mines if they did not act before the onset of cold weather, both Lewis of the United Mine Workers and S. D. Warriner, president of the Lehigh Coal and Navigation Company and chief spokesman for the anthracite operators, indicated a willingness to adjust their differences on the basis of the Reed-Pepper compromise. This willingness was enhanced by a personal telegram from Harding on September 1 stating: "The public interest transcends any partisan advantage that you might gain by further resistance. I urge you in the name of public welfare, to accede to the proposal that has been advanced by Senators Pepper and Reed."[76] Accepted the next day by both miners and operators, this compromise provided for the creation of a separate anthracite commission to study the hard-coal industry, new wage negotiations on the basis of a report by that commission, and the maintenance of the existing wage contract to August 31, 1923.[77]

What effect the Wilkerson injunction may have had in hastening a solution in the coal disputes is impossible to ascertain. Undoubtedly it encouraged recalcitrant operators and miners in the bituminous industry to adopt the Cleveland agreement, and it probably made the anthracite miners more amenable to a rapid solution of the hard-coal problem. Ironically, the injunction may have had more of an impact on the coal situation than on the outcome of the rail strike. The latter was already dying before Daugherty went to Chicago. By August 23, the chiefs of the non-striking railroad brotherhoods, concerned about the effect of the shopmen's strike on railroad unionism in general, began sounding out a score of roads about the possibility of the shopmen concluding "separate" agreements wherever possible. The shopmen publicly claimed that they would never consider such piecemeal action, but privately admitted that they would accept separate agreements if they could secure the reinstatement of strikers and the restoration of seniority rights. It was an open secret that Jewell was desperately seeking some way out of the strike in order to forestall a real debacle.[78]

The Wilkerson injunction gave the rail strikers a momentary lift—a sudden *esprit de corps*—which sometimes follows a shattering blow. But this passed quickly since it remained obvious that the strike was lost. Subsequently the injunction provided a convenient scapegoat for the unions to blame for their inability to win the rail struggle. There was never an admission by labor that the strike itself was a failure. Gompers liked to say that it was a success until the injunction altered the situation. Such claims were nonsense, of course, and the very vehemence with which labor assailed the Wilkerson injunction rested in part upon its own knowledge that the strike was already doomed.

In the long run the injunction undoubtedly stimulated the conclusion of separate agreements. Here Daniel Willard, president of the Baltimore and Ohio and one of the "moderate" operators, assumed an important role. He urged the carriers to make such agreements and indicated his own willingness to do so. This "Baltimore plan," as it was called, was not universally accepted by the executives; some believed, especially after the Wilkerson injunction, that if the carriers stuck together they could drive harder bargains.[79]

The shopmen, meanwhile, on September 13, issued a statement that they would enter into separate agreements, and on that basis the men would return to work. Within the next several weeks, numerous carriers with moderate tendencies, led by the Baltimore and Ohio, signed separate settlements which restored seniority rights but kept the wage reductions of July 1, 1922. These agreements represented face-saving settlements for the union and salvaged the rights of approximately 225,000 shopmen. Unfortunately the remainder of the shopmen (175,000) had to submit to separate agreements by harsh and vindictive managements led by the Pennsylvania Railroad which thereafter successfully herded them into company unions. In some instances, workers continued to strike rather than submit to such terms and as late as June 1923 were still holding out. But these were the exception and finally even they had to submit.

By any standards, railway labor had suffered a staggering defeat. There were some compensations. The Association of Railway Executives emerged less unified with moderate railway operators, such as Willard, gaining in prestige and importance. The strike helped to arrest management's drive for further wage reductions, not only in railway wages but in all of industry. Finally, the strike hastened a revision in procedures for negotiating interstate transportational labor-management conflicts. Specifically the strike eliminated the Railroad Labor Board as a factor in railway labor policy and created the circumstances for the subsequent passage of the 1926 Railroad Labor Act. As the *Nation* put it: "The only party to suffer an obvious and irrevocable defeat in the strike is the Railroad Labor Board."[80]

Of course, the ultimate loser in both strikes was the general public and this fact was politically crucial for the Harding administration. While the journals of opinion debated the success of the miners with their industrial union as opposed to the defeat of the shopmen's craft-type organization, all admitted that the cost of the strikes to American society was incalculable. The consensus was that "neither side [in the labor-management struggle] has made much of a pretense of caring for the public interest."[81] If the public was adversely affected and inconvenienced during the strikes, conditions in the immediate post-strike period were even worse. Throughout the fall and into the winter of 1922–23, there were dislocations of railroad cars, stalled trains, car shortages, and extreme inefficiency on the nation's railroads. Fruit shipments from the Pacific coast took twice as long in transit to eastern markets and millions of bushels of wheat waited to be moved. By mid-October coal production was again 70 percent of normal, but coal could not leave the mines because of a lack of transportational facilities. Prices began to soar and many a cellar was without coal as cold weather approached. Hoover's Fuel Administration, created during the strike and legalized by Congress in September, did what it could to relieve the worst conditions. But it could not forestall the anger of an irate citizenry. As one Massachusetts voter expressed his feelings in a brief note to the White House in mid-winter 1923: "May we have the pleasure of voting for Mr. Harding's opponent?" He signed it "Once a Republican." [82]

[8

WHATEVER chances the Harding administration possessed to build bridges of understanding between itself and organized labor, they vanished in the turmoil surrounding the 1922 strikes. As a result of the administration's actions, labor became irrevocably committed to the belief that Harding and his administration were unrelenting enemies of organized labor.

Labor's position was understandable. Harding's closest advisers were basically antilabor in their views. Mellon, Weeks, and Daugherty were extremely biased, while even those with "moderate" attitudes, such as Hoover and Fall, could hardly be called the friends of labor. Secretary Davis was a lightweight and exercised limited influence. Without any program for labor, the administration merely lurched from one labor problem to another, attempting to apply some soothing balm here and a bandage there, but never really coming to grips with the basic problems. As long as no real crisis existed, the administration could appear to be impartial. But once a serious labor-management struggle was fully joined and a stand had to be taken, Harding and his administration acted in a manner which was pro-management.

Perhaps it is too easily forgotten that Harding fell heir to all the unresolved post-World War I labor problems and that these were exacerbated by the Red Scare hysteria and a crippling depression shortly before he assumed office. Caught in this difficult situation Harding was naturally cautious with regard to labor matters, but he was not as timid as he might have been. His action on the twelve-hour day not only was successful, but under the circumstances may have been the only way to attack that problem. Presidential persuasion worked where force might have failed.

Also, Harding's concern for unemployment and his administration's program for relieving suffering, while meager by later New Deal standards, were nevertheless novel for their day. No such extensive or successful voluntary assault on unemployment and relief problems had been undertaken before. With regard to other labor-management disputes, besides those in coal and rails, Harding gingerly pushed the government into an expanding role as a nonpartisan mediator. Considering the many outspoken antilabor voices which surrounded him, his record in this regard was really better than could have been expected. From June 1, 1921, to June 1, 1923, some 1129 strikes or threatened strikes were handled by the Conciliation Service of the Labor Department and peaceful settlements were reached in 87 percent of the cases presented.[83]

Whatever else might be said, it must also be admitted that President Harding personally labored strenuously and conscientiously to try to achieve industrial peace during his tenure in office. He literally worked himself to exhaustion during the hectic strike-ridden summer of 1922. By Harding's own admission he devoted 90 percent of his time to the labor problem from July 1 to September 1. Reporters remarked on the frequency with which representatives of both sides came to the White House and how great was the pressure under which the president worked. As one reporter commented: "Twice a week, on Tuesdays and Fridays, we gathered around the President's desk for our regular press conferences to see his big frame begin to wilt gradually under the constant strain, to learn, in sometimes blunt answers, that his nerves were wearing raw."[84] Just before the issuance of the Wilkerson injunction, Mrs. Harding confided to an Ohio friend that the president found the coal and rail strikes "most trying." "And as to sleepless nights," continued the first lady, "I know all about them, too."[85]

Despite the administration's few successes and despite the president's sleepless nights in the summer of 1922, the administration's record simply represented too little as far as organized labor was concerned. Harding's laudatory patience in the coal and rail strikes finally turned into a

263

vice. When at last he decided to intervene, he provided no imaginative solutions. Whatever frustrations he suffered, his ultimate reliance on Daugherty and the Wilkerson injunction was an act of political stupidity. In view of the nature of the final settlements, it would have been better for the administration to have continued to procrastinate and temporize. Having not acted aggressively soon enough, Harding acted too aggressively too late.

Harding, although expecting some labor disaffection because of the Wilkerson injunction, was surprised and hurt by the virulence of labor's subsequent anti-administration stand. Reluctantly he came to realize that, regardless of the merits involved, he had largely alienated the labor vote. At the same time he was startled to perceive that he had also antagonized large segments of the general public, to say nothing of conservative business, with his moderate approach. Even the Wilkerson injunction, which rained down upon him the scorn of labor, did not fully rehabilitate him with the general public or with the conservative businessman. By the late fall of 1922 it was painfully apparent that Harding's knack for compromise not only had failed him in the labor field but had inadvertently forced him into actions which themselves were subject to controversy and misinterpretation. If his administration's labor policy offered only a little something for labor, it offered even less to Harding's own reputation as a skillful politician.

IX

America First

WHILE the Harding administration struggled during 1921–22 to compromise differences among competing economic blocs and strove to maintain some semblance of order, it also pushed ahead an avowed program of "America First." America First was a slogan which Harding had often used on the stump and he had appropriated it as one of his campaign themes in 1920. Certainly no other phrase, with the exception of "return to normalcy," was as descriptive of or as appealing to the Harding administration.

At a time of rising national chauvinism and one-hundred-percent patriotism, this sentiment had tremendous popular appeal. It represented a welcome change from the discredited Wilsonism which to many was the antithesis of an enlightened America First policy. Such a sentiment obviously encouraged a tendency toward political, though not necessarily economic, isolationism in foreign affairs. But its effect went far beyond external relations. This attitude also affected major aspects of domestic policy and conditioned a whole range of legislative and executive actions.

In the America First crusade, Harding was more often a follower than a leader. Still, he initiated numerous policies which entrenched America First attitudes more firmly in the political area. For example, he supported Hughes's efforts to conclude peace treaties and liquidate the war on the assumption that such action established the proper condition for a stronger America. For the same reason he pushed the seemingly contradictory goals of disarmament and military preparedness. His demands for economy in government, business expansion, tax revision, and aid for the farmer were based on a desire to create a prosperous and healthy nation which would be the envy of the entire world.

It would be an exaggeration to claim that this America First sentiment was the *primary* motivating force behind all these various events. However, in at least three cases before the fall of 1922, it was the chief triggering mechanism. In each of these situations a different pattern emerged. In the first—immigration restriction—there was almost universal congressional agreement and universal public support. In the second— the Fordney-McCumber Tariff—the customary congressional squabbling and logrolling accompanying a new tariff was evident. In the third—the ship subsidy bill—President Harding and the Congress bitterly divided on what constituted a proper America First program.

[2

THE nativist surge in the early years of the 1920's was far from new. It represented the continuation of prewar trends against aliens and Catholicism. During the war these had been submerged by anti-Hun feelings; but in the immediate postwar period they reasserted themselves along with a wave of antiradicalism. Adding to this resurgent nativism were the tensions arising from the economic depression and a swelling new wave of immigration. Already conditioned to wartime restrictive legislation, such as the Espionage and Sedition acts, the public was prepared to accept new legislative remedies to protect American society from this mass of arriving immigrants, especially those from southern and southeastern Europe, who were allegedly more susceptible to crime, to radical ideologies, to traitorous activities, and to alcoholism than "native" Americans.

By 1920 the demand for such restriction reached a peak. Strange bedfellows were made on the issue. Superpatriotic organizations such as the American Defense Society, the National Security League, the American Protective League, and the American Legion urged shutting off the flow of immigrants in order to curb radicalism. Organized labor, hard hit by the depression, joined the antialien crusade in order to protect natives' jobs and wages. Big business, consistently opposed to immigration restriction in the past, now began to support it, not so much for economic reasons as to ensure society against the ravages of foreign ideologies. Simultane-

ously, the Protestant clergy entered the fray by predicting a Catholic in-
undation if the door was left open, while sociologists voiced fears of cultural disintegration and decay.[1]

Actually, by 1920 the issue was not whether there was to be restriction, but what kind and to what degree. Support for a continuation of an
unrestricted policy had all but disappeared. Even liberal journals, such
as the *New Republic*, while quibbling about particular proposals, reluctantly agreed that "the democracy of today . . . cannot permit . . . social ills to be aggravated by excessive immigration." Presidential candidate Warren Harding merely expressed a widely held opinion when, in
September 1920, he proclaimed from his front porch that he favored
stronger immigration curbs. He was for an America First policy, he said,
that would admit only those aliens capable of "easy assimilation."[2]

Congress had already taken this matter under advisement. The foremost congressional champion of restriction was Albert Johnson, a rabid
nativist from the state of Washington and chairman of the House Committee on Immigration. Johnson and his like-minded House colleagues desired complete suspension of immigration. But the Senate balked at their
demands and supported instead a plan introduced by Senator William P.
Dillingham of Vermont. This measure, named the Per Centum Act, was
finally passed by both houses just before the end of the Wilson administration. It provided for the continued exclusion of Asiatics but permitted
a severely limited European migration, restricted annually to 3 percent of
any nation's nationals living in the United States in 1910. President Wilson, however, ignored this measure and it died without his signature. Immediately after the opening of Harding's special session in April 1921,
the bill was reintroduced in both houses. It cleared the House in a few
hours without a recorded vote and was sent to the Senate where, in early
May, it was endorsed 78–1—Senator Reed of Missouri being the only
person to vote against it. President Harding quickly signed it into law.[3]

The Per Centum Act was the first immigration measure to use the number of aliens already in the United States as a basis for determining those
yet to come. Unlike the Literacy Test Law of 1917, which it now superseded, the Per Centum Act was avowedly restrictive. Moreover, it was
designed to discriminate specifically against migrants from southern and
southeastern Europe. According to its proponents, its additional goals were
to restrict the spread of radicalism, protect the American worker from

267

foreign competition, help relieve the unemployment crisis of 1920–21, and hasten the assimilation of those aliens already in the country. As might be expected, the law was widely hailed in the press and the Harding administration was given credit for it even though the administration had done little more than follow public and congressional opinion.

The Per Centum Act accomplished some of its goals well. During the year ending June 30, 1921, 805,228 immigrants had come to the United States and more than 1,500,000 were expected for the year ending June 30, 1922. Instead, the act reduced the number of entering aliens for that year to 309,556. This reduction was of considerable significance in view of the existing depression and undoubtedly helped relieve the already congested labor market. As a factor in holding down unemployment during the difficult winter of 1921–22, its importance can be surmised although not accurately measured.[4] The law also did restrict that type of immigrant against whom Congress most wished to discriminate. Of the 335,480 aliens entering under the Per Centum Act during the year ending June 30, 1923, and the 357,642 during the following year, no more than 27 percent came from southern and southeastern Europe. On the other hand, more than 55 percent came from northern and western Europe. The remainder of the total came from unrestricted areas—immigration from the Western Hemisphere alone showing almost a sixfold increase by 1923–24. To the latter, of course, the Per Centum Act offered no barriers at all.

In other respects the law was not notably successful. Regardless of the change in the composition of the immigrant population, arriving aliens still crowded into the areas where the greatest congestion already existed. Under the Per Centum Act the states which had received the most immigrants before still received them—New York, Pennsylvania, New Jersey, Ohio, Massachusetts, Illinois, Michigan, and California. Despite the argument that the measure would curb radicalism, there was no evidence that it actually did so. Of the 13,731 aliens barred during 1921–22, none were rejected as "anarchists or radicals."[5]

Also there were severe problems encountered in administering the measure. Responsible for the law's enforcement was Secretary of Labor Davis who but forty years before had entered the country as an immigrant himself. As a result, he brought to the Labor Department a degree of sympathy for the arriving immigrant. In the first few months after the measure took effect, much sympathy was needed because of the hardships which occurred. For example, in June 1921 at the moment the Per Centum Act became operational, competing steamship companies raced to unload their human cargoes, thereby quickly oversubscribing the monthly quota (no more than 20 percent of the annual total could be admitted in any one month) and creating congestion at immigration centers. Thereafter such vessels lined up outside debarkation ports on the last day of every month so they could dart in on the next and disgorge their weary passengers. Much to the disgust of ardent restrictionists, Secretary Davis granted special dispensations to many of these immigrants who were stranded outside the quota. Harding, too, was lenient and intervened where necessary to alleviate truly deplorable conditions. His most expansive order came in mid-December 1921, when he saved almost 1000 immigrants from deportation. Even to the end of his term, Harding took pains to rectify obvious misfortune caused by the law. While in Florida enjoying a much needed rest in the spring of 1923, he received a wire from Fiorello LaGuardia notifying him that 300 Jewish immigrants were awaiting deportation simply because the quotas were filled. The Little Flower wanted Harding to delay their deportation on humanitarian grounds. The president readily complied.[6]

Nevertheless, both Harding and Davis were believers in restriction and recognized that constant exceptions would ultimately vitiate the purpose of the law. Therefore, while they acted to prevent hardships, they also endeavored to tighten the measure and make its operation more effective. They first attempted to secure better Bureau of Immigration personnel and eliminate the deadwood among the commissioners of immigration at the various ports of entry. In the spring of 1922, President Harding created the new post of assistant secretary in charge of immigration in the Labor Department and appointed Robe C. White to it. Also in early 1922 President Harding sent Meyer Bloomfield, a well-known lawyer and labor expert, to Europe to investigate the immigration situation there and lay the groundwork for the creation of United States immigration screening centers abroad.[7]

Because of the administration's attempts to enforce the law while at the same time being humane about it, considerable controversy arose. Both the White House and the Labor Department were often the recipients of irate communications, some of which complained because the law was being enforced and some because it was not. Simultaneously, thousands of individual hardship cases were brought before either the secretary or the president. To aid in screening these cases and to make recommendations, Davis created a Board of Review, one member of which was the old labor leader Terence V. Powderly. The difficulty in adjudicating all these cases fairly caused Davis to remark once in near despair: "The enforcement of the three percent Immigration law [is] one of the most difficult things that has come to the Bureau of Immigration in its history."[8]

Still, by mid-1922, the labor secretary felt confident enough of the department's over-all performance to claim that the law had been administered "with a great record of justice achieved against enormous odds, not the least of which is insidious propaganda."[9] Davis's pique concerning the latter was directed primarily toward those humanitarian groups, relief organizations, and churches which insisted on propagandizing the plight of new arrivals at the entry centers. Davis was not alone in his annoyance. Kenneth L. Roberts, a violent supporter of total exclusion, advised the nation through the pages of the *Saturday Evening Post* not to listen to the "sob stories" of these groups "whose members seemed far more interested in the welfare of foreign countries than in the welfare of the United States." Roberts's prescription for all such stories was to "dilute the tale with a weak carbolic solution and hand it to the ash man when he comes to remove the week's accumulation of trash."[10]

Like Davis, Commissioner General of Immigration William W. Husband, a vital force in the original passage of the Per Centum Act, never doubted the law's value or the effectiveness of the Labor Department in administering it: "I do not hesitate to say that the Per Centum limit law has accomplished the purpose for which it was obviously enacted with a degree of success which few anticipated."[11] Most qualified observers agreed and there was little congressional opposition when in the spring of 1922 the law came up for renewal. By joint resolution on May 11, 1922, Congress quickly extended the Per Centum Act to June 30, 1924. In so doing, a few new provisions were inserted which were intended to strengthen the measure. In every case these provisions made the law more restrictive and its operation more severe. At no time was there any congressional support for liberalizing the legislation and, while some humanitarian groups wailed and business elements indicated a desire to halt a further restrictive trend, the Harding administration strongly supported

270

the action of Congress. On the immigration issue Congress and the White House saw exactly alike.

[3

THE emergency tariff, passed by the special session of Congress and signed by Harding in May 1921, was intended as a temporary measure only. Granting more protection to farmers, the law was designed to lapse as soon as a permanent measure could be constructed which would assure increased protection for both agriculture and industry. It was generally assumed that the duties of the low Underwood-Simmons Tariff of 1913 would be markedly increased and that the nation would return to the Republican policy of high protectionism as last embodied in the Payne-Aldrich Tariff of 1909.

In the rush to reap the alleged benefits of such protection few persons realized what a drastic change had occurred in the trade and financial position of the United States. From being a debtor nation in the pre-1914 period, the United States had become the chief creditor nation in the world by 1920. From 1914 on, American exports had increased drastically and in 1919 stood at $9.5 billion. Although total exports suffered in the postwar economic depression, dropping to $5.2 billion in 1921, the relative position of the United States to the rest of the world did not alter. Obviously, the nation's economic health now depended in part on the continuation of exports and the expansion of external trade. Under such circumstances, any tariff policy which discouraged foreign contacts was both dangerous and short-sighted.

In 1921 Congress and the new Harding administration were only dimly aware of this danger. What they mainly saw was a threat from foreign competition and a deflating economy at home. In a reflex action they embraced increased protectionism as the solution and gave it a high priority on their list of legislative objectives. Even before the Harding administration was inaugurated, the House Ways and Means Committee under Chairman Fordney initiated hearings on a permanent tariff and, shortly after the Emergency Tariff was disposed of in May, introduced a bill in the House reinstituting across-the-board high protective rates. In drafting this bill, the House committee relied heavily on advice from Commissioner Thomas O. Marvin of the Federal Tariff Commission who was a strong

271

advocate of ad valorem duties based on the American value of products rather than on foreign values. As finally passed by the House on July 21, 1921, the measure not only raised rates in general but in the case of certain industrial "war babies," such as chemicals, rare ores, and dyestuffs, created virtually prohibitive duties.[12]

It was expected that the Senate would quickly endorse the House measure and that a permanent tariff would be agreed upon before the adjournment of the special session in November 1921. However, this did not materialize. Farm-relief legislation, tax revision, the peace treaties, and the soldier's bonus intruded on the Senate's time. There were other reasons as well, besides the state of the Senate calendar, which prompted a slowdown on a permanent tariff measure. Hearings on the Fordney tariff bill were begun by the Senate Finance Committee on July 25, 1921, and continued to January 9, 1922. During this time serious disagreements arose over American versus foreign valuation as the basis for determining rates. The former, of course, permitted a much higher level of protection and was championed by those who advocated a "Chinese Wall" theory of duties. Opponents believed such protection was too severe and, while they wished to protect domestic producers from unfair foreign competition, they did not wish to discriminate arbitrarily against all foreign imports. At the same time, bitter squabbling broke out between various competing interests over adequate protection for their products—between farmers and manufacturers, between representatives of East and West, and so forth.

Caution now became the watchword. Numerous observers warned that it was foolhardy to write a permanent law so soon after the war. They pointed to the unsettled conditions in industry, the fluctuation of production costs and prices, and especially the gyrations in the value of European money. Certain members of the Tariff Commission publicly took exception to the advice of Commissioner Marvin and stated that the statistical data currently available were too imperfect to sustain intelligent conclusions about duties. The Chamber of Commerce, meanwhile, watched with approaching panic the growing disunity in the Senate on the tariff question and, in fear of what might emerge, suggested that the whole thing ought to be delayed.

The Harding administration, although still regarding tariff revision as desirable, also began to waver and before the special session ended in

November indicated a willingness to downgrade the tariff in its own list of priorities. This brought forth charges from ardent tariff proponents that the administration was turning its back on permanent tariff revision. Not completely accurate, the charge was partially true in that the administration was vacillating on the proper form of tariff changes. Harding, for instance, was undecided about the feasibility of American valuation as the basis for determining new rates. At first he had championed this approach, influenced to a marked degree by Commissioner Marvin, but as other opinions began to be expressed he commenced to worry about how the nation could maintain adequate imports (and exports, too) if tariff duties were placed too high. In early December 1921 he wrote Marvin: "I am very much at sea in seeking to know what course is deserving of recommendation and support."[13] Actually, by late 1921 Harding was inclining more toward the moderate position held by Secretary Hoover that duties ought to represent only the difference between the cost of production at home and the cost abroad. This "equality-of-cost" principle would permit even the marginal domestic producer to compete with some assurance of success against the foreign producer although duties would still be low enough to encourage high-grade imports.[14]

Simultaneously, Harding's thinking on the tariff was also increasingly influenced by William S. Culbertson, a Wilson appointee and mild protectionist member of the Federal Tariff Commission. The holder of a Ph.D. in economics, Culbertson had for some time been plying Harding with lengthy memoranda on the foreign trade situation and arguing for the principle of tariff flexibility. He maintained that in view of the extremely fluid international situation, the only sensible solution was a flexible tariff which would permit a constant review and readjustment of rates. This review, he claimed, could be undertaken by the Federal Tariff Commission which already was charged with the responsibility of giving advice to the president and Congress on tariff matters. Culbertson believed that rigid rates, whatever the formula for their determination, would prove embarrassing in the long run and would require frequent congressional tampering with all the resultant squabbling and turmoil.[15]

As a result of his exposure to these various arguments, Harding became much more sophisticated in his own thinking on the tariff between election day 1920 and late 1921. He retained, of course, a strong protectionist bias. But he came to realize that an intelligent tariff policy could

273

not be capricious or arbitrary and that it had to take into account a complicated variety of other domestic and international economic factors. His state of the union message to the first regular session of the 67th Congress on December 6, 1921, reflected this awareness. While reiterating his desire for a permanent protective law, he added: "I hope a way will be found to make for flexibility and elasticity so that rates may be adjusted to meet unusual and changing conditions which cannot be accurately anticipated." He continued: "In this proposed flexibility, authorizing increases to meet conditions so likely to change, there should also be provision for decreases. A rate may be just today and entirely out of proportion six months from today. . . . frequent adjustment will be necessary for years to come." As to the proper procedure for accomplishing this, Harding said: "I know of no manner in which to effect this flexibility other than the extension of the powers of the Tariff Commission, so that it can adapt itself to a scientific and wholly just administration of the law." As for the constitutional problems involved, Harding concluded: "These can be met by giving authority to the Chief Executive, who could proclaim additional duties to meet conditions which the Congress may designate."[16]

Some hoped that the president's emphasis on the tariff in his December 1921 message would goad the Senate into immediate action. But still it dawdled. The Senate Finance Committee, which was responsible for all tariff legislation, refused to report out any bill until all the details were carefully considered. Strong protectionists, meanwhile, became impatient and warned of the dangers of continued delay. Representative Homer P. Snyder of New York wrote to George Christian in mid-January: "I dislike to bother you, but I am sure that you and the President want the real downright facts with regard to how the real people of this country feel. . . . the [tariff] delay is absolutely killing . . . the Republican party."[17]

Winter wore into spring and still there was no Senate action. Ardent protectionists became increasingly vociferous and deluged the White House with pro-tariff mail. Harding, in turn, indicated to senators that some move was mandatory if for no other reason than to redeem the campaign pledge of the party. Finally, on April 11, 1922, Senator McCumber, successor to Penrose as chairman of the Senate Finance Committee and a strong protectionist, reported a tariff bill to the Senate floor which was markedly different from the earlier House measure. The Senate version contained amendments embracing Harding's desire for flexibility and was, according to McCumber, a measure which did not rule out foreign competition yet gave American producers adequate protection. The majority of Republican senators greeted this measure without enthusiasm and, indeed, regarded it as a source of embarrassment. Congressional elections were not far off and few Republican senators desired to go before the electorate with a tariff fight fresh on their hands. The *Indianapolis News* correctly gauged Republican senatorial opinion when it said: "It is highly probable that many of them wish the bill had never been introduced or that, having been introduced, it could now be dropped."[18]

The main source of embarrassment was the appalling lack of Republican unity which the tariff debates betrayed and the further party fractionalization which they caused. The confrontation between the farm bloc and business interests was most bitter. Although Senator McCumber claimed that the Senate measure gave "the agricultural interests of the country a better standard of protection than has ever been given in any previous tariff bill," farm spokesmen declared that the farm rates were ridiculously low when compared with those given to industry. The question of rates on wool, hides, sugar, and even peanuts prompted violent debates as agricultural interests clamored for the highest possible duties. In this protection mania, the farmer indulged in economic idiocy. He often demanded exceedingly high rates on those items which he exported, such as wheat, and thus secured protection he did not need in exchange for agreeing to high duties on manufactured items which he customarily bought, such as clothes and building materials.[19]

There was also bitter wrangling over Harding's request for flexibility. Many senators, still suspicious of executive power, zealously guarded legislative prerogatives. Democratic Minority Leader Underwood, despite Harding's specific assurance that he had "no desire to enlarge the Executive's powers," characterized the flexibility provision as "an ignominious surrender to the Executive of one of the great functions of government that belong to the Congress." Surprisingly, some low-tariff advocates and ardent protectionists joined forces in attacking the flexibility idea. On the other hand, the United States Chamber of Commerce, which was anxious to increase export trade, endorsed this proposal. Secretary Hoover, who saw in periodic tariff adjustments a real aid in stimulating foreign markets, warmly supported the principle and even contributed some of the wording to the final legislative draft.[20]

But no one persisted in pushing the flexibility idea more vigorously than Harding himself. On a number of occasions he reminded individual senators that any tariff bill without a provision for flexibility would be a mistake. On August 11, in a letter to Senator McCumber, which was later published, he reiterated how interested he was in flexibility and added: "It has seemed to me that the varying conditions in the world and the unusual conditions following the World War make it extremely essential that we have this means of adapting our tariffs to meet the new conditions. Moreover, I believe it is a highly constructive and progressive step in retaining the good and eliminating the abuses which grow up under our tariff system."[21] This hope of eliminating abuses was exceedingly popular with some senators who saw in the flexibility principle the death knell for congressional logrolling and unscientific rates. Some low-tariff senators also believed that flexibility would bring about reductions from excessively high duties and supported the provision on that basis.

On August 19, 1922, the day after President Harding made his speech to Congress concerning the coal and rail strikes, the Senate finally passed the McCumber bill. There was a last-minute push for even higher duties on the part of both agriculture and industry and the closing four hours of debate were extremely lively. Charges of lobbying and manipulation filled the air, reducing the debate to name calling and several near fistfights. In the end, forty-eight senators voted for the measure and twenty-five against. Borah was the only Republican who responded in the negative. On the other hand, only three Democrats voted aye—Kendrick of Wyoming, and Ransdell and Broussard of Louisiana. The fact that more than twenty senators saw fit not to record their vote indicated a high degree of senatorial disenchantment.

The bill now went to a conference committee composed of ten members including Fordney from the House and McCumber from the Senate. For almost a fortnight this group labored to compromise here, adjust differences there, and logroll. The result was a fantastic hodgepodge of duties, many of which were devoid of economic significance. Both agriculture and industry continued to jockey for preference and their bitterness toward each other increased. When Senator Kellogg complained in the committee that many of the high industrial duties would be resented in the rural areas and might even cause him and other Republican farm colleagues to lose their seats, Representative Fordney retorted: "Well I would rather see the Senate lose you than American industry suffer."[22]

There was considerable disgruntlement in the House over the conference measure and some last-minute sparring occurred before weary representatives adopted it on September 15 by a vote of 210–90. Four days later, the Senate concluded its consideration of the measure. Senator Underwood continued his bitter fight against the bill to the very end. Senator LaFollette indicated that he would vote against the bill, while Borah, who was certainly not opposed to high tariffs for agriculture, railed against high tariffs for eastern manufacturers. Unlike most farm representatives, Borah would not support the one to get the other. The final Senate vote was 43–28, with five Republicans (Borah, LaFollette, Lenroot, Cameron, and Cummins) voting against and two Democrats (Broussard and Ransdell) voting for. Again more than a score of senators did not vote.[23]

At 11:07 A.M. on September 21, 1922, after sixteen months of waiting, President Harding signed the Fordney-McCumber bill into law. Both McCumber and Fordney were at the White House to witness the signing as were other members of the House Ways and Means and the Senate Finance committees. There was some levity as the president presented Fordney the gold-mounted fountain pen with which he signed the bill. But before he did, Harding evidenced his relief at its passage and expressed hope for its success in a brief comment: "Thank you for coming, gentlemen. This law has been long in the making. I don't know how many are in accord with me, but if we succeed in making effective the elastic provisions of the measure it will make the greatest contribution to tariff making in the nation's history."[24]

It was significant that Harding chose to direct his remarks at this particular aspect of a law which in its entirety filled an eight-page newspaper. His reason was not that he disagreed with the high duties, but that this flexibility provision was his major contribution and through it he hoped to spare himself and his party future grief. According to Section 315 of the law, the president was empowered to raise or lower rates up to 50 percent within the limits of equalizing foreign and domestic costs of production. If such rate revision proved insufficient, an escape clause permitted the president to change the basis of valuation from the foreign value to the American selling price, thus allowing a higher duty to be levied on

277

specific items. The Tariff Commission was charged with making recommendations to the president regarding such changes. But under the law only the president could announce them; the recommendations of the Tariff Commission were not intended to be binding on the president in any way.[25]

As for the new rates, the trend was upward and in the case of agricultural products they were the highest in history. The duty on corn was 15¢ per bushel (also 15¢ in 1909; free in 1913); hulled barley 20¢ per bushel (2¢ in 1909; 6¢ in 1913); oats 15¢ per bushel (15¢ in 1909; 6¢ in 1913); rye 15¢ per bushel (10¢ in 1909; free in 1913); wheat 30¢ per bushel (25¢ in 1909; free in 1913); beef 3¢ per pound (1½¢ in 1909; free in 1913). The sugar duty was raised to 2.206¢ per pound (1-1/3¢ in 1909; 1¼¢ in 1913); increases on wool for clothing averaged 50 to 100 percent over the 1909 rates. In the industrial area, duties on items such as fine cutlery and knives were set at 400 percent while the rates on chemicals and coal-tar products were virtually prohibitive. High rates were also established on such ores and metals as manganese, tungsten, ferromanganese, and molybdenum. The rates on iron and steel were restored to the Payne-Aldrich levels of 1909. Items which were lower than 1909 but as high as or higher than 1913 were photographic supplies, cameras, musical instruments, automobiles and automobile parts, bicycles, machine parts and tools, and tires. Transfers from the free to the dutiable list were numerous and reductions below the rates of 1913 were very rare. A few items were added to the free list; some were significant but most were meaningless. Agricultural implements were declared free (there was no competition anyway) as also were coffee (free in 1909 and 1913), leather (15 percent in 1909; free in 1913), and beets and shoes (15 percent in 1909; free in 1913). The latter three items were concessions to rural sentiment. Also on the free list were those perennial favorites horsehair, fossils, bristles, junk, lava, divi-divi, leeches, pulu, and spunk.[26]

Clearly, the Fordney-McCumber Tariff was a patchwork of compromise, political expediency, and economic greed. Farmers, businessmen, and even organized labor enthusiastically accepted protection for their own specific interests and opposed it for the other fellow. The tariff debates rarely involved principle and there were no great clashes as in the past between high- and low-tariff advocates. It was simply a bitter struggle between vested interest groups for economic preference. As the *New York*

Commercial described it: "The tariff now represents the composite selfishness of the country."[27]

Under such circumstances it was perhaps surprising that the law was no worse than it was. While the average of all rates was definitely higher than 1913, the average level of duties on manufactured items was actually lower than that of 1909. But even with the high agricultural rates figured in, the Fordney-McCumber Tariff was not the highest Republican tariff ever passed. If the average level of the 1913 act is estimated at 27 percent, then the comparative figures would be McKinley Tariff (1890) 49 percent; Wilson-Gorman Tariff (1894) 41 percent; Dingley Tariff (1897) 46 percent; Payne-Aldrich Tariff (1909) 40.7 percent; and Fordney-McCumber Tariff (1922) 38.5 percent. The 1922 law was, of course, unique in its flexibility provision. This innovation, however, would never achieve the success in creating "scientific rates" anticipated for it nor did it remove the tariff from politics.

The farmer, having hoped to benefit most from the new tariff, was the first to experience its adverse effect and quickly became disillusioned with it. Indeed, the measure was barely passed before the farmer began to attack the administration for what was his own doing. He blamed Harding and big business for the high industrial duties although it was farm representatives who had logrolled the manufacturer to these rates. As the *St. Louis Post-Dispatch* reminded disgruntled farm elements: "Had not the Senate farm bloc entered into a plundering partnership with other interests this 'tariff of abominations' could never have been passed." To his sorrow, the farmer quickly learned what most observers had claimed from the beginning—that he would lose several dollars in increased prices on manufactured items for every dollar he gained through the protection of farm goods.[28]

In the long run the most serious defect in the Fordney-McCumber Tariff was not its high rates, with their especially devastating effect on the farmer, but its total failure to recognize the changed economic role of the United States in the postwar world. This defect, however, became apparent only years later. For the moment even the disappointed farmer still clung to the notion that protectionism was absolutely essential to economic salvation. In his own protectionist views, therefore, Harding remained the spokesman for his day. Certainly he and his administration were not alone in advocating a protectionist course of action nor were they unique in

279

their failure to comprehend that the creditor status of the United States demanded a total reorientation of American tariff policy. From 1923 to 1935 three other administrations would attempt with equal enthusiasm to enjoy the privileges of a debtor nation and still reap the profits accruing to a creditor nation. During that whole era neither public nor congressional sentiment would permit otherwise.

[4

IF President Harding believed that immigration restriction and a protective tariff were essential to the welfare and prosperity of the country, he was equally convinced that a strong merchant marine was a *sine qua non* of national greatness. Harding did not adopt this view because he was influenced by shipping interests or because of any probusiness bias. An active and aggressive merchant marine was simply an integral part of his concept of America First. As a senator he had consistently advocated expanding the merchant marine and during the campaign of 1920 he had made numerous references to it. Even before his inaugural he exclaimed: "I want to acclaim the day when America is the most eminent of the maritime nations. A big navy and a big merchant marine are necessary to the future of the country."[29] In this regard Harding traced his lineage to Theodore Roosevelt and Admiral Alfred Thayer Mahan.

In the shipping field Harding inherited a sorry mess. Its origin rested in the Shipping Act of 1916 which had created the United States Shipping Board charged with encouraging, developing, and creating a merchant marine to meet the nation's commercial requirements. Placed under the executive branch, this board was composed of five members appointed by the president, and during World War I it operated and maintained a fleet of merchant vessels through a subsidiary known as the Emergency Fleet Corporation. Under contract with this corporation, private companies built ships for the government at premium prices and delivered them to the corporation upon their completion. However, of the 18 million tons scheduled to be completed for the war effort, only one-sixth, or approximately 3 million tons, were actually delivered before the armistice. Except for 4.5 million tons that were canceled, all the remainder were completed and delivered after the war was over. When the last vessel was finished in May 1922, the Shipping Board had received from private builders a total of 2311 ships aggregating 13,627,311 deadweight tons.

After the war this government-owned fleet was an embarrassment and it was expected that the Shipping Board would liquidate it in the interests of the privately owned merchant marine. This the board attempted to do. But in striving to secure top prices for these ships—Edward N. Hurley, chairman of the Shipping Board, wanted at least $150 a ton—the board found few buyers. Those who did buy made only small down payments with the result that after the onset of the depression of 1920–21 many of the ships were returned to the Shipping Board with regrets. Of the 426 ships sold by June 30, 1920, 121 were subsequently returned.

The period 1920–21 was an extremely difficult time for the shipping industry. International markets were glutted and the competition was keen. The carrying trade went to the swift and efficient; coal burners were losing out to oil burners; and steam was losing to the fast motor ship. Most of the ships held by the Shipping Board were clearly inadequate when compared with newer vessels built not for war but for postwar commercial competition. This fact, along with the depression, made disposal of the government fleet an almost impossible task. Indeed, a survey indicated that even the best ships owned by the board could not be sold at more than $30 a ton, which was far below the $200 per ton original cost or the $150 which Chairman Hurley wanted.[30]

On June 5, 1920, the 66th Congress passed the Jones Merchant Marine Act which was designed to make the Shipping Board more effective by increasing its membership to seven and also to make explicit the congressional desire that the liquidation of the government fleet to private owners be concluded as quickly as possible. But according to the law, if this proved impossible, the board was authorized either to charter the vessels to private companies or to operate them itself.[31] Although the board later operated some of the ships directly, at no time did it consider government operation permanent and concentrated its efforts on liquidation and on private charter contracts. As of January 1921, the Shipping Board had 1109 steel vessels in operation with 520 additional ships laid up—251 steel and 269 wood. At that time, according to Admiral William S. Benson, who had replaced Hurley as head of the Shipping Board, the government's operating deficit was running close to $15 million per month.[32]

The Shipping Board faced other problems. Throughout the wartime and postwar periods charges of graft and corruption were constantly hurled at the board by politicians who believed that the taxpayers' money was being squandered on the government's fleet. It was alleged that the board made secret deals with private shipping companies and that exceedingly high fees ($80,000 to $100,000) were paid to lawyers who handled the intricate chartering, receivership, and sale procedures of the board. Suspicion was also voiced that the current operating deficit masked other chicanery too widespread to believe. Such feeling was particularly strong among congressional farm representatives.

This was the situation when Harding took office in the spring of 1921. The Wilson administration had not developed any postwar plans or formulated any principles with regard to shipping, nor had it bothered to investigate the various charges against the board. Harding had made this Shipping Board mess a campaign issue; now its problems returned to haunt him. As Charles Piez, former chairman of the Emergency Fleet Corporation, warned Christian shortly after the inauguration: "The Shipping Board will prove a target of attack in this administration as it did in the last." Herbert Hoover advised Harding on March 17, 1921, that "for your own protection" the deplorable financial condition of the Shipping Board should be brought to light as quickly as possible and "in such manner as to admit no dispute from the previous administration." [33]

Shortly after taking office, President Harding requested Admiral Benson to continue temporarily as head of the Shipping Board while he launched a quest for a successor. His search was marked by frustration. Harding first offered the chairmanship to James A. Farrell, executive head of United States Steel, who had experience in running that company's large fleet of tankers. Farrell declined. Next he considered Philip A. S. Franklin who was president of the International Mercantile Marine, which operated a fleet of American ships but sailed them under the British flag. Fearful that the Senate might not confirm him because of his British connections, Harding finally dropped his name. Then Harding turned to Walter C. Teagle, president of Standard Oil of New Jersey and operator of one of the largest tanker fleets in the world. Teagle toyed with the idea although he feared hostile congressional reaction because of his association with Standard Oil. John D. Rockefeller, Sr., solved the problem by asking Harding not to appoint Teagle because he was badly needed at Standard which was momentarily short of top executives.

Almost in desperation Harding turned to Albert Lasker. Lasker had earlier hoped for the post of secretary of commerce and had been a candidate before Hoover took it. Will Hays, who admired Lasker for his publicity work during the 1920 campaign, had mentioned his name for a number of other jobs and now suggested him to Harding for the Shipping Board position. Aware that he was the president's fourth choice, Lasker was less than enthusiastic and certainly not flattered. But he was touched by Harding's frankness and by the president's direct appeal: "As the President of your country, I call upon you in the distressful position I find myself, with time pressing, to wire me your acceptance." Lasker finally agreed. With obvious relief, Harding replied: "To be honest about it, I have doubts about whether anybody who gets on the Shipping Board is entitled to congratulations, because you have now got tangled up with the 'damndest' job in the world."[34]

Lasker knew almost nothing about shipping. This fact caused some skittishness in Congress although shipping interests endorsed his appointment. Admittedly, he was a "human dynamo" and possessed the kind of take charge personality that was required to straighten out the shipping mess. Tall, taut, and slim, Lasker was the personification of efficiency and orderliness. He was also extremely egotistical. He had a "Judaic sense of righteousness" and could be obstinate to the point of immobility. He liked to play poker and was one of the common faces at the president's table, but he was puritanical in almost every other respect. He never learned to drive a car and hated the telephone. Almost vulgar in his disdain for the "mob," Lasker made no effort to hide his contempt for popular stupidity and proudly displayed the eccentric habits which had made him an extremely successful advertising executive. He had begun work for Lord and Thomas of Chicago in 1898 for $10 a week and left it in 1942 a multimillionaire, having become the "father of modern advertising." It was estimated that during his lifetime he made $45 million by, as he phrased it, being "an apostle of the obvious." Lucky Strike, Pepsodent, Kleenex, RCA, and Frigidaire were but a few of the products he popularized. He was a master of the tricky slogan, encouraging women to "Keep That School Girl Complexion" or "Reach for a Lucky Instead of a Sweet."[35] At the moment, however, his problem was to advertise an unwanted fleet of ships and get rid of it.

Along with Lasker, Harding appointed to the Shipping Board in June

1921 George E. Chamberlain, Meyer Lissner, Edward C. Plummer, T. V. O'Connor, Frederick I. Thompson, and Admiral Benson. This was an able board and its members worked well as a unit. All were devoted to the creation of a strong merchant marine and all held Lasker in high esteem, considering him to be an "extraordinary executive." At critical moments he always received their full support.[36]

In assuming the chairmanship of this board, Lasker told Harding that he would keep it for no more than two years by which time he intended to have the shipping problem solved. He began with a flourish. He moved into his Washington headquarters immediately upon his appointment and shocked Washingtonians by bringing along his "receptionist," Jim Sloane, who always wore a six-shooter. Lasker then hired the best legal and shipping talent he could find at unprecedented salaries—some as high as $25,-000 a year—while paying himself only $10,000. None of this endeared him to economy-minded congressmen but he produced quick results. He was instrumental in untangling a maritime tie-up by the Marine Engineers Union in June 1921. He began reevaluating all the contracts granted by the former board under which private business operated Shipping Board vessels. These contracts, which were ridiculously advantageous to private interests, were condemned by Lasker as representing "the most shameful piece of chicane, inefficiency, and of looting of the Public Treasury that the human mind can devise." In several cases he removed the best government ships from such contract arrangements and returned them to direct government operation. At the same time, in a controversial action, he ordered the reconditioning of the 59,597-ton former German liner *Leviathan* which the United States had seized during the war, in order to bring her into competition with the British *Aquitania* and *Olympic*.

In August 1921 Lasker completed his first assault on the surplus fleet problem by announcing the sale of 205 wooden vessels to a New York company for $430,500. This represented only $2100 apiece and all 205 ships brought less than the original cost of one. Even at this price there was only one bidder for the lot. Still, numerous congressmen, especially farm representatives, claimed Lasker was underpricing valuable government property. When asked about the low figure by a newspaperman, Commissioner Plummer replied: "The Board considers the Government lucky to get rid of them at this price." Supporting the administration, the *Chicago Tribune* said: "The shipping board has done a wise thing, we believe, in getting rid of 205 wooden ships at any price. In the hands of the board they are worthless."[37]

Lasker was much less successful in his drive to eliminate continuing government operational deficits. Poor private contractual arrangements, the continuing depression in the shipping industry, and the increasing obsolescence of the Shipping Board fleet contributed to this situation. Since 1916 the Congress had appropriated almost $3.5 billion in an attempt to build and operate a national merchant marine, yet the annual loss by late 1921 was running almost $150 million. At that time government-operated ships could not carry grain to starving Russia as cheaply as could American private lines, and the latter charged more than foreign competitors.[38] If American merchantmen, especially government-operated merchantmen, were losing the competitive battle, domestic passenger vessels were faring no better. Lasker tried everything to encourage travel on American lines. The fact that liquor was forbidden on American ships because of prohibition did not help, but Lasker compensated for this by supplying passengers with unlimited caviar, name bands like Paul Whiteman's and singers like Morton Downey, first-run movies, and the opportunity to drive free golf balls into the sea.

Because success was limited, there was considerable criticism of the Shipping Board by late 1921, and especially of Lasker. He had not liquidated the Shipping Board fleet nor had he eliminated operating deficits; and he seemed as addicted as his predecessors to employing high-salaried shipping experts and legal counselors. While he talked about taking the government out of the shipping business, he still attempted to revitalize government operations by such ventures as the *Leviathan*. Moreover, he had established no clear-cut guidelines for a permanent American merchant marine policy. President Harding nevertheless continued to support Lasker and warned his critics that it would take time to discover a way out of the shipping difficulty. Lasker, he said, was attempting to halt waste and bring losses to a minimum as a first step. Only when that was accomplished, said the president, "may [we] make gratifying progress toward the firm establishment of an American Merchant Marine."[39]

How much of the subsequent ship subsidy plan was the president's and how much was Lasker's is impossible to say. The impetus was certainly supplied by Harding. In the late fall of 1921, he began to prod Lasker to find a permanent solution to the shipping problem and Lasker ordered his experts to supply him with recommendations. Thereafter Lasker visited the White House frequently, seeking the president's views and informing him of his own progress. Lasker later claimed that "the ship subsidy plan, from beginning to end, was President Harding's personal plan."[40] No doubt this was an exaggeration, yet Harding did make suggestions and was directly involved in its development.

On February 28, 1922, Harding unfolded this plan in a special message before a joint session of Congress. First, he reiterated his desire for the United States to possess a great merchant fleet and the reasons why such a fleet was necessary. Then he traced the wartime need for ships, the activities of the Shipping Board, the postwar legacy, the various attempts of his administration to reduce costs and sell ships, and the current situation. He indicated that at that moment the government was losing $16 million per month through its private contract arrangements and on the operation of its own fleet. The immediate solution, he claimed, was for the government to sell the entire fleet to private interests for whatever it would bring and to substitute a direct subsidy formula for the private contract system. Under the plan, a merchant marine fund would be created to aid private shippers in building new ships as well as in buying the government fleet by setting aside 10 percent of the revenues from the tariff plus all the income from tonnage and various navigation taxes. Subsidies would be paid to private shippers in foreign trade on the basis of one-half cent per gross ton for every 100 miles with a further bounty for speed increasing upward to 2.6 cents per gross ton per 100 miles for 23-knot vessels. Shippers could make up to 10 percent annual profit, but any excess was to be divided between the owners and the government until the amount of the subsidy was paid back. The president estimated the total cost of such subsidies at $30 million per year. Harding's plan also called for the creation of a merchant marine naval reserve of 500 officers and 30,000 men, compulsory transportation of government officials and freight on American vessels, the creation of an army transport service, domestic control of marine insurance, preferential rail rates on through shipments in American vessels, and the extension of continental coastwise laws to the Philippine Islands. Harding concluded his presentation of the subsidy bill with the following admonition:

We have voiced our concern for the good fortunes of agriculture, and it is right that we should. We have long proclaimed our interest in manufacturing, which is thoroughly sound, and helped to make us what we are. In the evolution of railway transportation we have revealed the vital relationship of our rail transportation to both agriculture and commerce. We have been expending for many years large sums for deepened channels and better harbors and improved inland waterways, and much of it has found abundant return in enlarged commerce. But we have ignored our merchant marine. The World War revealed our weakness, our unpreparedness for defense in war, our unreadiness for self-reliance in peace.[41]

According to Harding, the time for a change was now.

Harding obviously saw the subsidy proposal as another facet of America First. He considered ship subsidies to be no different from the tariff. To Harding, such a proposal was in the national interest and while its immediate benefits might accrue to the advantage of some (i.e. the shippers), the ultimate result was of benefit to all. Harding never considered his subsidy proposal probusiness, or pro-shipping, or anti-agriculture. And he was surprised when opponents of the plan took this approach. Opposition to ship subsidies was no more understandable to him than opposition to protective rates on wheat or on steel. From his viewpoint, those who were hostile to ship subsidies were parochial in their outlook. Certainly they did not possess the dream of America as the great maritime nation which he, Mahan, and Roosevelt envisioned.

Whatever the merits of the specific provisions of the Harding plan, there was much to be said for ship subsidies. Great Britain traditionally had paid subsidies in order to maintain its commercial supremacy on the high seas. Canada was providing a $3 million annual subsidy to its shippers. France, too, paid a variety of direct and indirect subsidies to enhance the competitive position of her merchant vessels; so did the Union of South Africa, Spain, Portugal, and Japan. This fact of foreign subsidies, as well as the realities of the existing American shipping situation, caused many to announce immediate support for Harding's request. Said the *Philadelphia Inquirer*: "One thing is certain. If the day is to be saved and American service secured, it [the Harding plan] or something akin to it must be adopted." All the Hearst papers ultimately supported the proposal. Hearst, who really favored government ownership and operation, on March 19 declared: "The Hearst papers have never been in favor of a ship subsidy, but they will support the proposal of President Harding on the purely patriotic grounds that it is better to have a merchant marine created by a ship subsidy than not to have a merchant marine at all."[42]

287

Others came forward to support the plan. Secretary Hoover backed it although he would have retained a small fleet under government auspices to initiate new trade routes, even at a loss in operation. Senator Wesley Jones, chairman of the Senate Commerce Committee, also threw his weight behind it. Of course, shipping and industrial interests endorsed the proposal, especially ship companies, ship builders, exporters-importers, and dockyards. They all joined in a plethora of propaganda to make it a reality.[43]

There were those who just as readily opposed it. From the outset elements in organized labor voiced strong opposition. Not only did Samuel Gompers declare against the proposal but Andrew Furuseth, president of the International Seamen's Union, condemned it. The latter saw in the creation of a merchant marine naval reserve a potential strikebreaking force. Economic conservatives, especially those from the South, opposed the scheme on the assumption that subsidies of any kind were dangerous and represented little more than a form of public robbery. They questioned the plan's cost and disagreed with the *Washington Post* which claimed that the price of the subsidy was merely "a trifle" compared with the advantages involved.[44]

In the main, the earliest and most vigorous opposition came from spokesmen for the farmer. Secretary Wallace very much doubted the wisdom of the ship subsidy plan and conducted a hit-and-run debate with Lasker over it. Lasker resented Wallace's attitude and on numerous occasions attempted to poison Harding's mind against the agriculture secretary.[45] Senator Capper, despite direct pressure from the White House, announced his refusal to support the administration on this matter. Other important farm-bloc senators followed suit. Senator Borah unleashed a torrent of abuse on the administration for its subsidy suggestions. The majority of midwestern, southern, and Rocky Mountain newspapers railed against the proposal, maintaining it was designed to help the eastern seaboard and wealthy shipping interests at the expense of everyone else. Such journals warned that the other sections of the country would not tolerate such favoritism. This bird will come home to roost, said the *Louisville Courier-Journal*, "and a bird it is!—wide-mouthed, hooked-beaked, spear-taloned—as voracious a fledgling bird of prey as was ever brooded by cormorants who lived to gorge on the Government."[46]

288

It was a divided and unenthusiastic Congress which in the early spring of 1922 held joint hearings on the administration-sponsored ship subsidy bill. Lasker testified masterfully before the Senate Commerce and the House Merchant Marine and Fisheries committees, presenting an engrossing story of the shipping trouble and replying with ready knowledge to all questions. But it was soon obvious that the subsidy plan would have to be sold to more than the hearing committee if the bill was to pass Congress.[47]

From the beginning Lasker realized that his major opponent was the farmer and he sought immediately to neutralize this opposition. On April 7, 1922, he requested Harding "to get in touch with the gentlemen named on the enclosed sheet, who are leaders of the farm movement in America. . . . Their cooperation is of such great importance that if you could see your way clear to do them the honor to ask them to lunch with you, that act in itself would be most helpful."[48] Those named included Gray Silver, James Howard, Charles S. Barrett (president of the National Farmers' Union), and Thomas C. Atkeson (Washington representative of the National Grange). A private White House luncheon was arranged a few days later which Lasker also attended. Because of Lasker's persuasiveness and the president's pressure, Howard reluctantly crossed over to the administration's side and on April 22 wired Harding that "while the American Farm Bureau is opposed to a subsidy in principle," it recognized the necessity in this case. Concluded Howard: "We approve aid temporarily until our flag can be established on [the] high seas but no longer." As Howard later told Lasker, after he declared for the ship subsidy bill his job "wasn't worth a nickel."[49]

Throughout the remainder of the spring, Lasker conducted an intensive propaganda drive in the press and among farm-bloc congressmen. President Harding supplemented Lasker's activities with White House pressure. Harding was acutely aware of the opposition's rising criticism against the "saturnalia of graft" allegedly embedded in the Lasker Shipping Board and against the supposed collusion between the board and private shipping interests. Such claims circulated freely in rural areas and fitted neatly into the existing rural psychosis that a conspiracy against farmers was in operation. Realizing that in these areas time was not on his side, Harding on May 9 invited the Republican members of the joint

289

hearing committee to the White House where Lasker again carefully detailed the need for the ship subsidy bill and the president emphasized that he wanted it passed as quickly as possible.[50]

In late May and early June, Harding continued to exert pressure. On May 26 he wrote Representative Philip P. Campbell, chairman of the House Committee on Rules, requesting immediate consideration for the merchant marine proposal. He pointedly warned: "So much is involved and such a difficult and discouraging situation will follow if Congress fails to sanction the Merchant Marine Bill that I should feel myself obligated to call Congress immediately in extraordinary session to especially consider it if it went over through any neglect or delay beyond the present term." A week later, on June 3, Harding called a White House conference involving Speaker Gillett, Floor Leader Mondell, Campbell of the Rules Committee, Chairman Towner of the Republican caucus, and George W. Edmonds of the House Merchant Marine and Fisheries Committee to develop strategy for passing the ship subsidy bill. Again the president emphasized that he expected the party leadership to secure adoption of the bill and that he would tolerate no delay. Displaying unusual firmness, he rejected his guests' pleas for postponement and stated flatly that he wanted the ship subsidy bill "above everything else." The *New York Times* correctly gauged the situation: "Mr. Harding is bent on forcing the Ship Subsidy bill upon his weary party in Congress. . . . Neither the Congress nor the country seems to have anything like Mr. Harding's zeal for it."[51]

Indeed, Harding faced open rebellion among the House leadership over the ship subsidy bill. On June 11 Representative Mondell again argued with Harding about the wisdom of the move, pointing out that even if the House passed the bill, the Senate would never get to it because of its current preoccupation with the Fordney-McCumber Tariff. Why, asked Mondell, should the president risk splitting the party over an issue which could not possibly be resolved before the 1922 fall elections anyway? Harding replied on June 14 that he would not be dissuaded from pushing ahead and added: "I confess my amazement at much of the opposition in Congress. . . . I do not see how the party in power can escape its responsibility in doing everything possible to [create a strong merchant marine]." Two days later Mondell wrote to the president that because of his insistence the bill would be introduced but that the latest head count revealed only 159 Republicans and 6 Democrats who would vote for it as opposed to 100 Democrats and at least 80 Republicans who would vote against it.[52]

On the weekend of June 18 Speaker Gillett, Mondell, and other administration leaders, including Lasker, were guests of the president aboard the *Mayflower*. Further discussions were held on the impending fate of the ship subsidy measure and Mondell renewed his plea for postponement —at least until after the Fordney-McCumber Tariff passed the Senate. Faced with certain defeat in the House, Harding reluctantly agreed and on June 20 sent Mondell a letter indicating that he would accept a temporary postponement of the subsidy matter "until approximately such time as House members will be called in active attendance to send the tariff bill to conference." He warned, however, that he would then brook no further delay. The public, said the president, had already shown its attitude on a merchant marine by its vote for him in 1920 and the time had long passed for Congress to act.[53]

On June 30, 1922, the House recessed for six weeks, ostensibly to await final Senate action on the tariff, but really, as some said, to "carry the subsidy bill to the people." Most congressmen, however, had already made up their minds and home opinion merely reinforced their positions. Harding and Lasker, meanwhile, remained at work. On the day the House recessed, the president invited a group of farm leaders to the White House for dinner, again to have Lasker present the administration's case. Called at the suggestion of Howard, who felt increasingly isolated because of his pro-administration stand, this meeting was attended by such men as John L. Boland (Missouri Farm Bureau Federation), William S. Hill (South Dakota Farm Bureau Federation), C. W. Hunt (Iowa Farm Bureau Federation), Ralph Snyder (Kansas Farm Bureau Federation), D. A. Wallace (*Minnesota Farmer*), and John T. Orr (Texas Cotton Marketing Association). The meeting's avowed purpose was to convince the forces behind the farm bloc that the subsidy measure was in their long-range interests.[54]

This attempt, and all others like it, failed. First of all, the growing seriousness of the coal and rail strikes in July and August 1922 severely hampered the administration in pushing its ship subsidy campaign. Harding became increasingly involved in the labor disputes and devoted less and less time to the ship subsidy matter. Then, too, the administration dis-

covered no dramatic way by which it could convey to farmers how subsidies for a merchant marine would benefit them. Specifically it found no
antidote for the misleading information and emotional oratory which filled
western rural communities on the subsidy issue.[55]

To the end, it was this rural sentiment which kept the ship subsidy
proposal in a beleaguered position. On July 10 the Iowa Farm Bureau
Federation reported that a ballot among its Iowa membership indicated
sentiment was running thirty to one against the plan, and the federation
recommended that proponents of the measure not "waste their time" in
attempting to convince farmers of its value. Lasker, who kept a close check
on newspaper editorials during the summer of 1922, had to admit that
although industrial areas and the seacoast states were for the bill, the rural
areas and the Midwest remained heavily against it.[56]

When the House reconvened on August 15, Republican members were
now more than ever convinced that the administration should drop the
issue. Mondell and other House leaders again pressed Harding for postponement, maintaining that no point would be served in heightening dissension within the party so close to the fall elections. Besieged by the
labor turmoil and disturbed by the Senate's continued dalliance on the
Fordney-McCumber Tariff, Harding reluctantly agreed and on August 23
sent Mondell a letter accepting another postponement "until we can rivet
the attention of Congress on the ship subsidy matter alone."[57]

Temporarily, therefore, a breathing spell ensued on the question of
ship subsidies. The Wilkerson injunction, strike legislation, and the final
passage of the Fordney-McCumber Tariff subsequently engaged the attention of Congress and the president before the fall election recess. But
it was clear that Harding did not intend to abandon his pet measure permanently. Critics and later writers jumped to the conclusion that he reacted in this determined manner because he was a captive of predatory
capital and was in league with insidious shipping interests. This was nonsense. Only two factors could prompt Harding to adopt such a tenacious
stand in the face of vigorous congressional and party opposition—patriotism and a desire for economy. Harding's strong belief in economy
conflicted sharply with the continued loss of millions of dollars each year
through unprofitable government shipping operations. Simultaneously his
late nineteenth-century brand of patriotism fervently embraced American
supremacy on the high seas as a matter of national pride. These factors,

and not his capture by vested interests, forced him to hold fast to his subsidy position.

To return shipping to private hands was never Harding's *primary* goal, and he did not concentrate on this aspect either in his letters or in his speeches. Indeed, there were indications that he might have supported continued government operation if it could have been accomplished economically and if it would have resulted in a strengthened merchant marine. The creation of the latter was his primary goal and he never denied it. To place the American flag in a dominant trading position all over the world seemed to him to outweigh all detracting arguments. This was a mandate which sprang from his brand of America First. On this issue he was willing to wait and fight again another day.

X

Verdict at the Polls

[1

BY THE fall of 1922, the basic outline of the Harding program was clearly visible. The product of some planning and much compromise, the record was by no means a failure. In relation to Harding's 1920 campaign promises, the administration's achievements were rather impressive. In foreign affairs, it not only had normalized relationships with former enemy states, but had served as host to a successful international disarmament conference. At home the administration had encouraged a resurgence of business confidence by lowering taxes and stimulating trade. It had initiated a program of government savings and had established a system of budgeting. It had attacked the agricultural depression by supporting farm-relief measures as well as catering to rural demands for lower freight rates. It had made some headway against the unemployment crisis and had attempted to maintain industrial peace in the face of the intransigency of both capital and labor. It had endorsed further immigration restrictions and, in spite of congressional reluctance, had forced the adoption of a permanent tariff law which provided for flexibility while at the same time offering protection to both agriculture and industry. Only on the matter of strengthening the merchant marine had the administration failed to achieve its announced objectives.

This record, however, had been compiled at considerable cost. Representing the ultimate in compromise politics, the Harding program had contained something of benefit for everyone. But in certain particulars it had also antagonized everyone. Ironically, the most vociferous hostility had come from within the Republican party itself. Most of this opposition, as in the case of the farm bloc, arose not from any deep attachment to the national welfare—although the claim was often righteously made—but from the specific requirements of postwar sectional or occupational self-interest. Congress, meanwhile, showed itself to be merely a congeries of competing and conflicting regional and economic groupings, generating a collective wisdom no greater than the lowest common denominator would permit.

Congressional inadequacy and intraparty strife were only two of the public-relations problems, although perhaps the most important ones, confronting Harding vis-à-vis the electorate in the fall of 1922. Obviously the executive branch also possessed some weaknesses too glaring for the voters to miss. But in giving its verdict on the administration's program in 1922 the electorate offered a somewhat distorted clue to its acceptance or rejection of the Harding leadership. In the 1922 election, as in every congressional election, the defects of the incumbent administration received much greater attention than administration successes. Campaign oratory lent itself more to attack than to defense and the supercharged harangues of attackers always made more interesting press copy than the efforts of defenders. Significantly, in 1922 the administration's opponents steered clear of such customary favorites as foreign policy, taxes, and government spending, and concentrated instead on other more specific matters such as the soldier's bonus, ship subsidies, the activities of Harry Daugherty, the handling of the patronage, and "Newberryism." In each of these latter instances, the Harding administration was indeed vulnerable although perhaps not quite as vulnerable as opposition oratory professed.

[2

FROM the day of his appointment Harry Daugherty had been a focal point of much anti-administration criticism, and he filled that role proudly. Rough in personality and a tough fighter, Daugherty not only made enemies but encouraged them. Caring little for popular acclaim, he scorned public opinion and often antagonized it. In his treatment of the press, he was the opposite of Hughes and Hoover, going out of his way to confuse newspapermen. Moreover, he held many congressmen in contempt and, as one of his close friends remembered, kept them waiting in his outer office while he attended to minor business.[1] Appearing arrogant and high-handed, Daugherty inevitably affected the image of the entire administration adversely.

Some of this gruffness was deceiving. His close attachment to his invalid wife was touching, betraying a deep sensitivity behind his hard exterior. Crippled with arthritis, Mrs. Daugherty first lived with him in Washington in a Wardman Park Hotel apartment, but her worsening condition finally forced her to spend most of her time at the Johns Hopkins Hospital in Baltimore or at their winter home in Florida. Despite intensive treatment and an extremely painful operation in which the joints of both legs were broken to prevent rigidity, Mrs. Daugherty ultimately regressed to a state of complete helplessness. Through it all Daugherty spent much time shuttling back and forth between her sickbed and his Washington office.

Daugherty's attachment to his wife was matched only by his loyalty to Warren Harding. As already noted, Harding had repaid this loyalty by appointing him attorney general over almost universal opposition. Because of this, it was generally assumed that Daugherty held great power over Harding and numerous solons purposely "played up" to the attorney general in the belief that he was a sure way to the president.[2] Daugherty was closer to Harding than any other government officer or friend, but those who were involved in the inner workings of the administration knew that the attorney general, except on a few matters (such as political strategy), wielded no decisive influence over the president's actions.

As a lawyer Daugherty made a competent attorney general. The various legal opinions which he gave in that capacity were well argued and stood the test of time. Except for the controversial Wilkerson injunction and the war fraud cases, his official actions were correct and directed toward protecting the interests of the government. His performance strictly as a lawyer was at least skillful enough to receive the personal endorsement of Chief Justice William Howard Taft.[3]

The Justice Department under Daugherty did not undergo extensive renovation or reorganization, but a few salutary changes were made. Finding the department in chaos as a result of his predecessor's concentration on the radical menace, Daugherty immediately attempted to liquidate all remaining cases against radicals and cancel any outstanding warrants. He also pared the dockets of the federal courts which were clogged with untried wartime cases and brought some order out of the thousands of Volstead Act violations which were beginning to mount.

Contrary to later assertions, the Justice Department under Daugherty did not become a haven of refuge for all the low-life characters of Ohio. Although a spoilsman, Daugherty was relatively scrupulous in his appointments, especially in his top selections. Guy D. Goff, subsequently a senator from West Virginia, was his assistant attorney general; William D. Riter, a well-known lawyer of Salt Lake City, was another of his assistants as was Judge Robert H. Lovett of Illinois. James M. Beck, a recognized lawyer from Pennsylvania and a former assistant attorney general in Taft's administration, was his solicitor general. An indication of Daugherty's interest in acquiring top legal talent for the Justice Department was his assigning John M. Vorys, later a member of Congress from Ohio, to recruit promising young law graduates for government service. Daugherty was convinced that the Justice Department needed to be revitalized with young blood.[4]

Because of the Wilkerson injunction, much speculation later arose concerning Daugherty and the appointment of federal judges. It was later claimed that they were all his pawns or political hacks. Actually his record in this regard was no better or worse than that of his predecessors. Of the eighty-eight federal judges he recommended, not one was refused confirmation by the Senate. Among the eighty-eight, some were good and a few bad.[5] More controversial was his appointment of William J. Burns as head of the department's Bureau of Investigation. Burns was founder of the Burns Detective Agency and was a well-known national figure because of his antilabor activities in several labor disputes. Samuel Gompers, for instance, bitterly detested Burns. As Burns's assistant, Daugherty appointed J. Edgar Hoover, who at the time was only twenty-six and had already made a name for himself as A. Mitchell Palmer's special assistant in charge of matters relating to subversive activities. Burns and Hoover made a formidable team since both were dedicated to the expansion of the FBI. Daugherty, however, surprisingly did not permit empire building in this area despite his own penchant for red baiting. By 1922 he had halved the personnel of the budding FBI from approximately 1200 to 600.[6]

The greatest criticism of Daugherty in the first year of Harding's administration centered around his handling of certain war fraud cases. When Daugherty took office in March 1921, the government was supposed to press for the collection of overcharges from certain firms which allegedly had cheated on their earlier war contracts. Daugherty did not pursue such collections and, when this fact became known in the spring of 1922, the attorney general's congressional opponents elevated his lethargy to a campaign issue, charging that he was conniving with war profiteers to enable them to keep their ill-gotten gains.

Daugherty was open to these charges. He frankly considered many of the war fraud cases to rest on shaky legal grounds and he had little interest in pursuing them. Daugherty believed that now the war was over everything connected with it should be forgotten as quickly as possible. However, bitter congressional criticism caused him to exert some effort and ultimately the Justice Department recovered a few millions which the attorney general otherwise probably would have abandoned.

The war fraud charges opened the floodgates to intensified anti-Daugherty criticism. Before May 1922 such sniping had been sporadic and uncoordinated. Now it became constant and organized. Criticism reached a peak when labor joined the attack after the Wilkerson injunction. Samuel Untermyer, a well-known lawyer and friend of labor, made several scathing public assaults on Daugherty's record and called for a congressional investigation. Samuel Gompers, through the publications of the AFL, dredged up all of Daugherty's past and paraded it before the public's eyes, with suitable commentary. At its meeting in Atlantic City on September 14, 1922, the Executive Committee of the AFL boldly announced its intention to bring about Daugherty's removal, by means of impeachment if necessary. In Congress, Senator Thaddeus H. Caraway of Arkansas and Representative Oscar E. Keller of Minnesota assumed leadership of the anti-Daugherty forces and read one indictment after another into the *Congressional Record*, not too subtly using the attorney general as a whipping boy for the entire Harding administration. Simultaneously letters began to arrive at the White House from nervous Republicans who begged the president to "dump" Daugherty in the interest of protecting the party at the polls in the forthcoming congressional elections.[7]

Daugherty met all such criticism with snorts of scorn and told inquisitive reporters: "I wouldn't have given thirty cents for the office of Attorney General, but I wouldn't surrender it for a million dollars." Harding, of course, had no intention of asking him to resign. To each request for Daugherty's removal Harding replied that the attorney general was doing a "fine job." For those politicians who wanted to abandon Daugherty in order to enhance the party's chances at the polls, Harding had only contempt. The president indicated that he would welcome any investigation of the Justice Department which anyone might care to make and expressed confidence that the result would support the attorney general.[8]

Before the fall elections, no such investigation was made as the president's strong endorsement of Daugherty kept his attackers at bay. But many Republican candidates went into the congressional elections in November 1922 convinced that Harry Daugherty was a heavy burden to carry. Indeed, despite the president's constant assurances, the general public was, and remained, suspicious of Daugherty and was inclined to believe whatever his opponents said about him. Most citizens, if not believing that Daugherty was actually unfit for his high office, were in agreement with the *New York Times* "that the exportation of Mr. Daugherty from Columbus to Washington was not the most fortunate of Mr. Harding's acts." For many, as for the *New York World*, Harry Daugherty remained "the moral test of the Harding Administration."[9]

[3

NOT only Daugherty, but the whole matter of presidential appointments and party patronage severely plagued the Harding administration as it moved toward the 1922 fall elections. Critics were quick to claim that Harding had appointed a host of friends to high public office, many of them from Ohio and most of them unqualified. By mid-1922, under the pressure of such criticism, some sensitive Republican leaders openly fretted about the alleged political exodus from Ohio to Washington and particularly about the "hangers-on" who followed in Harding's wake.

Harding did not make an unconscionable number of appointments from Ohio and those he did make were clearly within the prerogatives of the chief executive. With the exception of Daugherty, none of these appointees brought Harding disgrace and some proved to be outstanding public servants. The political hangers-on from Ohio were a different matter. These persons, as we shall see, did not hold office and exercised their insidious influence entirely outside the official stream of governmental activity. The distinction between regular appointees and the hangers-on is important. It was these "unofficial" camp followers who ultimately disgraced the administration. Contemporary critics, however, indiscriminately lumped both groups together and later writers continued the practice.

Harding's major Ohio appointments were George Christian, Jr., as his private secretary; Charles Hard as Christian's assistant; Dr. Sawyer as White House physician; Ed Scobey as director of the mint; Daniel R. Crissinger as comptroller of the currency and later as governor of the Federal Reserve Board; Ora M. ("Reddy") Baldinger as presidential military aide; Rev. Heber H. Votaw as superintendent of federal prisons; and William Howard Taft as chief justice. In addition Harding made five diplomatic appointments from Ohio, the most important being Myron Herrick as ambassador to France.

The Christian, Hard, and Baldinger appointments were nonpolitical and noncontroversial. Christian and Hard had both been associated with Harding for many years, the former being Harding's secretary while he was senator. An honest and capable man, Christian was universally liked for his "tact and good taste." Baldinger was a former *Marion Star* newsboy who had served as a page in the Senate, had attended West Point, and during the war had risen to be a major in the air corps. "Reddy" had always been a favorite of the Hardings and his appointment was inoffensive to the nation.

The Herrick and Taft appointments were widely praised. Herrick served with distinction as America's ambassador to France while Taft brought to the high court outstanding legal qualities. Regardless of differing views concerning Taft's particular economic and constitutional biases, one could hardly deny the *New York World*'s assessment of his selection: "no man ever went on the Supreme Bench better equipped in learning and training and temperament." [10]

The Scobey, Crissinger, Sawyer, and Votaw appointments caused adverse comment. Votaw was Harding's brother-in-law. For a time he had been Harding's assistant secretary, but before that had served for twelve years as an Adventist missionary in India. As superintendent of federal prisons Votaw was ineffective, a fact which made the nepotism all the more glaring. There were rumors of narcotics peddling in federal prisons during his tenure, but there never was any indication that he was involved.

Ed Scobey, while actually from Texas, was regarded as an Ohio appointment because of his association with Harding in the early Ohio years. Harding felt a sense of obligation to Scobey for his campaign help and was determined to give him a government post which would permit him, because of his ill health, to remain in the West. Scobey's inclination toward heavy drinking gave Harding some pause for thought, but in the long run loyalty to a friend won out. The post of director of the mint was finally offered because it enabled Scobey to make Denver his home. This appointment was purely personal and the appointee possessed no special qualifications for the office. Fortunately, in the brief period he was director of the mint, Scobey did little damage.[11]

Daniel Crissinger had been a boyhood pal of Harding in Caledonia. Graduating from the University of Akron, Crissinger completed law school at the University of Cincinnati and returned to Marion to become one of its wealthiest businessmen-lawyers. Attorney for the Marion Shovel Company (Marion's largest business), Crissinger also was a stockholder or director in most of Marion's major enterprises. A lifelong Democrat, he nevertheless supported Harding for the presidency. His fellow townsman rewarded him first with the comptroller's position and then the Federal Reserve post. The business community rationalized the latter appointment by assuming that the traits of conservatism, communal pride, and thrift instilled by a small town more than offset Crissinger's lack of more formal qualifications. All things considered, Crissinger grew in the position and gave dedicated service to the Reserve Board, albeit of a decidedly conservative nature.[12]

Dr. Sawyer was taken to Washington because he was Mrs. Harding's personal physician. The first lady had absolute faith in him and believed no one else could keep her alive during her periodic bouts with a kidney malfunction. To give him status, Harding made him a brigadier general in the Medical Reserve Corps of the army. Dr. Sawyer, a diminutive man with a pointed white beard, loved to display all the trimmings of this rank, and the sight of him seated on his horse, Turco, in full dress uniform with shining epaulets, caused Washington to speak derisively of him as "the general." Although considered by some as a perfect example of the incompetent Harding appointee because of this absurd appearance, Sawyer was actually an honest man and an increasingly valuable and reliable presidential adviser. He was the first to warn the president of the Veterans' Bureau scandal.[13] Yet the general public and contemporary political pundits could never quite forget the image of the little Napoleon sitting on his horse.

If some of Harding's personal appointments from Ohio brought him criticism, those he did not make invited even greater hostility. No sooner had the "best minds" left Marion than the politicians and office seekers arrived, many of them from the Buckeye State. Despite such local pressure, Harding did not cater to Ohio men. Indeed, a minor rebellion occurred within the Ohio Republican party when the president refused to appoint Ohioans on a wholesale basis. Ohio's representatives and senators grumbled that their state was being by-passed and that the president had forgotten his old friends. Newton Fairbanks, chairman of the State Central Committee, became angry because Harding did not make him commissioner of internal revenue. Hoke Donithen, Harding's long-time Marion friend, hoped for a federal judgeship but was bluntly told by Harding, "your name will not be on the list." As late as March 1922, Senator Willis complained "we are having great difficulty in securing appropriate places for our Ohio men."[14]

Contrary to popular assumption, Harding was actually conscientious and relatively careful in dispensing the party patronage. Moreover, despite the fact that he had a hungry party at his back, he compiled a praiseworthy record in relation to civil service. He worked well with the Civil Service Commission and its members respected him as one who attempted to retain and expand the merit system. During his first year in office Harding had a better civil service record than any of the preceding four presidents except Taft (who, after all, followed a Republican president). Harding's record was infinitely superior to that of Woodrow Wilson.[15]

Compiling this record caused Harding great difficulty. Representatives and senators charged him with not accepting their recommendations and undercutting their support at home. Some congressmen even claimed that Harding was a "turncoat" Republican and was hatching a "big plot" to keep Republicans out of office. In the fall of 1921, Harding's sometime golfing partner, Senator Davis Elkins of West Virginia, stormed out of the White House and released a sharp blast to the press "expressing impatience and disappointment that so little progress had been made in the last eight months in calling to the support of the Administration men loyal to it and in full sympathy with it."[16]

How Harding achieved this record in view of the attitude of some of his cabinet officers was particularly surprising. Secretary of Labor Davis chafed under the merit system and so did Weeks, Denby, and Fall. Secretary Hubert Work, who replaced Hays in March 1922, and Secretary New, who replaced Work in March 1923, were also opposed to the civil service system. But none was so outspoken as Daugherty. He was thoroughly convinced that civil service was a "hindrance to the government" and openly advocated the abolition of the merit system. He particularly cautioned Harding about retaining any Democrats in office and warned him of creeping Republican party apathy if he did.[17]

On the other hand, Secretaries Hoover, Wallace, Mellon, and Hays were advocates of the merit system and supported its extension. Since neither Commerce nor Agriculture had many positions coveted by spoilsmen, the major battles over the merit system were waged in the Postal and Treasury departments. Mellon, who was attempting to introduce strict business procedures into his department, was especially adamant on the matter of merit appointments. He retained competent Democrats and remained insensitive to the political requirements of patronage. For example, Mellon's undersecretary, S. Parker Gilbert, Jr., had been Secretary Houston's righthand man during the last days of the Wilson administration. To Mellon, Treasury was not a political plum but an intricate business to be run by men who knew something about finance and fiscal affairs. Harding for his part was loath to cross Mellon on these matters and supported him, even against heavy pressure from Ohio. Once, when Senator Willis attempted to secure the appointment of an Ohio man to a Treasury position already held by a competent Democrat, Mellon protested directly to Harding with the result that Willis was informed no new appointment would be made.[18]

Because of Mellon's views, a bitter intraparty struggle developed by the spring of 1922 over appointments in the Treasury Department. Its focal point was Elmer Dover who had been appointed in November 1921 as assistant secretary of the treasury in charge of customs and internal revenue. Dover was a friend of Daugherty's and had been a regional campaign director for Harding in 1920 in the Northwest. Mellon had accepted Dover's appointment only reluctantly. An outspoken spoilsman, Dover immediately pushed the claims of hungry Republicans to Treasury positions. He ultimately became involved in a bitter conflict with his own subordinate, David H. Blair, commissioner of internal revenue, who was a Mellon appointee and an advocate of retaining competent men even if they were Democrats. When their squabbling reached Mellon's ear, he sided

303

with Blair. Dover then sought Daugherty's aid and finally the president's. But Harding, knowing Mellon intended to back Blair to the limit, indicated he would not intervene in the Treasury Department's business. The president pointedly warned Dover: ". . . it will be impossible to continue a satisfactory public service where responsible department heads are revealing a conflict of authority."[19] Dover, seeing the handwriting on the wall, resigned shortly thereafter.

Republican party leaders followed the Dover-Blair fight closely and expressed strong sympathy for Dover. Some 160 Republican members of Congress joined in a petition asking Harding to support the removal of all Democrats from the Treasury Department and effect their immediate replacement by Republicans. When Dover resigned, many stalwart Republicans, among them Daugherty, maintained that this would seriously damage the party at the polls in the upcoming congressional elections. Who would vote for a party which did not take care of its own, they asked? On the other hand, supporters of the merit system were delighted and applauded the stand of Mellon and the president. As the secretary of the National Civil Service Reform League put it: "Mr. Dover's resignation is significant of one thing—that the President and Secretary Mellon do not intend to have the service of the Treasury Department, one of the greatest business organizations in the world, debauched for the sake of 'rewarding the faithful.' "[20]

Like the Treasury Department, the Post Office Department also became embroiled in patronage problems. Unfortunately, these appointment difficulties tended to obscure the fact that Secretary Will Hays gave the department its most constructive leadership in more than two decades. He advocated higher wages for employees, increased worker morale and efficiency, and initiated with Dawes's help a program to reduce waste and eliminate duplicated efforts. Giving the appearance of being everywhere at once in his efforts to upgrade the postal service, Hays was referred to as "live-wire" Hays and the "human perpetual motion machine." But whatever image he conveyed, Hays's actions met with considerable success. The AFL at its convention in 1921 passed a resolution commending the 115-pound, five-and-one-half-foot Presbyterian elder for his postal reforms, while the National League of Postmasters called him "the best thing that ever happened to the Post Office Department."[21]

Hays was never happy dispensing patronage and relied on Harding and the merit system to protect the Post Office Department from its ravages. The problem was complicated. In 1913 when the Wilson regime took office, Republicans were thrown out of all first-, second-, and third-class presidential postmasterships and Democrats were appointed in their places. Then on March 31, 1917, President Wilson issued an executive order indirectly placing these positions under civil service by declaring that all future vacancies in these postmasterships caused by death, resignation, or retirement would be filled only by persons standing highest on the Civil Service Commission's eligibility list. By the end of Wilson's term, however, only one-fifth of these positions had been affected by this order. The remainder were still filled by Democrats appointed on a spoils basis before 1917. Republicans naturally resented this condition and heavy pressure was exerted on Harding and Hays to change it.

The normal reaction would have been to restore the status quo existing before March 31, 1917, thereby delivering the three presidential postmaster classes (approximately 12,000 jobs) back into the hands of Republican spoilsmen. Instead, on May 10, 1921, Harding issued an order which represented a neat compromise but disappointed many Republican office seekers. Under it, civil service rules were still to apply to all vacancies in the three classes, with the term of office now set at four years; but instead of the highest name being mandatory, the selection could be made from among the highest three. Those presidential postmasters who had been appointed before 1917 were given the opportunity to take competitive examinations rather than being summarily tossed out of their jobs. Obviously, the "highest three" principle provided some leeway for patronage politics to work.

Hays, having earlier urged Harding not to abandon the merit principle, regarded the president's order of May 10 as an admirable solution and set about to implement it. But in doing so he ran headlong into recalcitrant Republican congressmen who railed against the Harding compromise. Yet, with Harding's support, Hays achieved a measure of success. In a report on November 16, 1921, the National Civil Service Reform League complimented both Hays and Harding for their "gallant fight" against the spoilsmen even though the league itself opposed the "highest three" principle. Civil Service records showed that before the spring of 1922, 4165 presidential postmasters had been selected. Of these, 918 were promotions from fourth-class postmasterships. Of the remaining

3247, 2039 were highest on the list, 777 were second, and 431 third. The fact that some 60 percent of those appointed were highest on the list was viewed two ways. Harding and Hays believed that it indicated a marked success in protecting the postal service from the spoils system. The Civil Service Reform League, on the other hand, claimed in a report in April 1922 that it showed considerable political influence still existed in postal appointments.[22]

Hays's resignation on March 4, 1922, to become the morals czar of the film industry following the "Fatty" Arbuckle scandal, removed a friend of the merit system from an extremely sensitive area. Hubert Work's appointment as his replacement dealt a blow to further progress. Work immediately urged the president to revoke his May 10, 1921, order and remove postal appointments from the authority of the Civil Service Commission altogether. Harding, however, held fast and by doing so received some unexpected support from Democratic Senator Joseph T. Robinson of Arkansas who rose in the Senate to compliment the president for preventing inroads on the merit system.[23]

But compliments from a leader of the Democratic party were one thing Harding did not need in view of the bitterness of many Republicans. Certainly grumbling within the party over patronage was not conducive to election success in 1922 since, as Daugherty had prophesied, many workers did suffer a lapse in zeal. Meanwhile, Harding's opponents within the party used his performance on patronage as a means of undermining further his control over the party both in and out of Congress. Again, as Daugherty had predicted, those few votes which Harding gained by attempting to hold to middle ground on the merit system were undoubtedly more than offset by the alienation of party regulars. As for the Democrats —they stood to gain either way.

[4

IN 1918, Truman H. Newberry, a Republican candidate for the Senate from the state of Michigan, defeated the automobile magnate Henry Ford in an election which was the talk of the nation. A year later, in November 1919, Newberry was indicted by a grand jury at Grand Rapids on charges of fraud, corruption, and conspiracy in connection with this victory. In addition, 133 of his friends were indicted on similar charges.

On March 20, 1920, Newberry and sixteen others were declared guilty and given either jail sentences or fines under the Michigan Corrupt Practices Act which limited campaign spending to $3750. However, neither Newberry nor any of his friends went to jail or paid the fines since an appeal carried to the United States Supreme Court resulted in May 1921 in reversal of the lower court's decision.

In 1919, when Newberry first presented himself to the Senate to be sworn in, he found that body in angry disagreement over seating him. Senators such as Borah and Norris demanded his exclusion and prophesied that "Newberryism," a synonym in the Borah-Norris language for buying public office, would engulf the American political system unless strong action was taken. Allegedly Newberry, or, more accurately, his friends, had spent over $200,000 to prevent the election of Ford—a sum which was considerably higher than normal. Although wasting no love on Ford, farm-bloc senators seized upon Newberryism as an example of the "money power" in American politics and used it thereafter as a convenient strawman in their struggle with business interests.

Warren Harding, both as senator and as president, supported the claim of Newberry to his seat. Harding agreed with Senator Poindexter who contended that Newberry had not spent this money personally, that he often did not know it was being spent on his behalf, and that wealthy industrial opponents of Ford had financed Newberry's campaign from motives unknown to the candidate. Besides, Harding believed that the Supreme Court action reversing the lower court's decision had, in effect, exonerated Newberry and that there was absolutely no constitutional bar to seating him.

For over two years the Newberry case remained unresolved as the Senate intermittently continued to debate his fate. In the meantime, Newberryism, because of Harding's known attitude, was easily warped into an anti-administration issue by both Democrats and anti-Harding Republicans. Hence the final Senate vote on seating Newberry in January 1922 transcended in political significance the fate of one man. At that time forty-six senators upheld Newberry's right to a seat while forty-one voted to exclude him. The vote reflected not so much a judgment on Newberry's qualifications as the division within the Senate over current administration proposals and policies.

Upon hearing the final decision, President Harding sent Newberry a congratulatory letter on January 12, 1922, saying, "I am greatly pleased at the outcome."[24] Widely broadcast, this letter was taken as further proof by anti-administration groups that the Harding regime was controlled by wealthy predatory interests. Throughout the spring and summer of 1922 these anti-Harding elements did not allow the Newberry case to die and each mention of Newberry's name evoked the image not only of a tarnished personal reputation but of an administration which had defiled itself by supporting him. In the rural West, in particular, cries of "Newberryism" incited an emotional reaction which defied rational analysis. In the fall elections of 1922 Newberryism was worth its weight in votes for opponents of the administration.[25]

[5

ALTHOUGH the stiff opposition of President Harding to the soldier's bonus had forestalled congressional action in July 1921, bonus advocates revived the issue in the first regular session of Congress in December. Again Harding, backed by Mellon, made it clear that no bonus was possible unless Congress provided special funding. Yet the political pressure for passing a bonus without creating new taxes to support it was too insistent to ignore and, despite continued warnings from the White House, the Republican caucus on January 26, 1922, ordered the House Ways and Means Committee to hurry a bonus bill to the floor.

Administration supporters were once more in a dilemma. Unable to secure an agreement on special taxes to pay for the bonus, Republican leaders finally decided that the only solution was to break down Harding's intransigency. They begged him to accept deficit financing of a bonus through a bond issue and warned that the Democrats would make political capital out of either new taxes or a Republican failure to pass a bonus bill. Wrote Representative Horace M. Towner (Iowa) to the president: "I earnestly hope you can see your way clear to approve a bond issue to meet the bonus demands. . . . many members talk to me each day about the effect [a rejection of a bonus] will have upon their chances of being returned. Matters are so unsettled that each new embarrassment increases their apprehension."[26]

But Harding remained firm and prevented further bonus action during February. The press, meanwhile, overwhelmingly supported the administration's position. The *New York Times* expressed its anti-bonus opinion by saying: ". . . trade, commerce, agriculture, every industry, and every interest would suffer from this perilous gift, this addition to the cost of living, this reinflation, this enactment of bad times."[27] In a lighter vein the *Elmira Advertiser* summed it up this way:

> Now there remaineth Faith, Hope and Charity . . . and the greatest of these is the Bonus. . . .
> It never faileth! Banks may fail. The U.S. Treasury may have to stand in the corner with its hat in its hand, begging favors. Business may be busted higher than Gilroy's kite. The country can go hang.
> The bonus is like Charity. It never faileth.[28]

The public seemingly favored a bonus despite the fact it did not want to pay for it and despite prevailing press attitudes. In this respect, Congress, rather than the press, more accurately reflected general opinion. The trick, of course, was to get the bonus without its costing anything.

Bonus supporters could not believe that Harding would take the political risks involved in continuing to oppose some sort of payment to veterans. Their explanation was that the president was still under the evil influence of Mellon. Most of the tirades of bonus advocates continued to be directed against Mellon rather than the president. The American Legion was convinced that the Pittsburgh millionaire was the "mastermind" behind the bonus opposition and that he had simply "stuffed his ears against the voices and noises abroad in the land."[29] In the end, ran such thinking, Harding would come to his senses and not veto a bonus bill if one was passed.

During this impasse, bonus discussions in Congress continued backstage. A scheme joining the bonus to an insurance plan by which veterans would be issued certificates on which banks could lend up to 50 percent of their face value gathered congressional support in early March 1922. Immediately the banking fraternity attacked the proposal. When he was asked about it on March 6, Mellon characterized the plan as the "worst yet." Three days later Crissinger stated that as comptroller of the currency he would recommend to bankers that they not accept the insurance certificates. Meanwhile it was leaked to the press that Harding still adhered to his original views and that he was opposed to any plan that did not contain its own funding provisions.[30]

Despite the warnings of Mellon, Crissinger, the banking fraternity, and

Harding, the House Ways and Means Committee on March 14 reported the insurance bonus scheme to the floor. Nine days later the House passed the bill 333–70. Before the vote there was a display of bad temper on the part of bonus advocates, some of whom made wild charges against Secretary Mellon. At the same time bonus opponents contemptuously branded the measure "not a bonus bill, but a bogus bill," "wantonly vulgar," and "cheap."[31]

A titter ran through the Senate when the House bonus bill was laid before it on March 24. After some desultory debate, it was referred to the Finance Committee where the Senate's own bonus bill of the year before already lay buried. Senator McCumber, who was a strong bonus supporter, took immediate charge. His mail told him that the bonus was developing into a highly popular issue. Many other Republican senators believed likewise and on April 18 the Senate Republican caucus voted 26–9 for the Finance Committee to report the House bonus bill to the Senate floor "within a reasonable time."

With this backing, McCumber turned the attention of the Finance Committee to the bonus problem just as soon as it finished its work on the Fordney-McCumber Tariff. For the next two weeks, the committee hammered out its own version of the House bill, retaining the insurance aspects but adding a provision for some cash payments. Again no funding provisions were included. On May 6 McCumber rushed a copy of these Senate changes to President Harding with a covering letter soliciting his support. McCumber concluded his plea by stating that the bonus would cost less in the long run than many believed and that its passage was politically essential. To emphasize the point, McCumber, along with Lodge, Curtis, and Watson, called on the president in person and for over an hour urged him to accept any bonus proposition that could clear Congress. They pointed out that thirty-four senators and the entire House membership would shortly be campaigning for reelection. If the bonus was not passed, they said, the opposition of former servicemen and veterans' organizations might be fatal.[32]

Once again Harding held firm. He was well aware of the political danger but believed the fiscal integrity of the nation came first. Besides, he remained convinced that the more responsible segments of the public backed him in his views. In the face of such a firm presidential stand, confusion again reigned in Republican senatorial ranks. Finally, on May 31, the Senate Finance Committee voted by a 9–4 margin to report the Mc-Cumber bonus bill favorably to the floor despite the lack of Harding's support.

A test of wills now ensued. On the evening of June 8 McCumber introduced the bill in an extraordinary after-dinner session of the Senate. He characterized it as "nothing but an American bill" and set its cost at $3,845,659,481. Significantly, McCumber, who was one of those senators up for reelection in the fall, indicated this bill was so important that it ought to take precedence over all other pending legislation, including his own Fordney-McCumber Tariff bill. But from the White House came such violent objection that on June 16 McCumber dropped his plan to ask for such a substitution in the Senate calendar.[33]

While the Senate completed its consideration of the Fordney-McCumber Tariff, the bonus issue simmered amid much behind-the-scenes activity. Servicemen's organizations, especially the American Legion, conducted an extensive pro-bonus campaign and warned that those who did not support the bonus would shortly lose their political lives at the polls. Pro-bonus publications, such as the *Legionnaire* and the *Service Record*, printed cartoons and ran numerous articles to emphasize their feeling. As one striking cartoon pictured it: the wealthy industrialist was grasping government millions in his hand, the shipping magnate was raking in gold coins, and the foreign government was counting a wad of bills just given to him by Uncle Sam, while a blind serviceman with a cane, being led by a forlorn-looking Justice, received nothing.[34]

During this period the White House remained cautious and silent. George Christian turned aside all bonus inquiries by stating, "The President has authorized no statement of any kind in the matter." Meanwhile the presidential mailbox was full of letters supporting his position as well as many, especially from Legion chapters, condemning his stand. Senator Wadsworth later claimed that throughout this period Harding "greatly feared domination of the Government by an ever-growing veterans' lobby" and strove desperately to prevent it. Certainly on the bonus issue the president regarded the American Legion as a divisive force which separated the former soldier from the general population and worked against the national welfare.[35]

The Senate resumed debate on the bonus bill in late August. Numerous senators, among them McCumber, still believed that Harding would not block a bonus if one was passed. But on the evening of August 24 the president bluntly told Senator New that he would veto any bill which did not contain adequate funding and New announced this fact on the Senate floor the next day.[36] Now the question for the bonus advocates was this: Was it wise to pass a bonus only to have a Republican president veto it and thus dramatize party disunity just before an election? Perhaps more significantly, could a veto be overridden?

On the last day of August the Senate passed the McCumber bonus 47–22 and sent it to a conference committee. Twenty-seven Republicans and twenty Democrats voted for it; fifteen Republicans and seven Democrats voted against it. On this issue, Lodge, who was up for reelection, deserted the president. So did most other Republican senators who faced reelection. But Borah did not. When an American Legion post from Pocatello wired him that they would "drive him from office" if he opposed the bonus, Borah shot back that only "the most slimy creature . . . buys office by paying for it out of the public treasury."[37] Except for Borah, the farm bloc voted for the bill.

The House-Senate conference committee quickly adjusted the two versions and on September 14 the House passed the resultant product without a roll call. An hour's debate had been reserved for the measure but it was whooped through in twenty-five minutes. The next day the Senate adopted it by a vote of 36–17. Many senators were absent or did not vote. As finally passed, the bill provided that every honorably discharged veteran could request a service certificate, the value of which was $1 per day for home service and $1.25 per day for overseas service beyond sixty days. If the veteran did not cash this certificate immediately but held it for twenty years, the original value would increase about three times through compounded interest. The largest paid-up certificate would be worth about $1875.

Pressure now shifted to the president. Senator Lodge hurried to the White House and urged Harding to accept the measure. Other intimates, such as Senators Kellogg and Hale, begged him to follow the lead of Congress. Commander Hanford MacNider of the American Legion immediately asked for an audience with Harding to present the views not only of the Legion but of eleven other veterans' organizations as well.[38] Speculation mounted on whether the president would actually veto the bill. Democrats dared him to do so while Republicans held their breath.

On September 19 Harding vetoed the bonus measure in a message which was a joint product of himself and Mellon. It said:

With the avowed purpose of the bill to give expression of a nation's gratitude to those who served in its defense in the World War, I am in accord. [But] it is worth remembering that public credit is founded on the popular belief in the defensibility of the public expenditure as well as the government's ability to pay. Our heavy tax burdens reach, directly or indirectly, every element in our citizenship. To add one-sixth of the total sum of our public debt for a distribution among less than 5,000,000 out of 110,000,000, whether inspired by grateful sentiment or political expediency, would undermine the confidence on which our credit is builded and establish the precedent of distributing public funds whenever the proposal and the numbers affected make it seem politically appealing to do so.[39]

Both houses reacted swiftly. On September 20, the House voted 258–54 to override—forty-nine votes more than was necessary. That same afternoon the Senate vote was 44–28, four short of the required two-thirds. Interestingly, the effort to defeat the president was led in the House by Republican Floor Leader Mondell and in the Senate by Lodge. Almost every leader of the Republican party opposed the president on the veto vote. Of the Republican members of the House, 188 cast ballots to override and only 35 to sustain. In the Senate 27 Republican senators voted against Harding while only 21 gave him their support. Ironically, one of the four votes Harding needed to protect his veto was supplied by Senator Borah.[40]

Harding was the recipient of both praise and condemnation. Of course, the American Legion was especially resentful. At its convention in New Orleans in mid-October, it heaped scorn on the president for his veto as more than 1000 shouting delegates demanded the recall of those congressmen who had voted to uphold him. On the other hand, the *Philadelphia Public Ledger* asserted: "It took high and stubborn courage to hold out against the intercessions and pressures of the bonus-hunters. The President has met the acid test." Said the *Washington Post*: "President Harding's veto of the bonus bill is a logical conclusion from the premises on which he has so consistently stood. . . . The veto will create no surprise in those who have followed the President throughout his dealing with this subject." Concluded the *New York Times*: "By his long, prudent resistance to this measure, and at last by a tranquil courage that underlay his tact, Mr. Harding has . . . strengthened his hold upon the public confidence and respect, and laid his countrymen under an enduring obligation."[41]

As for Harding himself, he was well aware of the consequences of his act but was willing to accept them. He wrote to Charles Dawes a week after the veto: "I note what you say concerning the veto message . . . but I am very sure to be very much complained against for many months to come by a very considerable number of ex-service men. However, I can stand that without annoyance in view of the fact that I have the satisfaction of knowing I did the wise and best thing."[42] Few Republican congressmen who now had to face the voters agreed with him.

[6

RARELY had a party gone into an election more disunified, splintered, and confused than the Republican party in the fall of 1922. Primarily it was the fault of Republican congressmen, but Harding also shared some of the blame. His tendency to let matters drift in the hope that time would provide a satisfactory answer left Congress too much leeway in which to founder. Certainly he did not provide energetic and creative legislative leadership. His old Ohio friend Malcolm Jennings early saw this flaw in the administration and in late summer 1921 wrote Harding that effective "congressional action can only follow the establishment of dominant leadership upon your part. I know this is distasteful to you and I know how sincere [is] your belief that the executive should not trench upon the rights of the legislative branch." But, warned Jennings, to remain passive means "their getting together effectively under other leadership than *yours*."[43] Shortly thereafter the *New York Times* assessed the situation as follows: "There is no Republican leader in House or Senate. Confusion rules, varied only by partisan coalition. The agricultural bloc, drunk with its easy triumphs, presses on eagerly toward the most obnoxious, selfish class policies. So far as Congress is concerned, the Republican Party, after the stupendous vote of 1920, is feeble, sullen, demoralized, rent by schism, variously mutinous. . . . [Harding] has been very patient. But the time for non-action, or merely mild and genial suggestion, has passed."[44]

Before the summer of 1922, Harding steadfastly refused to adopt a more aggressive posture. During that summer, however, Harding began

314

to shift his position. Congressional inaction in the strike crisis and its dalliance on the tariff and ship subsidies angered him. The bonus situation was the final straw. By September the press began to notice Harding's mounting impatience. Numerous congressmen also commented on the president's growing toughness, and even his close senatorial friends found him less affable and more businesslike. Frankly, Harding was sick of Congress.[45]

But in view of the upcoming elections his disenchantment with that body had to be submerged in the greater party interest, and publicly he spoke glowingly of its achievements. In a letter to Mondell, who frequently as House floor leader had attempted to thwart the president's wishes, Harding wrote: "I doubt if any Congress in our history has accomplished so impressive a volume of work, touching so wide a range of national interest." Written for public consumption, this letter was circulated widely as a campaign document and irrevocably tied Harding and the 67th Congress together. Specifically, Harding complimented Congress for the Fordney-McCumber Tariff, the Budget Act, and the tax revision. Its deliberations, said the president, had been "so helpful to American welfare that they will not fail to appeal to the approval of the American people."[46]

Those Republican congressmen who were responsible for that record were not so sure. At 2 P.M. on September 22, when Congress adjourned *sine die*, members rushed home in an anxious mood. The usual end-of-session hilarity was missing. As the *New York Times* described the closing scene in the House: "During those last fifteen minutes a hundred or more worried members sat quiet, like children on the last day of school, waiting for the teacher to announce that Summer vacation was on."[47] Over in the Senate there was not even a quorum to witness the gavel pounding that brought the session to an end.

Republican members had cause to worry. Many hoped to shift the blame for their plight to the president. But Harding's stock was much higher with the general public than was that of Congress and his strong endorsement of congressional actions probably helped Republican congressmen more than it hindered them. Interestingly, the public's acceptance of Harding had remained strong throughout, while its acceptance of Congress had never been more than lukewarm. In February 1922 Mark Sullivan wrote in *World's Work*, "the public, at the present time, makes a sharp distinction between the two branches of what is loosely referred to as 'the Administration.' The public thinks that President Harding has done well. . . . But the same public, on the contrary, thinks that the Senate and House have done rather badly."[48] A month later the *New York Times* said: "Congressmen would be well pleased to have the country look at the President instead of too hard at themselves. Mr. Harding retains his popularity in a large degree. Congress has utterly lost whatever it had."[49] Despite the damaging effect of the strike situation in the summer of 1922, the president's popularity still held rather well, but that of Congress declined further. Looking toward the fall elections, the *Wall Street Journal* pointedly warned: "It will not do for the Republican party, as exhibited in the Senate and House of Representatives, to shelter itself behind the skirts of the administration and cast its own failures upon the broad shoulders of Mr. Harding and his Cabinet."[50]

Regardless of what they released for popular consumption, both the president and Republican congressmen were aware of the deteriorating political situation and prepared for the worst. The bonus fight, the ship subsidy struggle, and the squabbles over the permanent tariff had taken their toll. The tactics of the farm bloc, the Wilkerson injunction, Daugherty's activities, dissension over patronage, and Newberryism also added their weight. More important, the country had not yet experienced a return to prosperity and the public was restless. As Harding wrote to Crissinger, "A lot of people have persuaded themselves that the distressing agricultural situation and the widespread unemployment is chargeable to this administration. I do not know how we can correct this impression until time has joined in the argument."[51]

Being a practical politician, Harding knew that time had run out for the Republicans by the fall of 1922. Some months before, he had written to Malcolm Jennings: ". . . the party is not nearly so strong as it was last year. I may say to you, in the confidence which covers our correspondence, that the party is not much more than twenty-five percent as strong in my own estimate."[52] Harding was also enough of a realist to know that whatever were his differences with his congressional Republican colleagues, their fate was bound together. As one newspaper said on the eve of the voting: "It may be correct to say that the President is much more popular than his party, but it is impossible to torture election figures into making any such nice distinction. If his party were to be badly beaten, it would necessarily be a defeat also for him, and would cloud his political prospects."[53]

[7

ALREADY events had gone badly. Primaries in the spring and summer of 1922 had shown that the tide was running against the administration. In the Indiana primary on May 2, the first of the season, Senator Harry New was defeated for the Republican senatorial nomination by former Senator Albert J. Beveridge. New was intimately identified with the Harding administration, having voted against the bonus and for seating Newberry. On May 16 in the Pennsylvania primary, Gifford Pinchot won the gubernatorial nomination over the machine-backed regular Republican candidate, state Attorney General George E. Alter. Although Pinchot claimed that his selection represented no repudiation of the national administration, most observers considered it so.[54] In the Iowa primary on June 6, Smith W. Brookhart, a LaFollette follower and an outspoken critic of the administration, was nominated by the Republicans to the senatorial vacancy created by Senator Kenyon's elevation to the federal bench. Brookhart outdistanced his nearest rival 118,493 to 46,428. In Wisconsin Senator LaFollette easily won renomination as he attacked the ship subsidy bill, the bonus veto, and the Harding record in general.

But of all the primary results, none was more shocking than that in North Dakota. On June 28 Senator McCumber was defeated for renomination by Governor Lynn J. Frazier. McCumber had held his Senate seat for almost a quarter of a century while Frazier only eight months before had been replaced as governor of North Dakota in a recall election. McCumber was regarded by many as an errand boy for the administration even though he had opposed Harding on the bonus. Frazier, on the other hand, was openly anti-administration in his views. Political pundits later claimed that McCumber was defeated because of the association of his name with the tariff and his earlier vote for Newberry.

These primaries provided advance evidence that a political revolution was brewing, especially in the West. As a result the administration quickly arranged for barnstorming tours to send stump speakers, including cabinet members, into every area of the country before November to explain its position. Ultimately every cabinet member except Mellon took to the hustings. Hughes spoke in Boston and Cleveland; Hoover in Ohio and Michigan; Davis in the Rocky Mountain area and in the Far West; Weeks in Massachusetts and New Jersey; Wallace in the sensitive Midwest; Fall in the Southwest; Vice-President Coolidge in Minnesota and the border states; and Daugherty in Ohio and Illinois. Hughes emphasized successes in foreign policy; Hoover concentrated on economy in government; Wallace hammered away on the administration's record of benefits for the farmer; and Davis simply spread good-fellowship and good cheer.[55]

With this last-minute display of oratorical firepower, Republicans momentarily took heart. The White House and Republican campaign headquarters even put out a few rosy prophecies of victory. But at the grassroots level it was still evident that reelecting Republicans was going to be difficult. Just before the election it was predicted that the party would be lucky if it retained a House majority of 20 (instead of the 166 it then had) and a Senate margin of 12 (instead of 24). Harding wrote to Theodore Roosevelt, Jr.: "Undoubtedly we are going to have some notable Democratic gains. Such a reaction, after the overwhelming victory of 1920, [cannot] well be avoided."[56]

Election Day, November 7, fulfilled Republican fears. There were serious reverses. In Minnesota, Senator Kellogg was defeated by the Farmer-Labor candidate, Henrik Shipstead. Shipstead, elected on an anti-administration platform, became the first third-party senator since Populist days. In Iowa, Brookhart defeated his opponent handily and came into the Senate as an anti-administration radical. In Washington, Senator Miles Poindexter lost to his Democratic opponent, Clarence C. Dill. In Indiana, Beveridge, having beaten New in the primary, now lost to former Governor Samuel M. Ralston, a Democrat. Senator Frelinghuysen of New Jersey, one of Harding's close friends, lost to former Democratic Governor Edward I. Edwards. In Montana, Burton Wheeler, supported by a farmer-labor alliance, easily defeated his Republican opponent. In Wisconsin, La-Follette won a thumping victory with a 289,000-vote majority. In Michigan, Representative Fordney, a Republican member of Congress since 1899, was defeated, and in Wyoming, Representative Mondell, also a member of Congress since 1899, was turned out of office.

There were a few bright spots. Senator Lodge retained his seat in Massachusetts, although barely, and in Ohio Simeon D. Fess, a supporter of Harding, defeated Democratic Senator Atlee Pomerene. But these few successes did not soften the sharp pattern of reverses. In the Senate the Republicans lost 7 seats while the Democrats picked up 6, not including Farmer-Laborite Shipstead. The Republican majority was cut from 24 to 10. In the House, the Republicans lost 70 seats and the Democrats gained 76. The Republican majority was cut to 20, placing the balance of power in the hands of maverick Republicans and the farm bloc.

Immediately the post-mortems began. Mark Sullivan claimed that the chief reason for the Republican defeat was the lack of executive direction from the White House and an absence of congressional statesmanship.[57] Laborites proclaimed that the administration's labor policy had sealed its defeat and pointed to the Wilkerson injunction as the most damaging act of the Harding era. Newberryism and the activities of Daugherty were also mentioned as critical factors in the Republican downfall.

Most discussion, however, centered on the tariff and the bonus as the main ingredients in the Republican setback. Contemporary observers extended sympathy to the president on the bonus issue. They agreed that Republican congressmen had been cowardly in not providing the necessary taxes and had simply shoved the blame onto Harding. It was different with the tariff. Here most observers believed that the White House was culpable. *Current Opinion* estimated that the Fordney-McCumber law "lost the administration millions of votes."[58] The *Wall Street Journal*, which considered the measure "one of the most selfish, short-sighted and extravagant laws of its kind ever enacted," had no doubts that it was the chief culprit. For its passage alone, said the *Journal*, the Republicans "richly earned the licking they received."[59] The *New York Times* agreed. Said the *Times*: "A Spanish proverb says that no one but a fool breaks his leg twice over the same stone. The Republican Party broke its leg over the tariff stone in 1890 and again in 1910, but that remembrance did not deter it from going through the same stupid performance in 1922."[60]

In his own assessment of the election, President Harding was more philosophical than many of his Republican colleagues and accepted the verdict more calmly. To E. Mont Reily he wrote: ". . . there is nothing greatly serious to grieve about, except the loss of some very excellent men." Harding's main reaction was one of confusion rather than surprise. As he wrote to Gutzon Borglum just after the election, "I confess myself utterly unable to make a satisfactory diagnosis of the outcome." After considerable reflection, he finally thought he saw two basic trends in the voting: (1) farmer discontent and (2) labor opposition. In neither case, he asserted, would the administration alter its policy: it would let history judge its actions. To satisfy the farmer, said Harding, would involve "some artificial process which violates all economic laws" and to satisfy the laborer would mean "maintaining war levels of wage." To another friend, Harding admitted, however: "For such blame as the administration must assume I am willing to bear my share. . . . it is a very difficult thing to recover from the aftermath of war and get ourselves firmly on our feet. . . . However, I hope we shall do better in the two years before us."[61]

The election of 1922 was not really the staggering defeat for the administration which many contemporary observers claimed. While the numerical losses were large and serious, they were not catastrophic, especially when viewed in the context of American political history. The party in power kept control of both houses in 1922, which was not true for Arthur in 1882, Harrison in 1890, Cleveland in 1894, Taft in 1910, or Wilson in 1918. Moreover, the election of 1922 represented no genuine trial of strength on clearly definable issues. So much depended on local conditions or attitudes that a separate analysis was required to explain each victory or defeat. There was no unity among the administration's opposition except a general discontent. The manifestation of this discontent in one area centered on the tariff, in another on the Wilkerson injunction, in still another on Newberryism, and so on.

Further, despite claims to the contrary, the election was not a specific repudiation of Harding or the Harding policies. It certainly was not a mass protest against the economic orientation of the administration. Actually, the primary economic issue was the return of prosperity, not how to achieve it. In this respect the administration was simply unlucky. If the election had been six months later the result would have been far different. With the return of good times by mid-1923, most of the dissatisfaction and confusion of mid-1922 evaporated. Harding suspected that this would happen and for that reason had worked diligently for business and farm recovery before the election of 1922. Early in that year he had prophesied to Secretary Wallace: "If this process [business and farm recovery] will prove rapid enough to have a restoration by the middle of the year we shall have very little concern about anything. . . . If the more disappointing condition exists I do not suppose there is anything we can do that will ward off a very considerable modification of our majority in Congress." [62]

Whatever the election showed, it did not indicate a desire for a return to either progressivism or Wilsonism. Al Smith, who won the governor's race in New York, belonged to the anti-Wilson wing of the Democratic party. Ralston, who defeated Beveridge in Indiana, was firmly opposed to reopening the League question. Senator Hitchcock, a strong Wilson supporter, went down to defeat in Nebraska. In Massachusetts, Lodge was almost beaten by an anti-League, anti-Wilson Democrat. And in Missouri, Senator Reed, one of the most ardent irreconcilables, was reelected despite former President Wilson's personal intervention against him. Hence, Senator Walsh of Montana badly missed the point when writing to a friend in mid-November 1922: "I think the outstanding lesson [of the election] is that the country is radically inclined and has no stomach whatever for the standpat proclivities of the administration, either with respect to our foreign relations or our domestic problems." Walsh, like many other liberals, was wrong on both counts. Closer to the truth was Senator Hitchcock's appraisal: "I can see no national verdict in the result except a general expression of dissatisfaction with Government and with conditions. It hit the Republicans hardest, but it was, after all, a nonpartisan discontent." [63]

[8

REGARDLESS of the merits of the various election assessments, one fact clearly emerged. President Harding now more than ever was thrust into the spotlight as head of the governing party and forced into a position of having to exercise more direct control over congressional matters. He had been moving in that direction anyway and, having already survived one head-on collision with Congress on the bonus question, he was now prepared to act similarly on the single remaining issue which he believed involved the integrity of his administration and the welfare of the nation—the postponed ship subsidy bill.

As early as October 16, three weeks before the election, Harding wrote to a congressman friend that regardless of the election outcome he intended to call a special session of Congress "not later than November 20th, in order to get this exceedingly important legislation underway." [64]

321

On November 9, just two days after the election, Harding formally issued a call for an extra session to begin on November 20. At the time, he bluntly warned Congress that he would settle for nothing less than its acceptance of the ship subsidy bill.

This was a new and tougher Harding but his action represented the epitome of poor judgment and poor timing. Coming so soon after a difficult election, this call reinforced the schisms within his party and opened the administration to charges of ramming legislation through a lame-duck, discredited Congress before a new one could convene. Farm-bloc members and congressional radicals, especially, were incensed by the president's decision, and on November 19, the day before the special session convened, Senator LaFollette and Representative George Huddleston (Alabama) issued an invitation for the "progressive element" of all parties to meet in Washington, D.C., on December 1 to plan strategy. The immediate purpose was to discuss ways to discredit the Harding administration and defeat the ship subsidy bill. The motivating force behind this move, however, was a misguided belief that the election of 1922 showed the nation was still progressive and that the days of Teddy Roosevelt and Woodrow Wilson could be recaptured.

On December 1, thirteen senators and senators-elect and twenty-three representatives and representatives-elect met in Washington as planned. Under the direction of LaFollette and Norris, they endorsed a program which included abolition of the electoral college, direct primaries for all elective offices including the presidency, prompt convening of newly elected Congresses, and the elimination of "special privilege" from government. The following evening a banquet was held for the newly elected "progressive" senators and representatives. Among the speakers were La-Follette and Norris, but the most publicized speech was delivered by Samuel Untermyer who, among other things, violently attacked Attorney General Daugherty. However, neither these outbursts nor the meetings themselves met with much approval from the Republicans, the Democrats, or the general press. Most people remained suspicious of "this so-called bloc business." To regular Republicans, in particular, LaFollette was a "tearer-down, not a builder-up" who merely wanted to use this group "as a shock battalion . . . for his own purposes." [65]

This insurgent activity, whether sincere or not, dramatized the continuing schism within the Republican party and represented a direct challenge to Harding for party control. Little wonder, then, that Congress reconvened on November 20 amid much gloom. The Senate promptly adjourned for the day in recognition of the death of Senator Watson of Georgia while the House had only 291 of the 435 members present when Speaker Gillett gaveled it to order. Even before the first roll call was sounded, the insurgent and anti-administration forces had scored a victory of sorts. Knowing that his seat would again be challenged and not wishing to embarrass the administration further, Senator Newberry formally announced his resignation on November 19. President Harding immediately sent him a letter expressing his regret and concluded: "I think you have been outraged as no other man in public life."[66]

The only item of business before the special session was, of course, the delayed ship subsidy bill. On November 21, Harding stepped before a joint session and delivered a hard-hitting message. He was applauded only three times as, in an un-Harding-like manner, he attacked his enemies. He opened by admitting that opposition to the ship subsidy bill was severe. But, he said, its passage was absolutely necessary. The basic reasons were national prestige and dollars-and-cents. The alternatives, said the president, were to continue to lose supremacy on the high seas, face another $3 billion shipbuilding madness should war again come, continue to suffer a $150 million annual loss, and ultimately be left with a worn-out, useless fleet. Then, in a direct reference to the sectional aspects of the opposition, he stated that it would be discouraging "if a measure of such transcending national importance must have its fate depend on geographical, occupational, professional and partisan objections." In a parting shot at bloc elements he concluded: "Frankly I think it loftier statesmanship to support and commend a policy designed to effect the larger good of the nation than merely to record the too-hasty expressions of a constituency."[67]

This was the speech of a mild man whose patience was at an end and who was demanding action rather than requesting it. While many newspapers and journals applauded his firmness, they remained skeptical of Harding's wisdom in pushing the issue at this time. Even those who favored the legislation were apprehensive. Commented the *New York Times*: "Harding will have to fight harder than he has ever done since he became President if he is going to succeed in imposing his will upon Congress."[68]

The debate on the bill began in the House on November 23. Throughout, the White House checked carefully on the attitudes of all Republican members and applied strong pressure wherever necessary. As a result, the Republican majority remained fairly intact and both Democratic and insurgent leaders found their plans to make inroads on this majority stymied. By November 27 there were predictions that the bill might pass by as many as thirty votes. Two days later, as the roll call was taken, Lasker kept a list of the ayes and nays and later sent them to Harding with notations beside the names of those Republicans who voted against the measure but were currently seeking favors from the administration. The White House was playing rough. The final vote was 208–184, a margin of twenty-four votes.[69]

The bill was now sent to the Senate where it was referred to the Committee on Commerce under the chairmanship of Wesley Jones. Harding immediately expressed confidence that the Senate would also accept it, but privately he showed he possessed no delusions. On November 29 he wrote to a newspaper friend: ". . . we [will] have a more difficult contest in the Senate than we had in the House, because of the lack of limitation on debate and the inability to restrict debaters to the pending question." Advance rumblings from the Senate left little doubt of severe trouble ahead. However, when Senator Smoot wrote him on December 1 that it was going to be impossible to pass the bill, Harding shot back: "I am more deeply interested in the enactment of the Merchant Marine Bill than any one measure I have ever recommended to the Congress." His orders to Smoot were to push for its passage against all odds.[70]

On December 4 the extra session which Harding had called to consider ship subsidies automatically expired and the second regular (actually the fourth) session of the 67th Congress began. The ship subsidy bill now inevitably became entangled with the passage of other legislation in the waning months before final adjournment. Clearly the strategy of both the insurgent bloc and the Democrats was to prevent any vote at all on the subsidy measure before March 4 by forcing its displacement on the Senate calendar by as many bills as possible and, finally, by filibustering it to death when all else failed. By mid-January it was clear that such tactics were succeeding as other pending measures were moved ahead of the subsidy bill through skillful parliamentary maneuvering.

In desperation Harding decided on one last ploy. On February 7, in a bold move, the president again appeared before both houses of Congress, ostensibly to inform them of the results of the current debt-funding negotiations between the United States and Great Britain. However, a significant part of his speech was devoted to the ship subsidy bill and he expressed hope that it would not be killed by further delaying tactics. "I plead for a decision," he said. But the Senate turned a deaf ear. When the bill at last came to the top of the docket on February 19 a filibuster began. Senator Morris Sheppard of Texas talked for ten hours. Then Senator Reed of Missouri took over. In the midst of impossible parliamentary snarls the Senate recessed at 11:20 P.M. on February 20. The next day the filibuster continued with a number of senators participating, among them Borah who spent more time on a plea for recognition of the Soviet Union than discussing ship subsidies. The following day Senator Kenneth D. McKellar of Tennessee was the star performer. He proclaimed that it was his purpose to kill the subsidy bill "by any legitimate means."[71]

The situation was critical. The ship subsidy filibuster was creating an embarrassing logjam by preventing the passage of *any* legislation, and on Friday, February 23, as the filibuster entered its fifth day, Senator Curtis called on Harding and laid the harsh facts before him. Pro-administration leaders could foresee no break in the ship subsidy matter. Nevertheless, Harding ordered them to try to defeat the filibuster during the next several days. They failed. Hence, on February 28 at 2:11 P.M. the struggle ended as pro-administration senators, on orders from the White House, voted to drop the subsidy bill in favor of other pending legislation.[72]

Harding was bitter about the defeat. To a friend on the Shipping Board he wrote: "I think our nation has lost a beckoning opportunity which is not likely to come again. The pity of it is that the measure was defeated by a filibuster, and the defeat does not register the majority judgement of the Senate." Indeed, the president appeared to be more agitated by this loss than by the fall election. He simply could not understand the emotional reaction to the ship subsidy proposal which, from his point of view, was no more insidious or solicitous of special privilege than the tariff or farm relief. In despair he wrote to Albert Lasker: "It is a curious thing that men are almost universally opposed to a subsidy without realizing how many subsidies they are enjoying in the accepted things in government service."[73]

Of course the ship subsidy defeat was a direct outgrowth of the adverse fall election and represented the chief political event in its aftermath. The election had emboldened the farm-bloc and maverick Republican congressmen to defy the president and they got away with it. As for ship subsidies themselves, controversy continued in the public press and elsewhere on their merit, especially when it dawned on thoughtful persons that the only alternative now was to write off the government fleet.

But if there was continuing controversy in the United States about the wisdom of the ship subsidy bill's defeat, in one country there was absolutely no disagreement with the Senate's action. As one British newspaper, speaking for the rest, happily concluded: "Naturally, British shipping will benefit. . . . A new chapter now opens for the British Mercantile Marine."[74]

XI

New Approaches in
Foreign Policy

[1

IN VIEW of its importance in the campaign of 1920, it is ironic that foreign policy should have played such a minor role in the public assessment of the Harding administration by late 1922. This was not because the administration had ignored foreign affairs. On the contrary, the pace of international events had been so swift and the stakes of such significance that the administration had been compelled to participate in the international arena whether it wished to or not. To be sure, the resultant involvement was not the kind that President Wilson and League advocates had envisioned. But neither did it conform to the isolationist views of the League's opponents. It was a blend of the two which was typically Harding.

From the outset the Harding administration was confronted with Wilsonian hopes for internationalism and an equally virulent sentiment against foreign involvement. Harding's own position on the League in 1920, as well as his subsequent handling of the Washington Disarmament Conference, clearly reflected not only his ambivalence but that of the general public on a postwar role for the United States. On the one hand Harding desired through his America First programs to make America more self-reliant and self-sufficient; on the other he wished to encourage "proper" international participation. That he did not succumb completely to the postwar isolationist impulse was to his credit. The same may be said for

Hughes who acted throughout as the perfect implementer of Harding's sometimes perplexing, but always middle-of-the-road, approach.

Harding, after all, had traveled rather widely before becoming president and, as already mentioned, his various Senate committee assignments had long since introduced him to some of the nation's worldwide responsibilities. Harding first went to Europe in 1907 and two years later traveled to Egypt, the Mediterranean, Italy, and Germany. Nineteen eleven found him in Switzerland and also in the Caribbean. In 1915 he journeyed to Hawaii and, shortly before his inauguration, he went to Panama. Such travels did not automatically make him sympathetic to aggressive international action, but they did curb his inclination toward parochialism. Certainly they, along with prodding by Hughes, encouraged him to prevent the United States from withdrawing into its shell after 1921 and force it to remain on the international scene to protect its own interests if nothing else. Actually, Harding and Hughes injected again some reality into American foreign affairs by talking more about the nation's legitimate "national interests" than about universal humanitarian ideals. Under the watchful eye of a suspicious Congress, Harding and Hughes reconciled nonentanglement with the pragmatic requirements of playing the role of a dominant power, and they wrestled manfully, although not always successfully, with the imperatives imposed upon American foreign relations by the nation's expanding industrial and economic prowess.[1]

⌐ 2

IN NO area was the Harding-Hughes diplomatic effort more productive than in the Caribbean. And in no area was a change in policy from the Wilson years more needed. Here the Wilson legacy was a bitter one of military intervention and nonrecognition. The main trouble spot was Mexico. The murder of President Madero, the rivalry of Huerta and Villa, and the confiscatory aspects of the revolutionary Mexican Constitution of 1917 had conspired to make friendly relations with the United States virtually impossible during the Wilson years. Although American business concerns, especially oil companies, had loudly demanded some kind of definitive action, Wilson's ill-fated policy of nonrecognition and "watchful waiting" had supplied neither action nor a solution, and the Mexican problem was passed on to the Harding administration intact. Fortunately, the Mexican hero General Álvaro Obregón was elevated to the Mexican presidency in December 1920, and a new approach to American-Mexican relations suddenly became feasible. Obregón, who was violently anti-Wilson, made no secret of the fact that he was pleased by Harding's election and proclaimed that all problems between the two countries could now be adjudicated quickly.[2]

Tempering Obregón's enthusiasm, however, was the appointment of Albert Fall to the Harding cabinet. Fall's name was anathema in Mexico because of his constant demands for military intervention and his claim that the new Harding administration would pursue a hard line. Even so, in late March and early April, Obregón attempted to pave the way for a better understanding by setting aside some of the more objectionable Mexican land decrees and promised that the confiscatory clauses in the 1917 Constitution would not be applied to American businesses retroactively. Harding, meanwhile, was intensely interested in "closing the Mexico business" and encouraged informal contacts with Obregón through mutual friends who kept the White House informed of the Mexican president's state of mind and the possibility for negotiations. Reporting to Harding regularly were General James A. Ryan and Elmer Dover, both of whom were currently in Mexico City.[3]

Secretary of State Hughes did not like the Dovers and Ryans acting as "independent emissaries" and indicated as much to Harding who, beginning in June 1921, was careful to play down all such contacts. Despite Hughes's objections, however, the president continued to keep his private lines open. Hughes, using regular diplomatic channels, pursued a more cautious policy than was necessary and, as a result, prolonged the period before the two countries finally got together. Maintaining that Obregón's conciliatory actions were not sufficient to prompt recognition negotiations, Hughes demanded that Mexico first sign a formal Treaty of Amity and Commerce which would include guarantees concerning the property rights of American citizens. In addition Hughes demanded compensation for all losses sustained by Americans in Mexico as a result of the various internal upheavals since 1910. In substance, this was a restatement of the old Wilson policy.

Obregón was offended and flatly refused to consider such demands. Harding, fearful that Hughes's legalistic approach might jeopardize continued contact, urged the secretary of state to be more lenient. Because

329

of information he had received privately from Dover, the president knew that Obregón was truly desirous of cooperating but was "seeking to avoid the appearance of submission to our dictation." Harding therefore suggested to the secretary that the United States might "send a special commissioner to Mexico to negotiate . . . a speedy conclusion" to the whole affair.[4] In a letter from the State Department to Obregón, dated July 21, 1921, Hughes included a final paragraph, written by Harding himself, which stated: "It would be wholly pleasing to this Government to send a special commissioner to Mexico to negotiate [a proper settlement] . . . upon advice from you that such a treaty can be closed up."[5]

Still there was no immediate break in the impasse. The State Department continued to insist upon specific guarantees and a Treaty of Amity and Commerce before recognition could be discussed. Both Hughes and Undersecretary Henry Fletcher spent considerable time justifying this position to Harding who, although admitting its logic, more than once complained plaintively, "I wish we might recognize Mexico and reestablish helpful relationships."[6] Harding, meanwhile, received anguished letters from his contacts in Mexico who reported that "the extremely friendly feeling for the United States which has existed since Obregón's election is slowly giving way to the old time unfriendly feeling. A distrust and suspicion of our real friendship has arisen."[7]

Although the stalemate between the State Department and Mexico continued throughout late 1921, several events occurred which raised hopes for an early resumption of formal relations. The Mexican Supreme Court handed down the first of five decisions which softened the effect on foreigners of the controversial clauses of the Constitution of 1917, and the International Committee of Bankers negotiated a settlement with the Mexican government which recognized all her foreign debts.[8] Also in the summer of 1922, at General Ryan's suggestion, Harding invited Obregón's finance minister, Adolfo de la Huerta, to the White House for a series of friendly talks. Afterwards Ryan wrote the president: "You had a tremendous effect for good upon this man." After returning to Mexico, de la Huerta did work diligently to minimize the differences between the two countries and combat the growing anti-Americanism in Mexico.[9]

By early 1923, conditions for a rapprochement were further enhanced by the resignation of Fall from the Harding cabinet and the intensification of American business pressure for recognizing Mexico. Moreover, at

Harding's insistence Hughes finally modified his stiff stand by indicating that the settlement of American claims could wait until after recognition which might now be granted upon a simple Mexican guarantee of the protection of American property. General Ryan immediately suggested to both presidents that delegates from the two countries meet informally to work out such an agreement. Ryan's proposal was cleared by Harding through official State Department channels and on April 23 Secretary Hughes made a formal announcement that a joint Mexican-American commission would meet as soon as possible in Mexico City.[10]

The president appointed Judge John Barton Payne and Charles Warren as the American commissioners. Payne later recalled that before going to Mexico he asked Harding whether he wished a solution or merely a report on the legal circumstances affecting relations with Mexico. According to Payne: "President Harding responded *very emphatically* that he wanted a way to be found whereby the Government of the United States might recognize the Government of Mexico."[11] The ensuing Bucareli Conferences, named for the avenue in Mexico City on which the discussions took place, began on May 14, 1923, and were concluded on August 15, two weeks after Harding's death. They led to the result which Harding had desired—full recognition of Mexico and the exchange of ambassadors. While relations with Mexico continued stormy for a time and all difficulties did not immediately disappear, this resumption of normal contact represented the key step. More than any other person, President Harding had been responsible.[12]

The Mexican situation was but one of several arising from the earlier Wilson policy of nonrecognition and intervention in this area of the world. Relations with Cuba, Haiti, and Santo Domingo were all in disrepair and caused the Harding administration immediate anxiety. With respect to Cuba, the problem was to secure, without the use of armed force, a stable government which would be friendly to the United States. To this end, President Harding retained in Cuba as his personal representative General Enoch H. Crowder, who earlier, in January 1921, had been sent to Havana by President Wilson on a mission designed to prevent the presidential aspirations of several rival Cuban factions from exploding into civil war. As a result of Crowder's efforts, Alfredo Zayas, a pro-American moderate, was installed as president in May 1921.

Thereafter Harding kept Crowder in Havana to work with the Cuban

331

government in instituting legislative and economic reforms. Despite the opposition of some local Cuban politicos who derisively called him the "American Viceroy," Crowder initiated during 1921 and 1922 a series of beneficial changes. Finally realizing that the general's position in Cuba was subject to misinterpretation and anxious for better relations with all of Central America, Harding requested Congress in late 1922 to create an ambassadorial post at Havana and confirm Crowder's appointment to it. Thus, in February 1923, Crowder became the first American ambassador to Cuba.[13]

In other minor ways the Harding administration showed that it desired to normalize its relations with Cuba. In January 1922 Harding ordered the removal from Camagüey Province of a force of marines which had been sent there by President Wilson in July 1917 to protect railroad properties. In late 1922 Secretary Hughes, with the strong backing of Harding and despite anguished protests from certain American business interests, began a series of moves intended to recognize Cuba's claim to the Isle of Pines.[14] As a consequence, by the summer of 1923, Cuban-American relations took a decided turn for the better. The removal of the marines, the Crowder reforms, the promising negotiations over the Isle of Pines, and the creation of fiscal stability established an environment in which American influence could play a less obvious role. For the moment, civil war on the one hand and American military intervention on the other were forestalled. Concurrently, a more favorable climate for American business in the island was created. This latter was perhaps the most important result of the Harding-Hughes Cuban policy and was regarded by the administration as highly desirable. Both the president and the secretary of state much preferred this business "intervention" to any other kind.

A solution to the Haitian problem was not so easily found. American relations with this small country had played a role in the campaign of 1920. The Republican party had used the Haitian situation to influence the Negro vote and also to show Wilson's proclivity for "colonialism." Once during the campaign young Franklin Roosevelt boasted, "You know I have had something to do with the running of a couple of little republics. The [fact is] that I wrote Haiti's Constitution myself."[15] Harding subsequently replied:

If I should be elected president . . . I will not empower an Assistant Secretary of the Navy to draft a constitution for helpless neighbors in the West

Indies and jam it down their throats at the point of bayonets borne by the United States marines, nor will I misuse the power of the executive to cover with a veil of secrecy repeated acts of unwarranted interference in the domestic affairs of the little republics of the western hemisphere, such as in the last few years have not only made enemies of those who should be our friends but have rightfully discredited our country as their trusted neighbor.[16]

After assuming office Harding looked toward the ultimate elimination of the American military occupation in Haiti and had Hughes send Sumner Welles, chief of the Latin American Division of the State Department, to Haiti to conduct a careful survey. In July 1921 Welles recommended that an American loan be granted to relieve the country's financial instability, that the Haitian gendarmerie be improved, and that a marine officer be selected as the president's personal representative and empowered to effect various reforms. Hughes, who was already arranging a Haitian loan through the National City Bank of New York, endorsed these suggestions and sent them to Harding for his approval. At the same time, the secretary gave assurances to bank officials that "our troops will not be withdrawn so long as the maintenance of peace and tranquility in the Republic of Haiti require their retention." Harding, who was sincerely anxious to extricate the United States from the Haitian situation, gave his consent to Welles's proposals, but with respect to the bank loan told Hughes, "I doubt if we ought to convey the impression that we mean to maintain American supervision until the maturity of these obligations."[17]

Mainly on Secretary Denby's advice, Harding appointed Brigadier General John H. Russell as special commissioner and ambassador extraordinary to Haiti to implement Welles's recommendations. It was a mistake. Where Crowder had the respect of most Cubans, Russell was not even particularly acceptable to the pro-American clique which kept Haitian President Philippe Dartiguenave in power. Until shortly before, Russell had been the commander of the American occupation forces stationed in Haiti and was the author of certain "court martial" decrees against Haitian editors who had spoken out against American intervention. Moreover, his name was associated with several atrocities which had occurred during his tour as chief of military occupation.

Under heavy criticism, some of it coming from the National Association for the Advancement of Colored People in the United States, Russell attempted to stabilize Haitian finances, reorganize the functions of government, build up local police forces, and effect economic rehabilitation. After visiting the area in May 1922 Secretary Denby wrote to Harding that Russell was doing a good job under difficult circumstances. However, Denby concluded that the liquidation of military intervention was not yet possible. Said he, "The mere thought of withdrawing from Haiti is repulsive to any sane person who knows conditions there." Two months later a special bipartisan Senate committee headed by Senator McCormick completed a tour of Haiti and unanimously endorsed continued occupation.[18]

Harding was in a dilemma. He desired military withdrawal and often spoke of it. But, influenced by Denby, Hughes, and Russell, he permitted continued intervention although with such lack of enthusiasm that they found it necessary to submit constant reports to him on the wisdom of this action. In April 1923, after another visit to the area, Denby wrote him that the "situation in Haiti seems excellent at present," but maintained it was due solely to the continued American military presence. Hughes, in a thirteen-page report to Harding in June 1923, claimed "unhoped for success" from the occupation and maintained that because of it "peace and order have been established and safety of life and property exists in Haiti for almost the first time in its national existence." Hughes warned, however, that withdrawal would mean "revolution and bloodshed."[19] In late August, not long after Harding's death, Hughes reiterated his belief that continued occupation was still necessary. But, in language and tone reminiscent of Harding, he added: "[The United States] will welcome the day when it can leave."[20]

In the case of Santo Domingo, Harding's desire for military disengagement met with greater success. As with Haiti, the Dominican Republic had a history of instability and turmoil. In fifty years it had had fifty-three presidents, only two of whom had completed their terms. Even so, by its military occupation of that country in 1916 the United States had clearly violated international law, and the action was resented by other Latin powers. The American government thereafter salved its conscience by pointing to the many advantages—an updated school system, bridges, highways—which intervention had brought. Still it was foreign occupation and hated by the local populace.

Because he had chosen during the 1920 campaign to use the Dominican intervention as another example of Democratic diplomatic blundering, Harding also urged Hughes to liquidate this occupation as soon as possible. Hughes found a peculiar challenge in Santo Domingo, believing the prospects for a settlement here were much brighter than in Haiti. By June 1921 Hughes worked out a proposal whereby military rule could eventually be withdrawn and dubbed it the "Harding Plan." Rejected at first by Dominican leaders, it was reworked and modified until it met with their approval. According to this scheme, promulgated in June 1922, a provisional government was to take over the executive departments from the American military governor; American military forces were to concentrate in three places; order was to be maintained by the Dominican National Police; the provisional president was to provide for the holding of elections; a national assembly was to be convened which would supervise the creation of a permanent government; and, finally, American forces would leave.[21]

Sumner Welles was appointed in the spring of 1923 as envoy and minister plenipotentiary to the Dominican Republic to execute this evacuation plan. Welles was instrumental in allaying much American military discontent over the withdrawal program and urged both Harding and Hughes to stick to the plan despite numerous discouragements. In late May 1923 Welles reported to Hughes that the evacuation schedule was proceeding satisfactorily and predicted that American forces could be withdrawn completely by April or May 1924. He further stated that the evacuation move was "very favorably regarded in all the Latin-American Republics" and that the United States was successfully dispelling the belief that it "intended to pursue an imperialistic policy in the Caribbean."[22] Hughes passed this report along to Harding and received an enthusiastic reply: "It is a very gratifying report. I am more than pleased to know that the prospect of our withdrawal from Santo Domingo gives so much assurance of early fulfillment."[23]

Harding did not live to see the last marine leave on September 18, 1924. Still, it was the consummation of his earlier desire and owed much to his steadfast support. Significantly, Secretary Hughes thereafter claimed that the Dominican evacuation was the administration's most important diplomatic achievement in Latin America and provided positive proof that American policy was one of nonintervention.[24]

Puerto Rico offered a problem of a different sort. During the Wilson years, elements on the island had become increasingly vociferous in their demands for independence from the United States, and Wilson's governor general, Arthur Yager, had evidenced sympathy toward this sentiment. The incoming Harding administration was flatly opposed to independence and therefore, from the beginning, there was tension between Washington and various Puerto Rican leaders.

As Yager's replacement, President Harding appointed E. Mont Reily, one of the "original" Harding men and a western campaign manager during the election of 1920. According to Daugherty, Reily was "a queer duck" who constantly pestered Harding for a position after the election.[25] Reily later claimed that he really wanted an appointment to the Federal Reserve Board but as a consolation prize took the Puerto Rican post. As Reily told the story, Harding felt bad about not being able to give him what he desired but said: "Mont, I have got about a hundred friends who want to be Governor of Puerto Rico, but if you want it, you can have that."[26]

Harding appointed Reily purely on personal grounds and without consultation with Hughes, Daugherty, or anyone else. It was a miserable choice. From the day Reily made his maiden speech in Puerto Rico (July 30, 1921), he was in trouble. With such phrases as "Old Glory has come to stay" and "there is no sympathy or possible hope for independence," he not only alienated independence advocates but even embarrassed the American and pro-American population on the island. He compounded these errors by summarily removing from public office many Puerto Ricans who had leanings toward independence, replacing them with others whose views he approved. Moreover, he engaged in public and press debate with his opponents, often making wild and irresponsible charges. At the same time he deluged the White House with repeated and lengthy justifications of his course of action.[27]

When numerous protests from the island concerning Reily's performance made their way to Harding, the president was inclined to discount them. However, Secretary Weeks, who as secretary of war was Reily's immediate superior, took them seriously and wrote Harding in November 1921, "I think the Governor has lacked discretion in many of his acts . . . and some of his removals cannot be justified."[28] Under increasing fire both on the island and at home, Reily returned to Washington in late 1921 to convince Harding that his actions were what the situation in Puerto Rico required. He was successful. When, in mid-December, Secretary Weeks again wrote Harding about the continuing complaints from Puerto

Rico, the president replied with a curt letter, "I am frank to say [these complaints] do not impress me [and are] unworthy of any serious consideration."[29] The press took notice of the "row in Puerto Rico" but indicated by its comments that it was divided over Reily's activities. The *New York Herald* applauded the governor's "patriotic stand" and claimed that here was "a man who knows why he is in the palace at San Juan, and what he is about." But the *Independent* viewed the situation differently: "We admire in President Harding the quality of loyalty to those in whom he has once placed confidence, [nor should he] listen to idle gossip concerning his appointees. But here is a case where he has been shamefully imposed upon and the honor of America demands that he act promptly. Reily should be suspended at once."[30]

Despite a Harding admonition that he "be mindful to cure the indiscretions of utterance" which marked his earlier experience, Reily persisted in his headstrong manner upon his return to the island in early 1922, and as a consequence the Puerto Rican Senate passed a resolution in February demanding that he be removed. By now Reily had alienated even the moderates who joined with the independents to vote against the governor. In Washington, the Puerto Rican delegate to the United States House of Representatives, Felix Cordova Davila, became bitterly anti-Reily and in early March denounced the governor as "unprincipled, un-American and altogether unfitted to administer the affairs of Puerto Rico."[31]

Rumors now circulated that the United States Congress might investigate Reily. Harding, still voicing confidence in his appointee, indicated that he had no objection to such an investigation but worked behind the scenes to discourage it. Meanwhile a grand jury in Puerto Rico indicted Reily on charges of illegally appropriating island funds. By this time charges and countercharges so filled the air that the truth was impossible to find. Reily's enemies were busy conjuring up a host of unsupportable accusations against him while Reily, laboring under a severe persecution complex, found insidious cabals lurking behind every bush and tree. Quite understandably, on April 13, 1922, Harding wrote Reily: "I confess that with the information at hand the whole situation is more or less confusing to me."[32]

Throughout all this, Reily continued fighting with the Puerto Rican legislature, the courts, the grand jury, and even the island's attorney general whom he tried to remove. In exasperation Secretary Weeks finally wrote Harding, "I feel that we are not getting anywhere in this Puerto Rican situation and I hope you will conclude to take some early action in the matter."[33] But there were factors which caused Harding to move cautiously. There were indications that the grand jury charges against Reily were almost pure hokum (and they were) and that he was often the victim of double-crosses and local native politics (which he was). Moreover, to some island Americans he was still "a splendid man" and "a patriot" despite his lack of tact. American business interests particularly supported him.[34]

Nonetheless, Harding's patience was wearing thin. In May Harding wrote to a friend that although he was confident Reily was sincere, "I do wonder sometimes if we have not developed a situation [in Puerto Rico] which it will be quite impossible for him to cure." To Secretary Weeks, who kept badgering him about Reily, the president wrote in August, "I am well convinced that the Governor has very largely destroyed his usefulness by the series of blunders which have been brought to our attention." Late in that same month, he wrote to Reily himself, "I can not help but have the feeling, and it is very generally shared here, that you are acting with rather too much precipitation and are making the tranquilization of the Island vastly more difficult." Finally, in the first week in September, Harding admitted to Weeks, "I do not see but one cure for the situation in Puerto Rico, and that one cure I shall have to apply very shortly."[35]

Incredibly, Harding still procrastinated and in December 1922 permitted Reily once again to return to Washington and defend himself. Meanwhile, Secretary Weeks maintained pressure on Harding to act. Weeks even attempted to enlist the aid of Daugherty, suggesting that the attorney general go to Puerto Rico and investigate the situation personally for the president. But Daugherty claimed that it was not Justice Department business and bluntly said Weeks should "take care of his own troubles."[36] After listening to Reily in December, and despite Weeks's continuing plea for a change, Harding allowed Reily for a second time to return to his post in Puerto Rico.

In the end, it was Reily himself, not Harding, who solved the problem. While in the United States, Reily received a chest injury in an automobile accident and this injury was further aggravated by the return sea voyage to Puerto Rico in early February 1923. After his arrival on the island, his condition was complicated by a nervous breakdown. Hence, on February

16 Reily sent this cablegram to the president: "My physicians inform me it will be several months before I can recover and I must have complete change and rest, free from all care. This being the case I feel that I should resign and look after my health first. I would like for my resignation to become effective April first."[37] Harding eagerly accepted.

To succeed Reily, Harding now made an excellent appointment—Representative Horace M. Towner of Iowa, chairman of the House Committee on Insular Affairs. Harding had Towner in mind to replace Reily as early as January 1923, a month before Reily handed in his resignation.[38] Eschewing a belligerent stand and working amicably with all factions, Towner succeeded in reducing Puerto Rican tensions and within two months all visitors to the island reported substantial progress. In early May it was announced that Harding would visit Towner in Puerto Rico at the end of the president's projected Alaskan tour. Puerto Ricans were flattered. Even Antonio Barcelo, one of the foremost advocates of independence, sent a cable of appreciation to the president for "affording us an opportunity of offering you an affectionate and cordial welcome and of showing you the great progress of our people under the protection of the Glorious Flag of the United States."[39]

Harding of course never arrived. But Towner's tenure as governor of Puerto Rico continued as one of the most successful in the island's history. Reily lived out his years in Kansas City, defending his actions to the end and deluding himself that had Harding lived, the president "intended to go on to Puerto Rico, remove Governor Towner, and [send me] back there if my health permitted."[40] Reily could not comprehend that his original appointment was an error and that in retaining him in office the president had unnecessarily complicated Puerto Rican–American affairs for almost two years.

[3

FROM the beginning the Harding administration was determined to establish better relations not only with Mexico and the Caribbean republics but with all of the nation's neighbors to the South. For a start, Harding and Hughes catered specifically to Central and South American national pride. Shortly after his inauguration Harding journeyed to New York City to unveil the statue of Simón Bolívar which Venezuela had given to the city as a gift. On that same day, April 19, 1921, a park and an avenue in Caracas were dedicated to George Washington, symbolizing the common revolutionary heritage of the two countries. Skeptics later pointed out that all this attention was "necessary" in view of the recent discovery of oil in the Maracaibo region and the race between British and American oil companies for Venezuelan preferment. Obviously an improvement in United States–Venezuelan relations did not hurt the chances of American oil interests.

But Venezuela was not the only country which received the administration's attention. During 1921 and 1922 the United States sent delegations or naval escorts to all those South American countries which were celebrating independence centennials, among them Peru, Argentina, Chile, and Brazil. Hughes, upon Harding's direct orders, headed the American delegation to the latter country in August 1922, and used the occasion to emphasize the administration's friendship for all countries in the Western Hemisphere. At the dedication of the American Centennial Monument in Rio de Janeiro on September 8 Hughes declared: "We covet no territory; we seek no conquest; the liberty we cherish for ourselves we desire for others; and we assert no rights for ourselves that we do not accord to others. We sincerely desire to see throughout this hemisphere an abiding peace, the reign of justice and the diffusion of the blessings of a beneficent cooperation."[41] These were the sort of words which all South Americans desired to hear.

As salutary as these various celebrations and acts of attention proved to be, no single incident or event, including the resumption of relations with Mexico and the evacuation of Santo Domingo, so refurbished the image of the United States in the eyes of Latinos as the passage of the Colombian Treaty. For years the Democrats had been trying to do penance for Rooseveltian sins. A treaty worked out by Thaddeus A. Thomson, United States minister to Colombia in 1913, and Francisco J. Urrutia, Colombian minister of foreign affairs, was submitted to the two countries in mid-1914; it contained an expression of "sincere regret" for the earlier United States action in the Panama Revolution of 1903 and provided for a "heart balm" of $25 million to Panama's former owner Colombia. Colombia immediately ratified the treaty but a storm of protest arose in the United States. Although American oil interests were anxious for ratification in order to place them in a better competitive position in the Colombian oil fields, neither in 1914 nor in the succeeding six years was there any chance for its passage. Doubt concerning the long-range safety of American investment capital in Colombia and pro-Roosevelt sentiment of partisans such as Lodge combined to prevent ratification.[42]

By early 1921, however, it was clear that such a treaty was in the United States' best interests. Albert Fall, whose oil friend Edward Doheny had substantial holdings in Central and South America, urged Harding to resubmit it following his inaugural. Senator Lodge was also agreeable. To Elihu Root, Lodge privately admitted that a $25 million "heart balm" was a lot of money "but in the present condition of the world's trade it seems to me very important to get [the treaty] through."[43] The treaty as finally submitted was the same as the original Thomson-Urrutia proposal except for the removal of the "regret" clause, thrown out as a last-minute sop to the Roosevelt-worshipers.[44]

On March 9 Harding formally urged ratification of this document. He did not mention "oil" but based his request on a desire to adjust a longstanding international dispute and thereby enhance the United States' relations with all Latin American republics. In this respect Harding took the exact same approach which Wilson had in asking acceptance of the treaty. But where Wilson had failed, Harding succeeded. On April 12 Lodge reported the treaty to the floor and urged ratification, freely admitting that the primary reason he was for ratification was to strengthen the American position in the Colombian oil fields which might otherwise "pass into the hands of a powerful British combination." As for the $25 million "heart balm," Senator McCumber justified it by saying, "I am voting to stake $25,000,000 on the effort of the President to secure without an additional donation a supplemental agreement that will be worth to this country many times that sum."[45]

No such supplemental agreement was necessary. With the ratification of the treaty on April 20 (the day after the New York dedication of the Simón Bolívar statue), American relations with Colombia took an immediate turn for the better. Simultaneously, all Central and South American nations hailed the American action as "righting a great wrong." Colombia, subsequently, was wide open to American oil and business interests. American geologists, engineers, and petroleum experts quickly flooded the country and by 1923 exports from Colombia to the United States, alone, were greater than her entire foreign trade in 1913.[46]

341

In other less spectacular ways the Harding administration ingratiated itself with Central and South American nations, with resultant diplomatic and economic benefits. A boundary squabble between Costa Rica and Panama, which threatened the peace of that area shortly after Harding took over, was quickly de-fused by Hughes who virtually forced Panama to accept an arbitral award favoring Costa Rica. Costa Rica was surprised and pleased that the Colossus of the North should act thus against its own protégé, and Julio Acosta, the president of Costa Rica, immediately wired Harding his "assurance of profound gratitude for his act of equity in recognizing the lawful rights of Costa Rica." Somewhat later Costa Rica gave a nine-million-acre concession to American oil interests.[47]

Another dispute which the Harding administration helped solve was between Chile and Peru. These two countries had been wrangling over their respective claims in the Tacna-Arica area for almost forty years. Hughes wished to bring the two disputants together and in January 1922, with Harding's enthusiastic support, invited delegates from the two countries to Washington to discuss the matter. Chile, whose President Arturo Alessandri was a fellow Mason and very kindly disposed toward the Harding administration, accepted at once. Peru accepted shortly thereafter. Ultimately their delegates signed an agreement of arbitration in July 1922, naming the president of the United States as arbitrator. President Harding then selected an investigating commission, headed by General Pershing, to advise him, and arguments from the two countries were heard in February 1923. Harding died before the final award could be announced.[48]

The activities of the Harding administration in attempting to underwrite peace in the Western Hemisphere were carried one step further with the convening of the Central American Conference in Washington in late 1922. This conference grew out of a meeting in August of that year between the presidents of Nicaragua, Honduras, and Salvador aboard the U.S.S. *Tacoma*, where an agreement was reached to arbitrate any future conflicts between them. Hoping to broaden this pact and simultaneously provide a more stable political atmosphere in the area adjacent to the Panama Canal, Secretary Hughes, acting as an honest broker, issued invitations to Guatemala and Costa Rica to join the original three at Washington in December. Out of the ensuing deliberations came thirteen treaties, involving disarmament, free trade, cultural exchange, and social welfare, and plans for studying mutual labor, financial, educational, and transportational problems. Most significant was the creation of a Central American Tribunal as a court of arbitration to handle disputes between these five states.[49]

Even though the United States was not a signatory to twelve of the thirteen treaties, each of them contained a preamble implying the moral acquiescence of the United States. Moreover, some of the phraseology and provisions of these Central American treaties were found in all subsequent Pan-American peace pacts. Significantly, Sumner Welles, who represented the United States at the 1922 conference and was instrumental in fashioning these treaties, was later the United States delegate to the Pan-American meetings in 1936, 1939, 1940, and 1942, and was a chief architect of Franklin Roosevelt's Good Neighbor Policy.[50]

One final contribution of the Harding administration to better South American relations was a redefinition of the Monroe Doctrine. Secretary Hughes articulated on numerous occasions what both he and Harding felt: that the Monroe Doctrine was a policy of self-defense and not one of aggression or convenience. As Hughes expressed it, the Monroe Doctrine was not "a cover for extravagant utterances and pretensions" nor did it imply "unwarranted authority of visitation and superintendence, hostile to the proper recognition of the sovereignty of our sister Republics." At all times, said Hughes, the purpose of the United States "is to be co-workers with our sister Republics, and not masters, that our purpose is to resist aggression, not to commit it."[51] Such sentiment marked a break with the concept of the Monroe Doctrine as practiced during the Progressive Era. In that period the Doctrine had been employed to cure the disease of governmental instability after it had been contracted. Hughes hoped through cooperation to eliminate the causes for instability and thereby prevent the need for American action.

Hughes nevertheless admitted that there might be occasions when the United States would have to intervene on Latin soil. He believed that American investments in the area and the American position in the Panama Canal gave the United States a "special" responsibility. He once remarked that if the Monroe Doctrine did not exist the United States would have to invent it. This somewhat contradictory position was best disclosed at the Fifth Pan-American Conference at Santiago in March 1923. Here the United States supported the joint work of the conference in social, cultural, educational, health, and arbitration matters. But it discouraged

343

any attempt to limit its own unilateral powers under the Monroe Doctrine. Yet straws were in the wind and Hughes was wise enough to perceive it. For example, he endorsed a change in the organization of the governing board of the Pan-American Union whereby no longer was the United States secretary of state automatically chairman or United States recognition a *sine qua non* of membership.[52]

Taken together, the various actions of the Harding administration toward Central and South America from 1921 to 1923 represented a new and welcome diplomatic approach to that area of the world. Despite some failures, such as Reily's Puerto Rican fiasco and the continuation of Haitian intervention, the record was a decided improvement over the past. Together, Harding and Hughes did much to dismantle the philosophy and appearance, if not the actuality, of American imperialism which had blighted the Progressive Era. Specifically, their new departures led to a gradual liquidation of American military intervention by a series of calculated acts and to the elimination or reduction of much hemispheric friction.

In Central and South America the Harding-Hughes policies were widely accepted and highly praised. There was a marked increase in friendliness toward the United States and a concomitant reduction in suspicion. A new feeling of trust permeated dealings with the great neighbor to the north and, despite temporary lapses, such trust began to lay a basis for the later development of good-neighborism. For both Latin America and the United States it was, as Sumner Welles later claimed, "the dawn of a new era."[53]

[4

THE situation which faced the Harding administration on the other side of the world was strikingly dissimilar to that which it found in the Caribbean. While the Wilson administration had materially increased American involvement in the latter area, it had moved toward disengagement in the Philippines. In his message to Congress in December 1920 President Wilson had asked that consideration be given to "granting independence to the islands," while in the Philippines themselves Wilson's governor general, Francis B. Harrison, had actively encouraged independence hopes.

344

As chairman of the Philippine Committee in the Senate, Harding disagreed with this position. He did not believe that independence should be granted until a thorough investigation was made of the ability of the islands to succeed as an independent state. Hence, two weeks after his inauguration, Harding asked former Philippine Governor General W. Cameron Forbes (Harrison's predecessor and a Republican) and General Leonard Wood to act as a committee of two "to go to the Philippine Islands and to make there a study of the situation and to report thereon, in order that I may have a judgment on which I can base my action and my recommendations." [54] Both Forbes and Wood approached their mission seriously. Before sailing from Seattle on April 9, 1921, Wood wrote Elihu Root that his task as he saw it was to answer this question: "Is the educated minority in the Philippines capable of giving, and will they give, to the great inarticulate mass of the Philippine people . . . a government which, while not measuring up to our standards yet will fulfill certain basic requirements and be such a one that we can consider that we have discharged our duty to the people of the Islands, to our own people and to Civilization?" [55]

In the islands the two commissioners found a wide divergence of opinion. Independence leaders, such as Emilio Aguinaldo and Sergio Osmeña, claimed that it was time for the United States to honor its earlier promise to free them, that they had already absorbed American ideals of liberty, that the local government was stable, and, most important, that the majority of the people wanted independence. Others, and especially American citizens and American business interests, disagreed. They claimed that American withdrawal would be "a calamity for all of us alike, whether Americans or Filipinos." The final Forbes-Wood report, issued in the late fall of 1921, analyzed both these positions, and concluded: ". . . it would be a betrayal of the Philippine people, a misfortune to the American people, a distinct step backward in the path of progress, and a discreditable neglect of our National duty were we to withdraw from the islands and terminate our relationship there without giving the Filipinos the best chance possible to have an orderly and permanently stable government." [56]

This conclusion was undoubtedly the product of many subtle factors— national pride, the requirements of American investment capital, the "white man's burden," and so forth. But one obvious factor was American fear of Japan. Both Forbes and Wood were anti-Japanese. Forbes, especially, was convinced "that Japan wants the Philippine Islands."[57] Significantly, the Forbes-Wood mission was closely followed in Japan. That country was suspicious of American motives in the western Pacific and it openly supported Philippine independence. While Japan's desire may not have been to take the islands herself, she certainly looked with favor upon the liquidation of American control. Although there was some opposition to the Forbes-Wood report, a majority of politicians and editors in the United States supported it.

Harding sought a strong governor general to keep watch on affairs in Manila. He knew whom he wanted—General Wood. But the difficulty was in getting him to accept. Some of Wood's friends, such as Henry L. Stimson and Elihu Root, considered it a "damned insult" that this relatively minor post was offered the general. Wood himself was somewhat offended. However, upon Harding's insistence he agreed to serve as governor general of the Philippines for one year (to September 1922). Wood's sense of duty, his suspicion of Japan, and his deep conviction that the United States should not withdraw from the Philippines caused him to accept this position and then, despite his original one-year time limit, to remain in the islands indefinitely. What started as a limited commission in the spring of 1921 became a permanent task to which Wood dedicated the rest of his life. He died at his post in the Philippines in 1927.[58]

Wood's appointment was a real coup for Harding, but it contained some flaws. Wood tended to be dictatorial and pompous, traits which did not appeal to the independence-minded Filipinos. Wood also was inclined to run things "by the book" and permit little ingenuity or experimentation. His many rules and regulations were frustrating to those who were raised in a cultural atmosphere which was more permissive. Wood's rigid standards of public morality often brought him into conflict with native politicians and petty grafters. Still, his rectitude was an example for them and his incorruptibility a shield against slander. While they often opposed him, Filipinos were disarmed by his sincerity and honesty.

Of course, from the beginning the major point at issue was independence. Shortly after the announcement of the Forbes-Wood report, Osmeña, speaker of the Philippine legislature, requested the privilege of sending a delegation to the United States to present an opposing view. Harding indicated a willingness to hear such a group. Although he had already made up his mind, Harding did not wish to appear to be hasty.

Nor did he wish to offend the sensitivities of the islanders or make the situation worse by arbitrary statements. Sometime before the Philippine delegation arrived, he wrote to Jacob G. Schurman, United States minister to China and a mild supporter of Philippine independence:

I am frank to say that the decision as to a definite Philippine policy has given me very great anxiety. I have always had a reluctance to haul down the flag. Perhaps that is not a happy way to express it. I realize that so much has been promised in the way of Philippine independence that it would be a very dangerous program to completely reverse that policy. At the same time I am exceedingly reluctant to continue responsibility without the exercise of authority. . . . Under all these circumstances there does not seem to be any possible course other than to temporize and mollify, seeking to improve conditions there and establish a state of affairs and a readiness for self government which will give some promise of stability and security.[59]

After several unexpected delays, the Philippine delegation arrived in Washington in June 1922, and its meeting with Harding was highly successful. Aware of Harding's negative views, the members did not push for immediate independence although they indicated they expected it eventually. Both Manuel Quezon, representing the Philippine Senate, and Osmeña, representing the House, asked for greater Filipino control of local government and complained of Wood's autocratic proclivities. Harding's reply was masterly. He reiterated the promise of ultimate independence, claimed that the United States fully understood such aspirations, but alluded to "our larger responsibility" which demanded that for the time being the United States remain in control. Said he: "I must say to you that the time is not yet for independence. . . . Meanwhile, I can only renew the proven assurances of our good intentions . . . no backward step is contemplated. . . . Our relation to your domestic affairs is that of an unselfish devotion which is born of our fate in opening to you the way of liberty of which you dreamed."[60]

While satisfying the Filipinos for the moment, such temporizing did not make Wood's job any easier. Independence leaders pecked away at his authority in the islands and, indeed, during late July 1923 the Philippine legislature demanded the general's recall. Although Harding did not live to react to this situation, his position by mid-1923 was fairly clear. He backed Wood whenever Wood needed it, and he remained convinced that the time for Philippine independence was not yet ripe. Nevertheless, more than Wood, Harding was inclined to permit Filipinos wide latitude in

347

handling their own internal affairs. In this sense, the president was edging toward a more moderate approach to the Philippine problem. He was increasingly attracted to the views of E. A. Gilmore, vice-governor under Wood, who suggested that "the wisest solution for Congress and the Administration lies in an easy acquiescence to these gradual steps of elimination—to this gradual extinction of American sovereignty until only the shadow of it remains. . . . most of the Filipino leaders are willing to accept, for the present at least, the President's recent denial of [independence] if they can substantially eliminate the American executive from local control." [61]

To Wood's credit, it must be mentioned that while the Philippine legislature disliked him for his autocratic actions, he continued to push engineering, sanitation, and internal improvement projects of great benefit to the islands. At his best in planning roadways, hospitals, and schools, or organizing field teams to combat rinderpest, upgrade herds, or drain swamps, Wood can perhaps be forgiven his political limitations. Despite the intermittent furor, these limitations were not really prejudicial to the long-range friendly relationship between the United States and the Philippine Islands. Unlike the appointment of Reily in Puerto Rico, President Harding never had any serious cause to regret his selection and support of Wood.[62]

[5

AMERICAN-RUSSIAN relations during the Harding era provide an interesting study in the vicissitudes of constructing a rational foreign policy in the face of almost insurmountable emotional and ideological obstacles. President Wilson's posture of nonrecognition, American intervention in Siberia in 1919, and the Red Scare of 1919–20 had so poisoned relations with the emerging Soviet power that a new approach was extremely difficult. However, Harding had indicated on several occasions before his inauguration that he was willing to reopen the recognition question with the Soviets and consider the resumption of American-Russian trade relations. Hence, on March 22, 1921, shortly after Harding assumed office, Maxim Litvinov, Soviet representative in Estonia, transmitted to Harding an appeal from Mikhail Kalinin, president of the All-Russian Central Executive Committee, to reverse the Wilson policy and permit both countries to bury the hostility of the recent period.

Discussed at a cabinet meeting on March 25, this request had not a single supporter. Hughes was particularly opposed. He claimed that the Soviets would use American recognition to keep themselves in power, that they would employ their embassy in the United States to spread insidious propaganda, that they would not protect American property or life in the Soviet Union, and that they would not assume the debts and responsibilities which Russia had incurred before the Bolshevik revolution. Hoover, who usually allowed trade possibilities to influence his attitudes, agreed with Hughes in this case. Therefore, that very afternoon, with full cabinet backing and the acquiescence of Harding, Hughes replied to Kalinin that "this government is unable to perceive that there is any proper basis for considering trade relations" and that only after the Soviets guaranteed "the safety of life, the recognition by firm guarantees of private property, the sanctity of contract, and the rights of free labor" could there be any possibility of discussing recognition. Hence, despite Harding's pre-inauguration remarks, the administration's early Russian policy was no different from that of its predecessor.[63]

Russia, meanwhile, was engulfed in tragedy. Poor crops, the ravages of civil war, and the complete breakdown of her economic system caused famine to stalk the land in the late spring and summer of 1921 as millions verged on the edge of starvation. On July 15 the Russian author Maxim Gorky sent a plea to Hoover for American aid to combat the disaster. Hoover immediately recommended through Hughes that the United States meet the request on two conditions: (1) that all Americans held in Russia be immediately released and (2) that American relief workers have complete freedom of action. After some quibbling the Soviets agreed and signed a document to this effect in Riga on August 19. Ten days later advance units of American relief workers began arriving in Moscow.[64]

Support for Russian famine relief was widespread in the United States. Upon President Harding's authorization an American Relief Administration was created, headed by Hoover, to handle the distribution of such aid, and the public was asked to subscribe to it. Even Congress, despite the domestic economic depression, voted in December 1921 $20 million for Russian relief. The motivation was not all altruistic. Farm groups saw in famine relief an outlet for their crop surpluses; shipping interests saw cargoes in the holds of their idle ships; Hughes saw the American Relief Administration as a fact-finding agency; and Hoover saw it as an opportunity for American economic penetration. Aware of these various factors, the Soviets were always suspicious of the organization's activity and gave it less than enthusiastic cooperation. Still, by August 1922 the American Relief Administration had 200 Americans in Russia, overseeing some 18,-000 relief stations at which an estimated 10 million adults and children were fed. In the end, it expended over $60 million—$24 million from the United States government, $12 million in credits from the Soviet government, and $24 million from private and institutional sources in the United States. While there was some criticism of the program, especially the "high living" of some American relief workers and Hoover's uncooperative attitude toward those few private American relief organizations which conducted their own operations, the American Relief Administration project was an unqualified success. Even the suspicious Communists were impressed. Wrote the Bolshevik scholar Mikhail Pavlovich in late 1922: "The aid rendered Russia by the United States in relief to the starving was grandiose, even unprecedented. . . . The Soviet Government and the worker-peasant masses will never forget that great assistance." [65]

The American relief operation provided an excellent excuse for reopening the question of Russian-American trade relations and recognition. Raymond Robins, Senator Borah, Indiana's former Governor James P. Goodrich (who served with the American Relief Administration), and Alexander Gumberg (a fund raiser for it) were among those who advocated a change in policy. Certain American business interests, faced with the prospect of being squeezed out of Russian markets, also joined the protest. Hughes persisted in holding to his no-trade nonrecognition position, but Hoover began to think differently. Although he retained a deep visceral reaction against the Bolsheviks, his work with the American Relief Administration convinced him of their trade potential. By late 1921, he supported the idea that American companies should be allowed in Russia with some semblance of State Department support. Indeed, Hoover argued that American economic penetration might in the long run contribute to a Bolshevik downfall. Thus, where Hughes would eliminate the Bolsheviks by quarantine, Hoover would kill them through commercial and trade involvement. [66]

Before this question could be resolved the United States was reminded that Russia was not merely an American problem. On January 6, 1922, the Allied Supreme Council adopted a resolution to convene a conference of European powers, including Germany and Russia, to discuss "the economic reconstruction of Central and Eastern Europe." The date was fixed for March 8 at Genoa, Italy. The United States was invited to participate.

Washington hesitated. Some Republican leaders claimed that American acceptance would scare the Senate and jeopardize ratification of the Washington Conference disarmament treaties which were shortly to go before that body. On the other hand, leading business and banking interests urged participation and they were supported by elements of the press which declared: "Our present financial interests across the Atlantic are immense; in the future they may easily be even greater. We should be only looking after our own if we took part." [67] The cabinet was divided on the issue with practical economic considerations clashing with moral factors. Meanwhile, Richard Washburn Child, ambassador to Italy, advised against participation because the conference would not be able to ignore political questions, such as recognition of Russia, and the United States might find itself trapped. Influenced by Child's arguments and Hughes's opposition, Harding finally declined the invitation. Actually, Harding's own inclination was for the United States to attend and his final decision was based more on the advice of others than on his own conviction.[68]

Although scheduled for March 8, the Genoa Conference did not open until April 10. Three days before it convened, the State Department announced that Ambassador Child would attend as an "unofficial observer" and report to Washington on the conference's deliberations. In talking to the Associated Press in Rome, Child made it clear that he was *not* a representative. It was obvious, however, that the Hoover approach to the Russian problem had won a minor victory. American economic interest in the outcome at Genoa was too important to ignore. At the conference, Child avoided publicity, listened, watched, and rarely spoke. But when he did speak, he consistently emphasized that the United States could countenance no joint or separate agreements infringing on American economic rights. In a final report on his conference activities to Harding, Child claimed that his presentation of the American position had had "a good effect" but added incongruously: "I believe we escaped a most painful and costly experience by staying away from Genoa." [69]

The Genoa gathering was a failure. It bogged down over Allied demands that the Russians assume Czarist debts and the Russian counter-demand that the Allies pay for the damage caused by Allied intervention. The conference was thrown into further difficulties when, on April 16, the Russians and the Germans entered into a separate agreement at Rapallo restoring diplomatic and trade relations between them without any debt or compensatory arrangements being included. The solid front against Russia thus being broken, the Allies decided to salvage what they could by agreeing to hold another conference at The Hague on June 15. Again the United States was invited but again declined, this time not even bothering to send an "unofficial observer."

The Hague conference also ended in failure and, coupled with the Genoa debacle, reinforced the American nonrecognition position. Harding wrote to Child, "It is very apparent that we have done the wise thing," and Hughes took the occasion to reaffirm the original United States stand. In May in a brief speech to representatives of the Women's International League for Peace and Freedom, the secretary barred any immediate possibility of recognizing the Soviet Union because of Russian internal chaos, their debt-repudiation policy, their complete disregard for international agreements, and their insistence on world revolution.[70]

Rather than close the Russian question, Hughes's May 1922 statement intensified the nonrecognition debate. On May 15 Senator Borah introduced in the Senate a resolution "That the Senate of the United States favors recognition of the present Soviet Government of Russia." Knowing that this resolution had no chance of adoption, Borah had the sole purpose of forcing discussion and securing an airing of those views opposed to Hughes. At about the same time there were numerous statements from Americans inside Russia which also criticized the existing policy. Former Governor Goodrich sent voluminous reports both to the State Department and to Harding recommending a reexamination of nonrecognition and especially the State Department's opposition to trade relations. He concluded: "I believe that the continued policy of isolation and non-recognition of our Government is only delaying the economic reconstruction and the political development of this country. . . . I believe the time is near at hand when we should recognize the Revolution as an accomplished fact, resume relations with Russia, and give American capital a free opportunity to enter." Similarly, Meyer Bloomfield, who also was sending reports on the Russian situation to Harding and the State Department, wrote in

July 1922: "The old regime is done for. . . . I repeat the suggestion for contact with Russia. Other developments will follow as such contact proves desirable. . . . an infiltration into Russia of our best business elements working loyally with the Administration and guided by its policies will show Russia our economic practices and put it on its feet. No other country can do it." [71]

In the face of such views, Hoover reopened with Hughes the possibility of sending an American trade mission to Russia, and Hughes, after sounding out Harding on the matter, unenthusiastically agreed. The president was also skeptical of success, predicting that the Soviets would not accept such a mission except on the basis of equality—a condition which the administration felt it could not grant. In the end the Soviets took precisely this position, asking in return the right to send Russian commercial delegates to study the American economic system. Hughes peremptorily severed all further trade negotiations in mid-September. [72]

Throughout the remainder of 1922 and early 1923 Hughes held fast to his position. In general, public opinion and the press remained firmly behind the administration's policy and retained the naive view, espoused by Hughes, that somehow the American diplomatic and economic quarantine would bring the Russian Communist government to its knees. In the long run, even Hoover's emotional reaction to the Bolsheviks blunted his willingness to advocate further trade contacts and he, too, supported the secretary of state's action. On March 21, 1923, again in a speech to a delegation representing the Women's International League for Peace and Freedom, Hughes flatly declared that the United States would not modify its Russian policy until the USSR recognized Czarist debts, established adequate safeguards for life and property, agreed to abide by international conventions, and ceased its worldwide propaganda activities. *Izvestia* met this pronouncement with scorn, claiming Hughes was simply reiterating the old Wilson position. [73]

Harding publicly backed his secretary of state. But to assure such presidential support, Hughes found it necessary to exert considerable pressure. The secretary bombarded Harding with tales about Russian economic incompetence and continually wrote him letters justifying nonrecognition. Whenever a bit of information appeared which cast doubt on the wisdom of existing policy, Hughes would send it along to the president but with a covering letter saying: "This statement contains a good many inaccura-

353

cies." When Francis B. Loomis, after three months in Russia, sent a detailed report through Hughes to Harding in the spring of 1923 recommending "some kind of recognition," Hughes appended a letter stating: "I fear that Mr. Loomis, despite his recent contact with various Russians, has not gained a just understanding of the situation."[74]

In view of the many contrary opinions reaching Harding, Hughes could not prevent at least some erosion in the president's support for nonrecognition and by the summer of 1923 there were indications that Harding was moving toward a more flexible position. Some ten months before, he had written Ambassador Harvey concerning the latter's changing attitude toward Russian recognition: "Your views are very much in harmony with some which I have entertained for a long while on this important question. Of course, it is quite impossible to discreetly do anything or say anything at the present time."[75] In his correspondence with Hughes, Harding increasingly referred to the nonrecognition position as "State Department policy" rather than "administration policy." Then, in the spring of 1923, he quietly authorized Raymond Robins, a strong proponent of recognition, to go to Russia and report on the latest conditions directly to the White House, by-passing Hughes and the State Department.[76] Alexander Gumberg was so encouraged by this turn of events that he wrote to Borah on July 23, 1923, just ten days before Harding's death: "In spite of the stubbornness of some folks [the] struggle for world peace through rapprochement with Russia will be crowned with success in the near future."[77]

Whatever possibility existed of modifying the American nonrecognition policy, it died with Harding. To the end, the Hughes position *was* official policy. Therefore, despite a few signs of change, the new approach to Russian relations, hoped for by some persons as a result of the election of 1920, failed to materialize. In the eyes of the State Department the Soviet Union remained the Peck's bad boy of the international community.[78]

[6

ALTHOUGH they failed to do so in the Russian case, American economic expansion and trade requirements conditioned to a major extent the nature of the administration's diplomatic response throughout the

Harding era. Of course, neither Harding nor Hughes was responsible for the tremendous upsurge in American overseas economic activity in the immediate postwar years. But they did decide whether American foreign policy would hamper this development or facilitate it.

From the outset, both Hughes and Harding excluded the entry of the United States government into the foreign economic field. For example, the administration quickly reiterated the policy announced by Secretary Houston in the waning months of the Wilson era that no more foreign loans would be made directly by the United States government. Private loans were another matter. Yet even here the Harding administration worked out an arrangement with bankers whereby the State Department was to be kept informed of all private loans to foreign governments and could exercise a monitoring function. The feasibility of all such loan proposals was to be reviewed by the State, Treasury, and Commerce departments, with a decision in writing to be sent by the State Department to the prospective lender. As for the criteria, loans were to be discouraged to (1) foreign governments for balancing budgets, (2) foreign governments for military purposes, (3) foreign monopolies where their conduct adversely affected the American consumer, (4) foreign governments not recognized by the United States, and (5) foreign governments which had failed to pay their earlier obligations to the United States. In no case was a loan's inherent financial soundness to be the sole criterion.[79]

Under this arrangement a private loan could still be floated without government endorsement. Lenders, however, tended to shy away from ventures not "cleared" by the State Department. More especially, they shunned projects regarded as unsound by the Commerce Department. Commerce was generally more knowledgeable about foreign financial affairs than State and even Hughes consulted closely with Hoover on such matters. Surprisingly, Hoover and Commerce were far more careful in their assessment of foreign investments than was either State or Treasury. Commerce, on the other hand, encouraged sound foreign investments far more readily than did either State or Treasury.

On one matter there was common agreement throughout the Harding administration—there should be no discrimination by foreign governments against private American business interests anywhere in the world. In concluding a series of new commercial treaties from 1921 to 1924, Secretary Hughes made the acceptance of this "open-door" proposition his primary goal. As he phrased it in one typical note: "The policy of the Government with relation to foreign investments should be well understood. . . . [It] is the policy of the open door. We seek equality of opportunity for our nationals. We do not attempt to make contracts for them. . . . We do not favor one of our nationals as against another. Given the open door, all who wish are entitled to walk in. We resist policies of discrimination against American capital. This is true whether it relates to oil or telegraphs."[80]

Significantly it was oil and not telegraphs which caused the most crucial test of this open-door policy. Interest in oil was not a monopoly of the United States in the early twenties. The scramble for oil concessions had prompted all the major powers, especially England and France, to conclude separate economic arrangements with nations in the Far East, Middle East, and South America. American businessmen had also entered this competition. The Doheny, Mellon, and Sinclair interests had moved into the South American and Mexican areas while Standard and other groups invaded the Far and Middle East. Oil, after all, was a precious commodity and the lure of tremendous profits was enticing. But oil meant more than profits. Oil also meant national security—oil for the merchant marine and for the navy. The American craze for oil was all the more frenetic because there was an unfounded but growing fear that American domestic supplies would shortly run dry and that the United States in the meantime might find itself shut out of foreign fields, especially the oil-rich Middle East.

American oil diplomacy in the latter area was conditioned by an incredibly complicated patchwork of secret Allied agreements, Arab intrigue, and competing big-power interests.[81] From the beginning the Harding administration protested against exclusive grants of oil rights to foreign companies in those Middle Eastern areas where American companies also had a stake. This was especially true in Persia where Standard Oil was hoping to compete with well-entrenched British oil interests. The British and the French had already conspired to divide the oil-rich Middle East between them and freeze out foreign competitors through a secret arrangement reached at San Remo in April 1920. Following the San Remo agreement, however, Britain and France fell to bickering over their respective spheres of influence, a situation which was further complicated by a war in 1921–22 between Greece and Turkey. Within a few months, Turkey decisively defeated Greece, and Turkish Nationalists under Mustapha Kemal were in no mood to tolerate further outside interference by either Britain or France in areas now under Turkish Nationalist control. Specifically repudiating the Treaty of Sèvres which the Allies had forced upon the Sultanate at the end of World War I and which had established Allied spheres of influence in Turkish-dominated areas (such as Persia), the Nationalists now demanded a completely new peace treaty. The Allies agreed to negotiate one at Lausanne.

The Christian world meanwhile was shocked in mid-1922 by the burning of Smyrna and the atrocities against Christians in Anatolia committed by the Turks after the retreat of the Greek army. In the United States feeling ran particularly high. The White House was bombarded with demands that the United States "do something," some even suggesting American unilateral action to create a separate Armenian state for Christians in the Middle East. Missionary groups and private Middle Eastern relief organizations, especially, urged the State Department to assume "our share of responsibility."

Except for the dispatch of several destroyers to Constantinople in September 1922 to help evacuate women and children, the administration was not prepared to undertake further moves. Indeed, Harding did everything in his power to keep the United States from being overcome by the emotionalism surrounding the Christian massacres. More than once he reminded Hughes that since he had no intention of sending American forces there, the State Department ought not raise hopes by bellicose statements. He also requested Hughes to reply to the proponents of intervention that while the United States would remain interested in the Armenian-Turkish situation in a humanitarian way, it would under no circumstances become involved militarily.[82]

In view of the American emotionalism over Armenia and American oil companies' interest in oil, the proposed Lausanne Peace Conference presented the administration with a serious problem. In late October 1922 the United States, as a former Ally, was invited to attend along with Great Britain, France, Rumania, Yugoslavia, Japan, Greece, and Turkey. Hughes was suddenly faced with the task of accomplishing the impossible —protecting the American humanitarian and economic stake in the Middle East without assuming correlative political responsibilities. Immediately both American businesses and humanitarian and religious groups joined voices to urge American participation in the conference. Secretary Hoover, whose Commerce Department had often acted as consultant to American oil men in the Persian–Middle Eastern area, warned that non-participation would be a great mistake. Hoover saw the Lausanne Conference as an excellent opportunity to assert the open-door policy and help eliminate the last vestiges of Allied spheres of influence.[83]

In a fourteen-page position paper on American relations with the Middle East, Hughes told Harding on October 24 that American attendance at Lausanne was required "to present our own views" and "for the protection of our own interests." However, since the United States had no specific concern with the details relating to a new peace settlement between Turkey and the Allied powers, Hughes recommended an American role at Lausanne similar to that at Genoa, with Ambassador Child again representing the United States. Concluded Hughes:

In other words, I do not recommend that we should participate in the peace conference. . . . I do not think that we should be involved in negotiations rejecting policies and aims in which we have no share. I do think that we should be constantly in command of adequate information, keen for the protection of American interests, ready to throw the full weight of our influence to obtain assurances for the freedom of the Straits and the protection of minorities, candid as to our views, and in a position at any suitable time to make the separate agreement which at some time must be made with the Turkish Government recognized by the Allied Powers.[84]

The conference opened on November 20, 1922, with Ambassador Child in attendance, assisted by Joseph Grew, United States minister to Switzerland, and Admiral Mark L. Bristol, American high commissioner to Turkey. In contrast to Genoa, there was no attempt this time to minimize the American representatives' roles or emphasize their unique status. Indeed, the State Department went out of its way to indicate that they would participate actively on all matters affecting American interests and would "not be mere unofficial messenger boys." This soon became obvious. They spoke on most matters before the conference and were listened to with respect. The American delegation frequently supported Turkey, to the discomfort of the Allies, especially in Turkey's insistence on the full restoration of her sovereignty. Conversely, the delegation exercised a restraining influence on Turkish belligerency. The American delegation made it clear that the United States stood for freedom of the Straits without discrimination and for the protection of Christians within the Turkish state. In particular, Ambassador Child emphasized the necessity of an economic open door in the Middle East, a position which the Turks also supported.[85]

Because of Allied-Turkish arguments over the so-called capitulations (privileges reserved for the Allies in Turkey under the old Treaty of Sèvres), the Lausanne Conference broke down in January 1923. But it reconvened in April in the hope that the deadlock could be resolved. Ambassador Child did not return to this second conference and the American position was represented by Grew. Keeping both Hughes and Harding fully informed, Grew persistently backed the Turks in their resistance to Allied pressure concerning the capitulations. In the end the Allies had to abandon their claims to special privileges, a situation which made the Americans rejoice. The final treaty between Turkey and the Allies, signed in July 1923, provided for (1) the equal treatment of foreigners with regard to economic opportunities, (2) abrogation of the capitulations, (3) recognition of the philanthropic, educational, and religious institutions existing in Turkey before October 30, 1914, (4) Turkish protection for the life and liberty of minorities, and (5) freedom of transit in the Straits for all nations in peace and war. While the United States was not a signatory to this treaty, it regarded the final product as fully compatible with the open-door principle and strengthening the American position. Harding later said, "I firmly believe that the American influence at Lausanne played a becoming part, and an influential part, in making for peace." Grew got to the heart of the matter much more succinctly: "We won our fight." [86]

As Hughes had hoped, a by-product of the Lausanne Conference was the conclusion of a separate American-Turkish Treaty which ended the confusion in relations between the two countries occasioned by the termination of World War I. By this treaty the United States secured the same rights the Allies had received in the final Lausanne agreement. Also concluded were a separate extradition treaty, a separate statement concerning the treatment of American religious, philanthropic, and educational enterprises in Turkey, and a declaration concerning the administration of justice for Americans in Turkey. The Armenian question, much to the disgust of many partisans in the United States, was not mentioned for fear that it would jeopardize Turkey's acceptance of the final product. These various documents were signed on August 6, 1923.[87]

On a short-range basis, the Harding administration's success in the Middle East was considerable. Cordial relations between the United States and Turkey were reestablished and set a pattern for later contacts between the United States and other Middle Eastern countries. American oil companies thereafter found fewer barriers in their path and markedly increased their activities in that part of the world. The Harding administration's open-door policy became the foundation upon which their lucrative operations rested and belied the claim, despite American inaction over the Armenian massacres, that the United States followed a policy of "noninvolvement" in the Middle East. In reality, the State Department, with Harding's full approval, not only viewed with sympathy American business activity there but guarded it against encroachments by foreign powers. Beginning with Harding, American humanitarian interests in the Middle East became less and less important as economic considerations became increasingly more significant. This shift in emphasis did not advance the United States to the status of a major power in the area overnight, but by the time of Harding's death the trend in that direction was unmistakable.

[7

REESTABLISHING adequate American-European relations in the postwar years presented the Harding administration its greatest diplomatic challenge. The League fight had so poisoned the atmosphere that both Harding and Hughes found it very difficult to act on European matters. In view of intense congressional feelings, President Harding disliked having to create policy in this area. Once he shocked some reporters by off-handedly remarking, "I don't know anything about this European stuff." Such remarks betrayed as much cowardice as ignorance, and whenever possible he did leave European policy in the hands of Hughes and the various European ambassadors. He never demonstrated the same interest in Europe that he did either in Latin America or in the Middle East.

Harding was frankly confused by the complicated diplomatic and economic aspects of the European situation. He was not alone. Few Americans fully comprehended the altered circumstances between the United States and Europe which arose not only from American rejection of the League but also from the emergence of the United States as a creditor nation. Europe, for her part, while more sophisticated about the economic factors involved, persisted too long in dwelling on the political ramifications of America's nonparticipation in the League and failed abysmally in understanding American attitudes or American psychology. Europeans, for example, were offended when Harding's inaugural address mentioned neither France, nor England, nor Germany. And European statesmen too quickly and too naively assumed that the American loans granted in World War I would be forgiven, or at least funded in relation to all inter-Allied debts.

Even before Harding assumed office, the basic American position on the war-debt issue was clear. President Wilson had said in early 1920 that the United States would not participate in any general debt-funding scheme and Secretary of the Treasury Carter Glass, as well as his successor David Houston, repeatedly warned Europeans that the United States was concerned only with what was owed it, not with inter-Allied debts as a whole. To a British suggestion for a general debt cancellation, the Wilson administration gave a flat "No." President Wilson also established the policy that the United States "cannot consent to connect the reparation question with that of inter-governmental indebtedness."[88]

In taking this position the government was merely reflecting the attitudes of the average citizen. He did not regard the war loans, amounting to some $10 billion, as something to be borne by the American taxpayer. He fully expected that they would be repaid as soon as the war was over and any sign of European reluctance was immediately condemned. He failed to comprehend that these loans had really benefited the American economy and that Europe had not actually hired the money, as Coolidge later claimed, but that the American government had done so through wartime taxes and bond drives. In any case, the taxpayer easily translated the loan issue into a moral question which ultimately overshadowed both the economic and the political factors involved. Periodic European requests for cancellation merely reinforced his conviction of the complete moral bankruptcy of his former allies.

The Harding administration's debt policy was simply an extension of this feeling. At one of its first meetings in April 1921, the cabinet unanimously endorsed the full repayment of all war debts. The "big three" of the cabinet, Mellon, Hughes, and Hoover, joined forces on this matter. While each viewed the debts in a slightly different context—Hoover saw them as a trade problem, Hughes as a political problem, and Mellon as a fiscal problem—they agreed that they should be repaid. Of the three, Hoover was perhaps the most sophisticated in his views because he was dimly aware of the complicated economic ramifications involved. For that reason, he urged the widest possible flexibility in concluding final repayment agreements and saw the necessity of tying all such repayment schedules to the economic rehabilitation of Europe.[89]

Establishing precise procedures for repayment was difficult. The Wilson administration had not been able to arrive at a proper formula and offered few guidelines to its successor. Perhaps it was just as well since Mellon early despaired of any set rules because of the vast differences in solvency of the various debtor nations. Leaning toward Hoover's views, Mellon ultimately recommended to Harding that Congress be requested to grant full plenary powers to the Treasury Department to deal with the funding problem on a nation-by-nation basis.[90]

Harding forwarded Mellon's request but Congress flatly refused to grant the authority. Both the House Ways and Means Committee and the Senate Finance Committee concluded that the administration would be "too lenient" in concluding repayment agreements. As a result, after considerable debate and delay, on February 9, 1922, a Debt Funding Bill was approved by Congress which created a Debt Funding Commission, headed by the secretary of the treasury. This commission was empowered to make settlements but only within the framework of the following restrictions: (1) the time extension could not go beyond June 15, 1947, nor could the interest rate be less than 4.25 percent per annum; (2) the exchange of bonds or obligations of one foreign government for those of any other foreign government was forbidden as cancellation of any part of the debt; and (3) once agreed upon by the commission and a foreign government, the repayment settlement could not be revised or changed at a later date.[91]

Clearly the administration was prepared to be more lenient with the nation's debtors than was Congress. Nevertheless, believing a fight with Congress over the issue would be useless, Harding signed the measure and appointed as the commission's first members Mellon, Hoover, Hughes, Senator Smoot, and Representative Theodore Burton. Later, in 1923, Representative Charles R. Crisp, former Representative Richard Olney, and former United States Shipping Board Chairman Edward N. Hurley were added. Throughout its life to 1927, the commission's membership remained intact except for the substitution of Frank Kellogg for Hughes in 1925.

The commission held its first meeting on April 18, 1922. Immediately there was trouble. France quickly announced that she could not possibly adhere to the restrictions in the Debt Funding Act. Grumblings also came from other Allied governments. Indeed, Europe at the moment was being swept by a wave of anti-Americanism, prompted in no small measure by the passage of the Debt Funding Act. Simultaneously there was in Europe a resurgence of the suggestion that the debts be canceled altogether. Ambassador Harvey indicated from London that the British wanted the United States to "offer" cancellation, but their pride would not permit them to ask for it formally. France, of course, strongly favored cancellation, as did the other Allies. However, throughout the summer and fall of 1922, the administration made it clear that cancellation was unacceptable although Hoover, Mellon, Hughes, and Harding all realized that the Debt Funding Act would somehow have to be by-passed if any repayment agreements were to be concluded.

Since Great Britain was the other major holder of Allied debts, her reaction to the American position was a critical factor in a solution to the whole problem. During the summer of 1922 Ambassador Harvey encouraged the British to begin talks with the United States concerning her debt even though the Debt Funding Act made a successful outcome doubtful. Finally, on January 4, 1923, a British debt commission, headed by Stanley Baldwin, chancellor of the exchequer, arrived in Washington and a few days later negotiations were begun. Baldwin indicated that Britain intended to pay her debt and asked only that the arrangements be fair. American negotiators, desiring to meet the British halfway, simply chose to ignore the debt-funding measure. As a result, a settlement was reached on January 19 whereby the total British debt of $4,604,128,085.74 was to be paid off in sixty-two annual installments at an interest rate of 3 percent for the first ten years and 3.5 percent for the remaining fifty-two.[92]

Clearly contrary to the Debt Funding Act, this agreement now had to receive congressional approval. Even before it was presented to Congress, the settlement was condemned by a number of senators who called it a contract made "by the bond sharks of Wall Street." But Harding indicated that he wanted it passed and warned that he could not guarantee the success of any future debt negotiations if the British arrangement was rejected. Indeed he considered the matter so important that he appeared in person before a joint session on February 7, 1923, to urge its passage. "The call of the world today," he said, "is for integrity of agreements, the sanctity of covenants, the validity of contracts. Here is the first clearing of the war-clouded skies in a debt-burdened world."[93]

The House endorsed the British Debt Agreement two days later by a vote of 291–44. The next day, February 10, the Senate Committee on Finance reported the bill favorably to the Senate floor. Six days later it was approved by a vote of 70–13, but not before an amendment sponsored by Senator Robinson was added which made it mandatory for Congress to pass on each such debt agreement in the future. The majority of the press complimented the British for concluding the agreement and then applauded Congress's decision to accept it. The results were salutary. American good will toward Britain increased almost immediately, especially since the terms were regarded as "rather hard." Moreover, it removed from British-American relations a disturbing irritant which might have reached epidemic proportions in view of the subsequent activities of the Hearsts and other professional British tail-twisters in the late twenties. More important, the agreement had a helpful psychological effect upon other debtor countries in that it breeched the provisions contained in the Debt Funding Act of the year before.[94]

During its existence, the Debt Commission made funding agreements with fifteen other countries. The aggregate indebtedness was $11,522,354,-000 and the interest rate varied between 3 and 3½ percent. Although the British agreement was the only major one concluded before Harding's death, it was the most important one because it set the general pattern and procedures governing all the rest: (1) the required payment of the principal in full, (2) an adjustment based on an individual country's ability to pay through regulating the interest rate and not by any change in the principal, and (3) the principal plus accrued interest to be paid over sixty-two years.[95]

On the specific relationship between war debts and reparations, the United States consistently tried to deny the undeniable. Under the Versailles Treaty an Allied Reparations Commission had been saddled with the responsibility of defining the amount, method, and schedule of payment of German reparations. In April 1921 it set the total amount at $33 billion (or 132 billion gold marks). From 1921 to 1925 Germany was to pay $375 million annually and about $900 million thereafter.[96]

Almost immediately Germany defaulted and threats of force by the Allied powers, especially France, did not alter the situation. British leaders, slowly accepting Keynes's theory about the disastrous economic results of the Versailles Treaty, immediately urged the all-around cancellation of reparations as well as war debts. France, who was desirous of debt cancellation, hesitated on the question of reparations. The American position on war debts made the cancellation of reparations an academic question anyway.

While some journals, such as the *Nation* and *New Republic*, warned that it would be impossible for the United States to divorce reparations from the question of inter-Allied debts, overwhelming American sentiment demanded doing precisely that. When Great Britain in mid-December 1921 advocated the convening of a second Washington conference to deal with war debts and reparations together, Hughes was unenthusiastic and Harding torpedoed the suggestion by saying, "it is not possible to consider it." Later, in June 1922, when it was proposed that the United States accept the German indemnity in substitution for all American claims, Harding asked the opinion of his cabinet. The suggestion was unanimously opposed.[97]

Perhaps, as some critics later claimed, the Harding administration should have done something about the reparations problem in 1921–22, but at the time even those few who were agreeable to such action were cowed by popular and congressional fear of becoming needlessly involved in the "disputes of Europe." As the reparations crisis deepened in late 1922 and as the German economic system neared collapse, the administration continued to sit on its hands. There was some pious talk about "helping," but no concrete American action was taken. Neither Hughes nor Harding believed that much could be accomplished anyway in view of the harsh French attitude toward Germany.

That attitude was a crucial factor and when Germany finally defaulted on her reparation payments in January 1923, French and Belgian troops entered the Ruhr in retaliation. With the complete debasement of the German economy now in sight, Washington became truly scared. Talk of non-involvement in Europe's affairs subsided as it became obvious that Europe was again drifting into chaos and turmoil. Yet, for the moment, the administration pursued a confused course. In December, just before the Ruhr occupation, conflicting statements came from the White House indicating that the United States would "help find a solution" and that involvement with Europe was "unavoidable," but that "no specific action" would be taken. As the *New York Times* put it: "We appear to be in the negotiation, at the same time that we are endeavoring to keep out of it. . . . It would require a master of interpretation to extract a clear and consistent plan out of the confusing and contradictory intimations emanating from the White House."[98]

Actually the Harding administration was gradually moving away from its aloofness to Europe's dilemmas and was suffering the temporary inconsistencies resulting therefrom. Both Hughes and Harding had become convinced that some American response was necessary, especially since it was now obvious that America's ability to collect its war debts was, at least to some extent, tied to reparations. Harding had even asked Hughes to watch for a favorable opportunity to intervene, and that chance came in late December. The secretary had been invited to deliver an address on the Washington Disarmament Conference to the American Historical Association at New Haven on December 29, 1922. At the last moment, after securing clearance from the White House, Hughes inserted in his speech a proposal concerning the reparations impasse. To the assembled historians, he said, "The crux of the European situation lies in the settlement of reparations," and added, "There can be no economic recuperation in Europe unless Germany recuperates." Declaring that force was no solution, he concluded: "Why should [the affected parties] not invite men of the highest authority in finance in their respective countries—men of such prestige, experience and honor that their agreement upon the amount to be paid, and upon a financial plan for working out the payments would be accepted throughout the world as the most authoritative expression obtainable? . . . I have no doubt that distinguished Americans would be willing to serve in such a commission."[99]

This suggestion provided the basis for a new approach to the reparations question and opened new possibilities of contact between the interested parties. Significantly, Hughes's New Haven address marked the transition of American policy under Harding from one of calculated non-involvement in Europe's affairs to a cautious participation. Harding, with his skill at conciliation and his tact in handling the sensitivities of isolationist congressmen, had helped create the domestic political conditions which had made such a new approach possible, while Hughes had selected the timing and the issue for its implementation. Three months after Harding's death, the Allied governments issued invitations for the convening of a financial commission such as Hughes had proposed. Chairmaned by an American, Charles Dawes, this commission successfully stripped the reparations question of its political incrustations and, beginning in 1924, slowly led Europe back from the brink of economic disaster.

[8

IF DEBT funding and the reparations problem reflected the administration's increasing involvement in European affairs by 1923, other events demonstrated the fact even more clearly. In the first several months after March 1921, the Harding administration took almost no notice of the League. Then, beginning in late 1921, it began to move toward some cooperation with the League. Hughes believed that there was an advantage in maintaining contact, although on a tentative and selective basis. Harding, in turn, was decidedly friendly to the nonpolitical activities of the League and encouraged American participation in matters of health and social welfare. In reply to an invitation for the United States to participate in a League-sponsored international health conference at Brussels in late 1921, Harding stated his position to Hughes: "I can see no consistency in studied effort on our part to ignore the work of the League because we do not find it consistent to accept membership therein. I think we ought to maintain a position in which we may be able to commend the good which it accomplishes." This the United States should do, added Harding, in spite of "those who look upon the League with exceptional terror."[100]

In this connection, Joseph Grew, minister to Switzerland, played an increasingly significant role. Hughes left to Grew's discretion how far he should go in Geneva in maintaining contact with the League but cautioned him to be circumspect. As Grew wrote to a friend at the time: "[Hughes] emphasized the importance of avoiding publicity, and I cannot therefore run the risk of visiting the League's offices or of openly moving to Geneva during sessions of the Council or other bodies." However, Grew's presence was more than symbolic and as 1921 merged into 1922 he became less secretive and more direct in his relationship with League activities. Grew himself was an advocate of closer ties with the League and subtly worked in that direction. Still, his position was always ambiguous and the Allies at Geneva chuckled over this "subterranean channel between the State Department and the League of Nations."[101]

By mid-1922, the United States had developed a pragmatic relationship with the League, based largely on humanitarian interests. In keeping with Harding's wishes, the State Department began to send "unofficial observers" to the meetings of various League agencies. The ruse of the "unofficial observer" allowed the administration to by-pass the Senate's earlier injunction that the United States was not to be officially represented at League functions. In this way the administration was able to meet the demands of diplomatic reality while leaving the Senate to live in a world of its own making. Later, in explaining the role of these observers, Hughes made this interesting statement: "These representatives were unofficial only in the sense that they were not official members of the League committees or organs; they were official as far as the U.S. was concerned in the sense that they represented the Government for the purposes for which they were appointed. In effect, this system amounted to full American representation."[102]

Before his death, Harding authorized American participation on the Advisory Committee of the International Labor Office concerning anthrax control, on the Advisory Committee on Traffic in Opium, on the Commission for the Suppression of Traffic in Women and Children, and at the League Conference for the Suppression of Obscene Publications. At the time of his death, he and Hughes were toying with the idea of placing an American representative on the League's Finance Committee and sending Grew to represent the United States on the Temporary Mixed Commission relating to arms control. In short, by 1923 the United States had moved far afield from its 1921 position.[103] Had Harding lived and Hughes remained secretary of state there is reason to believe that this trend toward cooperation with the League would have continued at an accelerated rate.

The World Court offers an even better example of the Harding administration's attempt to establish a more direct relationship with Europe and the rest of the world by 1923. The United States had been a supporter of the World Court idea since the late nineteenth century. But because the Court of International Justice, created after World War I, was semi-attached to the League and the judges elected through the League bodies, it was claimed that American adherence would compromise the anti-League position of the United States. Certainly anti-League congressmen and irreconcilables wanted nothing to do with it.

Harding had never evidenced such antipathy. In connection with his "association of nations" idea in the campaign of 1920 he had always referred to "a world court." In his inaugural address he was even more specific: "We . . . would gladly join in that expressed conscience of progress which seeks to clarify and write the laws of international relationship, and establish a world court for the disposition of such justiciable questions as nations are agreed to submit thereto." [104] However, because of the various pressures on the new administration neither Harding nor Hughes was able to turn his attention to the Court problem for over a year. Then, on October 30, 1922, in a speech in Boston, Secretary Hughes declared: "We favor, and always have favored, an international court of justice for the determination according to judicial standards of justiciable international disputes. I believe that suitable arrangements can be made for the participation by this Government in the election of judges of the International Court which has been set up, so that this Government may give its formal support to that court as an independent tribunal of international justice." [105] The next day, in reply to inquiries about the Hughes speech, the White House disclosed that it fully backed the secretary's views and that the United States ought to "look toward participation." [106]

It was the intention of Hughes to push quickly for Senate consideration, but Harding counseled caution. The president had no desire to complicate further the upcoming congressional elections of November 1922, and he feared the effect of a struggle over the Court issue on the chances of his ship subsidy bill. He requested Hughes to wait until closer to the end of the 67th Congress before making a move. [107] Finally in February 1923, while home with the flu, Hughes worked out four reservations which he believed were necessary to assure American adherence, and he asked the president to submit them to the Senate. Harding agreed and on February 24 formally requested the Senate to endorse American membership on the basis of the Hughes reservations. Harding stated that "for a long period" the administration had been "considering methods whereby the United States could join without establishing any legal relation to the

League." The Hughes reservations, he said, accomplished this and there was "good reason to believe" that these reservations would be "acceptable to the signatory powers." He concluded: "I most earnestly urge your favorable advice and consent. I would rejoice if some action could be taken, even in the short period which remains of the present session."[108]

The proposal immediately went to the Senate Foreign Relations Committee where a split vote (8–8) permitted the chairman, Senator Lodge, to delay action until "further information could be obtained." A list of questions was compiled by Senator Borah which was then given to the president for reply. In handing this list to the president on February 27, Lodge pointedly remarked that there probably would be "some difficulty in making a detailed reply in time to have it brought to the attention of the Committee during the current session of Congress." But Harding quickly summoned Hughes, apprised him of the situation, and the secretary the next day handed the replies to Harding who fired them back to a surprised Lodge.[109]

The questions asked by the committee were designed to embarrass the administration, but Hughes handled them masterfully. He defended his four reservations as giving the United States all the protection and safeguards it needed: (1) American adherence to the Court would not bind the United States to the League, (2) the United States could participate in the selection of judges even though not an official member of the League, (3) the United States would pay its fair share of the Court's expenses as determined and appropriated by Congress, and (4) the protocol for the World Court could not be amended without the consent of the United States.

The committee was caught flatfooted by Hughes's quick answers and most observers agreed that Harding and Hughes had scored heavily against their opponents on the Court issue. As Harding wrote to Hughes on March 5, the day after Congress adjourned: "I am delighted to say to you that every newspaper reaction has been, to my mind, a favorable one, though it was not expected that the Senate would take any decisive action before adjournment. I think your prompt reply has put the Administration in a position of advantage."[110]

Neither Hughes nor Harding showed any inclination to lose that advantage and thereafter pressed the fight against the Court's opponents. On this issue Harding found himself at odds with some of his oldest Senate friends, such as Lodge, Brandegee, and McCormick, while receiving support from erstwhile Democratic enemies like Harrison, Robinson, and King. This obviously was a different Harding from the one who had so gingerly side-stepped irreconcilable belligerency in 1920 and 1921. Some commentators explained this by claiming that the president was merely a captive of Hughes on the Court issue. But Harding's own conviction was sincere. His determination to secure American participation was amply underscored in a letter to Malcolm Jennings in which he declared, "I should adhere to my [Court] position firmly even though the threat of political disruption were carried on to the utmost."[111] On April 24 in a luncheon speech to the Associated Press in New York City he took the opportunity to state this determination publicly. In this address he reiterated his opposition to the League, but defended the Court. In seeking American adherence he claimed that he was not creating conditions for American entry to the League "by the side door, the back door, or the cellar door." The League, he said, "is not for us." But he added, "we ought to be a party to the [Court] agreement, assume our part in its maintenance, and give to it the benefit such influence as our size and wealth and ideals may prove to be."[112]

Secretary Hughes, of course, was delighted by Harding's forthright stand and worked hand-in-glove with him throughout the spring of 1923. In a series of three speeches from April to June, the secretary supplemented the president's remarks by urging acceptance. Hoover also was active, claiming that American adherence was in keeping with traditional Republican party policy. Other advocates of the Court, whether Democratic or Republican, entered the lists to support the president. But they met a determined foe. The opposition fell into two groups: (1) irreconcilables or isolationists who thought Harding's action traitorous, and (2) all those anti-Harding Republicans who hoped to engineer his replacement in 1924. In the former category were men like Borah and Johnson; in the latter were LaFollette and his henchmen. These persons maintained that although they, too, wanted *a* Court, they did not want *this* Court. It was "sinister and subversive," said LaFollette; Johnson claimed it was a "trap." Public opinion, however, backed the administration and journals all across the political spectrum came to its defense. Harding's April 24 speech, especially, was widely applauded, at least partly because it showed a determination to stand up to the Borahs, LaFollettes, Johnsons, and Lodges.

371

The *Atlanta Constitution* reflected a common opinion when it claimed that Harding's courage "commands a deep citizen respect" and concluded: ". . . the American people today think more of Harding. They admire a firm leader and one whose conviction is not trimmed to political expediency."[113]

Unfortunately Harding did not quite live up to his billing. Although on more than one occasion he had indicated that his Court position was unshakable, his natural tendency to conciliate and to seek party harmony ultimately clouded his resolve. Harry Daugherty, who was very apprehensive about the impact of the Court battle on Harding's political future, begged him in late April to drop the issue. Barring that, said Daugherty, he at least should mollify the opposition by divorcing the Court *completely* from the League. John T. Adams, successor to Hays as chairman of the Republican National Committee, told the president the same thing in early June. Hence, as a trial balloon, Harding delivered another address on the Court in St. Louis on June 28, 1923, while traveling westward toward Alaska. It was a mistake. This speech was ambiguous and reminiscent of some of his 1920 campaign utterances on the League. In essence, he left the door open for the addition of other reservations besides those of Hughes to remake the Court "in theory and practice, in form and in substance, beyond the shadow of doubt, a World Court and not a League Court." At the same time, he reiterated his own belief that the four Hughes reservations alone would keep the United States "wholly free from any legal relations to the League."[114]

Borah and others like him immediately claimed that Harding's suggestion of a Court *completely* separate from the League was exactly what they had in mind. Hughes, Hoover, and other Court supporters simply chose to view the Harding speech on June 28 a temporary aberration dictated by political expediency. Harding died before he could elaborate on the matter himself. Maybe he had no intention of basically altering his position. But whatever he intended, it could not have produced a less favorable result than what actually happened. Harding's successor, Calvin Coolidge, was completely unable to hold the Senate in line and, some three years later, had to abandon the Court project altogether. To the end, such senators as Borah and Johnson engaged in their destructive tactics. As the *New York Times* had prophetically stated in May 1923: "The large supply of lethal weapons and poison gas which [the irreconcilables] accumulated for use against President Wilson is expected to hold out long enough to do President Harding's [Court] measure to death."[115]

[9

IN THE customary analysis of American diplomacy during the twenties, the actions of the Harding administration are never considered independently and are always submerged in the broad generalities which are reserved for the era as a whole. Although Hughes normally occupies a prominent place in such discussions, Warren Harding is only briefly mentioned. Usually he is described merely as the man who appointed Hughes secretary of state and convened the Washington Conference. Yet the record shows that during the most formative years of the 1920's, 1921–23, Warren Harding exercised considerable influence.

This influence represented a significant contribution, particularly in view of the disastrous diplomatic legacy left by the Wilson administration. Not only were American relationships throughout the world in a tangled mess when Harding took over, but the domestic political atmosphere was inimical to any diplomatic achievement. American politicians of both parties were wary of undertaking or sponsoring any new departures or risks. Unquestionably, Harding accurately gauged the feeling of the American people and their congressmen when he gingerly kept aloof from official participation in many of Europe's and the world's affairs. Yet, along with Hughes, he struggled to adjust foreign policy to the realities of American power.

By 1923 Harding and his administration had developed some satisfactory short-run solutions to many postwar problems despite the wariness of the public and the obstinacy of the Senate. The administration made significant progress toward better relations with Central and South America, began the liquidation of intervention in the Caribbean, protected American business interests in the Middle East, formalized debt-funding procedures, initiated a new approach to the reparations question, established a quasi-formal relationship with the League, and began moves for American adherence to the World Court. Looking back over this record, Secretary Hughes was prompted to exclaim in 1923: "I can see no reason to apologize for the accomplishments of this Administration in its foreign relations." He added, "I may venture to say that two years ago few would have believed that the measure of progress was possible that has actually been attained under the leadership of President Warren G. Harding."[116]

Whatever the verdict, it cannot be charged, as many writers later did, that this record represented a retreat into "a sullen and selfish isolation." Criticism of the record can, of course, be made, but it must be made on other than isolationist grounds. Leaving the moral question of international responsibility aside, certainly one of the main faults of the Harding-Hughes program was a lack of effective coordination between the nation's economic and trade requirements and its diplomatic-political goals. In this regard, the Harding administration's error was not in instituting isolationist policies but in attempting to retain traditional diplomatic caution while simultaneously working toward a privileged position in the markets of the world. Its relatively unsophisticated attitudes on such matters as war debts and reparations posed problems for the long-range future for both the United States and Europe, as did its acceptance of business requirements in certain others areas of the world as being the sole foundation upon which even a cautious American diplomatic involvement rested. Having effected a needed corrective from Wilsonian idealism in foreign affairs, the Harding administration unconsciously set up the conditions for an overemphasis in the opposite direction. If idealism, alone, would not undergird a successful American foreign policy, neither would mere self-interest or materialism. At the same time, the Harding administration often took only a restricted view of many diplomatic problems and geared its actions to achieve only remedial or interim goals. Also it possessed a dangerous naiveté about the ability of the United States to influence world affairs merely by example or by indirect methods and contacts.

Such weaknesses, however, cannot detract from the immediate overall success. Nor can they alter the fact that by 1923 President Harding had become aware of the need for more aggressive and dynamic diplomatic leadership. That this "new" Harding was something more than imaginary was reflected in the press comments at the time. As the *Atlanta Constitution* expressed it: "His record in reversing his own pre-election policy as to international relations—a position produced by the broader viewpoint of contact—was in the face of circumstances the highest example of true statesmanship, for he sacrificed political expediency to a great national duty and to a new world vision."[117] Perhaps more accurate and less sweeping was the statement by William Allen White shortly before Harding's death: "I believe that so far as it is humanly possible to enlarge and energize an American participation in [world affairs], President Harding is doing all that can be done."[118]

Typically, Harding himself remained outwardly unconcerned about contemporary verdicts on his administration's diplomatic performance and was convinced that the trend of events would justify its actions in this field just as in the domestic area. He firmly believed that the art of diplomacy could be no more successful than the art of politics would permit and that his administration was in each instance achieving what was politically attainable. In the end his diplomatic record displayed all the short-term successes and long-range drawbacks attendant upon such a belief.

XII

New Approaches in Domestic Policy

[1

IF SOME new approaches in foreign policy were visible by the end of the Harding administration, so also were some discernible shifts in domestic affairs. Certain of these developments, especially in the fields of economics and business, continued to reflect the basic conservatism of the administration. But others displayed a considerable degree of flexibility and even of progressive thinking. Unquestionably the fall election of 1922 was a potent conditioning factor for some of these changes. The emergence of the "new" Harding, increasingly independent of Congress and more self-assured in his presidential role, was also a significant element.

It would be a mistake, however, to assume that all the innovative reactions of the administration to domestic problems were the result of political expediency or occasioned by fear of further retribution at the polls. In his first congressional message in April 1921, Harding had assumed a number of liberal positions, recommending, for example, increased federal action in the fields of social welfare, radio regulation, aviation expansion, and highway development. This strong nationalistic outlook stood in marked contrast to some of the standpat aspects of the administration and represented one of the paradoxes of the Harding era.

From 1921 to 1923 there was a slow shift in administration concern from the postwar problems of economic depression to the ways of sustaining prosperity through cooperative state-federal and private-federal planning and action. This altered emphasis was plainly evident in Harding's last state of the union message, delivered to Congress shortly after the fall elections in December 1922. Billed as a "labor of love," this speech enlarged on some of Harding's suggestions of April 1921 and contained his sincere assessment of what was needed to maintain a vigorous and healthy nation. Yet it was more than that. It was a political manifesto designed to reaffirm his basic orthodoxy while at the same time presenting to his administration's critics a reflective and moderately progressive side.

Revised and edited almost to the moment of its delivery, this December message left no doubt that the administration was still a "business" administration. However, Harding raised conservative eyebrows by flatly stating that in any future war business should be conscripted along with all other resources. As for taxes, he indicated general support for Mellon's policies but declared the nation needed a more equitable income-tax structure, offering greater relief to all classes, not merely the wealthy. In the labor field, he urged the abolition of the Railroad Labor Board and suggested that its functions be transferred to the Interstate Commerce Commission. He strongly advocated the elimination of child labor by constitutional amendment. He suggested the compulsory registration of aliens and their indoctrination through federally sponsored Americanization programs. Indicating his concern for the continuing plight of the farmer, he urged a further expansion in rural credits and cheaper rural transportation. He also recommended an expansion in cooperative farm buying and selling. Gazing into the future, he suggested that the whole problem of transportation be studied immediately, especially the impact of the automobile, and emphasized the need for an integrated highway network. As for the railroads, Harding advocated their merger into larger and more logical systems, an interchange of freight cars, and the use of motor trucks as "feeders." Turning to internal improvements, he proposed the initiation of more reclamation, irrigation, and conservation projects through joint state-federal action. He further encouraged the rapid development of water-power sites and asked that plans be made for a unified system of distribution for steam, water, and electric power. On the question of prohibition, his position was clear. Despite the difficulties encountered, he supported the enforcement of the Volstead Act.[1]

As an "action" message for Congress, this address was virtually worthless. It contained few recommendations which the legislature could immediately adopt. But in view of the current ineffectiveness of Congress, this was perhaps not a serious defect. The speech was mainly the reflections of a frustrated president whose own thoughts were in flux about the primary domestic problems confronting the nation. As such, the message was favorably received by the country at large. Said the *New York Times* in an editorial: "The general spirit of his message is excellent," and added that it was a pity "it cannot all be at once crystallized into the statute book." Even liberal journals found the message "strikingly progressive" and admitted that it might ultimately provide "a constructive program of the first importance."[2]

[2

WHATEVER new directions the December 1922 state of the union message may have pointed to, it was clear that Harding did not contemplate any basic alteration in his administration's policy toward business. Throughout, the government's posture was one of a benevolent helpmeet. The administration frankly advocated "the least possible measure of Government interference with business [and] the largest cooperation." Harding never doubted that whatever aided business also benefited the nation. He was, however, keenly aware of the political and economic dangers of business malpractices and, as early as April 1921, had warned that "Government approval of fortunate, untrammeled business does not mean toleration of restraint of trade or of maintained prices by unnatural methods." For that reason Harding had asked the Federal Trade Commission, created by the Trade Commission Act of 1914, to continue to scrutinize business activities and watch for such abuses as open-price associations. Encouraged by this request and composed of Wilson appointees who believed that business competition was preferable to business cooperation, the Federal Trade Commission maintained an aggressiveness from 1921 to 1924 which wrung cries of anguish from the nation's businessmen.[3]

By 1923–24 the commission had won a number of significant victories. Upheld by the Supreme Court in 1922 in the Winsted Hosiery Company case, it temporarily slowed down the practice of misbranding products and false advertising.[4] Moreover, from 1921 to 1924, it conducted successful investigations of the tobacco, oil, steel, aluminum, and radio industries and issued complaints against the Aluminum Company of

America, against Bethlehem Steel, Lackawanna Steel, Midvale Steel, and Cambria Steel, and against the American Tobacco Company, P. Lorillard Company, and Liggett and Myers. It also initiated an investigation of the meat-packing industry which was instrumental in the passage of the Packers and Stockyard Act of 1921.[5]

The actions of the commission which caused the most furor in the business community related to trade associations. Throughout the early twenties, it took legal action under the Clayton Anti-Trust Law against such associations for price fixing and the suppression of competition. This brought it into immediate conflict with the Commerce Department. Hoover became an outspoken critic of the Federal Trade Commission, deploring its restrictive attitudes. Surprisingly, Daugherty upheld its decisions and in an extensive correspondence with Hoover warned that the Justice Department would continue to prosecute trade as well as open-price associations whenever necessary. This Daugherty-Hoover conflict persisted even after Harding's death. Daugherty's continued obduracy forced Commerce by 1924 to include with its publication of trade association statistics this statement: "The Department does not express any views as to the legal status of any association from which it receives information, or any approval of its activities."[6]

Although the courts in the early twenties generally supported the Daugherty position, time and changing circumstances were on Hoover's side.[7] Harding took no stand on this issue, preferring to release ambiguous statements that the administration supported all *legitimate* programs of business cooperation but would prosecute those adversely affecting the public interest. If one could interpolate, however, it appeared that Harding was more in sympathy with Hoover's position than with Daugherty's. By the time of his death Harding had the opportunity to appoint to the Federal Trade Commission only one new commissioner, Vernon W. Van Fleet, but this appointment was symbolic since Van Fleet was a former lobbyist for the National Association of Manufacturers. Within the next two years, President Coolidge replaced two of the four remaining Wilson appointees with two probusiness conservatives, one of whom he named chairman—William E. Humphrey. This signaled a final switch in the commission's attitudes. Humphrey had been an attorney for western lumber interests and was an outspoken advocate of trade associations. Shortly thereafter the Supreme Court also adopted a more favorable view of trade associations and began to modify the legal opinions of the earlier Harding years.[8]

If the ultimate fate of the Federal Trade Commission indicated the administration's continuing adherence to a probusiness philosophy, the case of the Federal Reserve Board was less obvious. Before 1921, Federal Reserve policy had been tied largely to Treasury Department requirements for war financing. But the postwar inflation and deflation had suddenly made the Federal Reserve Board the subject of much popular discussion and controversy. As we have seen, rural opinion attacked the board throughout the Harding era and the administration, in deference to rural sentiment, had finally agreed to an "agricultural representative" on the board. But the administration went farther than this. Through the person of Daniel Crissinger, who was an ex officio member of the board as comptroller of the currency, President Harding worked successfully for a relaxation in the tight money policy and a lowering in discount rates, both of which farmers desired. Crissinger constantly fed the president information on the attitudes of various board members and relayed to them the president's wish for a money policy which, while protecting business, would also satisfy the farmer.[9]

But by late 1922 strong signs of returning industrial prosperity conflicted sharply with the persisting depression on the farm, and there was momentary confusion on the board about its correct future course of action. As an apostle of low rates, Crissinger urged a continued downward trend while others thought the time had arrived to stabilize the situation by increasing rates. Mellon, for example, also an ex officio member of the board, disagreed with Crissinger and favored higher rates. Mellon temporarily won and, despite vigorous pressure for reductions, the board in early 1923 contracted its security holdings and ordered an increase in rates.

Along with its open-market operations, this decision of the board helped to make 1923 an unusually stable year economically and demonstrated that a controlled and mixed-rate policy could act as a hedge against either excessive inflation or deflation. At the moment, the balance between low- and high-rate advocates on the board proved to be healthy. However, by the end of the Harding period control definitely shifted toward the low-rate forces. The key factor was Harding's appointment of Crissinger to succeed W. P. G. Harding as governor of the board in May 1923. Along with the naming of a "farm representative" to the board in 1923, Crissinger's selection heralded the resumption of a low-rate policy which was mildly inflationary up to 1927, but thereafter became dangerously destructive. In the end business not only acquiesced in the Crissinger low-rate policy but with the beginning of the bull market in 1927 actually championed it. Simultaneously the gradual erosion on the Federal Reserve Board of the philosophy of applying restraints, as had wisely been done in 1923, rendered it impotent to take anti-inflationary action when circumstances again demanded it in 1928.[10]

In one other economic area—taxes—the Harding administration demonstrated by 1923 that although it was probusiness, it was not exclusively so. From the moment of the passage of the Revenue Act of 1921, Secretary Mellon wanted to change it. He remained convinced that a disproportionate tax burden was still borne by the wealthy and by the nonrural elements of the population. As a consequence, he continued to press for lower surtaxes. At the same time, as a sop to the forces opposing privileges for the wealthy, Mellon indicated his willingness to sponsor the elimination of tax-exempt securities, a favorite haven of refuge for the extremely rich. This latter action the president also advocated. On the matter of lower surtaxes, however, the secretary of the treasury met considerable resistance, even in the cabinet. Hoover, for example, doubted the wisdom of such reductions unless they were applied only to "earned income." Hoover also urged a marked increase in estate taxes, a stand which was anathema to Mellon.[11]

Before his death Harding never really capitulated to Mellon's desire to push additional surtax reductions through Congress. There is serious doubt that if he had lived Harding would have agreed to the submission of Mellon's tax plan of 1923. Earlier in that year Harding had indicated to Mellon that he would not sponsor any further surtax modifications without the simultaneous lowering of the entire tax structure so as to benefit everybody. As he wrote to Otto H. Kahn of Kuhn, Loeb and Company in mid-April 1923: "My own best judgment is that for a year or more to come we had better leave the question of modified income taxes alone. There are two schools of thought relating to the question, and no one can foretell at the present time what might be the result of opening up the question for revision. I am very sure that a proposal to reduce the surtaxes alone would meet with disfavor, and it is not altogether unlikely that such a proposal would result in increasing them."[12]

The death of Harding, together with an unexpectedly large treasury surplus in 1923, gave Mellon an opportunity to push more vigorously for surtax modifications. Coolidge not only supported him but, unlike Harding, encouraged him. Hence, in November, scarcely three months after Harding's death, Mellon presented Chairman William R. Green of the House Ways and Means Committee with a revised tax package known as the Mellon Plan of 1923. Interestingly, the Harding legacy to this proposal was a suffusion of moderation which Mellon inserted as a result of the earlier warnings of the dead president. Among other things, his plan now provided for a general reduction in the maximum normal tax rate for everyone from 8 to 6 percent. Even so, Harding's prophecy concerning what Congress would tolerate proved true, and the revenue bill that was ultimately passed in 1924 was not the Mellon Plan but more in line with what Harding had expected. Coolidge signed the measure reluctantly after publicly objecting to the fact that Congress reduced the maximum surtax to only 40 percent instead of Mellon's proposed 25 percent, raised the estate tax from 25 to 40 percent, and included a provision in the law which permitted publicizing income-tax returns.[13]

Whatever the temporary differences over such matters as Federal Reserve policy or surtax rates, the Harding administration to the end was regarded as completely sound by the business community. The reduction in the national debt of $2.4 billion, the decrease in government expenditures, the sympathetic attitude of the Commerce Department, the generally favorable tariff program—all filled the business world with confidence and expectancy. By the late summer of 1922, despite the coal and rail strikes, there was a general feeling that good times lay just ahead, and by early 1923 even the skeptics were convinced that business prosperity was returning and the postwar industrial depression was over.[14] Indeed, the year 1923 showed a marked rise in real earnings, in consumer expenditures, in production, in purchasing, in industrial payrolls, in the availability of work, and in profits. At the same time there was stability in the cost of living and no inflation. In 1923 many economic indexes reached levels which were not surpassed until the spring months of 1929. In 1923 the railroads moved the greatest volume of traffic in their history. In May 1923 payrolls in the basic manufacturing industries hit a high point for the decade. The same was true for employment. Average hourly earnings achieved an all-time high in October 1923. At the same time sales in relation to production reached such a peak that it was not surpassed even in 1929.[15]

This remarkable economic development in late 1922 and 1923 gave substance to the cult of prosperity which Hoover and the Commerce Department had been preaching since 1921. It inaugurated not only an era of good times but also the final enthronement of business philosophy. In this, President Harding and his policies had played a major role. Harding and his administration had supplied the political framework and general atmosphere which had made the postwar restoration of business confidence both rapid and inevitable. The so-called Coolidge boom which followed was obviously one of Harding's most important legacies to his successor.

[3

BUSINESS prosperity in 1923 overshadowed conditions on the American farm. Yet the administration continued to be impressed with the seriousness of the farm problem. The noisy activities of LaFollette and his followers acted as a constant reminder that a solution to rural distress was still not in sight. In reaction to this agitation, on December 2, 1922, the same day that the LaFollette progressives held their post-election strategy meeting in Washington, Harding announced that his administration intended to support additional relief measures for the farmer. Harding had already met with certain key senators such as Capper, McNary, and McCumber, and had secured their promise of support for more farm legislation.[16]

The primary result of this continued concern for the farmer was the passage of the Agricultural Credits Act of 1923. By this law several parallel programs of additional agricultural financing were created. First it established a system of twelve intermediate credit banks in association with the existing federal land banks, under the supervision of the Federal Farm Loan Board. These banks could make up to three-year loans to cooperatives, rural banks, and livestock associations. The act also authorized more liberal credit through the Federal Reserve System and extended the agricultural lending functions of the War Finance Corporation. In addition, the measure encouraged the creation of so-called National Agricultural Credit Corporations which were to be private agencies supported by private capital but receiving governmental support and supervision. Forty-three pages long, confusing, and extremely complicated, this act was symbolic of the frenetic condition of congressional and administrative thinking on the farm problem by the spring of 1923.[17]

Passed on the last day of the final session of the 67th Congress, the Agricultural Credits Act of 1923 received strong administration support. Harding's backing was especially important to its passage and it was more than flattery which prompted Secretary Wallace to write the president on March 10, 1923: "You will be glad to know that it is becoming quite well understood that it was your pressure which put through the farm credits bill."[18] Following its passage President Harding urged immediate implementation of the act, hoping that this further infusion of money would stimulate progress in rural areas. But despite high hopes, it soon became obvious that the mere expansion of farm credit was not going to solve the farm problem.

If the administration had failed in solving the farm problem by 1923, so had the farmer. In his attempts to underwrite his own salvation, he had placed heavy reliance on the creation of cooperatives and similar voluntary programs. One such movement, sometimes called the "California Plan," was widely propagandized in rural areas and Aaron Sapiro, founder of the movement, toured the country, making a fortune helping farmers establish this type of cooperative commodity control. Before 1923 the Farm Bureau Federation made the Sapiro brand of cooperative selling and buying one of its key tenets.[19]

By 1923, however, hopes for the cooperative movement began to fade. Gradually the Farm Bureau Federation deemphasized cooperatives while farm-bloc members retained only nominal enthusiasm for them. As many cooperatives failed and farmers lost their investment, support in local areas quickly disappeared. Nowhere was this turn of events more deplored than in Washington where the Harding administration, especially Hoover, had hoped that such self-help schemes would supplement the governmental programs already initiated for the farmer.

As confidence waned both in the efficacy of cooperatives and in government-sponsored credit measures to solve the farm problem, increasing interest was shown in certain quarters in the possibility of some form of farm subsidy. By 1923 this became a hot issue. The most popular plan was originated by George N. Peek, president of the Moline Plow Company, and Hugh S. Johnson, the company's general counsel, who advocated the restoration of farm-purchasing power by segregating exports from domestic supplies and dumping the exports at a supported disposal price abroad.[20]

Peek attended the Agricultural Conference of 1922 as a delegate and argued indirectly for his plan by demanding a "fair exchange value for all farm products with that of other commodities." Before returning home he talked briefly with Hoover about his export scheme and Hoover promised to study it. Accompanied by Johnson, Peek also visited Wallace's office where he found the reaction somewhat more favorable but not enthusiastic. Wallace was nonetheless sufficiently intrigued to ask Henry Taylor, chief of the Bureau of Agricultural Economics, to study the proposal further and report to him on the findings.[21]

Within the administration a hostile sentiment rapidly developed to the Peek-Johnson scheme. Hoover, already at odds with Wallace on a variety of matters, became the chief spokesman against the plan. Hoover remained an apostle of traditional approaches and persisted in his belief that the farm problem could best be handled by increasing savings in marketing and distribution. Specifically he continued to champion the cooperative movement, advocating that the government give more support to cooperatives and encourage their growth rather than become entrapped by subsidy schemes.[22]

Wallace was a slow convert to the subsidy idea. Merely intrigued by the Peek proposal at first, he also clung to more traditional solutions and as late as October 1922 told a group of Kansas farmers:

Government can not successfully fix prices on farm crops unless Government at the same time exercises arbitrary control over production and is prepared to take care of surplus crops grown. Government can see to it that the farmer has the credit facilities he needs. Government can see to it that the markets are open and that the farmer gets fair treatment. Government can collect and pass on to the farmers information as to crop production, probable demand, foreign competition, and the various things which influence prices. That is about as far as Government can safely go.[23]

But even as he made this statement Wallace was shifting away from traditional solutions. Partly instrumental in encouraging this change was his son, Henry A. Wallace, who assumed the editorship of *Wallace's Farmer* after his father went to Washington and advocated to his father all sorts of new ideas, including the Peek-Johnson scheme. From time to time young Henry attacked the economic conservatism of the administration in his editorials, causing his father, who was desperately trying to retain President Harding's confidence, to plead: "Have a heart."[24]

By the late spring of 1923, Secretary Wallace as well as Henry Taylor had become convinced that either the Peek-Johnson plan or something like it was worth a try. Wallace was actively engaged in wooing Harding to this position and when the president left on his western trip Wallace had received Harding's promise to keep an open mind. Just then anguished cries were coming from the rural areas because of a wheat crisis which was forcing prices below one dollar a bushel for the first time since 1914. Western journals and farm leaders spoke of "a national calamity" and some called for an extra session of Congress to meet the emergency. As he left Washington and headed west through the wheat states Harding certainly was amenable to considering some new solutions.[25]

Harding did not live to take a position on the subsidy proposal one way or the other. Yet before he died he had given Wallace sufficient encouragement so that the Agriculture Department continued working on it. As a result, in September, at one of the first cabinet meetings under Coolidge, Wallace broached the subject of subsidies but the new president was noncommittal. The next month, October, Wallace sent Taylor on a fact-finding mission through the Midwest and he reported back that there was strong support for the subsidy plan. Then in mid-November in a speech before the Chicago Association of Commerce, Wallace publicly announced for the Peek proposal and indicated that the Agriculture Department would submit such a plan to Congress. Shortly thereafter a draft bill emerged which was the joint product of department experts, Senator Charles L. McNary of Oregon, and Representative Gilbert N. Haugen of Iowa. These two men simultaneously introduced the measure in the House and Senate on January 16, 1924. Thus the first of many McNary-Haugen bills started on its tortuous road through Congress.

The fate of this first bill was the same as that of all those that followed. Despite strong agricultural support, they were either defeated in Congress or vetoed by President Coolidge.[26] Coolidge's attitude was naturally a grave disappointment to farm leaders and especially to Wallace. The new president proved to be far less responsive and malleable on the farm problem than Harding had been. Wallace felt that Mellon and a big-business bias dominated the Coolidge administration as they had never done under Harding. Worse, Wallace perceived that Hoover had rapidly become Coolidge's principal agriculture adviser and had undermined Wallace's position on the subsidy in order to advance his own hopes for reviving the lagging cooperative movement.[27]

By the fall of 1924, Wallace, more than any other cabinet member except Daugherty, had reason to wish Harding were still alive. The Iowan was virtually a secretary without portfolio and was almost totally ignored by the White House. Wallace's sudden death, as a result of complications following surgery in late October 1924, removed a growing embarrassment for the Coolidge administration. It also eliminated a strong advocate for a new approach to the farm problem and, together with Harding's earlier death, left the agricultural sector seriously weakened at the top level of government. Of course it is impossible to say what would have happened had Harding lived. Wallace himself believed things would have been different and at least one agricultural historian has recently stated that on the need for government subsidies Wallace and Harding "may have been approaching agreement when he [Harding] died."[28] George Peek later claimed, "[Harding] was sympathetic with the farmers demands and had he lived more favorable action might have been expected from him than was secured from his successor."[29] This much can be said: although not yet a supporter of the subsidy approach by the time of his death, Harding was at least willing to talk about it. Moreover, far better than Coolidge, he possessed the ability to fashion compromise out of disunity within his own official family on such controversial matters. This was a trait badly needed in the case of the continuing farm problem.

Unlike business, therefore, agriculture limped into the Coolidge years. Despite the fact that each American farmer by 1923 was providing enough food for himself, three members of his own family, twelve nonrural Americans, and two foreigners, he had not recouped his postwar economic losses. His net income had increased from the low of $5.5 billion in 1921 to slightly less than $8 billion by 1924, but remained at that relatively low level for the remainder of the decade. Agriculture's share of the national income, which had been 16 percent in 1919, had fallen precipitously to 10.3 percent by 1921 and continued downward to 8.8 percent by 1929. The purchasing power of the farm dollar, which stood at 75¢ in 1921, recovered to only 88¢ by 1923 and did not exceed that figure until 1928.[30]

As a result, regardless of how close Harding was to permitting new departures in handling the farm problem, he bequeathed to succeeding Republican administrations a lingering agricultural depression, a continuing threat of political revolt in the rural sections, and a growing demand for direct governmental intervention in agricultural affairs.

[4

WITH the Wilkerson injunction of 1922 the most virulent phase of the postwar reaction against organized labor came to an end. Based primarily on a fear of radicalism, this public and governmental attitude metamorphosed after 1922 into a search for a saner approach to labor problems and a rejection of massive antilabor antagonism. To labor, of course, the Harding administration had been permanently tainted by the Wilkerson injunction and this presented an almost insurmountable barrier to any kind of labor-government rapprochement. Nevertheless, numerous top Republican leaders, including Harding, attempted to recoup something by subsequently diverting governmental action into more constructive channels.

One of the most immediate results of the summer turmoil of 1922 was an undermining of the Harding administration's faith in the efficacy of compulsory arbitration or governmentally enforced labor-management decisions. As early as his senatorial days, Harding had toyed with the idea of compulsory arbitration as a means of preventing industrial chaos. After becoming president, on several occasions he broached the subject of creating an adjudicatory body with arbitrary power to settle strikes; and he was especially intrigued by the activities of the experimental Kansas Court of Industrial Relations. Created by the Kansas legislature in January 1921, this court was designed to prevent work stoppages in the food, clothing, and fuel industries, and was composed of a panel of three judges with broad powers to effect compulsory arbitration, fix wages, establish hours and working conditions, and examine and modify private contracts. During the rail strike of 1922, however, the Industrial Court failed miserably in its attempts to quell rail disturbances in Kansas and alienated many of its former supporters by its heavy-handed actions against strikers. One of these was newspaperman William Allen White who thereafter used the pages of his *Emporia Gazette* to ridicule the experiment, winning a Pulitzer Prize for one of his anti-court editorials.[31] The Kansas court's biased actions, together with its imprecise legal foundation, ultimately drove it into complete disrepute. Finally, the United States Supreme Court in two decisions, the first being the Wolff Packing Company case of 1923, mercifully put it out of business.[32]

By 1923, not only the Supreme Court but most employers and employees agreed on the wisdom of not attempting compulsory solutions to industrial disputes. The Harding administration followed suit. Although Harding ambiguously referred in his December 1922 state of the union message to the need for enforcing agreements reached between capital and labor, he thereafter dropped all discussion of compulsory arbitration. He was further disenchanted by the inability of the Railroad Labor Board to retain the support of either management or labor. By the spring of 1923 he was evidencing far more interest in establishing better procedures for aiding voluntary negotiations between capital and labor than in forcing the decisions of governmental boards upon them. By the time of his western trip in June, he was expressing strong sympathy for strengthening the conciliation and mediation services of the federal government.

This shifting government emphasis on voluntarism in labor-management negotiations had contemporary ramifications of considerable significance. In particular, business was able to garner both government and public sympathy for its own brand of voluntarism. For example, business firms were widely applauded when they initiated "voluntary" programs of their own which ranged all the way from the open-shop movement to welfare schemes for workers. Usually lost to view was the fact that the long-term advantages for labor from these "voluntary" actions were dubious because what capital could give it could also take away. Still, the ensuing surge of welfare capitalism, including the expansion of company unions, enlisted the enthusiasm of not only the general public but much of labor as well, and set the pattern for the remainder of the twenties. Labor militancy, in turn, drastically declined as returning industrial prosperity coupled with the apparent advantages of welfare capitalism lulled workers into a sense of security. By mid-1923 the average monthly number of industrial disputes had fallen by more than one-half. From 1923 to 1925 the annual number of strikes was only 37 percent of that in the years 1917–22 and only 48 percent as many workers were involved. Union membership, which had been approximately 5.1 million in 1920, had fallen to 3.5 million by 1923.[33]

This decline in union membership and the loss of labor militancy were accompanied by a concomitant erosion of labor's position at the hands of the courts, notably the Supreme Court. A key factor in this development was Harding's appointment of William Howard Taft as chief justice. Taft had coveted this position ever since he had left the presidency. Harding as early as December 1920 indicated that he intended to appoint Taft to the high court as soon as a vacancy occurred, and, after the death of Chief Justice White in the summer of 1921, selected him as White's successor.[34]

Although well received by the country at large, Taft's selection caused consternation in the ranks of labor. Labor had good reasons. Taft certainly was "not a friend." Although he believed that labor had a right to organize, to strike, and to bargain collectively, he denied that it had any special privileges or immunities under the law or that it could resort to intimidation of any kind to achieve its goals.

Taft dominated the Court until his resignation in 1930. Harding's legacy to the Court and to its later labor policy, however, did not end with Taft. In less than two years Harding appointed three more justices to that body. In September 1922 he appointed his old friend and speech writer, former Senator George Sutherland, to replace Justice John H. Clarke. Two months later he nominated Pierce Butler, a railroad lawyer and Roman Catholic Democrat from St. Paul, to succeed Justice William R. Day. In January 1923 he selected Edward T. Sanford, a Republican district judge from Tennessee, to supplant Justice Mahlon Pitney. Obviously, these three men—Sutherland, Butler, and Sanford—were eminently "safe" on economic matters and along with Taft represented a conservative and unimaginative phalanx which resisted change well into the thirties.[35]

It is only necessary to mention the major labor cases which came before the Court in the Harding years to show that Harding's appointments were definitely opposed to labor's interests. In the Duplex Printing Press Company case of 1921, involving a boycott by New York machinists against a Michigan press-making firm, the majority decided that no "new" guarantees had accrued to labor as a result of the passage of the 1914 Clayton Anti-Trust Act. In the Tri-City case, also in 1921, the majority opinion, written by Taft, seriously curtailed labor's ability to picket and to use other means of persuasion to enforce a strike. Again, in 1921, Taft wrote the majority opinion in *Truax v. Corrigan* in which an Arizona anti-injunction law was held unconstitutional as being contrary to the Fourteenth Amendment.[36]

It was in 1923, however, that the most celebrated labor decision of the twenties was delivered in *Adkins v. Children's Hospital*. Surprisingly, this time Taft dissented. By a 5–3 vote (Brandeis had disqualified himself), the majority held that a District of Columbia law fixing minimum wages for women was unconstitutional. In effect, this decision redefined labor as a commodity in direct opposition to the Clayton Act. Taft, believing the majority (including Harding's two new appointments, Butler and Sutherland) had drawn too rigid a view of liberty of contract, protested that employees were not always able to contract equally with employers.[37] Taft's Adkins decision, however, was one of the very few times he was in the minority. He concurred with the majority in the other major labor cases in 1922–23 (e.g., the Coronado case which declared unions to be suable, and the Drexel Furniture Company case which declared unconstitutional all congressional attempts to deal with child labor through the taxing power).[38]

In adopting this antilabor attitude, Taft and the majority of the Court were following not only public opinion but also the basic inclination of the Harding administration. Throughout, labor occupied a less critical or significant position than other elements of the economy in the administration's eyes. Although from time to time Harding evidenced sympathy for labor and even worked for better labor relations, he was prepared to sacrifice labor's interests, if necessary, in any showdown with either agriculture or business. Yet he sincerely hoped that such showdowns could be avoided and, except for the Wilkerson injunction, steered clear of openly antagonizing labor. His normal approach, used before the Wilkerson injunction and then again after it, was to encourage moderation and seek cooperation between labor and management. He sincerely believed that peace between labor and capital, even if purchased by the loss of labor's rights, would produce greater benefits for the worker in the long run than conflict. By securing widespread acceptance of this view by 1923, even among laborers, Harding and his administration gradually led the nation away from the turmoil of the Wilson period and into the soothing, although antilabor, tranquillity of the middle and late twenties.

[5

WITH regard to America First the Harding administration did not alter its stance by 1923. A protective tariff, immigration restriction, and the maintenance of a strong merchant marine remained cardinal principles which neither elections nor the passing of time affected. The march of events, however, did force the administration to adjust these principles to shifting circumstances after the fall of 1922.

The Fordney-McCumber Tariff with its flexibility provision was supposed to usher in a new era of scientific rate making. Unfortunately this did not happen. The Federal Tariff Commission, which was charged with adjusting duties to changing economic conditions, quickly discovered that it was almost impossible to use cost equalization as a yardstick for determining rates because foreign costs could not be pinpointed accurately. The commission, therefore, allowed such a wide margin for error that the result was hardly scientific, and increases in rates resulted from its deliberations more often than decreases.[39]

Nor was politics eliminated from the tariff issue. When Harding took office in 1921, all six members of the Tariff Commission were Wilson appointees, the majority being low-tariff advocates. However, by 1923 Harding had the opportunity to appoint four new commissioners. Three of his four appointees (Thomas O. Marvin, former editor of the *American Economist* and a well-known protectionist; William Burgess, a lobbyist for the pottery industry; and Henry H. Glassie, a Democrat with connections to the Louisiana sugar industry) were high-tariff men. The fourth was William S. Culbertson, a moderate tariff Republican of Emporia, Kansas, whom Wilson had appointed in 1917 and Harding reappointed in 1921. The two holdover commissioners were Edward P. Costigan, a Wilson low-tariff advocate from Denver, and David J. Lewis, also a Wilson low-tariff man.

The relationship of Harding to this commission was always interesting but never more so than in the few months before his death. At that time (beginning in March 1923) a controversy arose among the members of the commission whether it could initiate rate investigations itself or could act only on complaint or on authorization from the president. Culbertson and the two low-tariff men claimed that it could initiate action and advocated immediate inquiries into rates on wool, sugar, hosiery, and pottery.

Marvin, whom Harding had just elevated to the chairmanship of the commission, and his high-tariff colleagues maintained that it could not begin such inquiries and requested Harding, who at the moment was preparing to leave for a vacation in Florida, to issue a clarifying directive. Harding immediately notified all members of the commission that they should take no action of any kind until he returned from the South. To Burgess he wrote just before he left: "I am frankly opposed to entering upon a series of basic inquiries which is likely to precipitate an anxiety in the producing world."[40]

Clamor for review of certain rates continued nevertheless and these sounds reached Harding in Florida. Hence, in late March from St. Augustine, President Harding ordered the Tariff Commission to examine the rates on sugar so that he could "proclaim a reduction in duty, as provided by law" if a justification were found.[41] Before the commission fully completed its sugar investigation, however, Harding returned to Washington and summoned the commission members to the White House to reach agreement on its future action. After a two-hour conference in which both Culbertson and Marvin argued their positions persuasively, an uneasy compromise was effected. At first glance it seemed to be a victory for the Culbertson view since Harding decided that even in cases where no complaints had been filed the commission might "after conference with the President . . . order such formal investigations under [the 1922 tariff law] as the facts may warrant and the public interest require."[42] But upon more careful scrutiny Harding's compromise decision made it plain that the Tariff Commission was purely advisory, not quasi-judicial, and that its power of initiation was strictly limited by presidential approval.

Before his death Harding increasingly stressed this latter point. He warned the commission that it could not undertake a general revision of the tariff law by itself. In early May he told the commission "not to throw a monkey-wrench into the machinery" by making new investigations and stated bluntly that he would reduce rates only for "pronounced reasons." He reminded the commission that the expressed purpose of the 1922 law had been *protection* and that reductions could be justified only where rates were "obviously excessive." When Culbertson complained that except for sugar no major investigations had been undertaken since passage of the 1922 law, Harding agreed that the work of the commission needed to be accelerated. But he did not force Chairman Marvin to adopt a faster

393

pace nor did he indicate a willingness to order any new investigations himself.[43]

While Harding was alive Culbertson and the low-tariff advocates felt free to express their contrary ideas to the president and often did. With Coolidge it was different. Culbertson, who believed Harding had tried to be fair, found Coolidge intolerant and arbitrary. Costigan, one of the low-tariff supporters, resigned in complete disgust from the commission during Coolidge's term. The commission, meanwhile, did not effect a downward revision in high-tariff duties. By November 1923 the commission had received requests for decreases in 77 cases and increases in 48 cases. Of these 125 complaints the commission investigated 33 and Coolidge ultimately ordered rates lowered on 3 items and raised on 7. To moderate- and low-tariff advocates this represented a miserable record. Yet had Harding lived there is no reason to believe that his performance, despite his more congenial manner, would have been any better. To the end Harding remained a high-tariff man, and his attitude toward the commission in the spring of 1923 simply foreshadowed the trend in tariff rate making for the remainder of the decade.[44]

On the question of immigration restriction the Harding administration continued to follow public and congressional opinion. It urged greater efforts at Americanization and advocated tighter selection controls at the point of origin. In late 1922 Secretary Davis formulated several proposals for the compulsory education of immigrants in American citizenship and the English language. According to the Davis plan, an immigrant would be enrolled in such instruction immediately upon his arrival and would not be considered for permanent retention until he achieved a minimum competency. Davis also proposed an annual census of the alien population in order to maintain a check on newcomers and their assimilation progress.

At the same time, administration officials, led by Davis, reflected an increasing desire to restrict admissions even further than the Per Centum Act allowed. In the summer of 1923 Davis declared, "I am for selective immigration *or none*," and urged upon Harding a proposal for applying stiff physical and mental tests in addition to lowering the admission rate. Davis even suggested that consular officials investigate prospective immigrants and their family backgrounds in order to ascertain whether they would represent good risks if permitted to enter the United States.[45]

Davis's views were symptomatic of popular and congressional sentiment in 1922–23. In February of the latter year, for instance, Albert Johnson and his House Immigration Committee released a bill which would have reduced the influx of immigrants to 2 percent of the foreign-born residing in the United States in 1890, required immigrants to secure certificates of entry from American consuls abroad, and specifically excluded Japanese, Chinese, and low-caste Hindus.

Although widely supported, this bill fell by the wayside in the closing rush of the 67th Congress. Restriction, however, remained a topic of public conversation until the convening of the 68th Congress in December 1923 when Albert Johnson reintroduced his 2 percent bill. Before his death Harding had indicated that his administration would support the Johnson proposal, and Coolidge spoke of it favorably in his December 1923 state of the union message. With such widespread backing the Johnson bill quickly became law.[46] Under it the number of entering immigrants dropped from 357,803 in 1923–24 to 164,667 in 1924–25. The most drastic cuts were in the newer immigrant ranks: the British and Irish dropped only 19 percent; Germans 24 percent; but Italians declined over 90 percent.[47] This was in keeping with the pattern already set during the Harding years.

No such harmony of views existed between Congress and the Harding administration over the final solution to the merchant marine problem. The failure to pass the ship subsidy bill in February 1923 presented the administration with serious difficulties. As operating deficits on the government-owned fleet continued to mount, it appeared that only quick and complete liquidation at any price was now feasible. On April 14, 1923, after an agonizing conference between Harding and the Shipping Board, it was decided to offer all ships for sale on open bids, with government operation to continue only as a last resort.[48]

The results were disappointing. Even though the board publicly admitted that it would be happy with $30 a ton or $350 million for the whole fleet, there were only a few offers and then only for the very best ships, such as vessels of the "President" type which were ultimately sold to the Dollar Line in 1924. In the midst of this discouragement Albert Lasker retired from the Shipping Board on July 1, 1923. In a ten-page resignation letter, Lasker reminded Harding that he had agreed to serve for only two years and that time had now expired. He bitterly castigated Congress for its refusal to accept the ship subsidy bill and prophesied that something like it would finally have to be enacted. He suggested that a limited number of government routes might be maintained with approximately 250 of the best ships until their final sale to private owners could be arranged. The remainder of the fleet he now recommended selling for scrap. All this, Lasker admitted, was a bitter pill for him to swallow. After returning to Lord and Thomas in Chicago, Lasker thereafter avoided Washington completely and later claimed that his years on the Shipping Board were the "unhappiest" of his life.[49]

The Shipping Board continued to offer its ships for sale after Coolidge assumed office but by 1925–26 was still unable to find buyers even though it had knocked down its prices to as low as $30,000 for some vessels. By the end of 1927, the board still possessed 823 ships of 6,490,239 deadweight tons. During this same period, deficits on the remaining government-operated routes continued to rise as the Shipping Board, despite heroic measures, found no method of eliminating them. Congress, caught up in the investigatory fever accompanying the oil scandals, appointed a select committee to investigate the operations of the Shipping Board. After a year of hearings and twelve volumes of testimony, the committee produced a lackluster report. Aside from uncovering wartime waste (which was ancient history), rehashing Lasker's obvious bias for ship subsidies (which everyone knew), and reiterating the impossibility of getting rid of the fleet at a decent price (which was painfully obvious), the report had little to contribute and it reached no decision on the critical issue of whether the government should continue indefinitely to operate the remainder of the fleet at a loss.[50] By 1927, the problem of the merchant marine was no nearer solution than it had been in 1923.

The ship subsidy question was finally settled in 1936 with the passage of the New Deal's Merchant Marine Act. Interestingly, the same reasons advanced by Harding for ship subsidies in 1922 were used by Franklin Roosevelt in 1936. Although the 1936 law was not as lucrative to private interests and was more tightly controlled than the 1922 proposal, it was patterned along the same lines. Roosevelt was no more interested in government operation of shipping in 1936 than Harding had been in 1922. The main difference between them was merely the degree of government support to be given to private shipping companies. By the mid-thirties the question was how to construct a "scientific subsidy policy" not whether there should be a subsidy. As Harding had earlier maintained, the requirements of America First demanded a subsidy. It had been a wasteful and unnecessary fourteen years.

[6

IF THE Harding administration's approach to the shipping problem had attempted to chart a new course, the same was true of its handling of race relations. In this case, however, the administration, especially Harding himself, did not pursue the goal with a clearheaded consistency. Considerable confusion existed on the subject of Negro rights and seemingly sincere motivations were shot through with political expediency.

By the end of World War I large numbers of Negroes had migrated from the South into the North and this trend continued throughout the twenties. Although this movement increased northern racist feelings and promoted racial discrimination and unrest, it also catapulted the Negro into a new position of political importance. Crowded into the major northern cities and subjected to the new militancy of some Negro leaders and returning Negro war veterans, these Negroes began to ignore party labels and became increasingly susceptible to the blandishments of big-city Democratic machines whose goal was to break down the Negroes' traditional Republican orientation. Gone was the day when Republican politicians could say, as Mark Hanna once exclaimed, "I carry the Negro's vote around in my vest pocket."[51]

As an indication of the Negro's growing independence, in 1920 the NAACP demanded statements from all prospective Republican candidates on such matters as Negro patronage, Haitian independence, antilynch laws, and Negro suffrage. Although Harding was one of only three candidates who replied to the NAACP demand, he answered not a single question directly but merely said that he believed the party platform should make "every becoming declaration on behalf of the Negro citizenship, which the conscience of the Party and the conditions of this country combine to suggest."[52]

With some enthusiasm, the Negro, both officially and unofficially, supported Harding in the 1920 campaign. Harding, in turn, while promising the Negro "justice," steered clear of too many specifics. He assured Negro leaders that he would increase Negro patronage and work for an antilynching bill. As the campaign reached a climax and Harding pressed for Negro votes, he reiterated these two promises in a sufficiently forceful fashion that some southern Democrats raised the specter of "new force bills intended to strike at the heart of white supremacy" if Harding was elected. The late campaign attempt to brand Harding a Negro was partially spawned by this latent white supremacist fear.[53]

After his election Harding faced a difficult situation. It is unlikely that any president could have satisfied Negro desires in the immediate postwar period without alienating other, larger, and more influential segments of the population. Certainly no president could have satisfied the more vocal and more militant northern Negro leaders. Yet partly because of political expediency and partly because of a vague desire to promote a greater degree of racial justice, Harding tried to placate the Negro as much as possible.

True to his campaign promise, in his first message to Congress in April 1921 Harding requested the passage of an antilynching law. "Congress," he said, "ought to rid the stain of barbaric lynching from the banner of a free and orderly representative democracy." In the same speech, he also urged the creation of an interracial commission "to formulate, if not a policy, at least a national attitude of mind calculated to bring about the most satisfactory possible adjustment of relations between the races." This latter idea, along with the president's antilynching request, had the wholehearted support of Negro leaders such as James Weldon Johnson, executive secretary of the NAACP, and was enthusiastically received by the Negro community. Even the general press commented favorably on Harding's willingness to consider these controversial matters. Exclaimed the *Nation*: "This is in marked contrast to the attitude of the Wilson administration which sought, ostrich-like, to evade the whole quesion."[54]

But such evidence of the administration's interest in Negro welfare did not solve the Republican party's immediate political problem with respect to the black man. Since Taft's day, white southern Republicans had hoped to refashion the Republican party in the South into a potent political force by making it a "lily-white" organization. Harding's Texas friend Ed Scobey was one of those who deplored the party's historic reliance on the "black and tan" element and who opposed giving this group any of the party's patronage. By 1921 white Republican leaders in several southern states had already made considerable progress in eliminating the influence of the blacks and tans in order to enhance the Republican image among white southern voters. In Virginia the lily-white element virtually eliminated the Negro from the party. Obviously such action engendered bitter hostility not only among the politically impotent southern Negroes but among their politically influential northern brethren.

As leader of the party, Harding could not ignore this situation and cautiously groped toward some sort of compromise. To friends he wrote that he favored a strong two-party system in the South and admitted that it could be based only on white leadership. But he did not agree that either party membership or patronage should be lily-white. Harding warned one supporter of an "all-white" party that one could not "inconsiderately wave aside all those who have heretofore carried the party banner through years of adversity. Some of them are deserving."[55]

Such presidential comments did not appreciably clarify the situation and therefore Harding seized upon an invitation to speak on October 26, 1921, at the semicentennial celebration of the founding of the city of Birmingham as an opportunity to elaborate on his ideas for a revival of Republicanism in the South as well as to offer a blueprint for better race relations in the country as a whole. Addressing an attentive audience of both blacks and whites, he declared that in his judgment the race question was one of the most critical facing the United States. He admitted candidly that he believed there was an "eternal and inescapable difference" between the two races which made social equality impossible; but he added that there was no excuse for economic, political, or educational discrimination. He chided the South for keeping the Negro in ignorance and condemned local voting practices by saying, "let the black man vote when he is fit to vote; prohibit the white man voting when he is unfit to vote." At the same time, he warned his own party to "lay aside any program that looks to lining up the black man as a mere political adjunct." Prophetically he reminded his southern audience that the time had passed when the race problem was a southern problem only: it was a problem of the North and "of democracy everywhere." Nonetheless, he concluded by asking the South to take the lead in seeking solutions to the race problem because of its long association with the Negro so that there might at last "be an end of prejudice."[56]

Harding's Birmingham address was the most important presidential utterance on the race question since Reconstruction days and, regardless of motivation, required considerable courage. But his words were immediately misconstrued and condemned by the extremists among both blacks and whites. White supremacists blanched at his views on Negro suffrage and equal educational opportunity. Senator Pat Harrison of Mississippi was almost apoplectic in claiming the speech was "a blow to the white civilization." Conversely, Negro leaders such as W. E. B. DuBois claimed Harding's reference to the "eternal difference" between the races completely vitiated the more salutary aspects of the speech. Almost everyone erroneously concluded that his allusions to the Negro and the Republican party meant that he was inviting blacks to leave the party and that he had sided completely with the "lily-whites." Actually Harding had done no such thing. He merely desired a development in the South similar to that in the North where Negroes belonged to both parties and neither party had the Negro as its exclusive political or patronage problem. This condition, he felt, would be healthier not only for the two parties but also for the Negro.[57]

Although pleased by the many favorable comments made on his Birmingham address, Harding was distressed by these extremist attacks. He did not regard his private views on the impossibility of social equality as damaging to legitimate Negro aspirations. Nor did he understand the objection to having the Negro amalgamate into the political life of the nation through two parties rather than one. Moreover, Harding was sincere in his desire to act as a mediator between white and black on a whole range of racial problems, especially if this would enhance the political prospects of the Republican party in either North or South. He was at least willing to discuss publicly such controversial and politically dangerous matters. In this respect, alone, his Birmingham address was a notable event.[58]

The final relationship between the Harding administration and the Negro, however, was predicated not so much on campaign pronouncements or the Birmingham speech as on its patronage and legislative performance. Unfortunately in neither of these categories were the achievements great, although good intentions were again abundant. Hard-pressed over patronage demands in general, Harding attempted to increase the number of Negroes in government service as he had earlier promised. A month after taking office he urged cabinet officers to make places in their departments for qualified Negro Republicans and ordered them to report to him on their success. At the same time he indicated publicly that he

400

desired to appoint "leading Negro citizens from the several states to more important official positions than were heretofore accorded to them." Significantly, however, he assured southern white Republicans that he would not "add to the irritation there by the appointment of Negroes to federal offices."[59]

Harding did make one black appointment in the South which caused angry white protests—Walter L. Cohen as collector of customs at New Orleans. But Cohen was an exception. Indeed, by the summer of 1922, relatively few Negroes, in either North or South, had been appointed to positions paying more than $3000. The State Department had five, the most important being Solomon P. Hood, minister to Liberia. Treasury had three; Justice had one; Interior four; Agriculture one; Labor one; the Navy, Post Office, and Commerce departments none. The pressure of white office seekers and, according to Hoover, the lack of truly qualified black candidates conspired to make additional appointments impossible.[60]

The Negro community was bitterly disappointed. Harding's well-meaning calls for tolerance and his continued support of such measures as an antilynching bill were overshadowed by the administration's patronage record. Even Harding's courageous attacks on the politically powerful Ku Klux Klan did not impress Negro leaders as they groused about appointments.[61] For his part Harding was piqued by their criticism and believed he was being blamed unfairly for matters beyond his control. To his friend Malcolm Jennings he wrote: "The Negroes are very hard to please. If they could have half of the Cabinet, seventy-five percent of the Bureau Chiefs, two-thirds of the Diplomatic appointments and all the officers to enforce prohibition perhaps there would be a measure of contentment temporarily, but I do not think it would long abide."[62]

Ironically, it was the fate of the antilynching bill (Dyer bill), which Harding requested and supported, that caused the greatest Negro disenchantment. Passed by the House on January 26, 1922, the bill ran into immediate trouble in the Senate where it was bottled up by the Judiciary Committee. When several Negro lynchings occurred in the South in May 1922, pressure mounted on Harding to force it out of committee. But intense southern senatorial opposition caused him to move cautiously because of his fear of reprisal on other parts of the administration's legislative program. Not until the opening of the special session in November 1922 did the Dyer bill reach the Senate floor. When in late November

401

it became clear that the Republican Senate majority intended to pass the bill, the Democratic minority organized a filibuster. For a week southern leaders engaged in their talkathon, threatening to continue it indefinitely and block Senate consideration of all other pending legislation. Finally, on December 2, in order to clear the decks for the ship subsidy measure which had just passed the House, the Republican caucus, after three hours of soul searching and anguish, voted to drop the Dyer bill. As Lodge explained it to the press: "Of course, the Republicans feel very strongly, as I do, that the bill ought to become law [but] we had to choose between giving up the whole session to a protracted filibuster or going ahead with the regular business of the session."[63]

To blame Harding and his administration for the defeat of the Dyer bill was somewhat unfair. Such antilynching bills would be introduced in every session of Congress down to World War II and would be defeated by similar southern tactics. But this was of no consolation to Negro leaders in 1922 and 1923. They refused to accept Harding's expressions of regret and vented their wrath more on the administration than on the southern filibusterers. Wrote James Weldon Johnson to the White House: "The fate of the Dyer Bill comes as the culmination of a series of disappointments to the colored people during the present administration. . . . The present state of mind of the colored people will be far-reaching in its effects."[64]

The effects were far-reaching. When the Coolidge and Hoover administrations reinstituted the customary do-nothing policy toward Negroes, black citizens repudiated the Republican party by the droves. They increasingly concentrated on congressional and local elections and largely ignored the two major parties at the national level. Some Negro leaders, such as DuBois, became ever more radical and looked to other sources than either the Republicans or the Democrats, or even the NAACP, as a solution to the Negro's woes.

There was little question that during the twenties the Republican party completely bungled the chance to align growing numbers of northern Negroes behind its banner.[65] Still the fact remained that Warren Harding was the only president between the Square Deal and the Fair Deal who examined the question of race relations in a fresh way. If his achievements were meager, he was only partially to blame. His request for an interracial commission died in a congressional committee; his proposal for an antilynching bill was killed by a Senate filibuster; his hope for an early military withdrawal from Haiti, as demanded by the Negro community, was forestalled by Hughes and the State Department; his desire for an end to political and educational discrimination ran afoul of national and sectional folkways. Only in the matter of patronage could he be held culpable, and even here there were extenuating circumstances. In the area of race relations, Harding deserved more credit than he received.

[7

HARDING'S problems in working out a saner political approach to racial matters, frustrating though they were, were mild compared with his difficulties involving the Volstead Act. Inheriting from Wilson a skeletal enforcement system which had yet to work, Harding quickly discovered that prohibition was one of his administration's biggest headaches.

Under the Volstead Act, which inaugurated prohibition on January 17, 1920, enforcement was lodged in a Prohibition Unit headed by a commissioner of prohibition and housed in the Internal Revenue Division of the Treasury Department. Enthusiastic prohibitionists such as Wayne B. Wheeler, an Ohioan and general counsel of the Anti-Saloon League, immediately predicted that enforcement would be easy and that only $5 million annually would be required to keep the country "dry."[66] But even before the 1920 presidential campaign got underway, Wheeler's prediction had acquired a hollow ring as the flow of liquor continued, indicating that John Barleycorn was far from dead.

Despite his known drinking habits, Harding was more acceptable in 1920 to the drys than Governor Cox who, unlike Harding, had opposed prohibition and possessed a wet voting record. Harding's campaign promise to enforce the Volstead Act "as a fundamental principle of the American conscience" readily brought him the drys' support.[67] After becoming president, Harding held to this campaign promise with amazing consistency. Although plagued by enforcement failures, he kept trying and once he wrote Senator Edge, who had expressed the hope that he would support a relaxation in the prohibition law: "Prohibition is a constitutional mandate and I hold it to be absolutely necessary to give it a fair and thorough trial."[68]

It would have been virtually impossible for Harding to have acted otherwise. Not only was popular opinion in favor of enforcing the law (although many private citizens, like the president, maintained a double standard concerning their own conduct), but the pressure of prohibitionists on the administration was relentless. Primarily through Wayne Wheeler, who seemed to be everywhere, these self-styled guardians of public morals monitored the president and cabinet officers for lapses in enforcement zeal and alternately wheedled, badgered, and threatened whenever any backsliding occurred. Secretary Mellon, always somewhat of an embarrassment to the drys because of his distillery holdings, often ran afoul of their criticism. Once in the late fall of 1921, when Mellon, as administrative superior of the prohibition commissioner, ruled that light wines and beer could be allowed for medicinal purposes, Wheeler immediately protested in writing to Harding who wearily replied: "Somehow I had rather expected your letter." In late June 1922 when Secretary Weeks, who was personally opposed to prohibition, publicly stated he thought that beer ought to be legalized, the drys demanded his scalp. Other cabinet officials were similarly terrorized the moment they stepped out of line.[69]

At the same time, Wheeler and other dry leaders assumed the prerogative of screening all major political appointments for their dryness and peremptorily submitted their views to the White House. Appointments to judgeships and to the office of district attorney were especially sensitive from their point of view, but they even scrutinized candidates for diplomatic posts and bureau heads. Harding and some members of his official family were incensed at these pressure tactics, but they were helpless to do much about them because the drys were so politically potent.[70]

Naturally, the main interest of prohibition leaders centered on the Prohibition Unit. Wheeler and the Anti-Saloon League held virtual veto power over the appointment of the commissioner of prohibition and in May 1921, upon the recommendation of Wheeler, Major Roy A. Haynes, a fellow Anti-Saloon Leaguer from Ohio, was nominated by Harding for the post. Thereafter, Haynes and Wheeler were a dynamic team, expending their energies in the dual task of retaining popular support for enforcement and convincing everyone that it was successful. This was not easy. Since the Prohibition Unit was not covered by the merit system (the Volstead Act might not have been passed otherwise), spoilsmen often used it as a dumping ground for disgruntled Republicans who could not be accommodated elsewhere. The unit's caliber of appointee was therefore frequently low and the rate of corruption high. Although this was obvious even to prohibitionists, they resisted any change in the system and consequently enforcement suffered. Moreover, there was not close cooperation between the Prohibition Unit and the Department of Justice as the two often bickered over enforcement jurisdiction. Finally, the Prohibition Unit possessed an impossible logistical task. It had neither the manpower nor the organizational structure to cope with thousands of miles of unprotected border and coastline, millions of lawbreaking citizens, and hordes of ingenious liquor suppliers. As for money—the cost of prohibition enforcement jumped from the original appropriation of $2 million in 1920 to $6.3 million in 1923, and the end was nowhere in sight. As one disgusted senator exclaimed, not even $50 million a year would have been enough to enforce the Volstead Act.[71]

Ironically, while bootlegging and the smuggling of illicit liquor from "Rum Row" along the east coast or across the Great Lakes continued on unchecked during the Harding years, ardent prohibitionists concentrated their attention on such relatively minor matters as whether liquor could be served aboard American ocean-going passenger vessels, especially those operated by the Shipping Board. On April 30, 1923, the Supreme Court ruled that although the transportation of liquor into the territorial waters of the United States by both foreign and domestic vessels was illegal, the Volstead Act did not prevent ships flying the United States flag from carrying and selling liquor outside the three-mile limit.[72] Lasker, anxious to protect American lines from foreign competition, urged Harding to issue a presidential directive allowing liquor to be served on government-operated ships while the drys clamored for him to keep them dry. In the end even Harding's desire to advance the interests of the government fleet proved no match for his fear of prohibitionist political influence, and he retained a ban on liquor on the high seas in government-owned ships. Meanwhile, because of the Supreme Court's declaration that foreign as well as domestic vessels could possess no liquor inside the three-mile limit, Hughes was faced with an angry foreign reaction. Following negotiations which extended over seven months, a liquor treaty was finally signed with Great Britain in January 1924 which served as a model for similar treaties with other countries. By these treaties, foreign vessels were permitted to carry liquor on board under seal as sea stores within the three-mile limit, but in case of suspected liquor smuggling the United States had the right to board, search, and seize liquor on foreign vessels within an hour's run of American shores.[73]

Despite these and other attempts to clarify and systematize enforcement procedures, the over-all picture was one of inefficiency and confusion. In some localities jails soon ran out of space to house violators and the courts were so overwhelmed that jurists despaired of ever clearing their dockets. Attorney General Daugherty complained to congressmen in 1922 that the Justice Department was so overburdened with prohibition cases that it could get little else done. According to Daugherty, the number of pending cases had risen over 400 percent within the year. Chief Justice Taft deplored the mounting effect of prohibition on the work load of the Supreme Court by declaring in 1922, "I am discouraged about the liquor situation."[74]

Because of the growing failure of prohibition, some who originally supported it turned against it by 1923. This made enforcement even more difficult as open defiance of the law flourished in many areas. In New York, for example, the legislature indicated its collective disenchantment by repealing the state's enforcement act on May 4, 1923, and Governor Al Smith, an opponent of prohibition, signed the repeal on June 1 despite a public warning by President Harding that the federal government would continue to enforce the law "in every State within the Union."[75]

Although Harding's position was constitutionally impeccable, prohibition enforcement during his administration remained a farce. Yet prohibition leaders maintained the contrary. Haynes, a corpulent man with an expansive personality, was a fountain of enthusiasm and optimism. In January 1922 he declared that enforcement was approaching a high degree of efficiency and that it was more successful than its friends could have dreamed possible. From his Washington office he broadcast figures to show that since prohibition began over 17,500,000 Americans had stopped drinking—"a wonderful record." Just before the fall campaign of 1922, he claimed that the administration had at last solved the enforcement problem and the liquor question would soon be but a memory. He maintained that only 15 percent of former drinkers were still imbibing and that their sources of supply were drying up. At the same time he held that the competency of the personnel of the Prohibition Unit was rising and that only "carefully selected" persons "of proved ability" were being hired. In the spring of 1923, Haynes was still making optimistic claims, even stating that because of prohibition vice and crime were disappearing, children were healthier, and jails and asylums were emptier.[76] But by this time his claims were being discounted as the press began to laugh at him. Soon his name became a word to snicker at and vaudeville comedians always got a howl with it. Haynes finally realized that he was being lampooned everywhere and became more reluctant to talk with the press and reporters. Ultimately he suffered total disillusionment, as did other prohibition commissioners who followed him.

As prohibition turned into a national joke, Harding was increasingly disturbed about the matter. Never a strong believer in prohibition personally, he nonetheless deplored the wholesale breaking of the law which it encouraged. His concern was reflected in a change in his own habits in early 1923 when he decided to become an abstainer. Aside from the requirements of his health, it had gradually dawned on him that the example of the president in this matter was important. Dry leaders like Wheeler and Haynes, who for some time had been badgering the president to give up drinking, were delighted. Earlier Harding had told them that if he ever did "take the pledge" it would be only "as a contribution to the good of the state, because my personal scruples do not lead me in that direction."[77]

Presidential example notwithstanding, prohibition enforcement by the summer of 1923 was a dismal flop. The Harding administration had attempted by words, and a few deeds, to serve as a midwife for the birth of the new liquorless age which prohibitionists had envisioned. But the "reign of tears" which Billy Sunday claimed had ended with the passage of the Volstead Act was actually just beginning. Local and national corruption, increasing lawlessness, and a higher incidence of crime were already evident. Harding, who made his last pronouncement on prohibition while on his way to Alaska, was quite correct in worrying more about these side effects and their impact on the national moral fiber than the mere question of liquor itself. But he was wrong in not also realizing that the Volstead Act was an unenforceable law and that no amount of money from Congress or pious words from him could alter that fact. At the moment, however, neither he nor other public officials possessed the kind of political courage necessary to face the wrath of prohibitionists in asking for repeal or drastic enforcement modifications.

IF THE Harding administration could claim little success in prohibition enforcement, it could take credit for attempting to meet some of the nation's other emerging and pressing problems. For example, from the beginning of his administration, Harding talked about the need for greater federal participation in social welfare and, contrary to the advice of his Old Guard advisers, inserted in his first message to Congress in April 1921 a recommendation for the creation of a Department of Public Welfare. Harding believed such a department could unify the various welfare activities of the government, which were scattered through many departments, and could give added impetus to new programs in education, public health, sanitation, child welfare, and public recreation.[78] Congress never acted on this proposal, though Harding continued to urge it until his death.

Harding did achieve at least one notable success in the welfare area before 1923. He strongly supported the Sheppard-Towner bill which had first been introduced in the Wilson administration. Designed to encourage joint state-federal action in reducing the high death rate of infants and increasing sound hygiene among women and children, this measure had been passed over in the Wilson years but was resurrected in the 67th Congress. Immediately the medical profession condemned it as destroying the principle that "the care of the mother and child is a state and local, not a federal function."[79] Some congressional opponents claimed it violated states' rights. But Harding persisted in pushing the bill even though many of his conservative friends cautioned him not to do so. Harding's motivation was essentially humanitarian, but he was also influenced by the realization that the large numbers of women voters enfranchised under the woman's suffrage amendment were yet to be captured by either major party, and the Sheppard-Towner bill was one way to sway them in the Republican party's direction.[80] After several delays and after organized women's groups such as the League of Women Voters, the WCTU, the YWCA, and the National Federation of Business and Professional Women rallied to its support, the bill was finally passed and was signed by the White House. Hence, regardless of his motivation, Harding's signature committed the federal government to an experiment in welfare action with the states which laid the basis for the increasing use of federal money for such purposes.

This "matching" or cooperative activity between the states and the federal government on social welfare was carried even further by the Harding administration in the area of highway development. Harding was an automobile enthusiast from the day he bought his first car, a green Stevens-Duryea, in 1905. Naturally he was also a strong and consistent proponent of good roads. When he became president, federal support for road building rested on the Federal Aid Road Act of 1916 which permitted the secretary of agriculture to give limited aid to states in building or maintaining roads over which the mails were carried. In 1920 the federal government expended $19.5 million in this endeavor. Harding was of the opinion that this was far too little and, backed by the Agriculture Department which desired to "get the farmers out of the mud," he suggested in his first message to Congress in April 1921 that not only should these funds be increased, but better planning under federal auspices should be undertaken. Said he, ". . . it is important to exert Federal influence in developing comprehensive plans looking to the promotion of commerce, and apply our expenditures in the surest way to guarantee a public return for money expended. Large Federal outlay demands a Federal voice in the [highway] program." [81]

Harding's approach to highway development sprang from the same nationalistic spirit which sparked his interest in a merchant marine. Inevitably it meant a larger role for the federal government than most stand-patters relished. However, with Harding's backing, and under heavy pressure from farm groups and the American Automobile Association, Congress finally passed the Federal Highway Act of 1921 by which the various state highway departments designated a system of important interstate and intercounty roads upon which all future federal funds would be spent. This scheme helped to initiate a federal highway network, rescue road building from its chaotic condition, and prepare the way for handling the intrastate and interstate traffic of the future. The $75 million appropriated in 1921 represented a dramatic increase in federal aid which, when matched by state and local funds, resulted in a real spurt to planned road building. Two years later federal government appropriations under the Highway Act jumped to $88 million. Even so, Harding advocated still more federal activity. And his urgings came none too soon. By 1923 there were already 13.5 million cars and buses in operation in the United States.[82]

The Harding administration's keen interest in highways was accompanied by an equally enthusiastic and progressive attitude toward aviation and radio. Harding was of the opinion that the federal government should regulate fully all radio stations transmitting and receiving international traffic, and also establish rules and regulations necessary to prevent chaos on the domestic airwaves.[83] During his tenure, the basic policies concerning radio development and regulation were formulated, with Hoover being the prime mover. Quick action was necessary. When the Harding administration took over, only two stations were broadcasting experimentally. Within twelve months 320 stations were filling the air with jumbled transmissions. By 1922 three million homes possessed radio sets and even the women in the family had become used to such terms as "three-circuit regenerators" and "spiderweb windings." As Hoover correctly said, by 1922 the radio had passed "from the field of adventure to that of a public utility."[84]

Although he had no specific authority to do so, Hoover initiated the administration's drive for radio regulation by calling a meeting of radio broadcasters on February 27, 1922, at which time he got them to agree to an allocation of frequencies in the 500- to 1500-kilocycle range and to a system of voluntary licensing through the Department of Commerce until a permanent arrangement could be set up by Congress. Shortly thereafter, at the administration's insistence, a radio bill was introduced in Congress giving the Commerce Department broad powers over the airwaves, but it was sidetracked and ultimately lost in the rush to adjournment in March 1923. Undiscouraged, Hoover called a second conference of broadcasters two weeks after Congress adjourned and attempted to perfect his voluntary licensing program. Again he secured agreement from them on the need for temporary regulation. Hoover knew, however, that only congressional legislation could ultimately provide the authority necessary to police the airwaves properly and he continued to urge such legislation upon Congress after Harding's death. Coolidge was only lukewarm about the project and it was not until 1927 that a bill, almost exactly like the one Hoover first proposed in 1922, cleared Congress and provided the authority needed through the creation of a Federal Radio Commission.[85]

Aviation development and regulation provided a strikingly similar parallel. Harding's interest extended to all phases of aviation development and in his message to Congress in April 1921 he recommended the creation of a Bureau of Aeronautics in the Department of Commerce and an expansion in the air mail service. In December 1921 he reiterated his position by making a direct appeal to Chairman Samuel Winslow of the House Interstate Commerce Committee. Simultaneously, Harding received strong support from such persons as Ambassador Myron Herrick, who was president of the Aero Club of America, and Charles D. Walcott, chairman of the National Advisory Committee for Aeronautics which also had such important members as Michael Pupin and Orville Wright. But the key figure was Representative Frederick Hicks of New York, a member of the House Naval Affairs Committee, who was responsible for drafting a bill which embodied Harding's proposals. Introduced jointly in the House and Senate in mid-December 1921 this bill was shunted aside because of the press of other matters.

Secretary Hoover now picked up the ball. Always anxious to add new functions to the Commerce Department, he also was a sincere partisan of aviation and, as in the case of radio, sought temporary means to strengthen the situation while Congress dallied. In 1922 he convened the first national conference on commercial aviation and initiated a policy of government regulation even without congressional authorization. At the conference the discussion centered around the adoption of a common code for aids and safety devices, the systematic development of airways and airports, and the periodic inspections of planes and pilots.[86]

Despite continuing Commerce Department and White House pressure, Congress refused to act. It was not until 1926 that the Air Commerce Act finally established in the Commerce Department a Division of Aeronautics possessing full regulatory and developmental authority. In the meantime the Harding administration (and with somewhat less enthusiasm the Coolidge administration) continued to advance the cause of aviation in whatever ways it could. Further aviation conferences were held, and the air mail service was expanded. By 1922–23 the mail service was flying almost two million miles, most of it in the East and upper Midwest, with one route, New York to San Francisco, being transcontinental.[87]

The national outlook reflected in these activities was also apparent, although to a lesser extent, in the Harding administration's attitude toward navigation and power development. Under the Federal Water Power Act of 1920 a commission was created (composed of the secretaries of war, interior, and agriculture) "to provide for the improvement of navigation; the development of water power; and the use of public lands in relation

411

thereto." Further, this commission was authorized to issue licenses for power development or navigation improvement, regulate rates and services in particular cases, and publish the results of its activities and investigations in an annual report to Congress. Although this act was ostensibly a victory for those favoring strong government regulation, it actually functioned as a compromise. Wallace, Fall, and Weeks were not ardent regulationists but they did believe some regulation was necessary. Less strict in their licensing procedures for power sites than Senator Norris would have liked, they still believed in scrutinizing projects wherever the public interest seemed endangered. Meeting weekly, this commission by March 1923 had reviewed applications involving projects totaling an estimated 22 million horsepower, ranging from individual plants of less than 100 h.p. to large interconnecting systems.[88]

Throughout the period to 1923 Harding was both a strong advocate of intensified private activity in water-power development and an expansionist in federal activity in land conservation and irrigation projects. Again, however, it was Hoover who best reflected the administration's attitude. As chairman of the so-called Colorado River Commission, Hoover met with the representatives of seven western states and hammered out an agreement on November 16, 1922, which established a complicated formula for a fair division of water rights in the area, thus clearing the path for the long-discussed Boulder Dam project. This was the first time that more than two states had entered into such a compact with the federal government participating, and it signaled the opening of the great Southwest, at last freeing the Colorado River system from a generation of litigation and strife.[89]

Concerning the great controversial water-power issue of the day—the disposition of Muscle Shoals, a huge war-spawned nitrate-manufacturing facility built by the government at a cost of $100 million—the Harding administration offered nothing constructive. Like the Wilson administration before it, the Harding administration was in a quandary on how to use this installation for peacetime purposes. Public-power enthusiasts, such as Senator Norris, demanded that the government keep it; private-power supporters advocated selling it. Inclined toward the latter view, the Harding administration invited private bids in 1921, but contrary to expectations neither of the logical bidders (the Alabama Power Company and the Southern Power Company) made an offer. Instead, Henry Ford offered

412

to lease the installation for 100 years, pay $5 million for the government buildings, and produce nitrates and fertilizer at no more than an 8 percent profit. Secretary Weeks, who was in charge of the bids, was skeptical of the Ford offer. Surprisingly, President Harding also was not in favor of selling the installation to Ford and there was speculation that if Congress ever passed such a bill, Harding would veto it. Finally, in July 1922 the Senate Committee on Agriculture and Forestry, with Norris as chairman, rejected the Ford offer by a vote of 9–7. Simultaneously Norris's own proposal for operation by a government-controlled corporation was defeated 9–5. Thus the Muscle Shoals controversy continued as a problem for future Republican administrations.[90]

⌈ 9

OF ALL the areas in which the Harding administration evidenced a willingness to experiment, none was so obvious as government reorganization. In conjunction with Secretary Hughes, Harding early supported a revamping of the State Department by endorsing the Rogers bill. First introduced by John Jacob Rogers of Massachusetts in 1919, this measure advocated merging the diplomatic and consular services into a single foreign service of the United States. A culmination of several earlier ill-fated attempts to reorganize the State Department, this bill further specified that appointments would be made to the service only after a written and oral examination and a period of probation. Also, it systematized the service by creating nine classes of foreign service officers and increasing their stipends. Liberal retirement pay and disability allowances were also included, and promotions were to be made only through a foreign service Personnel Review Board composed of the undersecretary of state, two assistant secretaries, and three high-ranking foreign service officers.

The Rogers bill was placed on the congressional docket in late summer 1922, but not before both Hughes and Harding intervened directly with the House Foreign Affairs Committee and the Senate Foreign Relations Committee. Even then the bill was held over until after the fall elections; finally, in January 1923, the House accepted it by a wide margin after Harding again personally pressured congressmen to give it preferred status. After reaching the Senate the bill met further delays when some senators on the Foreign Relations Committee quibbled over its retirement features. Then, much to the dismay of Harding and Hughes, the bill was caught in the Senate's legislative logjam at the end of the 67th Congress in March 1923, and was not voted on before adjournment.

The Rogers bill was immediately exhumed in the 68th Congress in December 1923, and after again passing the House it was finally endorsed by the Senate by unanimous consent on May 15, 1924. President Coolidge signed it and the law went into effect on July 1, 1924. Although Harding had not lived to see this result, it was one which he had fervently desired and he must share some of the credit. The Rogers Act represented the end of a long struggle to reduce the influence of politics in the foreign service and upgrade the status of American diplomatic officials.[91]

Administration interest in upgrading the State Department was paralleled by a similar concern for the status of government employees in general. Specifically, Harding desired that federal employment have "all the stimulus of competition and reward that is offered elsewhere in private business."[92] As a result, a Government Reclassification Act, jointly sponsored by Representative Frederick R. Lehlbach (New Jersey) and Senator Thomas Sterling (South Dakota), was introduced into the first session of the 67th Congress in 1921. Passed by the House in December, it was reported favorably to the Senate in February 1922. But there it languished until just before adjournment in March 1923. Then its passage was the result of combined pressure from the White House and government employees.[93]

Signed by Harding on March 4, 1923, the bill provided badly needed relief. At the moment, the real earnings of government employees were no more than 86 percent of their income in 1914. The act not only raised pay scales, but also created a body known as the Personnel Classification Board which established a system of uniform pay rates, created new classes of positions, determined the actual duties and responsibilities of existing positions, prepared class specifications and the minimum qualifications for each class, passed on the requests of department officials for reallocations of positions, and collected and interpreted data relating to government salaries and their comparable scales in private employment. Obviously this act was a further attempt by the administration to create sounder operational practices and effect increased efficiency.[94]

But neither the Rogers Act nor the Reclassification Act was as grandiose in scope or conception as the administration's scheme for a reorganization of the executive branch. In the waning months of the Wilson administration, the Republican-controlled Congress passed a resolution creating a Joint Congressional Committee on Reorganization to study the problem and to report to Congress "not later than the second Monday in December, 1922." As a representative of the executive branch to work with this joint committee, President Harding appointed his old Ohio benefactor Walter Brown, who shortly thereafter was elected chairman of the group.

At the time of the committee's first meeting in May 1921, Harding emphasized his desire to weed out duplication of effort, combine similar functions under the same department, and effect a "common sense" reorganization. He also emphasized the need for speed. He was subsequently disappointed on almost all counts. Brown, who took the president seriously, immediately asked for "detailed suggestions" from the various departments on how reorganization might best be achieved. When after six months it became clear that the cabinet officers were dragging their feet and adopting a hostile attitude toward reorganization, Brown submitted to Harding in January 1922 a tentative scheme of his own. The most intriguing aspect was his recommendation that there be ten departments: State, Treasury, Justice, Agriculture, Interior, Commerce, Labor, Communications (instead of Post Office), Defense (instead of War and Navy), and Education and Welfare (new).[95]

Now began a series of intrigues which almost defy description. The Brown proposal, which also included interdepartmental transfer of numerous bureaus and agencies, immediately aroused great animosity. Commerce and Agriculture, already sparring over various functions, escalated their differences. Agriculture contested the idea of giving up any of its bureaus, especially the Forestry Division to Interior. Navy did not wish to be amalgamated with Army in a Department of Defense. Secretary Weeks, Secretary Denby, Secretary Hoover, Secretary Mellon, Secretary Wallace —all wrote Harding at one time or another protesting Brown's recommendations. In short, parochial interests took precedence in the minds of most cabinet officers over the general welfare. As Harding wrote to Gifford Pinchot in a moment of near despair: "It is a singular thing that even the broadest-minded Cabinet chief is naturally inclined to oppose the surrender of any of the government functions which have heretofore been committed to his Department. The task of reorganization is not easy."[96]

415

For almost a year the cabinet continued to argue over the Brown proposal. Harding did not intrude except on those occasions when it was necessary to apply soothing balm to injured feelings. He much preferred to have the cabinet officers work out their own differences and he made it clear that he did not intend to ride roughshod over any department head (he was referring mainly to Wallace). However, he also emphasized that he fully expected at some point to present a reorganization plan to Congress upon which there was general agreement. Through it all Harding sympathized with Brown and supported him whenever he could. As he wrote to Malcolm Jennings:

He [Brown] sailed in with high hopes. He had excellent ideas. He expected to work out a really great reformation. . . . I gave him all the backing that the presidential authority commanded. For awhile things ran smoothly. . . . Finally the rutted chaps began to conspire and get in their work. They pulled together. They erected barricades and stumbling blocks in every direction. He encountered the jealousies and greed for power. He found nobody willing to give up anything except here and there a disagreeable job, and found it necessary to appeal to me on many an occasion.[97]

As a testimony to Harding's skill at conciliation, on February 13, 1923, the cabinet submitted a counterproposal to the Brown Reorganization Committee which, except for a few minor details, corresponded to the original Brown plan. All ten of Brown's departments were endorsed although Navy still demurred on a Department of Defense. Actually the only major difference was the retention of Forestry in the Department of Agriculture. Immediately the Brown committee asked Congress to extend its time for filing a final report to July 1, 1924, by which time it hoped to iron out any remaining differences between the cabinet and itself.[98]

As with several other of Harding's new approaches, this one never progressed beyond 1923 and one can only speculate on what would have happened had Harding lived. As it was, Harding was gone and Coolidge had his hands full with the oil scandals by the time the July 1, 1924, deadline arrived. Congress, too, was in no mood in mid-1924 to implement the 1923 reorganization plan and Coolidge did not push it. Some few piecemeal changes were later made, but they did not come close to the imaginative and radical reorganization which Harding, the cabinet, and Brown had hammered out in 1923.

XIII

The Tragedy Begins

[1

FROM the summer of 1922 on, the presidency was an increasing burden for Warren Harding. He still liked the pomp, the ceremony, the attention, and the glitter of the office. But the strikes, protracted wrangling with Congress, continuing difficulties over patronage, prohibition enforcement problems, and concern over the fall elections provided ever-mounting pressures and by late 1922 he was almost overwhelmed with the magnitude of his presidential responsibilities. Becoming increasingly more solemn and serious, he worried some of his old friends who found him less buoyant around the poker table and less available for the golf course.

After little more than a year in office Harding discovered that the requirements of the presidency absorbed almost all his waking time. The summer strike months of 1922 were a particular nightmare. But those that followed were not much better. As he sought to establish more effective party leadership and as his battles with a recalcitrant Senate intensified, his White House engagement calendar was filled to capacity. He once remarked to the National Press Club, "I never find myself done. I never find myself with my work completed. I don't believe there is a human being who can do all the work there is to be done in the President's office. It seems as though I have been President for twenty years."[1]

Frankly, Harding wasted his energies on too many trivial matters. This was natural for a man who never before had had to account for his time carefully. Generally successful as president in his contacts with people, Harding had particular trouble with his correspondence and administrative paper work. Hughes later remarked that Harding dealt personally with a vast correspondence and was not content with mere perfunctory acknowledgments (as his papers amply show). Nicholas Murray Butler claimed that he once found Harding poring over a stack of a hundred letters and exclaimed, "Oh, come on, Mr. President, this is ridiculous," to which Harding wearily replied, "I suppose so," and added, "I am not fit for this office and should never have been here."[2]

This twin reaction of not liking the presidency and not feeling adequate to the task was expressed by Harding with some frequency beginning in the summer of 1922. He spoke increasingly of the day when he could return to his newspaper and once, in an off-the-cuff statement, declared: "A great many people think it is a fine thing to be President. . . . But I know better, and I would like nothing better than to be a Marionite again."[3] Later writers, viewing the Harding administration from the vantage point of the scandals, read deep significance into such statements. But almost every president—Washington and Lincoln included—had at one time or other expressed disillusionment about the job or their joy at retirement. Woodrow Wilson had once commented to Tumulty, ". . . how I wish this were March 4, 1921. . . . I tell you, my friend, it will be great to be free again."[4] Harding, therefore, was no exception. Still, his easygoing nature and his penchant for compromise and tranquillity made certain aspects of the presidency more painful for him than for most, especially the increasing need for exercising strong leadership and the necessity of making difficult decisions.

By the fall of 1922 Harding's general mental depression rested not merely on political factors or on the demands of the presidency. His own personal problems began to mount. In late August Mrs. Harding suddenly became ill with hydronephritis. Since February 1905, when she had had one kidney removed, severe uremic disturbances had periodically placed her life in danger. But, under Dr. Sawyer's care, she had managed to survive. Now, again, her life hung in the balance because of a kidney blockage, and for two weeks, during the height of the coal and rail strikes, Harding divided his time between concern over the strike situation and worry about his wife's health. On September 7 Mrs. Harding's condition became so grave that Dr. Sawyer summoned Dr. Joel T. Boone, assistant White House physician, and two specialists, Dr. John M. T. Finney of Baltimore and Dr. Charles H. Mayo of Rochester, Minnesota, to the White House for urgent consultation. Dr. Mayo later recalled that when he arrived Mrs. Harding was so ill that "it was impossible for her to carry on a conversation." Mayo, along with Drs. Boone and Finney, recommended immediate surgery. But Dr. Sawyer disagreed, claiming that an operation was too risky and that the first lady would live if they let nature take its course. The alternatives were presented to Mrs. Harding who, after learning of Dr. Sawyer's preference, said: "We will wait."[5]

The nation remained ignorant of Mrs. Harding's true condition until September 9 when her illness began to challenge strike news for front-page headlines. For three nights reporters chain-smoked cigarettes while sitting about the lobby of the executive offices maintaining a "death watch." Carefully they threw their stubs in the fireplace and put their burned matches back in their boxes; Mrs. Harding had once scolded them for littering in that very lobby. Finally, on September 13, they could report that Dr. Mayo was on his way home and that the crisis was over. Dr. Sawyer's gamble had paid off. But it was not until October 12 that Mrs. Harding was permitted up for a few brief moments and it was not until Thanksgiving Day that she was well enough to have dinner served to her in the dining room.

These were dark days for the president and he was visibly affected by his wife's illness. Close associates remarked on the intense strain under which he worked at this time. Dr. Boone claimed that Harding worried too hard and too long during his wife's illness with resultant damage to himself. Harry Daugherty, who was one of the few visitors to the living quarters of the White House during this period, indicated that the president came alive from the depths of despair when the crisis passed.[6]

As first lady, Mrs. Harding was extremely popular in the country and her recovery brought a collective sigh of relief. She was remembered fondly for having reintroduced some gaiety into the White House and was justly famous for her lawn parties for wounded veterans and Easter egg rolls for children. Interestingly, while the nation as a whole thought favorably of Florence Harding, "proper Washington society" did not. A bit too stiff and haughty, her hair marceled too tightly, the first lady seemed somewhat artificial and shallow to the social denizens who ruled the Washington scene. Mrs. Harding quickly sensed that she was not wholly accepted in these elite circles and this caused her to be too flamboyant in her relationship with such an undisciplined and showy person as Evalyn McLean. Mrs. Harding did not get along well with the high priestess of Washington so-

ciety, Alice Roosevelt Longworth. "Princess Alice" was frankly conde-
scending in her attitude toward Mrs. Harding and thought of her as merely
a provincial from central Ohio. Mrs. Harding, in turn, displayed a streak
of vindictiveness toward all those whom she regarded as "enemies." She
listened far too much to gossip and took silly tales much too seriously.
Addicted to the astrological prophecies of Madame Marcia, Washington's
famous R Street clairvoyant, she sometimes allowed her thoughts to be
colored by superstition, giving rise to false rumors that astrology really
ruled the White House.[7]

Clearly Mrs. Harding was an extremely ambitious and excitable
woman to whom the presidency came to mean fully as much as it did
to her husband. Florence Harding had not coveted the position for her
"Wurr'n," as her rasping voice called him, nor had she urged him to seek
it. But after he was nominated and elected she was intensely anxious for
him to succeed. His presidency thus became their joint venture. The old
maxim "The career of the woman is the man" certainly applied in this
case. In the process Mrs. Harding became even more of a nagger—prodding her husband, scolding him, even driving him. She often made suggestions which were adopted and she kept in close touch with administration
officials on a variety of questions. Florence Harding frankly made it her
business to know about major governmental developments.

There was never any outward indication that this wifely interference
unduly bothered Harding although he once remarked, "Mrs. Harding
wants to be the drum major in every band that passes." Still, if he quietly
tolerated her nagging and intrusions, it was also clear that Warren Harding had long since lost any intimate or physical attachment, if indeed he
ever had any, to Florence, described by one recent biographer as "sexless,
with the brittle quality of an autumn leaf after the chlorophyll has re-
ceded."[8] Mrs. Harding's hold on her husband had always rested more on
her tenacity and sense of purpose than on coyness or charm. Warren
seemed to draw a certain strength from her. She apparently provided the
resolve which at times he lacked. And, as the difficult months in the White
House slipped by, the two seemed to grow more dependent on each other
rather than less. Through her Warren Harding imbibed an increasing desire to exert stronger executive leadership and cut loose from weak friends.
Her frequent reminders that he was *president* acted as an antidote to his
own tendency to remain just "one of the boys." Her admonition that he

take *action* often overpowered his own inclination to do nothing or compromise. Such a husband-wife relationship could scarcely be described as blissful or loving, but in its strange way it was satisfactory to both partners. There was little doubt that Florence Harding always had her husband's best interests uppermost in her mind. He, in turn, despite her sexual limitations and her nagging, found the frustrations of the presidency somewhat easier to bear with her nearby.

[2

IF PERSONAL crises by the fall of 1922 had an effect on Harding's attitude toward the presidency, shifts in his relationship with his official family and his own political prospects for the future also played a part. From the beginning Harding had taken great pains to dispel the impression that he was controlled by a Senate cabal. In this endeavor he had been successful. But in placing primary reliance on his "best minds" cabinet to provide him, collectively, with solutions to the nation's problems, he met with only limited success. Certainly few presidents ever gave more thought to the selection of a cabinet and few had more respect for their cabinet than did Harding. Yet cabinet meetings were generally unproductive. Real policy and decision making was achieved by the president in private conferences with individual cabinet members rather than by the group as a whole. Hence, of great importance was the relative standing of the individual cabinet members with the president.

At first it was assumed that Daugherty and Fall would monopolize the president's ear. Daugherty always did retain quick physical access to the throne. A special private wire went directly from Daugherty's office in the Justice Department to the president's in the White House. Ordinarily Daugherty and Harding talked by phone several times each day. But Daugherty's influence was only relative and began to diminish by the spring of 1923 as a result of his ill health and the heavy attacks made on him by Congress. Still, there was never any indication that Harding consciously sought to replace or weaken his close personal ties with his attorney general. Fall was a different story. In 1921 his contacts with the president were frequent. By early 1922 these had declined markedly and there were rumors that Fall was dissatisfied with the growing importance of Hoover, Hughes, and Wallace in the cabinet. By late 1922 Harding had obviously cooled toward Fall and the New Mexican's influence with the president almost reached the vanishing point.

Increasingly Harding turned to Hoover and Hughes and, to a lesser extent, to Mellon and Wallace for advice. As early as January 1922 the press reported that the president's old Senate playmates were worried that "Warren is being spoiled by the high-brows Hughes and Hoover."[9] In the summer strike situation, most observers saw the hand of Hoover behind Harding's cautious and moderate approach before the Wilkerson injunction. In Harding's stiffening attitude toward Congress in late 1922 and early 1923 there were again unmistakable signs that the Hughes-Hoover combination was wielding dominant influence.

Harding's advocacy of the World Court in the late winter of 1923 was regarded by many political pundits as final proof of the emerging importance of the Hughes-Hoover element. Of course, this was too simple an explanation. But it did contain some truth. By the late winter of 1923 Harding decided to push for certain goals, such as the World Court, regardless of the attitude of Congress or of segments of his own party, and by so doing moved very close to the Hughes-Hoover position. As Henry A. Wallace later described the impressions his father got of Harding in this period: ". . . during the first year in the presidency [Harding] was not yet fully aware of the seriousness of the job. . . . During the last year of his life, however, Mr. Harding changed remarkably and became fully impressed with the extraordinary seriousness of the presidential job. . . . during the last year of his life [he] was desirous of rendering an unusual service to the American people."[10]

As already noted, both the press and the general public endorsed this apparent change, especially Harding's more aggressive attitude toward Congress. The public animus toward that body, clearly reflected in the voting patterns of the fall elections, remained to the end. The press, for example, welcomed the silence that final adjournment of the 67th Congress brought on March 4, 1923. In view of returning business prosperity, most journalists agreed that this was no time for Congress to rock the boat with its continued bickering. Now that prosperity seemed assured, there was a general desire to forget about politics altogether.

"The American citizen," said the *New Republic*, "to whom the passing of the old Congress is a source of the most unalloyed satisfaction is President Harding."[11] This was true. The president was anxious for a respite from congressional warfare and hoped that returning prosperity would mellow members of the new 68th Congress before it convened the next December. But actually, the 67th Congress had not treated the administration as badly as the frequent tension between the White House and Capitol Hill suggested. In fact, its record in passing administration-sponsored legislation was excellent. In the area of fiscal policy, debt reduction, and government economy, it had followed the administration's lead except for modifying certain particulars of the 1921 Mellon tax program. In agricultural matters it either pushed measures of its own, which the administration endorsed, or adopted White House recommendations. In foreign affairs it accepted every major treaty submitted to it. On the tariff and immigration the Congress and the White House saw generally alike. Although it did not rush to pass many of the administration's proposals for social welfare and internal improvements, Congress's failure was due more to lethargy than to antagonism. Even adherence to the World Court was left as an open question by the 67th Congress. Only in the case of the soldier's bonus and ship subsidies had the two ends of Pennsylvania Avenue found themselves in hopeless disagreement.

But by 1923 the appearance was more significant than the substance and both congressmen and the president were anxious to terminate their relationship and get away from Washington as quickly as possible. Harding immediately went to Florida for a golfing holiday. He needed it. Since July 1922 he had been confined to Washington by the strike situation, his wife's illness, and the closing sessions of the 67th Congress. In mid-January he had suffered a severe attack of the flu which ultimately swept the entire cabinet and rendered the top echelon of the Harding government helpless for a brief period of time. Refusing to remain in bed for more than a week, Harding had returned to his responsibilities too soon, although Dr. Sawyer forced him to reduce his work load. Even as late as March the president had not yet recovered his strength and hence sought the Florida sun as a restorative. From March 9 to 19 the presidential party, including assorted politicians and friends, sailed the Inland Waterway aboard Ned McLean's houseboat *Pioneer*, stopping at golf courses along the way. The president's flagging spirits appeared to revive under these conditions and some of his pessimism and disillusionment of the preceding fall and winter dissipated. However, he did not respond physically and by the time of his return to Washington he was still not up to par.

American politics does not take a vacation nor does it wait on tired bodies to restore themselves. No sooner had Congress adjourned and the president turned south than members rushed home to mend their political fences. Republicans were especially worried about their party's "image." Many felt that the administration's goals were still not being presented forcefully enough and party leaders, in particular, were upset by the continued existence of so much "misunderstanding." As one solution, Albert Lasker in late March suggested the creation of an Office of Administration Publicity with a director who would have the rank of assistant secretary. Supporting this proposal was Secretary Davis, himself a publicity enthusiast, who called Harding "the poorest advertiser in the United States." According to Davis, this publicity office would compensate for the fact that the president did not "blow his own horn enough."

Harding summarily vetoed the plan, claiming that the proposed office would quickly degenerate into a mere propaganda device. Anyway, said Harding, "the quiet sawer of wood gets further in the end than the beater of a drum." Press opinion overwhelmingly backed Harding in his opposition to the Lasker proposal, seeing in the publicity office a thinly veiled attempt at government censorship or at manufactured opinion. As for the administration's "image," said the New York Times: "the fact that President Harding does not blow his own horn is one of the characteristics which have commended him to steady-going Americans. . . . if his fellow countrymen do not like the way in which he sinks himself in his work, remains modest and unpretentious, and faces applause or blame with an equable temper, so much the worse for them." [12] On the other hand, even the New York Times had to admit that the president certainly would have to "go before the people" and make an extensive "swing around the circle" to buoy up Republican chances in the months ahead. Other newspapers agreed that "Mr. Harding, and Mr. Harding alone, can furnish the incentive for a Republican rally." [13]

Harding, too, realized this and, tired as he was, knew that he would have to carry his own case to the nation sometime during 1923. His political future depended on it, especially since there was already talk about the 1924 nominations. Amid speculation that he might not run again, Harding wrote to a friend in late January 1923, "if the present administration is not a success the nomination will not be worth having for me or anybody else in the Republican party. . . . My judgment is that the present administration will come to a full appraisal in the public mind by the beginning of 1924. . . . I have not a single worry about the situation."[14] Harding was counting heavily on prosperity to help stem the tide of anti-Republican criticism, and as the economy gathered momentum in the spring of 1923 he became increasingly optimistic. By that time he sensed that the administration was gaining in public favor and concluded that if current trends continued "there can not possibly be any doubt about renomination."[15]

Despite a few rumors concerning the possible candidacies of LaFollette and Johnson, the overwhelming majority of Republican politicians by March 1923 remained firmly behind Harding. They could already see that business growth was allaying most opposition and that the country genuinely "liked" the president. Moreover, it appeared by the spring of 1923 that Harding did not dislike the presidency as much as he had indicated a half year before. It was not a complete surprise, therefore, when on March 17 Harry Daugherty announced to a group of reporters in Miami, Florida: "President Harding will be a candidate for renomination. He will be opposed by no other candidate except by one man who always is and always has been a candidate [LaFollette]. The President will be renominated and re-elected because the country will demand it."[16]

There was immediate speculation on why Daugherty took this occasion, so far in advance of the convention of 1924, to make an announcement. However, the primary motive was obvious. Daugherty sought to remove any uncertainty regarding Harding and another term in order to isolate LaFollette and his brand of malcontents and prevent them from creating additional party disharmony during the summer. Moreover, the Daugherty statement was intended to place any other "hopefuls," such as Hiram Johnson, on notice that a bitter fight and political oblivion lay in their paths if they sought to block Harding's renomination. Johnson already sensed extreme dangers along this road and immediately disclaimed any intention of contesting Harding for the nomination. LaFollette, on the other hand, continued on his lonely way.

Interestingly, the Daugherty announcement was not cleared with Harding although the two men had reached a firm decision in early March that Harding would seek renomination. Harding obviously could not publicly repudiate Daugherty's statement but he wished it had been delayed. Harding's main concern was that the announcement compromised the effective-

425

ness of any "swing around the circle" because it now forced his listeners to think of him more as a candidate for renomination than as president. Sensing Harding's displeasure, Daugherty hastily wrote him that he had not intended to cause the president any embarrassment and that his statement had been designed more to reflect Daugherty's personal opinion than represent an official declaration. However, Daugherty added, since it happened he had received many telegrams and letters from all over the country suggesting that "my remarks were timely and had a good effect . . . because now everybody knew what they might expect when the time came."[17]

There were those, of course, who expressed immediate dismay at the Daugherty announcement. The *Nation* quickly appealed to all liberals of the "Borah, Brookhart, Johnson, LaFollette type" to prevent this "act of folly" and claimed that Americans would not tolerate four more years of "the utter ineptitude, inefficiency, economic folly, and diplomatic stupidity of the Harding regime." The *New Republic* also predicted Harding's overwhelming defeat and added: "It is a great pity that he does not withdraw." Some Democratic newspapers agreed that Harding would make an extremely weak candidate and be easy to beat. Others, remembering similar Democratic claims in 1920, were not so sure and admitted that the president's personal hold on the country was strong. But whatever the feeling, there seemed to be no adequate rebuttal to the *Washington Post*'s observation that "the opposition must show that there is no peace or prosperity if it attempts to make an issue of his Administration." These twin elements had always proven to be an unbeatable combination in American political history.[18]

[3

AT ALMOST the very moment political prospects were brightening for the Republicans in general and Harding in particular, a new disturbing factor appeared which, along with the president's health, began to command the center of the political stage. Scandals of serious import were widely rumored in the spring of 1923, an unsettling circumstance for the Republican party and all Republican politicians.

Attorney General Daugherty and his activities lay at the root of some of the concern. As previously noted, several attempts had already been made to saddle Daugherty with various misdemeanors and force his retirement from the government. But none was so serious as the drive by certain prolabor congressmen and labor lobbyists who, following the Wilkerson injunction, set out to "get" Daugherty. On December 1, 1922, Representative Oscar Keller of Minnesota filed fourteen charges of impeachment against the attorney general before the House Committee on the Judiciary. Keller claimed that Daugherty was not enforcing the antitrust laws, that he was undermining the activities of the Federal Trade Commission, that he had made some questionable appointments, and that he was using his office for personal gain. Samuel Untermyer was hired by Keller as special counsel to help him prove these charges.

The investigation began ten days later, but after two days of testimony, during which Daugherty answered his adversaries vigorously, Chairman Andrew J. Volstead of the Judiciary Committee declared that nothing had been uncovered to sustain the charges. At one of the sessions Volstead asked Keller's lawyer if he did not think it required "a lot of cheek" to attempt to obtain impeachment on such flimsy evidence. Indeed, Keller proved to be such an extremely inept leader in this whole affair that he went south after the hearings "for his health." The impeachment specifications were badly drawn and labor lawyers knew it. Gompers's own attorney, Jackson H. Ralston, quickly muted his support for the anti-Daugherty drive and ultimately crawfished on most of the charges.[19]

Labor elements subsequently liked to exaggerate the success of this assault on the attorney general, but it actually achieved little. On January 9, 1923, the Judiciary Committee voted 12–2 to dismiss the case and two weeks later the House voted 204–77 to sustain the decision of the committee. At the time most congressmen agreed that the impeachment attempt was merely a thinly veiled labor vendetta against Daugherty because of the Wilkerson injunction. The press took the same position. Although wasting little love on Daugherty, most newspapers branded the affair "a fiasco" and "merely a political move." As one paper summed up general feeling: "Mr. Daugherty should never have been extracted from Ohio, but . . . nothing was disclosed to give the slightest color of plausibility to the proposal for impeachment proceedings."[20]

Although successfully defending himself against such attacks, Daugherty showed the strain by becoming increasingly contentious and irritable. Throughout he fought alone and never asked Harding for any help. There was little doubt that presidential aid would have been forthcoming had it been requested. Harding was incensed at the Keller move and privately urged Daugherty to stand firm, promising him all assistance possible. To Harding this attack was an underhanded swipe at himself made by his labor opposition. In his eyes it was simply local Ohio gutter-level political tactics translated to the national scene. He and Daugherty had weathered such machinations before.

As during the fall election campaign, there were again many Republican leaders who urged Harding to dump Daugherty. They warned that he was becoming an increasing political liability and the president should get rid of him. But Harding would have none of it and on several occasions during the early spring of 1923 took pains to deny that he had any intention of asking Harry Daugherty to resign. At the time Harding was genuinely worried about Daugherty. The condition of Daugherty's invalid wife was growing worse, and his only son, Draper M. Daugherty, had shortly before degenerated into a hopeless alcoholic, finally being committed to a sanitarium in April 1923. Overcome by the same wave of influenza which had incapacitated Harding in January, Daugherty also had never fully recovered and had attempted to restore his health by traveling with the Harding party to Florida. Finding no relief, the attorney general then spent a fortnight at a rest center in Asheville, North Carolina, and finally convalesced for several weeks at Atlantic City and Washington Court House. Not until late May did Daugherty return to full-time duty in the Justice Department.

The Keller charges against the attorney general were merely the beginning of a sea of troubles which began to engulf the White House in the spring of 1923. Starting in late January rumors also began to circulate of scandalous activities by others close to the president. Discounted at first as malicious gossip in the wake of the bumbling Keller episode, these rumors gained credence as a web of suspicion slowly began to weave itself around the central core of the Harding government. Although nothing specific was known, shrewd observers sensed that the White House was increasingly disturbed by these rumors and that the president had more on his mind than the possibility of a second term or a presidential "swing around the circle." Indeed, the White House was worried. Not merely by coincidence had Florence Harding clipped a brief typed note to the entries in her household account book for February 1923: "The President is coming under some very powerful influence and needs to safeguard his health. . . . The opposition of the Moon to the Sun and Saturn in his horoscope shows that he cannot depend upon his friends. He would be suspicious of the ones he *should* trust and *trust* those he *should* be suspicious of."[21]

The first truly disturbing situation involved Charles Forbes, director of the Veterans' Bureau. Appointed by Harding on a whim, Forbes's past contained some unexplained and mysterious facets. Serving with distinction during World War I and discharged with both the Congressional Medal of Honor and the rank of lieutenant colonel, Forbes nonetheless had earlier once deserted the army and had been arrested although never brought to trial. Harding had first met "Charlie" Forbes in 1915 in Hawaii where Forbes was a Wilson appointee in charge of construction on the Pearl Harbor Naval Base. Acting as host for part of Harding's stay, Forbes had displayed to the future president a shrewd game of poker and an irresistible charm. Forbes's work for the Republican ticket in the Northwest during the campaign of 1920 had further ingratiated him with Harding. Yet Forbes's personal reputation among Republicans was unsavory. Neither Hays nor Daugherty, the two men most responsible for party patronage, endorsed Forbes's appointment to the Veterans' Bureau. Daugherty told the president at the time that it was a mistake.[22]

It was Brigadier General Sawyer, however, who distrusted and disliked Forbes most. Sawyer and Forbes clashed frequently over Veterans' Bureau policy and Sawyer early suspected Forbes's motives in handling bureau business. Sawyer confided his suspicions to Daugherty in late 1922 and suggested that Daugherty look into the matter. Meanwhile Senators Reed of Pennsylvania and Wadsworth of New York ran across rumors of Forbes's malodorous practices in early 1923 and warned Harding of the likelihood of their truth. Daugherty, after conducting a private investigation, told the president that Forbes was a crook and, with Sawyer's support, urged him to initiate some remedial action. At first Harding refused to listen, but then became increasingly alarmed as the evidence brought to him from a variety of sources began to mount. It was apparent that Forbes was selling government supplies from the medical supply base at Perryville, Maryland, to private contractors at ridiculously low prices and was also engaging in undercover deals relating to hospital building contracts and site selections.[23]

Shaken by these disclosures, Harding alternated between despondency and rage. Earlier, before he had become convinced of Forbes's guilt, he had called Forbes to the White House to explain his actions and had accepted his rather weak excuses and evasive answers. Now he summoned him to the White House again, this time, according to one contemporary story, shaking him "as a dog would a rat" and shouting at the frightened Forbes, "You double-crossing bastard!" No record remains of the rest of the conversation, but evidently Harding demanded his resignation, giving him the opportunity of leaving the country first. Emerging from this encounter "a confused and bewildered man," Forbes hastily booked passage for Europe and once there resigned on February 15.[24]

According to E. Mont Reily, President Harding "never recovered from the shock of Forbes's scoundrelism."[25] Maybe so. But the president certainly did not adopt a wise course in dealing with it. He did not publicly disassociate himself from Forbes or expose his crimes. He did not request immediate congressional help in a formal investigation or seek court action, undoubtedly fearing the advantages accruing to his opponents if he did. Instead, reverting to local Ohio political practice, he swept the situation under the rug. Harding was foolish. Already rumors about Forbes had reached such proportions that some congressmen were becoming restive and two weeks after Forbes's resignation, the Senate on March 2, on its own initiative and without encouragement from the White House, ordered a full-scale investigation into the Veterans' Bureau.

The Forbes rumors acquired a much deeper significance when, on March 14, Charles F. Cramer, general counsel of the Veterans' Bureau, committed suicide. Standing before a bathroom mirror in his home at 2134 Wyoming Avenue (which incidentally had been Harding's home while he was a senator), he put a .45-caliber bullet through his right temple. Cramer was an old friend of Forbes and had worked closely with him in his various schemes to plunder the Veterans' Bureau. At the time, however, all the public and the press knew was that Cramer was depressed by the rumors about bureau activities and by "recent financial reverses." Significantly, at the moment of Cramer's death, a clipping on the projected Senate investigation lay on his desk in his bedroom.[26]

The Forbes resignation and the Cramer suicide provided sufficient grist for the rumor mills, but their impact was eclipsed by the sudden death of Jess Smith ten weeks later. Smith was an enigma. A diabetic, he was a large man, loose-jointed and awkward, with flabby jowls, double chin, scraggly mustache and large, almost pleading brown eyes. He wore black, round shell-rimmed glasses with the ear pieces coming out of the center of the lens circle, giving him the appearance of a sad old owl. Smith was basically naive, extremely friendly and gregarious, and customarily shouted out a "Whaddayaknow?" as he hummed his favorite tune, "My God, How the Money Rolls In." His cultural tastes did not elevate him above the mass of his fellows. He rarely, if ever, read anything but the newspaper and then only the political news, the sports page, and the funnies. He was fond of clothes, which he did not wear particularly well, and had closets full of suits. He also was addicted to jewelry, especially flashy rings, his favorite being set with diamonds and two large rubies.[27]

Smith's connection with the administration was mainly through Harry Daugherty. Daugherty had befriended Smith when the latter was a boy in Washington Court House, and after Smith's father died Daugherty acted as his adviser, even helping him get started as a department store owner. Smith showed his gratitude by being available thereafter for any kind of job Daugherty needed done. Smith worked diligently for Harding's nomination and was with the Harding entourage at the 1920 convention. He fully intended to return to his Washington Court House store, but Daugherty had come to depend so much on Jess to handle details and keep disgruntled politicians happy that, according to Daugherty, "it became absolutely necessary to take Jess Smith with me wherever I went." Henceforth the two men were inseparable. Smith served as Daugherty's valet, his private secretary, his messenger, and his accountant. During the 1920 campaign they shared buses, trains, and hotel suites together. Jointly they owned a bachelor's camp along Deer Creek in Ohio where they often went to relax and to plan Daugherty's next political moves.[28]

After Harding's election, Smith moved with Daugherty to Washington, D.C. Daugherty at first rented a house from Ned McLean at 1509 H Street, halfway between the White House and the Justice Department. He used the upstairs as a residence but reserved the ground floor for receiving people who came to talk about patronage. Because of the incessant turmoil there and his desire to have his wife with him, Daugherty finally moved his private quarters in October 1921 to an apartment in the Wardman Park Hotel. In the short time that Daugherty lived at the H Street address men of standing called there—Secretary Fall, General Sawyer,

Ambassador Richard Washburn Child. Even President and Mrs. Harding dined there on two occasions. Jess Smith was always in attendance.

Although Smith never presumed to speak for Daugherty or represent him officially, he quickly became a permanent fixture in the Justice Department. He had a desk near Daugherty's office on the sixth floor and handled some of Daugherty's routine mail. Smith was never at any time on the government payroll although he used Justice Department secretaries and wrote notes and letters on official Justice Department stationery. He never typed a title under his name and simply scrawled at the bottom "Jess W. Smith." He had free run of the building and the files, carried a badge and a card from the FBI, commonly referred to the president as "Warren," and, according to newspapermen who covered the Justice Department, "was in a higher position than any of the assistant Attorneys General."[29]

Smith loved all this but, unlike his friend Daugherty, was out of his depth in the political big time. Mixing among the great and near great, Smith quickly developed a sense of importance which he communicated to others who for one reason or another were seeking favors from the administration. Fancying himself a smart "fixer," he began peddling "influence" and plucking off some of the easy money floating around Washington in the early prohibition days. His basic motivation was to cover margin accounts with Samuel Ungerleider, a Columbus stockbroker who had opened offices in Washington in 1921 and who included among his clients such men as Harry Daugherty and Warren Harding.

In pursuing his illegal activities Smith did not act alone. He had the help of several other Ohio men, especially Howard Mannington who occupied a greenstone-faced house at 1625 K Street. Mannington was an Urbana, Ohio, newspaper editor and sometime politician who had held a minor state office when Daugherty was in the Ohio legislature. Mannington later had helped in Harding's campaign for senator in 1914 and had served as a majordomo in handling delegations to Marion during the presidential campaign of 1920. After the inauguration he had stayed on in Washington to help Jess Smith weed through tons of mail addressed to Daugherty from office seekers. At no time did Mannington hold a government position.

With the aid of Fred A. Caskey from Marietta, Ohio, and an Illinois friend, M. P. Kraffmiller, Smith and Mannington ran the "little green house on K Street" as a kind of racket headquarters. Contrary to later assertions, affairs there were not rowdy, but commercial, and aroused no suspicion from the neighbors. Mannington was the "bag man" and handled the money; Caskey took care of what little paper work was necessary. Jess Smith came around to grab his share of the profits and to handle any "big stuff," such as immunity from prosecution or deals involving access to Justice Department papers and files. Peddling influence to the gullible, selling permits to withdraw liquor from bonded government warehouses, and arranging for the illegal sale of government property were but part of the repertory of this crew. They always had a brisk business. If Smith and Mannington were willing to sell, there were the greedy who were willing to buy. George L. Remus, a Chicago lawyer who abandoned a lucrative practice in 1919 to become a multimillionaire czar of bootlegging, later claimed that he supplied Smith with more than $250,000 in order to enjoy immunity from Justice Department arrest and prosecution. In another instance, the General Drug Company paid the K Street group as high as $20,000 for a liquor withdrawal permit. Smith also allegedly received $224,000 in Liberty Bonds to help arrange the transfer of a German-held firm from the alien property custodian's care to that of a private financial combine.[30]

In the spring of 1923 these specific deals, of course, were unknown and only unsubstantiated rumors floated about. The fact, however, that these persons were all connected with Harry Daugherty, and through Daugherty to Harding, created an ugly situation. As in the case of Forbes, Senator Wadsworth and other close Republican friends worried about the K Street rumors and on several occasions warned Harding about them. As Wadsworth later recalled, "I seldom if ever met these men myself," but it was common knowledge that they were around and were exercising an evil influence. When Harding was asked about this group he would invariably "get very angry," especially if the suggestion was made that they might be engaged in something crooked.[31]

Later, after the scandals broke, much misinformation was written in the press about this so-called Ohio Gang, and there was much conjecture about the relationship of Daugherty and Harding to its activities. Despite later claims, this much is clear. The Ohio Gang had very few of the characteristics of a gang because it had no concrete form, no cohesion, and no plan. If it had any leadership, it was provided by Jess Smith. The Ohio Gang was simply a collection of rank opportunists who worked together as a matter of expediency. Each was jealous and distrustful of the other; they owed no allegiance to anyone. They looked for the quick buck, not sustained graft. Each new batch of boodle was from a completely separate operation or deal. Division of the profits occurred on a haphazard basis. Compared with the great bosses and professional grafters in American politics, these men were amateurs and their actual take was relatively small.

Smith was a friend of Harding's, but through Harry Daugherty. Occasionally he bought dry goods for Mrs. Harding because of his knowledge of materials gained as a department store operator. In addition, he handled a few special jobs for the president—for example, he arranged for the undercover investigation of Professor William Chancellor and the Negro-blood story—but these were intermittent chores and indicated neither a presidential reliance on nor a deep personal attachment to Smith. Jess was one of the common faces around Harding's poker table and he regarded him as a "good fellow." But, again, the president accepted him in the inner circle mainly because he was so close to Daugherty.[32]

After the Forbes episode and the Cramer suicide, Harding became much more suspicious toward such persons as Smith and Mannington. When, in mid-March, Crissinger suggested to the president that Mannington be named receiver of a bank in Springfield, Ohio, Harding notified him that the appointment was not to be made under any circumstances. Not long after, when the guest list for the presidential trip to Alaska was undergoing final revision, Harding personally ordered Smith's name deleted. Moreover, he told Daugherty to send Smith back to Ohio because he believed that Jess was running around Washington with "a gay crowd."[33]

Daugherty had been responsible for Smith's name being on the guest list and knew that Jess was looking forward to the Alaskan trip. Reluctantly Daugherty told him that he could not go and suggested that he leave Washington, return to Ohio, and get help for his diabetes which was growing worse. Smith was utterly demoralized by this action. His health had been declining for some time and his state of mind was already precarious. The year before, he had been operated on for appendicitis; but because of his diabetes, the incision had never healed, requiring him to wear an uncomfortable trusslike belt. Smith also had become increasingly afraid of exposure for his K Street activities. Harding's refusal to take him to Alaska was ominous and Daugherty's intimation of an Ohio exile was like

434

a death sentence. Smith now began to brood. For solace he returned to Washington Court House where he sought out his divorced wife, Roxy Stinson, and disclosed some of his fears to her. According to Roxy, by May 1923 Smith was living in mortal terror, could not bear being alone, constantly suspected that he was being followed, was afraid of the dark, and repeated over and over, "They are going to get me." It was in this condition that Daugherty found him when he, too, returned to Washington Court House for a few days in late May. Daugherty urged Jess to get a few days' rest by accompanying him to the shack they owned along Deer Creek. Shortly after arriving there, an argument occurred between the two men, after which Smith went into town, bought a gun, and the following night, May 28, took a train for Washington, D.C.[34]

Smith immediately went to the Daugherty apartment in the Wardman Park Hotel. Daugherty, meanwhile, also returned to Washington but went to the White House where he stayed as a guest for several nights. Daugherty, however, was sufficiently worried about Smith to ask Warren F. Martin, a special assistant to the attorney general, to stay in the apartment with Jess as long as he (Daugherty) remained at the White House. Martin moved in that day, May 29. Smith left the apartment that morning and during the forenoon talked briefly with a few old Ohio friends, one of whom later remembered his acting peculiarly and mumbling something about "hanging together for Harding's sake." That afternoon he played golf at Ned McLean's "Friendship" in a foursome with Martin, Dr. Joel Boone, and Major Peyton Gordon, the federal attorney of the District of Columbia. During the late afternoon or early evening, after gathering up a briefcase of papers in the Justice Department, he went to the White House and there was confronted by Harding who displayed a general knowledge of his misdeeds. Returning to the apartment sometime before 9 P.M., Smith told Martin that he was tired and went to his own room. The next morning, May 30, at about 6:30 A.M., Martin heard a crash, rushed into Smith's bedroom, and found him slumped on the floor, still in his pajamas, with his head in a wastebasket, pistol in hand, and a bullet through his right temple. Martin immediately notified William Burns who occupied the apartment directly below. Burns and Martin then called the White House which hurriedly dispatched Dr. Boone to the scene. After examining the body, Dr. Boone told the press that Smith had had a very severe case of diabetes, had not fully recovered from an appendicitis opera-

435

tion a year before, and in a state of depression, customary to diabetics, had killed himself.[35]

Smith's body was placed in the custody of Burns and shipped off to Washington Court House for burial. No autopsy was performed. Moreover, no records, diaries, papers, or accounts of any kind were ever found. Before his death Smith had burned everything. Only two wills were left. One had been made just before his appendicitis operation in 1922, leaving some $200,000 to twenty-five different persons, including $25,000 to Harry Daugherty, $25,000 to Mal Daugherty (who, along with Harry, had helped finance Smith's early business ventures), and $25,000 to Roxy Stinson. The other will, on his desk but unwitnessed at the time of his death, left everything to only five persons (the two Daughertys, Roxy, and two of Jess's cousins) on a share-alike basis. The first will was probated.[36]

Smith's suicide had a disastrous effect on the White House. Harding received the call from the Wardman Park death scene and issued the order which sent Dr. Boone on his way. Harding did not tell Daugherty about the tragedy until after Boone returned with the full particulars. Harding's own reaction to the event was more distress than sorrow, although he had liked the dead man. The Smith suicide offered him final proof that his administration was deeply tainted with corruption and this fact now began to sap the president's morale: he lost some of the optimism with which he had greeted the return of prosperity and the prospects of future Republican victories. Not even the mounting assurance of his own renomination and reelection could blot out the dangerous and bizarre events that had begun with Forbes's resignation.

Harding's increasing distress was sensed by a few. William Allen White later recalled that Harding had remarked to him: "My God, this is a hell of a job! I have no trouble with my enemies. I can take care of my enemies all right. But my damn friends, my God-damn friends, White, they're the ones that keep me walking the floor nights!"[37] Hoover later maintained that Harding suffered increasing mental anxiety over these betrayals and in the last several months of his life could hardly conceal his disillusionment. Nicholas Murray Butler subsequently claimed that Harding desperately wanted to talk with someone about it, but could not bring himself to utter the unpleasant facts which were facing him. Butler recounted how one weekend in early May 1923 Harding begged him to come to the White

House as an overnight guest because he had matters of grave importance to discuss with him. Butler arrived to find Harding very nervous and distraught. Yet throughout Butler's stay, during which the president seemed several times on the brink of blurting out terrible secrets, Harding remained silent and said nothing significant enough to warrant the Columbia president's long trip from New York.[38]

Although Jess Smith's suicide was more eloquent than words in indicating the creeping malaise affecting the administration, both Harding and Daugherty pretended that nothing serious was wrong. They turned aside queries about the rumors of corruption by claiming that Smith's death was due to a mentally unbalanced condition brought on by diabetes, and nothing more. Even to their closest friends the pair would not admit otherwise. Several days after Smith's suicide Daugherty wrote to Ned McLean: "Poor old Jess—he was a great friend of yours. I know the whole story now and some day I will tell you enough of it to convince you that he did not commit an act of cowardice; what he did is traceable to his sickness." Later, even after the full glare of publicity revealed the sordid activities of the "little green house on K Street," Daugherty persisted in claiming that Smith was actually an "innocent" who had been led into evil paths by others, momentarily lost his sense of right and wrong because of his illness, and was basically upright and honest.[39]

These were the faces which Harding and Daugherty turned to the press and the public. But the real situation was different. The night after the announcement of Smith's death, Harry Daugherty could not bring himself to return to the Wardman Park apartment and stayed on at the White House. Mrs. Harding, herself nervous and upset, attempted to change the mood by inviting a couple in from the outside to dine. It was to no avail. Neither Harding nor Daugherty could be raised from their gloom or their own silent thoughts. At dinner only a few words were spoken and there were frequent awkward pauses. Afterwards a private showing of a motion picture was held in the upstairs hall, but even this offered no real diversion. From time to time Daugherty could be heard uttering a long low "O-o-o-o-o-o," while the president remained uncommunicative. After the movie the two guests, sensing the situation, quickly departed, leaving the White House and its occupants alone with their fears and apprehensions.[40]

437

BY THE spring of 1923, Harding's health was definitely declining. Later it was claimed that he was literally worrying himself to death because of the scandals. Anxiety did fill the last few months of his life, and the fear of exposure was unquestionably present. However, his health problems were not psychosomatic, but physiological. Moreover, they predated the presidency.

From the time he was a young man Harding had had mysterious bouts with indigestion which were somehow connected with his nervous system. Five times in his pre-senatorial days, and especially after his first exposure to the Duchess's nagging following their marriage, he had gone for treatment to the Seventh-Day Adventist sanitarium in Battle Creek, Michigan, run by vegetarian Dr. J. P. Kellogg of cornflakes fame. In between, his medical problems were handled by his father, but once the symptoms disappeared Harding returned to eating and smoking too much and sleeping too little. By early 1919, however, he suspected that he had some sort of heart ailment and later in that year confessed to Senator Watson that he had traces of sugar in his urine and his blood pressure was sometimes as high as 175. Throughout 1920 and 1921 his health apparently gave him little trouble although observers noticed that the campaign and the burdens of the presidential office placed an obvious physical strain on him. Beginning in early 1922 he was much more easily exhausted and occasionally complained of a chest pain which fortunately vanished after several moments. Both he and Dr. Sawyer maintained the fiction that it was nothing more than a recurrence of his earlier digestive disorder, but secretly they suspected angina pectoris. The strike days of 1922 were especially wearing and Mrs. Harding's illness compounded the president's own health problems. While newspapers were expressing concern over Mrs. Harding's condition the president's blood pressure soared into the 180's. At about this time, Dr. Emanuel Libman, a famous New York heart specialist, happened to see Harding at a dinner party. The next day he confided to a friend his private opinion that the president would be dead in six months from coronary complications.[41]

The flu attack which felled Harding in mid-January 1923 unquestionably was the triggering factor in the subsequent rapid deterioration in his health. One medical expert later claimed this flu attack was actually accom-

438

panied by an undiagnosed coronary thrombosis followed by myocardial infarction. Thereafter Harding did experience great difficulty sleeping at night. Arthur Brooks, the president's personal valet, confided to Edmund Starling in the late winter that the president could not lie down because if he did he could not breathe. Although Harding gave up drinking he did not curtail his smoking and in March persisted in going to the golf course in good weather. Yet after the first few rounds he complained to Starling: "Colonel, why after playing eleven or twelve holes do I drag my feet and feel so tired?" Starling suggested he should play only nine holes. "Hell!" said the president. "If I can't play eighteen holes I won't play at all!"[42]

By late spring it was obvious to all those around him that Harding was ill. His normal ruddy color had become a pallor and his energies were always at low ebb. He told Hughes at the time that his blood pressure was consistently above 175 which caused Hughes in alarm to tell his wife: "We have been worrying about Mrs. Harding, but I think it is the President we should be more concerned about." E. Mont Reily reported eating dinner with him in the late spring and hearing him despondently claim: "I am sick—I am all in. . . . I am very weary and tired, and I need rest." In early June, Senator Willis went to the White House with five items on a slip of paper which he wanted to discuss with the president. But when Willis returned to his office and handed the slip to his private secretary only two items were checked off. Asked why, Willis replied, "Warren seemed so tired."[43]

The president's declining health certainly did not provide an auspicious background for his much-publicized trip to Alaska in mid-June 1923. The decision to make this trip rested on both medical and political grounds. The president obviously required a rest and Dr. Sawyer thought the trip might be beneficial if the politicking was kept to a minimum. But Harding and his cabinet officers regarded the jaunt somewhat differently. A trip to Alaska had long been considered necessary in order to resolve an administrative headache—no fewer than five cabinet officers and twenty-eight bureaus exercised authority over the territory. Many of these were in bitter conflict on how and by whom the natural resources of the area should be developed. Secretary Fall, for example, had consistently advocated concentrating the administration of Alaska into one department (obviously Interior) and allowing private enterprise to exploit its natural resources immediately. Wallace, for one, had objected strenuously. Harding was torn between these conflicting opinions and desired to go to Alaska and investigate for himself before making up his mind.

Republican politicians saw the trip as an excellent opportunity for the president to "stump the country." Malcolm Jennings urged him to cash in on his rising popularity, lambast Congress for its ineffectiveness, and not let modesty "prevent your doing yourself, your party and your country a great service in your western trip."[44] Tired as Harding was, it was not too difficult for such men to convince him to combine a "swing around the circle" with the Alaskan venture. The president was vain about his speaking ability and often sought to release his tensions this way. "I like to go out into the country and 'bloviate,' " he would say. Hence, he ordered Walter Brown west ahead of the presidential party to make the necessary arrangements. When, just before leaving, the president saw the crushing speaking schedule that Brown had arranged for him, he blanched and ordered it cut back. Even as revised it still required a killing pace.

A few close friends now counseled against the Alaskan trip; Senator Watson told Harding directly that it might kill him. Dr. Sawyer also opposed the venture after he saw the final itinerary. Although excited about the trip, Mrs. Harding had premonitions about it and just before leaving told Starling: "Wherever we are to stop I want the doctors, General Sawyer and Captain Boone, as close to the President's room as possible. . . . You understand?"[45]

Later, these facts were marshaled as evidence that the whole Alaskan party was suffused with a sense of foreboding and that there was morbid talk of death. The Forbes, Cramer, and Smith tragedies added credence to these contentions. But nothing seemed as conclusive as Harding's selling the *Marion Star* and making a new will just before he left. The *Star* was the president's most prized possession. The fact that he would sell it was, in the eyes of later observers, Harding's final capitulation to the hopelessness of his situation. This was nonsense. The sale actually represented a desire on Harding's part to provide for his post-presidential future and not a death wish based on the past. Two Ohioans, Louis H. Brush and Roy D. Moore, had earlier offered $550,000 for the *Star* and Harding now accepted. Under the terms of the sale Harding was to be a contributing editor to the *Star* for ten years after leaving the presidency. At the moment Harding faced extensive plant renovation and the acquisition of new printing machinery, and he did not have the money to invest. The sale was therefore a shrewd move. All Harding really cared for was writing editorials and this was assured by the agreement. Similarly, there was nothing unusual about his making a new will. The *Star*'s sale necessitated it. Daugherty drew it up and Harding signed it the day before he left. It provided for a $100,000 life estate for Mrs. Harding along with their home in Marion; a $50,000 life estate for his father; various provisions for his brother and sisters; a $25,000 bequest to the Marion Park Commission; some cash gifts to various nieces, nephews, and Mrs. Harding's grandchildren; $2000 to the Baptist Church of Marion; and sums of $1000 and $2000 to old employees of the *Marion Star*.[46]

If there was no air of morbidity about the presidential party, it was nevertheless subdued by the realization that the president was tired and that he appeared to be nervous and worried. As the presidential car *Superb* left Washington on June 20, correspondents commented privately on the contrast with previous presidential jaunts. Missing was a certain spirit of lightheartedness as well as some of the president's favorite cronies. This time more sober men were along and there seemed to be a greater sense of purpose. Among the guests were Speaker of the House Gillett, Secretary of Agriculture Wallace, Dr. Hubert Work (who had succeeded Fall as secretary of the interior), and Secretary of Commerce Hoover (who was already on the west coast and joined the party there). Harry Daugherty was left behind in Washington although he planned to meet the group in Los Angeles on its way back from Alaska. Also along, besides Mrs. Harding and Drs. Sawyer and Boone, were Mrs. Hoover, Mrs. Work, Mrs. Sawyer, Mr. and Mrs. George Christian, Jr., Mr. and Mrs. Malcolm Jennings, and assorted secretaries, stenographers, newspapermen, and secret-service agents.

The plan was to travel westward through St. Louis, Kansas City, Denver, Salt Lake City, Helena, Spokane, and Portland to Tacoma where the party on July 5 would board the U.S.S. *Henderson* for passage to Alaska. Returning to Seattle on July 27, after a brief stop at Vancouver, the party would then travel by train down the west coast to San Francisco, Los Angeles, and San Diego where on August 4 the group would board ship for the return trip to Washington via the Panama Canal and Puerto Rico. Harding was slated to be back at the White House on August 26 or 27. All along the way Harding was scheduled to make speeches and engage in political haymaking by explaining the administration's record. He was, he claimed, "trying to learn more about the United States of America and seeking to have the people of the United States know more about their Government." It was, he said, a "voyage to understanding." [47]

At first the crowds were small and not particularly responsive. But as Harding moved farther west the crowds became larger. And despite a torrid heat wave which plagued the journey all the way to Denver, the president doggedly stuck to his "voyage to understanding" theme and to his schedule. In St. Louis his face became severely sunburned and in Kansas City he had to apply ice compresses to his lips before delivering a speech in Convention Hall. That same evening he talked privately for almost an hour with Mrs. Emma Fall, wife of the former interior secretary. William Allen White later claimed that Harding returned from this visit visibly shaken and the next day on the train again made reference about his enemies not bothering him, only his friends. [48] After the Teapot Dome scandal broke, this story was widely circulated and was assigned deep meaning. Yet Senator Capper, who was also with the president that night and saw him after Mrs. Fall's visit, specifically contradicted White's claim about Harding's nervousness and stated that there was nothing at all dramatic about the incident. Mrs. Fall subsequently maintained that the White version was a complete fabrication. She said that she was in Kansas City quite by chance, talked with Harding only about general matters, later accompanied the Hardings to hear his Convention Hall speech, after which they returned her to her hotel. [49]

So the president continued across the country, meeting old friends and trying to make new ones. In the sun-seared farm states he made a special effort to please the rural citizenry. Six miles from Hutchinson, Kansas, he stopped to help cut grain on the farm of Chester O'Neal. Improperly dressed in a blue coat and white flannel trousers, he won the admiration of the crowd by taking his turn at the tractor. Pleased with himself, Harding turned to Senator Capper and asked if this did not qualify him for membership in the farm bloc. Somewhat abashed, Senator Capper assured him that it did. In Denver, an automobile accident, involving two correspondents of the presidential party in which one was killed, momentarily plunged the group into sadness. But a side journey through Zion Park and a warm welcome in Salt Lake City rapidly dispelled the gloom. A day later Harding was in Yellowstone feeding the bears. Then it was on to

Helena, Montana, and Meacham, Oregon, where he reviewed a Pioneer Pageant, led a grand march, powwowed and smoked a peace pipe with Indian chiefs, and dedicated the Oregon Trail by unveiling a monument in memory of the first wagon train to arrive in the Willamette Valley. Finally he reached Spokane and Tacoma where rain fell for the first time since the party had left Washington two weeks before. On July 5, the president prepared to board the *Henderson* for four days' rest at sea.

In the drama and excitement that surrounded this presidential pilgrimage, the words which were spoken were oftentimes ignored or obfuscated. Neither the contemporary public nor commentators thereafter paid much attention to what Harding was saying and the philosophy of government he was trying to convey. In a little over two weeks he delivered fourteen major addresses besides innumerable short off-the-cuff whistle-stoppers. Some of these speeches were excellent, not so verbose as earlier efforts, and suffused with the sincerity and convictions of a man who believed in what his administration had accomplished and what it stood for. His first major address, on the World Court, was delivered in St. Louis on June 21. Thereafter Harding spoke in Kansas City on railroad and transportation problems; in Hutchinson, Kansas, on agriculture; in Denver on prohibition and law enforcement; in Cheyenne on the coal problem; in Salt Lake City on taxation and government expenditures; in Idaho Falls on cooperation in production and distribution; in Butte on business conditions; in Helena on social justice and labor; in Spokane on internal improvements, land reclamation, and water-power development; in Portland on immigration and Americanization; and in Tacoma on the merchant marine. No such series of presidential speeches again occurred until the fireside chats of Franklin Roosevelt.[50]

In the main these speeches were enlargements on his state of the union message of December 1922, and represented Harding's political and economic beliefs as of mid-1923. In them he indicated his continued support of the World Court. "My hope is in the great court," he said. "My mind is made up." He also advocated continued remedial legislation and credit extension for the farmer without intimating that he favored any radical solutions. He warned of future crises in transportation and prophesied that unless the railroads increased their efficiency and consolidated into a smaller number of systems, government ownership would become inevitable. He reiterated his belief that labor unions were beneficial and that

443

workers had the right to organize and strike. But he rejected any domination of the economy by labor unions. He expressed a belief that no successful arbitration was possible between capital and labor unless both sides would accept joint responsibility for policing the outcome. "I do not hope," he said, "for compliance on the part of employees so long as decisions are ignored by the managers."

With respect to the coal problem, Harding expressed hope that an equitable solution could be found which would skirt the pitfalls either of nationalization of the mines or of continued anarchy in the coal fields. He also indicated his growing interest in cooperative experiments of all kinds—in production, transportation, distribution, and purchasing. He reaffirmed his administration's dedication to business progress and to business-government cooperation, but he warned that business had to remain responsive to public needs. He confidently predicted a "new era" of long-term prosperity and he exhibited pride in the accomplishments of his administration in government economy, tax decreases, and debt reduction—three achievements which he believed had contributed greatly to economic recovery.

With regard to conservation, Harding urged a change in policies which would permit the wise development of the nation's natural resources so that they would not be subject either to reckless exploitation or to statutory nonuse. In this respect he advocated more planning between the various states and the federal government in the areas of land reclamation, irrigation, and water power. "The Government comes in," he maintained, "neither as an interloper nor as a benevolent carry-all." Harding also urged the better conservation of human resources and to this end suggested the retention of immigration restriction coupled with a carefully controlled local-federal program of Americanization. He left no doubt that he intended to enforce the prohibition law, as well as all laws, because it was his constitutional duty. If laws were bad, he said, the recourse was to repeal them, not ignore them. Finally, he reaffirmed his belief in the necessity of a strong merchant marine. Just before setting foot on the *Henderson* in Tacoma, he stated: "I do not for one moment believe in Government ownership and operation as a permanent policy. But I prefer that hazardous venture to the surrender of our hopes for a merchant marine."

It was clear that by the time Harding reached Tacoma, he had spoken not only as president but also as the leader of the Republican party and had set the framework for the 1924 campaign. Most newspapers commented on how silent his Republican opponents became as he moved westward, and the press remained more convinced than ever that his renomination was "a foregone conclusion." His western speeches, many agreed, showed a much abler Harding than the one the nation had overwhelmingly elected in 1920. Observers were especially struck by his independence and his courage. Through his western speeches he had personally written the Republican platform for 1924 and had presented both his party and the nation, as the *Minneapolis Tribune* said, with a "take it or leave it."[51]

Harding arrived at Tacoma satisfied. Everywhere he spoke he seemed to gather strength. By the time he reached the west coast, he sensed that the public and the press were behind him and that he was scoring heavily against his opponents. Seeing crowds of people buoyed his confidence and some of his nervousness and anxiety temporarily slipped away. He had come a long way from Washington, D.C., to the state of Washington, but it had been worth it. As he told a group shortly before boarding the *Henderson*: "We have been having a wonderful trip across the Continent. . . . Everywhere we have met a confident and a seemingly happy people, although as yet they may not be wholly satisfied with the conditions which require correction after the deflation incident to the war. Everywhere, however, they are hopeful and confident of the future and manifestly glad to live in this wonderful republic of ours. . . . I am very much more proud of our country than when I started westward."[52] For Harding, the first leg of his voyage to understanding was over.

[5

THE *Henderson*, which had been one of the first transports to carry American troops to Europe in 1917, was the largest ship yet to sail the inland waters to Alaska and there was a holiday spirit about the venture. Down Puget Sound she carried the presidential party to the roar of a twenty-one-gun salute, two destroyers steaming along slowly in convoy. As the ship got underway, the navy band aboard played "Yes, We Have No Bananas" and "I-o-wa, I-o-wa, That's Where the Tall Corn Grows." Then for four leisurely days the *Henderson* headed northward. On the fourth evening those aboard saw their first Alaskan sunset—at 10 P.M. The next morning they made their first Alaskan landfall at Metlakatla, a town of some 400 native Indians of Mongolian origin, where Governor Scott C. Bone of Alaska greeted them.

Now began what Harding called "the Discovery of Alaska." From Metlakatla the party went to Ketchikan, then to Wrangell, and finally to Juneau, the capital. There it rained fiercely as Harding delivered an address in front of the governor's residence. From Juneau, a thriving metropolis of 2000, the group traveled to Skagway and afterwards began a cold three-day voyage across the Gulf of Alaska to Seward. Here they embarked on an arduous two-and-one-half-day overland journey via the government-owned Alaskan Central Railway to Anchorage, McKinley Park, and Fairbanks. Traveling farther north than any other American president, Harding on July 15 piloted the locomotive for twenty-six miles. Arriving in Fairbanks in an amazing 94-degree heat he addressed almost all the town's 1500 inhabitants in the ball park. A few in his audience drove in jalopies almost 300 miles to hear him.

Scheduled to return from Fairbanks to Seward by way of the Richardson Trail, both the president and Mrs. Harding were clearly too exhausted to undertake this trip and returned by rail. At Seward they reboarded the *Henderson* and arrived at Sitka on July 22. Here Harding attended a local mission church service, visited the government's agricultural experiment station, and delivered a brief speech. After Sitka, the *Henderson* headed south for Vancouver and home.

Harding had looked forward to the Alaskan portion of the journey and, according to Hoover, left Tacoma on July 5 with "the atmosphere of a school boy entering on a holiday." He was constantly awed by the majestic scenery which he watched by the hour. But as the presidential party moved farther and farther north and the days lengthened, Harding found it increasingly difficult to sleep and kept such irregular hours walking the deck or playing cards that it caused comment. Later it was claimed that he was so worried he could not sleep. Actually his worsening heart condition, the excitement of the journey, and the almost constant daylight were the primary factors. As for his mental health, Herbert Hoover remembered: "His whole outlook was forward-looking. During conversations on his Alaskan trip there was no indication of the supposed apprehension of his early end which has been circulated. . . . In fact conversations on many occasions [were] on the general line as to what we should undertake and what should be done as to this, that, and the other.

446

Many of the questions discussed stretched into actual action in the future over periods of years; he sometimes put in the reservation that 'we will carry through this, that, or the other, if we are reelected.' "[53]

On the other hand, it was obvious that something was bothering the president and that his mind was often preoccupied. Hoover recalled that on the way north from Tacoma Harding once asked him in the privacy of the presidential cabin what Hoover would do if he were president and knew of a scandal brewing. Hoover replied: "Publish it, and at least get credit for integrity on your side." When Hoover asked for particulars, Harding said that he had discovered some irregularities in the Justice Department involving Jess Smith, that he had sent for Smith and had told him that he was to be arrested the following morning, but Smith had burned his papers and then killed himself. When Hoover attempted to probe deeper and asked whether Harry Daugherty was also involved, Harding "abruptly dried up and never raised the question again."[54]

As long as the party remained on the Alaskan leg of the journey, Harding's spirits remained good even though his sleeping habits continued to be irregular. But when the *Henderson* turned south toward home, the president became noticeably more morose and his nervousness again increased. Hoover later claimed that everyone on board was saddened by the necessity of going back to problems and responsibilities and that Harding was not alone.[55] However, to sleep at all the president now began to take heavy sedatives, and when these failed he stayed awake and played cards endlessly, much to the discomfort of his partners. By the time the *Henderson* arrived at Vancouver on July 26, even reporters remarked on his condition, one of them stating: "[The president] is not just tired or worn out. He is beyond being merely fatigued. He is an entirely exhausted man, and the sort of rest he requires is not that of a day, or two or three, but of weeks."[56]

The first hint of serious trouble occurred after an official luncheon at Vancouver when Harding retreated to the golf course for some relaxation. He played the first six holes but became so tired that he moved over to the seventeenth, finishing out the eighteenth so that there would be no suspicion. He returned to the hotel and lay down for about an hour before attending a formal dinner that evening given by the Canadian government. He ate little and made only a fifteen-minute speech without the usual force, although the Canadians received it with enthusiasm because he was the first American president to speak on Canadian soil. Retiring to the main ballroom, he stood for twenty-five minutes shaking hands, but excused himself long before the line had passed, and returned to the *Henderson* where he went to bed.[57]

The *Henderson* left Vancouver that night and was due in Seattle the next morning, July 27. But dense fog delayed her arrival until early afternoon. Greeted by a local reception committee, the president motored through the Seattle business district where thousands lined the streets to see him. In mid-afternoon he entered the University of Washington Stadium for a major speech. Hatless in a fierce sun, Harding spoke of the future of Alaska from a text which Hoover had helped him write and indicated that he believed no radical changes in its administration were necessary. Rejecting the idea of a sudden exploitation of Alaskan resources such as Secretary Fall had advocated, Harding maintained that a slow, planned evolution was required which would first protect the territory's natural wealth and then permit its gradual use. He concluded: "Alaska is destined for ultimate statehood. . . . Mine is pride and faith in Alaska."[58]

It was a good speech but the president delivered it listlessly. Once he made a slip, calling Alaska Nebraska, and his voice fell several times. Some members of the presidential party urged him to return at once to his train which was waiting to take him down the coast to San Francisco. But he insisted on following the established schedule. Not until 7:30 P.M. did he arrive at his private car and go instantly to bed. Later that night, as the train moved down the coast, the president called for Dr. Sawyer, complaining of nausea and pains in the upper abdominal region. Dr. Sawyer, who had treated Harding for a brief dietary upset just before his arrival in Vancouver, thought it was merely a recurrence. But Dr. Boone immediately suspected a cardiac malfunction since the president's pulse rate had shot to 120 and his respiration to 40. Dr. Work agreed with Boone and privately urged Hoover to wire ahead for Dr. Ray Lyman Wilbur, president of Stanford and a later president of the American Medical Association, to meet the train in San Francisco and bring a heart specialist (Dr. Charles M. Cooper) with him. All scheduled stops between Seattle and San Francisco were canceled and the train was ordered to proceed to San Francisco as rapidly as possible.[59]

En route the next day, July 28, the president felt much better and Dr.

Sawyer permitted him to get up, telling the press that Harding's illness was probably only an "acute gastrointestinal attack" brought on by tainted crabmeat. Upon the train's arrival in San Francisco at 8 A.M. Sunday, July 29, Harding felt well enough to dress himself, shunned a wheelchair which had been provided for him, and, despite the protests of his doctors, walked unaided to a waiting automobile which drove him to reserved rooms in the Palace Hotel. He was again put to bed. By nightfall he was worse. Now it was abundantly clear that Harding had had a cardiac collapse. Through a blood count and chest X-rays it was also quickly determined that the president had bronchopneumonia. But even as his doctors outlined an intensive program of treatment, Harding refused to take the matter seriously, insisted on going to the bathroom himself, and told them that he absolutely had to be back on his feet by Tuesday when he was scheduled to give a major foreign policy address.

Through Monday and Tuesday the doctors gave Harding a steady flow of digitalis and caffeine, and by Tuesday night there was a decided improvement. The president's lungs were clearing up and the doctors began to be optimistic. On that same day Harding's foreign policy address was released to the press by Herbert Hoover. It represented a strong defense of the administration's overseas record and was favorably received. Listing no fewer than fifteen major achievements in foreign policy, Harding reiterated his desire to add one more—membership in the World Court. In answer to those critics who claimed that he would ultimately have to capitulate to the irreconcilables on this question, Harding replied that he would accept Court adherence on any basis which could pass the Senate. "All else is mere detail," he said.[60]

On Wednesday and Thursday there was again continued improvement and by late Thursday afternoon the president was permitted to sit up in bed. George Christian, Jr., saw him like this just before he left to read an address on "The Ideals of Christian Fraternity" which Harding had prepared earlier for delivery to the Grand Commandery of Knights Templars in Hollywood. At about the same time, Starling of the secret service dropped in and chatted with Harding about the relatively poor fishing in Alaska before he went out to make arrangements for the president's return to Washington. Somewhere around dinner time, Harding talked by phone with Malcolm Jennings and told him that he was "out of the woods" but was still "so tired, so tired."

449

About 7:30 P.M., propped up by pillows, he was listening to Mrs. Harding who was reading aloud from a favorable article about him in the *Saturday Evening Post*, entitled "A Calm Review of a Calm Man." Sue S. Dauser, a night nurse, was standing by while the day nurse, Ruth Powderly, momentarily disappeared for a glass of water to give the president his medicine. At that moment Mrs. Harding interrupted her reading to plump up his pillows, when the president remarked: "That's good, read some more." As Mrs. Harding began to read again, the president twisted convulsively. At first she thought a piece of gum he was chewing had lodged in his throat and started to run her finger in his mouth to get it out, but then she rushed from the room calling frantically for the doctors. Drs. Work and Wilbur reached the bedroom within seconds, followed closely by Boone and Sawyer. Sawyer immediately listened to his heart, grabbed a hypodermic needle, and offered stimulants—but to no avail. Dr. Wilbur whispered to Sawyer to keep trying, even though it was useless, for the sake of Mrs. Harding. At the same time Dr. Sawyer called to her to hold herself together. Mrs. Harding replied quietly, "I won't break down."[61]

Stephen Early, an Associated Press reporter, happened to be in the hall when Mrs. Harding came bursting out calling for the doctors. Realizing something was wrong, he ran down to the next floor and called the AP's San Francisco office, telling them to stand by for a bulletin. Then he rushed back upstairs. A nurse was standing by the president's door which had been left open; inside sitting by the bed was Florence Harding saying to herself over and over, "Warren, Warren, Warren!" Two secret-service men were just arriving to seal off the entire floor in order to prevent news leaks. Early raced downstairs and again phoned his office, giving the AP a news beat on the president's death of some twenty-five minutes.[62]

The nation was stunned. From the first report of Harding's illness on July 29, the press had followed his progress in great detail. On July 31 the true seriousness of his condition was first revealed and called forth a wave of sympathy and deep concern. Not even the most ardent of the president's opponents failed to show genuine anxiety over his condition, for he was universally liked as a man. Harding's health became the single topic of national conversation for four days and a sigh of relief went up on August 1 as the headlines announced that the crisis was passed. August 2 found most newspapers talking of his impending return to Washington and the necessity of decreasing the presidential work load. On August 3 the nation's papers were edged in black.

As the nation reeled with the news, the first lady was ordered to bed by Dr. Sawyer and she remained there through the next morning. A few friends were allowed to see her and help her prepare for the long journey back to Washington. The doctors in attendance agreed that the president's death was probably caused by cerebral hemorrhage. They pleaded with Mrs. Harding to permit an autopsy but she steadfastly refused. Hence they could only guess that the final blow was the bursting of a sclerotic blood vessel in the brain. But it could also have been a massive rupture in the wall of the heart in view of the president's high blood pressure and his physical activity during the critical period in the first few days after the original seizure. In any event, a death certificate of apoplexy was finally signed by Drs. Boone, Wilbur, Cooper, Sawyer, and Work.[63]

Early the next morning, August 3, the president's body was surrendered to the embalmers, dressed in a cutaway coat and black trousers, and placed in a casket in the big drawing room of the hotel's presidential suite. By mid-morning the room was banked with flowers—the bright California sun streaming through the windows bathing the scene in a glow of warmth rather than funereal sadness. Callers were permitted to pass by the casket and observe the calm and unworried look on the president's face.

[6

THE ordeal of a cross-country funeral procession now lay ahead. San Francisco, which the day before had displayed gay-colored bunting in honor of the president's arrival, was draped in black as the presidential party with the hearse at its head journeyed the half mile to the railroad station. The casket was placed in the car *Superb* and was mounted so that it could be seen through the windows. Almost exactly twenty-four hours after the president's death the funeral train left heading east. Harry Daugherty, who had hurried west as soon as the news of Harding's illness had reached him, remained close by Mrs. Harding to comfort her. On the train she bore up well, but constantly spoke of her dead husband in doleful tones. "He did too much," she would say, and then sob, "I warned him . . .

451

again and again I begged him to take a rest and not try to see every-body." [64]

It was a memorable trip. Reporters on the train were awed by the outpouring of people. The crowds were immense. Every town, every city, every hamlet turned out mourning people, standing silently or kneeling by the tracks and on the station platforms. Even in the sparsely settled West there were those who came to watch as the train rolled by. Arriving in Chicago on August 6, some two and one-half hours late, the train had to put on a pilot engine to force the crowds off the track. It required five policemen to keep people off the car in which the president's body rested. It was estimated that over a million and one-half persons lined the rails through Chicago and in one section it required two hours for the train to travel nineteen miles.

As the funeral procession continued into Ohio, Mrs. Harding re-quested that it make frequent stops. One reporter claimed that the crowds in Ohio were "so close together as to virtually suggest an aisle of mourn-ers extending across the entire commonwealth." All night long Ohioans slept or rested at stations, in autos, or on lawns to catch a glimpse of their fallen leader. Hundreds placed pennies on the tracks and scrambled for them as souvenirs after they had been flattened by the passing wheels. At some places the crowds sang softly or hummed hymns as the funeral cortege inched silently by.

Arriving in Washington at 10:22 P.M. on August 7, the train backed into the station so that the *Superb* was near the exit. Mrs. Harding alighted first, being supported by George Christian and Dr. Sawyer. They were met by President Coolidge. In the concourse a band played "Nearer My God to Thee" while the casket was removed through a special door cut in the side of the *Superb*. A huge flag was draped over the coffin and a single wreath laid on it. Escorted through the station by a military guard it was placed on a waiting caisson and in column formation was marched to the White House.

Harding's coffin was placed in the center of the East Room, just as McKinley's had been, and a marine was stationed at each corner. Mrs. Harding selected from the mass of flowers that had been sent those which she said Warren had particularly liked and placed them near the casket. That night she maintained a lonely vigil beside the body and, according to some observers, spoke to it from time to time. Later, after the scandals

452

broke, these expressions of wifely grief were said to indicate that Mrs. Harding was losing her mind or was near prostration.[65] She was neither. Throughout the whole ordeal she was always the master of her emotions.

At 10 A.M. on the morning of August 8, the casket was moved from the East Room and placed on a caisson for the slow march to the Capitol. Behind it came the honorary pallbearers, led by Senator Lodge. Mrs. Harding moved through the doorway on the arm of Christian and disappeared into an automobile. Behind her in the procession came President Coolidge, Chief Justice Taft, and Woodrow Wilson. Following the three living presidents came the cabinet with Hughes in front. Ahead, the army band played a funeral dirge while farther down the line the marine band played "Onward, Christian Soldiers." As the procession moved along Pennsylvania Avenue guns at Fort Myer boomed out every sixty seconds. In front of the Congressional Library, a wall of humanity gathered to watch the marchers make their turn into the Capitol grounds. There, enterprising small boys, completely unaware of the drama going on around them, were filling up bottles with water from the library fountain and selling them for a nickel to refresh parched throats.

Upon reaching the Capitol the casket was placed in the center of the rotunda at the exact spot where Lincoln had laid in state. Ten truckloads of flowers were arranged around the walls. As President Coolidge stepped forward to lay a wreath on the bier, four male singers, stationed by the great sculptured head of Lincoln, sang "Lead, Kindly Light." Mrs. Harding entered the rotunda from the Senate passage and walked to her place near the casket, accompanied by George Christian. A brief service began, led by the Reverend Dr. J. Freeman Anderson of the Calvary Baptist Church. Halfway through, a loud report slammed down from the ceiling above; eyes shot upward but could see nothing. Unknown to those below a free-lance writer had sneaked into the balcony to view the ceremony better and had allowed a pail on which he was standing to slip out from under him.

After the service the casket was opened and immediately a line of people four abreast began to form. Starting at 12:30 P.M. more than 35,000 filed by before the doors closed at 4:30. Outside in two long lines another 20,000 waited in vain. At 5 P.M. President Coolidge, the honorary pallbearers, and the cabinet entered to pay their last respects. Daugherty was visibly moved, momentarily overcome with grief. The casket was then placed on the caisson and borne to Union Station where it again was transferred to the *Superb* for the final trek to Ohio.

The trip to Marion was a repetition of the cross-country journey—people lined the tracks at Baltimore, York, Harrisburg, everywhere. Because of the necessity of frequent stops, the train did not reach Marion until noon on August 9, hours behind schedule. From the train the president's body was taken to the home of his father, Dr. George Harding, on East Center Street. Even though it was insufferably hot, the great bronze casket was placed in a small sitting room where all the windows remained closed as hundreds of Marion friends, whispering and weeping, filed by. Taft, who was present, fully expected someone to faint—as it was, Daugherty collapsed into a chair.

On the next day, August 10, came the burial. A green carpet was laid from the street to the steps of Dr. Harding's porch and as a gun boomed, the flag-draped coffin appeared in the doorway. Ohio national guardsmen lined the curbs, and behind them on the lawns, sidewalks, and porches stood thousands of Marion's citizens. A group of bemedaled enlisted men stepped smartly forward and bore the coffin to a waiting gray hearse. Ahead of them marched Major Baldinger who not too many years before had carried papers down this same street as a *Marion Star* newsboy. Behind the casket came Coolidge, then Taft, six members of the cabinet including Daugherty, and assorted other officials. Last came Florence Harding, again accompanied by George Christian.

Before arriving at the cemetery, the hearse wound through Marion, past the *Star* building where the presses were silent, past the local Elks lodge whose purple and black crepe indicated its grief at the loss of a brother, and across Church Street down which delegations had trouped on their way to 380 Mount Vernon Avenue in the late summer of 1920. At the cemetery the hearse halted. Again the line of dignitaries formed; again Mrs. Harding relied on the support of George Christian. The iron gates of the arched Victorian stone vault were opened and in front of them the bearers placed the coffin on a velvet catafalque. As government officials lined up in two rows, the Trinity Baptist Girls' Choir, dressed in white robes, began "Lead, Kindly Light." The Reverend Dr. George Landis, pastor of Trinity, took his place between the coffin and the mausoleum. After a brief prayer service, the bearers lifted the casket up the single step into the tomb. Beside the empty catafalque a soldier with a shiny

454

silver cornet played "Taps." Mrs. Harding was then beckoned into the tomb by Major Baldinger. She stepped in alone, and for several minutes was lost from view. The president of the United States and others patiently waited. Then she reappeared, walking firmly, her chin lifted. For her, too, the voyage to understanding was at last over.[66]

XIV

The Final Disaster

[1

"IN THE inscrutable wisdom of Divine Providence, Warren Gamaliel Harding, twenty-ninth President of the United States, has been taken from us." So read the first proclamation issued by President Calvin Coolidge on August 4, 1923. Designating a period of national mourning to last until Harding's final interment at Marion on August 10, this proclamation heralded an outpouring of testimonials and eulogies to the dead leader.

Both the great and the small stopped to mourn Harding's passing. Special services were held in churches of all denominations; in some areas schools were dismissed; state legislatures held commemorative programs; and even foreign governments memorialized the fallen president. In South America, where Harding's new approach in foreign policy was widely acclaimed, there was a general wave of sympathy. The Congress of Peru declared August 10 a national day of mourning. President Alessandri of Chile ordered the country's flag to fly at half-mast for a period of eight days. In Panama, President Porras suspended all business and closed the schools for twenty-four hours. The government of Mexico lowered its flags for three days.[1]

The world's press everywhere deplored the loss of a "man of peace" and claimed, "Harding's death is a blow to us all." European newspapers, especially, remarked on Harding's contributions in allaying international tensions and his rising interest in international cooperation. The American press, which had always felt a kinship with the dead president, extended itself upon his death. Treating his administration sympathetically, the majority of newspapers emphasized the severe problems which he had faced on March 4, 1921, and the calm manner in which he had attempted to solve them. Even those critics who remained opposed to his specific policies attested to his sincerity and high-minded purpose. Many remarked on the increasing devotion he had given to his job and some spoke of him as a martyr to the presidency. All agreed on his gentleness, his patience, and his tolerance. He was, they said, "an ideal American," "the greatest commoner since Lincoln," and "a Man of the people." Concluded the *Atlanta Constitution*, "President Harding had endeared himself to the people of all classes as few executives have in the history of this government."[2]

For those who had worked closely with Harding and who knew him intimately, these various testimonials were not sufficient to convey their own feelings or their sense of personal loss. From the solitude of his cabin on Deer Creek, Daugherty wrote to E. Mont Reily, "I can hardly write about it or allow myself to think about it yet." To the McLeans he confided: ". . . at times for a second it seems like it must be a horrible dream."[3] Other administration officials experienced a similar, although less shattering, reaction. Strangely enough, Secretary Hughes appeared to be more deeply affected than any other cabinet member except Daugherty. To George Harvey he wrote: "I cannot bring myself to speak of the tragic experience through which we have just passed; I cannot realize that our beloved Chief is no longer with us."[4]

Naturally, mingled with these expressions of personal sorrow were observations designed to place Harding and his administration in a favorable light. Administration officials sought in this way to impart luster not only to Harding's image, but also to themselves. Secretary Wallace, for example, maintained that Harding had assumed power at an extremely critical period and had successfully led the country into an era of peace and prosperity. "Only those who have been privileged to see behind the scenes," said Wallace, "can fully value the great service President Harding gave to his country and, indeed, to the entire world."[5] Shortly after the president's death, Hoover told a group of engineers: "When he came into responsibility as President he faced unprecedented problems of domestic rehabilitation. It was a time when war-stirred emotions had created bitter prejudices and conflict in thought. Kindly and genial, but inflexible in his devotion to duty, he was strong in his determination to restore confi-

dence and secure progress. All this he accomplished through patient conciliation and friendly good will for he felt deeply that hard driving might
open unhealable breaches among our people. We have all benefited by
the success of his efforts."[6] Speaking somewhat more personally, Secretary Davis told one audience: "He labored without fuss or feathers. He
was a poor publicist for himself, but a powerful one for those who worked
with him. He gave the glory of achievement to others and took the criti-
cisms when they came, for himself."[7]

But the best and most complete contemporary official assessment of
Harding and his administration's contributions came more than six months
after his death in a formal eulogy by Secretary Hughes. In accordance with
an earlier agreement, both houses of Congress met on February 27, 1924,
in a joint memorial service for the dead president. The secretary of state
was assigned to deliver the main address. All important officials of government were present and Mrs. Harding, as well as such close friends as Dr.
Sawyer and George Christian, was seated in the galleries. In a moving
tribute Hughes traced Harding's ancestry, his boyhood, his work as an
editor, and his political career. He spoke fondly of Harding's sincere desire for peace, his calm courage, his compassion, and his friendliness. Then
Hughes enumerated the basic achievements of the Harding administration
and prophesied that they would stand the test of time. According to the
secretary of state, Harding had liquidated the leftover problems of war;
he had regularized relations with enemy governments; he had cemented
relations with America's neighbors to the south; he had established the
requirements for a lasting peace; he had placed the operation of the government on a business basis; and in the face of almost insurmountable
obstacles he had restored economic prosperity. In conclusion, Hughes
offered a warning to those who wished to denigrate Harding's value or
downgrade his efforts because of the corrupt actions of a few of his friends:

> We, who look on with critics' eyes,
>   Exempt from action's crucial test,
> Human ourselves, at least are wise
>   In honoring one who did his best.[8]

[2

BUT best is sometimes not good enough. Already, by the time of the
Hughes eulogy, the general outlines of the famous scandals were known

to the public and as a result the reputation of Harding was beginning to suffer. Shortly, it became all too obvious that such qualities as gentleness and friendliness when combined with the machinations of false friends were as much liabilities as assets.

On October 22, 1923, not quite three months after Harding's death, the Veterans' Bureau investigation began. Resulting from a resolution passed by the 67th Congress, this investigation was conducted by Major General John F. O'Ryan, the Senate committee's chief counsel. For over six months he had gathered facts and sifted information before opening formal hearings. Then, on October 23, he presented his key witness, Elias H. Mortimer, one of Charlie Forbes's chief partners in crime. For the next three weeks testimony disclosed a sordid tale of bribery and corruption. Forbes, who had returned from Europe to appear before the committee in his own behalf, vehemently denied all knowledge of these activities and denounced Mortimer as a liar, bootlegger, and wife beater. Nevertheless, by the close of the investigation in December it was clear that the Veterans' Bureau had been used by Forbes and his cronies for personal gain, a conclusion which Harding had reluctantly reached almost a year before but had failed to do anything about.[9]

From the testimony it did not appear that there was any master plan for this chicanery or that Forbes was controlled by anyone above him. It was simply an opportunistic patchwork of individual bribery and greed. The circumstances were favorable for it. The Veterans' Bureau was a hodgepodge of diverse functions relating to the welfare of the veteran, and all these, even control of hospitals and hospital construction, were concentrated in the hands of the bureau's director. This had not always been the case. Originally the Treasury Department had exercised jurisdiction over veterans' hospitals and medical facilities, even being responsible for selecting sites and letting contracts for hospital construction. But in August 1921, Forbes had begun a crusade for all such authority to be assigned to his bureau and skillfully enlisted the support of the American Legion which charged the Treasury Department with incompetency. Both Forbes and the Legion beseeched the White House to shift full responsibility to the Veterans' Bureau. Dr. Sawyer, suspicious of Forbes's motives, sided with the Treasury Department in this struggle and won the undying enmity of the Legion which thereafter howled for his scalp. Secretary Mellon also was a recipient of Legion scorn because he, too, strenuously opposed the change. Harding, extremely sensitive to the needs of wounded veterans, taken in by the blandishments of Forbes, and cowed by the vociferousness of the Legion, decided in the bureau's favor and by executive order in late April 1922 decreed that the control, management, and construction of all veterans' hospitals would thereafter rest with the Veterans' Bureau. Simultaneously, the president also gave jurisdiction over medical supplies, including the huge supply depot at Perryville, Maryland, to the same bureau.

Shortly before this presidential action, Forbes had met Mortimer who was an agent for Thompson-Black Construction Company of St. Louis. Mortimer was interested in landing hospital construction contracts for his firm. Throughout February and March 1922 Forbes often visited Mortimer and his wife, Kathryn, in their apartment in the Wardman Park Hotel and once went with them on a vacation to Atlantic City. Then in April, and again in June, the Mortimers accompanied Forbes on a hospital-site inspection tour of the West during which Mortimer paid all bills and arranged for several conferences between John W. Thompson and Forbes. At one of these meetings Forbes was given a "loan" of $5000 in exchange for preferential treatment for the Thompson-Black Company. Concurrently Forbes worked out an arrangement with the Hurley-Mason Company (which was owned by Charles F. Hurley, a close friend of Forbes in Tacoma, Washington) whereby it would enter a closed system of bidding and contract letting with the Thompson-Black firm so that all profits from the construction of veterans' hospitals could be split three ways: one-third to Thompson-Black, one-third to Hurley-Mason, and one-third to Forbes. Seeing further opportunity for graft, Forbes also became involved in speculation on land sites for the hospitals. In one case in San Francisco he authorized the government to pay $105,000 for land that was worth less than $20,000. At least $25,000 of the difference was split between Forbes and Cramer, the bureau's chief counsel who had arranged the deal.

Still not sated, in November 1922 Forbes began negotiations on another coup. Stored in some fifty buildings at the medical supply depot at Perryville, Maryland, were huge quantities of sheets, towels, gauze, drugs, liquor, pajamas, paper, moleskin, and even hardware and some trucks. No complete inventory had ever been made of all the items, some of which had been damaged by leaky roofs, but the value was estimated at between five and seven million dollars. Forbes now arranged for a Boston firm, Thompson and Kelley, to make a bid on these goods even though there was no public advertisement of sale. Needing clearance from the budget coordinator before any sale of government property could be made, Forbes submitted a three-page list of damaged supplies for that office's approval. It was given. Then Forbes appended to this list a second list of undamaged goods which was three times as long, never sought specific clearance for it, and on November 15 signed a contract with Thompson and Kelley, giving them $3 million worth of undamaged supplies for only $600,000. The following day pajamas, towels, sheets, gauze, etc., began to move out of Perryville.

It was this action which had caused Forbes's banishment by Harding. But it was Mortimer's testimony on the hospital construction deals which finally sealed his fate. Forbes's increasing attention to Kathryn Mortimer in the late spring of 1922 had aroused Mortimer's ire and had caused Mrs. Forbes, shortly before, to go to Europe with all of Forbes's available assets. She later divorced him. Mortimer and his wife, in turn, separated just after they accompanied Forbes on the western inspection trip in June 1922. Seeking revenge on Forbes, Mortimer was more than willing to talk to the Senate investigating committee.

As a result of the disclosures of October and November 1923, Charles Forbes and J. W. Thompson were tried in Chicago in 1924 for conspiracy to defraud the government. Again the star witness was Elias Mortimer. The trial lasted nine weeks and after five hours the jury found both defendants guilty. Neither Forbes nor Thompson took the stand in his own defense. Each received two years in jail and a $10,000 fine. Forbes began his term at Leavenworth on March 21, 1926. Thompson, at the time seriously ill with a bad heart, never served his sentence, dying in St. Louis on May 3, 1926.[10]

[3

THE Veterans' Bureau scandal was hardly news before a much more complicated and subtle plot to defraud the government seized the headlines. One of the unconfirmed rumors circulating in Washington before Harding's death related to alleged "oil deals" involving top administration officials. The basis for such rumors was certain actions taken by Albert

Fall while he was secretary of the interior. These rumors were further fed by a bitter struggle between Fall and ardent conservationists over a proper conservation policy.

In most respects Albert Fall was an able cabinet officer. While he operated his department largely on the spoils system, he recruited some very able men. With the aid of these men, Fall reorganized the loosely structured Interior Department, reduced the number of land offices, combined various bureaus, and introduced such efficiency, especially in the Pension Bureau, that Harding wrote him in the spring of 1922, "I am immensely pleased that you have been able to accomplish such gratifying results." H. Foster Bain, director of the Bureau of Mines and long-time department employee, later recalled that Secretary Fall had the respect of all those who worked under him and Bain, himself, considered him "the best secretary under whom I served."[11]

The early attacks on Fall centered on his conservation ideas and not his administrative ability. Gifford Pinchot, then commissioner of forestry in Pennsylvania, and other ardent conservationists, such as Henry A. Slattery, secretary of the National Conservation Association, were dismayed by Fall's appointment. They feared that Fall, who was not in sympathy with the existing policy of wholesale withdrawal of natural resources from immediate use, would undermine the conservation system, and their fears were heightened when it became known that under the Brown reorganization plan the Forestry Division was slated to be transferred from Agriculture to Interior.[12]

But it was not in timber that Fall first attempted to implement his ideas about greater utilization of resources. Shortly after assuming office, Fall and Secretary Denby discussed the possibility of a more effective use of naval oil reserve lands in view of nearby private exploitation and the emerging Japanese naval threat in the Pacific. Between them it was agreed that the Interior Department, because of its greater experience in such matters, could better develop a suitable long-range policy for the oil reserves than the Navy Department. Therefore, Fall wrote a letter to Harding on May 11, 1921, requesting him to concur in transferring the naval reserves to the Interior Department. Harding talked personally with both Fall and Denby about the matter. Viewing Fall's request merely as a question of proper departmental jurisdiction, Harding asked for Denby's agreement to the change in writing. On May 26, 1921, Denby wrote Harding his approval and Harding accepted it as an amicable settlement between two cabinet officers over claims to a specific function. On May 31 the president formally transferred the reserves by executive order No. 3474 which was carried to the White House for Harding's signature by Assistant Secretary of the Navy Theodore Roosevelt, Jr.[13]

This reserve-transfer story was hardly newsworthy; indeed, only the major papers reported it at all, the *Washington Evening Star* giving it only seven lines. But even this meager coverage was enough to catch the eye of militant conservationists who immediately shifted their concern from timber to oil. As soon as he saw the announcement, Henry Slattery sought an audience with Theodore Roosevelt, Jr., and disclosed his alarm at this action. Roosevelt assured Slattery that there was nothing to worry about, that Fall had fought with his father in the Rough Riders, and that Fall was "a great, good friend." Slattery next went to see Senator LaFollette, telling him that he believed Fall intended to give the oil reserves to private exploiters. Thus, even before any wrongdoing occurred, conservationists like Slattery, whom Harold Ickes later caustically dubbed "Sir Galahad of the Woodlands," were prepared to believe the worst.[14]

Private exploitation was indeed very much on Secretary Fall's mind. By the General Leasing Act of February 1920, Congress had authorized the secretary of the navy to make private leases on reserve land if he thought such action wise. The purpose was to prevent drainage from the reserves through private drilling, which continually occurred on the boundaries of the government's holdings. Throughout the remainder of the Wilson years, Navy Secretary Josephus Daniels authorized a few isolated private leases but never considered leasing all the reserves. On the other hand, Wilson's secretary of the interior, Franklin K. Lane, strongly advocated the private development of all government oil lands and deplored Daniels's niggardly use of the General Leasing Act.

Harding's secretary of the navy, Denby, was very much worried about the drainage problem and for this reason had first sought Fall's advice and afterwards had proved receptive to Fall's overtures about long-range development. To Denby it seemed logical that Fall's Interior Department handle any leasing details. Denby's sole concern was to prevent drainage and realize the full potential of the reserves for national defense purposes. As Denby pointed out at the time, in the event of war the oil was useless if it was still in the ground. It had to be refined and in accessible storage tanks ready for use. In the minds of both Fall and Denby, the May transfer of the oil reserves was specifically intended as a prelude to the further development of the reserves under the General Leasing Act of 1920.[15]

On July 12, 1921, the Interior Department granted a private lease to Edward Doheny in Naval Reserve No. 1 which was located in Elk Hills, California. This award occasioned little comment since it resulted from open competitive bidding and was duly recorded in the press. By the following April, however, rumors circulated that other leases, secret and unpublished, had been awarded both in Elk Hills and in Naval Reserve No. 3 near Salt Creek, Wyoming, commonly called Teapot Dome. Senator John Kendrick of Wyoming, after receiving telegrams from constituents claiming Teapot Dome had been privately leased, asked the Interior Department for confirmation. When he received no satisfaction, he rose in the Senate on April 15, 1922, and introduced a resolution demanding the information. The day before, the *Wall Street Journal* had carried a routine business announcement that a lease had been granted for all of Teapot Dome to the Harry F. Sinclair interests and that "the arrangement . . . marks one of the greatest petroleum undertakings of the age and signalizes a notable departure on the part of the government in seeking partnership with private capital for the working of government-owned natural resources." [16]

The Kendrick resolution was not part of the conservationists' war on Fall, but they quickly appropriated it. At the moment Fall was on an inspection tour in the West and Acting Secretary Edward C. Finney was left to explain the department's actions. On April 18 he admitted that a lease had been granted to Sinclair's Mammoth Oil Company to develop all of Teapot Dome and also indicated that an additional lease was about to be awarded to Doheny's Pan-American Petroleum and Transport Company in Elk Hills in exchange for storage tanks and pipelines to be built on the west coast and at Pearl Harbor. Three days later, in compliance with the Kendrick resolution, the department sent to the Senate a copy of the Sinclair lease along with a flat admission that there had been no competitive bidding in this case because naval preparedness and national security were involved.[17]

These events received relatively little press coverage and, after the Department's explanation, the matter seemed to be closed. However, Slattery, Pinchot, LaFollette, and others were not placated and immediately

464

questioned why so much secrecy had surrounded the Sinclair lease, why no public announcement of it had been made, and why a lease had been granted for the whole reserve. Hence, on April 21, LaFollette introduced a new resolution in the Senate calling for additional clarification from the Interior Department about Teapot Dome. Then on April 28, LaFollette abruptly modified his resolution to request an official inquiry by the Committee on Public Lands into *all* leases on the naval reserves and "to report its findings and recommendations to the Senate."[18] Secretary Fall was at his ranch in Three Rivers, New Mexico, when the Senate approved the LaFollette resolution and he immediately hurried back to Washington to gather materials to defend himself.

LaFollette badgered Senator Thomas Walsh of Montana into assuming responsibility for this investigation. Walsh was a member of the Public Lands Committee which included within its ranks not only Kendrick but such Republican insurgents as Ladd, Norbeck, and Norris. Motivated at first only by duty, Walsh found his task unenlightening and burdensome, especially when he was deluged in June 1922 by the truckload of materials which Fall dumped on the committee as justification for his actions. Accompanying this mass of data was a letter from Harding, dated June 7, 1922, which said that the Fall and Denby oil policy "was submitted to me prior to the adoption thereof, and the policy decided upon and the subsequent acts have at all times had my entire approval."[19]

Senator Walsh was an Irish-American Catholic, born in Two Rivers, Wisconsin, a year before the Civil War began. Raised as a small-town boy, he secured a law degree from the University of Wisconsin and "practiced" his way west through the Dakotas into Montana. He soon became recognized as the ablest lawyer in the Big Sky country and in 1913 left Helena for Washington and the United States Senate. Thereafter his fellow Montanans made his Senate seat a life tenure. In public Walsh appeared to be austere, his sharp eyes peering out from under heavy Celtic eyebrows, a smooth western accent flowing from beneath a stubby mustache. Observers considered him a relentless prosecutor and he did possess an uncanny ability to smell out the basest motivation in any act. At this time, however, Walsh had no reason to doubt Harding's affirmation of faith in Fall and plodded through the maze of technicalities relating to leasing, oil drainage, and private contracts without enthusiasm.[20]

But just enough suspicious events popped up to keep Walsh at his

465

task. Not long after the LaFollette resolution was passed, the Wisconsin senator's office was ransacked by someone who obviously was not keen about the impending investigation. Later, Walsh's own past in Montana was secretly checked and he suspected that his phones were tapped and his mail opened. At the same time, he began to receive all sorts of information about "oil deals." Of particular interest were rumors that after the granting of the oil leases Fall's Three Rivers ranch had experienced a sudden burst of affluence.[21]

Meanwhile Fall resigned from the cabinet. On January 2, 1923, the White House announced that after March 4 the secretary would devote full time to his private business affairs. His resignation was not a surprise. It was common knowledge that Fall had become increasingly unhappy in the cabinet. Moreover he had had severe financial and family worries in recent years. He had lost two of his four children, one a thirty-two-year-old son, in the 1918 influenza epidemic. Soon after he had been gored through the lung by a pet stag at his New Mexican ranch. When he entered the cabinet he was already eight years in arrears in his taxes and did not intend to remain in politics very much longer. Now he resigned to accept employment with the Sinclair oil interests and in the spring of 1923 accompanied Harry Sinclair to Russia to arrange for oil concessions on the island of Sakhalin. Harding replaced Fall with Dr. Hubert Work whom he transferred from the Postal Department to Interior. Work, incidentally, was the first cabinet officer ever to be selected from Montana, Senator Walsh's home state, and his appointment was enthusiastically hailed throughout the Northwest.

Fall's departure brought joy not only to conservationists but to many Republicans who had come to regard the interior secretary as a political liability. William Allen White claimed in the columns of the *Emporia Gazette* that his resignation was a good start and hoped that Daugherty would be next. But with many of his colleagues, and certainly with some of his fellow cabinet members, Fall's stock was still high. Senator Borah defended Fall as "open, candid, and courageous," while Herbert Hoover sent him a "farewell" note saying, "In my recollection, that department [Interior] has never had so constructive and legal a headship as you gave it."[22]

After his last cabinet meeting on March 2, Fall remarked to reporters, "I have tried to impress upon my friends and associates that my leaving Washington is not a case of saying good-bye, but until we meet again."[23] He had reason to remember these words when seven and one half months later, on October 24, just two days after the Veterans' Bureau investigation began, Fall appeared as a lead-off witness in the oil lease investigation.[24] Walsh opened the hearings even though he did not yet have anything specific against Fall. For two days these two products of the western frontier faced each other as Walsh grilled Fall about all aspects of the leases. Walsh got nowhere. Fall took full responsibility, claimed he had not published the leases because of the need to be discreet about naval policy, maintained that there was nothing sinister in his motives, asserted that before his resignation he had never been in either Sinclair's or Doheny's employ, and swore that he had never received any money from these interests while he had been in government service. Most observers came away convinced that Walsh was on the wrong track.

Denby was the next witness. He made a miserable showing—indecisive, unclear, confused, and scared. Denby betrayed ignorance of many details relating to the leases. It was obvious he had left most of these matters to Fall. Next came a flood of witnesses: naval officers, mining and geological experts, H. Foster Bain, Theodore Roosevelt, Jr., Edward Finney, Sinclair, and Doheny. It appeared that there was considerable disagreement among the experts whether oil drainage was actually occurring at the reserves and there was certainly no unanimity among naval officers that the development of the reserves was in the navy's best interests. Doheny indicated that his company expected to get as many as 250 million barrels from its various government leases and make perhaps $100 million in profits. But it was Harry Sinclair who answered the key question. In querying the oilman about his exact relationship with Fall, Senator Lenroot asked whether the secretary had received "any benefits or profits, directly or indirectly, in any manner whatsoever" through the awarding of the leases. Sinclair replied flatly, "No, sir, none." With this, the investigation seemed to have reached a dead end.

Now came the first break. Through information supplied by Carl C. Magee, editor of the New Mexico *State Tribune* and an old enemy of Fall, it was learned that in November 1921 Fall had purchased a neighboring ranch for $91,500 and other land costing $33,000. A little later Fall had built an irrigation reservoir and a hydroelectric plant at a cost of $40,000. It was also discovered that Sinclair had visited Fall's ranch

467

during this period and had sent him a few head of blooded Holstein cattle and two prize hogs.

The press, which up to this point had been reporting the investigation without much interest, now began to follow the committee's actions more closely. The smell of oil money was in the air. Fall, who was again at his New Mexico ranch, was ordered to reappear and answer questions about this sudden prosperity. Slowly he made his way back to Washington via Chicago, New York, and Atlantic City. Upon reaching the capital he entrenched himself in the Wardman Park Hotel where he pleaded poor health, and on December 26 sent the committee a long letter protesting his innocence by claiming that he had been loaned $100,000 by Edward McLean. Walsh immediately summoned McLean who was vacationing in Palm Beach. He corroborated Fall's statement on the loan through his attorney but avoided appearing before the committee under oath. McLean wrote letters, sent telegrams, and finally dispatched two lawyers (Wilton J. Lambert of his own staff and Wilson's attorney general, A. Mitchell Palmer) to seek immunity for him because of his "poor health" and "bad sinuses."

A sinus sufferer himself, Walsh could see no legitimate physical reason for McLean's nonappearance and as a subcommittee of one traveled to Palm Beach in mid-January to see the millionaire. Under oath, McLean now denied loaning Fall the money and claimed that he had said he had in order to "go down the line for a friend." At that moment Fall was also in Palm Beach "for his health," and Walsh quickly got in touch with him. But Fall refused to see him, sending Walsh a letter instead in which he admitted he received no money from McLean, but from "other sources." Fall refused to divulge these sources but vehemently denied the money came from either Sinclair or Doheny.

Walsh hurried back to Washington where disclosures now came thick and fast. Archibald B. Roosevelt, younger brother of the assistant secretary of the navy, volunteered testimony to the committee on January 21 that while he was in the employ of Sinclair as a vice-president of a subsidiary oil company, he had overheard Sinclair's private secretary, Gustav D. Wahlberg, say that Sinclair had "advanced" $68,000 to the foreman of Fall's ranch. Walsh immediately placed Wahlberg on the stand who denied ever mentioning $68,000—insisted that young Roosevelt had misunderstood. What he had said, claimed Wahlberg, was "six to eight cows" not "sixty-eight thous'."

Next appeared an even more sensational volunteer witness—Edward Doheny. A millionaire many times over, this little sixty-seven-year-old man with mild blue eyes and a white mustache could easily have been mistaken for a "professor of philosophy at some small backwater college." Much of his early life he had spent as a prospector wandering about the limitless expanse of the West looking for gold and silver. There he had become fast friends with another young prospector, Albert Fall, but while Fall had become a politician and senator, Doheny had shifted from ore to oil and struck it rich. Both the Southwest and Mexico had yielded up its black treasure to him and he had organized companies to produce and market it. Even though very wealthy, he was not ostentatious like the forty-seven-year-old Harry Sinclair and was living out his final years in California quietly and simply.

When Doheny heard of the McLean testimony he went to see his lawyer, a husky Scotchman named Gavin McNab, who advised him to return to Washington at once. Doheny agreed but first attempted to get in touch with Fall who was finally located wandering aimlessly about in New Orleans. En route to the capital Doheny stopped there and urged Fall to return to Washington also. Two days later, on January 24, 1924, Doheny stepped before the committee. He said that he was the one who had "loaned" Fall $100,000 on November 21, 1921, not because of any interest he had in oil leases but because of their old friendship. This sum, Doheny insisted, "was a bagatelle to me . . . no more than $25 or $50 perhaps to the ordinary individual." The money, he said, had been delivered to Fall by his son, Edward, Jr., in a little black satchel. "It was my own money," claimed the oilman, "and did not belong in whole or in part to any oil company with which I am connected." For that reason, he added, what he had told the committee earlier—that Fall had not in any way profited from the oil leases—was still true.

Fall arrived in Washington from New Orleans a few hours after the Doheny testimony. To newspapermen he announced merely, "I am a sick man," and went immediately to the home of Colonel J. W. Zevely, law partner of A. Mitchell Palmer. For the next several days, while Fall remained incommunicado, the committee heard additional testimony indicating that Sinclair also had provided Fall with a considerable sum of

469

money in Liberty Bonds. At this point Doheny was recalled to testify and, nettled by the committee's questioning, dropped a few bombshells. Apparently seeking revenge against Walsh for his pestering, Doheny indicated that Fall was not the only politician with whom he had had monetary dealings. Doheny indicated that over the years he had contributed as heavily to the Democratic party as to the Republican party and mentioned that several former members of Wilson's cabinet, such as William G. McAdoo, Franklin K. Lane, and Thomas W. Gregory, had been on his payroll at one time or another. "I paid them for their influence," snapped Doheny. In McAdoo's case, Doheny said that he had retained him as a counsel at $25,000 per year. At the moment McAdoo was one of the top contenders for the 1924 Democratic nomination and was strongly supported by Walsh.

Barely had the reverberations from these disclosures died when it was again Fall's turn to testify. The committee had earlier requested him to appear on January 29, but Fall's lawyer presented instead a statement from four doctors who claimed that he could not leave his bed. The committee then sent its own physicians to examine Fall and they reported back that he was able to testify. As a result a subpoena was issued and on February 2 Fall, who had taken to drinking heavily and was a trembling wreck, finally appeared in a jam-packed Senate caucus room, leaning on a cane, his blue suit wrinkled and baggy, his shoulders bent, face sagging, mouth dropping, and his gold-framed glasses hanging limply from his ears.[25] To many observers he looked more worried than ill. Taking the stand, eyes downward, he read: "I decline . . . to answer any questions on the ground that it may tend to incriminate me." Without looking at his former Senate colleagues, he took the arm of his lawyer with one hand, gripped his cane with the other, and made his way to the door. According to Mark Sullivan the room was so silent that all one could hear was the tapping of his cane.[26]

The rest was hectic but anticlimactic. While the press engaged in a Roman holiday of sensationalism and reveled in the tarnished reputations besmirched by oil, Senator Walsh, stung by the Doheny revelations about top Democrats, turned childishly partisan and momentarily overplayed his hand by attempting to link Republican cabinet members and Coolidge with Fall's crimes. Walsh even tried to connect Harding's nomination in 1920 with Teapot Dome. All such attempts misfired and it soon became

470

clear that only Secretary Fall was the culprit—but not before considerable damage had been done to Republicans and Democrats alike. McAdoo, for example, who cleared himself by showing that his services had been purchased by Doheny only after he was out of public office, found his road to the Democratic nomination just that much rougher, while the taciturn Vermonter in the White House had to exert himself even harder to demonstrate that he would not countenance further corruption in Republican ranks.

Indeed, when Coolidge became convinced that only Fall was guilty and that the Walsh investigation would provide no further embarrassing revelations concerning Republicans, he moved aggressively. On January 27 he announced that as soon as the facts warranted, and because members of both parties had been splattered by the oil investigation, he would appoint a special commission of two men, one from each party, to handle any prosecutions which were necessary. Shortly thereafter he designated former Ohio Senator Atlee Pomerene (Democrat) and Philadelphia lawyer Owen J. Roberts (Republican) as the two men.

Meanwhile a great clamor arose from Republican and Democratic congressmen alike for Secretary Denby's resignation. Coolidge remained silent for the moment, thereby indicating his refusal to bow to such pressure. However, on February 18, protesting his innocence but claiming he could stand no more personal abuse, Denby volunteered his resignation. Coolidge replied, "It is with regret that I am to part with you." Herbert Hoover wrote in retrospect that Denby "was a good and able man; and he was driven from the Cabinet by political persecution and public hysteria." The majority of the press agreed that although his resignation did remove an embarrassment for the administration, Denby's only crime was a misplaced trust in a fellow cabinet officer.[27]

As the Walsh investigation came to an acrimonious close in the spring of 1924 the two-man team of Pomerene and Roberts took over. They unearthed new evidence that Doheny's "loan" of $100,000 was made concurrently with Fall's decision to lease Elk Hills to Doheny and that a number of other secret leases through December 1922 were granted to Doheny by Fall. They also uncovered deposits of some $200,000 in Liberty Bonds made by Sinclair either to Fall's or to Fall's son-in-law's account in several western and southwestern banks. It appeared that Fall had received a total of about $400,000 in one way or another from both Sinclair and

471

Doheny. Armed with these facts as well as those of the Walsh investigation, the two-man counsel initiated prosecutions in early June 1924. Fall and Doheny were charged with conspiracy to defraud; Fall and Sinclair with conspiracy to defraud; and Fall and both Dohenys (father and son) with bribery.

The resultant trials and legal maneuvering went on for almost six years. At one time or other Sinclair was represented by no fewer than nine lawyers. Doheny also armed himself with an array of legal talent. The outcome was ludicrous. Doheny and Fall were acquitted on December 16, 1926, of the charge of conspiracy. During the Sinclair trial in November 1927 prosecutor Roberts proved that the jury was being shadowed by agents hired by Sinclair and a retrial was ordered. On April 21, 1928, a new jury inexplicably acquitted Sinclair and Fall of conspiracy. On October 25, 1929, after deliberating a day and a half, a jury declared Fall guilty of accepting a bribe from Doheny, but recommended mercy. Fall was sentenced to a year in jail and a $100,000 fine, and began serving his sentence in July 1931. Sinclair meanwhile was charged with contempt of court in connection with his jury tampering and was sentenced to six months in jail. Then in March 1930 Doheny was acquitted of the charge of bribing Fall, a ridiculous verdict in view of Fall's earlier conviction of bribe taking. This verdict caused Senator Norris to remark that it is "very difficult, if not impossible, to convict one hundred million dollars."[28]

The Teapot Dome scandal was certainly the most famous of the Harding era and thereafter commanded the major attention of commentators, popular writers, journalists, and historians. Yet the scandal's historical significance was really very limited. Even the contemporary public quickly tired of it, and, despite numerous attempts on the part of investigators to broaden its scope, the scandal remained essentially the evil doings of one unscrupulous cabinet officer and two opportunistic oilmen. In the end, as quixotic juries permitted one acquittal after another, the only scapegoat for all the furor was Albert Fall. He, of course, persisted in proclaiming his innocence, maintaining that he had done nothing wrong except deny to the committee that he had received any money from Sinclair or Doheny. This, he said, was his only crime. He admitted that such a lie deserved condemnation and that his "borrowing" the money "may have been unethical [but] I certainly did not realize it at the time." Even so, concluded

Fall, none of this justified the charge "that I was disloyal or dishonest as Secretary of the Interior and as a member of Harding's Cabinet."[29]

Whatever the precise degree of Fall's guilt, certainly Teapot Dome was not the broadly conceived, underhanded, sinister plot to bargain away the nation's resources that some writers later liked to contend. The leasing action was in keeping with Fall's own ideas concerning the private development of conservation areas. On the basis of his philosophy, Fall might have turned over the reserves to some private company for development willingly; bribery would not have been necessary. His crime was his own greed and the secretive manner in which he selected the particular companies for the job. Fall made the mistake of attempting to do business for the government as he might for a private corporation—negotiating directly with a company or companies believed best qualified to handle the task and arranging a suitable bargain with them. At a time when oil companies were expanding into worldwide complex operations and the quest for oil was corrupting international conferences and shaping foreign policies, it was not surprising that one American official succumbed to the temptation to take personal advantage of the situation. As for Fall's skill as a bargainer and the profitability of the oil leases to the government, these questions were left unanswered. Senator Walsh later admitted that such matters had not concerned him and were never a subject of discussion. Quite properly Walsh claimed that it would have been shocking "to condone the fraudulent transfer of the Nation's resources upon the ground that the government had in fact profited, or would profit."[30] Yet there is reason to believe that in the long run the leases may have been in the national interest. On December 7, 1941, those pipelines, storage facilities, and refined oil then available to the navy on the west coast and at Pearl Harbor were partially, at least, a direct outgrowth of the Fall leases of 1921–22.[31]

[4

IN LATE January 1924 Rollin Kirby, cartoonist for the *New York World*, depicted for his readers a fat and sweaty GOP, sitting in a chair, one hand gripping an armrest and the other clutching his chest, being forced to take a large dose of "Oil" from a huge spoon. Captioned "Ugh!" it was an accurate representation of the Republican party in the late winter and spring of 1924.[32]

Specifically, the oil scandal provided a springboard for launching attacks on the Harding administration's record in general and reopening the case of Harry Daugherty in particular. Convinced that the Veterans' Bureau and Teapot Dome affairs were only the beginning of other more sensational revelations, old Daugherty enemies quivered at the possibility of connecting the attorney general with all such wrongdoing. In the eyes of these people, Fall and Daugherty represented an evil team and Fall's name was rarely mentioned without Daugherty's being coupled with it.

Whatever Daugherty's faults and whatever he may have had to hide, they did not relate to Albert Fall. The two men were not friends and went their separate ways, rarely conferring with one another. Daugherty always considered Fall disloyal because of his pro-Roosevelt leanings and Fall was basically jealous of Daugherty's close personal relationship with Harding. Fall did not consult Daugherty on the legality of the oil leases or ask his opinion on any leasing matter. But because both were old friends of Harding, they were linked together in the public mind and what affected one was assumed to affect the other.[33]

As head of the Justice Department, Daugherty was naturally in the line of fire for any administration scandal. Moreover, his unsavory past and his already tarnished public image made an adverse public reaction almost inevitable. After Denby's resignation, voices were immediately raised demanding Daugherty's removal. While President Coolidge held off taking such action, one of the primary reasons for his appointment of Pomerene and Roberts to investigate the Teapot Dome scandal was his doubt about permitting the Justice Department under Daugherty to do so. Daugherty meanwhile became increasingly defiant, claiming that he was still being hounded by the "labor lobby."

Daugherty was wrong. By 1924 his opposition was much more broadly based than labor. One of Senator Borah's earliest admonitions to Coolidge in the fall of 1923 was "remove Daugherty from your cabinet." Numerous other Republican senators had expressed similar feelings. Both Hughes and Hoover indicated to Coolidge that Daugherty should be dropped in due time. Even Chief Justice Taft, who regarded Daugherty as "one of the finest fellows I know," sadly admitted in early 1924 that perhaps the time had arrived for Daugherty to go. Democrats, of course, capitalized on this anti-Daugherty feeling to drive wedges into Republican ranks wherever possible.[34]

The movement for Daugherty's removal began seriously on February 19 when Senator Wheeler delivered a blast in the Senate against the attorney general and introduced a resolution calling for a thorough investigation of the Justice Department. In his resolution Wheeler followed the unusual procedure of naming the senators who should serve on the committee because he wanted "a real investigation." Those named were Brookhart, Jones, McLean, Ashurst, and, of course, Wheeler. The next day a frightened group of Republican senators, among them Lodge, called at the White House and begged Coolidge to ask Daugherty to resign. But Coolidge took no action, and Daugherty hotly denied Wheeler's accusations.

For the next ten days, innuendo, false statements, rumors, and personal insults were common as the clamor for Daugherty's head reached a crescendo. The Democrats busily blew their horns while most Republicans scrambled on the "dump Daugherty" bandwagon in fear. Finally, on March 1, 1924, by a vote of 66–1, the Senate adopted a revised investigating resolution which was like the original except it did not name the committee members. Instead, the Senate elected the membership from the floor. LaFollette immediately nominated the inexperienced and radical Brookhart (Iowa-R.) as chairman. Other members nominated and elected were Wheeler (Montana-D.), Ashurst (Arizona-D.), Jones (Washington-R.), and Moses (New Hampshire-R.). During this process the Senate erupted into bitter debate with charge and countercharge being fired off indiscriminately as Democratic Senators Heflin, Caraway, and McKellar unloosed a barrage of denunciation against Republicans in general and Daugherty in particular. For such men, the investigation was already over.[35]

Wheeler at once assumed the role of prosecutor and dominated the proceedings. A freshman senator from Montana and only forty-two years old, he possessed a driving political ambition which caused him to see this investigation as his springboard to fame. Having served earlier as a federal district attorney, Wheeler fancied himself a great lawyer and relished the thought of bringing Daugherty to his knees. Of liberal persuasion in the manner peculiar to the Northwest, Wheeler possessed an ill-disguised contempt for the Harding administration and considered "normalcy" merely a sellout to eastern capitalists. Encouraged by the success

475

of his fellow Montanan in the oil investigation, Wheeler hoped to duplicate Walsh's effort in the case of the Justice Department.

But Wheeler was no Walsh. He had neither Walsh's patience for detail nor his normal sense of balance and propriety. From the beginning Wheeler acted as Walsh came to act only at the very end of the Teapot Dome affair. Sensationalism was Wheeler's watchword. When the public hearings began on March 12, 1924, Wheeler called as the first witness Roxy Stinson, divorced wife of Jess Smith. Roxy was only nineteen and Jess thirty when they had first started going together. Roxy's mother, a widow who shortly before had moved from Marion to Washington Court House, had just set up a music studio over the Smith department store. According to local gossip, the stylish Roxy was interested in a good time, and Jess provided it. They were married in 1908. Their marriage had lasted only a little more than a year when Roxy applied for a divorce, charging Jess with extreme cruelty. There were those, however, who claimed that Jess had not been able to fulfill his husbandly duties well enough to suit the high-stepping, red-haired Roxy. In any event, even after the divorce Jess remained strangely attached to her and upon becoming a "big shot" in Washington sent her money and intermittently returned to Washington Court House to see her. Harry Daugherty thought Roxy was not a good influence on Jess and was interested only in his money. Roxy, in turn, detested Harry Daugherty.

Wearing rimless glasses and looking somewhat like a schoolmarm—a contrived image which enhanced the credibility of her testimony—Roxy now appeared before the committee and, amid frequent outbursts of tears and with the press hanging on every word, told an amazing story.[36] For two days she recounted her relationship with Jess, chronicled his fears and his last movements in Washington Court House just before his death, and alluded darkly to "big deals" involving stock, oil, and liquor engineered at the "little green house on K Street." She claimed that Harry Daugherty knew of these activities and was in on the final division of the spoils. She testified that Smith possessed as many as seventy-five $1000 bills at one time which he and Daugherty allegedly shared as their "take." Roxy claimed that at least some of this money went into stock accounts at the brokerage house of Ungerleider and Company. Roxy said that even she had an account there under the name of "William R. A. Hays No. 3."

Roxy Stinson's testimony placed Daugherty, already under intense

476

pressure to resign, in an even more precarious position. He immediately issued a categorical denial, claiming her stories were those of a "disappointed and malicious woman." She blamed him, Daugherty said, "because her divorced husband did not make her sole legatee under his will." [37] Indeed, Roxy had been miffed at the terms of the Smith will and had sued for a larger share, specifically for $11,000 in the "William R. A. Hays No. 3" account which she claimed was hers alone and not a part of the estate. Both Harry and Mal Daugherty had contested this action and had antagonized her further by having her shadowed, perhaps, as she claimed, in order to "frame" her.

A parade of witnesses now followed, each telling of scandals and corruption, always linking Jess Smith with the action and through him, Harry Daugherty. Wheeler made the most of these disclosures and whenever the connection between Smith and Daugherty was merely implicit, he attempted to make it explicit. Howard Mannington, who had skipped to Europe sometime before, reluctantly returned to testify, but Wheeler got little out of him. Remus, the bootlegger, represented better game and told the committee of huge sums in protection money paid directly to Smith and, he supposed, indirectly to Daugherty. Besides Roxy, however, the star witness was Gaston B. Means. Means had an interesting record. Born in North Carolina in 1879 of an aristocratic southern family, Means left the University of North Carolina before completing a degree and thereafter became a self-styled detective skilled in bribery, swindling, cheating, and peddling influence. His various exploits had a Munchausen quality as this rogue experienced everything from being a secret agent in World War I to being indicted for murdering a wealthy widow who died of a gunshot wound while alone with him in a North Carolina woods in 1917. Because of lack of evidence he was never convicted. In 1921 he was appointed as an FBI agent upon the recommendation of William Burns. [38]

Gaston Means was not known personally to Daugherty and the attorney general approved his appointment routinely, just as he did hundreds of others. Indeed, Daugherty had no contact with Means until March 1922 when rumors came to him that Means was involved in bribe taking and liquor violations. Somehow Means managed on his $7.00 a day Justice Department pay to employ a house staff of three servants and travel about in his own chauffeur-driven Cadillac. Daugherty immediately suspended him from his FBI job, finally discharged him, and in 1923 secured indictments against him for conspiracy and bootlegging. In July 1924 Means was convicted and sentenced to two years in jail and a $10,000 fine. Six months later, in another trial, he was also convicted of obstructing justice and received another two-year sentence and $10,000 fine. Under such circumstances Means's testimony against Daugherty before the Wheeler committee was hardly unbiased.

In his testimony Means connected Daugherty directly with the K Street activities and portrayed Smith as Daugherty's henchman. Means also stated that he had often spied on top government officials for Jess Smith who, he assumed, got his orders from Daugherty. For example, Means admitted that he was the one who had broken into LaFollette's office shortly after the oil investigation began. Means also detailed the Ohio Gang's procedures, the manner in which it secured clients, and his own role in arranging for payoffs. All in all, his testimony revealed a Justice Department which was engaged in wholesale intrigue and corruption and an administration burdened with the guilt of this knowledge. No one in the administration was exempt from Means's charges. In one burst of vitriol he named Secretary Mellon as "the arch enemy of the Government, the arch traitor," and, if it was any consolation to Daugherty, once remarked that the attorney general was "a much higher class and finer man than Mr. Mellon."

From such testimony Wheeler extracted much sensationalism, but it is questionable how much truth he gleaned. Obviously the fatal flaw in Wheeler's investigation was the nature of his important witnesses—Remus, a bootlegger; Roxy Stinson, a divorcee of questionable motives; Gaston Means, a swindler and a known liar. Possibly Wheeler was sincerely deluded by the testimony of these witnesses; there was just enough truth hidden among all the lies to cause legitimate suspicion.

In the end it was the attorney general's and the Justice Department's reactions to the Wheeler investigation, rather than the specific disclosures themselves, which proved really damaging. From the beginning Wheeler was personally subjected to harassment, threats, espionage, and vilification. During the investigation, witnesses had their rooms rifled, papers stolen, and a concerted effort was made to keep some witnesses from testifying. Finally, a trumped-up charge of bribery was brought against Wheeler in Montana in early April 1924 which was so patently fraudulent that it was later laughed out of court. All of this was the work of William

Burns and his FBI agents who, with Daugherty's blessing, hoped to counteract Wheeler's efforts.

Throughout this shabby affair the voices demanding Daugherty's resignation naturally became more strident while Coolidge found fewer and fewer reasons to continue to protect him. Finally, on March 27, when Daugherty indicated that he would refuse the Wheeler Committee access to Justice Department files, C. Bascom Slemp, Coolidge's private secretary, told Daugherty that the president "expects your resignation." The attorney general supplied it the next day "solely out of deference to your [Coolidge's] request and in compliance therewith," but protested: "I can not escape the conviction, Mr. President, that your request for my resignation is also most untimely. It comes at a time when . . . I have not as yet had an opportunity to place upon the witness stand before the Senate Committee a single witness in my defense or in explanation or rebuttal of the whispered and gossipy charges against me." In contrast to the friendly note he had sent Denby, Coolidge wrote: "I hereby accept your resignation effective at once."[39] Not long after, William Burns also resigned under presidential pressure and his assistant, J. Edgar Hoover, took his place.

Surprisingly, once the Daugherty resignation was consummated, considerable dissension arose over its wisdom. Many journals, even liberal ones, charged Coolidge with cowardice and claimed Daugherty was made a scapegoat. Although virtually all these journals agreed that Daugherty was "a misfit every day of the three years" he was in office, they pointed out that he had not been tried or convicted in a court of law and had not been given the opportunity to defend himself. A few journals, mainly Republican, predicted that by asking for Daugherty's resignation Coolidge had opened the door to further resignation demands and "would soon have no Cabinet at all." Daugherty's dismissal did spark a new series of wild charges. Senator McKellar called for a Senate investigation of Andrew Mellon and made veiled threats that after Mellon, Wallace and Hoover would be next. Senators Caraway (Arkansas) and Couzens (Michigan) were especially eager for Wallace's scalp, while Senator Reed (Missouri) was anxious to bring Hoover down. Investigation hysteria was rampant.[40]

The legal aftermath of the Justice Department investigation, as with the Teapot Dome affair, was confused and inconclusive. Partly because of the slipshod methods used by Wheeler, and partly because relatively little was uncovered which was provable, only one successful prosecution resulted. During the investigation it was discovered that the biggest payoff to Jess Smith involved a deal concocted with the aid of the alien property custodian. Colonel Thomas W. Miller, a war hero and former congressman from Delaware, had been appointed to this post by Harding and, like Charlie Forbes, succumbed to using his position for personal gain. One of the original incorporators of the American Legion, with memberships in the Union League Club, the Yale Club, the National Press Club, and the Wilmington Country Club, Miller appeared to be incorruptible. But, under pressure from Smith and John T. King (Wood's first campaign manager in 1920), Colonel Miller agreed in September 1921 to arrange for the illegal transfer of a German-owned American subsidiary company, the American Metal Company, to a syndicate headed by a Richard Merton. To bind this transfer Merton gave King $441,300 of which $391,300 were in Liberty Bonds. Of these, $50,000 ultimately found their way into the hands of Miller and $224,000 into the hands of Jess Smith who deposited $50,000 of them in Mal Daugherty's Washington Court House Midland National Bank in an account called "Jess Smith Extra No. 3." This account supposedly was a "political account" and was used jointly by both Smith and Harry Daugherty. The Senate Committee tried to gain access to the bank records but both Harry Daugherty and his brother Mal blocked all attempts.

It was assumed that Harry Daugherty was at least indirectly involved in this payoff through "Jess Smith Extra No. 3," and therefore he was indicted along with King and Miller on charges of defrauding the government. Since King died before the case came to court in September 1926, only Daugherty and Miller stood trial. Daugherty remained defiant throughout and reiterated what he had claimed ever since the Wheeler investigation had begun: the "labor lobby" and the "Reds" were after him; Means and the other witnesses had lied; he had never been in the "little green house on K Street"; he knew nothing about Howard Mannington or the so-called Ohio Gang; he had never promised anybody anything in order to place Harding in the White House; and Jess Smith's corrupt activities had not been known to him until just before Smith's death.

The whole case against Daugherty, of course, revolved around "Jess Smith Extra No. 3," and he was finally called to the witness stand to testify under oath about it. Instead of appearing he wrote out the following statement:

Having been personal attorney for [Warren Harding, Mrs. Harding, the Midland National Bank of Washington Court House, and Mal S. Daugherty],

And having been Attorney General of the United States during the time that President Harding served as President,

And also for a time after President Harding's death under President Coolidge,

And with all of those named as attorney, personal friend and Attorney General, my relations were of the most confidential character as well as professional,

I refuse to testify and answer questions put to me . . .[41]

No action Daugherty might have taken could have been more damaging to his already battered reputation. Shortly thereafter it was learned that he and his brother Mal had destroyed the ledger sheets of the Midland National Bank relating to the "Jess Smith Extra No. 3" account and no trace of it remained. The bribery question therefore had to be surrendered into the hands of the jury with the critical issue still unresolved. After arguing for almost sixty-six hours, it remained hopelessly deadlocked and a retrial was ordered. At that trial, in February 1927, Miller was convicted and sentenced to eighteen months in jail and fined $5000. But the jury was still in sufficient doubt about Daugherty's guilt that it failed to convict him. The indictment was thereafter dropped. Miller ultimately served thirteen months in jail, joining Fall and Forbes as the three officials of the Harding administration to stand trial for their crimes and be convicted.

Ever after, controversy raged over the motivation behind Daugherty's refusal to testify and his destruction of the Midland Bank records. Some persons, such as Senator Heflin, darkly suggested that Daugherty's action masked unspeakable crimes and that Jess Smith had probably been murdered to hide what he knew. Even those who supported Daugherty had to admit that his unwillingness to take the stand was unfortunate and placed him in a very bad light. Mark Sullivan, who basically liked Daugherty, thought the real reason for his refusal could not be money since money had never meant that much to Daugherty. Some other factor, perhaps the protection of Harding's personal reputation, seemed more plausible. This latter theory gained credence when, shortly after the first trial, Daugherty's lawyer, Max D. Steuer, told the press: "It was not anything connected with this case that impelled him to refrain from [testifying].

. . . If the jury knew the real reason for destroying the ledger sheets they would commend rather than condemn Mr. Daugherty."[42] As for Daugherty, he maintained both his silence and his truculence. Continuing to claim that the whole business was a Red-labor-inspired plot against him personally, Daugherty insisted that he had "done nothing that prevents my looking the whole world in the face." "If anybody does not like my position," he once wrote a friend, "you can tell them to go to hell."[43]

[5

ALL the investigations—Veterans' Bureau, Teapot Dome, and the Daugherty affair—automatically raised speculation about the culpability of the entire Harding cabinet, and even the president and the vice-president, in the various scandals. At the height of the investigation fever in the late winter and spring of 1924 no one seemed immune from suspicion. Coolidge and cabinet officers scurried to assure the public and Congress that they neither knew about nor were involved in the chicanery, especially the activities of Albert Fall. On January 26, 1924, Coolidge announced that while he was vice-president he had never heard the oil leases discussed at any cabinet meeting. Five days later, Secretary Hughes also issued a press release that the oil leases were never brought before the cabinet and that he, personally, had never been asked about them either in or out of cabinet meetings. On that same day, Hoover was quoted as supporting Hughes's recollection of the matter. On February 1, Secretary Weeks issued a statement that he had missed very few cabinet meetings and if there had been a discussion of the leases he did not remember it. "My recollection," he said, "is exactly the same as expressed by Secretary Hughes." Their memories were undoubtedly accurate. As already noted, each member in the Harding cabinet kept relatively aloof from the internal departmental activities of his fellows and, except for Hoover, generally minded his own business. It was quite possible for a Wallace or a Hughes to sit next to a Daugherty or a Fall and not know of any corruption until it was exposed. Besides, as Doheny testified in the Teapot Dome investigation, the actual negotiation on the oil leases, for example, was done by lesser officials—technicians—and not by the secretary of the navy, the secretary of the interior, and himself. The cabinet men, he said, "had little to do with the details."[44]

In the case of the Justice Department there was no real reason for any of the cabinet officers to suspect Daugherty of any wrongdoing. Indeed, when the Justice Department investigation broke with its attendant sensationalism, most cabinet officers were confused and did not know whom to denounce. Generally it fell to Secretary Hughes to uphold the integrity of the cabinet by acting as its spokesman whenever he could. In one address in April 1924, shortly after the Stinson and Means disclosures, Hughes agreed that all those involved in corruption should be summarily punished, but he pointedly warned: "Neither political party has a monopoly of virtue or of rascality. There are crooks in every community and in every party. Now and then, one gets into office. Let wrongs be exposed and punished, but let not partisan Pecksniffs affect 'a holier than thou' attitude. . . . Guilt is personal and corruption knows no party."[45]

Harding's possible role caused even greater, but less open, speculation. Many persons were loath to link the dead president's name publicly with the corruption even though they discussed it privately. At first even the newspapers were careful not to report rumors of Harding's involvement. Likewise, partisan Democrats steered clear of making assaults on Harding personally, although they raked his administration and his appointees. But rumors of presidential involvement circulated anyway and were fed by the testimony of such persons as Mortimer, Stinson, Remus, and Means.

At no time was there any evidence that Harding was connected with the corruption in any direct way. In the case of Forbes it was obvious that Harding had made an error in judgment in appointing him, and then a far more grievous error in permitting him to run for his life rather than exposing him and bringing him to trial for his misdeeds. Again, in Fall's case, Harding's crime was not collusion, but placing his trust in a faithless friend. In this instance, however, the president probably went to his death unaware of having been betrayed. His letter to the Walsh Committee in June 1923, in which he claimed all oil actions had been taken with his complete knowledge, was the natural reaction of a president who wished to support a presumably faithful but beleaguered subordinate. Harding regarded the congressional attacks on Fall, especially by LaFollette, as being politically inspired and to the end displayed confidence in his former secretary of the interior.[46]

Harding definitely knew about some of Jess Smith's actions and had attempted to scare him away from Washington in order to forestall his arrest and imprisonment. No one will ever know how many specific details Harding had uncovered about the house on K Street, but it was enough to make him realize Smith's culpability. Again, Harding did not take the necessary punitive action and his own reputation had to suffer as a result. Whether Harding secretly suspected that Daugherty might also be involved and whether this caused him to move more cautiously, we will likewise never know. It is almost inconceivable, however, that the many activities of Smith, especially his involvement with the alien property custodian, could have remained completely hidden from Daugherty. This thought probably occurred to Harding and heightened his anxiety over the consequences should Smith be exposed. Aside from a desire to protect Daugherty, it is most likely that Harding's main worry concerning Smith's crimes centered more on a fear of what his congressional enemies would do with such information politically than on any potential damage to his own personal reputation.

Harding should have been more concerned with his own reputation. The instinct for self-preservation should have caused him to throw the scoundrels to the dogs and then withdraw behind a cloak of presidential rage. But in some illogical way Harding sought to save his own reputation, as well as that of his friends, by inaction. In the process, he lost everything. After his death, as one disclosure succeeded another, speculation on his involvement in the scandals inevitably increased. The first public airing of such speculation came in mid-February 1924 when a publicity-seeking retired New York banker, Frank A. Vanderlip, questioned the validity of the sale of the *Marion Star* by claiming that $550,000 was too much to pay for a local daily and hinted that the price may have masked presidential skullduggery. Vanderlip was careful not to charge Harding with anything specific, slyly remarking "no one wants to look under the edge of a shroud." The Walsh committee, at the time indiscriminately probing all rumors, immediately hailed Vanderlip before it but soon traced his story to his own imagination. Brush and Moore, the two newspapermen who had purchased the *Star*, later sued Vanderlip for slander and ultimately collected $100,000 in damages. Both Republican and Democratic leaders were disgusted by this episode, but that did not prevent the rumor mills from continuing to concoct and circulate numerous intriguing variations on the Vanderlip theme.[47]

However, it was not idle gossipmongers or political enemies who did as much to undermine Harding's personal reputation as his old friend, Harry Daugherty. This was certainly not Daugherty's intention. But the manner in which he hid behind the dead president in his refusal to testify at his trial in 1926 did little to allay suspicions. What was Harding's connection with the "Jess Smith Extra No. 3" account? What were the funds in this account used for? If not for political purposes, as Daugherty's words and actions seemingly implied, then what sort of personal use was made of them that disclosure might prove embarrassing to the dead president? The most common speculation centered on "woman trouble."

[6

AFTER the president's burial, Florence Harding returned to the White House where she remained in virtual seclusion for almost a week. President Coolidge continued to make temporary headquarters in the Willard Hotel. On August 17, 1923, Mrs. Harding moved to the McLean estate, "Friendship," and then, on September 5, accompanied by Major Baldinger and Dr. and Mrs. Sawyer, left Washington for Marion. She spent the remainder of September and October in Marion setting her affairs in order and finally returned to Washington in November with the intention of living in the capital permanently. During the winter of 1923–24 she occupied a suite on the top floor of the Willard Hotel, rarely going out, but seeing and receiving old friends. On one occasion she did go out—she attended the funeral of Woodrow Wilson.

The various investigations into her husband's administration gave Florence Harding intense anguish and she became extremely bitter toward all those officials, including President Coolidge, who did not openly fight and condemn the Walshes and the Wheelers. Her contempt for such persons as Means, Stinson, and Remus was fathomless. On several occasions she was on the point of appearing as a voluntary witness to deny certain of their charges which she knew to be untrue. But she resolved that as a president's widow she ought not become the subject of sensational newspaper copy or dignify the slander.

Her Washington residence was an unhappy time and in the summer of 1924 Florence Harding returned to Marion to the White Oaks home of Dr. Sawyer. She was still there in late September when Dr. Sawyer sud-

485

denly died of a cerebral hemorrhage. His death was a crippling blow to Florence Harding. Her thoughts thereafter became morose. "My world is going to bits," she once commented and on another occasion said, "I do not see much in life for me." Intensifying her somber mood was the news of the sudden death in a motor accident of Mrs. Hubert Work who had accompanied her to Alaska and was a close friend. Next came the announcement of Secretary Wallace's untimely death on October 25, after which she took to her bed and never left it alive. Indeed, with her husband's administration under attack, with Fall disgraced, with Daugherty removed, and with these other tragedies happening to people whom she knew and liked, she appeared to lose the will to live. By early November friends described her as being "extremely distressed" and anxious for the end. On November 21, 1924, not quite two months after Sawyer's fatal attack, Mrs. Harding died at White Oaks of chronic nephritis and myocarditis. Two days after Florence Harding's death, Harry Daugherty's wife, Lucie Daugherty, died in her Town Street home in Columbus, Ohio. Mrs. Daugherty had contracted pneumonia and had not been told of the death of Florence Harding for fear of the effect which this news might have on her own precarious condition. Florence and Lucie had been intimate friends since girlhood.[48]

Scarcely had Mrs. Harding been lowered into the grave beside her husband than rumors circulated that she had destroyed all her husband's correspondence in order to protect dark secrets about the administration and, especially, about their own private lives. As early as October 1923 the Manuscripts Division of the Library of Congress had asked Mrs. Harding about the president's papers, but she had put them off by saying that when she was ready she would get in touch with them. She never did, although during the last year of her life she employed secretaries to trace Harding's correspondents, furiously gathered up every scrap of her husband's letters, and cleared out the files of the *Marion Star*. When in early 1924, she refused an offer from Doubleday, Page to publish a volume of Harding's letters, Frank N. Doubleday charged that she had burned them all. In December 1925 Dr. Charles Moore, acting chief of the Manuscripts Division of the Library of Congress, also claimed that Mrs. Harding had destroyed all her husband's correspondence. Just two days after the Moore charge, George Christian issued a brief denial, which passed almost unnoticed, and stated that under the terms of Mrs. Harding's will the letters were in the possession of the Harding Memorial Association. Christian claimed that only "unimportant correspondence" had been eliminated by Mrs. Harding and that the Memorial Association would "dispose of them [the letters] in such manner as it believes they will be of the greatest benefit to posterity and the nation."[49]

Rumors of letter burnings, the death of many of the major participants, and Daugherty's refusal to testify at his 1926 trial set the stage for the appearance in 1927 of a 440-page book entitled *The President's Daughter*.[50] Privately published under the imprint of the Elizabeth Ann Guild, Inc., this work shocked the publishing world. Many booksellers refused to handle it and reviewers at first ignored it. Still it sold some 90,000 copies at $5 apiece, being traded under the counter and read omnivorously not only by the original purchasers but by countless others who borrowed it.

This book told a sensational story of extramarital presidential love, replete with syrupy poems, fervid embraces, secret meetings, breathless remarks (such as "Isn't this g-r-a-n-d?" and "What rapture!"), numerous pictures of an eight-year-old girl who looked like the dead president, and a dedication to unwed mothers. The author, Nan Britton, was the daughter of Dr. Samuel Britton, a moderately successful Marion doctor and a friend of the Hardings. At age fourteen Nan had fallen in love with the town's handsome editor. In her book she carried her story from this first infatuation with the future president, through numerous amorous trysts with him in New York and elsewhere, to the climax on October 22, 1919, when at age twenty-three (Harding was fifty-four at the time) she gave birth to a daughter at Asbury Park, New Jersey, which she claimed belonged to him. According to Nan, Harding came to her for *real* love because he did not get along well with Florence, often sighing, "She makes life hell for me, Nan!" To Nan, Warren Harding was "such a darling," "my hero," and "sweet." To be the mother of his child, said Nan, was simply "glorious."

In the book Nan stated that while the 1920 convention was in session, Harding visited her several times at her sister's Chicago apartment. After his nomination she went to the Adirondacks for a rest, leaving the baby behind with her sister. During the campaign Harding sent her money, as much as $100 to $150 a week, via a secret-service agent named "Tim Slade." Nan claimed that after Harding's election she visited him several times, usually masquerading as his niece, and in June 1921 even sneaked into the White House to be alone with him in a small closet. Thereafter she visited the White House intermittently and continued to receive money from him. During their last meeting in 1923, she said the president talked wistfully of marrying her and of adopting the child. But he also talked of death. "Really, dearie," he complained, "my burdens are more than I can bear," and begged her to keep their secret: "I would rather die than disappoint my party!"

Nan was on a trip to France—at Harding's expense, so she claimed—when he died. Meanwhile, the child, Elizabeth Ann, had formally been adopted by Nan's sister in January 1922. As Nan concluded the story: After Harding's death she returned to live in New York, finally marrying a Norwegian sea captain in January 1924, who not long after abandoned her. In debt and desiring to reclaim her child, as well as secure $50,000 which she claimed Harding had promised her in the event of his death, she returned to Marion and confessed the whole story to Harding's sister, Abigail. Abigail believed her and so did another sister, Carolyn, both of whom gave her a few hundred dollars to help out. But when Harding's brother, Dr. George ("Deac") Harding, heard of this, he demanded an interview with Nan at which she was supposed to supply letters, dates, specific names, places, etc. Alas, she could produce no letters because she had burned them all. When Deac Harding thereafter summarily refused to deal with her, Nan said she hit upon the idea of writing *The President's Daughter* as a means of raising money to provide for herself and her child.

That was the extent of the story. Nan finished the manuscript in mid-January 1927 with the help of a friend, Richard Wightman, whose wife later sued him for divorce, naming Nan as corespondent. Together Nan and Richard sought a publisher, submitting it first to Boni and Liveright, then to Knopf, then to Simon and Schuster, all of whom rejected it. Finally, finding that no reputable publisher would touch it, Nan published it herself. Certainly she possessed a strong motivation of some sort, whether financial or otherwise, to get her story into print. Certainly, too, her ambition was somewhat abnormal. In a day when such things were not readily admitted, Nan publicly branded herself an adulteress by publishing her memoir, forever stigmatized her child as illegitimate, and created the conditions for destroying completely the reputation of her lover whom she still claimed she "truly worshipped." At no time did she evidence any trace of guilt and she displayed a hopelessly romantic view of illicit love triumphing over all obstacles. The enormity of her wrong, or that of Harding's, if true, simply never fazed her.

Despite the "conspiracy of silence" which greeted her book, Nan's name quickly became a household word. There were many who immediately believed her story. Incredible in certain respects—the number of mutual friends who knew of this clandestine relationship but never talked, the elusive secret-service man, "Tim Slade," who arranged meetings for the two lovers, the impossible trysts under the very noses of relatives and friends—her claims and descriptions contained enough authenticity to confirm suspicions. In July 1927, in the *Baltimore Sun*, H. L. Mencken, under the title "Saturnalia," pilloried the Harding administration through snide references to *The President's Daughter*. Others were convinced that here at last was the reason for Daugherty's silence at his 1926 trial. Nan's disclosures seemingly fleshed out Daugherty's skeletal implications in his refusal to testify. Many Marionites, knowing both the president and Nan Britton, were quite willing to accept at least a portion of Nan's story and, although they thought she exaggerated, especially about the relationship while Harding was president, considered an occasional earlier liaison between Nan and Harding as not impossible. Perhaps more significant was the fact that Harding's sisters had indeed, as reported by Nan, accepted her claims that some sort of intimate relationship had existed between herself and their brother.[51]

In the ensuing years there were, of course, ardent defenders of the president. Some claimed that Harding could not be a father because he was sterile, which was possibly the truth: he and Mrs. Harding had been unable to have children even though she had conceived during a previous marriage. Patrick Kenney, the president's private doorkeeper at the White House, stated that he "never had heard of Nan Britton," that he had "never admitted any woman by such a name," and that "*no* strange woman ever came to see President Harding." W. Frank Gibbs, who opened Harding's mail while he was a senator, claimed that no correspondence ever existed between the president and this woman. Ike Hoover, White House usher, bluntly stated: "There was never a gadabout by that name or any other name in the White House. Nan Britton is a liar." Shortly after the Britton book appeared, Ed Scobey wrote to a friend in Piqua, Ohio: "I never heard of this woman and I know a great deal of that book is untrue." Of all the defenders, however, none was more outspoken than Dr. Joseph

DeBarthe, a former editor of the *Buffalo Times* and self-taught physician, who wrote a rejoinder to Nan's book, entitled *The Answer*, in which he charged her with sexual fantasies, deliberate falsehoods, and criminal libel. Nan filed a $50,000 suit against Charles A. Klunk, a hotel proprietor in Marion, for subsidizing and distributing *The Answer* (DeBarthe had died suddenly in a fall down a flight of stairs), but in 1931 Judge John M. Killits of the Federal District Court in Toledo and a highly prejudiced jury ruled against her. Nan's case foundered on the fact that she could produce no letters or other documentary evidence.[52]

The Harding reputation, already sufficiently battered by Nan Britton's disclosures, was further damaged by the publication in 1930 of another book—this one by Gaston Means, entitled *The Strange Death of President Harding*.[53] Ghostwritten for Means by Mrs. May Dixon Thacker, this work was a compendium of Means's alleged relationship with Harding and the Harding administration. Mrs. Thacker, who was the sister of Thomas Dixon, the famous author of *The Klansman*, gathered the material from Means while he was an inmate in Atlanta Penitentiary. The result was a runaway best seller.

Undocumented and nonspecific, the book was both libelous and ridiculous. Yet the gullible were willing to believe it. Means told of secret spying missions for Mrs. Harding, of amorous trysts and love letters to strange women by General Sawyer, and of gross sexual infidelities by the president. He described frequent meetings with Jess Smith at Daugherty's H Street address where drunken orgies were attended by Harding at which chorus girls were sometimes injured by flying glass. Means claimed that he had handled as much as $500,000 at one time for the Ohio Gang, that Daugherty was the evil mastermind behind it all, and that Daugherty got to be attorney general by blackmailing Harding through his knowledge of Nan Britton. He further claimed that he had investigated the Britton affair for Mrs. Harding, stole Nan's diaries and letters, and gave them to Mrs. Harding who after reading them murmured: "I ought to kill them both. . . . That's what I ought to do. . . . They deserve it. . . . They are not fit to live." Thereafter, said Means, Mrs. Harding used the Britton letters to terrorize her own husband in a vicious struggle with Daugherty to dominate him. Jess Smith, who was the "weak link" in the Ohio Gang, was murdered because he knew too much. Mrs. Harding's illness in the early fall of 1922 was triggered, stated Means, by her sudden discovery of the Britton affair, and her adoration of Warren Harding gradually turned to hate. In her fear that her husband would be either exposed or impeached, and with "her brain on fire" from both the prattlings of soothsayers and the knowledge that she was a discarded wife, Mrs. Harding planned the Alaskan trip along with General Sawyer, her chief accomplice. By implication, Means established the conditions for Sawyer and Mrs. Harding to slip the president poison rather than medicine on the return journey down the west coast. The lack of an autopsy, Means said, represented prima facie evidence of foul play.

The Means book delivered a final blow to the Harding image. The seeds of suspicion that Harry Daugherty had inadvertently planted by not testifying in 1926 now came to bitter fruition. It apparently mattered little that President Harding had never met Means or that Means was a perjurer, a thief, a convict, and a swindler. Submerged by sensationalism was the fact that Means did not know Mrs. Harding, that he had never been in the White House, that he had not been present at the places and on the dates he mentioned. Not surprisingly, on November 7, 1931, in *Liberty Magazine* in an article entitled "Debunking the Strange Death of President Harding" May Dixon Thacker wrote "with humiliation . . . and in justice to the dead" that she now believed she had been duped by Means and that the book was nothing more than a "colossal hoax—a tissue of falsehood from beginning to end."[54] Unfortunately, in the publishing world repudiations seldom rate the same publicity as original accusations and Mrs. Thacker's article did not counteract the effect of the Means book. The damage had been done.

[7

IN REVIEWING *The Strange Death of President Harding* for the *Nation* in 1930, Oswald G. Villard made a telling point. Admitting that the work was vicious and libelous, Villard nevertheless claimed that until such men as Hoover and Hughes came forward to challenge the charges, "Mr. Means and his book will hold the field; he will profit by its phenomenal and unchecked sale; and the volume will spread throughout the country the belief that his allegations are in the main correct."[55]

During this whole period, most of Harding's co-workers were cowering in fear and wished not to be too directly associated with the Harding name. Indeed, after Hughes's eulogy in 1924 their silence was monumental. Some of them, especially Hoover, had strong political ambitions and quickly sensed the political dangers of too close an identification. Such officials ran the risk of being compromised not only by the corruption and suspected presidential philandering, but more specifically by the leakage of scandal money into the coffers of the Republican party. Through the various oil trials and a subsequent Senate investigation in the spring of 1928, it became painfully clear that some of the profits Sinclair enjoyed on his leases ultimately made their way into the hands of Chairman Will Hays and Treasurer Fred Upham to defray the party's 1920 campaign debt. Although no collusion was involved between these party officials and Sinclair, such a situation caused Republicans like Borah to wail that the entire party needed to be purged. Prospective presidential aspirants like Hoover knew that they were high on Borah's purge list. Borah attempted to convince the Republican National Committee that it ought to begin a fund-raising campaign to replace the Sinclair contributions dollar for dollar, and when the committee refused to do so Borah began solicitations on his own for a so-called Conscience Fund. It was a grandstand play—even conscience-stricken Republican newspapers ridiculed the idea —and in the end the Idaho senator collected only $8000. By 1928, the public was obviously far more interested in the former president's alleged sexual peccadilloes than in the purity of the Republican treasury.[56]

Throughout the remainder of the twenties and into the thirties the general pattern remained unchanged: Republican leaders sought to ignore Harding. It had not started out that way. Shortly after his death and while the eulogies were still flowing, the Harding Memorial Association was created to raise money for a suitable presidential tomb and monument. President Coolidge accepted the honorary chairmanship and top government officials, including all the cabinet members, were on the association's executive board. In mid-1924 Dr. Sawyer resigned his White House post to act as full-time coordinator. At that time the association had some $900,000 in cash and pledges and a committee of Mellon, Weeks, and Charles Schwab was appointed by Coolidge to determine the location, plans, and allotment of funds for the memorial. The site selected was Marion and the ground was broken in 1926. However, by that time Republican leaders were seeking excuses for not remembering Harding, and on the occasion of the laying of the memorial's cornerstone only Vice-

President Dawes could be found who was willing to go to Marion and deliver an endorsement of his former boss.[57]

Formal dedication of the completed memorial, a circle of forty-six Tuscan and Ionic columns in white Georgia marble, was scheduled for July 4, 1927. Obviously no less than a president could deliver this address. But Silent Cal was "too busy" and to the end of his term, according to Hoover, "expressed a furious distaste" at any mention of dedicating the memorial. Hoover was not much better. Shortly after he was inaugurated in 1929, Hoke Donithen, secretary of the association, requested him to suggest a new date for the dedication, but Hoover's office replied that the president could not "suggest any date for the dedication when he might be present." In a closing paragraph, there was this revealing statement: "If, under the circumstances, the Association feels that it should go ahead with the arrangements for the dedication without his presence, the President will, of course, understand. In fact, he thinks that perhaps that would be the best course to pursue."[58]

So the memorial stood undedicated. Clearly it was an embarrassment, more a monument to Republican political cowardice than a tribute to a dead president. Even the *Baltimore Sun,* which had never been friendly to Harding, scoffed: "that he [Harding] was unworthy of so much as an oration by any member of Mr. Hoover's Cabinet is not believed by anybody outside the Administration itself."[59] Finally, in January 1931, Hoover indicated that he would dedicate the memorial after all, and the date was set for June 16. At last the gathering was held. Chief Justice Hughes spoke first, saying little. Former President Coolidge, accepting the memorial on behalf of the American people, said less. Then President Hoover stepped before a battery of microphones and, with Harry Daugherty sitting directly behind him, squarely faced the issue. After tracing Harding's humble beginnings, recounting his political career, and mentioning his winning qualities, Hoover stated bluntly: "Here was a man whose soul was seared by a great disillusionment. . . . Harding had a dim realization that he had been betrayed by a few of the men whom he had trusted, by men whom he believed were his devoted friends. It was later proved in the courts of the land that these men had betrayed not only the friendship and trust of their staunch and loyal friend but that they had betrayed their country. That was the tragedy of the life of Warren Harding."[60]

493

It was not Harding's tragedy alone. For all the major participants, the tragedy was both personal and collective. Stung by Hoover's remarks at the dedication in 1931, Daugherty vowed to vindicate himself, and also Harding, by writing a book of his own, which he published in 1932 under the title *The Inside Story of the Harding Tragedy*. Interestingly, his collaborator was Thomas Dixon, who shortly before had condemned his sister's literary relationship with Gaston Means. Daugherty hoped his book would be an antidote to all the previous slanders and lies about the Harding administration. The result was something less than spectacular. Mainly an unabashed justification for his every move, Daugherty's book shed little light into the dark corners of the administration. Of course, he denied any involvement in the scandals, dealt kindly with both Smith and Fall, was harsh in his treatment of Forbes, labeled Roxy Stinson a liar, and dismissed Means and Nan Britton with utter contempt. Until Nan Britton's book came out, Daugherty claimed, he had never heard of her. But he did not offer specific evidence to destroy her claims. As for his former senatorial enemies, Daugherty blistered them with stinging rebukes, calling Wheeler "the little lawyer from Butte" and charging him with being a Wobbly and a Communist sympathizer. The most serious defect in the book, however, was his failure to explain his refusal to testify about the "Jess Smith Extra No. 3" fund in 1926. He merely implied that his silence was not to forestall exposure of any presidential sexual escapades but to protect contributors to the campaign fund of 1920.[61]

Daugherty's effort had little effect on the snowballing tendency to believe the worst about Harding and his administration. Daugherty came to realize this not long after his book was published and wrote Charles Hard that any attempt to right the record was futile since "the public would not stand for it, because the public liked what is racy, sensational and ruinous to somebody."[62] Thereafter Daugherty gave up trying and retired to live in Florida, ultimately outlasting most of his enemies. On the occasion of his eightieth birthday in January 1940, he told a group of reporters: "I am a conservative—a standpatter. I'm not a progressive at all—never been nervous enough." Then, musing about old enmities, he remarked: "Wheeler—I guess there was a place in this world for Wheeler and a place for me." Upon his death in the fall of 1941 his estate amounted to only $175,000, disclosing no vast hidden fortune or the residue of great spoils.[63]

494

Others connected with the Harding tragedy did not end their days so benignly. On May 9, 1932, Albert Fall was released from prison without paying his fine because he was penniless. He had lost his ranch at Three Rivers through foreclosure and now retired to a small, shabby home in El Paso. His health, poor while in prison, deteriorated rapidly after his release. Yet he clung to life in a pathetic struggle which wore out Mrs. Fall, who died in 1943. A year later, Fall died virtually unnoticed in a Santa Fe hospital at age eighty-three. Edward Doheny, living in quiet retirement in California, never fully recovered from the tragic death of his only son, Edward, Jr., who was shot and killed in a senseless quarrel with his secretary just before the Doheny trial in 1930. Doheny died at age seventy-nine in 1935, spending the last three years in bed, a helpless, half-insane invalid. He divided among his relatives a fortune estimated at $75 million. Harry Sinclair, on the other hand, continued to live a life of adventure and luxury, finally retiring to a sumptuous Pasadena home where he died in 1956 at age eighty, an extremely wealthy man.

Charles Forbes, the first of the miscreants to be convicted, was released from prison in November 1927. His first action was to give an exclusive interview to the *New York World* disclosing "new," highly colored secrets about Harding, explaining how he was railroaded to jail, and naming Harry Daugherty and General Sawyer as the two evil geniuses of the Harding administration.[64] But he soon tired of this crusade and next attempted to clear the name of Dr. Frederick A. Cook, the explorer, who had been Forbes's cellmate at Leavenworth, serving time for using the mails to defraud. Forbes sought to prove that Cook, not Admiral Peary, had actually been the first to reach the North Pole. However, it was not long until Forbes, like Thomas Miller who was also released from jail in the late twenties, became lost in the mists of obscurity.

The major witnesses at the various investigations possessed diverse subsequent careers. Ned McLean and his wife, Evalyn, battled their way through the courts after 1925 in an effort to divorce one another and McLean ultimately lost control of both his newspapers, the *Washington Post* and the *Cincinnati Enquirer*. In 1933 a lunacy commission declared him insane because of excessive use of alcohol and he became a patient in the Sheppard-Pratt Hospital in Towson, Maryland, dying there in July 1941, at age fifty-five. Evalyn continued to live until 1947, an aging Washington hostess, still wearing the Hope diamond. George Remus, the bootlegger, ultimately served five short prison sentences for his many illicit activities. Upon his last release in April 1927, he returned to his home in Cincinnati where he accused his wife of infidelity and in October shot her to death in a Cincinnati park. At his murder trial he conducted his own defense, was judged guilty but insane, and was committed to an asylum. Howard Mannington escaped the net of the law altogether and became wealthy through various sugar deals in Cuba. Roxy Stinson, frightened and forlorn, returned to Ohio where she was shunned by her neighbors and generally ignored by the world. Gaston Means, after leaving Atlanta Penitentiary in 1930, was arrested a year later for beating his wife and assaulting an officer and as a result spent more time in jail. Then, in the days immediately following the Lindbergh kidnapping, Means gulled Evalyn McLean into giving him $104,000 to find the Lindbergh child. He proceeded to use the money for his own purposes. Indicted and convicted for fraud, he was sentenced to fifteen years. Even while in jail, he again attempted to defraud Mrs. McLean and drew an additional sentence of two years and a fine of $10,000. Fittingly, Means died in a federal penitentiary.

As for Nan Britton, her goal of providing for herself and her daughter, whoever was the real father, was achieved. Not only did she make a small fortune from *The President's Daughter*, but at one point she had to hire eight secretaries to handle the flood of letters which poured in from all over the country. No longer feeling the restraints which had bothered them in the first instance, Boni and Liveright published a second edition of *The President's Daughter*, hoping to cash in on some of the profits. Nan, meanwhile, gave interviews, wrote a few insipid articles, and even entered into negotiations in October 1930 with a film company to make a movie of her book. It was later claimed that film czar Will Hays stepped in and prevented it.

In an attempt to stretch her luck, Nan published a second book in 1932, entitled *Honesty or Politics*, but it was neither as sensational nor as interesting as her first effort.[65] Largely a description of how *The President's Daughter* came to be written and published, this account demonstrated the same naiveté, the same round-eyed adoration, the same physical affinity for Harding as the earlier volume showed. As a moneymaker it was barely a success. The depression year of 1932 was not a propitious moment to hawk new books. Besides, the public had finally tired of the subject and had other more pressing matters on its mind. Slowly Nan drifted into near obscurity, living in Evanston, Illinois, only to be sought out from time to time by eager professors or free-lance writers who hoped to bolster academic careers or make money by unearthing new information on the Harding scandals and the president's secret love life. But Nan had offered all she knew in her own books and still could not provide documentary evidence.[66]

XV

The Myth and the Reality

[1

"PRESIDENT HARDING is dead and I have a telegram for the Vice-President." So shouted a delivery man to Colonel John Coolidge whose head popped out of a bedroom window in the small white cottage where his son was vacationing in Plymouth, Vermont. It was after midnight on the morning of August 3, 1923. Calvin Coolidge was quickly awakened by his father and with mingled feelings read the brief message from Attorney General Daugherty which urged him immediately to "Take the oath of office as successor to the Presidency." In a dramatic and homey scene, Colonel Coolidge administered the presidential oath to his son on the spot. It mattered little that the legality was dubious and the ceremony had to be repeated later in Washington, D.C.[1]

Technically the Harding era was over and the Coolidge years had begun. But not really. Until his election in his own right in 1924, Coolidge actually served as caretaker for the Harding program, and for the time being he belonged more to the Harding period than to his own. No more unlikely person could have been saddled with such custodial responsibility. Often described as "a small, hatchet-faced, colorless man, with a tight-shut, thin-lipped mouth," Coolidge had not been impressive during the Harding era. William Allen White had referred to him in the *Emporia Gazette* as a "runty, aloof, little man, who quacks through his nose when he speaks," while Mark Sullivan had found Harding to be much "the bigger man, the larger personality."[2]

Aside from presiding over the Senate, Coolidge's contributions to the Harding administration had been minimal. He had not participated in policy making or in administration decisions. He stuck close to the Capitol end of Washington and consorted neither with Harding's cronies nor with the aristocracy of the cabinet. There is no record of his suggesting anything significant and the Harding Papers do not disclose any attempt on the president's part to consult regularly or purposefully with him. To Harding, Coolidge was simply "that little fellow from Massachusetts." Indeed, Harding apparently did not even consider him a permanent member of the administration. As early as 1922 there was some discussion of retiring Coolidge in 1924 and sending him back to Massachusetts to run against David Walsh for the Senate. Certainly there was no thought that Coolidge would ever succeed to the presidency.[3]

Ironically, considering his lack of loquaciousness and his general parsimonious attitudes, Coolidge's primary importance to the Harding administration was social. He may have been "weaned on a dill pickle" (which Alice Roosevelt Longworth later denied ever having said about him), but he faithfully showed up at the many functions which Harding could not attend. He became "the official diner-out of the administration." Once, asked why he accepted so many dinner invitations, he allegedly replied: "Got to eat somewhere." Only his wife, Grace, whose charm and graciousness made him more bearable, knew how miserably restless he was in this role and how useless he felt. Coolidge's personal letters during this time were filled with uncertainty, pessimism, and irritation, and he frequently spoke of his "barren life." Yet in his later *Autobiography* he called this "a period of most important preparation" and revealed that presiding over the Senate was fascinating to him. In any event, despite his restlessness, he apparently was proud to be included as a member of the Harding cabinet and had no thought of giving up the vice-presidency.[4]

Coolidge's sudden succession to the presidency was a shock. "Imagine—Calvin Coolidge, President! My God!" was the first reaction of veteran newspaper reporters. Somehow Harding, with all his shortcomings, seemed suited to the job—but Coolidge? Then began an amazing metamorphosis. Newspapers created a Coolidge image and a Coolidge myth. According to newspaperman Thomas L. Stokes, "It was one of the greatest feats of newspaper propaganda that the modern world has seen. It was really a miracle. He said nothing. Newspapers must have copy. So we grasped little incidents to build up human interest stories and we created a character."[5] Frank R. Kent, *Baltimore Sun* correspondent, later commented on the phenomenon: "Not in the memory of anyone now living has there been a President who leaned so heavily on this newspaper tendency to praise and protect, who profited by it so much, who would shrivel so quickly if he lost it, as Calvin Coolidge."[6]

Coolidge was neither as silent nor as wise as the artificially created popular belief thereafter suggested.[7] But because of the scandals, the presidential office needed bolstering and this was hardly the time for the press to undermine the incumbent, whoever he was. Fortunately certain facets of the Coolidge personality fitted neatly into the desired image. Being less gregarious and affable than Harding, Coolidge naturally tempered the open and easy atmosphere surrounding the White House. This "change" was quickly heralded as a conscious effort on his part to get rid of the poker players and the "carousing" that went on during the Harding years. But this shift would have occurred anyway, regardless of the scandals. Immediately upon assuming office Coolidge told the chief usher, Ike Hoover, "I want things as they used to be—before!" Notice was served that the occupants of the White House were no longer "just folks" nor could people casually "drop in." The habitual tolerance of Harding gave way to Coolidge's inscrutable aloofness. Unlike Harding, Coolidge "slapped no man on the back, he pawed no man's shoulder, he squeezed no man's hand."[8] A kind of puritanism descended which was certainly worthy of respect, but was not exciting. And just as they had earlier made Harding's affability a virtue, now newspapers praised Coolidge's restraint.

This Coolidge "change," however, only extended to superficialities and did not affect the Harding administration's program, or its top personnel. The claim by some that the death of Harding ushered in "a new period in American politics" was simply not true. The Harding cabinet was kept intact until public and congressional pressure forced out Daugherty and Denby. Coolidge retained all Harding appointees on regulatory boards and commissions until 1925. In the diplomatic corps the only significant change was the appointment of Frank Kellogg to replace George Harvey as ambassador to Great Britain and this was occasioned by Harvey's resignation, not Coolidge's initiative. Coolidge retained Wood in the Philippines and Crowder in Cuba. He even reappointed Dr. Sawyer as White House physician. Besides Harvey, the only major resignation following Harding's death was that of George Christian as private secretary, who left to handle Mrs. Harding's personal affairs and who was replaced by former Representative C. Bascom Slemp of Virginia.

As for Harding's policies, Coolidge's support was immediate. In officially announcing Harding's death he stated: "It will be my purpose to carry out his polices which he has begun for the service of the American people." After his first cabinet meeting on August 14, 1923, Coolidge stated that all the policies of the Harding administration, not just some of them, would be continued. Hence, despite the cries for change from insurgent Republicans, Coolidge early staked his political future on the Harding program. Among those policies which he listed as receiving his wholehearted support were (1) the collection of all war debts, (2) participation in the World Court, (3) prevention of Soviet recognition, (4) the improvement of relations with Latin and South America, (5) further restriction of immigration, (6) continuation of economy in government, (7) maintenance of the protective tariff system, and (8) additional remedial legislation for the farmer. Two weeks later in a press conference, the new president also announced that, like his predecessor, he would oppose a soldier's bonus and enforce the Volstead Act.[9]

In his first message to Congress in December 1923, Coolidge reaffirmed these policies and added a few more: the return of all shipping to private ownership, railroad consolidation along the lines suggested by Harding, and the maintenance of naval strength up to Washington Treaty limits. Instead of Coolidge's high-pitched voice, it could have been Harding's mellifluous tones for the hour and four minutes it required to stake out these positions. Except for his unequivocal endorsement of the Mellon tax plan of 1923, not one straying step did Coolidge take from Harding's orthodoxy, not one new idea did he advance. Strangely, the press did not remark on this fact; indeed, newspapers avoided mentioning it. They talked instead of Coolidge's "constructive policy" and his "emergent wise leadership." But it had all been advocated before and represented well-known Harding views. The Ohioan had cleared the path; now a new president walked down it with the approval of the nation.[10]

Until 1925 Coolidge followed the Harding pattern remarkably well. He declared the League a dead issue, but retained the tenuous ties with that organization that had been established during the Harding years. He resisted all pressure for debt cancellation and, although he was willing to

501

be malleable on interest terms and time schedules, he insisted that the debts be paid. He restated Harding's proposal for joining the World Court and supported it in the face of a recalcitrant Senate. He encouraged the rapid completion of recognition negotiations with Mexico and endorsed the removal of troops from the Dominican Republic. He reinforced the Harding decision against immediate Philippine independence and supported General Wood against the demands of Filipino politicians. Toward Russia, Coolidge at first appeared to adopt the same conciliatory tone which Harding had shown in the last months before his death, but not long thereafter, mainly under the guidance of Hughes, embraced the same intransigent position which had characterized the Harding years.

On the domestic front Coolidge's actions were also distinctly Hardingesque. In the brief anthracite coal strike in the late fall of 1923, he insisted on remaining neutral and relied on outside mediators to bring the disputants together. His hope rested primarily on local action and ultimately Governor Pinchot of Pennsylvania provided the tact and the drive which produced a favorable settlement. Like Harding, Coolidge encouraged Secretary of Labor Davis to overhaul the immigration system and endorsed the Johnson bill which was designed to curb the incoming flow even further. He strongly upheld Mellon's hand in continuing to reduce the national debt and supported the Budget Bureau. He exhorted the states to tighten their prohibition enforcement procedures, but evidenced little more interest than Harding in expending large sums of federal money on enforcement. On the bonus question, Coolidge proved to be as adamant as Harding. When in mid-May 1924 the Congress presented him with a new bonus law, he immediately vetoed it. Unlike Harding, however, Coolidge was not able to hold Congress in line as it hurriedly passed the bill over his veto.

The bonus struggle highlighted yet another striking similarity between Harding and Coolidge. Coolidge, no less than his predecessor, continued to experience difficulty with Congress. Coolidge tried various tacks in dealing with the Republican insurgents who were either elected or reelected in the fall of 1922. His most elaborate and naive attempt to placate them was his announcement in September 1923 that LaFollette was welcome at the White House and that the president hoped he could rely on the Wisconsin senator to support his program. LaFollette, whose presidential ambitions were predetermining his actions, was not impressed. At the same time, other insurgents indicated that they intended to monitor the administration carefully and pointedly warned that on certain issues they held the balance of power.

During the first session of the 68th Congress (December–June 1924), Coolidge was treated shabbily. In the first four months after his December message not one executive proposal was acted on. Not only did Congress run roughshod over his opposition to the bonus, it ignored his plea for adherence to the World Court. It manhandled the Mellon tax plan. It even squabbled over his appointment of Harlan F. Stone to succeed Daugherty as attorney general. In the end the public felt rather sorry for Coolidge and, just before the nominating conventions in June, newspapers caught the general mood by declaring that the "public rejoices at Congress passing its resolution to adjourn." As one editor summed up its work: "a Republican Congress has devoted itself to bloodying the President's nose, boxing his ears, and otherwise maltreating him."[11] The Harding pattern was repeating itself.

In one respect, however, the situation was markedly different—the scandals. Here Coolidge operated under a severe handicap. He had to remain pure himself while leading a party which was obviously tainted by corruption. As already noted, throughout February, March, and early April, newspapers wallowed delightedly in the muck churned up by the various investigations. The reading public was fascinated and devoured rumors with even greater relish than the facts. In mid-March the *New York Times*, not noted for sensational reporting, was devoting three and four full pages daily to investigation matters.[12]

Fortunately for Coolidge and the Republicans there was a limit to public credulity. By late March there were those who began to complain about excesses and especially about Wheeler's "grandstanding." Editorials began to warn readers that much of the testimony was dubious and cautioned against anything but tentative conclusions. Even the *New Republic* admitted that most of the Stinson-Means charges in the Daugherty investigation were "intrinsically improbable."[13] More important, there were increasing complaints by businessmen and local chambers of commerce that the constant round of investigations was hurting the economy. Coolidge, recovering from his earlier fright regarding the disclosures, by mid-April began to show impatience at the Wheeler-Walsh drive to uncover more dirt. Surprisingly the public, while still intrigued by the scandals, apparently agreed with him. As April moved into May and there were no new disclosures, the scandals disappeared into the inner recesses of the newspapers. By May 8 not a single spectator attended the dying hearings of the Teapot Dome investigation.

In the case of the Justice Department investigation, as Wheeler ultimately failed to deliver on his constant promises of other revelations of an "almost unbelievable nature," public interest not only waned but turned against him. By May both Walsh and Wheeler were receiving angry letters condemning them for their actions, and some Democrats found it necessary to explain to irate constituents why their two Montana colleagues were so zealous. It became increasingly obvious, in view of the upcoming presidential nominating conventions, that the Walshes, LaFollettes, and Wheelers were less avenging angels than ambitious politicians with personal axes of their own to grind. In June, when the final Walsh report admitted that only Fall, Sinclair, and Doheny were culpable in the Teapot Dome affair, it was greeted with derision. One editor remarked: "After the thunder and the earthquake, the still small voice . . . the report of Senator Walsh." Said another, "If this is all that Senator Walsh had to recommend, we might as well not have undertaken the investigation at all." Concluded the *American Federationist*: "The single, solemn truth is that the Walsh report is a flat fizzle."[14]

Thus the investigation mania ran its course and Coolidge, by doing nothing more than appointing a two-man special counsel and waiting for public reaction to set in, emerged virtually unscathed. He did not tamp down the fires of public discontent or party insurrection by shrewd and calculated maneuvering. He simply did what was natural for him—kept quiet and waited. The fires of discontent had never burned brightly enough to demand careful attention anyway and ultimately flickered out of their own accord. Coolidge was further aided by the fact that the electorate was still generally distrustful of Congress and observed all its actions with a jaundiced eye. Moreover the public's sense of morality had been blunted by the war and, as Will Rogers said, it was difficult to convince a jury of serious wrongdoing when most of the jurors secretly admired those who committed the crimes. Then, too, it was impossible to sustain interest in a few government scandals when several times each year the nation was witnessing other events which the headline-hungry press blew up into gigantic proportions. In the late spring of 1924 the Bobby Franks kidnapping and murder quickly supplanted the more mundane crime of Albert Fall, and not many months later the public was infinitely more concerned with the lonely plight of Floyd Collins in a cave in Kentucky than in the honesty of its government officials. The Hall-Mills murder, with its "pig woman" and various other revelations, had far more emotional impact than malfeasance in the Veterans' Bureau or the alien property custodian's office. The precise topography of De Russey's Lane in New Jersey where the murdered rector and his choir-singer mistress were found dominated the news while a Forbes and a Miller were quickly forgotten.

But of all the factors in the rapid decline of public interest in the scandals perhaps none was so important as the return of business prosperity. Throughout the spring of 1924, the scandal disclosures had to compete on the front pages of the newspapers with bold evidence of increasing dividends, profits, and spiraling sales. On the very day, March 24, that the oil investigating committee voted to charge Harry Sinclair with contempt, one of the front-page headlines in the *New York Times* read: "U.S. Steel Gained Half Billion in 1923; Profit $108,707,064."[15] Such indications of an expanding economy not only turned the public mind away from the scandals but encouraged the continuing defection of the middle and upper-middle classes from the tenets of progressivism. These groups rapidly embraced the new buoyant philosophy of welfare capitalism whose chief exponent was the large efficient business corporation and whose goals were full employment, relatively high wages, widespread consumption, mass production, increased leisure time, and mounting profits. In the midst of burgeoning optimism and ample evidence of affluence, these middle- and upper-middle-income groups (the professional classes, the small manufacturer, the tradesman, the businessman, and even the white-collar worker) had money in their pockets, and the feeling that soon they would have more. This rising expectation, coupled with the outward signs of prosperity, robbed progressivism of much of its relevancy. Die-hard liberals might long to combat existing pockets of poverty or right society's social wrongs, but these middle-group Americans were generally satisfied with their lot. From their point of view, the scandals notwithstanding, there was no need to be disturbed about the state of the nation.

Hence, it was not only public apathy, moral insensibility, emotional satiety, Democratic ineptitude, or Coolidge's purity which rendered the impact of the Harding scandals less significant. It was also the amazing postwar economic success of the Harding program. Ironically, if Harding bequeathed to his successor the awesome liability of the scandals, he also left him an asset in the form of returning industrial prosperity which politically more than made up the deficit.

[2

THE election campaign of 1924 actually began in 1922. The opening battle was the fall congressional campaign of that year and the outcome caused insurgents, Democrats, and anti-Harding opponents of all types to conclude that the Harding program was unacceptable to the public and that their own hazy plans could be substituted.

From the beginning the Republican insurgent group, in particular, miscalculated both the nature of the public discontent in mid-1922 and the actual support for its own ideas. Resting primarily on western farm dissatisfaction, this insurgency did not have the broad national appeal necessary for permanence. Instead of possessing a truly enlightened political philosophy, most of the insurgents embraced a hodgepodge of relatively unsophisticated and outmoded beliefs. Too much myth and lore of a bygone day encrusted their attitudes; they inadequately understood modern economic development; and they insisted on repeating the clichés and slogans of the late nineteenth century. By 1923 this group, in spite of LaFollette, possessed poor leadership and could not rely on any substantial help from either of the major parties. Indeed, as the economic picture brightened slightly on the farm in early 1924, this element even began to lose some of its rural support.

While LaFollette insurgents and remnants of the earlier farm bloc continued to blow their anti-Harding horns, especially during the scandal investigations, other anti-administration elements quietly sought new political alignments. As early as 1919, a group of die-hard liberals met in New York City to examine the possibility of forming a national progressive political organization. This group included labor men, Socialists, old Populists, single-taxers, Bull Moosers, intellectuals, and a few LaFollette insurgents. The meeting dissolved after passing a few resolutions and calling for a second gathering in St. Louis later in the year. This latter conference then created a "Committee of Forty-Eight," which was not a new political party but was intended to be a step toward one. Among the

506

forty-eight were such divergent personalities as J. A. H. Hopkins (a former Bull Mooser), McAlister Coleman (a Debsian Socialist), Gilbert E. Roe (a LaFollette lieutenant), Arthur Garfield Hays (a prominent liberal intellectual), and Frederic C. Howe (a former Tom Johnson supporter).[16]

There matters stood until February 1922 when, in a separate move, fifteen railroad brotherhoods convened a Conference for Progressive Political Action in Chicago to "bring about political unity" and promote "a better understanding" among prolabor liberals. Representatives of the Committee of Forty-Eight attended as did members of various socialist and farmer-labor parties. It was agreed to meet again after the 1922 fall elections to establish a third-party organization if that seemed feasible. All these various elements united in their efforts to oppose the Harding administration at the polls in 1922, denouncing "the invisible government of plutocracy and privilege." Especially effective was the work of the Committee of Forty-Eight in several western states.[17]

The fall election returns provided the impetus for further action. As planned, a second meeting of the Conference for Progressive Political Action was held in Cleveland in December, two weeks after the Washington gathering of the newly elected progressive senators and representatives under the aegis of LaFollette and Norris. There was no official connection between these two groups, although some who attended the Washington meeting also turned up in Cleveland. The Cleveland affair was certainly no love feast. First, the Communists under William Z. Foster created dissension by attempting unsuccessfully to gain representation. Then a cleavage appeared between the farmer elements and the labor groups. The intellectuals were disowned by both. Finally, there was a squabble over the advisability of creating a third party. The farm groups wanted to move very slowly and perfect state organizations first. The unions also dragged their feet. Only the Socialists and more militant elements argued for immediate third-party action. A final decision was postponed until 1923.[18]

Again in 1923 no consensus was reached and not until 1924 was it finally decided to create a third party. There was a constant struggle, meanwhile, to prevent infiltration by the Communists and to hold the various diverse elements together. Important in the final decision to create a third party were the emergence of the Harding scandals, the political demise of McAdoo as a Democratic nominee (before the Doheny disclosures he was

507

the favorite of the railway unions), and LaFollette's willingness to be a third-party candidate. Six hundred delegates flocked to the nominating convention of the Progressive party in July 1924 and agreed unanimously on the Wisconsin senator as their presidential nominee. For vice-president they selected the *bête noire* of the Justice Department—Senator Wheeler. Their platform condemned the Mellon tax program, denounced protective tariffs, favored a soldier's bonus, called for the abolition of injunctions in labor disputes, and rejected the current "mercenary system of degraded foreign policy." [19] In short, the Progressives' position represented a direct challenge to the Harding program and an indictment of almost everything for which it stood. Significantly, in the eyes of these dissident elements it was Harding who was on trial in the election of 1924, not Coolidge. Coolidge was still merely the custodian of the Harding program.

Coolidge was certainly not ashamed of that program nor was he reluctant to run on it. No sooner had Harding died than Republican politicians speculated on who would be the party's nominee in 1924. Hughes told Taft as they rode back from the station after Harding's funeral that under no circumstances would he make the race. Taft declared the same thing. There were others not so self-effacing. LaFollette would eagerly have taken the nomination if the party had asked him. Hiram Johnson was waiting in the wings, as were other hopefuls. But it was clear that they could wrest the nomination from Coolidge only with great difficulty. Coolidge wanted it and intended to have it.

As early as December 8, 1923, Coolidge formally announced his candidacy. From that time forward the issue was never in doubt. One by one Harding's cabinet members endorsed him. By the spring of 1924 Hiram Johnson dropped his presidential aspirations. By mid-April Coolidge had 530 of the 555 delegates necessary for the nomination already pledged to him. It was freely predicted that by convention time he would have over 1000. [20]

Coolidge possessed certain obvious advantages which became the favorites of historians thereafter—his incumbency, his integrity, his honesty, his silence, and so forth. Often overlooked, however, was the fact that Coolidge decided to stand on the Harding program and the 1920 platform. By so doing he automatically garnered the support of all former Harding supporters. The Harding organization now became a factor in keeping Coolidge in the White House. It was a marriage of mutual interest. As Taft wrote to Root in June 1924, "The only hope of the party is in Coolidge."[21] Conversely, the only hope of Coolidge was in the Harding record, scandals notwithstanding.

The Republican convention was anticlimactic. Rigidly organized by Coolidge's hand-picked manager, William M. Butler, and his ubiquitous secretary, C. Bascom Slemp, the convention quickly nominated him and endorsed a reiteration of the 1920 platform. The only suspense came in the selection of a vice-presidential nominee. Various names were proposed, even Borah's. When the latter's name came up, Butler turned to Mellon and said, "Mr. Secretary, what do you think of Borah?" Looking off in the distance and taking his little black cigar from his mouth, Mellon replied: "I never think of him unless somebody mentions his name."[22] Significantly, the convention settled on Charles Dawes as Coolidge's running mate, a man whom Harding had once mentioned as his own presidential successor and who, even during the height of the scandals, did not hide his admiration for the dead Ohioan.

Rarely before had the Democrats been so hopelessly divided as they were in 1924. That party was experiencing the first ground swell of cataclysmic change which confronted it with an entirely new set of circumstances. The bitter cleavage between the emerging northern urban wing and the conservative southern element marked the beginning of a fierce internal struggle over such matters as immigration restriction, religion, and prohibition, and symbolized the cultural and ideological schism between the older and the newer America. In the midst of such turmoil, the party's ability to combat the Republicans was limited. The Democrats attempted to paper over their disunity and displayed righteous indignation at the Harding scandals by making Senator Walsh permanent chairman of their 1924 convention. On opening day 12,000 of them jammed into Madison Square Garden to hear Senator Pat Harrison scream about the saturnalia of corruption in Washington. Then followed the shattering experience of twenty-nine sessions and 102 ballots to arrive at the selection of John W. Davis, a conservative lawyer and former ambassador to Great Britain, as presidential nominee. This folly was compounded by naming western radical Charles W. Bryan, brother of William Jennings Bryan, as Davis's running mate. By this action, as one wag said, the Democratic party had succeeded in "snatching defeat from the jaws of victory."[23]

Victory was never in sight. Neither the Democrats nor the Progressives were able to mount a sustained offensive against the incumbent Republican party. The alternative represented by LaFollette was obviously not acceptable to the public, while the Democrats, with the conservative Davis at the helm, were unable to offer any alternative at all. In some matters, such as prohibition and Negro rights, neither of the opposing parties presented anything novel or genuinely liberal. And while Davis lapsed into a pattern of dull campaigning, LaFollette succumbed to the same regional and class orientation which in the past had proved the undoing of other third-party movements. Mouthing old Populist shibboleths, LaFollette tried to energize the country with warnings about "Wall Street," "bloated plutocrats," and "money piracy." What he got for his pains was largely apathy. LaFollette's political philosophy was almost as archaic as that of bona fide reactionaries. Moreover, he found himself the leader of competing groups which possessed little basis for harmony. LaFollette had to be different things to too many different men. For example, caught between labor on the one hand and the farmer on the other he often had no alternative but to utter absolute economic nonsense. He had to preach "high beef on the hoof and low beef on the table."

Surprisingly neither the Progressives nor the Democrats concentrated their fire on the one area where the Republicans were the most vulnerable —the scandals. The Republicans expected this attack and at the time of the nominating conventions many believed the scandals would cost the party the election. But events showed differently. Embarrassed by their own indirect involvement through Lane, McAdoo, and others, and fearful of a public backlash, the Democrats generally steered clear of the scandals. Here Coolidge's own purity was important. As between Davis and Coolidge there was no issue of corruption.

The Progressives were more aggressive on the subject, but even they fell short of expectations. While LaFollette attacked both major parties by claiming that "fraud, graft and corruption under the last Democratic administration [Wilson's] equaled in magnitude, if not in venality, that of the administration now in power," he was too busy raking Wall Street for its "gigantic robberies" to be particularly bothered with such peripheral thievery as that committed by Fall. Of all the candidates, only LaFollette's running mate, Senator Wheeler, made corruption the hallmark of his campaign. His favorite tactic was to debate an empty chair, representing Calvin Coolidge, at which he would fire demands such as "tell the people of New York City why you kept Harry M. Daugherty as Attorney General." Of course there would be no response, after which he would quip, "There, my friends, is the usual silence that emanates from the White House."[24]

The Republican strategy was inevitable—perhaps masterful as some claimed—considering the personality of their candidate. The scandal issue was met with silence. Coolidge stuck to the theory that no candidate was ever injured by not talking too much. Coolidge knew that public-opinion polls showed him ahead and that all he had to do was avoid mistakes. In July the *Wall Street Journal* was already proclaiming a Coolidge victory. Charles Michelson, a veteran Washington reporter, later stated he could not "recall anybody who thought John W. Davis had a chance." There was even talk that LaFollette might lose Wisconsin and the Northwest. By late October the *Literary Digest* poll showed Coolidge outstripping his closest rival by more than two to one and receiving a minimum of 327 electoral votes. Even such a Democratic stalwart as Senator Walsh despaired of his party's winning and began to hold a post-mortem long before the votes were counted.[25]

Of the 28,647,000 votes cast, Coolidge received 15,275,000 or 54 percent in a three-way race, a phenomenal showing. Davis collected a little over 8,385,000 and LaFollette 4,826,000. Coolidge carried thirty-five states with 382 electoral votes; Davis twelve with 136; and LaFollette one (Wisconsin) with 13. Later it was fashionable for historians, striving to show the continuance of the progressive spirit, to emphasize LaFollette's vote. But, by any test, his showing was poor. Of his 4,826,000 votes, 3,798,000 were cast as Progressive; 858,000 as Socialist; and 170,000 as Farm-Labor. Roughly 2,500,000 of his votes came from agrarians and a little over 1,000,000 from labor. In other words, even in the Midwest fewer than one-third of all the votes cast went to LaFollette. The election results in Kansas, Iowa, and Nebraska represented a complete LaFollette collapse. Here neither farmers nor laborers voted for him in the numbers expected. In the nonindustrialized, sparsely populated regions of the country, where his vote was greatest, he never ran higher than second, and only in Wisconsin was he first. Thus in no area, except in the senator's own home state, was the only real alternative to the Harding program endorsed by the electorate.[26]

In analyzing their own defeat, Democrats, and some later historians, claimed the major factor was the suicidal Madison Square Garden convention fight and sighed, "if only McAdoo had been nominated." This was wishful thinking. As Josephus Daniels wrote to Franklin Roosevelt in 1927: "I believe that [if McAdoo] had been nominated in 1924 before the bitter feeling of Madison Square [Garden], that he would have pulled the labor vote and . . . have won the party many of the dissatisfied farmers in the West, but I do not think he could have been elected."[27] Few persons really believed that Smith could have beaten Coolidge either, but most agreed that Davis was certainly the wrong candidate. Even this, however, can be debated. In view of returning prosperity and the general conservatism of the public at that moment, Davis may have made a better, not a worse, showing than the other available Democratic candidates.

As for LaFollette, the reasons for his defeat were obvious. Labor support was not wholehearted, the public was suspicious of many of the groups that championed him, his agrarian support was not unified, he had little monetary backing, he possessed no effective party organization, he harped on worn-out issues, and, most important, his program had no popular appeal. The rapid demise of the Progressive party after the election attested to the impermanency of his support and the quixotic political behavior of the elements that made up his following. Immediately after the defeat, the Socialists, agrarians, and labor groups came to a parting of the ways. Progressive congressmen who had supported LaFollette quickly scurried back into the Republican or Democratic fold. In February 1925, amid considerable wrangling, the Conference for Progressive Political Action was formally liquidated. Four months later, in June 1925, LaFollette followed it into the grave.[28]

Coolidge's victory was ascribed to various factors—his political shrewdness, his honesty, his silence, and so on. Some observers went so far as to claim that his victory was purely a personal one and did not represent a public endorsement of his party. This conclusion belied the facts. Republicans gained in both houses and increased their control in state and local communities. The election of 1924 was actually a repetition of 1920 —it demonstrated a continued public desire for "normalcy," but with this significant difference. In 1920 the voting public had no point of reference to what constituted "normalcy"; in 1924 it had such a reference—the Harding policies, which Coolidge had promised to continue. Therefore, voter endorsement was not made in the dark in 1924, nor was it the result of the campaign magic of one silent, honest man. Harding and his administration had constructed a program which by 1924 was so basically acceptable that even the shock effect of scandal could not affect it.

Business prosperity was probably the major campaign factor. Prosperity represented the consummation of the Harding policies and gave them validity. Without such prosperity the election prospects for Coolidge would have been far different. Prosperity did several things. It justified conservatives in their beliefs and it convinced many others, even some liberals, that whatever caused such outstanding economic advance had to possess some "progressive" qualities. Old doctrinaire labels became blurred in the glow of economic progress, and even some former Progressives after 1924 embraced the new economic order as a logical extension of Wilsonian liberalism.[29]

In any case, Coolidge's election marked the true end of the Harding era. Henceforth American politics carried Coolidge's special stamp and he no longer lived so directly under the shadow of his predecessor. Beginning in 1925 several changes were made in the cabinet, especially in State and Agriculture, which permitted Coolidge to influence more personally both foreign affairs and domestic economic matters. After 1925 Coolidge rapidly packed regulatory boards and agencies with his type of men. Thereafter he openly showed a big-business bias in contrast to Harding who had struggled to maintain some kind of balance between business and agriculture. As Coolidge's most recent biographer said, he stood in awe of the Dodsworths and respected his fellow Babbitts. Just after Harding's death, William Gibbs McAdoo prophesied that Coolidge would prove to be "a more useful servitor of the interests than Harding was." Indeed, from the beginning, the *Wall Street Journal* enthusiastically hailed Coolidge's elevation to the presidency and proclaimed that he was "sound from every angle." Clarence W. Barron, who accurately reflected the feelings of big business, greeted the opening of Coolidge's administration with "He has never made a mistake in action or in his public utterances on economic questions." Coolidge's lackluster message to Congress in December 1924, which was not even delivered in person but was read in a monotone by disinterested clerks, was highly praised in business circles precisely because it recommended nothing more than the status quo. Chief Justice Taft

513

uttered a widely held business opinion when he wrote to Elihu Root: "It isn't essential that we should have a great amount of legislation. . . . What we need is stability and not movement at the present time."[30]

Business could well afford to be satisfied. In contrast to the Harding era, Secretary Mellon emerged after 1925 as the single most important presidential adviser. Coolidge thereafter rested his political life on Mellon's economics and consulted closely with him before making any moves. Hoover continued as secretary of commerce and also played a part in enhancing the business image, but he was never in as much presidential favor as he had been under Harding. Coolidge often referred to Hoover as the "Wonder Boy" and in a fit of pique in 1928 remarked: "that man has offered me unsolicited advice for six years, all of it bad!"[31] Along with others, Hoover was oftentimes in sharp disagreement with Mellon's theories. For example, after 1925 Mellon reversed his earlier stand and increasingly supported easy money policies while Hoover constantly warned of their dangers. In cases involving such opposing opinions, Coolidge would customarily admonish: ". . . if I were in your position, I think I would yield my views to that of the Treasurer [Mellon]."[32]

"Business seems to be in the saddle," said *Harper's* in early 1925. "Let us see what it can make of the job."[33] If there was any real change after Harding, this was it. A business civilization emerged triumphant and the Harding era of conciliation, consensus, and accommodation gave way to the business-dominated "wonderful nonsense" of the subsequent period with its growing stock speculation, bull market, ticker-tape parades, Mayor Jimmy Walker, Peaches Browning, flagpole sitting, and bunion derbies. But still it must be remembered that in this mad race for pleasure, quick riches, and affluence the Harding era had supplied the starting gun, loaded the cartridge, and pulled the trigger.

Through it all the taciturn little man in the White House could "sit tight." He could do so because, despite the momentary danger and aggravation of the scandals, his predecessor had provided him with an economic and political philosophy which was well suited to the times, and had bequeathed him mainly settled problems rather than unsettled ones. This was a much different legacy from the one left Harding by his predecessor.

514

"THE accurate historian will rank Warren G. Harding as one of the really great Presidents of the United States of America. No other historical verdict will be possible."[34] So wrote George Christian in an article for *Current History* in September 1923, just a month after Harding's death. Almost forty years later, Arthur M. Schlesinger published the results of a poll of seventy-five American historians who were asked to rate the presidents, and with "little dissent" they agreed that Warren G. Harding was a flat failure. Scandals, suspected personal immorality, and ineffective leadership were mentioned as the chief factors which prompted such an adverse verdict.[35] Thus, despite Christian's high hopes of 1923, historians, in whom he had placed such supreme confidence, by mid-century had relegated Warren Harding to the bottom of the pile as the worst president ever to hold that high office. How this came about represents a final irony in the Harding story.

In August 1923 the *Outlook* in its obituary of Harding wrote this epitaph: "Among American Presidents Harding will be one of the least misunderstood. No myth will obscure his personality."[36] Except for Washington and Lincoln, no American president has been surrounded by as many myths, as much misunderstanding, and as many inaccuracies as Harding. Immediately after his death, well-meaning but highly emotional eulogies crowded the pages of magazines and newspapers, bestowing on him attributes which he did not possess and which he would have been the first to deny. The years 1923–24 saw the appearance of no fewer than four full-length biographies deifying him. All were hopelessly sentimental and generally useless except for demonstrating one fact: Harding was briefly remembered as one of the nation's most loved presidents.[37]

The corrosive effect of the scandals, Nan Britton's disclosures in *The President's Daughter*, and Gaston Means's compendium of lies, *The Strange Death of President Harding*, prompted a devastating reaction. This set the pattern for much subsequent mythmaking and muckraking. Throughout the thirties and forties, pulp magazines such as *True Detective Stories* continued to titillate readers with wholly fictional exposés of Harding's private life, while tabloids like the *New York Daily News* discovered that sensational tales about the former president still sold newspapers. Even as late as 1963, such publications as *Inside Story* and *Fact* carried reports which "proved" that Harding was "America's First Negro President," while Clare Booth Luce loaned her prestige to an article in *McCall's*, entitled "All for the Love of a Lady," in which she gave millions of modern housewives a warmed-over version of the Britton episode direct from the pages of Nan's own book.[38]

Never at any time after the onset of the thirties did the works of Harding's apologists, such as Daugherty's *The Inside Story of the Harding Tragedy*, offset the cumulative effect of this muckraking activity and, as Oswald Villard had prophesied, the muckrakers continued to capture public attention. To Harding's friends this appeared as rank injustice. But in terms of historical accuracy, justice would not have been served if only apologists like Daugherty had emerged victorious. Inaccuracies, gross errors, and faulty conclusions were shared by apologists and muckrakers and both groups contributed to a clouded picture of the twenty-ninth president.

Ultimately, neither of these groups proved to be the most significant element in creating a mythical Harding for posterity. From the outset the main bulk of lasting impressions concerning the Ohioan and his administration came from the journalistic world—especially from the so-called liberal journalists. Representing only a small minority of the working press, these men were extremely articulate and were mainly political mavericks or Roosevelt-Wilson followers. In their treatment of Harding, they made him the last major victim of their own wartime and postwar disillusionment. In him they discovered a convenient outlet for all their own frustrations arising from a feeling of ideological betrayal and defeat. Harding became their scapegoat for the wartime and postwar degeneration of Wilsonian liberalism.

Nowhere was this attitude more obvious than in the pages of the *New Republic* or in the bombast of H. L. Mencken. While Mencken was certainly no Wilsonian liberal, he served as the high priest for all those who found idiocy rampant in the existing order. In Mencken the nation possessed an arrogant self-righteous urban counterpart to the parochial bigotry of rural America and through him sophisticated elements vicariously hooted and howled at Harding and the Harding years. By the middle and late twenties, many liberals looked to Mencken as the source of much inspiration and agreed with him that Warren Harding was the perfect example of the "booboisie" who infested the American countryside and the small towns. Mencken's caustic analysis of "Gamalielese," with its "trombone phrases" and "wet sponge" style, was quickly adopted as holy writ by those who preferred Menckenese.[39]

Mencken was soon joined by others. Naturally the various scandals of 1924 provided an almost inexhaustible supply of fuel for anti-Harding fires, and no one stoked them more vigorously than Bruce Bliven. In 1920 Bliven was managing editor of the *New York Globe*, but shortly thereafter became managing editor of the *New Republic*. In February 1920 Bliven interviewed Harding in New York City during the preconvention campaign. His initial interview article was written "in the friendliest spirit," although Bliven found himself opposed to Harding both philosophically and politically. His assessment of Harding upon the latter's death was somewhat less friendly, but not harsh.[40]

However, in 1924, after the scandals came to light, Bliven began in the *New Republic* a series of five devastating articles on the Harding administration. Concentrating on the theme of the Ohio Gang (a term which Bliven did not invent but helped to popularize), he manufactured a conspiracy thesis which was at once appealing and logical. Prefacing many of his controversial statements with "fair-minded persons will agree," Bliven contended the following: the Ohio Gang was a definable group of political cronies headed by Harry Daugherty; the Gang had its origins in the "cynical, sordid and corrupt" machine politics of Ohio; Harding was "taken in hand" by Daugherty as early as 1912 and was thereafter managed "on behalf of the state machine"; the Republican party in 1920 "with brazen impudence forced upon the country Daugherty's man"; the "best minds" cabinet was largely a hoax with Harding serving merely as a figurehead; and there was a gigantic plot to turn over the Justice Department to Daugherty and to the Gang for booty, and surrender the nation to Mellon and to big business for swollen profits. In summation, Bliven colorfully claimed that the Harding era ". . . was one of gum shoes and whispering; of night-blooming gentlemen who were perpetually 'seeing' Jim or Joe or Jack and 'fixing things up'; perpetually conferring in hotel rooms, with bell boys coming in relays to locked doors with cigars and cracked ice. . . . It was an era of incessant telegrams in code, an era of regiments of key-hole listeners, letter thieves, wire tappers, an era of spies themselves spied upon, of double-crossers double-crossed."[41]

Unlike the muckraking writings, these Bliven articles possessed the sheen of truth plus the skill of the journalistic pen. Yet fact was so mingled with fiction and error so masked by moral indignation that the net result was a mélange of distortion and prejudice which passed for critical insight. Relying on journalistic license, Bliven added together numerous slight inaccuracies to arrive at a great big one—that Harding was part of a calculated and sinister plan to plunder the American people.[42]

The Harding image could ill afford the shock effect of such writings by a reputable journalist. Ironically, though, even more crippling blows were struck, not by Bliven, who had been a consistent opponent of Harding, but by a supposed friend. In the summer of 1926, Brand Whitlock suggested to William Allen White that the Kansas editor write a book about Harding. White replied: "The story of Babylon is a Sunday School story compared with the story of Washington from June, 1919, until July, 1923. . . . And the whole thing is epitomized by the rise of Harding. If ever there was a man who was a he-harlot, it was this same Warren G. Harding. But I suppose it ought not to be written now. It would hurt too many hearts."[43] Two years later White did publish a book, *Masks in a Pageant*, which contained, among other things, his personal assessment of Harding and his administration. What soured White so completely on Harding is not clear. The scandals were certainly a factor. But the virulence of his attack perhaps revealed more about White than about Harding. Undoubtedly the former Bull Mooser felt that he had been duped by Harding and thus struck blindly at the dead president in chagrin and anger. In some way this assault may have served as expiation for White's own political "sin" of having supported such an un-Roosevelt-like character.

In any event, White's treatment of Harding in *Masks in a Pageant* was in the form of a Greek morality play studded with the political jargon and imagery of turn-of-the-century midwestern populism. Poker games were "bacchanalian orgies," strings were pulled in Washington by the "oil kings," and raids were committed on the public treasury by the "Wall Street crowd." White ridiculed the Harding cabinet, devoted not a single page to any constructive aspect of the Harding administration, and employed over half of his narrative in describing the corruption of the Ohio Gang. White's suggestion that Jess Smith was murdered was lifted directly from Gaston Means's testimony and the articles of Bruce Bliven, as was his treatment of the Gang as a conspiracy. White's dramatic de-

518

scription of Harding's last days and his exaggeration of the president's fears on the Alaska trip contained a considerable amount of fiction.[44]

Masks in a Pageant was a popular book, but its impact was not as great as that of another book, also written by a journalist, which appeared three years later, in 1931. Few college history students have missed reading *Only Yesterday* or fail to respond to the name of Frederick Lewis Allen. Allen was a Harvard graduate and later overseer, assistant editor of *Atlantic Monthly*, editor of *Century Magazine*, and, finally, in 1941, editor of *Harper's Magazine*. Highly successful in recapturing the flavor of the twenties in his *Only Yesterday*, Allen was alarmingly defective on the Harding years. Journalistically oriented, he relied too heavily on headlines to tell his story and concentrated more on the chaff than on the wheat of historical gleaning.

Allen perpetuated a growing number of Harding myths for those tens of thousands of young readers whose total exposure to the twenties came through the pages of his *Only Yesterday*. Pro-Wilson and pro-League, Allen included in his book his personal biases, nostalgically remembering the twenties socially, but deploring the period's political and economic "immorality." For Allen, Harding was the prime symbol of national decay. He repeated the belief that the party bosses had early settled on Harding and later sealed his fate in a smoke-filled room. From both Mencken and White he borrowed the contention that Harding was a hopelessly ill-informed dupe and that his mind was utterly incapable of grasping difficult situations. He subscribed in general to the conspiracy thesis expounded by Bliven, and reiterated White's claim that Hughes and Hoover were appointed to the cabinet merely as window dressing. Moreover, Allen left his readers with the impression that Harding's private life was a succession "of cheap sex episodes," that he paid little attention to the affairs of state, that he gave offices away "like a benevolent Santa Claus," and that he was president because of an "ambitious wife [who] had tailored and groomed him into outward respectability." Allen described Harding's Washington in Blivenesque terms as being infested with "blowzy gentlemen with cigars stuck in their cheeks and rolls of very useful hundred-dollar bills in their pockets." He even suggested that Means's allegation that Harding's death was the result of either suicide or poison was "very plausible." In his coverage of the Harding era, Allen devoted fewer than four pages to the constructive activities of the administration—two lines on the German peace treaty, seven lines on the Budget Bureau, one line on the tariff, six lines on tax policy, four lines on war debts and reparations, four lines on labor problems, and so on. Conversely, he devoted twenty-two pages to the scandals. As an editor, Allen should have been the first to recognize this as a flagrant case of slanted reporting.[45]

There were still other journalistic writers who helped fix attitudes on the Harding period. One, Mark Sullivan, was responsible for what was unquestionably the best popular treatment yet to appear on the Harding years. Sullivan, editor of *Collier's Weekly*, free-lance contributor to many periodicals and newspapers, and, like Allen, a Harvard graduate and later overseer, published the sixth, and last, volume of his *Our Times* in 1935. Subtitled *The Twenties*, this volume covered the years 1920–25 and dealt mainly with Harding and the Harding era. Unlike those journalists who preceded him, Sullivan made a serious attempt not to rely on his own memory or partisan contemporary accounts, but to unearth sources not yet tapped. He urgently requested the Harding Memorial Association to permit him access to the Harding Papers, assuring them that he had "no axe to grind" and maintaining that his book would be "a more accurate and truthful account of Harding's Presidency than any which has yet been published." To Dr. Carl Sawyer, son of General Sawyer and president of the association, Sullivan wrote: "It is my conviction, growing out of the immense amount of research I have done, that Harding has been misjudged and that he was a much abler man than he has ever been given credit for being."[46]

Dr. Sawyer foolishly refused Sullivan's request. Had Sullivan gained access to the Harding collection in 1935, many of the earlier distortions might have been corrected and much subsequent mythmaking prevented. Instead, Sullivan was left to shift as best he could; he interviewed many close personal friends of Harding, but never got at the important manuscript materials. Still, Sullivan went about his work in a craftsmanlike manner, marking an important departure from the past. The result was a narrative which contained little of the animus or prejudice of earlier accounts. Although displaying the same unfortunate myopia on the scandals which had plagued White and Allen, Sullivan nevertheless devoted some space to other aspects of the administration and thus initiated a needed corrective. Even so, lacking the cooperation of the Harding Memorial Association, Sullivan repeated a fair share of inaccuracies and myths which by now were deeply embedded in the Harding story.

This move by Sullivan toward a more careful examination of the early twenties made less impact than it might have because of the contemporaneous publication of other less favorable works. M. R. Werner, a freelance writer and sometime correspondent for the *New York Tribune*, published his *Privileged Characters* in the same year that *Our Times* appeared. Supposedly a "factual" exposé of the corruption of the Harding period, this work merely repeated, in most cases verbatim, the testimony which had been given before the various congressional investigating committees. Werner made no attempt to establish the credibility of witnesses and utilized only the most sensational and controversial portions of the hearings to prove his points.[47] Similarly, William Allen White's breezy biography of Coolidge, *A Puritan in Babylon* (1938), used the Harding administration as a vehicle for moralizing about American politics in the 1920's. The title alone carried the message. In exaggerated form, White drew a sharp contrast between Coolidge's incorruptibility and his predecessor's venality. In so doing, White managed to reiterate all the Harding myths contained in his earlier *Masks in a Pageant* and used them as a counterpoint to enhance the importance of his current subject.[48] Significant also in perpetuating an adverse Harding image was Alice Roosevelt Longworth's *Crowded Hours* (1933). This work provided juicy reading in thousands of homes whose occupants wished to view the recent past through the eyes of Theodore Roosevelt's daughter. Always pungent and frank, Mrs. Longworth wasted few kind words on Harding. In one famous passage, she compared Harding's study in the White House to a back room in a speakeasy: "the air heavy with tobacco smoke, trays with bottles containing every imaginable brand of whisky stood about, cards and poker chips at hand—a general atmosphere of waistcoat unbuttoned, feet on the desk, and the spittoon alongside." Most readers, of course, were unaware that Alice's husband, Nicholas, often sat at Harding's poker table in that very study and that even Alice had been known to take a hand. Alice's final judgment on Harding was: "I think every one must feel that the brevity of his tenure of office was a mercy to him and to the country. Harding was not a bad man. He was just a slob."[49]

In 1939, however, the most influential, and damning, work yet to be published on the Harding period appeared. In that year Samuel Hopkins

Adams brought out his *Incredible Era: The Life and Times of Warren Gamaliel Harding*. From the preface to the concluding chapter, Adams spun a highly dramatic yarn of desperate villains, evil deeds, dupes, clever manipulators, dark secrets, and darker plots. Adams had the proper background for it. A reporter and special writer for the *New York Sun*, Adams had already published a novel in 1926, entitled *Revelry*, which was the story of a weak and degenerate president, Willis Markham (Harding), who possessed such shady friends as Dan Lurcock (Daugherty) and Jeff Sims (Jess Smith), and who habituated the Crow's Nest on Blue Street (the "little green house on K Street"). Predictably, Markham turned the bedrooms of Washington into his sexual playground and ultimately committed suicide after being disgraced and betrayed by his corrupt friends.

Incredible Era had all the trappings of scholarship but little of the substance. Footnotes appeared occasionally citing Sullivan's *Our Times*, Nan Britton's *The President's Daughter*, White's *Masks in a Pageant*, Daugherty's *The Inside Story of the Harding Tragedy*, Means's *The Strange Death of President Harding*, and so on. Sometimes a footnote for a particularly dubious bit of information would read: "Statement to the writer by the Good Samaritan who chooses to remain anonymous." The net result was an incredible potpourri of all the facts and myths which could be amassed about the Harding era up to that time. Adams evidently hoped to reduce it all to intelligibility, but failed to apply critical analysis to this accumulation of data. While he dismissed Gaston Means as a fraud, he proceeded to quote him as an expert on the Harding period no fewer than sixteen times. He accepted Nan Britton's story as *positively* true, but supplied no additional or corroborative proof. Although Adams did not himself believe the charge that Harding had Negro blood in his veins, he devoted so much space to it that the reader comes to the opposite conclusion. In evaluating the activities of the Harding administration, he destroyed any claim to objectivity by his selection of chapter headings alone: "An Ohio Group," "Daugherty Grooms His Entry," "A Smoke-Filled Room: 2:11 A.M.," "Big Job, Little Man," "Ohio, Here We Come!" "Oil," "Menace," and "The Strange Burial of President Harding." This preoccupation with the sensational and the hearsay caused Cyril Clemens, son of Mark Twain and a collector of Harding letters, to fire off an angry note to Adams, enclosing several pages of factual errors and faulty interpretations. This book, said Clemens, ought to be called "Malice toward All," and he charged Adams with transferring "too many fiction particles" with him to "the stern and exacting and prosaic, if you will, field of history." "Please," begged Clemens, "return to your delightful fiction writing."[50]

Still Adams's prose was superb, his book received wide circulation, and it was quickly adopted as *the* authoritative work on Harding. Along with Allen's *Only Yesterday* and White's *Masks in a Pageant*, it thereafter served as the primary transmission belt by which all the various slanted accounts and oft-repeated myths were carried to later generations.

[4

PERHAPS one should be tolerant toward these early "impressionistic" writers. Most of them were born in the late nineteenth century, grew to adulthood during the Progressive Era, and were liberal in their political orientation. They reported history as they saw it and lived it. More specifically, most of them were practicing journalists with a natural tendency to overstate, to create stark differences of black and white, to compress and simplify rather than elaborate, and to rush to meet deadlines. Moreover, they were obviously affected by that style of journalism typical of the 1920's. They found it difficult to eschew the spectacular, sensational, or dramatic. Just as they groped for colorful adjectives to describe a Bobby Jones or a Babe Ruth, so they sought similar adjectives to characterize a politician. They were equally at home with the Headline Hero or the Headline Bum. Jones was the Galileo of the Links, Ruth was the Sultan of Swat, and Harding was the King of Scandals.

But what of the trained historian? What about these learned men whose collective wisdom ultimately judged Harding as a total failure? Frankly, the historian's record in this instance is also poor. The first examination of the Harding period by a person trained in historical methodology was undertaken in 1928 by Harold F. Alderfer, later a professor of political science at the Pennsylvania State University, but then a fledgling Ph.D. candidate at Syracuse University. His dissertation, "The Personality and Politics of Warren G. Harding," was insufficiently documented and placed too much reliance on contemporary newspaper accounts, yet it attempted to strike a balance on the Harding years and clear away some of the misconceptions. Although Alderfer found little to admire in Harding as president, he treated him without rancor or moral indignation and reached the conclusion that in many respects Harding was a victim of circumstances.

Unfortunately Alderfer did not expand or publish his study, nor was his spadework continued by others. Instead retrogression ensued. In 1930 Preston W. Slosson, then associate professor of history at the University of Michigan, published a short article in *Current History* entitled "Warren G. Harding: A Revised Estimate." Slosson strove for impartiality but his final judgment was harsh. Parroting Mencken, Slosson claimed that "the quality of Harding's mind as revealed in his public address is appalling" and, following White's *Masks in a Pageant*, peremptorily maintained that Harding was completely ignorant of national and foreign affairs, that Hughes and Hoover spent much of their time holding their noses, and that "not a single act of creative statesmanship was born in the Harding brain." Concluded Slosson: "After Cromwell, Charles II; after Washington, Aaron Burr and his ilk; after Lincoln, the carpetbaggers; after Wilson, Harding."[51]

This caustic view was followed in two years by the "official" *Dictionary of American Biography* article on Harding by Allan Nevins. Nevins had been an editorial writer for the *New York Evening Post* and the *Nation,* and in the middle twenties was on the staff of the *New York World.* In 1927, however, he started his career as a historian at Cornell, and in 1932 was a newly minted professor of history at Columbia. His Harding article attempted to be factual but its tone was disapproving, especially when he referred to the president's "dissipated habits." Nevins blamed Harding, not Congress, for the political ineffectiveness during the period, gave Borah sole credit for calling the Washington Conference, perpetuated the smoke-filled-room theory together with its tangential myths, left open the possibility that Jess Smith was murdered, and repeated from White some of the more dramatic events surrounding Harding's last days. In this process Nevins made some glaring errors. He claimed, for example, that Colonel Harvey narrowly missed being made secretary of state and that Fall was widely opposed for secretary of the interior.[52]

Both Slosson and Nevins suffered from a malaise which afflicted all early historians in their handling of the Harding era. Their source materials were exceedingly thin or nonexistent; and their conclusions slavishly copied those of the journalists and popular writers whom they quoted. Yet, paradoxically, historians were currently castigating these same popu-

524

lar accounts for their lack of research and their heavy reliance on opinion and prejudice. Even Sullivan's *Our Times* drew the historians' ire. A review of this work in the *American Historical Review* in 1936 depicted Sullivan as one who "wanders through the postwar years, touches a few matters in detail, mentions others barely, and deals with most political and public happenings not at all."[53] More severe was the historians' judgment of White's book. In evaluating *Masks in a Pageant*, the *Mississippi Valley Historical Review* described the work as merely "the impressions of one man" which reflected personal bias and represented no attempt to judge events by the accepted standards of historical analysis.[54] Even more bitterly denounced was Adams's *Incredible Era*. In a review for the *American Historical Review* in 1940, Professor Frederick L. Paxson said the Adams book was little more than an amalgam of prejudice, myth, contradiction, and fiction. He refuted Adams's contention that journalists were "highly qualified specialists" of the historical scene and asked how such "specialists" could write one thing about Harding while he was alive and another after his death. Concluded Paxson sarcastically: "There is something wrong with the critical apparatus of this *Incredible Era*."[55]

There was also something wrong with the historians. Despite the recognized shortcomings of these popular sources, historians persisted in using them and adopting their views. Claude M. Fuess, in his biography of Harding's successor, *Calvin Coolidge: The Man from Vermont* (1940), depended almost exclusively for his assessment of Harding on Allen's *Only Yesterday*, Sullivan's *Our Times*, and Adams's *Incredible Era*. In 1947, William Allen White's biographer, Professor Walter Johnson, somewhat limply attempted to explain away the Kansan's earlier sympathy with Harding in his *William Allen White's America*, and for his own view of Harding relied heavily on Allen, Adams, and Sullivan. The next year, 1948, Karl Schriftgiesser, whose background was mainly journalistic, reached a kind of plateau in writing subjective history in his *This Was Normalcy: An Account of Party Politics during Twelve Republican Years, 1920–1932*. Admitting in his foreword that the work's biases "come from a reading of [the history of the twenties] against a background of the definite and purposeful leadership of Franklin Delano Roosevelt," Schriftgiesser even out-Aliced Alice Longworth on Harding: "Poker games played in short sleeves by men sipping highballs in defiance of the law of the land, filling the ancient rooms with cigar smoke and raucous laughter, became an almost nightly spectacle in the old house on Pennsylvania Avenue. The soft, paunchy, slouching Harding, his jaw packed with chewing tobacco, presided there over a motley crew. Any night might see him playing for high stakes with drunken Charles Forbes, reckless Senator Brandegee, simpering Jess Smith, thieving Secretary Fall, incompetent Ned McLean, to name but a few."[56] Schriftgiesser's conclusions, like the statement above, contained just enough truth to be believed: Harding was nominated in a smoke-filled room by vested interests seeking booty in the form of oil and natural resources; he fastened an idiotic isolation on the country thereby creating a moral vacuum in foreign policy which later trapped the United States into World War II; through Mellon, Harding established an economic system which made inevitable the Great Depression that followed; he was a little man "whose prepossessing façade was a false mask for the emptiness inside"; and he was killed by the treason of his friends and the fear that his sexual peccadilloes would be exposed.

The year 1948 also witnessed a temporary break in this chain of quoting and requoting with the publication of Frederick L. Paxson's *Postwar Years: Normalcy, 1918–1923*. Using the materials and the tools of analysis available to him at the time, this University of California professor attempted to modify Adams's *Incredible Era* and adjust the balance in favor of the non-scandalous activities of the Harding administration. Concentrating on politics and economics, Paxson eschewed the temptation to moralize on the personality and private behavior of the president, and strove to show the problems he faced and the solutions presented. Especially good on congressional affairs and the last stages of the Wilson administration, Paxson's work naturally suffered from a lack of intimate knowledge which only a perusal of manuscript materials can impart. More a summary of facts than a work of insight or interpretation, Paxson's book represented a step in the right direction but failed to initiate a new departure. Hence, despite Paxson's efforts, the basic pattern with regard to Harding continued for almost two decades more. For those historians handling the early twenties it was easier and more natural to refer to White, Allen, Sullivan, and Adams. By this time these works had begun to acquire with age and repeated use a validity which few historical reviewers at the time of their publication claimed for them. Gradually they became the historical "gospel," rarely contested and widely accepted.[57]

As with the journalists whom they copied, the historians cannot be entirely blamed for their actions. Their errors were not consciously committed. Obviously their most damning sin was their willingness to adopt indiscriminately the views of memoir writers or journalists and pass them along to each other without reexamination and verification. Historians waited too long to compare these views with the new material (archival and manuscript holdings) which was slowly making its way into service. Moreover, historians, like journalists, were affected by the strictures of their own profession and their own times. Early historians writing on the Harding period received their graduate training at the hands of mentors who were sympathetic to the Progressive Era, while they, in turn, lived to experience personally the devastating effects of the Great Depression. This conditioned most of them to react unfavorably to the twenties, causing them to treat the era with disdain. As a result, Theodore Roosevelt and Woodrow Wilson emerged in their eyes somewhat bigger than they actually were historically, while Harding and Coolidge became, by contrast, the drab foreground over which these luminaries cast their shadows. The thirties was again a decade when powerful and exciting men walked the stage, especially Franklin Roosevelt. The era sandwiched in between did not stand out in their minds and automatically seemed of less historical importance.

Also, during the thirties and forties there was a distinct tendency on the part of historians to belabor the "Golden Calf" attitude of the 1920's as an *inevitable* prelude to economic disaster. The majority of American historians, while not Marxian determinists, nonetheless found it convenient to detect a scapegoat for the depression in the economic conservatism of the twenties, and read into the actions of those who advanced that philosophy all sorts of malevolent motives. Simultaneously, from the vantage point of the forties, with a world again at war, it was easy to assume that the foreign policy of the twenties had also been sadly at fault. From 1930 to 1950, Americans were fed this historical diet—including budding historians then being educated in the graduate schools. Thus there was a natural transfer of negative attitudes toward the decade of normalcy from the older generation of historians, who had been trained in the Progressive Era, to their students, and then to their students' students who were trained in the pre-1950 period.

Times change. Historians educated in the 1950's generated less enthusiasm for the older historical interpretations and frames of reference.

In an age of global American responsibility and amazing economic affluence, it became increasingly difficult to regard the post-World War I economic revival of the twenties as a failure or the decade's constant, although relatively naive, quest for disengagement and disarmament as twin follies. A historical credibility gap developed as the 1920's seemingly had more to say to the 1950's and 1960's than did the Progressive Era or the 1930's. Mentors, as well as their graduate students, now were forced to reexamine the twenties in an altered perspective. Articles in historical journals began to reflect this new interest in the Roaring Decade.[58]

The 1960's saw one development of monumental significance for reevaluating the early twenties and the Harding story. In 1964, the Harding Memorial Association, at last rectifying an error which, had it been done earlier, could have saved both the Harding family and the historical profession much grief, presented to the Ohio Historical Society a voluminous collection of Harding papers which were immediately opened to scholars. Once rumored to have been burned, this collection proved to be a gold mine of information. If any sizable portion of it had been destroyed by Mrs. Harding or others, it was difficult to detect since the collection seemed virtually intact.[59] Other collateral collections appeared simultaneously and, along with the opening of the Hoover Papers at West Branch, Iowa, at last made a thorough reassessment of the Harding period possible. One pilot study quickly emerged—Andrew Sinclair's *The Available Man: The Life behind the Masks of Warren Gamaliel Harding*. Somewhat thin because of the limited time Sinclair spent in the Harding collection, the work nonetheless contained enough new information to shatter some myths and damage others. Relying more on shrewd deduction than painstaking research, Sinclair established guideposts for new approaches and left to others the task of more detailed digging.

[5

MYTHS surrounding historical figures are never fully dispelled nor is the truth ever completely ascertained. The Harding Papers illuminated most dark corners but they did not, for example, shed any light on the Nan Britton affair. Perhaps this was to be expected if the papers were culled at all by Florence Harding as alleged. The only mention of Nan in the Harding Papers appears in a letter pledging campaign support to

Harding from a Louise Beiderhase of New York City, dated October 30, 1920, in which Miss Beiderhase referred to a brief visit made three years before by the Ohio senator to a secretarial school classroom in the Fifteenth Street YWCA where she and Nan were classmates.[60] The Marion campaign headquarters' reply was a short note simply thanking Miss Beiderhase for her good wishes. There was no indication that Harding saw the Beiderhase letter or the reply. Still, the almost complete lack of any mention of Nan Britton in the Harding Papers, rather than allaying suspicion, served only to heighten it. In this instance, at least, the truth still is elusive.

Less elusive is the evidence relating to another "woman affair" which throughout all these years had received little publicity and, indeed, to most people remained unknown. Unknown, that is, until 1964 when the Carrie Phillips letters exploded on the scene. Originally discovered in 1956 in a shoebox in Mrs. Phillips's Marion home by her guardian and lawyer, Don Williamson, these letters were from Harding to the beautiful wife of James E. Phillips, owner of the Uhler-Phillips Department Store in Marion. Carrie Phillips's relationship with Warren Harding had earlier caused some local Marion gossip. Both White in his *Masks in a Pageant* and Adams in his *Incredible Era* made veiled comments about a possible affair between the two. But Nan Britton's disclosures so overshadowed this speculation that the Harding-Phillips connection was all but forgotten until the emergence of the Phillips letters. These letters, ninety-eight of them covering the years 1910–20, revealed a rather pathetic and lonely Harding who was sexually starved at home and who sought love and sexual fulfillment elsewhere. These letters indicated without question that in the Carrie Phillips case Warren Harding, for whatever reasons, had been consistently unfaithful to his wife before his election as president and that the Nan Britton allegations were to some extent also probably true.[61]

Carrie, a Bucyrus (Ohio) girl who had acquired a suavity and urbanity that made men notice her, had first been thrown together with Harding in 1905 when Florence was in a Columbus hospital for removal of a kidney and Phillips was in the Battle Creek Sanitarium in Michigan for nervous disorders. For the following fifteen years their clandestine liaison continued, while the two families remained friendly. The Hardings and the Phillipses, for example, visited Europe together in 1909. There Carrie fell in love with Germany and before World War I spent much time in that country; but she always returned to Marion and to her rather stormy and secret relationship with the future president. If Florence Harding suspected anything she did not make an issue of it. Jim Phillips first learned of his wife's infidelity in 1920, but evidently harbored no lasting resentment toward Harding. In the Harding Memorial program he purchased space to inscribe to the dead president his own testimonial: "In Memory of Our Esteemed Friend and Neighbor."[62] After Harding's election in 1920 Carrie resumed her travels in Europe, became increasingly estranged from her husband, and ultimately settled down in Marion to live as a recluse, an eccentric alone with her dogs, from 1939 to 1956. At that time her declining physical condition forced her into a home for the aged where she died in 1960.

Unfortunately, properly controlled restricted scholarly access to the Phillips letters could not be arranged before the major parties involved in the discovery and those responsible for a bumbling newspaper disclosure of their contents in 1964 were enjoined in a million-dollar lawsuit brought by the Harding heirs. The letters were, of course, immediately impounded by the courts. Once more a curtain of secrecy was drawn about the facts with the result that Harding's reputation was again left to the mercy of rumor, misinterpretation, and fanciful exaggeration.[63]

The inevitable was not long in coming. Francis Russell, a Harvard-trained free-lance writer and one of those involved in the Phillips letters controversy, published a book in 1968 entitled *The Shadow of Blooming Grove: Warren G. Harding in His Times*. By this one stroke, attempts to redefine the early twenties and construct a more balanced account of the Harding administration were severely jolted. Claiming to have read the Harding Papers carefully, Russell wrote an excellent Foreword for his book and then ignored it completely. Stating that Harding was a most misunderstood president and "was neither a fool nor a tool," he led the reader through 663 pages of elaborate detail to believe just the opposite. Curiously comparing Harding with Dwight D. Eisenhower, "the President who most resembled him," Russell used the Phillips letters as his major point of departure.[64] Under the guise of having made startling new historical discoveries (as *historical* documents the Phillips letters are of very limited value despite Russell's claims),[65] Russell aimed his book at the prurient interests of the general public and reaped the desired reward—much publicity and a Book-of-the-Month Club selection. But as one of his re-

530

viewers correctly said, good writing and wide acceptance by the reading public is no excuse for bad history.[66] The Russell book contained no footnotes and the bibliography consisted only of a few sources for each chapter, many of which were old and outdated. Again, gossip was elevated to fact, conversations were reported which might or might not have taken place, old myths were reincarnated, and minor details of marginal significance became central themes. For example, reflecting the preoccupation of his own times with the race problem, Russell seized upon the Negro-blood story as the primary conditioning factor in the development of Harding's personality and ridiculously called it the "shadow" which hung over Harding's entire life. Such a transparent and clumsy attempt to psychoanalyze the former president did little to qualify Russell as a psychiatrist.

While maintaining that Harding was a complete misfit in the White House, Russell failed to examine Harding's presidency critically. Four pages were devoted to labor, ten lines to the tariff, a dozen to the bonus, a half-page to prohibition. Agricultural policy was handled in a short paragraph and it took only eight lines to distort completely Harding's connection with Kenyon, Capper, and the farm bloc. The election of 1922 was glossed over and almost nothing appeared on the relationship between Harding and the various members of his cabinet. There was more on Nan Britton and her alleged wrigglings in a White House closet than on the nation's South American policy. More coverage was given to the burial of the unknown soldier than to the entire Washington Conference. No mention was made of Russia or war debts and reparations. Indeed, once again, the recounting of Teapot Dome and the scandals required more space than all the other events of the presidency combined.

Of course, Russell spent much time on the amorous aspects of Harding's life, especially the Britton and Phillips liaisons. Unable to quote directly from the Phillips letters, he teasingly employed dashes to heighten the reader's imagination—and to stay out of jail. By appropriating large chunks of *The President's Daughter*, he injected Nan's story into his own narrative wherever he believed it was applicable. His resultant conclusion that Warren Harding was intimately involved with at least two women other than his wife, particularly in the decade before he became president, was certainly not new. Nor were many of the other bits and pieces of information which he "found." As with earlier writers, he relied far too heavily on the congressional investigations of the various scandals without weighing the character and motivation of the witnesses, and he persisted in accepting at face value the dubious veracity of persons like George Harvey on the smoke-filled room and Charlie Forbes on events occurring in the Harding White House. Worse, Russell's failure to use such important supplementary materials as the voluminous Hughes and Hoover papers caused him to give his readers only an incomplete and one-dimensional view.

As with other popular writers on Harding, Russell was quite willing to spend countless hours gathering gossip, examining love letters, and checking hotel registers, but quickly tired of plowing through State Department reports, position papers, departmental memoranda, policy-making conferences, bureau decisions, presidential briefings, and those million-and-one unsensational day-to-day activities which delimit a president and his presidency. Instead he moved over the Harding story, picked up titillating kinds of minutiae, and presented them artfully to the reading public, thereby blurring again the image of the twenty-ninth president. If Adams's *Incredible Era* could be called "Malice toward All," as Cyril Clemens claimed, Russell's effort might be labeled "Malice toward Central Ohio." In the Boston-born Russell the same streak of disdain and of condescension toward the "dull, flat Ohio countryside" and its political offspring, which both Allen and Adams had also displayed, again showed through. Repelled by his exposure to the Ohio scene during his researches, Russell dourly noted in his conclusion that Marion was certainly not his favorite small city.[67]

[6

ALTHOUGH such sensational matters as sexual escapades and mixed-blood stories continue to appeal to popular writers and to the prurient-minded public, they remain of peripheral value in any over-all historical assessment of the Harding era. While Carrie Phillips hinted darkly several times at "exposing" Harding if he did not do her bidding and Nan Britton claimed that she received some "spending money" from him, there is absolutely no evidence of any aberrant political activity on Harding's part which can be traced to his extramarital dalliances. His relationship with Nan, whatever the facts, in no way altered the pattern of his political beliefs or the character of his political life. Even Carrie's angry and violent pleas in 1917 that he vote against the war with Germany, a situation on which she expended most of her threats, did not prevent him from speaking out in favor of it on the Senate floor.[68] These amorous detours apparently had no impact on his senatorial career, his nomination or election, or his presidency. With or without their existence, the Harding administration's agricultural, labor, business, conservation, marine, immigration, tariff, fiscal, and overseas policies would have remained the same. This latter is also true in relation to Harding's other personal habits or traits—his drinking, smoking, swearing, card playing, and golfing had little to do with his administration's success or failure. Too long have Harding's detractors obscured his contributions by stirring up emotional dust over these personal activities; conversely, too long have Harding's relatives and friends struggled to whitewash his personal immorality. Ultimately, his historical significance, if any, lies in the nature and effectiveness of his presidency.

Over the years that presidency has almost become a cliché. The "Harding administration" has been used in virtually every presidential election since 1924 as an example of evil and the epitome of a bankrupt "do-nothing" political philosophy. On the basis of the record, this picture is grossly unfair. Coolidge exaggerated when he claimed, "It would be difficult to find two years of peacetime history in all the record of our republic that were marked with more important and far-reaching accomplishments."[69] But he was closer to the truth than William Allen White, who once claimed: "President Harding's administration from 1921 to 1923 was an episode, a sort of intermezzo between President Wilson with his illusion of world peace unfairly negotiated and President Coolidge with his speculative boom."[70]

Taken separately, the Harding administration's achievements were rather impressive—the peace treaties, the Budget Bureau, the Washington Conference, agricultural legislation, economy in government, debt reduction, and business recovery—but the total was more important than any of the parts. The Harding administration acted as a cushion against the friction and the acrimony of the Wilson days and eased the transition of the nation to a prosperous peacetime existence. The period 1921–23 was one of crisis and readjustment—these were years of tremendous economic and social change. Harding was able to secure a general consensus during this period which facilitated national progress rather than blocked

533

it. By all standards of political compromise, the Harding administration was a success. Harding's personal contribution as an emollient and mediator was immense.

If the net effect was restorative for the nation, contrary to contemporary appearances, it was also constructive for the Republican party. Out of office for eight years, that party had no policy and no program. The Harding administration provided it with both. Partly the result of conscious endeavor and partly accidental, this program proved so adaptable that it was retained with only minor variations throughout the rest of the twenties and elicited the support of two succeeding presidents. Endorsed wholeheartedly by the public in 1924 and again, indirectly, in 1928, this "normalcy" program in longevity alone has to be classified as highly significant. In a very real sense the entire decade was the "Harding era."

In terms of honesty and frankness of purpose, the Harding administration was relatively unique. This seems like a ridiculous statement in view of the scandals. However, rarely has an administration been so open about its goals and proceeded so rapidly to achieve them. In 1920 Harding was no unknown quantity and represented no political surprise. Everything for which he stood he had articulated in his campaign speeches and few presidents have so conscientiously attempted to translate campaign promises into reality. That many of these were "conservative" and at variance with the thinking of numerous "liberals" is beside the point. If a criterion for political success is that the electorate receive almost exactly what it has been told to expect, then in Harding's case the criterion was fully met.

The Harding administration also deserves considerable credit in view of the recalcitrant role of Congress. Not since the Reconstruction period had Congress been so obstreperous as during the immediate post-World War I years. In opposing Wilson this Republican-controlled body had gotten so used to trampling on the prerogatives of the chief executive that it could not stop even after a Republican was elected to that office. Harding, of course, was no strong executive, but in view of congressional attitudes it was perhaps just as well. More often than not he handled Congress masterfully and, since that body was not prepared for domination by the executive anyway, it probably gave him as much as, if not more than, it would have given to a more aggressive president. Yet Harding sometimes displayed unusual political courage, especially when congressional intransigency threatened his ability to maintain economy in government or undergird a sound America First.

Perhaps more important, the Harding administration represented a momentary salutary balance between the various competing forces in the American economic system. In this respect Harding was able to accomplish what neither Coolidge nor Hoover could do after him. Under Harding, business had not yet succeeded in infiltrating government to the exclusion of other interests. Harding, more than his two successors, was actually "president of all the people" and a champion of no specific interest. Too, Harding remained remarkably open-minded and malleable on most questions. During his administration, although they did not then realize it, liberals and progressives alike had a greater opportunity to influence decision making at the top level of government than at any other time during the rest of the decade. Despite the scandals, Harding's administration was less controlled by vested interests or by pressure groups than the administrations of either of his successors. Furthermore, the economy was in better balance under Harding by 1923 than it was thereafter under either Coolidge or Hoover.

Obviously, the Harding administration possessed serious defects. No amount of new manuscript materials or reevaluations can alter this fact. Its solutions to pressing domestic problems were oftentimes shallow and makeshift. Its economic philosophy, particularly in relation to the tariff and war debts, was outmoded and no longer fit realities. Its lack of sensitivity to the needs of the working man was patently clear. Its economic conservatism precluded any real experimentation in dealing with the grave problems of agriculture. While it showed some interest in the social and welfare sectors, it moved only gingerly and without the required enthusiasm. Its various attempts at international cooperation were less than aggressive and its approach to the problems of war and peace was relatively unsophisticated.

But of all the administration's defects perhaps none was so crippling as the qualities of Harding himself. Certain of his virtues—his gentleness, his humaneness, his affability, and his gregariousness—so highly prized in Marion, became faults in Washington, D.C. Undoubtedly a more discriminating mind than Harding's would have detected the unworthy men among his associates and blocked them from securing high office. Harding's particular friends and acquaintances represented a heavy burden for any president to bear. The president himself obviously had a number of skeletons in his own closet—skeletons which, if not affecting his administration while he was alive, plagued it after his death.

In the American political system there is no such thing as an innocent bystander in the White House. If Harding can rightly claim the achievements of a Hughes in State or of a Hoover in Commerce, he must also shoulder responsibility for a Daugherty in Justice and a Fall in Interior. Especially must he bear the onus for his lack of punitive action against such men as Forbes and Smith. By his inaction he forfeited whatever chance he had to maintain the integrity of his position and salvage a favorable image for himself and his administration. As it was, the subsequent popular and scholarly negative verdict was inevitable, if not wholly deserved.

It is perhaps to Harding's credit that he had few illusions about himself. He was "small town" and unsophisticated and he knew it. He was a conservative whose political values came from a bygone day when men looked more to themselves for their salvation than to Washington. This he freely admitted. Not long before his death, in words highly reminiscent of a later, younger, and more liberal president, he exhorted one audience, "think more of what you can do for your government than what your government can do for you."[71] Moreover, his intellectual talents were not outstanding and his mental capacity was not enriched either by a first-class education or by rigorous self-discipline. This he also admitted. He once said: "I know my limitations; I know how far removed from greatness I am."[72] Such laudable frankness cannot be accepted as a substitute for ability nor can it compensate for the many errors made or the opportunities lost. Yet Harding was not, as one New York editor once called him, "an indistinguished and undistinguishable unit in the ruck of Republican Senators."[73] And, as Harry New later put it, "he was a much abler man than he thought himself."[74]

Still, as many observers later claimed, Harding probably should never have been president. Possibly that was the key mistake which, in view of his personal shortcomings and his past, Harding's own native intelligence should have prevented. But he *was* president and as such he was certainly the equal of a Franklin Pierce, an Andrew Johnson, a Benjamin Harrison, or even a Calvin Coolidge. In concrete accomplishments, his administration was superior to a sizable portion of those in the nation's history. Indeed, in establishing the political philosophy and program for an entire decade, his 882 days in office were more significant than all but a few similar short periods in the nation's experience.[75] Yet the Harding era is still mainly remembered for its smoke-filled room, its Nan Britton, and its Teapot Dome. The record notwithstanding, its myths still command more attention than its realities.

NOTES

ABBREVIATIONS

AHR	*American Historical Review*
HMD	Harry M. Daugherty
HP	Harding Papers (in Ohio Historical Society Library)
JAH	*Journal of American History*
MVHR	*Mississippi Valley Historical Review*
NYPL	New York Public Library
OSAHQ	*Ohio State Archaeological and Historical Quarterly*
WGH	Warren G. Harding

Notes

CHAPTER I. THE MAKING OF A PRESIDENT

1. For a detailed report of the convention see George L. Hart, reporter, *Proceedings of the Seventeenth Republican National Convention* (New York, 1920).

2. For an accurate account of the maneuvering see Wesley M. Bagby, "The 'Smoke-Filled Room' and the Nomination of Warren G. Harding," *MVHR*, XLI, No. 4 (March 1955), 657–674.

3. William T. Hutchinson, *Lowden of Illinois: The Life of Frank O. Lowden*, II (Chicago, 1957), 466; Bagby, "The 'Smoke-Filled Room' and the Nomination of Warren G. Harding," 665–666.

4. Harry M. Daugherty, *The Inside Story of the Harding Tragedy* (New York, 1932), 51–55.

5. Nicholas Murray Butler, *Across the Busy Years*, I (New York, 1940), 279; Mark Sullivan, *Our Times: The United States, 1900–1925*, VI (New York, 1935), 66–67.

6. Harding genealogy is in Warren G. Harding Papers (Ohio Historical Society Library, Columbus, Ohio), Box 801. These are hereafter cited as HP. For a standard account of the Harding family see Ray B. Harris, "Background and Youth of the Seventh Ohio President," *OSAHQ*, LII (1943), 260–264, 269. The most recent book which covers the early Harding years is Francis Russell, *The Shadow of Blooming Grove: Warren G. Harding in His Times* (New York, 1968), 17–81.

7. C. Remsberg to R. B. Harris, June 6, 1938, Ray Baker Harris Papers (Ohio Historical Society Library, Columbus, Ohio), Box 9, Folder 1.

8. Frank M. Warwick, *Growing up with Warren Harding* (n.p., n.d.). Originally published as eighteen installments in the *New York Evening Post* in 1920, this work possesses the friendly bias of a man who had the future president as a friend from the time they were "six or eight."

9. For Harding's life at Ohio Central College see letters of Charity Remsberg to Ray B. Harris, Harris Papers, Box 9, Folder 1. Ohio Central College burned down in 1894.

10. Harris, "Background and Youth of the Seventh Ohio President," 274. For manuscript accounts of Harding's life to age eighteen see letters of Charity Remsberg to Cyril Clemens, Cyril Clemens Papers (Ohio Historical Society Library, Columbus, Ohio), Box 3, Folder "Remsberg"; and a 217-page typescript by George B. Christian, Sr., in HP, Box 792. Romanticized published accounts can be found

in Thomas H. Russell, *The Illustrious Life and Work of Warren G. Harding, Twenty-Ninth President of the United States* (Chicago, 1923), 49–55; and Joseph M. Chapple, *Life and Times of Warren G. Harding, Our After-War President* (Boston, 1924), 11–38.

11. For a sample of the vicious exchanges between the *Independent* and the *Star* see editorials in the *Marion Star*, April 7, 1886, and *Marion Independent*, October 12, 1894.

12. Harding's courtship, marriage, and father-in-law difficulties are amply covered in Russell, *The Shadow of Blooming Grove*, 82–113; and Harold F. Alderfer, "The Personality and Politics of Warren Harding," Ph.D. dissertation (Syracuse University, 1928), 108–111.

13. Sullivan, *Our Times*, VI, 96.

14. William A. White, *Masks in a Pageant* (New York, 1928), 397. Business papers relating to the *Star* and its management are in HP, Boxes 705–752.

15. For the best analysis of Harding's booster activities see Andrew Sinclair, *The Available Man: The Life behind the Masks of Warren Gamaliel Harding* (New York, 1965), 13–24.

16. For a similar analysis of the political importance of Harding's background see *ibid.*, 3–24.

17. Several writers, among them Sinclair in his *The Available Man*, claim that Harding accepted graft. For proof Sinclair mentions that Harding received railroad passes. This is surely an extremely broad view of graft. There is no evidence that Harding was a "grafter" in the *restricted* sense of the word.

18. Alderfer, "The Personality and Politics of Warren G. Harding," 90–91, 92, 133–134. For early opinions on the tariff, labor unions, and anarchists see editorials, *Marion Star*, May 6, 1886, May 14, 1886, May 27, 1886.

19. Alderfer, "The Personality and Politics of Warren G. Harding," 135.

20. *Marion Star*, editorial, January 22, 1908.

21. Hoyt L. Warner, *Progressivism in Ohio, 1897–1917* (Columbus, Ohio, 1964), 258–262.

22. Alderfer, "The Personality and Politics of Warren G. Harding," 153.

23. Alice Roosevelt Longworth, *Crowded Hours* (New York, 1933), 202–203; Butler, *Across the Busy Years*, I, 243; Harding quotations are from Alderfer, "The Personality and Politics of Warren G. Harding," 154.

24. Forrest Crissey, *Theodore E. Burton: American Statesman* (Cleveland, 1956), 235–238; Warner, *Progressivism in Ohio*, 470. For an exaggeration of Daugherty's role see Sullivan, *Our Times*, VI, 28; cf. Sinclair, *The Available Man*, 52.

25. Warner, *Progressivism in Ohio*, 471.

26. Sullivan, *Our Times*, VI, 27, n. 4b. Sinclair is mistaken in his *The Available Man*, 69, in claiming the speech was a "failure."

27. Boxes 683–692 and 753–762 in HP cover Harding's senatorial years. His complete senatorial voting record is in Box 796, Folder 1. For a quorum call analysis see Alderfer, "The Personality and Politics of Warren G. Harding," 162–163.

28. Sinclair in *The Available Man*, 76–77, for example, presents an oversimplification of Harding's relations with Wall Street. For a better analysis see Alderfer, "The Personality and Politics of Warren G. Harding," 166–167.

29. Russell and Sinclair both oversimplify Harding's antiradical views. Harding, for example, strongly opposed the expulsion of the New York Socialists. See Robert K. Murray, *Red Scare: A Study in National Hysteria, 1919–1920* (Minneapolis, 1955), 243.

30. *Cong. Record*, 65 Cong., 1 Sess., 5648.

31. WGH to Scobey, March 13, 1919, HP, Box 757, Folder 4, items 321069–321071.

32. Harding's questions angered Wilson. See David F. Houston, *Eight Years with Wilson's Cabinet, 1913–1920,* II (New York, 1926), 15–17.

33. *Cong. Record,* 66 Cong., 1 Sess., 5219–5225; WGH to Scobey, September 2, 1919, F. E. Scobey Papers (Ohio Historical Society Library, Columbus, Ohio), Box 2, item 279.

34. WGH to Hard, HP, Box 464, Folder 3720-2, item 217003.

35. WGH to Malcolm Jennings, September 12, 1919, Malcolm Jennings Papers (Ohio Historical Society Library, Columbus, Ohio).

36. Longworth, *Crowded Hours,* 292.

37. Daugherty's own account of his early career is in a 13-page letter, dated June 7, 1938, to Ray B. Harris in Harris Papers, Box 9, Folder 3.

38. For the best description of Daugherty's talents see Sullivan, *Our Times,* VI, 22–23.

39. HMD to R. B. Harris, June 7, 1938, Harris Papers, Box 9, Folder 3; Sullivan, *Our Times,* VI, 16–17.

40. For the purest statement of this myth see Sullivan, *Our Times,* VI, 26.

41. WGH to Hard, December 12, 1918, HP, Box 464, Folder 3720-3, items 217126–217130; WGH to HMD, December 20, 1918, HP, Box 686, Folder 4945-4, items 314266–314270.

42. Hard to WGH, August 9, 1918, Charles E. Hard Papers (Ohio Historical Society Library, Columbus, Ohio), Box 1.

43. Charles E. Hard, "The Man Who Did Not Want to Become President," *Northwest Ohio Quarterly,* XXXI, No. 3 (Summer 1959), 121–122.

44. Examples are in the Scobey Papers. These papers are extremely useful on Harding's decision to run.

45. Scobey to WGH, November 27, 1918, Scobey Papers, Box 1, items 205–206.

46. He even mentioned it in his biography in *Who's Who in America,* XVII (1932–33).

47. E. Mont Reily to Fellow Republicans, January 20, 1919, Warren G. Harding Papers (New York Public Library, New York).

48. See Sinclair, *The Available Man,* 101–121.

49. E. Mont Reily, "Years of Confusion," unpublished manuscript (Ohio Historical Society Library, Columbus, Ohio), 111–120; WGH to Scobey, January 14, 1919, HP, Box 756, Folder 2, items 321042–321044.

50. For sample Reily-Harding exchanges see Harding Papers, NYPL; for sample Scobey-Harding exchanges see HP, Box 757, Folder 6, especially WGH to Scobey, June 4, 1919, items 321074–321075, and October 26, 1919, Box 759, Folder 3, items 321116–321118.

51. Hard, "The Man Who Did Not Want to Become President," 125.

52. Daugherty, *The Inside Story,* 28.

53. WGH to Jennings, November 4, 1919, Jennings Papers.

54. WGH to Scobey, November 22, 1919, HP, Box 759, Folder 5, items 321130–321132.

55. Scobey to WGH, November 25, 1919, Scobey Papers, Box 2, item 320.

56. WGH to Brown, December 15, 1919, Walter F. Brown Papers (Ohio Historical Society Library, Columbus, Ohio), Box 1; Brown to Procter, December 2, 1919, *ibid.* The maneuvering between Brown and Procter is seen in letters in late 1919 between Arthur L. Garford, Walter L. Brown, and Colonel Procter in the Arthur L. Garford Papers (Ohio Historical Society Library, Columbus, Ohio) and in the Brown Papers, Box 1.

57. WGH to Scobey, December 16, 1919, HP, Box 759, Folder 6, items 321134–321136.

58. WGH to H. M. Sewall, December 16, 1919, HP, Box 690, Folder 4973-1.

59. Sullivan, *Our Times*, VI, 33.

60. WGH to Scobey, December 30, 1919, Scobey Papers, Box 2, item 347.

61. HMD to G. B. Christian, Jr., November 2, 1919, HP, Box 685, Folder 4945-2, item 314050.

62. Hard to WGH, December 15, 1918, HP, Box 464, Folder 3720-3, items 217121–217125; Scobey to WGH, December 24, 1919, Scobey Papers, Box 2, items 338–339.

63. HMD to WGH, December 26, 1919, HP, Box 685, Folder 4945-1, item 313991.

64. G. B. Christian, Jr., to Scobey, November 29, 1919, Scobey Papers, Box 2, item 323.

65. WGH to Scobey, December 30, 1919, HP, Box 759, Folder 6, items 321138–321140.

66. HMD to Scobey, January 19, 1919, Scobey Papers, Box 2, item 358. For other insights into Daugherty's role during the preconvention campaign see Harry M. Daugherty Papers (Ohio Historical Society Library, Columbus, Ohio), and HP, Box 685, Folder 4945-2, and Box 686, Folders 4945-3 and 4945-4.

67. Sample comment, HMD to R. B. Harris, June 29, 1938, Harris Papers, Box 9, Folder 3.

68. Sample letter, WGH to J. H. Rossiter, January 20, 1920, HP, Box 690, Folder 4972-1, item 316124.

69. Daugherty's constant anguish over the lack of funds is reflected in letters to E. Mont Reily, Daugherty Papers. See also Alderfer, "The Personality and Politics of Warren G. Harding," 22; Reily, "Years of Confusion," 408.

70. WGH to Jennings, January 20, 1920, Jennings Papers.

71. The best treatment of the Ohio primary is Robert Hauser, "Warren G. Harding and the Ohio Presidential Primary of 1920," unpublished M.A. thesis (Pennsylvania State University, 1967).

72. *New York Times*, April 29, 1920, p. 12.

73. See Harding-Hays correspondence in Will H. Hays Papers, February–April 1920 (Indiana State Historical Library, Indianapolis).

74. WGH to Scobey, May 10, 1920, HP, Box 760, Folder 9, items 321180–321181; WGH to Hard, May 18, 1920, HP, Box 464, Folder 3720-1, item 216872. Daugherty in his *The Inside Story*, 30–31, claims he had a difficult time restoring Harding's confidence after the Ohio primary. Harding's letters reveal no such trauma.

75. For a discussion of Lowden's irregularities in Missouri see Hutchinson, *Lowden of Illinois*, II, 452–455. Campaign expenditures are in Senate Committee on Privileges and Elections, 66 Cong., 3 Sess., *Senate Report No. 823* (Washington, D.C., 1920), 2943.

76. Wesley M. Bagby, *The Road to Normalcy: The Presidential Campaign and Election of 1920* (in *Johns Hopkins University Studies in Historical and Political Science*, LXXX, No. 1, Baltimore, 1962), 25–27, 29, quoting Villard on Wood.

77. It was Mark Sullivan in *Our Times*, VI, 34ff, who made popular Daugherty's claim that the "strategy of conciliation" was his idea.

78. Hutchinson, *Lowden of Illinois*, II, 423.

79. Kathleen Lawlor Manuscript in HP, Box 797, Folder 2, quoting Fall.

80. Philip C. Jessup, *Elihu Root*, II (New York, 1938), 410.

81. *New York Times*, June 11, 1920, p. 1; Hutchinson, *Lowden of Illinois*, II, 459; William A. White, *The Autobiography of William Allen White* (New York, 1946), 585.

82. Alderfer, "The Personality and Politics of Warren G. Harding," 34–35.

83. Sullivan, *Our Times*, VI, 51.

84. William Allen White is totally inaccurate in his *A Puritan in Babylon: The Story of Calvin Coolidge* (New York, 1938), 201, in claiming that Willis nominated Harding "as an afterthought."

85. Hutchinson in his *Lowden of Illinois*, II, 461, claims that the Lowden group really wanted a recess. However, Lowden was closing the gap on Wood by the fourth ballot and the actual voting on the adjournment motion showed much dissatisfaction among Lowden delegates.

86. Butler, *Across the Busy Years*, I, 279; White, *Autobiography*, 584; "Reminiscences of James W. Wadsworth" (Oral History Research Office, Columbia University), 273. No other commentator except White ever mentioned Harding as either drinking or being unkempt.

87. Mrs. Harding probably would not have permitted him to give up at this late date. One rumor at Chicago claimed that she tore the phone from his hands when he once began to tell Daugherty to withdraw his name. Charles Michelson, *The Ghost Talks* (New York, 1944), 229.

88. Hermann Hagedorn, *Leonard Wood: A Biography*, II (New York, 1931), 356; G. T. Harding III to R. B. Harris, July 26, 1937, Harris Papers, Box 9, Folder 1; *New York Times*, June 11, 1921, p. 3.

89. HMD to R. B. Harris, July 7, 1936, Harris Papers, Box 9, Folder 4; G. B. Harris to HMD, August 7, 1935, *ibid.* Mark Sullivan leaves the impression that Mrs. Harding was *against* his filing for the Senate, *Our Times*, VI, 45–48.

90. HMD to Cyril Clemens, June 20, 1940, Clemens Papers, Box 1.

91. Sullivan, *Our Times*, VI, 35–36.

92. *New York Times*, February 21, 1920, p. 3.

93. For the complete version of this undocumented and unsubstantiated story, as well as an exaggerated picture of Harvey's preconvention and convention role, see Willis F. Johnson, *George Harvey: A Passionate Patriot* (Boston, 1929), 273–281. For an elaborate repetition of this account see Sullivan, *Our Times*, VI, 59–64.

94. "Reminiscences of James W. Wadsworth," 271.

95. J. Wadsworth to R. B. Harris, October 8, 1932, Harris Papers, Box 2, Folder 6.

96. Daugherty was keenly aware of this senatorial antipathy to Harding and regarded it as one of the chief obstacles to a Harding nomination. See HMD to R. B. Harris, June 29, 1938, Harris Papers, Box 9, Folder 3.

97. J. Wadsworth to R. B. Harris, October 8, 1932, Harris Papers, Box 2, Folder 6.

98. Bagby, "The 'Smoke-Filled Room' and the Nomination of Warren G. Harding," 664.

99. James Watson to Cyril Clemens, October 26, 1939, Clemens Papers, Box 3.

100. HMD to R. B. Harris, June 30, 1939, Harris Papers, Box 9, Folder 5. The best account of the "smoke-filled room" episode is in Ray B. Harris, *Warren G. Harding: An Account of His Nomination for the Presidency by the Republican Convention of 1920* (Washington, D.C., 1957). Also excellent is Bagby, "The 'Smoke-Filled Room' and the Nomination of Warren G. Harding," 657–674.

101. "How the Press Size up Harding," *Literary Digest*, LXV, No. 13 (June 26, 1920), 13, quoting *New York Evening World*.

102. For a demolition of the "oligarchy" myth by one of its own members, see Harry S. New, "The Senatorial Oligarchy," *Saturday Evening Post*, CCIV (May 28, 1932), 84. For Penrose's role see Bagby, "The 'Smoke-Filled Room' and the Nomination of Warren G. Harding," 669; HMD to R. B. Harris, May 24, 1934, Harris Papers, Box 9, Folder 3. Precise details vary somewhat in these accounts.

103. There are various versions of the Coolidge nomination. The significant fact is that he was not Harding's personal choice. Hiram Johnson later claimed Harding

offered him the vice-presidency. This is doubtful. See "Reminiscences of Albert D. Lasker" (Oral History Research Office, Columbia University), 130–131; Johnson to Cyril Clemens, September 19, 1942, Clemens Papers, Box 2; and Hagedorn, *Leonard Wood*, II, 362. The best evidence indicates that Harding was prepared to go along with Lenroot.

104. The chief popularizer of the "money and oil deal" theory was William Allen White. See his *Autobiography*, 584, and his *Masks in a Pageant*, 407. Hamon's convention role is told in Daugherty, *The Inside Story*, 32–40, and Reily, "Years of Confusion," 179–183. For recent refutations of the oil deal charges see Bagby, "The 'Smoke-Filled Room' and the Nomination of Warren G. Harding," 670–671, and Burl Noggle, *Teapot Dome: Oil and Politics in the 1920's* (Baton Rouge, 1962), 2–4, 141–143.

105. "Reminiscences of James W. Wadsworth," 275; James Wadsworth to Cyril Clemens, November 14, 1947, Clemens Papers, Box 3.

106. *New York Times*, June 13, 1920, p. 5, quoting various newspapers.

107. *Atlanta Constitution*, June 13, 1920, Section C, p. 4.

CHAPTER II. NOT NOSTRUMS BUT NORMALCY

1. James M. Cox, *Journey through My Years* (New York, 1946), 229–231; Wesley M. Bagby, "Woodrow Wilson, a Third Term, and the Solemn Referendum," *AHR*, LX, No. 3 (April 1955), 567–575. An assessment of Cox as governor is in Warner, *Progressivism in Ohio*, 385–435. For FDR see Frank Freidel, *Franklin D. Roosevelt: The Ordeal* (Boston, 1954), 51–69.

2. Sinclair, *The Available Man*, 152.

3. Sullivan, *Our Times*, VI, 106.

4. For the full text of the speech see *Republican Campaign Text-Book, 1920* (New York, 1920), 37–40.

5. *New York Times*, July 23, 1920, p. 2, quoting various newspapers and Senator Johnson.

6. Democratic National Committee, *Governor Cox's Speech, August 7, 1920* (n.p., 1920). See also Cox, *Journey through My Years*, 266.

7. White to WGH, July 10, 1920, HP, Box 536, Folder 4220-1, items 244710–244712.

8. *New York Times*, July 2, 1920, p. 5; Hagedorn, *Leonard Wood*, II, 373; Raymond Robins to WGH, July 17, 1920, HP, Box 579, Folder 4382-1, items 263660–263774.

9. Bagby, *The Road to Normalcy*, 123; "Reminiscences of Albert D. Lasker," 132–133; "The 'Little Presbyterian Elder' in the Cabinet," *Literary Digest*, LXIX, No. 12 (June 18, 1921), 36–38.

10. HMD to WGH, July 1, 1920, HP, Box 763, Folder 3, items 184162–184163.

11. For press rumors that Hays and Daugherty were not compatible see *New York Times*, June 20, 1920, p. 1.

12. For early Wallace-Harding contacts see HP, Box 533, Folder 4197-1, especially items 243784 and 243793.

13. Daugherty, *The Inside Story*, 57–58. Mrs. Harding to Evalyn McLean, October 31, 1920, HP, Box 789, Folder 1, item unnumbered.

14. This correspondence is in HP, Boxes 498–692, 777–778, 782–788, 792.

15. Cox makes such a charge in Cox, *Journey through My Years*, 272.

16. Edge to WGH, June 14, 1920, HP, Box 559, Folder 4320-1, items 254906–254907.

17. *New York Times*, June 14, 1920, p. 2.

18. See *ibid.*, issues July 11, 1920, p. 1; July 12, 1920, p. 2.

19. See Lasker letters, HP, Box 520, Folder 4137-1, and Box 559, Folder 4354-1, items 260040–260046.

20. Reily, "Years of Confusion," 308.

21. Sinclair, *The Available Man*, 164.

22. White to WGH, October 5, 1920, HP, Box 536, Folder 4220-1, item 244703.

23. Clinton Gilbert, *Behind the Mirrors: The Psychology of Disintegration at Washington* (New York, 1922), 145. See also "Front Porching with Harding," *Nation*, CXI (September 25, 1920), 342–343. Samples of tailoring remarks for delegations are in HP, Box 501, Folder 3991-1 and 3991-2.

24. Lodge to WGH, July 8, 1920, HP, Box 544, Folder 4270-1, item 248019; Lodge to WGH, July 15, 1920, HP, Box 544, Folder 4270-1, item 248027. See also WGH to Edge, June 22, 1920, HP, Box 559, Folder 4320-1, item 254908.

25. WGH to Dover, August 6, 1920, HP, Box 501, Folder 3991-2, items 231489–231491.

26. Joel F. Paschal, *Mr. Justice Sutherland: A Man against the State* (Princeton, N.J., 1951), 106.

27. Hoover to WGH, August 2, 1920, HP, Box 502, Folder 3995-2, items 231918–231920; WGH to Hoover, August 7, 1920, *ibid.*

28. Lodge-Harding correspondence in HP, Box 544, Folder 4270-1.

29. Harding's request for Knox's advice is in WGH to Knox, August 10, 1920, Philander C. Knox Papers (Library of Congress), Vol. 23; Johnson, *George Harvey*, 281; Hiram Johnson to WGH, HP, Box 502, Folder 3997-1, item 232039.

30. WGH to Brandegee, August 10, 1920, HP, Box 694, Folder 1, item 148689.

31. See Herbert C. Hoover Papers (Hoover Presidential Library, West Branch, Iowa), Box AK I-7 and Box 1-Q/89.

32. Various letters, Elihu Root to Lodge, Elihu Root Papers (Library of Congress), Box 161, Folders "1919" and "1920"; Root to Harvey, no date, HP, Box 421, Folder 3245-1, item 198437.

33. For various Taft letters to Harding see HP, Box 448, Folder 3619-1, items 209550–209564.

34. *Speeches of Senator Warren G. Harding from His Acceptance of the Nomination to October 1, 1920* (n.p., n.d.), 92–93, 94.

35. Lodge to WGH, August 28, 1920, HP, Box 700, Folder 1, item 151742; Weeks to WGH, August 29, 1920, HP, Box 546, Folder 4277-1, item 248882; White to WGH, September 10, 1920, HP, Box 536, Folder 4220-1, item 244705; Herbert Hoover to a friend, September 2, 1920, Hoover Papers, Box AK I-7.

36. WGH to F. H. Gillett, August 30, 1920, HP, Box 543, Folder 4267-1, item 247579.

37. WGH to Hiram Johnson, September 6, 1920, HP, Box 502, Folder 3997-2, item 232652.

38. Fall to WGH, September 20, 1920, HP, Box 696, Folder 1, items 149780–149783.

39. Hoover to WGH, September 27, 1920, HP, Box 573, Folder 4360-2, items 260915–260916.

40. *New York Times*, September 21, 1920, p. 7.

41. "Reminiscences of Albert D. Lasker," 133a.

42. *New York Times*, October 8, 1920, p. 1.

43. *Ibid.*, October 12, 1920, p. 3.

44. Hoover to Hays, October 23, 1920, Hays Papers.

45. Crissey, *Theodore E. Burton*, 269–270.

46. *New York Times*, October 15, 1920, pp. 1–2.

47. Johnson, *George Harvey*, 280, quoting letter from WGH dated October 25, 1920.

48. WGH to F. H. Gillett, August 9, 1920, HP, Box 543, Folder 4267-1, items 247577–247578.

49. Cox, *Journey through My Years*, 271.

50. Allan Nevins, ed., *The Letters of Brand Whitlock* (New York, 1936), 309.

51. The quotations are from Lawrence W. Levine, *Defender of the Faith; William Jennings Bryan: The Last Decade, 1915–1925* (New York, 1965), 176–177, and Nevins, ed., *The Letters of Brand Whitlock*, 304.

52. Coolidge to WGH, September 14, 1920, HP, Box 536, Folder 4265-1, item 247322.

53. Comments are in Reily to WGH, September 23, 1920, HP, Box 555, Folder 4308-1, item 253069; Dover to WGH, October 9, 1920, HP, Box 501, Folder 3991-1, items 231467–231468; Penrose to WGH, October 11, 1920, HP, Box 617, Folder 4513-1, item 282712; Forbes to WGH, October 12, 1920, HP, Box 628, Folder 4555-1, item 287793; Hays to W. H. King, October 29, 1920, Hays Papers.

54. Sullivan to Walsh, September 17, 1920, Thomas J. Walsh Papers (Library of Congress), Box 373.

55. For Daugherty's fears see HMD to Reily, September 25, 1920, Daugherty Papers.

56. For the panic among local workers see George H. Clark to Hard, October 13, 1920, Hard Papers, Box 2, Folder 1. Although a Democrat, Edward L. Doheny, the oil millionaire, helped raise money for full-page portraits of Harding's parents to refute the Negro-blood story. See James E. Pollard, *The Presidents and the Press* (New York, 1947), 700–701.

57. Evalyn Walsh McLean, *Father Struck It Rich* (Boston, 1936), 242.

58. Comment on George H. Clark's letter to Charles Hard, October 13, 1920, Hard Papers, Box 2, Folder 1.

59. Michelson, *The Ghost Talks*, 227.

60. Mrs. Harding to Mrs. Harry New, November 2, 1920, HP, Box 789, Folder 1, unnumbered; see also Daugherty, *The Inside Story*, 61–62.

61. Francis Russell, *The Great Interlude: Neglected Events and Persons from the First World War to the Depression* (New York, 1964), 61.

62. For the best coverage of the Negro-blood story see Randolph C. Downes, "Negro Rights and White Backlash in the Campaign of 1920," *Ohio History*, LXXV, Nos. 2–3 (Spring–Summer 1966), 85–107.

63. Mrs. Harding to George Harvey, October 25, 1920, HP, Box 353, Folder 2521-1, item 146753; Mrs. Harding to a friend, October 25, 1920, HP, Box 353, Folder 2521-1, item 146749.

64. *New York Times*, November 3, 1920, p. 1; Freidel, *Franklin D. Roosevelt: The Ordeal*, 91. The Roosevelt statement did not seem so humorous against the backdrop of his fight for life at Campobello less than a year later.

65. Under state laws 17,500,000 women already had the suffrage.

66. The various figures are from Bagby, *The Road to Normalcy*, 130; James K. Pollock, *Party Campaign Funds* (New York, 1926), 27; and *New York Times*, November 12, 1920, p. 32.

67. *New York Times*, November 12, 1920, p. 32. This deficit ultimately was partially liquidated by tainted Teapot Dome oil money.

68. Pollock, *Party Campaign Funds*, 111–142, especially 127–128.

69. Hoover to Mrs. Robert A. Burdette, September 29, 1920, Hoover Papers, Box AK I-7.

70. Bagby, *The Road to Normalcy*, 160, quoting the *New York Post* and the *New York Tribune*.

71. William G. McAdoo, *Crowded Years: The Reminiscences of William G. Mc-Adoo* (Boston, 1931), 388–389.

72. *New York Times*, July 21, 1920, p. 7. Confusion still exists on how the word "normalcy" originated. The best guess is that Harding meant normality but said normalcy.

CHAPTER III. THE WILSON LEGACY

1. "Wilson's Legacy to Harding," *Nation*, CXII (February 23, 1921), 282–283.

2. Hutchinson, *Lowden of Illinois*, II, 397.

3. The story of demobilization is in Benedict Crowell and Robert F. Wilson, *Demobilization: Our Industrial and Military Demobilization after the Armistice, 1918–1920* (New Haven, 1921); Paul A. Samuelson and Everett E. Hagen, *After the War, 1918–1920: Military and Economic Demobilization of the United States* (n.p., 1943); and James R. Mock and Evangeline Thurber, *Report on Demobilization* (Norman, Okl., 1944).

4. Mock and Thurber, *Report on Demobilization*, 100; Samuelson and Hagen, *After the War*, 5 and fn. 1 and 2.

5. Mock and Thurber, *Report on Demobilization*, 109–110.

6. *Ibid.*, 95.

7. Seward W. Livermore, *Politics Is Adjourned: Woodrow Wilson and the War Congress, 1916–1918* (Middleton, Conn., 1966), *passim*. This book explodes the myth that a wartime truce existed between Republicans and Democrats.

8. Mock and Thurber, *Report on Demobilization*, 40–83, 151–157, 168, 174–181; also National Industrial Conference Board, *Problems of Industrial Readjustment in the United States* (Report No. 15, Boston, 1919).

9. Gene Smith, *When the Cheering Stopped: The Last Years of Woodrow Wilson* (New York, Time edition, 1966). This is the best work on this subject and handles Wilson's illness exhaustively.

10. *Ibid.*, 92.

11. *Ibid.*, 153.

12. *Ibid.*, 107.

13. *Ibid.*, 126–128.

14. *Ibid.*, 116, 119.

15. *Ibid.*, 119.

16. *Ibid.*, 137.

17. *Ibid.*, 149. The degree of ineffectiveness was indicated by Joseph C. Grew, minister to Denmark, who complained that the only instruction he got from Colby's State Department was "Don't send in too much stuff."

18. *Ibid.*, 152.

19. Edward G. Lowry, "Before the Curtain Rises," *New Republic*, XXV, No. 325 (February 23, 1921), 374.

20. Smith, *When the Cheering Stopped*, 161.

21. *Washington Post*, March 4, 1921, p. 10.

22. Wilson F. Payne, *Business Behavior, 1919–1922: An Account of Post-War Inflation and Depression* (in *Studies in Business Administration*, University of Chicago, XII, No. 4, Chicago, 1942), 207; John D. Hicks, *Rehearsal for Disaster* (Gainesville, Fla., 1961), 1–32; Samuelson and Hagen, *After the War*, 15–35; George Soule, *Prosperity Decade: From War to Depression, 1917–1929* (New York, 1947), 81–95.

23. For statistics see National Industrial Conference Board, *Changes in the Cost of Living, July, 1914–March, 1922* (Report No. 49, New York, 1922), 31, 33; cf.

Paul H. Douglas, *Real Wages in the United States, 1890–1926* (Cambridge, Mass., 1930), 55. The latter used Bureau of Labor statistics in which December 1914 represented 100. On this index, the cost of living in December 1918 was 169.3 and in June 1920 was 210.2. For the reliability of these various figures see Douglas, *Real Wages in the United States*, 49–51.

24. Disagreement exists among authorities over the low point; some say July or August 1921, others March 1922. Close agreement exists on the percentage decline in prices and cost of living. National Industrial Conference Board, *Changes in the Cost of Living, July, 1914–July, 1923* (Report No. 63, New York, 1923), viii, 4; National Industrial Conference Board, *Changes in the Cost of Living, July, 1914–March, 1922*, 31, 33; Douglas, *Real Wages in the United States*, 58–59.

25. Hicks, *Rehearsal for Disaster*, 65; James H. Shideler, *Farm Crisis, 1919–1923* (Berkeley, 1957), 11, 15, 19. This last work is the best on the postwar farm crisis.

26. Shideler, *Farm Crisis*, 46; R. R. Enfield, *The Agricultural Crisis, 1920–1923* (London, 1924), 3–5; Hicks, *Rehearsal for Disaster*, 78–79.

27. Daniel J. Ahearn, *The Wages of Farm and Factory Laborers, 1914–1944* (in *Studies in History, Economics and Public Law*, No. 518, Columbia University, New York, 1945), 91; Soule, *Prosperity Decade*, 96, 99–100; Kenneth C. MacKay, *The Progressive Movement of 1924* (in *Studies in History, Economics and Public Law*, No. 527, Columbia University, New York, 1947), 41–42; Hicks, *Rehearsal for Disaster*, 70–71, 73, 80.

28. National Industrial Conference Board, *Wages, Hours, and Employment in American Manufacturing Industries, July, 1914–July, 1923* (Report No. 62, New York, 1923), 33, Chart I; Douglas, *Real Wages in the United States*, 241–243, 382–383, 386; Ahearn, *The Wages of Farm and Factory Laborers*, 128–129, 223.

29. National Industrial Conference Board, *The Unemployment Problem* (Report No. 43, New York, 1921), 9–10; Douglas, *Real Wages in the United States*, 408; Soule, *Prosperity Decade*, 96; National Industrial Conference Board, *Wages in the United States, 1914–1930* (New York, 1931), 208.

30. Mock and Thurber, *Report on Demobilization*, 28–29.

31. For a complete analysis of the Red Scare see Murray, *Red Scare*. For the steel strike see Robert K. Murray, "Communism and the Great Steel Strike of 1919," *MVHR*, XXXVIII, No. 3 (December 1951), 445–465. For the Centralia Massacre see Robert K. Murray, "Centralia: An Unfinished American Tragedy," *Northwest Review*, VI, No. 2 (Spring 1963), 7–18.

32. For an interesting analysis see Arthur S. Link, "What Happened to the Progressive Movement in the 1920's?" *AHR*, LXIV, No. 4 (July 1959), 839.

33. Paul Sann, *The Lawless Decade: A Pictorial History of a Great American Transition* (New York, 1957), 64.

34. "Wilson's Legacy to Harding," *Nation*, CXII (February 23, 1921), 282–283; Nevins, ed., *The Letters of Brand Whitlock*, 321; and Edmund W. Starling, *Starling of the White House* (New York, 1946), 174.

CHAPTER IV. THE NEW ADMINISTRATION BEGINS

1. Portions of this chapter were first published as Robert K. Murray, "President Harding and His Cabinet," *Ohio History*, LXXV, Nos. 2–3 (Spring–Summer 1966), 108–125.

2. Ten other presidents served in the Senate but no other president was currently a senator when elected president. *Cong. Record*, 66 Cong., 3 Sess., 4.

3. Fola and Belle LaFollette, *Robert M. LaFollette*, II (New York, 1953), 1020.

4. *New York Times*, February 22, 1921, p. 1.

5. Invitations, arrangements, etc., in HP, Box 405, Folder 3089-1.

6. WGH to Jennings, December 14, 1920, Jennings Papers; WGH to Mr. Leffing-well, January 12, 1921, HP, Box 360, Folder 2563, item 170935; Butler, *Across the Busy Years*, I, 403.

7. These were Harding's views as of December 18, 1920. In an article entitled "The Men of the Cabinet," *World's Work*, LXII, No. 1 (May 1921), 81, Mark Sullivan claimed that "If Harding had chosen his Cabinet the day after his election, it would have been much more clearly a Cabinet of politicians than it now is." No doubt the Marion discussions influenced Harding in a number of ways, but it is an exaggeration to say that Harding changed his whole view of cabinet making in a little over three weeks' time.

8. See *Our Times*, VI, 147, n. 7.

9. Hughes to WGH, December 13, 1920, Charles E. Hughes Papers (Library of Congress), Box 4A, Folder "1920"; Hughes to R. B. Harris, April 3, 1934, Harris Papers, Box 4, Folder 4.

10. Claudius O. Johnson, *Borah of Idaho* (New York, 1936), 258; Jessup, *Elihu Root*, II, 415; *New York Times*, January 20, 1921, p. 1, and January 22, 1921, p. 1. Butler's contention in his *Across the Busy Years*, I, 397, 403, that Harding offered the post to him on December 18 is erroneous. So also is Johnson's statement in *George Harvey*, 282, that Harding offered the job to Harvey.

11. WGH to Wallace, November 1, 1920, HP, Box 535, Folder 4197-1, item 243803.

12. For an able discussion of Wallace see Russell Lord, *The Wallaces of Iowa* (Boston, 1947), 214–215.

13. Brandegee to WGH, December 28, 1920, HP, Box 694, Folder 1, item 148691.

14. *New York Times*, January 19, 1921, p. 2; New to WGH, December 22, 1920, HP, Box 701, Folder 8, items 152559–152560; WGH to HMD, February 9, 1921, HP, Box 368, Folder 2601-1, item 174897; also Box 695, Folder 1, items 149279–149283.

15. WGH to Hoover, HP, Box 389, Folder 2865-1, item 184821.

16. WGH to HMD, February 9, 1921, HP, Box 368, Folder 2601-1, items 174897–174900.

17. Hughes Papers, Box 173, Folder 45, Beerits memo, "Fall Scandals," p. 1; telegram from Hoover to WGH, February 23, 1921, Hoover Papers, Box AK I-7. To take the Commerce post Hoover turned down an offer from Daniel Guggenheim of a full partnership and a guaranteed income of $500,000 a year. See Eugene Lyons, *Herbert Hoover: A Biography* (New York, 1964), 144.

18. Henry L. Stoddard, *As I Knew Them: Presidents and Politics from Grant to Coolidge* (New York, 1927), 521–522; Bascom N. Timmons, *Portrait of an American: Charles G. Dawes* (New York, 1953), 201; Charles G. Dawes, *The First Year of the Budget of the United States* (New York, 1923), 1.

19. Philip H. Love, *Andrew W. Mellon: The Man and His Work* (Baltimore, 1929), 33–37; Harvey O'Connor, *Mellon's Millions: The Biography of a Fortune* (New York, 1933), 117–119; Mellon to R. B. Harris, Harris Papers, Box 4, Folder 4.

20. Lyons, *Hoover*, 144; Stoddard, *As I Knew Them*, 521–522; for the clearest account see Daugherty, *The Inside Story*, 92–100. As an example of how badly facts can be garbled see Karl Schriftgiesser, *This Was Normalcy: An Account of Party Politics during Twelve Republican Years, 1920–1932* (Boston, 1948), 85.

21. Timmons, *Dawes*, 203.

22. For problems relating to Mellon's acceptance see Love, *Mellon*, 35–37; Knox Papers, Box 7, various letters; Mellon to R. B. Harris, Harris Papers, Box 4, Folder 4; O'Connor, *Mellon's Millions*, 109, 121.

23. Wallace to WGH, February 10, 1921, HP, Box 655, Folder 4714-1, item 300357. See also Hagedorn, *Wood*, II, 374–375; *New York Times*, February 16, 1921, p. 1.

24. Lodge to WGH, December 24, 1920, HP, Box 655, Folder 4715-1. See also Box 487, Folder 3944-1, numerous items.

25. New to WGH, December 22, 1920, HP, Box 701, Folder 8, items 152559–152560.

26. Wadsworth to WGH, January 22, 1921, HP, Box 655, Folder 4715-1, items 300425–300429.

27. James J. Davis, *The Iron Puddler: My Life in the Rolling Mills and What Came of It* (Indianapolis, 1922), Introduction. Also James J. Davis Papers (Library of Congress), Box 38, Book I, p. 214. See HP, Box 486, Folder 3932-1, endorsements for Davis.

28. Davis to R. B. Harris, April 2, 1934, Harris Papers, Box 4, Folder 7.

29. Telegram from Gompers to WGH, February 7, 1921, HP, Box 656, Folder 4720-1, items 300952–300954.

30. Wadsworth to R. B. Harris, June 20, 1938, Harris Papers, Box 2, Folder 6. Schriftgiesser in his *This Was Normalcy*, 88, conjures up the myth that Harding wanted to appoint Charles M. Schwab as secretary of labor.

31. Hays to WGH, February 4, 1921, HP, Box 655, Folder 4716-1, item 300586; WGH to Hays, February 9, 1921, Hays Papers.

32. Hutchinson, *Lowden of Illinois*, II, 484–485, and 485 n. 5.

33. Sullivan, *Our Times*, VI, 295–296; "Denby, the 'Dark Horse' of the Harding Cabinet," *Current Opinion*, LXX, No. 4 (April 1921), 471–473; *New York Times*, February 27, 1921, p. 1.

34. "A Cabinet Member Whose Life Story Reads Like a Dime Novel," *Current Opinion*, LXXI, No. 1 (July 1921), 34–36. Various issues of *New York Times*, January 27–February 1, 1921, especially January 28, 1921, p. 1. See also *New York Times*, March 2, 1921, p. 1.

35. Shaw to R. B. Harris, November 19, 1933, Harris Papers, Box 3, Folder 4. For early conservation opposition to Fall see Noggle, *Teapot Dome*, 6–30.

36. Wadsworth to R. B. Harris, June 20, 1938, Harris Papers, Box 2, Folder 6.

37. This quotation and Mark Sullivan's account of Daugherty's appointment is in *Our Times*, VI, 147–152.

38. Finley Peter Dunne, "A Look at Harding from the Side Lines," *Saturday Evening Post*, CCIX, No. 11 (September 12, 1936), 76.

39. Sullivan, *Our Times*, VI, 151. Sullivan claims Harding added: "You can set that up in a block on your first page." Actually, this was said by Harding in a different connection and did not relate to Daugherty's appointment. See *New York Times*, February 22, 1921, p. 1.

40. *New York Times*, February 22, 1921, p. 1.

41. Sullivan, *Our Times*, VI, 152.

42. *Ibid.*, 150.

43. *Ibid.*

44. *Ibid.*, n. 9.

45. For Daugherty's own story of his selection see Daugherty, *The Inside Story*, 85–91.

46. Sullivan, "The Men of the Cabinet," 81.

47. William B. Munro, "Two Years of President Harding" *Atlantic Monthly*, CXXXI, No. 3 (March 1923), 384–393.

48. WGH to McLean, January 2, 1921, HP, Box 476, Folder 3853-1, item 221328.

49. Starling, *Starling of the White House*, 163; Josephus Daniels, *The Wilson Era: Years of War and After, 1917–1923* (Chapel Hill, 1946), 587–588.

50. Daniels, *The Wilson Era*, 587–588; Starling, *Starling of the White House*, 164; Smith, *When the Cheering Stopped*, 166, 172–177. Wilson's statement on Harding is in Clemens Papers, Box 2, recollections of Bishop James E. Freeman.

51. Every newspaper carried full accounts of the inauguration ceremonies and Harding's address.

52. *New York Times*, March 5, 1921, p. 12.

53. Elbert F. Baldwin, "Exit Wilson: Enter Harding," *Outlook*, CXXVII, No. 12 (March 16, 1921), 415.

54. *New York Times*, March 5, 1921, p. 1; Johnson, *Borah of Idaho*, 288; La-Follette and LaFollette, *Robert M. LaFollette*, II, 1024.

55. Mary Randolph, *Presidents and First Ladies* (New York, 1936), 229.

56. The quotation is from Clinton Gilbert, *The Mirrors of Washington* (New York, 1921), 6; Edward G. Lowry, *Washington Close-Ups: Intimate Views of Some Public Figures* (Boston, 1921), 14–15.

57. Lowry, *Washington Close-Ups*, 21–22; Pollard, *The Presidents and the Press*, 703–705, 712.

58. Pollard, *The Presidents and the Press*, 701, 708; WGH to Raymond T. Clapper, no date, HP, Box 354, Folder 2524-1, item 147022.

59. Sullivan, *Our Times*, VI, 102, n. 10.

60. Starling, *Starling of the White House*, 175.

61. Irwin H. Hoover, *Forty-Two Years in the White House* (Boston, 1934), 254–255; "Reminiscences of James W. Wadsworth," 142; HMD to Cyril Clemens, April 29, 1940, Clemens Papers, Box 1.

62. Hoover, *Forty-Two Years in the White House*, 249–250; Herbert Hoover, *The Memoirs of Herbert Hoover: The Cabinet and the Presidency, 1920–1933* (New York, 1952), II, 48.

63. Sullivan, *Our Times*, VI, 100.

64. Starling, *Starling of the White House*, 169.

65. Mrs. E. J. Parmelee to WGH, March 28, 1921, HP, item 78181.

66. W. D. Hines to Cyril Clemens, July 31, 1939, Clemens Papers, Box 2.

67. HMD to Cyril Clemens, October 25, 1938, Clemens Papers, Box 1; Starling, *Starling of the White House*, 169; Sullivan, *Our Times*, VI, 244.

68. Starling, *Starling of the White House*, 174; Sullivan, *Our Times*, VI, 103.

69. There are 36 boxes and crates of Harding's books in the Ohio Historical Society Library, besides those still on the shelves in his Marion home. Many of these were complimentary copies which he obviously never read. The library in his home runs to history and biography.

70. "Reminiscences of James W. Wadsworth," 142.

71. Sullivan, *Our Times*, VI, 417, quoting Mencken; Houston, *Eight Years with Wilson's Cabinet*, II, 148, quoting Wilson.

72. Reily, "Years of Confusion," 195; John Barrett to Cyril Clemens, August 18, 1938, Clemens Papers, Box 1; Calvin Coolidge, *The Autobiography of Calvin Coolidge* (New York, 1929), 158; *New York Times*, April 24, 1921, Section II, p. 2.

73. Mark Sullivan, *The Great Adventure at Washington: The Story of the Conference* (New York, 1922), 225.

74. James E. Watson, *As I Knew Them* (New York, 1936), 226.

75. Michelson, *The Ghost Talks*, 229.

76. Davis to Cyril Clemens, June 29, 1939, Clemens Papers, Box 1.

77. *New York Times*, March 18, 1921, p. 2, and March 20, 1921, p. 1.

78. *New York Times*, March 22, 1921, p. 1.

79. For the complete text of Harding's message see Warren G. Harding, *Speeches as President* (Columbus, Ohio, n.d.), "Address of the President of the United States, April 12, 1921," pp. 3–19.

80. Walter Lippmann, *Men of Destiny* (New York, 1928), 109.

81. Harding, *Speeches as President*, "Address of the President of the United States, April 12, 1921," p. 17.

82. WGH to Malcolm Jennings, July 14, 1921, HP, Box 699, Folder 1, item 151332.

83. WGH to Jennings, January 6, 1922, Jennings Papers.

CHAPTER V. LIQUIDATING THE WAR

1. Gilbert, *Behind the Mirrors*, 150.

2. Gilbert, *The Mirrors of Washington*, 82–83.

3. For reporters' appreciation see Charles C. Hyde, "Charles Evans Hughes," in Samuel F. Bemis, ed., *The American Secretaries of State and Their Diplomacy*, X (New York, 1929), 259–260. See also Merlo J. Pusey, *Charles Evans Hughes*, II (New York, 1951), 423–424.

4. Graham H. Stuart, *The Department of State: A History of Its Organization, Procedure and Personnel* (New York, 1949), 278, quoting Brandeis.

5. Edward G. Lowry, "Mr. Harding Digging In," *New Republic*, XXVI, No. 337 (May 18, 1921), 342.

6. Hoover's comment in Hoover, *Memoirs*, II, 36.

7. Evidence for their relationship is found in HP, Boxes 42–45.

8. Deduced from evidence contained in HP. Cf. Pusey, *Charles Evans Hughes*, II.

9. Hughes to WGH, January 28, 1921, Hughes Papers, Box 4A, Folder "1921."

10. For Harvey's diplomatic career see Johnson, *George Harvey*.

11. Herrick's career is in T. Bentley Mott, *Myron T. Herrick: Friend of France* (New York, 1929).

12. Stuart, *The Department of State*, 262–263.

13. *Ibid.*, 264.

14. Pusey, *Charles Evans Hughes*, II, 411.

15. John A. Garraty, *Henry Cabot Lodge: A Biography* (New York, 1953), 399.

16. Paschal, *Mr. Justice Sutherland*, 107.

17. Taft to C. H. Kelsey, November 8, 1920, William H. Taft Papers (Library of Congress), Box 503.

18. Harding, *Speeches as President*, "Address of the President of the United States, April 12, 1921," p. 7.

19. Denna F. Fleming, *The United States and World Organization, 1920–1933* (New York, 1938), 76.

20. Hughes Papers, Box 172, Folder 25, Beerits memo, 14.

21. *Ibid.*, 16, 18.

22. Hughes to G. W. Wickersham, March 28, 1923, HP, Box 370, Folder 2608-1, items 175582–175598.

23. Smith, *When the Cheering Stopped*, xiv.

24. *Cong. Record*, 67 Cong., 1 Sess., 865, 2547, 3262, 3299.

25. Hughes Papers, Box 172, Folder 25, Beerits memo, 21a–21d; Pusey, *Charles Evans Hughes*, II, 440–444.

26. *Cong. Record*, 67 Cong., 1 Sess., 5769.

27. *Ibid.*, 5791.

28. *New York Times*, September 28, 1921, p. 1.

29. *Ibid.*, September 25, 1921, p. 1.

30. *Cong. Record*, 67 Cong., 1 Sess., 6438; *New York Times*, November 15, 1921, p. 21.

31. Background material on the naval race can be found in C. Leonard Hoag, *Preface to Preparedness: The Washington Disarmament Conference and Public Opinion* (Washington, D.C., 1941); Raymond L. Buell, *The Washington Conference* (New York, 1922); and Harold and Margaret Sprout, *Toward a New Order of Sea Power: American Naval Policy and the World Scene, 1918–1922* (Princeton, 1946).

32. WGH to Lodge, February 20, 1921, HP, Box 700, Folder 2, item 151802.

33. *Cong. Record*, 66 Cong., 3 Sess., 3171. Discussion of the congressional naval debate is in Sprout and Sprout, *Toward a New Order of Sea Power*, 88–149.

34. *New York Times*, February 18, 1921, p. 3, quoting Borah.

35. Press opinion is in Hoag, *Preface to Preparedness*, 41–43; John C. Vinson, *The Parchment Peace: The United States Senate and the Washington Conference, 1921–1922* (Athens, Ga., 1955), 80. Borah's personal crusade was but a part of a much larger and very vocal peace movement in the United States.

36. Butler, *Across the Busy Years*, I, 394; Sprout and Sprout, *Toward a New Order of Sea Power*, 123; Harding, *Speeches as President*, "Address of the President of the United States, April 12, 1921," p. 8.

37. WGH to Hoover, May 14, 1921, Hoover Papers, Box 1-I/242; memo from Hoover to WGH, May 11, 1921, HP, Box 5, Folder 3-1, item 2087.

38. Harding, *Speeches as President*, "Address of the President at Hoboken, N.J., May 23, 1921," p. 3.

39. WGH to Poindexter, May 14, 1921, HP, Box 368, Folder 2601, item 174876.

40. S. G. Porter to WGH, June 4, 1921, HP, Box 170, Folder 172-1, items 82030–82031.

41. WGH to Mondell, June 25, 1921, HP, Box 368, Folder 2601-1, items 174878–174879.

42. WGH to Raymond Robins, May 19, 1921, HP, Box 368, Folder 2601-1, item 174875.

43. WGH to F. W. Mondell, June 25, 1921, HP, Box 368, Folder 2601-1, items 174878–174879.

44. For this reason some authors have drawn erroneous conclusions. See Hoag, *Preface to Preparedness*, 62–63.

45. Yamato Ichihashi, *The Washington Conference and After* (Palo Alto, Calif., 1928), 6; Butler, *Across the Busy Years*, II, 130–139; other informal contacts are in Vinson, *The Parchment Peace*, 97–114.

46. The Imperial Council's discussions are analyzed in J. Bartlet Brebner, "Canada, the Anglo-Japanese Alliance and the Washington Conference," *Political Science Quarterly*, L, No. 1 (March 1935), 45–58; H. C. Allen, *Great Britain and the United States: A History of Anglo-American Relations, 1783–1952* (New York, 1955), 734–735; Sprout and Sprout, *Toward a New Order of Sea Power*, 88–103; Vinson, *The Parchment Peace*, 104–108.

47. Hughes Papers, Box 169, Folder 3, Beerits memo, 6–8; *U.S. Foreign Relations, 1921* (Washington, D.C., 1921), 18; Charles E. Hughes, *The Pathway of Peace: Representative Addresses Delivered during His Term as Secretary of State, 1921–1925* (New York, 1925), 34.

48. The best over-all treatment of these factors is found in Vinson, *The Parchment Peace*, especially 97–114.

49. *New York Times*, July 11, 1921, p. 10.

50. Johnson, *George Harvey*, 351–352.

51. The work of the Advisory Committee is discussed in Hoag, *Preface to Preparedness*, 126–141.

52. Harding, *Speeches as President*, "Address of the President of the United States, November 11, 1921," p. 6.

53. Sann, *The Lawless Decade*, 61, quoting Simpson.

54. Harding's speech is in *Conference on the Limitation of Armaments, Washington, November 12, 1921–February 6, 1922* (Washington, D.C., 1922), 44–48.

55. Allen, *Great Britain and the United States*, 737.

56. The complete text is in *Conference on the Limitation of Armaments*, 50–65.

57. White, *Autobiography*, 598.

58. Hughes's own description of Harding's role and of planning the "surprise" is in Hughes Papers, Box 170, Folder 10, "Treaty for the Limitation of Naval Armament," Beerits memo, 1–8. Not knowing of Harding's desire to center attention on Hughes, reporters were disappointed in the president's efforts on opening day. See White, *A Puritan in Babylon*, 233.

59. Hughes's statement is in his *The Pathway of Peace*, 32.

60. Full texts of all plenary sessions and treaties are in *Conference on the Limitation of Armaments*.

61. For early discussions see National Archives, Record Group 59, State Department Files, 741.9411/94, Harvey to Hughes, May 23, 1921; 741.9411/95, Harvey to Hughes, May 23, 1921; 741.9411/136A, Hughes to Harvey, July 6, 1921.

62. For the text of the Four-Power Treaty see *Conference on the Limitation of Armaments*, 1612–1616. Best on the Four-Power Treaty is J. Chal Vinson, "The Drafting of the Four Power Treaty of the Washington Conference," *Journal of Modern History*, XXV, No. 1 (March 1953), 40–47.

63. Rumors are aired in Sullivan, *The Great Adventure at Washington*, 204–205.

64. Hughes Papers, Box 169, Folder 7, "Four Power Treaty," Beerits memo, p. 29.

65. *U.S. Foreign Relations, 1922*, I, 45–48; *Conference on the Limitation of Armaments*, 1619–1620.

66. *Conference on the Limitation of Armaments*, 182–276, 340–356, 1368–1432.

67. The Yap Treaty is best treated in Ichihashi, *The Washington Conference and After*, 323–339; for the text of the Nine-Power Treaty see *Conference on the Limitation of Armaments*, 1621–1629.

68. Hearst opposition is in Hoag, *Preface to Preparedness*, 45; *Conference on the Limitation of Armaments*, 248, quoting Hughes; Ichihashi, *The Washington Conference*, 112, quoting Kato.

69. Harding's involvement is seen in HP, Boxes 43, 45.

70. Sullivan, *The Great Adventure at Washington*, 224–225.

71. *Conference on the Limitation of Armaments*, 404.

72. Harding, *Speeches as President*, "Address of the President of the United States, February 10, 1922," pp. 9–10.

73. *Cong. Record*, 67 Cong., 2 Sess., 3552, 3710–3713; *Literary Digest* poll in Hoag, *Preface to Preparedness*, 146; *Washington Post*, February 11, 1922, p. 6.

74. *New York Times*, December 17, 1921, p. 1, and December 22, 1921, p. 1.

75. *Ibid.*, January 5, 1922, p. 2.

76. John C. Vinson, *William E. Borah and the Outlawing of War* (Athens, Ga., 1957), 40. The best recent article analyzing Borah's motives is Robert J. Maddox, "William E. Borah and the Crusade to Outlaw War," *Historian*, XXIX, No. 2 (February 1967), 200–220.

77. *Cong. Record*, 67 Cong., 2 Sess., 2391–2392.

78. Johnson, *George Harvey*, 332.

79. Examples of the Senate debate are in *Cong. Record*, 67 Cong., 2 Sess., 3551–3552, 4486–4497; *New York Times*, March 9, 1922, p. 2.

80. *Cong. Record*, 67 Cong., 2 Sess., 4496–4497; comment by Johnson in *New York Times*, March 25, 1922, p. 10. Best on Four-Power Treaty debates is J. Chal Vinson, "The Parchment Peace: The Senate Defense of the Four Power Treaty of the Washington Conference," *MVHR*, XXXIX, No. 2 (September 1952), 303–314.

81. *New York Times*, March 21, 1922, p. 2, and March 25, 1922, p. 3; WGH to Harvey, March 22, 1922, HP, Box 361, Folder 2569-1, items 171552–171553.

82. WGH to Harvey, February 18, 1922, HP, Box 361, Folder 2569-1, item 171547.

83. William A. White, *Forty Years on Main Street* (New York, 1937), 244–245.

84. Allen, *Great Britain and the United States*, 739, 741–744; Mark Sullivan, "Afterthoughts on the Conference," *World's Work*, XLIII, No. 5 (April 1922), 596; Hughes Papers, Box 170, Folder 10, "Treaty for the Limitation of Naval Armament," Beerits memo, 35.

85. Henry M. Robinson, *Fantastic Interim: A Hindsight History of American Manners, Morals, and Mistakes between Versailles and Pearl Harbor* (New York, 1943), 55.

86. Jessup, *Elihu Root*, II, 465; Hughes, *The Pathway of Peace*, 6–9, 39–40.

87. "Silly pacifists" statement is in *New York Times*, October 24, 1922, p. 1. To the end Harding claimed that there were limits in reduction beyond which the administration would not go "even in the praiseworthy name of economy."

88. Latest work on Mitchell is Alfred F. Hurley, *Billy Mitchell: Crusader for Air Power* (New York, 1964). For Poindexter and Hicks see Samuel F. Wells, Jr., "William Mitchell and the *Ostfriesland*: A Study in Military Reform," *Historian*, XXVI, No. 4 (August 1964), 557; another recent general article is Lester H. Brune, "Foreign Policy and the Air Power Dispute, 1919–1932," *Historian*, XXIII, No. 4 (August 1961), 449–464.

89. Gerald E. Wheeler, *Prelude to Pearl Harbor: The United States Navy and the Far East, 1921–1931* (Columbia, Mo., n.d.), 71–80, 187–188. Best general treatment of the naval and military consequences of the Washington Conference is Sprout and Sprout, *Toward a New Order of Sea Power*, 122–296.

90. See HP, Box 363, Folder 2575-1, items 172236–172238. Also Vinson, *The Parchment Peace*, 140–148.

91. H. H. Kohlsaat, *From McKinley to Harding: Personal Recollections of Our Presidents* (New York, 1923), 232.

92. Ray Ginger, *The Bending Cross: A Biography of Eugene Victor Debs* (New Brunswick, N.J., 1949), 405.

93. J. Coxey, Sr., to WGH, March 30, 1921, HP, Box 154, Folder 111-1, items 74394–74395; Norman Thomas to WGH, March 12, 1921, HP, Box 154, Folder 111-2, items 74401–74402.

94. Ginger, *The Bending Cross*, 407–408.

95. *Ibid.*, 408; Sullivan, *Our Times*, VI, 216–219.

96. *New York Times*, February 2, 1921, p. 10, and August 28, 1921, Section II, p. 1.

97. HMD to WGH, December 17, 1921, HP, Box 154, Folder 111-2, items 74527–74528.

98. WGH to HMD, December 19, 1921, HP, Box 154, Folder 111-2, item 74531. Cf. Ginger, *The Bending Cross*, 412; Lincoln Steffens, *The Autobiography of Lincoln Steffens* (New York, 1931), 843–844.

99. Ginger, *The Bending Cross*, 415. For Daugherty's account of Debs's release see *The Inside Story*, 115–121. Debs's own account is in Eugene V. Debs, *Writings and Speeches of Eugene V. Debs* (New York, 1948), 468–472. Samuel Gompers exaggerated his role in Debs's release in his *Seventy Years of Life and Labor: An Autobiography*, II (New York, 1925), 416.

100. *New York Times*, December 26, 1921, p. 12; Malcolm Jennings to WGH, no date, HP, Box 699, Folder 1, item 151318; WGH to Malcolm Jennings, January 6, 1922, Jennings Papers.

CHAPTER VI. RESTORING PROSPERITY

1. Editorial, *Emporia Gazette*, October 8, 1922; White, *Masks in a Pageant*, 428.

2. *New York Times*, February 26, 1920, p. 25.

3. WGH, "Less Government in Business and More Business in Government," *World's Work*, XLI, No. 1 (November 1920), 26.

4. *Wall Street Journal*, March 5, 1921, p. 1; Harding, *Speeches as President*, "Address of the President of the United States, April 12, 1921," p. 6.

5. For statistics see Committee on Public Debt Policy, *Our National Debt: Its History and Its Meaning Today* (New York, 1949), 9–10, 24, 168, Appendix Table 10; National Industrial Conference Board, *Tax Burdens and Exemptions* (Report No. 64, New York, 1923), 16.

6. W. F. Willoughby, *The National Budget System: With Suggestions for Its Improvement* (in *Studies in Administration*, Institute for Government Research, Baltimore, 1927), 4–31, 32, n. 10. For an excellent analysis of the Budget Act see Fritz M. Marx, "The Bureau of the Budget: Its Evolution and Present Role," *American Political Science Review*, XXXIX, No. 4 (August 1945), 653–684. See also 42 *Statutes at Large* 20.

7. WGH to Charles Dawes, HP, June 9, 1921, Box 695, Folder 4, item 149397.

8. Sullivan, *Our Times*, VI, 205. Timmons in *Charles G. Dawes*, 193, states that Dawes may have said "Helen Maria." The public liked "Hell and Maria" better.

9. A contemporary view of Dawes is found in Donald Wilhelm, "Wielding the Budget Broom in Washington," *Independent*, CVI, No. 3782 (September 3, 1921), 91–92.

10. Timmons, *Charles G. Dawes*, 203; *New York Times*, June 24, 1921, p. 1, quoting Dawes.

11. Timmons, *Charles G. Dawes*, 204–205; Dawes, *The First Year of the Budget*, 2.

12. Dawes, *The First Year of the Budget*, 4; Timmons, *Charles G. Dawes*, 206; Sullivan, *Our Times*, VI, 209, quoting Harding.

13. On Harding's pique at disagreements see HP, Box 38, Folder 19-7, items 17859–17861.

14. Dawes, *The First Year of the Budget*, 86–87, 96. *New York Times*, December 6, 1921, p. 1. Dawes's first report is *Report to the President of the United States by the Director of the Bureau of the Budget* (Washington, D.C., 1922).

15. Dawes, *The First Year of the Budget*, 94.

16. *Commercial and Financial Chronicle*, December 10, 1921.

17. Dawes, *The First Year of the Budget*, 164–165.

18. *New York Times*, February 4, 1922, p. 1.

19. Figures vary slightly depending on the sources consulted. Statistics here are from Dawes, *The First Year of the Budget*, 86, n. 1. Timmons, *Charles G. Dawes*, 209, gives a different set. See also the Committee on Public Debt Policy, *Our National Debt*, 168.

20. Dawes, *The First Year of the Budget*, 223.

21. *Ibid.*, 55, 69, 237.

22. WGH to HMD, HP, Box 29, Folder 10-7, item 12926.

23. *New York Times*, October 14, 1922, p. 1.

24. Love, *Andrew W. Mellon*, 33–34; O'Connor, *Mellon's Millions*, 121. Neither book is an adequate biography.

25. J. W. Harriman to WGH, HP, Box 697, Folder 1, item 150326.

26. "Mr. Mellon," *Outlook*, CXXVIII, No. 12 (July 20, 1921), 472–473; Hoover, *Memoirs*, II, 60.

27. Gilbert, *Behind the Mirrors*, 111.

28. Lowry, *Washington Close-Ups*, 155–157; Thomas L. Stokes, *Chip Off My Shoulder* (Princeton, 1940), 75.

29. For example, O'Connor in *Mellon's Millions* claims that Mellon was "boss" of the Harding regime and that Harding was in "awe" of Mellon. For samples of the president's true reaction see HP, Box 46, Folder 21-1 and 21-2, various items.

30. Gilbert, *Behind the Mirrors*, 111–112.

31. For an insight into Mellon's views see Andrew W. Mellon, *Taxation: The People's Business* (New York, 1924), 9, 11, 16–21, 31.

32. Mellon's proposal is in HP, Box 46, Folder 2, items 21702–21710; also *Report of the Secretary of the Treasury, 1921* (Washington, D.C., 1922), 353–354.

33. Roy C. and Gladys Blakey, *The Federal Income Tax* (New York, 1940), 200, 204–206.

34. Arthur Mann, *La Guardia: A Fighter against His Times, 1882–1933* (Philadelphia, 1959), 235.

35. National Industrial Conference Board, *Tax Burdens and Exemptions*, 29, Table 10; 119, Table 31; 128.

36. White, *Autobiography*, 616.

37. *Cong. Record*, 67 Cong., 1 Sess., 3353.

38. Harding, *Speeches as President*, "Address of the President of the United States to the Senate, July 12, 1921," *passim*.

39. *New York Times*, July 14, 1921, p. 14.

40. *Ibid.*, September 4, 1920, p. 1, quoting *Stars and Stripes*.

41. Blakey and Blakey, *The Federal Income Tax*, 211; O'Connor, *Mellon's Millions*, 127.

42. *Cong. Record*, 67 Cong., 1 Sess., 7524.

43. *New York Times*, November 18, 1921, p. 1.

44. *Cong. Record*, 67 Cong., 1 Sess., 8175.

45. For a contemporary analysis see Roy G. Blakey, "The Revenue Act of 1921," *American Economic Review*, XII, No. 1 (March 1922), 75–108. Blakey claims that the smaller taxpayer was proportionately more benefited than the wealthy one by the law. O'Connor claims just the reverse and maintains that the Mellon interests saved one million dollars by its passage. O'Connor, *Mellon's Millions*, 129.

46. Blakey and Blakey, *The Federal Income Tax*, 218.

47. Hicks, *Rehearsal for Disaster*, 67, quoting *Wallace's Farmer*.

48. Gilbert, *Behind the Mirrors*, 132.

49. Gilbert, *The Mirrors of Washington*, 113.

50. For the Hoover-Mellon correspondence see Hoover Papers, Box 1-I/311.

51. For some typical Hoover-Hughes correspondence see Hoover Papers, Box 1-I/288; also Hughes Papers, Box 26, Folder "Hoover."

52. Mrs. Albert Fall to Cyril Clemens, no date, Clemens Papers, Box 2.

53. For examples see Harding-Hoover correspondence in Hoover Papers, Box 1-I/242; 1-I/243; 1-I/244.

54. Hoover, *Memoirs*, II, 47–48.

55. Reily, "Years of Confusion," 264.

56. Hoover, *Memoirs*, II, 42.

57. Joseph Brandes, *Herbert Hoover and Economic Diplomacy: Department of Commerce Policy, 1921–1928* (Pittsburgh, 1962), 9. This is an excellent book on Hoover's Commerce Years. See also Hoover, *Memoirs*, II, 41.

58. Figures given in Hoover, *Memoirs*, II, 44; for a synopsis of Hoover's Commerce activities see Lyons, *Herbert Hoover*, 159–173, and David Henshaw, *Herbert Hoover: American Quaker* (New York, 1950), 121–145.

59. Insights into the Agriculture-Labor-Commerce disputes are found in Hoover Papers, Box 1-I/185, folder marked "Labor Department Re Transfer of Labor Statistics Bureau," and Box 1-I/2, Box 1-I/311, and Box 1-I/242, various items.

60. Klein's appointment is in HP, Box 5, Folder 3-9, item 2617; interview by the author with C. A. Jones, November 2, 1966.

61. Brandes, *Herbert Hoover and Economic Diplomacy*, 42, for an example of State-Commerce difficulty.

62. Ray L. Wilbur and Arthur M. Hyde, *The Hoover Policies* (New York, 1937), 80–83. For Hoover's support of trade associations see various items in "Public Statements," XIII, Hoover Papers, especially item 319; Brandes, *Herbert Hoover and Economic Diplomacy*, 15–21; Harris G. Warren, *Herbert Hoover and the Great Depression* (New York, 1959), 28–29.

63. Wilbur and Hyde, *The Hoover Policies*, 109, 115.

CHAPTER VII. HELP FOR THE FARMER

1. For examples of Wallace's memos, etc., to Harding see HP, Box 1, Folder 1-3.

2. Shideler, *Farm Crisis*, 124.

3. Lord, *The Wallaces of Iowa*, 171–173.

4. Henry C. Wallace, *Our Debt and Duty to the Farmer* (New York, 1925), 95–96.

5. Murray R. Benedict, *Farm Policies of the United States, 1790–1950* (New York, 1953), 180.

6. Shideler, *Farm Crisis*, 129.

7. Gutzon Borglum to E. F. Ladd, October 26, 1920, HP, Box 360, Folder 2563-1, item 170960.

8. Arthur Capper to Cyril Clemens, March 23, 1949, Clemens Papers, Box 1.

9. For an analysis of this opposition see Theodore Saloutos and John D. Hicks, *Agricultural Discontent in the Middle West, 1900–1939* (Madison, Wis., 1951), 331.

10. *Ibid.*, 255–285, 323–324.

11. Stokes, *Chip Off My Shoulder*, 83, quoting Wilson.

12. *Cong. Record*, 67 Cong., 1 Sess., 1288.

13. Benedict, *Farm Policies*, 183, n. 25.

14. Saloutos and Hicks, *Agricultural Discontent*, 326.

15. For Wallace's support see HP, Box 1, Folder 1-4, various items, especially 327.

16. Benedict, *Farm Policies*, 183, n. 25.

17. Lowry, *Washington Close-Ups*, 110.

18. For Norris's own feelings see George W. Norris, *Fighting Liberal: The Autobiography of George W. Norris* (New York, 1961), 281.

19. White, *A Puritan in Babylon*, 237.

20. Norris, *Fighting Liberal*, 282–283.

21. Benedict, *Farm Policies*, 183, n. 28; HP, Box 1, Folder 1-4, item 339.

22. Philip P. Campbell to WGH, January 3, 1922, HP, Box 197, Folder 227-2, item 93614.

23. WGH to Wallace, January 24, 1922, HP, Box 703, Folder 12, items 168515–168516.

24. Wallace to WGH, January 10, 1922, HP, Box 197, Folder 227-2, item 93610.

25. Lord, *The Wallaces of Iowa*, 219, 236; *New York Times*, December 31, 1921, p. 6.

26. Joint Commission on Agricultural Inquiry, "The Agricultural Crisis and Its Causes," Part 1 of the *Report of the Joint Commission on Agricultural Inquiry*, House Report 408, 67 Cong., 1 Sess. (Washington, D.C., 1921), 9–25.

27. Harding, *Speeches as President*, "Address of the President of the United States, January 23, 1922," pp. 4–11; *New York Times*, January 24, 1922, p. 1. The two words "or bloc" do not appear in the official proceedings.

28. HP, Box 1, Folder 1-4, item 331; *New York Times*, January 24, 1921, p. 14, and January 25, 1922, p. 8.

29. There was some dissension among "radical" elements at the conference. See R. G. Tugwell, "Reflections on Farm Relief," *Political Science Quarterly*, XLIII, No. 4 (December 1928), 488; "What the Farmer Wants," *Literary Digest*, LXXII, No. 6 (February 11, 1922), 10.

30. *Report of the National Agricultural Conference, January 23–27, 1922*, House Document 195, 67 Cong., 2 Sess. (Washington, D.C., 1922), *passim*.

31. *New York Times*, January 29, 1922, p. 21.

32. Wallace to WGH, February 6, 1922, HP, Box 310, Folder 1363-1, item 132163.

33. HP, Box 1, Folder 1-4, item 330.

34. For the compromise see *ibid.*, items 343–344.

35. *New York Times*, January 20, 1922, p. 14; the Senate vote is in *Cong. Record*, 67 Cong., 2 Sess., 1270; WGH to Hays, January 17, 1922, HP, Box 130, Folder 90-2, item 64174.

36. *New York Times*, February 1, 1922, p. 1; WGH to Kenyon, February 4, 1922, HP, Box 699, Folder 6, item 151538; Kenyon to WGH, February 6, 1922, HP, Box 699, Folder 6, item 151539.

37. Homer E. Socolofsky, *Arthur Capper: Publisher, Politician and Philanthropist* (Lawrence, Kan., 1962), 145–146, 149–151.

38. WGH to W. P. Dillingham, November 28, 1921, HP, Box 197, Folder 227-1, item 93541.

39. For Hoover's farm philosophy see James H. Shideler, "Herbert Hoover and the Federal Farm Board Project, 1921–1925," *MVHR*, XLII, No. 4 (March 1956), 710–729.

40. E. G. Nourse, *Legal Status of Agricultural Cooperation* (New York, 1927), 252–266.

41. Saloutos and Hicks, *Agricultural Discontent*, 335; Benedict, *Farm Policies*, 183, n. 27; *Annual Report of the Department of Agriculture, 1922*, 38–39.

42. Carroll H. Wooddy, *The Growth of the Federal Government, 1915–1932* (New York, 1934), 278–280.

43. Benedict, *Farm Policies*, 205–206; Leverett S. Lyon *et al.*, *Government and Economic Life: Development and Current Issues of American Public Policy* (Washington, D.C., 1939), II, 890–891; Lord, *The Wallaces of Iowa*, 236.

44. For an example see the memo of December 18, 1922, HP, Box 1, Folder 1-4, item 400; WGH to F. E. Warren, January 4, 1923, HP, Box 1, Folder 1-5, item 525.

45. For a detailed description of the ICC and its relation to the Esch-Cummins Act see I. L. Sharfman, *The Interstate Commerce Commission: A Study in Administrative Law and Procedure*, 4 pts. (New York, 1931–37), Pt. I, 177–244, and Pt. III-B, 102–112.

46. Gorham Dana to WGH, April 28, 1921, HP, Box 62, Folder 31-12, item 30063.

47. For samples of farm opinion see HP, Box 60, Folder 31-4, items 28366–28382.

48. Campbell to WGH, May 19, 1921, HP, Box 62, Folder 31-13, items 30168–30169.

49. Meeting resolution, HP, Box 8, Folder 5-1, item 3493.

50. Harding's interest in this legislation is in HP, Box 63, Folder 31-16, various items; also HP, Box 62, Folder 31-13, especially item 30209 and letters from businesses, items 30216–30275.

51. Hoover to WGH, September 23, 1921, HP, Box 5, Folder 3-2, item 2158.

52. HP, Box 1, Folder 1-2, copy of Wallace speech of April 28, 1922.

53. WGH to Mrs. E. C. Hoagland, September 28, 1921, HP, Box 363, Folder 2577-1, item 172440.

54. WGH to Capper, July 15, 1921, HP, Box 63, Folder 31-14, items 30372–30373; for examples of Harding's opinion see HP, Box 8, Folder 5-1, item 3519; Box 63, Folder 31-15, item 30411; Box 697, Folder 1, item 150334.

55. HP, Box 8, Folder 5-2, various items.

56. *New York Times*, May 21, 1922, p. 1; *ibid.*, May 22, 1922, p. 1.

57. *Ibid.*, May 25, 1922, pp. 1, 4; for an analysis and full report on the decision see Interstate Commerce Commission, *Reduced Rates, 1922*, No. 13293 (Washington, D.C., 1922); railroad protests to Harding are in HP, Box 60, Folder 31-4.

58. For a full review of agricultural legislation in the Harding administration see Henry C. Wallace, *U.S. Department of Agriculture Yearbook, 1921*; *Yearbook, 1922*; *Yearbook, 1923*. For a recent misinterpretation of Harding and the farm bloc see John D. Hicks, *Republican Ascendancy, 1921–1933* (New York, 1960), 54–55.

CHAPTER VIII. A LITTLE SOMETHING FOR LABOR

1. See Desk Diaries, Davis Papers, Box 1; other details on his life are in Davis, *The Iron Puddler, passim*. The quotes are from *The Iron Puddler*, 269, 270.

2. WGH to Moore, May 11, 1921, HP, Box 700, Folder 9, item 152149.

3. HP, Box 23, Folder 6-2, item 10210.

4. WGH to Davis, March 23, 1922, HP, Box 362, item 171508.

5. Charles W. Thompson, *Presidents I've Known and Two Near Presidents* (Indianapolis, 1929), 338–339; Mrs. Charity Remsberg to R. B. Harris, June 6, 1938, Harris Papers, Box 9, Folder 1.

6. See samples in Harding's senatorial correspondence, HP, Box 753–762.

7. For the quotes and Gompers's reactions see Samuel Gompers, *Seventy Years of Life and Labor*, I, 553–555.

8. Davis to WGH, July 2, 1923, HP, Box 32, Folder 15-6, item 14728.

9. For such opinion see various issues of *American Federationist* from July to November 1921.

10. HP, Box 792, Christian mss., 157; Gompers, *Seventy Years of Life and Labor*, I, 556–557.

11. WGH to Hoover, August 24, 1921, HP, Box 285, Folder 804-1, items 122681–122683.

12. Harding, *Speeches as President*, "Address of President Harding, September 26, 1921," p. 3; Lyons, *Herbert Hoover*, 166.

13. Lyons, *Herbert Hoover*, 166; Warren, *Herbert Hoover and the Great Depression*, 27.

14. For a sample letter to the departments see WGH to Hoover, January 26, 1922, Hoover Papers, Box 1-I/243.

15. Sample letter, dated May 22, 1922, Hoover Papers, Box 1-I/243.

16. Hoover to Davis, October 4, 1921, HP, Box 285, Folder 804-1, item 122761.

17. Gilbert, *Behind the Mirrors*, 141.

18. Selig Perlman and Philip Taft, *Labor Movements*, in John R. Commons, ed., *History of Labor in the United States, 1896–1932*, IV (New York, 1935), 494–514, on the early Harding era strikes.

19. Harding, *Speeches as President*, "Inaugural Address, March 4, 1921."

20. Davis Papers, Box 38, Book 1, p. 257.

21. Hoover to WGH, April 8, 1922, Hoover Papers, Box 1-I/313; Hoover's proposed draft is in HP, Box 363, Folder 2575-1, item 172171; Harding's letter to Gary is in HP, Box 363, Folder 2575-1, items 172168–172169.

22. A statement by Gary is in HP, Box 360, Folder 2565-1, item 171162.

23. *New York Times*, May 20, 1922, p. 14.

24. Federated American Engineering Societies, *The Twelve Hour Shift in Industry* (New York, 1922), Foreword. For Hoover-Harding correspondence over the foreword see Hoover Papers, Box 1-I/313.

25. *New York Times*, May 26, 1923, p. 1.

26. Davis Papers, Box 39, Book 4, p. 1503.

27. Hoover to WGH, June 13, 1923, Hoover Papers, Box 1-I/313; WGH to Hoover, June 18, 1923, Hoover Papers, Box 1-I/313.

28. Copy of letter, Gary to WGH, June 20, 1923, Hoover Papers, Box 1-I/313; Gary to WGH, June 27, 1923, HP, Box 365, Folder 2584-1, item 173198.

29. Harding, *Speeches as President*, "Address at Tacoma, Washington"; Lyons, *Herbert Hoover*, 167.

30. *New York Times*, July 7, 1923, p. 1. Hoover's role in the 12-hour day episode has often been exaggerated while Harding's has been neglected. Of critical importance in any evaluation of Hoover's and Harding's roles is Box 1-I/313 in the Hoover Papers, Folder "Twelve Hour Day." Before this present work, only Ida Tarbell had used this file (in August 1925).

31. David Friday, "Railway Wages and the Farmer," *American Review of Reviews*, LXVI, No. 2 (August 1922), 185–187.

32. WGH to Capper, June 15, 1921, HP, Box 63, Folder 31-14, item 30372.

33. WGH to F. G. Lyman, October 11, 1921, W. G. Harding Papers (Library of Congress), Box 1.

34. *New York Times*, October 17, 1921, p. 14; *ibid.*, October 22, 1921, p. 12.

35. WGH to Weeks, October 24, 1921, HP, Box 54, Folder 25-4, item 25565; WGH to Hoover, October 24, 1921, Hoover Papers, Box 1-I/242. See also Hoover Papers, Box 1-I/253, Folder "Railroads-Strikes, 1921."

36. *New York Times*, October, 29, 1921, p. 1.

37. Perlman and Taft, *Labor Movements*, 482; Saul D. Alinsky, *John L. Lewis: An Unauthorized Biography* (New York, 1949), 36–38.

38. See report, HP, Box 173, Folder 175-4, items 83462–83463.

39. *New York Times*, March 31, 1922, p. 1.

40. For an analysis of work rules see National Industrial Conference, *Railroad Wages and Working Rules* (Report No. 46, New York, 1922), 22–69.

41. Copy of strike announcement, HP, Box 63, Folder 31-18, item 30876. For Jewell's own account see B. M. Jewell, "The Railway Strike: Strikers' Viewpoint," *Current History*, XVII (November 1922), 202–207.

42. McMenimen to WGH, July 20, 1922, HP, Box 95, Folder 58-80, items 45449–45452; *New York Times*, July 4, 1922, p. 1; *New York Times*, July 5, 1922, p. 1; *New York Times*, July 7, 1922, p. 1.

43. For contemporary accounts of the Herrin massacre see *Chicago Tribune* for June 22, 23, 24, and 25, 1922. For a good secondary account see Alinsky, *John L. Lewis*, 42–48.

44. For material on the Hoover-Davis roles see Hoover Papers, Box 1-I/360, Folder "Coal Strikes: 1921–March, 1922," and various items Box 1-I/185. Also see desk diaries, Davis Papers, Box 1.

45. Conference memo, HP, Box 174, Folder 175-8, items 83818–83820.

46. Lewis to WGH, July 15, 1922, HP, Box 174, Folder 175-9, items 83921–83929; *New York Times*, July 14, 1922, p. 15; *New York Times*, July 18, 1922, p. 1.

47. Telegram, July 18, 1922, HP, Box 174, Folder 175-8, items 83861–83864.

48. WGH to Consolidated Coal and Coke, July 27, 1922, HP, Box 174, Folder 175-8, item 83907.

49. Christian to Alice L. Daly, July 24, 1922, HP, Box 174, Folder 175-11, items 84136–84137.

50. WGH to G. S. McElroy, August 7, 1922, HP, Box 174, Folder 31-8, item 29463. See also WGH to Gutzon Borglum, September 5, 1922, HP, Box 693, Folder 6, item 148538.

51. Copy of the proposal, July 31, 1922, HP, Box 64, Folder 31-19, item 30926.

52. Copy of rejection, August 1, 1922, HP, Box 62, Folder 31-11, items 29833–29836.

53. Union acceptance, August 2, 1922, HP, Box 62, Folder 31-11, items 29691–29696.

54. WGH to Harriman, August 5, 1922, HP, Box 370, Folder 2610-1, item 175799; WGH to Timothy Shea, August 4, 1922, HP, Box 62, Folder 31-11, item 29738; sample telegram, August 4, 1922, HP, Box 62, Folder 31-11, items 29702–29704.

55. Cuyler to WGH, August 11, 1922, HP, Box 357, Folder 2548-1, items 169327–169338; Jewell to WGH, August 11, 1922, HP, Box 699, Folder 2, items 151389–151392.

56. WGH to C. B. King, August 10, 1922, HP, Box 365, Folder 2587.

57. Clipping, HMD to WGH, August 16, 1922, HP, Box 30, Folder 10-12, items 13506–13508.

58. Harding, *Speeches as President*, "Address of the President of the United States, August 18, 1922."

59. "The President's Plan for Industrial Peace," *Literary Digest*, LXXIV, No. 10 (September 2, 1922), 10; "The President's Strike Message," *New Republic*, XXXII, No. 404 (August 30, 1922), 3–4; H. O. Dunkle to WGH, August 19, 1922, HP, Box 365, Folder 2585-1, item 173262.

60. 42 *Statutes at Large* 1025.

61. *Washington Post*, August 19, 1922, p. 6, quoting the *Bulletin*.

62. For an example see *Wall Street Journal*, August 19, 1922, p. 2.

63. Norbeck to WGH, August 8, 1922, HP, Box 59, Folder 31-1, item 27948; Wallace speech, August 15, 1922, HP, Box 1, Folder 1-3, item 257.

64. *New York Times*, September 2, 1922, p. 2; Daugherty, *The Inside Story*, 128–131.

65. Daugherty, *The Inside Story*, 127; Daugherty's reports on violence and radicalism in HP, Box 61, Folder 31-9, items 29553–29574; HP, Box 61, Folder 31-8, *passim*.

66. The telegrams are in HP, Box 62, Folder 31-10, items 29622–29623.

67. The full text is in Felix Frankfurter and Nathan Greene, *The Labor Injunction* (Gloucester, Mass., 1963), 253–263.

68. Hoover, *Memoirs*, II, 48; Lyons, *Herbert Hoover*, 167.

69. Daugherty, *The Inside Story*, 148–150; HMD to R. B. Harris, September 19, 1936, Harris Papers, Box 9, Folder 4.

70. Oswald G. Villard, *Prophets True and False* (New York, 1928), 70, quoting Dawes; examples of impeachment resolutions in HP, Box 28, Folder 10-3.

71. Foster R. Dulles, *Labor in America: A History*, 2nd rev. ed. (New York, 1960), 240, quoting the *World* and *Evening Post*; *Washington Post*, September 3, 1922, p. 6.

72. See Daugherty, *The Inside Story*, 148ff.

73. WGH to Dawes, September 5, 1922, HP, Box 363, Folder 2578-1, item 172542.

74. For Mellon's influence see HP, Box 370, Folder 2611-1, items 175905–175909.

75. Perlman and Taft, *Labor Movements*, 485–487; Ellis Searles, "The Victory of Coal Miners," *Current History*, XVII (November 1922), 218–221.

76. HP, Box 704, Folder 11, item 154011.

77. For an analysis see Edward W. Parker, "The Anthracite Strike of 1922," *Current History*, XVII (November 1922), 208–212.

78. *New York Times*, August 25, 1922, p. 1; Hoover to WGH, July 20, 1922, HP, Box 95, Folder 58–80, items 45448–45460.

79. Willard to Hoover, August 7, 1922, Hoover Papers, Box 1-I/ 253.

80. "The Railroad Strike—Defeat or Victory?" *Nation*, CXV (September 27, 1922), 297.

81. "The Anthracite Strike Ends," *Outlook*, CXXXII, No. 2 (September 13, 1922), 45–46.

82. "Public Loses the Shop Strike," *Nation*, CXVI (January 3, 1923), 14; E. J. Allard to WGH, February 22, 1923, HP, Box 173, Folder 175-3, item 83403. The Coal Commission, authorized by Congress in September 1922, was appointed by Harding in December and was successful in extending the coal contracts to April 1, 1924. After Harding's death it submitted a five-volume report to Congress on conditions in the coal fields. Few of its recommendations were ever enacted. See *Report of the United States Coal Commission*, Senate Doc. 195, 68 Cong., 2 Sess., 5 pts. (Washington, D.C., 1924).

83. Davis to WGH, June 1, 1923, Davis Papers, Box 39, Book 4, p. 1501.

84. Stokes, *Chip Off My Shoulder*, 96.

85. Mrs. Harding to Mary E. Lee, August 28, 1922, Mary E. Lee Papers (Ohio Historical Society Library, Columbus, Ohio), Box 9, Folder 4.

CHAPTER IX. AMERICA FIRST

1. For an excellent analysis of the background of restriction see John Higham, *Strangers in the Land: Patterns of American Nativism, 1860–1925* (New Brunswick, N.J., 1955), 234–270; for labor and immigration see *Hearings: Immigration and Labor*, House Committee on Immigration, 67 Cong., 4 Sess. (Washington, D.C., 1923), *passim*. Other information is in *Hearings: Biological Aspects of Immigration*, House Committee on Immigration, 66 Cong., 2 Sess. (Washington, D.C., 1921), *passim*.

2. Higham, *Strangers in the Land*, 302, citing the *New Republic*; *New York Times*, September 15, 1920, p. 3, quoting Harding.

3. *Hearings: Emergency Immigration Legislation*, Senate Committee on Immigration, 66 Cong., 3 Sess. (Washington, D.C., 1921), *passim*; *Cong. Record*, 67 Cong., 1 Sess., 589, 968; 42 *Statutes at Large* 5.

4. Roy L. Garis, *Immigration Restriction: A Study of the Opposition to and Regulation of Immigration into the United States* (New York, 1927), 147–148. Higham in *Strangers in the Land*, 312, doubts that immigration restriction helped fight the depression.

5. Garis, *Immigration Restriction*, 78, 82, 150–152, 158, 167; see also National Industrial Conference Board, *The Immigration Problem in the United States*, Report No. 58 (New York, 1923), 70, Table 9.

6. Higham, *Strangers in the Land*, 312; Garis, *Immigration Restriction*, 150; Davis to WGH, December 17, 1921, HP, Box 31, Folder 15-3, items 14482–14486; *New York Times*, March 24, 1923, p. 1.

7. For examples of tightening see HP, Box 33, Folder 15-13, *passim*; HP, Box 32, Folder 15-4, items 14567–14576; WGH to H. P. Fletcher, January 11, 1922, National Archives, Record Group 59, State Department Files 102.9102/19.

8. See HP, Box 156, Folder 114-1, items 75063–75073, containing the opinions of Harding and Davis.

9. James J. Davis, "How the Immigration Laws Are Now Working," *American Review of Reviews*, LXV, No. 5 (May 1922), 515.

10. Kenneth L. Roberts, "Shutting the Sea Gates," *Saturday Evening Post*, CXCIV, No. 31 (January 28, 1922), 11.

11. William W. Husband, "Immigration under the Per Centum Limit Act," *Monthly Labor Review*, XV, No. 2 (August 1922), 235.

12. For a discussion of American vs. foreign valuation see J. Marshall Gersting, *The Flexible Provisions in the United States Tariff, 1922–1930* (Philadelphia, 1932), 17–36.

13. WGH to Marvin, December 6, 1921, HP, Box 107, Folder 60-3, item 52174.

14. Wilbur and Hyde, *The Hoover Policies*, 181.

15. Culbertson to WGH, October 28, 1921, HP, Box 107, Folder 60-3, items 52155–52161; John D. Larkin, *The President's Control of the Tariff* (Cambridge, Mass., 1936), 21, n. 20.

16. Harding, *Speeches as President*, "Address of the President of the United States, December 6, 1921," pp. 1–8.

17. Snyder to Christian, January 14, 1922, HP, Box 110, Folder 60-16, item 53814.

18. *Washington Post*, May 19, 1922, p. 6, quoting the *News*.

19. *New York Times*, April 13, 1922, p. 6, and April 15, 1922, p. 17; for the farmer's tariff mania see "Who Wants a High Tariff?" *World's Work*, XLII, No. 4 (August 1921), 322.

20. *New York Times*, August 20, 1922, Section VII, p. 2; HP, Box 107, Folder 60-3, items 52164–52168.

21. WGH to McCumber, August 11, 1922, HP, Box 701, Folder 7, items 152534–152535.

22. Frank W. Taussig, *The Tariff History of the United States*, 8th ed. (New York, 1931), 457; *New York Times*, September 10, 1922, p. 1.

23. *New York Times*, September 16, 1922, p. 6; Oscar W. Underwood, *Drifting Sands of Party Politics* (New York, 1931), 235; Johnson, *Borah of Idaho*, 260; La-Follette and LaFollette, *Robert M. LaFollette*, II, 1062; *Cong. Record*, 67 Cong., 2 Sess., 12907.

24. *New York Times*, September 22, 1922, p. 1.

25. 42 *Statutes at Large* 941, for flexibility provision.

26. For a comparison of tariff rates see House Committee on Ways and Means, *Comparison of Tariff Acts of 1909, 1913, and 1922*, 68 Cong., 1 Sess. (Washington, D.C., 1924), *passim*.

27. "The Farmer and 'His' New Tariff," *Literary Digest*, LXXV, No. 1 (October 7, 1922), 13. See also Abraham Berglund, "The Tariff Act of 1922," *American Economic Review*, XIII, No. 1 (March 1923), 27; Frank W. Taussig, "The Tariff Act of 1922," *Quarterly Journal of Economics*, XXXVII (November 1922), 28–30.

28. American Academy of Political and Social Science, *The Agricultural Situation in the United States* (in *Annals*, CXVII, Philadelphia, 1925), 167–176, for attitude of agricultural elements; "The Farmer and 'His' New Tariff," 64, quoting the *Post-Dispatch*.

29. *New York Times*, December 5, 1920, p. 1.

30. For shipping background to 1920 see Darrell H. Smith and Paul V. Betters, *The United States Shipping Board: Its History, Activities and Organization* (in *Service Monographs of the United States Government*, No. 63, Washington, D.C., 1931), *passim*; Paul M. Zeis, *American Shipping Policy* (Princeton, 1938), 106–112; Smith and Betters, *The United States Shipping Board*, 54–56.

31. 41 *Statutes at Large* 988.

32. For the full story see Smith and Betters, *The United States Shipping Board*, *passim*.

33. Piez to Christian, March 16, 1921, HP, Box 64, Folder 40-1, items 31519–31521; Hoover to WGH, March 17, 1921, HP, Box 67, Folder 40-12, item 33020.

34. John Gunther, *Taken at the Flood: The Story of Albert D. Lasker* (New York, 1960), 127–137, 140–144; Hays to WGH, February 19, 1921, HP, Box 655, Folder 4716-1, item 300594; WGH to Lasker, June 10, 1921, HP, Box 65, Folder 40-6, item 32090.

35. Gunther, *Taken at the Flood*, 4–5, 11–13, 109. Gunther is excellent on Lasker, but atrocious on the era.

36. For sample opinion, see Thompson to WGH, November 1, 1922, HP, Box 65, Folder 40-5, item 31994.

37. *New York Times*, August 22, 1921, p. 1, quoting Plummer; *Washington Post*, August 22, 1921, p. 6, quoting the *Chicago Tribune*.

38. For statistics on Shipping Board operations see Smith and Betters, *The United States Shipping Board*, Appendix 7, pp. 303–307.

39. See sample, WGH to Jones, August 20, 1921, HP, Box 66, Folder 40-8, items 32219–32221.

40. *New York Times*, March 1, 1922, p. 3.

41. The full text is in Harding, *Speeches as President*, "Address of the President of the United States, February 28, 1922," pp. 1–11.

42. *Washington Post*, March 2, 1922, p. 8, quoting the *Inquirer*; *Washington Times*, March 19, 1922, p. 4; for a jaundiced view of the *Tribune*'s motives see Morris R. Werner, *Privileged Characters* (New York, 1935), 337. In general, Werner's account of the Lasker Shipping Board, 319–379, is distorted and unreliable.

43. For Hoover's various positions see HP, Box 5, Folder 3-1, item 2054; Hoover to WGH, February 2, 1923, Hoover Papers, Box 1-I/243; Hoover Papers, Box 72, Vol. III, Public Statements; James W. Prothro, *The Dollar Decade: Business Ideas in the 1920's* (Baton Rouge, 1954), 160.

44. Lasker tried to win labor's support but failed—see HP, Box 65, Folder 40-4, item 31780; *Joint Hearings before the Senate Committee on Commerce and the House Committee on Merchant Marine and Fisheries to Amend the Merchant Marine Act of 1920*, 67 Cong., 2 Sess. (Washington, D.C., 1922), *passim*; "A $30,000,-000 Bonus for Shipping," *Literary Digest*, LXXII, No. 11 (March 18, 1922), 14, quoting the *Post*.

45. For examples of the Lasker-Wallace feud see HP, Box 1, Folder 1-3, items 212–248.

46. Johnson, *Borah of Idaho*, 261; "A $30,000,000 Bonus for Shipping," 15, quoting the *Courier-Journal*.

47. For shipping hearings see *Joint Hearings . . . to Amend the Merchant Marine Act of 1920*. For the dissenting report see 67 Cong., 2 Sess., House Report No. 1112, pt. 2.

48. Lasker to WGH, April 7, 1922, HP, Box 65, Folder 40-4, item 31776.

49. Howard to WGH, April 22, 1922, HP, Box 147, Folder 99-3, item 71778; Howard to Lasker, June 20, 1922, HP, Box 147, Folder 99-6, item 71988; "The Ship Subsidy and the Farmer," *American Review of Reviews*, LXVI, No. 2 (August 1922), 199–200.

50. Lasker to WGH, May 10, 1922, HP, Box 699, Folder 11, item 151704; *New York Times*, May 9, 1922, p. 1.

51. WGH to Campbell, May 26, 1922, HP, Box 147, Folder 99-4, item 71792; *New York Times*, June 4, 1922, p. 1, and June 14, 1922, p. 18.

52. Mondell to WGH, June 12, 1922, HP, Box 147, Folder 99-4, item 71865; WGH to Mondell, June 14, 1922, HP, item 71867; Mondell to WGH, June 16, 1922, HP, Folder 99-6, items 72036–72039.

53. WGH to Mondell, June 20, 1922, HP, Box 700, Folder 10, items 152200–152204; *New York Times*, June 21, 1922, p. 1.

54. *New York Times*, July 1, 1922, p. 4; see also HP, Box 147, Folder 99-5, items 71942–71980, concerning the dinner.

55. Both Hoover and Colonel McCormick of the *Chicago Tribune* advocated tying the proposed St. Lawrence Seaway to the subsidy proposal as a means of wooing the farmer. Lasker and Harding should have listened to this advice.

56. HP, Box 147, Folder 99-6, item 72025; see sample polls, HP, Box 147, Folder 99-6, items 72053–72067.

57. WGH to Mondell, August 23, 1922, HP, Box 700, Folder 10, items 152205–152206.

CHAPTER X. VERDICT AT THE POLLS

1. Interview with C. A. Jones, Columbus, Ohio, November 2, 1966.

2. Example seen in J. R. Clark to Knox, April 9, 1921, Knox Papers, Volume 23.

3. For sample briefs see HP, Box 9, Folder 5-4, items 3801–3808, and Box 29, Folder 10-9, items 13239–13249. The Taft endorsement is in Taft to HMD, February 25, 1921, Harris Papers, Box 4, Folder 6.

4. See Harris Papers, Box 4, Folder 6.

5. See Appendix to Daugherty, *The Inside Story*, for a list.

6. Wooddy, *The Growth of the Federal Government*, 91.

7. Samples of removal petitions in HP, Box 28, Folder 10-3.

8. WGH to J. Williams, June 13, 1922, HP, Box 29, Folder 10-10, items 12605–12606.

9. *New York Times*, April 28, 1922, p. 16; "Mr. Daugherty as an Issue," *Literary Digest*, LXXIII, No. 11 (June 10, 1922), 13, quoting the *New York World*.

10. Herbert S. Duffy, *William Howard Taft* (New York, 1930), 310, quoting *New York World*.

11. For correspondence between WGH and Scobey see HP, Box 368, Folder 2598-1, items 174567–174569, and numerous items in Box 758. For references to Scobey's intemperate drinking see Scobey Papers, Box 2, item 270.

12. "Crissinger: A Graduate of the Little Red Schoolhouse," *Current Opinion*, LXXIV, No. 9 (March 1923), 283–284. Conservatives thought Crissinger was excellent but John K. Galbraith, *The Great Crash 1929* (New York, 1962), 32, claims the

Federal Reserve Board under Crissinger's direction was "a body of startling incompetence."

13. Interview with Dr. Warren Sawyer, Marion, Ohio, August 3, 1966.

14. Various letters, March 1921, Newton H. Fairbanks Papers (Ohio Historical Society Library, Columbus, Ohio); WGH to Donithen, February 6, 1923, Alfred W. (Hoke) Donithen Papers (Ohio Historical Society Library, Columbus, Ohio); Willis to WGH, March 31, 1922, HP, item 127165.

15. A recent example of an inaccurate assessment is in George H. Mayer, *The Republican Party, 1854–1964* (New York, 1964), 380. Examples of Harding's relationship with the commission are in HP, Box 2, Folder 2-2, various items. "Report of First Year's Civil Service Activities of Four Presidents," made by the Civil Service Commission, in HP, Box 2, Folder 2-3, items 842–852.

16. *New York Times*, October 15, 1921, p. 1.

17. Alderfer, "The Personality and Politics of Warren G. Harding," 215.

18. WGH to W. Abernethy, May 27, 1922, HP, Box 46, Folder 21-6, item 22101.

19. WGH to Dover, May 5, 1922, HP, Box 48, Folder 21-16, item 22915. The best analysis of the Blair-Dover fight is found in Alderfer, "The Personality and Politics of Warren G. Harding," 193–200.

20. Alderfer, "The Personality and Politics of Warren G. Harding," 203.

21. " 'Good Will' in the Post Office," *Literary Digest*, LXX, No. 10 (September 3, 1921), 40; testimonial, February 11, 1922, National League of Postmasters, Hays Papers.

22. The figures vary slightly among the sources. See HP, Box 38, Folder 19-5, items 17641–17644, for the report of the Civil Service Commission.

23. Alderfer, "The Personality and Politics of Warren G. Harding," 209, 214, 216; HP, Box 2, Folders 2-4 and 2-5, various items, and Box 39, Folder 19-10.

24. WGH to Newberry, January 12, 1922, HP, Box 701, Folder 8, item 152573.

25. It is revealing that Senator Norris in his autobiography, *Fighting Liberal*, 221–239, should have devoted the major part of his discussion on the Harding administration to the scandals *and* the Newberry case.

26. Towner to WGH, February 13, 1922, HP, Box 142, Folder 95-8, item 69736.

27. "The Bonus and the Taxpayer," *Literary Digest*, LXXII, No. 6 (February 11, 1922), 8, quoting the *New York Times*.

28. *Elmira Advertiser*, February 20, 1922.

29. "The Bonus and the Taxpayer," 9.

30. *New York Times*, March 7, 1922, p. 1; *ibid.*, March 10, 1922, p. 1; *ibid.*, March 8, 1922, p. 1.

31. *Cong. Record*, 67 Cong., 2 Sess., 4447.

32. McCumber to WGH, May 6, 1922, HP, Box 143, Folder 95-10, items 69945–69946.

33. *New York Times*, June 1, 1922, p. 1; *ibid.*, June 9, 1922, p. 1; *ibid.*, June 16, 1922, p. 1; *ibid.*, June 17, 1922, p. 1; and *ibid.*, June 21, 1922, p. 1.

34. Cartoon, *Service Record*, I, No. 4 (November 1922), 25.

35. Wadsworth to Harris, June 13, 1933, Harris Papers; for samples of Legion pressure on the president see HP, Box 113, Folder 64-1 to 64-3, and Box 114.

36. *New York Times*, August 26, 1922, p. 1.

37. *Ibid.*, April 23, 1922, p. 1, quoting Borah.

38. For Lodge pressure see HP, Box 369, Folder 2606-1, items 175341–175342. MacNider's request is in HP, Box 143, Folder 95-11, item 70057.

39. *Soldiers' Adjusted Compensation Message of the President of the United States*, 67 Cong., 2 Sess., House Doc. 396 (Washington, D.C., 1922). For Mellon draft see HP, Box 46, Folder 21-5, items 22080–22084.

40. *Cong. Record*, 67 Cong., 2 Sess., 12999 and 13004.

41. "The Death of the Bonus Bill," *Literary Digest*, LXXIV, No. 14 (September 30, 1922), 8, quoting the *Public Ledger*; *Washington Post*, September 20, 1922, p. 6; *New York Times*, September 22, 1922, p. 14.

42. WGH to Dawes, September 26, 1922, HP, Box 127, Folder 79-5, item 62739.

43. Jennings to WGH, August 11, 1921, Jennings Papers.

44. *New York Times*, January 7, 1922, p. 12.

45. Samples of Harding's impatience in HP, Box 368, Folder 2601-1, item 174863; *New York Times*, June 5, 1922, p. 1.

46. WGH to Mondell, October 11, 1922, HP, Box 366, Folder 2589-1, item 173717.

47. *New York Times*, September 23, 1922, p. 1.

48. Mark Sullivan, "National Politics in 1922," *World's Work*, XLIII, No. 4 (February 1922), 361–369.

49. *New York Times*, March 4, 1922, p. 14.

50. *Wall Street Journal*, May 19, 1922, p. 1.

51. WGH to Crissinger, January 19, 1922, HP, Box 47, Folder 21-8, item 22250.

52. WGH to Jennings, January 1922, Jennings Papers.

53. *New York Times*, October 17, 1922, p. 18.

54. A footnote to "Newberryism": Pinchot and his followers spent over $120,000 to gain the Pennsylvania gubernatorial nomination.

55. *New York Times*, issues October 11–November 2, 1922.

56. WGH to Roosevelt, October 19, 1922, HP, Box 35, Folder 18-9, items 16058–16059.

57. Mark Sullivan, "Two Years of President Harding," *World's Work*, XLV, No. 1 (November 1922), 31–38.

58. "The Revolt of November 7," *Current Opinion*, LXXIII, No. 6 (December 1922), 702.

59. *Wall Street Journal*, November 9, 1922, p. 1.

60. *New York Times*, November 8, 1922, p. 14.

61. WGH to Reily, November 22, 1922, HP, Box 362, Folder 2571-1, item 171808; WGH to Borglum, November 9, 1922, HP, Box 693, Folder 6, item 148544; WGH to David Pugh, November 16, 1922, HP, Box 366, Folder 2588-1, items 173548–173549.

62. WGH to Wallace, January 24, 1922, HP, Box 703, Folder 12, items 168515–168516.

63. Senator Walsh to Gavin McNab, November 15, 1922, Thomas J. Walsh Papers, Box 373; *New York Times*, November 14, 1922, p. 4, quoting Senator Hitchcock.

64. WGH to B. L. Rosenbloom, October 16, 1922, HP, Box 148, Folder 99-7, item 72124.

65. LaFollette and LaFollette, *Robert M. LaFollette*, II, 1067–1068; "Big Possibilities of the Progressive Bloc," *Literary Digest*, LXXV, No. 11 (December 16, 1922), 5–7.

66. WGH to Newberry, November 18, 1922, HP, Box 701, Folder 8, items 152579–152581.

67. Harding, *Speeches as President*, "Message of the President of the United States to Congress, November 21, 1922."

68. *New York Times*, November 24, 1922, p. 16.

69. Lasker to WGH, December 1, 1922, HP, Box 148, Folder 99-8, items 72279–72286; *Cong. Record*, 67 Cong., 3 Sess., 429.

70. WGH to J. T. Williams, Jr., November 29, 1922, HP, Box 704, Folder 7, item 168677; WGH to Smoot, December 1, 1922, HP, Box 370, Folder 2610-1, item 175741.

71. *New York Times*, issues February 21–23, 1923. The president's speech is in *Cong. Record*, 67 Cong., 4 Sess., 3212–3214.

72. *Cong. Record*, 67 Cong., 4 Sess., 4852.

73. WGH to F. I. Thompson, March 5, 1923, HP, Box 148, Folder 99-10, item 72478; WGH to Lasker, January 15, 1923, HP, Box 65, Folder 40-10, item 32455.

74. *New York Times*, March 1, 1923, p. 4, quoting the *London Daily Chronicle*.

CHAPTER XI. NEW APPROACHES IN FOREIGN POLICY

1. A concise treatment of foreign affairs during this period is Dexter Perkins, *Charles Evans Hughes and American Democratic Statesmanship* (Boston, 1956); another is Betty Glad, *Charles Evans Hughes and the Illusions of Innocence: A Study in American Diplomacy* (Urbana, Ill., 1966), but it is flawed by bias and moral hindsight.

2. Eugene P. Trani, "Harding Administration and Recognition of Mexico," *Ohio History*, LXXV (Spring and Summer 1966), 139. For oil and Mexico see Ludwell Denny, *We Fight for Oil* (New York, 1928), 53–57.

3. Examples of contacts are in HP, Box 701, Folder 9, various items, and Box 167, Folder 163-2, items 80487–80488, 80515, 80534–80536.

4. WGH to Hughes, July 21, 1921, HP, Box 167, Folder 163-1, item 80468.

5. For comparison of text see HP, Box 701, Folder 9, items 152601–152605, and WGH to Hughes, July 21, 1921, National Archives, Record Group 59, State Department Files, 812.00/25109½.

6. For a Fletcher argument see HP, Box 167, Folder 163-1, item 80368; Harding's typical reply, HP, Box 167, Folder 163-1, item 80398.

7. Dover to WGH, October 20, 1921, HP, Box 695, Folder 7, items 149620–149621.

8. Trani, "Harding Administration and Recognition of Mexico," 144–145.

9. Ryan to WGH, August 22, 1922, HP, Box 167, Folder 163-4, items 80720–80721.

10. Ryan to WGH, April 13, 1923, HP, Box 167, Folder 163-1, item 80439.

11. Interview, September 11, 1933, Harris Papers, Box 3, Folder 4.

12. For Hughes on Mexico see Hughes Papers, Box 172, Folder 37, Beerits memo, "Relations with Mexico." Hughes makes little mention of Harding's efforts.

13. For a favorable biography of Crowder see David A. Lockmiller, *Enoch H. Crowder: Soldier, Lawyer and Statesman* (Columbia, Mo., 1955). See also Hughes on Cuba in Hughes Papers, Box 173, Folder 41, Beerits memo, "Latin American Intervention"; HP, Box 163, Folder 150-1, various items, especially 78673–78680, 78745–78749.

14. Robert F. Smith, *The United States and Cuba: Business and Diplomacy, 1917–1960* (New York, 1960), 103–112.

15. Freidel, *Franklin D. Roosevelt*, II, 81.

16. D. A. Graber, *Crisis Diplomacy: A History of U.S. Intervention Policies and Practices* (Washington, D.C., 1959), 200.

17. Hughes to WGH, July 19, 1921, HP, Box 182, Folder 180-1, items 86746–86749; Hughes to WGH, August 20, 1921, HP, Box 182, Folder 180-1, item 86754; WGH to Hughes, August 20, 1921, HP, Box 182, Folder 180-1, item 86755.

18. Protests against Russell are in HP, Box 182, Folders 180-1 and 180-2, various items; Denby to WGH, May 25, 1922, HP, Box 34, Folder 18-7, items 15954–15960. For discussion of Senate report see " 'White-Wash' on the Black Republic," *Literary Digest*, LXXIV, No. 3 (July 15, 1922), 15.

19. HP, Box 182, Folder 180-3, items 86998–87000; for a typical Russell report see *ibid.*, items 87002–87018; Hughes to WGH, June 13, 1923, *ibid.*, items 86998–87000.

20. Hughes, *The Pathways of Peace*, 131–134, speech of August 30, 1923. American troops were not finally removed from Haiti until 1943.

21. Hughes Papers, Box 173, Folder 41, Beerits memo, "Latin American Intervention," 2–7; Hughes, *The Pathway of Peace*, 129–131; Sumner Welles, *Naboth's Vineyard: The Dominican Republic, 1844–1928* (New York, 1928), II, 841–845.

22. Welles's report, HP, Box 261, Folder 409-2, items 113931–113933.

23. WGH to Hughes, June 2, 1923, HP, Box 261, Folder 409-2, item 113934.

24. For Hughes's final assessment see Charles E. Hughes, *Our Relations to the Nations of the Western Hemisphere* (Princeton, 1928), 77, 83. Also Hughes Papers, Box 173, Folder 41, Beerits memo, "Latin American Intervention," 1.

25. HMD to R. B. Harris, September 13, 1939, Harris Papers, Box 9, Folder 5.

26. Reily to HMD, January 15, 1932, Daugherty Papers.

27. For Reily's early troubles see Luis Munoz Marin, "A 'Ninety-Eight Percent American' in Puerto Rico," *New Republic*, XXIX, No. 370 (January 4, 1922), 151–153.

28. Weeks to WGH, November 12, 1921, HP, Box 252, Folder 400-643, item 111642.

29. WGH to Weeks, December 16, 1921, HP, Box 252, Folder 400-644, item 111688.

30. "The Row in Puerto Rico," *Literary Digest*, LXXI, No. 11 (December 10, 1921), 12, quoting the *Herald*; "Act at Once, Mr. Harding!" *Independent*, CVIII, No. 3804 (February 11, 1922), 137.

31. Puerto Rican Senate resolution, HP, Box 252, Folder 400-644, items 111654–111658; *New York Times*, April 8, 1922, p. 3.

32. WGH to Reily, April 13, 1922, Warren G. Harding Papers, NYPL.

33. Weeks to WGH, June 26, 1922, HP, Box 253, Folder 400-646, item 111939.

34. Samples of support in HP, Box 252, Folders 400-643, 400-644, and 400-645.

35. WGH to W. L. Kessinger, May 24, 1922, HP, Box 253, Folder 400-646, item 111897; WGH to Weeks, August 11, 1922, HP, Box 704, Folder 2, item 153709; WGH to Reily, August 25, 1922, HP, Box 702, Folder 2, item 152839; WGH to Weeks, September 5, 1922, HP, Box 253, Folder 400-647, item 112000.

36. HMD to R. B. Harris, September 13, 1939, Harris Papers, Box 9, Folder 5.

37. Reily to WGH, February 16, 1923, HP, Box 253, Folder 400-649, items 112168–112173.

38. WGH to A. B. Cummins, January 15, 1923, HP, Box 253, Folder 400-648, item 112142.

39. Barcelo to WGH, May 16, 1923, HP, Box 253, Folder 400-649, item 112230.

40. Reily to Clemens, August 7, 1939, Clemens Papers, Box 3.

41. Hughes speech in Bemis, ed., *The American Secretaries of State*, X, 263.

42. E. Taylor Parks, *Colombia and the United States, 1765–1934* (Durham, N.C., 1935), 440–451; J. Fred Rippy, *The Capitalists and Colombia* (New York, 1931), 104–107, 115.

43. Fall to WGH, February 21, 1921, HP, Box 696, Folder 1, item 149788; Lodge to WGH, February 21, 1921, HP, Box 656, Folder 4717-1, items 300704–300705; Lodge to Root, March 15, 1921, and April 6, 1921, Root Papers, Box 161, Folder "1921."

44. *Cong. Record*, 67 Cong., 1 Sess., 487.

45. *New York Times*, April 13, 1921, p. 3; Rippy, *The Capitalists and Colombia*, 116.

46. Parks, *Colombia and the United States*, 465–466.

47. Acosta to WGH, March 23, 1921, HP, Box 75, Folder 43-1, item 36136; Denny, *We Fight for Oil*, 97–98.

48. For official record see *Arbitration between Peru and Chile* (Washington, D.C., 1924). The Tacna-Arica matter was not fully settled until 1929.

49. For official proceedings see *Conference on Central American Affairs, Washington, December 4, 1922– February 7, 1923* (Washington, D.C., 1923).

50. Samuel F. Bemis, *The Latin American Policy of the United States: An Historical Interpretation* (New York, 1943), 207–208.

51. Hughes, *The Pathway of Peace*, 142–163; Hughes, *Our Relations to the Nations of the Western Hemisphere*, 17; see also Hughes Papers, Box 173, Folder 41, Beerits memo, "Latin American Intervention."

52. Report on Conference, submitted to Harding, June 4, 1923, HP, Box 334, Folder 1933-1, items 140665–140676.

53. Bemis, *The Latin American Policy of the United States*, 204.

54. HP, Box 156, Folder 113-1, item 74974, and Box 57, Folder 25-17, item 26647.

55. Wood to Root, March 31, 1921, Root Papers, Box 169, Folder "1921."

56. Manuel Quezon, "Why the Filipinos Desire Independence," *Current History*, XV (November 1921), 239–245; example of American sentiment, HP, Box 251, Folder 400-638, items 111012–111016, and Folder 400-639, item 111116; Forbes report, HP, Box 251, Folder 400-639, item 111021.

57. Forbes to WGH, November 10, 1921, HP, Box 696, Folder 3, items 149922–149931.

58. Sample correspondence on Wood's appointment is in HP, Box 702, Folder 7, items 153086–153087, 153089–153090. See also Hagedorn, *Leonard Wood*, II, 378, 402–403, *passim*.

59. WGH to Schurman, April 19, 1922, HP, Box 702, Folder 7, items 153111–153112.

60. Reply to delegation, June 22, 1922, HP, Box 251, Folder 400-641, items 111324–111333.

61. Gilmore to Towner, September 26, 1922, HP, Box 251, Folder 400-641, items 111411–111412.

62. For survey of American-Philippine relations see Gerald E. Wheeler, "Republican Philippine Policy, 1921–1933," *Pacific Historical Review*, XXVIII (November 1959), 377–390.

63. *New York Times*, March 26, 1921, p. 1.

64. Frederick L. Schuman, *American Policy toward Russia since 1917* (New York, 1928), 205; William A. Williams, *American Russian Relations, 1781–1947* (New York, 1952), 201.

65. Robert P. Browder, *The Origins of Soviet-American Diplomacy* (Princeton, 1953), 20–21. The most complete work on the American Relief Administration is H. H. Fisher, *The Famine in Soviet Russia, 1919–1923: The Operations of the American Relief Administration* (New York, 1927). The Soviets had short memories. In 1947, Soviet historian N. L. Rubinstein called the American Relief Administration "condensed milk diplomacy" aimed at filling Russia with "a whole army of spies and undercover agents."

66. Brandes, *Herbert Hoover and Economic Diplomacy*, 29–30; also Hoover's letters to Hughes, December 6, 1921, June 15, 1922, and July 26, 1922, Hoover Papers, Box 1-I/ 288.

67. *New York Times*, January 28, 1922, p. 12.

68. Child to Hughes, January 30, 1922, HP, Box 307, Folder 1275-1, items 131036–131037; for Harding's doubt see WGH to Harvey, March 22, 1922, HP, Box 361, Folder 2569-1, item 171552.

69. Report to Harding, May 22, 1922, HP, Box 362, Folder 2574-1, items 172046–172060; for intimate Child-Harding correspondence see Box 694, Folder 5.

70. *New York Times*, May 2, 1922, p. 1.

71. For Borah see *Cong. Record*, 67 Cong., 2 Sess., 6945–6948; for Goodrich and Bloomfield reports see HP, Box 265, Folder 471-1, items 115445–115458, and Box 164, Folder 156-1, items 79239–79240, 79270–79274.

72. Williams, *American Russian Relations*, 195–198.

73. For opinion on recognition policy 1920–24 see James G. Hodgson, *Recognition of Soviet Russia* (New York, 1925); "Russian Comment on America's Attitude," *Current History*, XVIII (May 1923), 290.

74. Hughes to WGH, May 3, 1923, HP, Box 165, Folder 156-2, item 79484; Hughes to WGH, May 3, 1923, HP, Box 165, Folder 156-2, item 79484. Loomis report is in HP, Box 165, Folder 156-2, items 79488–79498.

75. WGH to Harvey, April 11, 1922, HP, Box 363, Folder 2574-1, item 172101.

76. For an early example see WGH to Hughes, May 20, 1922, National Archives, Record Group 59, State Department Files 761.62 119 R18/ 17; Williams, *American Russian Relations*, 203–204.

77. Williams, *American Russian Relations*, 204.

78. In the long run, economic imperatives of the kind Hoover envisioned did stimulate a new departure in American-Russian relations. See Browder, *The Origins of Soviet-American Diplomacy*, 25–48.

79. Herbert Feis, *The Diplomacy of the Dollar: First Era, 1919–1932* (Baltimore, 1950), 10–14, 18–20; Hoover, *Memoirs*, II, 86–91.

80. Hughes, *Our Relations to the Nations of the Western Hemisphere*, 68–69.

81. Best coverage of the United States stake in Middle Eastern oil is John A. De-Novo, *American Interests and Policies in the Middle East, 1900–1939* (Minneapolis, 1963), 167–209.

82. WGH to Hughes, May 20, 1922, National Archives, Record Group 59, State Department Files, 867.4016/ 498.

83. Hoover's interest in Middle Eastern oil was explicit. See Hoover Papers, Box 1-I/ 288 and Box 1-I/ 551, for examples.

84. Hughes to WGH, October 24, 1922, HP, Box 369, Folder 2603-1, items 175100–175113.

85. Hughes was not always happy with the delegation's pro-Turkish stand. See Hughes to WGH, December 20, 1922, and WGH to Hughes, December 21, 1922, HP, Box 44, Folder 20-15, items 20858–20870. See also Joseph C. Grew, *Turbulent Era: A Diplomatic Record of Forty Years, 1904–1945* (Boston, 1952), I, 514, 517.

86. For the negotiations see Grew, *Turbulent Era*, I, 475–600; Harding, *Speeches as President*, "Address Prepared by President Warren G. Harding, July 31, 1923"; Grew, *Turbulent Era*, I, 584.

87. *U.S. Foreign Relations, 1923*, II, 1153–1171. For Hughes on Armenia see Hughes Papers, Box 172, Folder 35, Beerits memo, "Relations with Turkey," 14. The Senate rejected the Turkish treaty in 1927 because of no provision concerning Armenia. It made little difference—good relations with Turkey had already been restored.

88. Harold G. Moulton and Leo Pasvolsky, *War Debts and World Prosperity* (New York, 1932), 53–57, 64, 69.

89. For Hoover's differences with Hughes see Hoover Papers, Box 1-I/ 551, various letters to Hughes.

90. Copy of Mellon's request in HP, Box 88, Folder 57-2, item 41899.

91. *Cong. Record*, 67 Cong., 2 Sess., 1978.

92. Final agreement is in HP, Box 88, Folder 57-3, items 42060–42062.

93. Harding, *Speeches as President*, "Address of the President of the United States, February 7, 1923," p. 3.

94. For the best treatment of British debt funding see Henry G. Hendricks, *The Federal Debt, 1919–1930: A Chapter in American Public Finance* (Washington, D.C., 1933), 99–160.

95. For various debt-funding agreements see Moulton and Pasvolsky, *World War Debt Settlements*, 221–409.

96. An exhaustive treatment of reparations is Carl Bergmann, *The History of Reparations* (Boston, 1927).

97. WGH to Hoover, December 16, 1921, Hoover Papers, Box 1-I/243; Hoover to WGH, June 9, 1922, *ibid.*

98. *New York Times*, December 14, 1922, p. 16.

99. Hughes, *The Pathway of Peace*, 57. Hughes Papers, Box 172, Folder 27, Beerits memo, "Dawes Plan."

100. WGH to Hughes, July 27, 1922, National Archives, Record Group 59, State Department Files, 512.4 U1/1.

101. Grew, *Turbulent Era*, I, 458, 459–461.

102. Hughes Papers, Box 172, Folder 25, Beerits memo, 27.

103. Fleming, *The United States and World Organization*, 231–236. See also Clarence A. Berdahl, "Relations of the United States with the Assembly of the League of Nations," *American Political Science Review*, XXVI, No. 1 (February 1932), 99–112; HP, Box 119, Folder 74-2, items 58645–58671.

104. Harding, *Speeches as President*, "Inaugural Address, March 4, 1921."

105. Hughes Papers, Box 172, Folder 25, Beerits memo, 35.

106. *New York Times*, November 1, 1922, p. 1.

107. Hughes Papers, Box 172, Folder 25, Beerits memo, 35.

108. Copy of message, February 24, 1923, HP, Box 345, Folder 2274-1, item 144037.

109. Committee memo to WGH, no date, HP, Box 345, Folder 2274-1, items 144033–144034; WGH to Hughes, February 28, 1923, HP, Box 345, Folder 2274-1, item 144067; *New York Times*, March 1, 1923, p. 1.

110. WGH to Hughes, March 5, 1923, HP, Box 345, Folder 2274-1, item 144032.

111. WGH to Jennings, May 5, 1923, Jennings Papers.

112. Harding, *Speeches as President*, "Address of the President of the United States, April 24, 1923," pp. 4–5.

113. *New York Times*, March 9, 1923, p. 1, quoting Johnson; *ibid.*, April 26, 1923, p. 1, quoting LaFollette; "Starting the Fight to Join the Peace Court," *Literary Digest*, LXXVI, No. 10 (March 10, 1923), 8; *Atlanta Constitution*, April 25, 1923, p. 8.

114. Harding, *Speeches as President*, "Address of the President of the United States at St. Louis, June 28, 1923."

115. *New York Times*, May 21, 1923, p. 16. For complete coverage of World Court matters see Denna F. Fleming, *The United States and the World Court* (New York, 1945).

116. HP, Box 45, Folder 20-18, items 21212–21235, for Hughes on the Harding foreign policy. See also HP, Box 370, Folder 2608-1, item 175598.

117. *Atlanta Constitution*, August 3, 1923, p. 8.

118. *New York Times*, June 3, 1923, p. 5, quoting White.

CHAPTER XII. NEW APPROACHES IN DOMESTIC POLICY

1. Harding, *Speeches as President*, "Address of the President of the United States to Congress, December 8, 1922."

2. *New York Times*, December 9, 1922, p. 12; "Harding's Fight to Keep the Reins," *Literary Digest*, LXXV, No. 12 (December 23, 1922), 5.

3. Harding, *Speeches as President*, "Address of the President of the United States, April 12, 1921," p. 7.

4. FTC v. Winsted Hosiery Company, 258 US 483 (1922).

5. Thomas C. Blaisdell, Jr., *The Federal Trade Commission: An Experiment in the Control of Business* (New York, 1932), 177, 195.

6. Hoover-Daugherty correspondence is in Hoover Papers, Box 1-I/179. For Daugherty and trade associations see Robert F. Himmelberg, "Relaxation of the Federal Anti-Trust Policy as a Goal of the Business Community during the Period 1918–1933," unpublished Ph.D. dissertation (Pennsylvania State University, 1963), 91–109.

7. Examples are American Column and Lumber Co. v. U.S., 257 US 377 (1921); U.S. v. American Linseed Oil Co., 262 US 371 (1923).

8. On Humphrey see "Helping, Not Hindering, Business," *NAM Proceedings of the Thirtieth Annual Convention* (New York, 1925), 161–170. Excellent on the shift is G. Cullom Davis, "The Transformation of the Federal Trade Commission, 1914–1929," *MVHR*, XLIX, No. 3 (December 1962), 450–51. Sample Supreme Court decisions are Maple Flooring Manufacturers' Association v. U.S., 268 US 563 (1925); Cement Manufacturers' Protective Association v. U.S., 268 US 588 (1925).

9. Crissinger to Harding, November 2, 1921, HP, Box 47, Folder 21-8, items 22232–22234; also Box 130, Folder 90-2, various items.

10. Harold L. Reed, *Federal Reserve Policy, 1921–1930* (New York, 1930), 25–26, 33–35, 37–38, 40–41; for a general treatment see Seymour E. Harris, *Twenty Years of Federal Reserve Policy*, 2 vols. (Cambridge, Mass., 1933); Elmus R. Wicker, "Federal Reserve Monetary Policy, 1922–33: A Reinterpretation," *Journal of Political Economy*, LXXIII, No. 4 (August 1955), 325–343. Federal Reserve Board decisions are in *Digest of Rulings of the Federal Reserve Board, 1914–1927* (Washington, D.C., 1928).

11. Hoover's views in Hoover Papers, Box 1-I/242. Mellon's views in Mellon, *Taxation*, 74–77, 111–122.

12. WGH to Kahn, April 16, 1923, HP, Box 370, Folder 2611-1, item 175916.

13. 43 *Statutes at Large* 253. Not until 1926 did Mellon and Coolidge receive a tax measure they approved. To say that the twenties were ruled by Mellon economics is accurate only for the years 1926–29.

14. Statement of July 7, 1922, Davis Papers, Box 39, Book 3, pp. 945–946; "The March of Events," *World's Work*, XLV, No. 5 (March 1923), 5.

15. Statistics vary slightly: M. Ada Beney, *Wages, Hours, and Unemployment in the United States, 1914–1936* (New York, 1936), 30, 44–47; National Industrial Conference Board, *Wages in the United States, 1914–1930*, p. 59, Table 13, p. 211, Table A; National Industrial Conference Board, *Wages, Hours, and Employment in American Manufacturing Industries, July 1914–January 1924* (New York, 1924), p. 10, Table A, p. 15, Table C; Frederick C. Mills, *Economic Tendencies in the United States: Aspects of Pre-War and Post-War Changes* (New York, 1932), p. 243, Table 105, p. 393; Douglas, *Real Wages in the United States*, 426–427, 470–477, 551–567.

16. HP, Box 1, Folder 1-4, items 398–399.

17. G. C. Henderson, "The Agricultural Credits Act of 1923," *Quarterly Journal of Economics*, XXXVII (May 1923), 518–522.

18. Wallace to WGH, March 10, 1923, HP, Box 49, Folder 21-23, item 23642.

19. For the cooperative movement see Saloutos and Hicks, *Agricultural Discontent*, 286–320; Shideler, *Farm Crisis*, 99–104; Grace H. Larsen and Henry E. Erdman, "Aaron Sapiro: Genius of Farm Co-operative Promotion," *MVHR*, XLIX, No. 2 (September 1962), 242–268.

20. Gilbert C. Fite, *George N. Peek and the Fight for Farm Parity* (Norman, Okla., 1954), *passim*.

21. *Ibid.*, 44–49.

22. Shideler, "Herbert Hoover and the Federal Farm Board Project, 1921–1925," 711–712.

23. Publicity release, October 26, 1922, HP, Box 1, Folder 1-4, item 333.

24. Lord, *The Wallaces of Iowa*, 232–233.

25. Wallace had reviewed Harding's main speeches on agriculture before the president left and had made numerous suggestions which Harding had accepted. See especially HP, Box 1, Folder 1-5, items 515–518.

26. For discussion of the struggle for farm parity after 1923 see Fite, *George N. Peek*, 63–220.

27. For later Wallace-Hoover difficulties see Wallace to Hoover, April 8, 1924, Hoover Papers, Box 1-I/2; Shideler, "Herbert Hoover and the Federal Farm Board Project, 1921–1925," 713, 718–719.

28. Shideler, *Farm Crisis*, 129.

29. Peek to Clemens, October 30, 1939, Clemens Papers, Box 3.

30. Soule, *Prosperity Decade*, 229, 231.

31. Best on the Kansas court is National Industrial Conference Board, *The Kansas Court of Industrial Relations* (Report No. 67, New York, 1924). White's observations are in Walter Johnson, ed., *Selected Letters of William Allen White, 1899–1943* (New York, 1947), 22; White, *Autobiography*, 610–612.

32. Wolff Packing Co. v. Court of Industrial Relations, 262 US 522 (1923).

33. The figures vary somewhat. See President's Research Committee on Social Trends, *Recent Social Trends in the United States*, 2 vols. (New York, 1933), II, 841; Perlman and Taft, *Labor Movements*, IV, 581. From 1923 to 1929 union membership dropped only 148,000 more. In a most interesting analysis of labor see Irving Bernstein, *The Lean Years: A History of the American Worker, 1920–1933* (Cambridge, Mass., 1960), *passim*.

34. Henry F. Pringle, *The Life and Times of William Howard Taft: A Biography*, 2 vols. (New York, 1939), II, 951–952, 955–959.

35. By the time of Harding's death, the membership of the Court was as it would remain until 1930 except for Justice Harlan F. Stone who was added by Coolidge in 1925 to replace Justice McKenna.

36. Duplex Printing Press Co. v. Deering, 254 US 443 (1921); American Steel Foundries v. Tri-City Central Trades Council, 257 US 184 (1921); Truax v. Corrigan, 257 US 312 (1921).

37. Adkins v. Children's Hospital, 261 US 525 (1923).

38. United Mine Workers v. Coronado Coal Co., 259 US 344 (1922); Bailey v. Drexel Furniture Co., 259 US 20 (1922).

39. Larkin, *The President's Control of the Tariff*, 5–6, 113–131, 184; Gersting, *The Flexible Provisions in the United States' Tariff*, 87–88; *Sixth Annual Report of the United States Tariff Commission* (Washington, D.C., 1922), 59–63.

40. For various views see HP, Box 108, Folder 60-7, various items.

41. WGH to Marvin, March 27, 1923, HP, Box 108, Folder 60-8, item 52681.

42. Agreement is in HP, Box 108, Folder 60-9, item 52923.

43. *New York Times*, April 23, 1923, p. 5, and May 7, 1923, p. 21; HP, Box 109, Folder 60-11, items 53124–53132, and Box 694, Folder 12, items 149249–149251.

44. Colin B. Goodykoontz, "Edward P. Costigan and the Tariff Commission, 1917–1928," *Pacific Historical Review*, XVI, No. 4 (November 1947), 410–419; *Eighth Annual Report of the United States Tariff Commission* (Washington, D.C., 1924), 9. Most illuminating are *Minutes of Meetings of the United States Tariff Commission from September 19, 1922 to January 26, 1926*, Senate Doc. No. 83, 69 Cong., 1 Sess. (Washington, D.C., 1926).

45. HP, Box 31, Folder 15-3, items 14490–14494, and Box 32, Folder 15-5, items 14702–14710; Davis Papers, Box 39, Book 4, pp. 1499, 1529.

46. For background on the Johnson bill see Higham, *Strangers in the Land*, 270–299, 313–315, 320–322; also House Committee on Immigration, *Hearings, Analysis of America's Modern Melting Pot*, 67 Cong., 3 Sess. (Washington, D.C., 1923).

47. Garis, *Immigration Restriction*, 170, 183 n. 20, 261–262.

48. *New York Times*, April 15, 1923, p. 1.

49. Lasker to WGH, June 7, 1923, HP, Box 65, Folder 40-5, items 31897–31906; Gunther, *Taken at the Flood*, 143.

50. House Report No. 2, 68 Cong., 1 Sess. (Washington, D.C., 1924).

51. Elbert L. Tatum, *The Changed Political Thought of the Negro, 1915–1940* (New York, 1941), 72.

52. WGH to J. R. Shillady, February 20, 1920, HP, Box 690, Folder 4975-1, item 316285.

53. For the Negro and the 1920 campaign see Downes, "Negro Rights and White Backlash in the Campaign of 1920," 85–107.

54. Harding, *Speeches as President*, "Address of the President of the United States, April 12, 1921"; "A Race Commission—A Constructive Plan," *Nation*, CXII (April 27, 1921), 612.

55. HP, Box 215, Folder 300-98, items 100850–100853.

56. Harding, *Speeches as President*, "Address of the President of the United States, October 26, 1921."

57. *New York Times*, October 28, 1921, 4, quoting Harrison; W. E. B. DuBois, "President Harding and Social Equality," *Crisis*, XXIII, No. 2 (December 1921), 53–56; WGH to ex-Gov. O'Neal, November 7, 1921, HP, Box 361, Folder 2569-1, items 171588–171589.

58. For a harsh view of Harding and the Birmingham speech see Richard B. Sherman, "The Harding Administration and the Negro: An Opportunity Lost," *Journal of Negro History*, XLIX, No. 3 (July 1964), 159–160.

59. Sample order to cabinet officers in HP, Box 1, Folder 1-1; WGH to Brascher, October 5, 1921, HP, Box 694, Folder 2, items 148776–148777.

60. For the Cohen case see *New York Times*, May 17, 1923, 1; HP, Box 140, Folder 93-4, items 68433–68442; Commerce Department report to Harding, Hoover Papers, Box 1-I/ 243.

61. Sample attack on the Klan in *New York Times*, May 18, 1923, 1. Harding asked Daugherty to keep a close eye on Klan activities.

62. WGH to Jennings, January 6, 1922, Jennings Papers.

63. For filibuster see *Cong. Record*, 67 Cong., 3 Sess., 288–450; *New York Times*, December 3, 1922, p. 1, quoting Lodge.

64. Johnson to Christian, December 21, 1922, HP, Box 205, Folder 266-6, items 97160–97161.

65. The most detailed treatment of the Negro in the twenties is Mary A. Miller, "The Political Attitude of the Negro, 1920–1932," unpublished M.A. thesis (Pennsylvania State University, 1968).

66. Charles Merz, *The Dry Decade* (New York, 1931), 52.

67. Andrew Sinclair, *Prohibition: The Era of Excess* (Boston, 1962), 256–257.

68. WGH to Edge, August 17, 1921, HP, Box 695, Folder 9, item 149703.

69. For samples of Wheeler's pressure see HP, Box 119, Folder 75-1. Except for Hays and Hoover the Harding cabinet was not noted for its teetotaling.

70. Examples in HP, Box 370, Folder 2608-1, item 175611, and Box 28, Folder 10-5, item 12785; Peter H. Odegard, *Pressure Politics: The Story of the Anti-Saloon League* (New York, 1928), 196.

71. For comments on caliber of appointees see Laurence F. Schmeckebier, *The Bureau of Prohibition: Its History, Activities and Organization* (Washington, D.C., 1929), 46, and *passim*; report of National Civil Service Reform League in *New York Times*, November 17, 1921, p. 17; House Committee on Civil Service, *Hearings, Extension of Civil Service Regulations to Prohibition Agents*, 68 Cong., 1 Sess. (Washington, D.C., 1924), *passim*.

72. Cunard Steamship Company v. Mellon, 262 US 100 (1923).

73. Hughes Papers, Box 173, Folder 48, "Treaties to Prevent Liquor Smuggling," Beerits memo, 10–11, on negotiations.

74. Pringle, *The Life and Times of William Howard Taft*, II, 981.

75. Sullivan, *Our Times*, VI, 214.

76. Merz, *The Dry Decade*, 123; Schmeckebier, *The Bureau of Prohibition*, 46–47; Herbert Asbury, *The Great Illusion: An Informal History of Prohibition* (New York, 1950), 188; Sinclair, *Prohibition*, 248.

77. WGH to William F. Anderson, January 2, 1922, HP, Box 370, Folder 2608-1, items 175569–175570.

78. Harding, *Speeches as President*, "Address of the President of the United States, April 12, 1921," p. 13.

79. Editorial, *American Medical Association Journal*, February 5, 1921.

80. WGH to Hays, August 16, 1920, Hays Papers.

81. Harding, *Speeches as President*, "Address of the President of the United States, April 12, 1921," pp. 8–9.

82. 42 *Statutes at Large* 212; President's Research Committee on Social Trends, *Recent Social Trends in the United States*, I, 173.

83. Harding, *Speeches as President*, "Address of the President of the United States, April 12, 1921," p. 11.

84. Wilbur and Hyde, *The Hoover Policies*, 211.

85. Hoover, *Memoirs*, II, 141–142.

86. Wilbur and Hyde, *The Hoover Policies*, 215–216; Hoover, *Memoirs*, II, 132–133.

87. Typescript report, HP, Box 39, Folder 19-9. The Hays Papers also contain much information on the early air mail routes.

88. Typed report of the commission, HP, Box 139, Folder 92-1, items 68045–68050. At all times this commission was under very heavy pressure from private utilities.

89. Hoover, *Memoirs*, II, 115–117; Hoover Papers, Box 1-I/172, various items.

90. Judson King, *The Conservation Fight: From Theodore Roosevelt to the Tennessee Valley Authority* (Washington, D.C., 1959), 95–98. King, 106, erroneously claims Harding was favorable to the Ford offer. See C. H. Huston to Hoover, February 21, 1923, HP, Box 5, Folder 3-5, item 2466.

91. Benjamin H. Williams, *American Diplomacy: Policies and Practices* (New York, 1936), 461–462; Graham H. Stuart, *American Diplomatic and Consular Practice* (New York, 1936), 185–189; 43 *Statutes at Large* 140. Key documents on the Rogers bill are 67 Cong., 2 Sess., House Report No. 646 (Washington, D.C., 1923), and *Hearings on the Foreign Service of the United States*, 68 Cong., 1 Sess. (Washington, D.C., 1924).

92. Alderfer, "The Personality and Politics of Warren G. Harding," 217–218.

93. See HP, Box 222, Folder 303-2 and 303-3, various items.

94. 42 *Statutes at Large* 1488. See also Paul V. Betters, *The Personnel Classification Board: Its History, Activities and Organization* (Washington, D.C., 1931).

95. Brown Report of January 21, 1922, Brown Papers, Box 1.

96. WGH to Pinchot, November 18, 1922, HP, Box 701, Folder 10, items 152682–152683.

97. WGH to Jennings, January 6, 1922, Jennings Papers.

98. For the cabinet plan see *Reorganization of the Executive Departments*, Senate Doc. No. 302, 67 Cong., 4 Sess. (Washington, D.C., 1923).

CHAPTER XIII. THE TRAGEDY BEGINS

1. White House calendar sheets are in Hard Papers, Box 2, Folder 6; *New York Times*, March 5, 1922, p. 1, quoting Harding.

2. Hughes, *The Pathway of Peace*, 302; Butler, *Across the Busy Years*, I, 411.

3. HP, Box 359, Folder 2560-1, items 170649–170652.

4. Joseph Tumulty, *Woodrow Wilson as I Know Him* (New York, 1921), 506–507.

5. Dr. Mayo to R. B. Harris, June 27, 1933, Harris Papers, Box 7, Folder 8; *New York Times*, November 22, 1924, p. 3.

6. Dr. Boone to R. B. Harris, June 27, 1938, Harris Papers, Box 8, Folder 5; Daugherty, *The Inside Story*, 171.

7. Ishbel Ross, *Grace Coolidge and Her Era: The Story of a President's Wife* (New York, 1962), 89; Hoover, *Forty-Two Years in the White House*, 274–275; Longworth, *Crowded Hours*, 324; McLean, *Father Struck It Rich*, 256; Mrs. Fall to Clemens, June 19, 1940, Clemens Papers. See also Madame Garcia, "When an Astrologer Ruled the White House," *Liberty Magazine*, April 9, 1938.

8. The band quotation is from Hoover, *Forty-Two Years in the White House*, 275. The autumn leaf quotation is from Russell, *The Shadow of Blooming Grove*, 5. Russell is severe on Florence Harding.

9. *New York Times*, January 22, 1922, Sec. III, p. 6.

10. H. A. Wallace to R. B. Harris, September 11, 1933, Harris Papers, Box 4, Folder 5.

11. "The Dilemma of the Party Politicians," *New Republic*, XXXIV, No. 433 (March 21, 1923), 82.

12. *New York Times*, April 4, 1923, p. 16.

13. *Ibid.*, February 5, 1923, p. 6.

14. WGH to G. Christian, Sr., January 29, 1923, HP, Box 369, Folder 2606-1, items 175436–175437.

15. WGH to Carmi Thompson, March 5, 1923, HP, Box 703, Folder 9, item 153602; WGH to C. C. Fisher, May 19, 1923, HP, Box 69, Folder 8, item 150132.

16. *New York Times*, March 18, 1923, p. 1.

17. HMD to WGH, April 16, 1923, HP, Box 695, Folder 3, items 149364–149368.

18. "Mr. Harding and a Second Term," *Nation*, CXVI (April 4, 1923), 380; "The Dilemma of the Party Politicians," *New Republic*, XXXIV, No. 433 (March 21, 1923), 84; "Harding's Chances for Another Term," *Literary Digest*, LXXVI, No. 13 (March 31, 1923), 7, quoting the *Post*. Russell in his *The Shadow of Blooming Grove*, 563–564, claims that Harding's popularity was declining rapidly in the spring of 1923. Russell is wrong.

19. For Daugherty's testimony see HP, Box 30, Folder 10-15, also published separately as *Reply by the Attorney General of the United States, Hon. Harry M. Daugherty, to Charges Filed with the Committee on the Judiciary of the House of Representatives, December 1, 1922.*

20. "Uncle Sam's Prosecutor Prosecuted," *Literary Digest*, LXXV, No. 11 (December 16, 1923), 11.

21. Accounts book, HP, Box 790, Folder 1.

22. Raymond Benjamin to Hays, November 16, 1920, Hays Papers; Daugherty, *The Inside Story*, 179–184. For Forbes's background see Carl C. Dickey, "Plundering the Wounded Men," *World's Work*, XLVIII, No. 2 (June 1924), 167–174.

23. "Reminiscences of James W. Wadsworth," 294; HMD to Clemens, July 8, 1940, Clemens Papers, Box 1; Daugherty, *The Inside Story*, 184.

24. For several colorful accounts, somewhat fictionalized, see Samuel H. Adams, *Incredible Era: The Life and Times of Warren Gamaliel Harding* (Boston, 1939), 294–297; Russell, *The Great Interlude*, 67; Stokes, *Chip Off My Shoulder*, 124; Starling, *Starling of the White House*, 192; and Sullivan, *Our Times*, VI, 238–242.

25. Reily, "Years of Confusion," 317.

26. *New York Times*, March 15, 1923, p. 1.

27. The best description of Smith is in Sullivan, *Our Times*, VI, 24.

28. Daugherty, *The Inside Story*, 68–69; interview by Robert K. Murray with C. A. Jones, November 2, 1966.

29. Forbes interview, *New York World*, December 4, 1927; Daugherty, *The Inside Story*, 231–233; *New York Times*, May 31, 1923, p. 2.

30. For a detailed, and highly colored, description of the Ohio Gang's activities see Adams, *Incredible Era*, 231–241.

31. "Reminiscences of James W. Wadsworth," 279.

32. Interview by Robert K. Murray with C. A. Jones, November 2, 1966.

33. Christian to Crissinger, March 10, 1923, HP, Box 47, Folder 21-9, item 22344. For an unverified account of Harding's throwing Smith out of the White House see Russell, *The Great Interlude*, 69.

34. Daugherty, *The Inside Story*, 248–249; Stimson testimony is in *Investigation of the Honorable Harry M. Daugherty*, U.S. Senate Select Committee, 68 Cong., 1 Sess. (Washington, D.C., 1924), I, 538–545 and *passim*.

35. Interview by Robert K. Murray with C. A. Jones, November 2, 1966; *New York Times*, May 31, 1923, p. 1.

36. *New York Times*, June 10, 1923, p. 7.

37. White, *Autobiography*, 619.

38. Butler, *Across the Busy Years*, I, 411–412.

39. HMD to McLean, June 4, 1923, Evalyn Walsh McLean Papers (Library of Congress), Box 5, Folder "Daugherty"; Daugherty, *The Inside Story*, 245–250.

40. Sullivan, *Our Times*, VI, 236–237.

41. Rudolph Marx, *The Health of the Presidents* (New York, 1960), 326; Dr. Marx to R. B. Harris, January 19, 1962, Harris Papers, Box 10, Folder 3; Watson, *As I Knew Them*, 210; Russell, *The Great Interlude*, 68.

42. Marx, *The Health of the Presidents*, 330; Starling, *Starling of the White House*, 189.

43. Pusey, *Charles Evans Hughes*, II, 562; Reily, "Years of Confusion," 449; interview by Robert K. Murray with C. A. Jones, November 2, 1966.

44. Jennings to WGH, April 13, 1923, Jennings Papers.

45. Watson, *As I Knew Them*, 231; Starling, *Starling of the White House*, 196.

46. For the most exaggerated account of the morbidity see Adams, *Incredible Era*, 333–340. The will and estate papers are in W. G. Harding Papers (Library of Congress), Box 2.

47. See sample remarks in HP, Box 151, Folder 101-2.

48. White, *Autobiography*, 623–624; White, *A Puritan in Babylon*, 239.

49. Capper to Clemens, August 23, 1949, Clemens Papers, Box 1; Mrs. Fall to Clemens, no date, Clemens Papers, Box 2.

50. These addresses are published in Harding, *Speeches as President*.

51. "Mr. Harding Foreshadows His 1924 Platform," *Literary Digest*, LXXVIII, No. 3 (July 21, 1923), 9, quoting the *Minneapolis Tribune*.

52. Speech at Dallas, Oregon, July 3, 1923, HP, Box 151, Folder 101-4, item 73360.

53. Alaskan notes, Hoover Papers, Box 1-I/ 546, provide one of the best eyewitness accounts available on the Alaskan trip. These notes, written immediately after the events, vary in a number of details with Hoover's *Memoirs*, II, 48–52, written many years later. Another excellent eyewitness account is a 21-page report of Ernest Chapman, a railroad policeman who accompanied the presidential party. See HP, Box 765, dated September 11, 1923.

54. Hoover, *Memoirs*, II, 49; Lyons, *Herbert Hoover*, 169.

55. Alaskan notes, Hoover Papers, Box 1-I/ 546. One of the most repeated stories of the Alaskan trip was that a seaplane caught up with the *Henderson* as it turned south, delivering to Harding a long, coded message from Washington which upset him terribly. The contents of the message were never known or revealed; indeed, there is some doubt about the authenticity of the entire episode.

56. "The President and the People," *Outlook*, CXXXIV, No. 12 (August 8, 1923), 535.

57. See Alaskan notes, Hoover Papers, Box 1-I/ 546.

58. Harding, *Speeches as President*, "The Territory of Alaska."

59. Hoover Papers, Box 1-I/546, "Last Illness: Hoover's Recollection"; Marx, *The Health of the Presidents*, 333–334. Dr. Work later claimed the digestive disturbance before Vancouver was not connected with Harding's later difficulty. Others on board the *Henderson* had also complained of some gastrointestinal distress before Vancouver. Work to Hoover, August 16, 1923, Hoover Papers, Box 1-I/ 172.

60. *New York Times*, August 1, 1923, p. 1; Harding, *Speeches as President*, "Address on Our Foreign Relations."

61. Starling, *Starling of the White House*, 198–199; Malcolm Jennings, "A Journey and Its Ending," pamphlet, n.p., n.d., 14; Ray Lyman Wilbur, "The Last Illness of a Calm Man," *Saturday Evening Post*, CXCVI, No. 15 (October 13, 1923), 64; S. Dauser to Reily, January 22, 1932, "Years of Confusion," 364; Hoover Papers, Box 1-I/ 546 "Last Illness: Hoover's Recollection." The article being read was Samuel G. Blythe, "A Calm Review of a Calm Man," *Saturday Evening Post*, CXCVI, No. 4 (January 28, 1923), 3–4, 73–76. The exact positions of the death-room occupants and the whereabouts of the doctors are subject to some debate. What is described in the text is the best that can be pieced together.

62. Starling, *Starling of the White House*, 201.

63. Marx, *The Health of the Presidents*, 335–336.

64. Reily, "Years of Confusion," 368.

65. The primary source for much of this gossip is McLean, *Father Struck It Rich*. A recent repetition of these stories is in Arthur M. Schlesinger, Jr., *The Crisis of the Old Order, 1919–1933* (in *The Age of Roosevelt*, I, New York, 1957), 53. For a contrary view see Hoover, *Forty-Two Years in the White House*, 114.

66. For the events between August 3 and August 11, the contemporary press is the best source. The *New York Tribune* carried the most colorful descriptions of the train trips and the Marion funeral. See also "Warren Harding's 4000 Mile Funeral," *Literary Digest, LXXVIII*, No. 8 (August 25, 1923), 36–40. Best on the Washington ceremonies is the *Washington Post*.

CHAPTER XIV. THE FINAL DISASTER

1. "What Harding's Passing Means in Other Lands," *Literary Digest*, LXXVIII, No. 7 (August 18, 1923), 21.

2. *Atlanta Constitution*, August 3, 1923, p. 8.

3. HMD to Reily, August 23, 1923, Daugherty Papers; McLean Papers, Folder "Daugherty."

4. Johnson, *George Harvey*, 399.

5. Russell, *The Illustrious Life and Work of Warren G. Harding*, 32, quoting Wallace.

6. Speech, October 23, 1923, Hoover Papers, Box 1-I/244.

7. Speech, August 10, 1923, Davis Papers, Box 39, Book 4, p. 1524.

8. *Cong. Record.*, 68 Cong., 1 Sess., 3318–3323.

9. Except where indicated, all the information on the Veterans' Bureau scandal is taken from *Investigation of Veterans Bureau*, Hearings before the Select Committee, U.S. Senate, 67 Cong., 4 Sess. (Washington, D.C., 1923).

10. The most highly colored account of Forbes and the Veterans' Bureau is in Werner, *Privileged Characters*, 193–228.

11. WGH to Fall, April 17, 1922, HP, Folder 6-4, item 10612; Bain to Clemens, April 14, 1940, Clemens Papers, Box 1.

12. Burl Noggle, "The Origins of the Teapot Dome Investigation," *MVHR*, XLIV, No. 2 (September 1957), 237–266, is excellent on the attacks on Fall and the events leading to Teapot Dome. Also excellent for understanding the event is J. Leonard Bates, *The Origins of Teapot Dome: Progressives, Parties, and Petroleum, 1909–1921* (Urbana, Ill., 1963), especially 200–244.

13. Harris Papers, Box 15, Folder 3. A copy of the transfer order is in *Leases upon Naval Oil Reserves*, Hearings before the Committee on Public Lands and Surveys, U.S. Senate, 68 Cong., 1 Sess., I (Washington, D.C., 1924), 177–178.

14. Noggle, *Teapot Dome*, 19, 25–26.

15. Bain to Clemens, October 18, 1939, Clemens Papers, Box 1; Hughes Papers, Box 173, Folder 45, Beerits memo, "Fall Oil Scandals," p. 3.

16. *Cong. Record*, 67 Cong., 2 Sess., 5567–5568; *Wall Street Journal*, April 14, 1922, p. 1.

17. For Fall's reaction to the Kendrick resolution see *Leases upon Naval Oil Reserves*, I, 296–298.

18. *Cong. Record*, 67 Cong., 2 Sess., 5792, 6041–6050, 6097.

19. For Harding's letter see *Leases upon Naval Oil Reserves*, I, 25.

20. Josephine O'Keane, *Thomas J. Walsh: A Senator from Montana* (Francestown, N.H., 1955), must be used with care, but provides the basic facts on Walsh's background.

21. Walsh's papers contain endless letters from informants filled with rumors, nonsense, fiction, etc., Walsh Papers, Boxes 208–214.

22. White, *Forty Years on Main Street*, 111–112; Johnson, *Borah of Idaho*, 287; Schlesinger, *The Crisis of the Old Order*, 55.

23. *New York Times*, March 3, 1923, p. 2.

24. Unless otherwise noted, the subsequent narrative material on the oil scandals is drawn from *Leases upon Naval Oil Reserves, passim*.

25. *New York Times*, February 3, 1924, p. 1.

26. Sullivan, *Our Times*, VI, 329. For a scholarly treatment of Fall and Teapot Dome consult David H. Stratton, "Albert B. Fall and the Teapot Dome Affair," unpublished Ph.D. dissertation (University of Colorado, 1955).

27. "Denby Out, But Not Down," *Literary Digest*, LXXX, No. 9 (March 1, 1924), 10; Hoover, *Memoirs*, II, 54.

28. Norris, *Fighting Liberal*, 237. For a caustic analysis of the various trials see M. R. Werner and John Starr, *Teapot Dome* (New York, 1959), 194–277. By 1927 all of the Fall leases were set aside by court order. See Mammoth Oil Company v. U.S., 275 US 13 (1927), and Pan American Petroleum Company v. U.S., 273 US 456 (1927).

29. Fall's statement appears in Russell, *The Shadow of Blooming Grove*, 500.

30. Walsh to R. B. Harris, April 7, 1932, Harris Papers, Box 4, Folder 8.

31. For interesting comments on the wisdom of the leases see Werner and Starr, *Teapot Dome*, 79; "Yes—But What Are the Facts," *Outlook*, CXXXVI, No. 14 (April 2, 1924), 555–558.

32. *New York World*, January 30, 1924, cartoon.

33. Daugherty, *The Inside Story*, 77–78, 193–194; HMD to Willis, February 22, 1924, Hoover Papers, Box 1-I/551 (copy).

34. White, *A Puritan in Babylon*, 266; Hoover, *Memoirs*, II, 54; Pringle, *The Life and Times of William Howard Taft*, II, 1022.

35. *New York Times*, issues February 20, 1924, p. 1; February 21, 1924, p. 1; February 28, 1924, p. 1; March 2, 1924, p. 1. For Wheeler's own account of his crusade against Daugherty, which must be taken with a grain of salt, see Burton K. Wheeler, *Yankee from the West* (Garden City, N.Y., 1962), *passim*.

36. Unless otherwise indicated the information in the subsequent narrative is from *Investigation of the Honorable Harry M. Daugherty*, Senate Select Committee on the Investigation of the Attorney General, 68 Cong., 1 Sess. (Washington, D.C., 1924), *passim*.

37. *New York Times*, March 15, 1924, p. 1.

38. A recent biography of Means which strives to separate truth from fiction is Edwin P. Hoyt, *Spectacular Rogue: Gaston B. Means* (Indianapolis, 1963).

39. *New York Times*, March 29, 1924, p. 1, quoting Daugherty and Coolidge.

40. "Mr. Coolidge Dismisses Mr. Daugherty," *Nation*, CXVIII (April 9, 1924), 386; "Why Daugherty Is Out," *Literary Digest*, LXXX, No. 2 (April 12, 1924), 5–8.

41. For the complete statement see Sullivan, *Our Times*, VI, 354.

42. *Ibid.*, 355.

43. HMD to N. H. Fairbanks, April 3, 1924, Fairbanks Papers. For a highly colored treatment of the Daugherty investigation and its aftermath see Werner, *Privileged Characters*, 229–318.

44. Various cabinet members' statements are in *New York Times*, January 26, 1924, p. 1, and February 1, 1924, p. 1. See also Arthur Pound and Samuel T. Moore, eds., *More They Told Barron: Conversations and Revelations of an American Pepys in Wall Street* (New York, 1931), 194. The only evidence to suggest that the cabinet may have discussed the leases appears in Lord, *The Wallaces of Iowa*, 241–242. Lord claims Wallace tried unsuccessfully to air the oil leases in cabinet meetings. Lord gives no sources.

45. Address, April 15, 1924, Hughes Papers, Box 173, Folder 45, Beerits memo, "Fall Oil Scandals," 6–7.

46. Daugherty unequivocally claims that Harding died without knowing about Fall. See *The Inside Story*, 202.

47. The final sale price for the *Star* was actually $423,000. Harding's death eliminated that portion of the agreement which provided for his services as a contributing editor. It was generally agreed that this price was "fair."

48. Undated letter to "Charlie," Harris Papers, Box 1, Folder 2; *New York Times*, November 23, 1924, p. 1.

49. Dr. Charles Moore to Mrs. Harding, October 12, 1923, HP, Box 789, Folder 5, item unnumbered; *New York Times*, December 27, 1925, p. 2.

50. Nan Britton, *The President's Daughter* (New York, 1927). Unless otherwise indicated the information in the following narrative, including quotations, comes from the book.

51. Even today in Marion various interpretations of the Britton affair can be heard. There are those who claim that George Christian, Jr., admitted many times

in private that the Britton story was all true. See K. Lawler to Hard, January 27, 1932, Hard Papers, Box 2, Folder 4.

52. Reily, "Years of Confusion," 371–372, 379, 385; Scobey to W. K. Leonard, November 14, 1927, Scobey Papers, Box 3, item 686.

53. Gaston B. Means, *The Strange Death of President Harding (as told to May Dixon Thacker)* (New York, 1930). The following narrative, including quotations, is from the book.

54. Daugherty, *The Inside Story*, 238.

55. "The Death of Harding," *Nation*, CXXX, No. 3386 (May 28, 1930), 631.

56. The 1928 Senate investigation was *Leases upon Naval Oil Reserves. Activities of the Continental Trading Company of Canada*, Hearings before the Committee on Public Lands and Surveys, U.S. Senate, 70 Cong., 1 Sess. (Washington, D.C., 1928).

57. *New York Times*, May 31, 1926, p. 17.

58. George Akerson to Hoke Donithen, April 8, 1929, Hoover Papers, Box 1-G/915.

59. *Baltimore Sun*, October 8, 1930, p. 8.

60. *New York Times*, June 17, 1931, p. 1.

61. Daugherty, *The Inside Story, passim*. For Daugherty's explanation of his refusal to testify see p. 257.

62. HMD to Hard, January 12, 1932, Hard Papers, Box 2, Folder 4.

63. Interview, *Columbus Citizen*, January 26, 1940; for Daugherty's will see Harris Papers, Box 9, Folder 5.

64. Interview, *New York World*, December 4, 1927.

65. Nan Britton, *Honesty or Politics* (New York, 1932).

66. In 1964 Nan was 68 and Elizabeth Ann, the mother of three children in Glendale, Calif., was 44. Russell, *The Shadow of Blooming Grove*, 658.

CHAPTER XV. THE MYTH AND THE REALITY

1. Copy of telegram, HP, Box 30, Folder 10-14, item 13723; for the best version of the oath taking see Claude M. Fuess, *Calvin Coolidge: The Man from Vermont* (Boston, 1940), 307–311.

2. Fuess, *Calvin Coolidge*, 285, 317.

3. Michelson, *The Ghost Talks*, 232. Fuess says "Harding had great confidence in Coolidge, consulted him frequently, and was influenced by him to a marked degree." Fuess is wrong.

4. Fuess, *Calvin Coolidge*, 288, 290, 293, 300, 307; Ross, *Grace Coolidge and Her Era*, 73–74.

5. Stokes, *Chip Off My Shoulder*, 139.

6. Pollard, *The President and the Press*, 718.

7. The most recent work on Coolidge is Donald R. McCoy, *Calvin Coolidge: The Quiet President* (New York, 1967). McCoy is sympathetic yet balanced.

8. White, *A Puritan in Babylon*, 247; White in *Masks in a Pageant*, 448, places much emphasis on the Coolidge "change."

9. *New York Times*, August 15, 1923, p. 1, and August 27, 1923, p. 1.

10. *Ibid.*, December 7, 1923, p. 1.

11. Fuess, *Calvin Coolidge*, 342.

12. See issues March 13–15, 1924.

13. "How to Estimate the Daugherty Evidence," *New Republic*, XXXVIII, No. 486 (March 26, 1924), 112–113.

14. *Literary Digest*, LXXXI (June 21, 1924), 14–15; *American Federationist*, XXXI (July 1924), 577–578. The Walsh report is *Leases upon Naval Oil Reserves*, 68 Cong., 1 Sess., Senate Report No. 794 (Washington, D.C., 1924).

15. *New York Times*, March 24, 1924, p. 1.

16. Russel B. Nye, *Midwestern Progressive Politics: A Historical Study of Its Origins and Development, 1870–1950* (East Lansing, Mich., 1951), 323–325.

17. *Ibid.*, 326; MacKay, *The Progressive Movement of 1924*, 60–64.

18. MacKay, *The Progressive Movement of 1924*, 67; Nathan Fine, *Labor and Farmer Parties in the United States, 1828–1928* (New York, 1928), 402–407.

19. Fine, *Labor and Farmer Parties in the United States*, 409–410. The best coverage of the Progressives is in this book, 398–438.

20. For sample opinion see *New York Times*, April 14, 1924, p. 1.

21. Taft to Root, June 9, 1924, Root Papers, Box 166, Folder "1923–1928."

22. Butler, *Across the Busy Years*, I, 281.

23. For the convention see *Official Report of the Proceedings of the Democratic National Convention . . . 1924* (Indianapolis, 1924).

24. *New York Times*, November 2, 1924, p. 2; Burl Noggle in his *Teapot Dome*, viii, claims that Teapot Dome was more of a liability for the Democrats than for the Republicans. See also J. Leonard Bates, "The Teapot Dome Scandal and the Election of 1924," *AHR*, LX, No. 2 (January 1955), 303–322.

25. Michelson, *The Ghost Talks*, 235; "2,386,052 Straws Forecast Tuesday's Tempest," *Literary Digest*, No. 5 (November 1, 1924), 5–7; O'Keane, *Thomas J. Walsh*, 165–167.

26. MacKay, *The Progressive Movement of 1924*, 219–221, 274, for election statistics; for LaFollette's appeal in eastern cities see Fine, *Labor and Farmer Parties in the United States*, 414.

27. Noggle, *Teapot Dome*, 171.

28. MacKay, *The Progressive Movement of 1924*, 235, 243.

29. For two recent analyses of prosperity and progressivism see Link, "What Happened to the Progressive Movement in the 1920's?" 833–851; Paul W. Glad, "Progressives and the Business Culture of the 1920's," *JAH*, LIII, No. 1 (June 1966), 75–89. It is clear that this connection between prosperity and progressivism was important in the Republican coalition during the twenties. Only when prosperity faltered did the pendulum swing toward the Democrats and a new type of liberalism. See J. Joseph Huthmacher, *Massachusetts People and Politics, 1919–1933* (Boston, 1959).

30. Noggle, *Teapot Dome*, 59, quoting McAdoo; *Wall Street Journal*, December 7, 1923, p. 1, and August 4, 1923, p. 1, quoting Barron; Taft to Root, September 19, 1924, Root Papers, Box 166, Folder "1923–28."

31. White, *A Puritan in Babylon*, 400.

32. *Ibid.*, 394.

33. Nye, *Midwestern Progressive Politics*, 348, quoting *Harper's*.

34. George B. Christian, Jr., "Warren Gamaliel Harding," *Current History*, XVII (September 1923), 903.

35. Arthur M. Schlesinger, "Our Presidents: A Rating by 75 Historians," *New York Times Magazine*, July 29, 1962, 12–13, 40.

36. "President Harding and His Administration," *Outlook*, CXXXIV, No. 13 (August 15, 1923), 575.

37. Chapple, *Life and Times of Warren G. Harding*; W. F. Johnson, *The Life of Warren G. Harding* (Philadelphia, 1923); Russell, *The Illustrious Life and Work of Warren G. Harding*; C. Asher, *He Was "Just Folks"* (Chicago, 1923). The Chapple book is the best.

38. See "The Unpublished Truth about President Harding's Death," *True Detective Stories*, February 1932; Clare Booth Luce, "All for the Love of a Lady," *McCall's*, XCI, No. 2 (November 1963), 28, 178–180. For a "new" slant on Harding's death see Frances W. Schruben, "An Even Stranger Death of President Harding," *Southern California Quarterly*, XLIII, No. 1 (March 1966).

39. H. L. Mencken, "A Short View of Gamalielese," *Nation*, CXII (April 27, 1921), 621–622. As late as 1934 Mencken admitted, "I met Harding only once and knew little of him personally." Mencken to R. B. Harris, February 1, 1934, Harris Papers, Box 10, Folder 2.

40. Letters between Bliven and Harding, HP, Box 684, Folder 4936-1, items 313401–313407; Bruce Bliven, "Two Presidents," *New Republic*, XXXV, No. 454 (August 15, 1923), 321–322.

41. The Bliven articles are "The Ohio Gang," *New Republic*, XXXVIII, No. 492 (May 7, 1924), 276–277; "The Ohio Gang," *ibid.*, XXXVIII, No. 493 (May 14, 1924), 305–308; "The Ohio Gang: Money Changers in the Temple," *ibid.*, XXXVIII, No. 494 (May 21, 1924), 334–336; "Charlie, Warren and Ned," *ibid.*, XXXIX, No. 495 (May 28, 1924), 9–11; "The Era of Good Fellows," *ibid.*, XXXIX, No. 496 (June 4, 1924), 40–42.

42. Still writing in 1965, Bliven was still committing the same errors, still relying mainly on his memory. See Bruce Bliven, "Tempest over Teapot," *American Heritage*, XVI, No. 5 (August 1965), 20–23, 100, 105.

43. Johnson, ed., *Selected Letters of William Allen White*, 260.

44. White, *Masks in a Pageant*, 402ff.

45. Frederick L. Allen, *Only Yesterday: An Informal History of the Nineteen-Twenties* (New York, 1931), 42, 126–127, 127–129, 135, 150, 152–154.

46. Sullivan to Dr. C. Sawyer, July 19, 1935, HP, Box 802, Folder 1.

47. Werner was a self-styled popular historian, authoring such works as *Barnum* (1923), *Brigham Young* (1925), and *Bryan* (1929).

48. White relied mainly on his own *Masks in a Pageant*, Allen's *Only Yesterday*, and Sullivan's *Our Times*, VI, in his handling of Harding.

49. Longworth, *Crowded Hours*, 324–325.

50. Clemens to Adams, no date, Harris Papers, Box 4, Folder 8.

51. Preston W. Slosson, "Warren G. Harding: A Revised Estimate," *Current History*, XXXIII, No. 2 (November 1930), 174, 178–179. Slosson also published *The Great Crusade and After, 1914–1928* (New York, 1930) in which his few references to the Harding administration merely parroted White's *Masks in a Pageant*.

52. Dumas Malone, ed., *Dictionary of American Biography*, VIII (New York, 1932), 252–257.

53. Review of *Our Times*, VI, *The Twenties*, by Theodore C. Smith, *AHR*, XLI, No. 4 (July 1936), 784.

54. Review of *Masks in a Pageant* by Lester B. Shippee, *MVHR*, XV, No. 4 (March 1929), 575–577.

55. Review of *Incredible Era* by Frederick L. Paxson, *AHR*, XLVI, No. 1 (October 1940), 179–180.

56. Schriftgiesser, *This Was Normalcy*, 81.

57. Arthur Link in 1947 stated that Adams's *Incredible Era* was "a tolerant and sympathetic biography, and the result is about as good as we are entitled to expect." That Adams's work should finally have been enthroned by a biographer of Link's stature was ludicrous. See Link, "A Decade of Biographical Contributions to Recent American History," *MVHR*, XXXIV, No. 4 (March 1948), 643.

58. For examples see Henry F. May, "Shifting Perspectives on the 1920's," *MVHR*, XLIII, No. 3 (December 1956), 405–427; John D. Hicks, "Research Op-

portunities in the 1920's," *Historian*, XXV, No. 1 (November 1962), 1–2. In 1960, John D. Hicks made a new attempt at a new overview of the twenties, in his *Republican Ascendancy*. Unfortunately, for the Harding years Hicks still relied on Allen, White, Sullivan, and Adams. Other recent books which also repeat many of the old myths are William E. Leutchenburg, *The Perils of Prosperity, 1914–32* (Chicago, 1958); and Schlesinger, *The Crisis of the Old Order*.

59. For the best description of the Harding collection see Donald E. Pitzer, "An Introduction to the Harding Papers," *Ohio History*, LXXV, Nos. 2–3 (Spring–Summer 1966), 76–84. See also Kenneth W. Duckett, "The Harding Papers: How Some Were Burned . . ." *American Heritage*, XVI, No. 2 (February 1965), 25–31, 102–109. Controversy still exists over what and how much Mrs. Harding actually destroyed. It appears that little of importance is missing from the presidential years.

60. Louise Beiderhase to WGH, October 30, 1920, HP, Box 564, items 256761–256762.

61. The Phillips letters are presently in the custody of Byron E. Ford of Vorys, Sater, Seymour, and Pease, a law firm in Columbus, Ohio.

62. This information is found in Edwin K. Gross, *Vindication for Mr. Normalcy: A 100th Birthday Memorial* (Buffalo, 1965), 51. On the whole this book is ridiculously eulogistic and unhistorical.

63. For the newspaper disclosure see *New York Times*, July 10, 1964, p. 1. For a discussion of the events leading to the pending lawsuit against McGraw-Hill, Francis Russell, Kenneth W. Duckett, *American Heritage*, and the *New York Times* see Francis Russell, "The Harding Papers . . . and Some Were Saved," *American Heritage*, XVI, No. 2 (February 1965), 25–31, 102–110.

64. Russell, *The Shadow of Blooming Grove*, xiv.

65. Russell maintains that there are 105 letters covering the years 1909–20. Actually, the period covered is 1910–20 and there are only 98 letters from Harding to Mrs. Phillips (most of them concentrated in the years 1912–18) plus a few fragments of letters, several notes in Mrs. Phillips's own hand, and assorted poems. I have read the Phillips letters carefully and in their entirety. Many are tedious and boring in their length and repetition, several running to 20 pages and one to 40 pages. As insights into Harding's sexual frustrations they are interesting, and the letters do indicate that Harding actually loved Carrie Phillips. But love poems, romantic daydreams, suggestive remarks, and references to intimate embraces are hardly of great historical significance. None of the letters, for example, deal with public figures or contemporary political activity and only a few touch on any policy matters (mainly, war with Germany). All are singularly lacking even in personal, family, or local Marion information or details.

66. Review of *The Shadow of Blooming Grove*, by John A. Garraty, *New York Times Book Review*, November 24, 1968, pp. 1, 56–58.

67. Russell, *The Shadow of Blooming Grove*, 663.

68. Russell exaggerates Harding's anxiety on this occasion, *ibid.*, 281–284. The Phillips letters do not reveal any trauma or drastic reaction on his part. Indeed, he indicated that he was prepared for exposure if necessary in order to preserve his political honor.

69. Coolidge, *The Autobiography of Calvin Coolidge*, 180.

70. White, *A Puritan in Babylon*, vi.

71. *Washington Post*, April 7, 1923, p. 1. On another occasion he wrote: ". . . we must have a citizenship less concerned about what government can do for it and more anxious about what it can do for the nation."

72. "Warren Harding's 4000 Mile Funeral," *Literary Digest*, LXXVIII, No. 8 (August 25, 1923), 36.

73. Sullivan, *Our Times*, VI, 28, quoting Charles R. Miller of the *New York Times*.

74. *Ibid.*, 95, n. 9.

75. For a recent reassessment of Harding's administration see Thomas A. Bailey, *Presidential Greatness: The Image and the Man from George Washington to the Present* (New York, 1966), 312–315.

SOURCES AND INDEX

Sources

IT WOULD be superfluous to list here all the materials used or consulted in the preparation of this book. For specific references the footnotes should be utilized. They were designed to provide the reader with detailed information and make an elaborate bibliography unnecessary. This note is appended, however, to indicate those sources which proved particularly valuable for me and to demonstrate the scope and magnitude of the research and writing already extant on the 1920's.

Unpublished Sources

MANUSCRIPT COLLECTIONS

The manuscript collections pertaining to this era of history are now rather numerous and multiplying rapidly. The most important, of course, are the Harding Papers in the Ohio Historical Society Library at Columbus, Ohio. Embracing some 804 boxes, those most significant for the presidential years are boxes 1–497, 693–704, 763, 765, and 779–780. Boxes 693–704 are especially significant because they contain typed copies of the most important letters written during the years 1921–23.

The Harding Papers are currently being microfilmed by the Ohio Historical Society under a grant from the National Historical Publications Commission. This has necessitated some reorganization of the Harding Papers from the form in which they were received from the Harding Memorial Association and in which I found them. Future researchers should consult the guide to the microfilm edition, published by the Manuscripts Department of the Historical Society. This guide will contain a box conversion table, making cross-references with my footnotes easily possible. Both the guide and the microfilming will be completed by March 1970.

Besides the Harding Papers in Columbus there are three other minor collections of Harding manuscript materials. The W. G. Harding Papers in the Library of Congress consist of two containers and a scrapbook, but are of marginal value. The Papers of Warren Harding in the Princeton University Library contain no surprises and the most important letters are duplicated in the Ohio collection. The Warren G. Harding Papers in the New York Public Library consist of eighty letters to George H. Van Fleet, editor of the *Marion Star*, and 125 letters to and from E. Mont Reily. Some of the latter are also duplicated in the Ohio holdings.

Supplementing the voluminous Harding materials in the Ohio Historical Society

Library are fifteen other manuscript collections which are housed there and are of crucial importance in understanding Harding and the Harding era. They are the Walter F. Brown Papers (4 boxes); Cyril Clemens Papers (3 boxes); Harry M. Daugherty Papers (1 folder); Alfred (Hoke) W. Donithen Papers (1 folder); Newton H. Fairbanks Papers (86 pieces); Simeon D. Fess Papers (39 boxes); Arthur L. Garford Papers (130 boxes); Charles E. Hard Papers (2 boxes); Ray Baker Harris Papers (16 boxes); Malcolm Jennings Papers (1 box); Mary E. Lee Papers (10 boxes); E. Mont Reily Papers (467-page typed manuscript); F. E. Scobey Papers (3 boxes); James C. Woods Papers (1 box); and Frank B. Willis Papers (39 boxes).

Other manuscript collections (all in the Library of Congress) which were consulted and which contain valuable information on the Harding years are the William E. Borah Papers (boxes 201–236); Edward T. Clark Papers (boxes 3–4, 7, 10, 17–18, and 21–22); Calvin Coolidge Papers (reel 188); James J. Davis Papers (containers 1, 38–39, and 52); Charles E. Hughes Papers (boxes 4A, 4B, 15–47, and 169–173); Philander C. Knox Papers (bound volumes 23 and 24); Evalyn Walsh McLean Papers (boxes 5–6, general correspondence); Elihu Root Papers (boxes 138–139, 161, 166–167, and 169); William H. Taft Papers (series 3, boxes of "General Correspondence" 1920–23); and the Thomas J. Walsh papers (boxes 183–185, 200–203, 208–214, 266, 275, and 311).

The Will H. Hays Papers in the Indiana State Historical Society Library at Indianapolis, Indiana, were a disappointment. Although containing over 200,000 pieces and some significant material on the campaign of 1920, the collection is weak on the years 1921–23. Also of limited value for this present study were the Joseph S. Frelinghuysen Papers in the Rutgers University Library (New Brunswick, N.J.), the Albert B. Fall Papers in the University of New Mexico Library (Albuquerque, N.M.), and the Edwin Denby Papers in the Detroit Public Library (Detroit, Mich.), all of which contain some scattered correspondence with Harding. Of much greater importance were the Herbert C. Hoover Papers in the Hoover Presidential Library at West Branch, Iowa. This is truly a staggering collection. Department of Commerce materials alone comprise over 580 boxes. With the archivists' help I finally isolated those specific boxes most useful for Harding and the Harding era: 1-I/185, 1-I/242, 1-I/243, 1-I/244, 1-I/253, 1-I/257, 1-I/311, 1-I/313, and 1-I/360.

The controversial Phillips letters are presently under the control of the courts in Ohio and are physically in the custody of Byron E. Ford of Vorys, Sater, Seymour, and Pease of Columbus, Ohio. They are not now available to scholars. As explained in the text and the footnotes, the letters are of little real importance historically. They do not revise any previously held views about Harding nor do they shed significant new light on his political career, his attitudes, his actions, or his administration's policies. They do, of course, prove beyond doubt his intimacy with Carrie Phillips.

NATIONAL ARCHIVE MATERIALS

Although I carefully mined the available manuscript collections, I make no pretense at having more than scratched the surface of the materials in the National Archives. The real work in this field still remains to be done. My own ardor was somewhat cooled by the fact that I found the Archives less than satisfactory in adding substantially to the Harding story. Perhaps if one could gain access to all of the Justice Department and FBI materials for the early and middle twenties, the end product might be worth the effort. As it was, the available records of such government units as Agriculture, Labor, and Commerce were not particularly enlightening. The only sources which proved of considerable value were the records of the Navy and Interior departments and Record Group 59 of the Department of State.

ORAL HISTORY

Fortunately, I was able to interview a number of persons who were personally acquainted with Harding or participated in some of the events of the period. Not all of these would permit the use of their names. Most of them, however, proved to be surprisingly cooperative. Unfortunately, their memories were not always clear, were sometimes clouded by obvious bias, or were vitiated by contradictions. Especially helpful both in supplying information and in gaining access for me to new areas of oral information were C. A. Jones, Paul D. Michel, and Dr. Warren C. Sawyer.

In the Oral History Research Office of Columbia University there are two collections which proved of value for this present study. "The Reminiscences of James W. Wadsworth" is a rather voluminous memoir which frequently mentions or refers to Harding and events in the Harding era. "The Reminiscences of Albert D. Lasker" is useful in delimiting his relationship with Harding during the Shipping Board fiasco.

Published Sources

PUBLIC DOCUMENTS, GOVERNMENT PUBLICATIONS, AND SPEECHES

Basic for an understanding of the 1920 convention is George L. Hart, reporter, *Proceedings of the Seventeenth Republican National Convention* (New York, 1920). All of Harding's speeches while he was president have conveniently been collected by the Ohio Historical Society into a single volume, entitled *Speeches as President* (Columbus, n.d.). Also under a separate cover are all of Harding's campaign speeches entitled *Speeches of Senator Warren G. Harding* (n.p., n.d.). Together these two compilations provide a concentrated picture of Harding's thought process, aspirations, and political reactions.

In developing this study constant recourse to the *Congressional Record* and to many congressional hearings and investigations was of course necessary. Of the latter, the most important were the Senate hearings on campaign expenses in 1920 and the subsequent Kenyon report; the 1922 House investigation of Keller's charges against Attorney General Daugherty and the subsequent report; the 1923 Senate investigation of the Veterans' Bureau and the final report; the 1924 Senate investigation of the oil leases and the Walsh report; the 1924 Senate investigation of Daugherty and the Justice Department; and the 1928 Senate investigation of the final disposition of the oil "bribe money." Besides these, use was made of published hearings on such matters as the tariff, ship subsidies, tax legislation, immigration, prohibition, and government reorganization. For specific citations the footnotes should be consulted.

Valuable, too, were the annual reports of the Tariff Commission, the Federal Trade Commission, the Interstate Commerce Commission, and the Federal Reserve Board. Also important were the annual reports of the departments of the Treasury, Agriculture, Commerce, Labor, Interior, Navy, and the Post Office. Special reports involving the Conference on Central American Affairs and the Washington Conference on the Limitation of Armaments were likewise significant. Again, for specific citations the footnotes should be used.

MEMOIRS, WRITINGS, AND AUTOBIOGRAPHIES

Especially helpful to me were the memoirs, writings, and autobiographies left by the many firsthand observers of the Harding period. Of the journalists leaving their impressions I found the most pertinent to be Clinton Gilbert, *The Mirrors of Washington* (G. P. Putnam's Sons, New York, 1921); H. H. Kohlsaat, *From McKinley to Harding: Personal Recollections of Our Presidents* (Charles Scribner's Sons, New York, 1923); Edward G. Lowry, *Washington Close-Ups: Intimate Views of Some Public Figures* (Houghton Mifflin Company, Boston, 1921); Charles Michelson, *The Ghost Talks* (G. P. Putnam's Sons, New York, 1944); Henry L. Stoddard, *As I Knew Them: President and Politics from Grant to Coolidge* (Harper and Brothers, New York, 1927); Thomas L. Stokes, *Chip Off My Shoulder* (Princeton University Press, Princeton, 1940); Charles W. Thompson, *Presidents I Have Known and Two Near Presidents* (Bobbs-Merrill Company, Indianapolis, 1929); and William A. White, *The Autobiography of William Allen White* (Macmillan Company, New York, 1946).

Among the writings of political leaders, the most germane to this study were Nicholas M. Butler, *Across the Busy Years*, 2 vols. (Charles Scribner's Sons, New York, 1940); James M. Cox, *Journey through My Years* (Simon and Schuster, New York, 1946); William G. McAdoo, *Crowded Years: The Reminiscences of William G. McAdoo* (Houghton Mifflin Company, Boston, 1931); George W. Norris, *Fighting Liberal: The Autobiography of George W. Norris* (Collier Books, New York, 1961); Oscar W. Underwood, *Drifting Sands of Party Politics* (Century Company, New York, 1931); and James E. Watson, *As I Knew Them* (Bobbs-Merrill Company, New York, 1936).

Other contemporary observers who left important observations are Samuel Gompers, *Seventy Years of Life and Labor: An Autobiography*, 2 vols. (E. P. Dutton and Company, New York, 1925); Irwin H. (Ike) Hoover, *Forty-Two Years in the White House* (Houghton Mifflin Company, Boston, 1934); Alice Roosevelt Longworth, *Crowded Hours* (Charles Scribner's Sons, New York, 1933); Evalyn Walsh McLean, *Father Struck It Rich* (Little, Brown and Company, Boston, 1936); and Edmund W. Starling, *Starling of the White House* (Simon and Schuster, New York, 1946).

Foremost among the writings of the members of Harding's cabinet are Calvin Coolidge, *The Autobiography of Calvin Coolidge* (Cosmopolitan Book Corporation, New York, 1929); Harry M. Daugherty (in collaboration with Thomas Dixon), *The Inside Story of the Harding Tragedy* (Churchill Company, New York, 1932); James J. Davis, *The Iron Puddler: My Life in the Rolling Mills and What Came of It* (Bobbs-Merrill Company, Indianapolis, 1922); Charles E. Hughes, *The Pathway of Peace* (Harper and Brothers, New York, 1925); Herbert Hoover, *The Memoirs of Herbert Hoover: The Cabinet and the Presidency, 1920–33* (Macmillan Company, New York, 1952); and Andrew W. Mellon, *Taxation: The People's Business* (Macmillan Company, New York, 1924).

NEWSPAPERS AND PERIODICALS

For contemporary newspaper opinion, embracing both Democratic and Republican views, I consulted the *Atlanta Constitution, Chicago Tribune, New York Herald Tribune, New York Times, New York World, Wall Street Journal*, and *Washington Post*. Contemporary periodicals which proved most useful were *American Review of Reviews* (New York), *Atlantic Monthly* (Boston), *Current History* (New York), *Current Opinion* (New York), *Independent* (New York), *Literary Digest* (New York), *Nation* (New York), *New Republic* (New York), *Outlook* (New York), *Saturday Evening Post* (Philadelphia), and *World's Work* (New York).

Secondary Sources

SCHOLARLY JOURNALS

Of extreme value for this study were numerous articles, many just recently published, in a variety of scholarly journals. Foremost among these were articles in the *Mississippi Valley Historical Review* and the *Journal of American History* by Wesley M. Bagby, Robert L. Daniel, G. Cullom Davis, Paul W. Glad, Henry F. May, Burl Noggle, James H. Shideler, J. Chal Vinson, and Allen M. Wakstein. Full citations are provided in the footnotes. Besides these articles there are many others, each significant in its own way, in such journals as *American Historical Review*, *Historian*, *American Heritage*, *Agricultural History*, *Journal of Modern History*, *Journal of Political Economy*, *American Political Science Review*, *Political Science Quarterly*, *American Economic Review*, *Quarterly Journal of Economics*, *Pacific Historical Review*, *Business History Review*, *Journal of Negro History*, *Northwest Ohio Quarterly*, *Ohio State Archaeological and Historical Quarterly*, and *Ohio History*.

BIOGRAPHIES

Perhaps the best work on the last days of Wilson, and especially on the role of Mrs. Wilson, is Gene Smith, *When the Cheering Stopped: The Last Years of Woodrow Wilson* (Morrow, New York, 1964; the edition I used for this study was the Time, Inc., paperback published in 1966). The most recent and detailed, but still too impressionistic, biography of Harding is Francis Russell, *The Shadow of Blooming Grove: Warren G. Harding in His Times* (McGraw-Hill, New York, 1968). Too superficial, but nevertheless provocative, is Andrew Sinclair, *The Available Man: The Life behind the Masks of Warren Gamaliel Harding* (Macmillan Company, New York, 1965). The best known, but badly flawed, biography of the Ohio president is Samuel H. Adams, *Incredible Era: The Life and Times of Warren Gamaliel Harding* (Houghton Mifflin Company, Boston, 1939). The other significant analysis of Harding, also defective, is in William A. White, *Masks in a Pageant* (Macmillan Company, New York, 1928).

Helpful biographies on the various members of Harding's official family are Bascom N. Timmons, *Portrait of an American: Charles G. Dawes* (Henry Holt and Company, New York, 1953); Russell Lord, *The Wallaces of Iowa* (Houghton Mifflin Company, Boston, 1947); Harvey O'Connor, *Mellon's Millions: The Biography of a Fortune* (John Day Company, New York, 1933); Merlo J. Pusey, *Charles Evans Hughes*, 2 vols. (Macmillan Company, New York, 1951); Eugene Lyons, *Herbert Hoover: A Biography* (Doubleday and Company, New York, 1964); and the two standard biographies of Coolidge—William A. White, *A Puritan in Babylon* (Macmillan Company, New York, 1938), and Claude M. Fuess, *Calvin Coolidge: The Man from Vermont* (Little, Brown and Company, Boston, 1940). The most recent, and the best, biography of Coolidge is Donald R. McCoy, *Calvin Coolidge: The Quiet President* (Macmillan Company, New York, 1967). Unfortunately there are no acceptable biographies of Albert Fall, Will Hays, James Davis, Edwin Denby, Hubert Work, or John Weeks.

Other important biographies consulted were Henry F. Pringle, *The Life and Times of William Howard Taft: A Biography*, 2 vols. (Farrar and Rinehart, New York, 1939); Ray Ginger, *The Bending Cross: A Biography of Eugene Victor Debs* (Rutgers University Press, New Brunswick, 1949); Saul D. Alinsky, *John L. Lewis: An Unauthorized Biography* (G. P. Putnam's Sons, New York, 1949); Elliott M. Rudwick, *W. E. B. DuBois: A Study in Minority Group Leadership* (University of Pennsylvania Press, Philadelphia, 1960); Gilbert C. Fite, *George N. Peek and the Fight for Farm Parity* (University of Oklahoma Press, Norman, 1954); Homer E.

Socolofsky, *Arthur Capper: Publisher, Politician, and Philanthropist* (University of Kansas Press, Lawrence, 1962); T. Bently Mott, *Myron T. Herrick: A Friend of France* (Doubleday, Doran and Company, New York, 1929); David A. Lockmiller, *Enoch H. Crowder: Soldier, Lawyer and Statesman* (University of Missouri Press, Columbia, 1955); Willis F. Johnson, *George Harvey: A Passionate Patriot* (Houghton Mifflin Company, Boston, 1929); Hermann Hagedorn, *Leonard Wood: A Biography*, 2 vols. (Harper and Brothers, New York, 1931); Forrest Crissey, *Theodore D. Burton* (World Publishing Company, Cleveland, 1956); John A. Garraty, *Henry Cabot Lodge: A Biography* (Alfred A. Knopf, New York, 1953); John Gunther, *Taken at the Flood: The Story of Albert D. Lasker* (Harper and Brothers, New York, 1960); William T. Hutchinson, *Lowden of Illinois: The Life of Frank O. Lowden*, 2 vols. (University of Chicago Press, Chicago, 1957); Philip C. Jessup, *Elihu Root*, 2 vols. (Dodd, Mead and Company, New York, 1938); Claudius O. Johnson, *Borah of Idaho* (Longmans, Green and Company, New York, 1936); Fola and Belle C. LaFollette, *Robert M. LaFollette*, 2 vols. (Macmillan Company, New York, 1953); Josephine O'Keane, *Thomas J. Walsh: A Senator from Montana* (Marshall Jones Company, Francestown, N.H., 1955); and Joel F. Paschal, *Mr. Justice Sutherland: A Man against the State* (Princeton University Press, Princeton, 1951).

SPECIAL STUDIES AND MONOGRAPHS

I found no lack of monographic materials or special studies available on virtually every aspect of life during the Harding years. Only a limited number can be suggested here.

Most useful on public opinion and the policy-making process relating to foreign affairs are Selig Adler, *The Isolationist Impulse: Its Twentieth Century Reaction* (Abelard-Schuman, New York, 1957); Selig Adler, *The Uncertain Giant, 1921–1941: American Foreign Policy between the Wars* (Macmillan Company, New York, 1965); and Frank H. Simonds, *American Foreign Policy in the Post-War Years* (Johns Hopkins Press, Baltimore, 1935). Disappointing is Betty Glad, *Charles Evans Hughes and the Illusions of Innocence: A Study in American Diplomacy* (University of Illinois Press, Urbana, 1966).

On the relationship between the United States and the Soviet Union in the twenties the following works are the most pertinent: Robert P. Browder, *The Origins of Soviet-American Diplomacy* (Princeton University Press, Princeton, 1953); H. H. Fisher, *The Famine in Soviet Russia, 1919–1923: The Operations of the American Relief Administration* (Macmillan Company, New York, 1927); and James G. Hodgson, *Recognition of Soviet Russia* (H. W. Wilson Company, New York, 1925). By far the best work on the United States and Great Britain is H. C. Allen, *Great Britain and the United States: A History of Anglo-American Relations, 1783–1952* (St. Martin's Press, New York, 1955). On South American affairs the following seem most valuable: D. A. Graber, *Crisis Diplomacy: A History of U.S. Intervention Policies and Practices* (Public Affairs Press, Washington, D.C., 1959); Gordon K. Lewis, *Puerto Rico: Freedom and Power in the Caribbean* (MR Press, New York, 1963); E. Taylor Parks, *Colombia and the United States, 1765–1934* (Duke University Press, Durham, 1935); J. Fred Rippy, *The Capitalists and Colombia* (Vanguard Press, New York, 1931); Robert F. Smith, *The United States and Cuba: Business and Diplomacy, 1917–1960* (Bookman Associates, New York, 1960); and Sumner Welles, *Naboth's Vineyard: The Dominican Republic, 1844–1928*, 2 vols. (Payson and Clarke, New York, 1928).

Numerous works are available on the Washington Conference: Raymond L. Buell, *The Washington Conference* (D. Appleton and Company, New York, 1922); C. Leonard Hoag, *Preface to Preparedness: The Washington Disarmament Confer-*

ence and Public Opinion (American Council on Public Affairs, Washington, D.C., 1941); Yamato Ichihashi, *The Washington Conference and After* (Stanford University Press, Palo Alto, 1928); and John C. Vinson, *The Parchment Peace: The United States Senate and the Washington Conference, 1921–1922* (University of Georgia Press, Athens, 1955). On the general problem of disarmament Denys P. Myers, *World Disarmament: Its Problems and Prospects* (World Peace Foundation, Boston, 1932), provides valuable hindsight while John C. Vinson, *William E. Borah and the Outlawry of War* (University of Georgia Press, Athens, 1957), is excellent on the continuing American interest. On naval affairs and their relationship to world peace and disarmament the two best works are Gerald E. Wheeler, *Prelude to Pearl Harbor: The United States Navy and the Far East, 1921–1931* (University of Missouri Press, Columbia, n.d.) and Harold and Margaret Sprout, *Toward a New Order of Sea Power: American Naval Policy and the World Scene, 1918–1922* (Princeton University Press, Princeton, 1946).

The works most useful on the confused and complicated story of American oil diplomacy are Sidney R. Cooke and E. H. Davenport, *The Oil Trusts and Anglo-American Relations* (Macmillan Company, New York, 1924); Ludwell Denny, *We Fight for Oil* (Alfred A. Knopf, New York, 1928); John Ise, *The United States Oil Policy* (Yale University Press, New Haven, 1926); and John A. DeNovo, *American Interests and Policies in the Middle East, 1900–1939* (University of Minnesota Press, Minneapolis, 1963).

The following works are the most significant on the war debts and reparations question: Harold G. Moulton and Constantine E. McGuire, *Germany's Capacity to Pay: A Study of the Reparation Problem* (McGraw-Hill Book Company, New York, 1923); Harold G. Moulton and Leo Pasvolsky, *War Debts and World Prosperity* (Brookings Institution, New York, 1932); and Harold G. Moulton and Leo Pasvolsky, *World War Debt Settlements* (Macmillan Company, New York, 1926). The most exhaustive study of the reparations problem, translated from the German, is Carl Bergmann, *The History of Reparations* (Houghton Mifflin Company, Boston, 1927).

Although too moralistic and disorganized, the two books by Denna F. Fleming are the best on the World Court and American relations with the League: *The United States and the World Court* (Doubleday, Doran and Company, New York, 1945), and *The United States and World Organization, 1920–1933* (Columbia University Press, New York, 1938).

On demobilization, inflation, and postwar depression, the studies most significant are Benedict Crowell and Robert F. Wilson, *Demobilization: Our Industrial and Military Demobilization after the Armistice, 1918–1920* (Yale University Press, New Haven, 1921); James R. Mock and Evangeline Thurber, *Report on Demobilization* (University of Oklahoma Press, Norman, 1944); Paul A. Samuelson and Everett E. Hagen, *After the War, 1918–1920: Military and Economic Demobilization of the United States* (National Resources Planning Board, n.p., 1943); Frederick C. Mills, *Economic Tendencies in the United States: Aspects of Pre-War and Post-War Changes* (National Bureau of Economic Research, New York, 1932); and Wilson F. Payne, *Business Behavior, 1919–1922: An Account of Post-War Inflation and Depression* (in *Studies in Business Administration*, XII, No. 4, University of Chicago Press, Chicago, 1942).

Invaluable on the political events of the early twenties are Wesley M. Bagby, *The Road to Normalcy: The Presidential Campaign and Election of 1920* (in *Johns Hopkins University Studies in Historical and Political Science*, LXXX, No. 1, Johns Hopkins University Press, Baltimore, 1962); Kenneth C. MacKay, *The Progressive Movement of 1924* (in *Studies in History, Economics and Public Law*, No. 527, Columbia University Press, New York, 1947); and Nathan Fine, *Labor and Farmer*

Parties in the United States, 1828–1928 (Rand School of Social Science, New York, 1928). Important for its analysis of campaign expenses is James K. Pollock, Party Campaign Funds (Alfred A. Knopf, New York, 1926). The most balanced works on Teapot Dome are J. Leonard Bates, The Origins of Teapot Dome: Progressives, Parties, and Petroleum, 1909–1921 (University of Illinois Press, Urbana, 1963), and Burl Noggle, Teapot Dome: Oil and Politics in the 1920's (Louisiana State University Press, Baton Rouge, 1962). The most colorful, but distorted, contemporary account of the scandal is Marcus E. Ravage, The Story of Teapot Dome (Republic Publishing Company, New York, 1924). Badly flawed is M. R. Werner and John Starr, Teapot Dome (Viking Press, New York, 1959). Morris R. Werner, Privileged Characters (R. M. McBride and Company, New York, 1935) is an entertaining exposé of all the scandals in the Harding administration but has to be used with extreme caution.

Good on business attitudes during the early twenties is James W. Prothro, The Dollar Decade: Business Ideas in the 1920's (Louisiana State University Press, Baton Rouge, 1954). Still the best on labor matters is Selig Perlman and Philip Taft, Labor Movements (in John R. Commons, ed., History of Labor in the United States, 1896–1932, IV, Macmillan Company, New York, 1935). A recent biased, but interesting, handling of labor during the twenties is Irving Bernstein, The Lean Years: A History of the American Worker, 1920–1933 (Houghton Mifflin Company, Cambridge, Mass., 1960). Other valuable books on specific aspects of the labor problem are Marion C. Cahill, Shorter Hours: A Study of the Movement since the Civil War (in Studies in History, Economics and Public Law, No. 380, Columbia University Press, New York, 1932); Elias Lieberman, Unions before the Bar: Historic Trials Showing the Evolution of Labor Rights in the United States, rev. ed. (Oxford Book Company, New York, 1960); Felix Frankfurter and Nathan Greene, The Labor Injunction (Macmillan Company, New York, 1930); National Industrial Conference Board, The Kansas Court of Industrial Relations (Report No. 67, National Industrial Conference Board, New York, 1924); and Arthur E. Suffern, The Coal Miners' Struggle for Industrial Status (Macmillan Company, New York, 1926).

On the farm problem unquestionably the most comprehensive work is The Agricultural Situation in the United States (in American Academy of Political and Social Science Annals, CXVII, Philadelphia, 1925). Also good are R. R. Enfield, The Agricultural Crisis, 1920–1923 (Longmans, Green and Company, London, 1924); James H. Shideler, Farm Crisis, 1919–1923 (University of California Press, Berkeley, 1957); and Robert L. Morlan, Political Prairie Fire: The Nonpartisan League, 1915–1922 (University of Minnesota Press, Minneapolis, 1955). General works of benefit are Theodore Saloutos and John D. Hicks, Agricultural Discontent in the Middle West, 1900–1939 (University of Wisconsin Press, Madison, 1951); Russel B. Nye, Midwestern Progressive Politics: A Historical Study of Its Origins and Development, 1870–1950 (Michigan State College Press, East Lansing, 1951); and Murray R. Benedict, Farm Policies of the United States, 1790–1950 (Twentieth Century Fund, New York, 1953).

Besides the various works of Frank W. Taussig, useful on the tariff are John D. Larkin, The President's Control of the Tariff (Harvard University Press, Cambridge, Mass., 1936) and J. Marshall Gersting, The Flexible Provisions in the United States' Tariff, 1922–1930 (University of Pennsylvania Press, Philadelphia, 1932). Of primary importance on the immigration question are John Higham, Strangers in the Land: Patterns of American Nativism, 1860–1925 (Rutgers University Press, New Brunswick, 1955). One of the best contemporary works on immigration is Roy L. Garis, Immigration Restriction: A Study of the Opposition to and Regulation of Immigration into the United States (Macmillan Company, New York, 1927).

There are a host of popular and scholarly studies available on prohibition. Herbert Asbury, *The Great Illusion: An Informal History of Prohibition* (Doubleday and Company, New York, 1950); Peter H. Odegard, *Pressure Politics: The Story of the Anti-Saloon League* (Columbia University Press, New York, 1928); Charles Merz, *The Dry Decade* (Doubleday, Doran and Company, New York, 1931); and Clark Warburton, *The Economic Results of Prohibition* (in *Studies in History, Economics and Public Law*, No. 379, Columbia University Press, New York, 1932). The most recent, and in many respects the best, treatment of the whole subject of prohibition is Andrew Sinclair, *Prohibition: The Era of Excess* (Little, Brown and Company, Boston, 1962).

The most complete compendium of data on all phases of American social life in the decade is President's Research Committee on Social Trends, *Recent Social Trends in the United States*, 2 vols. (McGraw-Hill Book Company, New York, 1933). David M. Chalmers, *Hooded Americanism: The First Century of the Ku Klux Klan, 1865–1965* (Doubleday, Garden City, N.Y., 1965), is best on the Klan while Norman F. Furniss, *The Fundamentalist Controversy, 1918–1931* (Yale University Press, New Haven, 1954), is excellent on religious intolerance. The most readable and entertaining work on customs, habits, and manners is Charles Merz, *The Great American Bandwagon* (Literary Guild of America, New York, 1928). An analysis of the postwar anticommunist phenomenon is found in Robert K. Murray, *Red Scare: A Study in National Hysteria, 1919–1920* (University of Minnesota Press, Minneapolis, 1955). Little of significance has been done on race relations during the era. The only work which deals with the subject specifically is Elbert L. Tatum, *The Changed Political Thought of the Negro, 1915–1940* (Exposition Press, New York, 1951). Two books of some value for their general coverage are Robert L. Jack, *History of the National Association for the Advancement of Colored People* (Meador Publishing Company, Boston, 1943), and Maurice R. Davie, *Negroes in American Society* (McGraw-Hill Book Company, New York, 1949).

A wide variety of studies exist on all aspects of American economic policy during the twenties. Among the most useful are Leverett S. Lyon, *et al.*, *Government and Economic Life: Development and Current Issues of American Public Policy*, 2 vols. (Brookings Institution, Washington, D.C., 1939); Ray L. Wilbur and Arthur M. Hyde, *The Hoover Policies* (Charles Scribner's Sons, New York, 1937); Joseph Brandes, *Herbert Hoover and Economic Diplomacy: Department of Commerce Policy, 1921–1928* (University of Pittsburgh Press, Pittsburgh, 1962); Herbert Feis, *The Diplomacy of the Dollar: First Era, 1919–1932* (Johns Hopkins University Press, Baltimore, 1950); Committee on Public Debt Policy, *Our National Debt: Its Meaning Today* (Harcourt, Brace and Company, New York, 1949); and Roy G. and Gladys C. Blakey, *The Federal Income Tax* (Longmans, Green and Company, New York, 1940). Federal Reserve activities are best explained in Harold L. Reed, *Federal Reserve Policy, 1921–1930* (McGraw-Hill Book Company, New York, 1930), and Seymour E. Harris, *Twenty Years of Federal Reserve Policy*, 2 vols. (Harvard University Press, Cambridge, Mass., 1933). Best on the postwar shipping crisis is Paul M. Zeis, *American Shipping Policy* (Princeton University Press, Princeton, 1938), and Darrell H. Smith and Paul V. Betters, *The United States Shipping Board: Its History, Activities and Organization* (in *Service Monographs of the United States Government*, No. 63, Brookings Institution, Washington, D.C., 1931).

Among the most significant works on the operation of various bureaus of the federal government during the early twenties are W. F. Willoughby, *The National Budget System: With Suggestions for Its Improvement* (in *Studies in Administration*, Institute for Government Research, Washington, D.C., 1927); I. L. Sharfman, *The Interstate Commerce Commission: A Study in Administrative Law and Procedure*, 4 pts. (Commonwealth Fund, New York, 1931–37); Thomas C. Blaisdell, Jr., *The Federal Trade Commission: An Experiment in the Control of Business* (Columbia

University Press, New York, 1932); and Laurence F. Schmeckebier, *The Bureau of Prohibition: Its History, Activities and Organization* (in *Service Monographs of the United States Government*, No. 57, Brookings Institution, Washington, D.C., 1929). For other titles the footnotes should be consulted.

Fortunately many statistical studies are available on the early twenties. Besides those published by the federal government, especially by the Bureau of Labor Statistics, the most valuable for this present work were sponsored by the National Industrial Conference Board: *Wages in the United States, 1914–1930* (National Industrial Conference Board, New York, 1931); M. Ada Beney, *Wages, Hours, and Unemployment in the United States, 1914–1936* (Report No. 229, National Industrial Conference Board, New York, 1936); *Changes in the Cost of Living, July, 1914–July, 1923* (Report No. 63, National Industrial Conference Board, New York, 1923); *Wages, Hours and Employment in American Manufacturing Industries, July, 1914–July, 1923* (Report No. 62, National Industrial Conference Board, New York, 1923); *The Cost of Living among Wage Earners: Anthracite Region of Pennsylvania, February, 1922* (Special Report No. 21, National Industrial Conference Board, New York, 1922); *Wages, Hours and Employment of Railroad Workers* (Report No. 70, National Industrial Conference Board, New York, 1924); and *The Unemployment Problem* (Report No. 43, National Industrial Conference Board, New York, 1921). Of a more general, but illuminating, nature are the following statistical studies: Paul H. Douglas, *Real Wages in the United States, 1890–1926* (Houghton Mifflin Company, Cambridge, Mass., 1930); Lazare Teper, *Hours of Labor* (in *Johns Hopkins University Studies in Historical and Political Science*, L, No. 1, Johns Hopkins University Press, Baltimore, 1932); and Daniel J. Ahearn, *The Wages of Farm and Factory Laborers, 1914–1944* (in *Studies in History, Economics and Public Law*, No. 518, Columbia University Press, New York, 1945).

GENERAL HISTORIES, THESES, AND MISCELLANEOUS

Among the theses and dissertations used in this study were the following: Harold F. Alderfer, "The Personality and Politics of Warren G. Harding" (Ph.D. dissertation, Syracuse University, 1928); J. Leonard Bates, "Senator Walsh of Montana, 1918–1924: A Liberal under Pressure" (Ph.D. dissertation, University of North Carolina, 1952); Robert E. Hauser, "Warren G. Harding and the Ohio Presidential Primary of 1920" (M.A. thesis, Pennsylvania State University, 1967); Frank G. Krautwater, "The Senatorial Career of Warren G. Harding" (M.A. thesis, Ohio State University, 1950); Mary A. Miller, "The Political Attitude of the Negro: 1920–1932" (M.A. thesis, Pennsylvania State University, 1968); John L. Nether, "Simeon D. Fess: Educator and Politician" (Ph.D. dissertation, Ohio State University, 1964); Gerald E. Ridinger, "The Political Career of Frank B. Willis" (Ph.D. dissertation, Ohio State University, 1957); James H. Shideler, "The Neo-Progressives: Reform Politics in the United States, 1920–1925" (Ph.D. dissertation, University of California, 1945); and David H. Stratton, "Albert B. Fall and the Teapot Dome Affair" (Ph.D. dissertation, University of Colorado, 1955).

Valuable as background for this study and as examples of the treatment given to the early twenties by previous historical writers were these books: Frederick L. Allen, *Only Yesterday: An Informal History of the Nineteen-Twenties* (Harper and Brothers, New York, 1931); Mark Sullivan, *Our Times: The United States, 1900–1925*, VI (Charles Scribner's Sons, New York, 1935); Frederic L. Paxson, *Postwar Years: Normalcy, 1918–1923* (University of California Press, Berkeley, 1948); William E. Leuchtenburg, *The Perils of Prosperity, 1914–1932* (University of Chicago Press, Chicago, 1958); Arthur M. Schlesinger, Jr., *The Crisis of the Old Order, 1919–1933* (in *The Age of Roosevelt*, I, Houghton Mifflin Company, New York,

1957); Karl Schriftgiesser, *This Was Normalcy: An Account of Party Politics during Twelve Republican Years, 1920–1932* (Little, Brown and Company, Boston, 1948); and George Soule, *Prosperity Decade, from War to Depression: 1917–1929* (Rinehart and Company, New York, 1947).

Finally, significant for their bias and tone, if not always for their content, are those two most famous muckraking writings on Harding: Nan Britton, *The President's Daughter* (Elizabeth Ann Guild, New York, 1927), and Gaston B. Means, *The Strange Death of President Harding* (Guild Publishing Corporation, New York, 1930).

Index

Children's Bureau, 228
Childs, William H., 46
Chile, 133, 134, 340, 342
China: and Washington Conference, 148, 155–156; mentioned, 135, 191
Christian, George B., Jr., 21, 23, 26, 27, 47, 117, 118, 231, 247, 274, 300, 311, 441, 449, 452, 453, 454, 458, 486, 501, 515
Christian, Mrs. George B., 441
Cincinnati Enquirer, 64, 495
Civil service: record in State Department, 135; cabinet attitude toward, 302–303; Wilson's March *1917* order, 305; Harding's May *1921* order, 305
Civil Service Commission, 302, 305
Clark, Edgar C., 239
Clayton Anti-Trust Act, 218, 379, 390
Clemens, Cyril, 522
Clemens, Samuel (Mark Twain), 121, 522
Cleveland, Grover, 320
Cleveland (Ohio) formula, 258
Coal Distribution and Control Bill, 252–253
Coal Inquiry Bill, 252
Coal strikes. *See* Strikes
Cohan, George M., 116
Cohen, Walter L., 401
Colby, Bainbridge, 79, 130
Coleman, McAlister, 507
Collective bargaining, Harding and, 54
Collier, William M., 134
Collier's Weekly, 48
Collins, Floyd, 505
Colombia, relations with, 340–341
Colorado River Commission, 412
Columbia University, 87
Columbus Dispatch, 29, 121
Commerce, Department of: appointments to, 192; strengthened by Hoover, 195–198; reviews loans, 355; interest in Middle Eastern oil, 358; as prophet of prosperity, 383; mentioned, 410, 411. *See also* Business policy; Economic policy; Foreign and Domestic Commerce, Bureau of; Hoover, Herbert C.
Commission for the Suppression of Traffic in Women and Children, 368
Committee of Forty-Eight, 506
Commons, John R., 220
Communications, Department of, 415

Communist party (U.S.A.), 88
Communists, in election of *1924*, 507
Compulsory arbitration, 388–389
Conference for Progressive Political Action, 507–511, 512
Congress: makeup after election of *1920*, 66; Harding's relations with, 127–128, 534; lack of leadership and public apathy toward, 314–316; record by *1922*, 315; general record, 423
   Sixty-Sixth: composition and actions of, 74; opening of third session, 94; and disarmament, 142–143
   Sixty-Seventh: ineffectiveness of, 128; analysis of work of, 190; special session, November *1922*, 323; last regular session, December *1922*, 324
   Sixty-Eighth, treats Coolidge shabbily, 503
Conservation: Harding's views on, 54; Fall opposed to, 106; Harding supports on western trip, 444; and Teapot Dome, 461–465
Conventions. *See* Republican Convention of *1920*; Democratic Convention of *1920*
Cook, Dr. Frederick A., 495
Coolidge, Calvin: nominated vice-president, 40; used little in campaign, 48–49; and Boston police strike, 87; and World Court, 372–373; and farm subsidies, 386–387; appoints two-man team to investigate Teapot Dome, 471; accepts Denby's resignation, 471; and Daugherty, 474, 478–479; denies knowledge of scandals, 482; made honorary president of Harding Memorial Association, 492; refuses to dedicate memorial, 493; reputation in Harding era, 498–499; creation of Coolidge myth, 499–500; nature of Coolidge "change," 500; continues Harding program, 500–502; waits out scandals, 503–504; runs on Harding program in *1924*, 508; reasons for success in *1924*, 512–513; puts own stamp on period, 513–514; mentioned, 31, 42, 62, 112, 122, 150, 209, 231, 318, 361, 379, 382, 394, 396, 402, 410, 414, 416, 453, 454, 456, 470, 485, 527, 533, 535, 536
Coolidge, Grace (Mrs. Calvin), 499
Coolidge, John, 498

Haiti: relations with, 332–334; mentioned, 397, 402–403
Hale, Frederick, 15, 117, 118, 312
Hall-Mills murder, 505
Hamilton, Alexander, 171
Hamon, Jake, 40–41
Hanna, Dan, 13
Hanna, Marcus A. (Mark), 10, 13, 397
Hard, Charles E., 18, 20, 21, 23, 26, 27, 47, 64, 300, 494
Harding, Abigail (Daisy), 488
Harding, Carolyn, 488
Harding, Florence Kling (Mrs. Warren): early life and marriage, 8; helps with *Star*, 9; opposes Harding's candidacy, 23; attitudes at Republican convention, 35; asset in *1920* campaign, 49; reacts to Negro-blood story, 64; predicts victory, 65; alters atmosphere of White House, 113; insists Harding go to church, 120; opposes Debs's release, 167; illness in *1922*, 418; at odds with Washington high society, 419–420; relations with husband while president, 420–421; fears of future, 428–429; reaction to Smith's death, 437; concerned about Alaska trip, 440; funeral trips and Harding's burial, 451–455; reaction to scandal investigations, 485; death, 486; mentioned, 5, 18, 94, 115, 148, 150, 441, 458, 486, 490, 528, 529
Harding, Dr. George Tryon, 6, 65–66, 454
Harding, George T., III (Deac), 28, 35, 488
Harding, Warren G.: final balloting on nomination, 3–5; birth and early life, 5–7; runs *Marion Star*, 9; early political philosophy and activities, 10–12; Senate race of *1914*, 13–14; senatorial years and attitudes, 15–16; and League fight, 16–18; relationship with Daugherty before *1919*, 18–19; drawn into presidential race, 22–23; announces candidacy, 25; enters Ohio primary, 28–30; preconvention activities, 31–32; name presented at *1920* convention, 34; and smoke-filled-room myth, 36–39; reasons for nomination success, 41–42; acceptance speech and unity drive, 44–46; controls campaign of *1920*, 49; cam-

paign promises, 54; and League issue, 55–61; wins Maine election, 62; Negro-blood story, 63–65; election returns, 66; reasons for campaign success, 69–70; legacy from Wilson, 89–92; bids farewell to Senate, 94–95; selects cabinet, 95–109; inauguration, 109–112; relations with press, 113–114; physical and personality traits, 114–120; mental abilities, 120–122; work habits, 123; relations with Congress, 125–128; relationship with Hughes, 131–133; policy toward League of Nations, 136–138, 367–368; and Washington Disarmament Conference, 143–162; final attitude on association of nations, 165–166; releases Debs and other prisoners, 166–169; economic philosophy, 170–171; supports Dawes and Budget Bureau, 174–179; relations with Mellon and tax policy, 181–191, 381–382; relations with Hoover, 194–195; relations with Wallace, 201; basic views on agriculture and relations with farm bloc, 201–205; signs emergency tariff, 207; opposes Norris Farm Relief Bill, 209; credibility gap with farmers, 210–211; and Agricultural Conference, 211–214; compromises on membership of Federal Reserve Board, 216; relationship with Kenyon and Capper, 217–218; supports Wallace reorganization plans, 220; attitude toward railroads and freight rates, 222–224; agricultural policy, 226, 383–388; basic attitudes on labor, 229–230; relations with Davis and Gompers, 229–231; supports Unemployment Conference, 232; and twelve-hour day, 235–238; and railroad workers' wages, 238–241; and threatened rail strike of *1921*, 240–241; and coal situation in *1921*, 243–244; and strikes of *1922*, 246–264; attitude toward immigration, 267–269; signs Fordney-McCumber Tariff, 277; supports merchant marine and advocates subsidies, 280–293, 321–325; outline of program by *1922*, 294; Ohio appointments, 299–301; attitude toward merit system, 302; and

612